Text smart

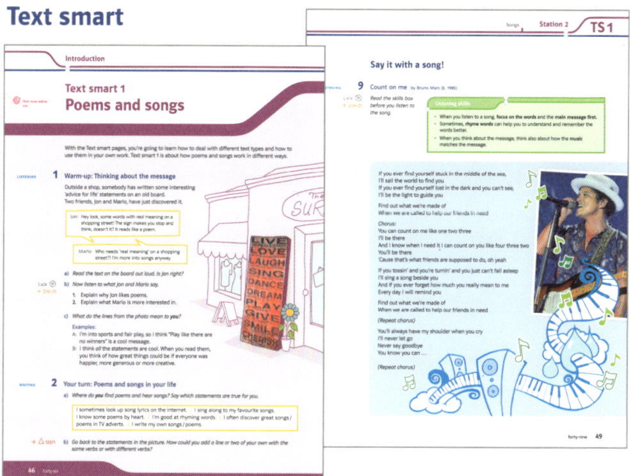

Auf den neuen Text smart-Seiten lernst du, wie du mit authentischen Texten (z. B. Sachtexten, Erzählungen, Songs und Gedichten) umgehst und sie im Anschluss für deine eigenen Arbeiten nutzen kannst.

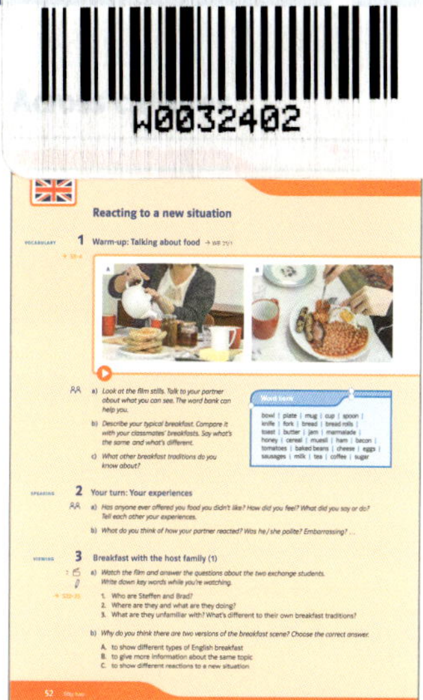

Vergleiche auf diesen Seiten deinen Alltag mit der Alltagskultur in Großbritannien und lerne, mit verschiedenen Begegnungssituationen umzugehen.

Diff pool

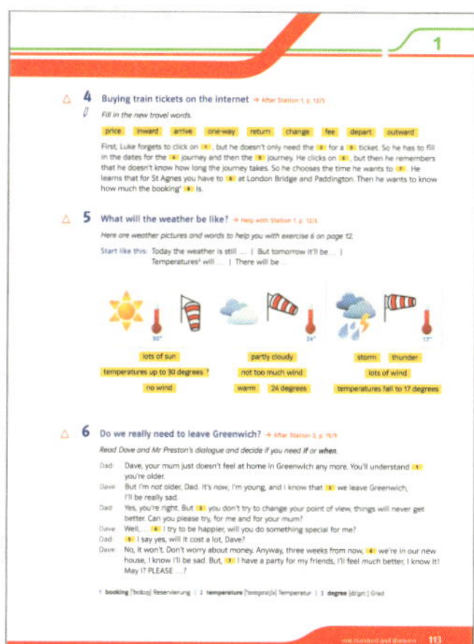

Skills

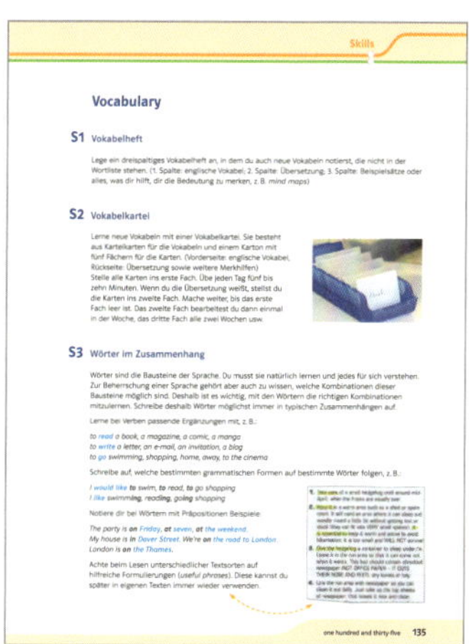

Grammar, Vocabulary

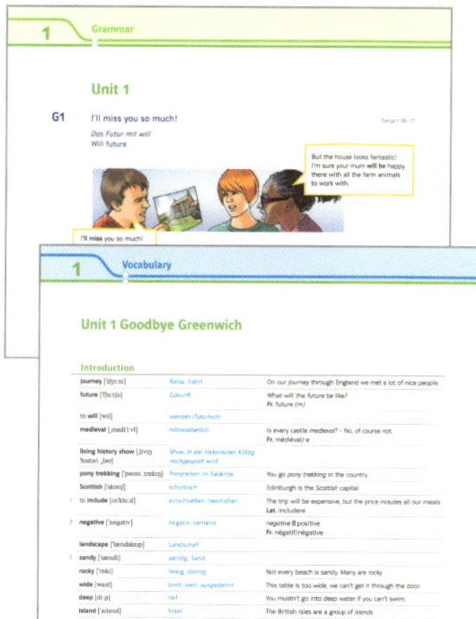

Im hinteren Buchteil stehen dir hilfreiche Anhänge zur Verfügung. Achte auf die Verweise in den Units, die dir sagen, in welchem Anhang du nachschlagen kannst.

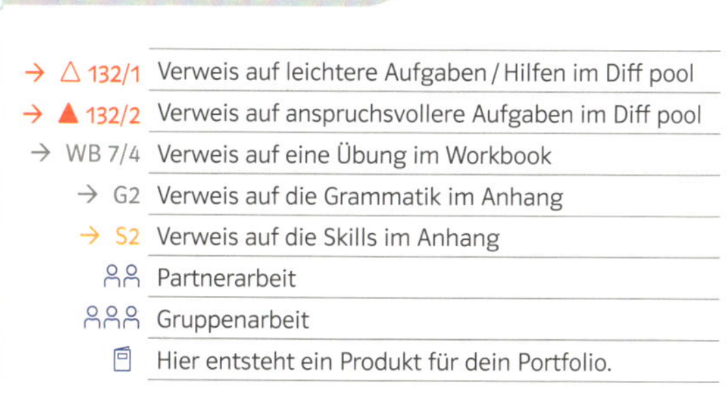

→ △ 132/1	Verweis auf leichtere Aufgaben / Hilfen im Diff pool
→ ▲ 132/2	Verweis auf anspruchsvollere Aufgaben im Diff pool
→ WB 7/4	Verweis auf eine Übung im Workbook
→ G2	Verweis auf die Grammatik im Anhang
→ S2	Verweis auf die Skills im Anhang
	Partnerarbeit
	Gruppenarbeit
	Hier entsteht ein Produkt für dein Portfolio.
	Schreiben (geschlossen / einfach)
	Schreiben (offen / kreativ)
S1/14	Verweis auf die Schüler-CDs im Workbook (Audio)
L1/19	Verweis auf die Lehrer-CDs (Audio)
	Verweis auf die Lehrer-DVD (Film)
	Code auf www.klett.de eingeben und Zusatzmaterial nutzen
	Übungen, die die Unit task besonders vorbereiten
	Across cultures

Green Line 3 G9 für Klasse 7 an Gymnasien

Herausgeber: Harald Weisshaar, Bisingen

Autorinnen und Autoren: Carolyn Jones, Beckenham; Jon Marks, Ventnor; Harald Weisshaar, Bisingen; Alison Wooder, Ventnor sowie Jennifer Baer-Engel, Göppingen; Cornelia Kaminski, Fulda; Elise Köhler-Davidson, Friedrichsdorf

Beratung: Paul Dennis, Lahnstein; Cornelia Kaminski, Fulda; Nilgül Karabulut, Aachen; Hartmut Klose, Seevetal; Antje Körber, Merseburg; Jörg Nieswand, Berlin; Jörg Schulze, Dresden

Zusätzliche Informationen in der Lehrerausgabe:

Produktiver Lernwortschatz · Rezeptiver Wortschatz · Neue Grammatik

△→ ▲→ **Help with/Instead of/After …:** Verweis auf unterstützende/alternative/weiterführende Aufgaben im Diff pool des Schülerbuchs für leistungsschwächere bzw. -stärkere Schüler/innen.

HA: Vorschlag zur Hausaufgabe

Transfer: Einbeziehung der Lebenswelt der Schüler/innen

Folie 1: Hier können Sie Folie 1 des Folienordners einsetzen.

WB 4/1: Hier können Sie im Workbook Seite 4, Aufgabe 1 einsetzen.

KV 1: Hier können Sie Kopiervorlage 1 des Lehrerbands einsetzen.

Voc.: Hier sind Verweise auf Wortschatzhilfen im Schülerbuch und Workbook (WB) angegeben.

Lösung: Hier finden Sie Lösungen zu den geschlossenen Aufgaben.

1. Auflage

1 5 4 3 2 1 | 2020 19 18 17 16

Redaktion: Michael Mattison; Anette Mohamud; Martina Reckart; Lektorat editoria: Cornelia Schaller, Fellbach sowie für die Lehrerfassung: Juliane Rebstock
Herstellung: Anita Bauch; Anne Leibbrand, Cristina Dunu

Gestaltung: Petra Michel, Essen
Umschlaggestaltung: know idea, Freiburg; Koma Amok, Stuttgart
Illustrationen: Peer Kramer, Düsseldorf; jani lunablau, Barcelona sowie Christian Dekelver, Weinstadt *(Karten)*; Denise Drews, Zürich *(Time line)*
Satz: Satzkiste GmbH, Stuttgart; Fotosatz Kaufmann, Stuttgart
Reproduktion: Schwaben-Repro, Stuttgart
Druck: Mohn Media Mohndruck GmbH, Gütersloh

Printed in Germany
ISBN 978-3-12-854232-4

Green Line 3 G9

Lehrerfassung

von
Carolyn Jones
Jon Marks
Harald Weisshaar
Alison Wooder
Jennifer Baer-Engel
Cornelia Kaminski
Elise Köhler-Davidson

herausgegeben von
Harald Weisshaar

Ernst Klett Verlag
Stuttgart · Leipzig

Inhalt

Inhalt

Inhalt

Legende

 Kompetenzaufgabe

 Across cultures

 Across cultures

〈 〉 fakultativ

Die in diesem Band aufbereiteten Inhalte stellen ein Angebot dar, sie sind nicht obligatorisch durchzunehmen. Maßgeblich für die Auswahl der Texte und Übungen ist der Lehrplan Ihres Bundeslandes bzw. Ihr schulinternes Curriculum.

Unit 1
Goodbye Greenwich

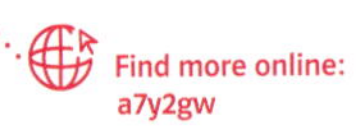

A A beach in Cornwall, in the south-west of England

B A medieval 'living history' show at Caerphilly Castle in Wales

Folie 2/32: Reaktivierung von Vorwissen, Orientierung auf Landkarte
Folie 2/33: Vorentlastung des Wortschatzes und Bildbeschreibung

SPEAKING

1 Parts of the British Isles

→ △ 112/1

112/1 Talking about places
△→ Help with ...

Look at the pictures and find the places on the map at the back of your book. Which part of the British Isles do they belong to? Which part of them looks most interesting to you and why?

Lösung: *A: England B: Wales C: Ireland D: Scotland*

Across cultures

The United Kingdom includes Great Britain and Northern Ireland.
Yes, and most of Ireland is a separate country: the Republic of Ireland.

LISTENING

2 Come on Dave, don't be so negative!

L1/1

→ S19–21

S19–21 Listening

a) *Dave is talking about his parents' plans and his mum's vet surgery. What is the problem from Dave's point of view? Listen and take notes.*

b) *Now talk about the different places that Dave and his friends discuss. Make a grid for your answers with these headings:*

Place* | *Landscape* | *Things to do* | *Other information

Pony trekking in Ireland

In Unit 1 you learn

… how to talk about places in the British Isles. You learn:

- to describe places
- to talk about plans for a journey
- to talk about the future with will
- to make conditional sentences

D The Edinburgh Festival in the Scottish capital

WB 2/1 Vocabulary (Cornwall)
WB 2/2 Vocabulary (Scotland)

BULARY

3 Places → WB 2/1–2

laces and what you there, p. 169

a) *Collect vocabulary in different categories like landscapes, sights, things to do.*

b) *Each of you does the following: Take four cards and write* ***one*** *of your words / phrases from a) on each card. Shuffle all the cards and pick four. Choose a place in the British Isles and take turns to talk about it, with the words on your cards.*

Transfer

c) ***Your turn:*** *Find information about a German region (e.g. the North Sea). Write a short text and present it.*

Word bank

high mountain | field | forest | sandy / rocky beach | wide river | deep lake | island city | village | harbour | visit a castle | go hiking / climbing / mountain biking / (wind) surfing / pony trekking

Across cultures

Did you know that palm trees grow in the south-west of England? Some call it the **English Riviera**. Are there any surprising facts about the region where you live?

Lösung: a) ***Landscapes:*** *high mountain, field, forest, sandy/rocky beach, wide river, deep lake, island;* ***Sights:*** *city, village, harbour;* ***Things to do:*** *visit a castle, go hiking/climbing/mountain biking/(wind)surfing/pony trekking*

Folie 2/34: Unterstützung des Hörverstehens und Möglichkeit zum Perspektivwechsel

L1/2

Moving to the middle of nowhere

Dave's parents have found a beautiful house near St Agnes, in the Cornish countryside. Dave is very sad to leave.

Dave: Oh no, why do we have to move to the middle of nowhere? London is just fine. And I'll miss you so much!

Olivia: But the house looks fantastic! And your mum never wanted to live in the city. She'll be happy there with her new surgery and all the farm animals and pets to work with, won't she?

Dave: Yes, but will I be happy? Has anyone ever asked *me*? If I want to see farm animals, I can go to Mudchute Farm.

Luke: What about your dad? Will he find work there?

Dave: Well, he travels a lot anyway. He'll stay in London with Aunt Frances when he has to work there. I think it'll be OK for *him*. But me?

Holly: Oh Dave, I'll miss you too! I'm so sorry you won't be able to go to the park with us any longer.

Jay: And we won't be able to play video games together.

Gwen: Come on now, it's not the end of the world. There are games you can play online. Oh, and we'll text you and have lots of video chats together.

Olivia: And we'll come to visit you! Cornwall is a great place. Most British people go there for a holiday. I've been there with my mum.

Dave: That's nice for people on holiday – but *I'll* be in a new school, and there'll be nobody I know. It'll be horrible. And I'm sure Sid will hate it too.

Jay: Don't worry, you'll make lots of new friends. But what about Olivia's idea? We could go to Cornwall to visit you.

Holly: All of us together, in Cornwall? Wow! I'll ask my mum.

Luke: Well, maybe. I'll think about it. But we'll have to find the money first, won't we?

Gwen: I'm sure we'll find a way to get there.

Olivia: Will it be OK for us to stay with Dave?

Luke: I'm sure it will. His parents are cool.

Dave: That's a wonderful idea. It'll be great to see you all there.

WB 3/3 Pronunciation (sounds)

READING

1 Questions about the future → WB 3/3

1. What does Dave say about the Prestons' future in Cornwall?
2. What do his friends say to make him feel better?
3. What will the friends need to do before they go to Cornwall? Think about these things: parents, dates, transport, money.

Examples:

1. He'll miss his friends. His mum will be happy …
2. They'll miss him too. They'll text him …
3. They'll have to ask their parents …

WB 3/4 Listening (correct answers)
KV 1: Working with language
KV 2: Language (will future)

LANGUAGE

2 Rules for the *will* future → WB 3/4 → G1

Find 4–5 sentences with **will** *or* **won't** *in the text. Say if they're predictions about the future or spontaneous reactions / decisions. You see some examples on the right.*

Prediction	Spontaneous reaction / decision
I'll miss you. She'll be happy there.	I'll ask my mum. We'll text you.

LANGUAGE

3 How will we get there?

KV 3: Language (Dave's future in Cornwall)

→ △ 112/2
→ ▲ 112/3

Frequently asked ...ions
After ...
Mediation: ...German station
After ...

Luke goes to a travel agent's to ask about the journey to St Agnes.

a) *Complete dialogue A with forms of the* **will future** *and read it with a partner.*

b) *Now do the same with dialogue B.*

Train + bus: London Paddington to St Agnes
Time: 6 – 7 hours
Prices: £50 – £70
Children under 12 must travel with an adult.

Coach + bus: London Victoria to St Agnes
Time: 8 hours
Prices: £65 – £75
Children under 14 must travel with an adult.

A

Luke: My friends and I want to go to Cornwall, but we're worried that tickets (be) expensive.

Assistant: Don't worry. It (not be) too expensive. But it depends on the date. Give me your dates and I (check) for you.

(a few minutes later)

Yes, on those dates, train tickets per person are £5 cheaper than by coach. – Oh, but now I see better prices for the next day. Between £10 and £15 cheaper by train.

Luke: £15 cheaper per person? Cool! My friends (like) that.

Assistant: Well, I can't promise £15, but it (be) a better price than a day earlier. – Oh, and children under 12 need to travel with a person who is 16 or older.

Luke: Oh, that (not be) a problem. – Anyway, I (talk) to my friends and come back.

Lösung: a) *will be – won't be – I'll/I will check – will like – it'll/it will be – won't be – I'll/I will talk;* **b)** *Will we – we'll/we will go – It'll/It will be – won't take – won't have – will I get*

B

Olivia: (we go) by train or by coach?

Luke: I think we (go) by train. It (be) cheaper and (not take) so long.

Gwen: And we (not have) to find an adult to go with us.

Holly: There's just one problem: Where (I get) the money?

WB 3/5 Language (farm holidays)
KV 4: Listening (comprehension)

LISTENING

4 Preparing for the trip → WB 3/5

L 1/5

Listen to the dialogue and answer the questions.

a) *What's Holly's problem? What can she do and who can help her?*

b) *What will these people do? Say one sentence about each person: Dave, Granny Rose, Luke, the girls, the boys, Luke's grandparents, Holly, Amber.*

Folie 2/35: Festigung und Anwendung des neuen Wortschatzes (Ticketbuchung)
WB 4/6 Language (booking tickets)

VOCABULARY

5 How to: Book train tickets on the internet → WB 4/6

Luke wants to book tickets for the five friends and Granny Rose online. They want to leave next Sunday morning and return a week later.

→ △ 113/4
→ S10

a) *Help him to fill in the form (1). He clicks on "Buy train tickets". Then he chooses a connection and clicks on it. A new window shows details for this connection (2).*

Lösung: a) *From Greenwich to St Agnes – Return: Sunday – one adult, five children*

113/4 Buying train tickets on the internet △→ After …

S10 Reading (Umgang mit neuen Wörtern)

Voc.: Travel words, p. 171

Useful phrases

One-way/single ticket | return ticket | fee | to depart | to arrive | to change at … | outward journey | inward journey | price/fare | platform

1

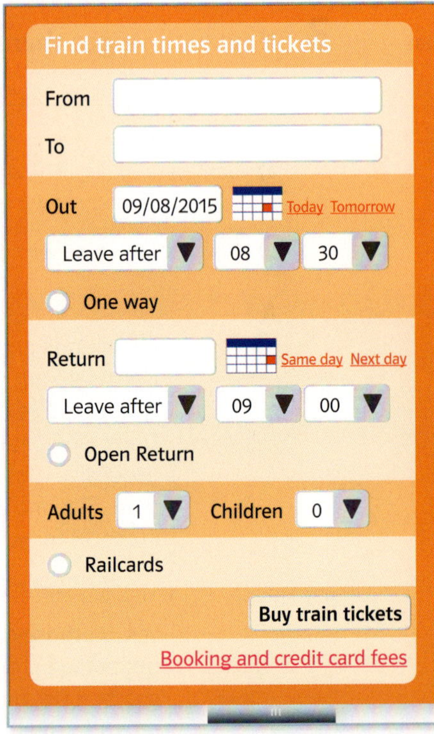
Find train times and tickets
From
To
Out 09/08/2015 Today Tomorrow
Leave after 08 30
One way
Return Same day Next day
Leave after 09 00
Open Return
Adults 1 Children 0
Railcards
Buy train tickets
Booking and credit card fees

2

Journey Summary — Outward Journey (9 Aug 2015)

Depart		Arrive		Travel by	Duration
09:32	Greenwich	09:43	London Bridge	Train	00h 11 Calling Points
09:53	London Bridge	10:23	London Paddington	Tube	00h 30
10:43	London Paddington	16:46	Redruth	Train	06h 03 Calling Points
17:12	Redruth	17:46	St Agnes	Bus	00h 34

Text me these details   Add to calendar

b) *Match words and phrases from the phrases box with these definitions.*

1. to leave
2. to leave one train and get on another
3. a ticket to go to a place and back
4. going away to a place
5. this tells you what a ticket costs
6. to get to a place
7. a ticket to go to a place
8. going back to your starting place
9. extra money you have to pay

Lösung: b) 1. *to depart* 2. *to change at …* 3. *return ticket* 4. *outward journey* 5. *price/fare* 6. *to arrive* 7. *one-way/single ticket* 8. *inward journey* 9. *fee*

Tip

You often hear *will future* in weather forecasts.

MEDIATION

6 The weather forecast → WB 4/7

Folie 2/36: Festigung und Anwendung des neuen Wortschatzes (Wetter)
KV 5: Writing (weather)   WB 4/7 Writing (weather forecast)

→ △ 113/5
→ S18

A British tourist who wants to do a 5-hour mountain climbing tour shows you this weather forecast for tomorrow. He asks you to tell him if he can go on his tour. What is your advice?

S18 Mediation

113/5 What will the weather be like? △→ Help with …

Voc.: Weather words, p. 171 / Weather, Word bank (WB), p. 15

Wettervorhersage Oberallgäu: Während es heute bei Höchsttemperaturen über 30 Grad noch sehr heiß mit viel Sonne ist, zieht morgen eine Schlechtwetterfront von Südwesten herein. Es ist mit starken Unwettern und Hagel zu rechnen, vor allem Samstagnachmittag und -abend. Im Bergland besteht Gefahr durch orkanartige Windböen mit Geschwindigkeiten bis zu 105 km/h. Durch starke Niederschläge kann es zu Überflutungen kommen.

How to get information

→ S11–14 S11–14 Writing

For the Unit task you'll need information about different parts of the British Isles: England (e.g. Cornwall, or maybe London), Scotland, Wales and Ireland (Northern Ireland or the Republic of Ireland).

1 Where to get information

If you want to collect pictures and facts about interesting places, you can write to a tourist board and ask for free material. What else can you do?

WB 5/8 Writing (internet contact form)
WB 5/9 Writing (e-mail)
WB 5/10 Activity (getting information)

2 Asking for information

→ WB 5/8–10

Make four groups, one for each of the regions you learned about on pages 8–9.
Find out e-mail addresses of organisations that have interesting material. Then write a polite e-mail to ask for the material. Some of them don't give you their e-mail addresses but ask you to fill in an internet contact form. Make sure you don't write to the same organisation about the same material more than once!

Writing skills

Before you send off your e-mail or contact form, **remember**:

- Don't forget your greetings.
- Who are you?
- What do you want to do?
- What do you need?
- How do you ask for it politely?
- What information about yourselves do you need to give?

Dear Sir or Madam,

We are students of a German grammar school. We would like to do a project about the British Isles and need information about Scotland for it.
Could you please send us some free material about interesting places in Scotland, Scottish history and things to do in Scotland?
Here is our address:
…-Gymnasium
Class …
…straße (XX)
D-(XXXXX) …

Thank you very much for your help.

Best wishes,
The students of Class (…)

3 Working with the material

When you have enough material, go through it together in your group.
Make notes of interesting ideas for a presentation, and look for the best photos.

L1/6

Visit Cornwall – You'll love it!

Where is Cornwall?

If you look at a map of Great Britain, you'll find Cornwall in the far west. Look north, west or south of Cornwall and you'll find the same 'neighbour': the Atlantic Ocean. Cornwall's coastline is almost 300 miles long and gets more sun than any other part of the UK.

Why do more than 3 million tourists visit Cornwall every year?

If you like dramatic landscapes, beautiful fishing harbours and wonderful beaches and if you're into water sports, you'll find that Cornwall is just the right place for your holiday.
But Cornwall has more to offer than its coastline and water sports. There are lots of other outdoor activities, like adventure sports, pony trekking or golf. And if you aren't into sports at all, you can visit a lot of very interesting sights.
If you go to Bodmin Moor, you'll get to know a wild landscape with prehistoric monuments that you can explore on great walking trails. And if you visit the Eden Project near St Austell, you can look at beautiful and useful plants from around the world and learn about the environment. It's the most popular tourist attraction in Cornwall.
If you visit one of the museums, you'll learn a lot about Cornwall's Celtic past or its mining history. You can still see Celtic culture in Bronze Age monuments, Celtic crosses and Cornish place names. Like Irish, Scottish Gaelic or Welsh, Cornish is a Celtic language and a few people in Cornwall still speak it besides English – but you'll be very lucky if you hear it.
If you want to eat real Cornish food, you should try pasties[1]. (And if you're still hungry, try cream tea[2] with scones[3], clotted cream[4] and jam[5]!)
When you're here, don't forget to come in and say 'hello' at one of our many visitor centres!

KV 6a: Pre-viewing (mind map/pictures)
KV 6b: While-viewing (right/wrong)

DVD 2/11

Mehr zum Thema Cornwall

READING 

7 Tourist information about Cornwall → WB 6/11

WB 6/11 Listening (holiday plans)

Olivia has found this text about Cornwall on the internet. Say what information there is about the geography, tourism, things to do, sights, history and food.

LANGUAGE

8 What will happen if ...? → WB 6/12 → G2

KV 7: Language (conditional clauses)
KV 8: Language (conditional clauses)
WB 6/12 Language (conditional clauses)

*Collect all the sentences with **if** from the text. They have two parts: an **if-clause** and a **main clause**. There are three basic patterns, but in one example the order is different:*

If ..., ... will ...	If ..., ... can ...	If ..., ... should ... If ..., try ...

Lösung: 1. If you look at ..., you'll find Cornwall ... If you like ..., you'll find that Cornwall is ... If you go to ..., you'll get to know ... If you visit ..., you'll learn ...; ... but you'll be lucky if you hear it. 2. And if you aren't into ..., you can visit ... If you visit ..., you can look at ... 3. If you want to eat ..., you should try ... And if you're still hungry, try ...

1 **pasty** ['pæsti] Pastete | 2 **cream tea** [ˌkri:m 'ti:] Nachmittagstee | 3 **scone** [skɒn] brötchenartiges Buttergebäck | 4 **clotted cream** [ˌklɒtɪd 'kri:m] Sahne *(aus erhitzter Milch)* | 5 **jam** [dʒæm] Marmelade

READING 9

Find the rule

WB 6/13 Language (Scotland)

→ WB 6/13 → G2

a) *Match the three patterns with the meanings. Then write the rule and put it in your folder.*

1. If you go to Cornwall, you'll see a lot of beautiful beaches.
2. If you go to Cornwall, you can do water sports.
3. If you go to Cornwall, you should try cream tea.

A Advice
B Prediction
C Possibility

Lösung: a) 1. B 2. C 3. A

→ △ 113/6
→ ▲ 114/7

b) *In German, there's only one word for* ***if*** *and* ***when****. Can you explain the difference between sentences 1 and 2 with the information in brackets?*

A If I go to Cornwall, I'll go surfing. (I don't know if we'll go to Cornwall or to Italy.)

B When Dave goes to Cornwall, he'll miss his friends. (We know he'll go there, but we don't know when.)

o we really need to
ireenwich?
fter …
erman tourist
ions
fter …

NGUAGE 10

Go on with the story

Play a game in class: One student starts with an if-sentence. The next student uses the main clause as an if-clause and makes a new sentence, and so on.

Example: If I go on holiday, I'll take my dog. → If I take my dog, he'll be happy.
→ If my dog is happy, he'll … → …

EAKING 11

Languages in Britain

Look at the photo. Which of the Cornish words can you understand?

Across cultures 

Everybody in the British Isles speaks English. But Cornwall, Ireland, Scotland, Wales and the Isle of Man still have their own **Celtic languages**. What languages do people in your class speak besides German? Do people speak in a local dialect or with an accent?

TENING 12

Announcements

KV9: Listening (right/wrong)

L1/8–11

→ S21

ning (Typische
ehenssituationen)

a) *Mr Preston travels a lot. Listen to four little dialogues and find out this information for each scene. Take notes:*

1. where he is
2. where he wants to go
3. what sight they talk about
4. what the announcement is about.

b) *Say in what way the fourth dialogue is different from the other three.*

Lösung: a) *1: 1. Wales, station; 2. London; 3. Cardiff; 4. train to London is arriving; 2: 1. Scotland, ticket office; 2. London (King's Cross); 3. Edinburgh Castle; 4. passengers must keep their bags with them at all times; 3: 1. Cornwall, train; 2. Redruth; 3. Eden Project; 4. the next station is Redruth, train terminates there, passengers have to get off the train; 4: 1. Ireland, airport; 2. London (Heathrow), Greenwich; 3. Dublin, Jeanie Johnston; 4. flight to Heathrow will depart at 19.30 instead of 18.20.*
b) *dialogues 1–3 > station/train; dialogue 4 > airport*

WB 7/14 Speaking (holiday ideas)
WB 7/15 Writing (holiday plans)
WB 7/16 Mediation (information for tourists)

SPEAKING

13 Role play: At the travel agent's → WB 7/14–16

→ S17

S17 Speaking (Mündliche Aufgaben)

One of you is an assistant at a travel agent's. The other chooses one of these roles:
A: A father who wants to travel with his wife and young children; B: A teenager who wants to travel with her mum; or C: a young couple who is interested in sports. They all want to go to Cornwall. Use the useful phrases to make dialogues. (You can also look back at Ex. 3 on p. 11.)

Useful phrases

Assistant:
Hello, what can I do for you?
How long would you like to stay?
If you're into …, you'll …
Do you want to go by car, by train or by coach? Do you need a ticket?
Would you like to book a room / a flat / a house?
If you want to …, you can …

Customer:
I'd like to travel to … with …
Over the weekend / two weeks / …
We love … / We're into …
How long does it take?
We need … tickets.
How much is it?
Oh, I think that's too expensive.
Yes, that's fine. Thank you.

READING

14 British history: A poem about the Romans

KV 10: Writing (poem)

→ 114/8

114/8 A poem about your home town → After …

a) *Explain what the poem says about the Romans and what they did in Britain.*

The Romans in Britain
(A history in 40 words)
by Judith Nicholls

The Romans gave us aqueducts
fine buildings and straight[1] roads,
where all those Roman
legionaries
marched with heavy loads[2].

They gave us central heating[3],
good laws[4], a peaceful[5] home …
Then after just four centuries
they shuffled back to Rome.

Useful phrases

to build (a bridge, a road, a town) | to supply somebody (with water, food) | to rule (a country)

b) *Think of how you could complete this little poem about Britain.*

Great Britain is an island.
It is in the North …
It's got green fields and mountains.
It's where I'd like to …

The biggest city is …
It's got a lot to show.
There's always something happening.
It's where I'd like to…

1 **straight** [streɪt] gerade | 2 **heavy load** [ˌhevi ˈləʊd] schwere Last | 3 **central heating** [ˌsentrl ˈhiːtɪŋ] Zentralheizung | 4 **law** [lɔː] hier: Gesetz | 5 **peaceful** [ˈpiːsfl] friedlich

Our big British Isles quiz

You're going to work in four groups. You're going to make question cards for a quiz about the British Isles (Wales, England, etc.). You can use information in this book and from other sources. When you're finished, you'll be able to play a quiz game.

/17 Before you start
ng out information)
/18 Pictures of places
ts)

Step 1

Get organised

→ WB 8/17–18

Make four groups of 4–6, one for a different part of the British Isles. In your group, agree on 16 interesting sights or places in your region. Each of you makes 2–4 question cards so you have one for each sight in the end.

Step 2

Prepare your cards

Make cards that look like this on the back. But don't finish them until you've done Step 3.

(A question about the sight / place / thing)
Which of these animals never lived at the Tower?

(Three answers, two of which are wrong)

a) a polar bear that loved to fish;
b) a raven that was able to talk;
c) a zebra that liked beer

(The right answer)

Step 3

WB 9/19 Example cards (multiple choice)

Test your cards

→ WB 9/19

a) *Show a picture of the sight / place / thing you want to use for the front of your card. Read the question and the three answers. The others guess which answer is right. Correct them if they're wrong. You can give tips to help them.*

b) *Are the questions, answers and tips OK? If a quiz question is too difficult, make changes or give more tips.*

c) *Now make your cards.*

Useful phrases

Ideas for tips:

In this place you can …
It's famous for …
One of the attractions here is …
If you want to …, you will … here.
If you're interested in history, you should …
It's in the north / east / south / west.
… built it.

Step 4

WB 9/20 Speaking (questions)

Play the quiz game in your groups

→ WB 9/20

- *Shuffle the 16 cards for your group and place them on a table face down.*
- *Each group draws four cards from each group.*
- *In each group, shuffle all the cards again.*
- *Every player draws the same number of cards. One player starts and uses a card for the person next to him / her. If the person gets the answer right, he / she can keep the card.*
- *When you've used all the cards once, the person with the most cards wins!*

polar bear [ˈpəʊlə ˌbeə] Eisbär | **to fish** [fɪʃ] Fische fangen | **zebra** [ˈzebrə] | **beer** [bɪə] Bier

S1/4–8 L1/12–16

Things will get better

A Come in, come in!" Mrs Preston said from the hall of the big old house by the sea. "I'll make some tea."

"We can't have tea, Mum," Dave said. "There's no electricity, remember?"

"Oh, yes," she answered. "Well, a glass of water then?"

"Er … OK, yes please, Mrs Preston," Olivia said.

"Hi," Dave said to his friends and his granny. "Thanks for coming. Good journey?"

"Yeah, the journey was fine, thanks," Luke answered. "But *you* don't look fine. What's the matter? Is everything OK?"

"No, not really," Dave said. "We've been here a week, and there's no electricity yet. Dad is in London, the cat has run away, I haven't got any friends and I'm really missing my old life in Greenwich. It's awful here. I hate it."

"Oh, Dave!" Granny Rose said. "Don't be sad. You've only been here a week. Things will get better. You know they will."

B "Here are your glasses of water," Mrs Preston said. Then she looked at one of the glasses. "Oh dear," she said "Why is this water brown? I think we've got a problem with the water now too."

"Let's go out," Dave said to his friends. "We'll go up to the coastal path, to the old mine. Is that OK, Mum?"

"Yes, that's fine," Dave's mum answered. "See you later. I'll call a plumber."

"But it's Sunday," Granny Rose said. "If you call a plumber on a Sunday, it'll be *really* expensive."

C The friends were standing on a hill by an old building. It had a tall chimney, but no roof. There was a strong wind from the sea, and it brought lots of big black clouds.

"This old building looks a bit scary," Holly whispered.

"Don't be silly. It's just one of many old mine buildings in this area. Tin was really important here," Olivia said. "Going right back to Celtic times. Tin from Cornwall went all over the world. But now there's almost no tin left."

"Looks like a great place for geocaching!" Luke said excitedly as he grabbed his smartphone. "Let's see if there's a cache somewhere near here. – Yes, there must be a difficult puzzle cache."

"Really?" Dave asked, "Let's solve the puzzle and get to that cache!"

Suddenly a deep voice behind them boomed, "Hey you, what are you doing here?! Keep away from MY treasure!"

The friends were scared. They turned around and saw a big man with a serious face. He was wearing a kind of skirt and trousers. He had wild hair and looked dangerous, not only because of the long spear in his hand.

"I'm sorry, we – we didn't want to steal anything from you. We didn't know the cache was yours," Dave said. He was really scared.

Suddenly the sun came out again and the man's face went from scary to much friendlier.

"Hello!" he said to Dave. "I was only joking. Have you just moved into number 7?"

"Er, yes," Dave said. "And you are a Celtic warrior?"

"I'm Bob," the man said. "Your new neighbour."

"Ah," Dave said. "So you're on your way to a fancy dress party, aren't you?"

The others just looked at Bob's strange clothes and said nothing.

"Oh, don't worry!" Bob laughed. "I don't always wear these clothes. I'm in the local history society. We do shows about the history of Cornwall. These are clothes from Celtic times."

"Right," Dave said. "Nice to meet you."

"I just came up to say hello," Bob said. "Tea at my house anyone?"

D "This is my wife, Helen," Bob said.

The friends were standing in the kitchen of Bob's house. "And these are my children, Jago and Tamara." The boy and girl were both about 13. "Good old Cornish names."

"Hello Dave. I'm Jago," the boy said.

"We're twins," the girl said. "Do you like computers, Dave?"

"Not now, Tamara," Bob said. "I'm sure Dave doesn't want to hear about your new computer games."

Then Olivia saw a big bag of tools on the kitchen floor.

"What do you do, Mr … er …?

"Call me Bob. I'm a plumber. And Helen here's an electrician. We do the plumbing and electrics for half the village. Well, the *whole* village, really."

Then Bob's bag of tools moved. A cat came out of it.

"That's the cat that moved in here last week," Bob said.

"Sid!" Dave shouted. "There you are!"

E An hour later, there were thirteen people and a cat in Dave's garden. The friends, Bob and his family, Granny Rose and Dave's parents were all sitting around a big garden table. There was tea and a cake.

"We were on the train before you," Granny Rose said to Dave's dad. "I didn't know you were coming today."

"Change of plan at work," Dave's dad said. "I can be here all this week."

"Thanks again for fixing the water," Dave's mum said to Bob. "Are you sure I can't pay you for …"

"No, no," Bob said. "It was a five-minute job, and we're neighbours. But I'll have another piece of Rose's cake, if that's OK."

"And I'll have a look at your electrics tomorrow morning," Helen added.

Dave turned to Luke. "I think it'll be OK here after all," he said.

KV 11: Writing (visit in Cornwall)
WB 10/21 Reading (correct order/multiple choice)

READING → S5-8

S5–8 Reading

1 Understanding the text → WB 10/21

a) *Find headings for parts A–E of the story.*

b) *Answer these questions.*

Voc.: More jobs, p. 175

1. What problems do the Prestons have in their new home?
2. What do the friends think of Bob at first? What do we get to know about him?
3. Think of what Granny Rose said at the end of part A. At the end of the story, was she right? Explain.

SPEAKING

2 Help for Dave

Talk about what everyone can do to make Dave happier in his new home.

Example: Tamara and Jago can play computer games with him.

KV 12a+b: Creative writing (diary entry/postcard)
WB 10/22 Writing/Speaking (options)

WRITING → S11-14

S11–14 Writing

3 Creative writing → WB 10/22

a) *Write a diary entry for one of the characters about what happened on their first day in Cornwall and what he/she felt.*

b) *Write a postcard from one of Dave's friends to his/her parents at home.*

Writing skills

A **diary entry** is a very personal text. Usually nobody else reads it. It's like writing to a close friend. Put the date at the top and start writing about what happened, what was important and how you feel about it. You can also write about your hopes and plans for the future.

Dear Mum and Dad,

How are you? We arrived in St Agnes yesterday. There is a beautiful harbour with nice sailboats, and we're camping really close to the sea. The weather is great,
and we've spent a lot of time at the beach.

See you soon,

Megan

The caves → S22–24 S22–24 Film skills/Viewing

SPEAKING **1** **Things to do in the country**

→ △ 114/9

Things to do in the
try
Help with ...

Talk about which of these activities are interesting for you.

1. feeding animals
2. milking cows
3. exploring a cave
4. swimming in a lake
5. playing in an adventure playground
6. reading ghost stories
7. walking
8. geocaching

VIEWING **2** **Themes** → WB 11/23 KV 13: Viewing (film stills) WB 11/23 Vocabulary (matching)

DVD 2/12

Watch the film. Then say which themes below play a role in the film. Explain why / why not. Which of them are more important / the most important?

1. food
2. city and country life
3. school
4. children and adults
5. stories
6. sports
7. love
8. ghosts

Lösung: *Doesn't play a role:* 3. school; ***Not really important:*** 1. food, 6. sports, 7. love; ***Important:*** 2. city and country life, 4. children and adults, 8. ghosts; ***Very important:*** 5. stories

VIEWING **3** **Suspense: What's going to happen?** KV 14: Viewing (suspense)

Watch the film again, find examples of the ideas below and take notes. They can help you to talk about elements that create suspense in a story.

Story: What about ...
- *Laura's grandpa?*
- *ghosts?*
- *getting lost?*
- *phones, maps and torches?*

Acting: What about ...
- *people's faces?*

Audiovisual effects: What about ...
- *darkness?*
- *strange sounds, a voice in the caves?*
- *dramatic music?*

Film skills

Elements that create suspense:
- clues in the story about what could happen
- acting
- music
- light
- sounds

WRITING **4** **Laura and her grandpa**

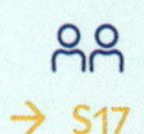

→ S17

Write a scene that comes after the last scene in the film: Laura and her grandpa talk about what has really happened and why. Act it and film it.

aking
chene Sprache)

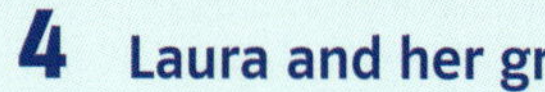

KV 15: Vocabulary (Unit 1)
WB 11/24 Across cultures (Celtic languages)

<Revision A> ist fakultativ und dient der Festigung/Wiederholung. Es werden keine neuen Sprachmittel eingeführt.

VOCABULARY

1 Offline for a month

KV 16a+b: Test yourself
KV 17–19: Speaking cards

a) *Sally is a 14-year old blogger from London. Last month she was offline for four weeks. Read about her experience. Fill in the gaps. Put the verbs in the right tense.*

to spend | to send | face-to-face | to post | to download | to stay in touch | to watch | offline | social networks | to see | challenge | phone | media mad | to get

Lösung: a) 1. *media mad* 2. *spend* 3. *offline* 4. *stay in touch* 5. *social networks* 6. *sent* 7. *phone* 8. *posted* 9. *see* 10. *watched* 11. *downloaded* 12. *got* 13. *face-to-face* 14. *challenge*

SALLY'S BLOG

MY MONTH OFFLINE – A REAL CHALLENGE!

I'm 1 ! I use the computer and the internet *very* often. I've got a smartphone, a tablet and a laptop – yes, I 2 a lot of time online. "When I was young we didn't have all those things," my Aunt Elizabeth told me one day. "I bet you can't live for a week 3 ." "Ha," I said. "Of course I can. I can even do it for a month! You'll see!"

Well, that's how it started. I wasn't able to 4 with my friends on my phone or on 5 for four weeks. When my friends met in town they 6 me texts but I wasn't able to read them because I didn't have my 7 anymore. They 8 photos I wasn't able to 9 , and when they 10 videos or 11 new music and then talked about how great it all was, I didn't know what they were talking about. And once, my friend Anne forgot that I was offline. At school, she asked me angrily, "Why didn't you come to my party?!" "*What* party?" I replied. "My birthday party!" Anne answered. Oops, I never 12 her invitation! So that wasn't so great.

But I also discovered that I had more time for other things when I was offline. I read more books, I did more sports and I talked to people 13 more often. But now I'm happy to be online again and tell you about this experience. Try it. It's a real 14 !

b) *Would you be able to stay offline for a month? Say why/why not.*

MEDIATION

2 A new computer game

Your little brother has a new computer game, but the instructions are in English and he doesn't understand everything. Explain the game to him. (Remember: In mediation, you don't need to know every word when you explain something; just the main ideas!)

Welcome to **Jungle World**, where Jolly Joe and his monkey friends swing from tree to tree and try to grab as much fruit as they can! But they have to be careful – the jungle is a dangerous place full of wild animals who want the fruit *and* you! Choose which monkey you want to be and give him/her a name. Then start your adventure through the jungle. With S-P-A-C-E your monkey jumps. Press ← → if you want to move left or right and press ↑ ↓ to go up or down. Try to grab as much fruit as you can – the more you get, the more points you get! You find different kinds of small fruit in the trees – but watch out: There are snakes in the trees too! The fruit on the ground is bigger, but be careful there too: Before you can grab some fruit, a tiger or lion could grab *you*! Enjoy **Jungle World**.

WRITING

3 A postcard from …

Have a look at the material you collected for the Task in Unit 6. Imagine you've been to one of the places. Write a postcard to your friend / your grandma / … . Tell them …

- what you did
- what the weather was like
- anything special about the place where you are (landscape, sights, events, etc.)

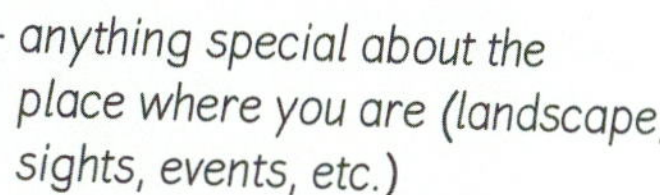

- anything strange / interesting / exciting that happened to you
- any special food you ate

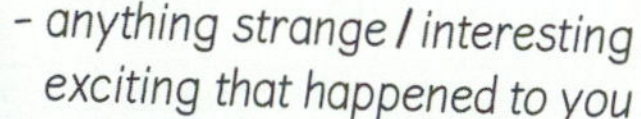

ISTENING

4 Travelling around the world: Announcements

L1/17

a) *Listen to five announcements and say where the people are. Which words helped you to find out about where they are?*

b) *Listen again. Who is the announcement important for? What is the most important information for these people?*

Transfer

c) *Your turn: Write your own announcement and read it to your partner. Your partner has to guess where you are.*

Lösung: a) 1. *at a train station (delayed; platform; tickets)*; 2. *in an airport terminal (boarding call; British Airlines; gate; captain; aircraft)*; 3. *on a ferry (captain; on board; ferry; cruise; knots)*; 4. *on the Tube (station; Bond Street; change; Jubilee Line; Central Line train; mind the gap; train; platform)*; 5. *in a train station (information desk; entrance hall; train station)*

WRITING

5 The world 50 years from now

In a short text, make predictions about the future. What will life be like 50 (or 100, 200) years from now? Use the ***will*** *future in your text, and think of these ideas:*

how people will live / travel | what people will eat / drink | what school / nature / technology will be like | how people will communicate with each other

forest skyscrapers to live in

robots for cleaning the house

British stories and legends

Every country has special places where famous historical people lived or important events happened. When we don't know all the facts, we like to hear strange and wonderful stories about them. But how much is really true?

SPEAKING

1 Warm-up

Talk about famous historical people you know about in your country or in Britain.

READING

2 Typical ingredients of legends

Folie 2/38: Wortschatzvorentlastung und Bildbeschreibung

a) *Read the text. Which ingredients do you like in a story or legend? Why?*

Legends are stories about people in history – but usually they aren't completely true. Often, writers have taken historical events and changed them a bit to make the stories more exciting, or maybe to show the difference between right and wrong more clearly. Legends have colourful characters like brave kings and cruel queens, or magical characters like wizards. There are heroes ('good guys') and villains ('bad guys') who have dangerous fights – of course, the good guy usually wins! Popular heroes are often brave knights, but sometimes they're just normal men who do brave things to help other people. Villains can be dangerous criminals or very powerful people who use their power in a bad way. And finally, there are more modern legends from popular books, like Sherlock Holmes, a private detective who solved mysterious crimes. He never lived at all, but people all over the world love to think he did!

b) *Look at the stills of Jinsoo and Marley. They're playing the roles of three famous British legends. What do you think the stories are about? What do you know about them?*

Word bank

Nouns: king | queen | wizard | hero / heroine | villain | knight | robber | outlaw

Adjectives: colourful | magical | brave | cruel | dangerous | powerful | mysterious

Phrases: to have a fight | to hide in the forest | to use your power | to solve a crime

VIEWING **3**

Stories and legends (1)

KV 20: Activity (card game)

DVD 2/13 

ng: b) 1a), d), g); 2c), 3b), e)

a) *Watch the film and take notes about the three legends.*

b) *Match the sentence parts. Find the correct statements for each character.*

1. Sherlock Holmes was a private detective.
2. Robin Hood was a famous outlaw.
3. King Arthur was a powerful king.

a) Dr Watson was his assistant.
b) Many people think Tintagel was his castle.
c) He lived in Sherwood Forest, near Nottingham.
d) He lived in Baker Street in London.
e) His knights sat at the Round Table.
f) He loved Maid Marian.
g) He solved many mysterious crimes.
h) He stole from the rich and gave to the poor.

KV 21: Role play (useful phrases)
WB 13/1 Vocabulary (word puzzle)
WB 13/2 Speaking (famous characters)

VIEWING **4**

Stories and legends (2)

→ WB 13/1–2

g: a) *Sherlock* *s: typical outfit:* *nd cap, magnifying* *Robin Hood: green* *th a feather, green* *ow and arrow;* *rthur: crown*

a) *Watch the film again. Which characters have which props?*

bell | castle | bow and arrow[1] | gloves | cape[2] | crown[3] | lucky charm | magnifying glass[4] | cap[5]

b) *Your turn: Read the skills box. Then find out about another character from a legend or story, maybe a woman (like Boudicca, a Celtic queen who fought against the Romans; Vivien, the Lady[6] of the Lake who gave King Arthur his sword[7] Excalibur; or Miss Marple, a detective in Agatha Christie's crime stories.) Which costume, props or set could you give that character in a film? Why?*

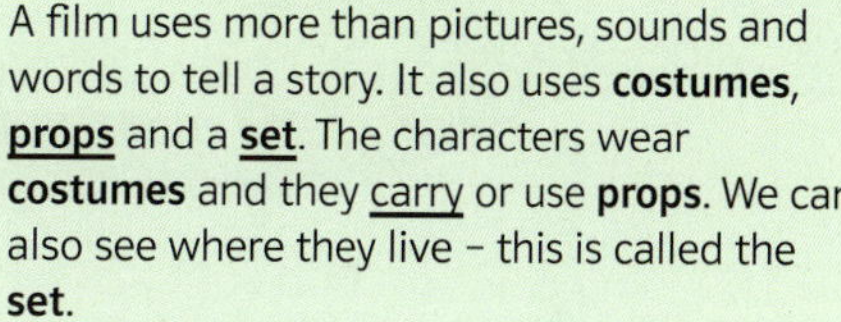

Film skills

A film uses more than pictures, sounds and words to tell a story. It also uses **costumes**, **props** and a **set**. The characters wear **costumes** and they carry or use **props**. We can also see where they live – this is called the **set**.

Example:
If you want to show that a woman is a queen, she can wear a crown and beautiful clothes and live in a castle.

c) *Role play: In groups of three, each of you chooses to be one of the characters. Your characters meet. Talk to each other about*

1. where you live
2. what you do
3. what you wear and carry
4. what's good and bad about your life.

Example:
A: Hi there. I'm Robin, I help the poor.
B: And I'm Miss Marple. I love to solve mysterious crimes.
C: …

1 **bow and arrow** [ˌbəʊ‿ən‿ˈærəʊ] Pfeil und Bogen | 2 **cape** [keɪp] Umhang | 3 **crown** [kraʊn] Krone | 4 **magnifying glass** [ˈmægnɪfaɪŋ ˌglɑːs] Lupe | 5 **cap** [kæp] Kappe; Mütze | 6 **lady** [ˈleɪdi] Herrin; Dame | 7 **sword** [sɔːd] Schwert

Unit 2

Find your place

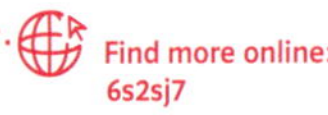

SPEAKING

1 Everyone is different

Folie 3/1: Thematische Einstimmung/Bildbeschreibung

a) *Look at the photos above. What do you think the different people are thinking? Say why.*

b) *Now look at the photos again and the sayings below. Say which ones match, and why. What's the main idea behind each saying?*

Across cultures

"Practice makes perfect" or "You can't judge a book by its cover" are examples of **popular English sayings**. Are there any sayings in German which describe the ideas and pictures on this page? Which ones?

Voc.: Musical instruments, Tools, WB (Word bank), pp. 11–12

- You can't judge a book by its cover.
- Everyone is good at something.
- Practice makes perfect.
- Life is a competition!
- I don't care if I'm in or out, as long as I've got my friends.
- It doesn't matter if you win or lose, but how you play the game.
- You'll never know until you try.
- Don't follow the crowd.

Transfer

HA

c) *Your turn: Do any of the sayings above match your personality? Or do other ones describe you better? Write down your ideas in 8–10 sentences.*

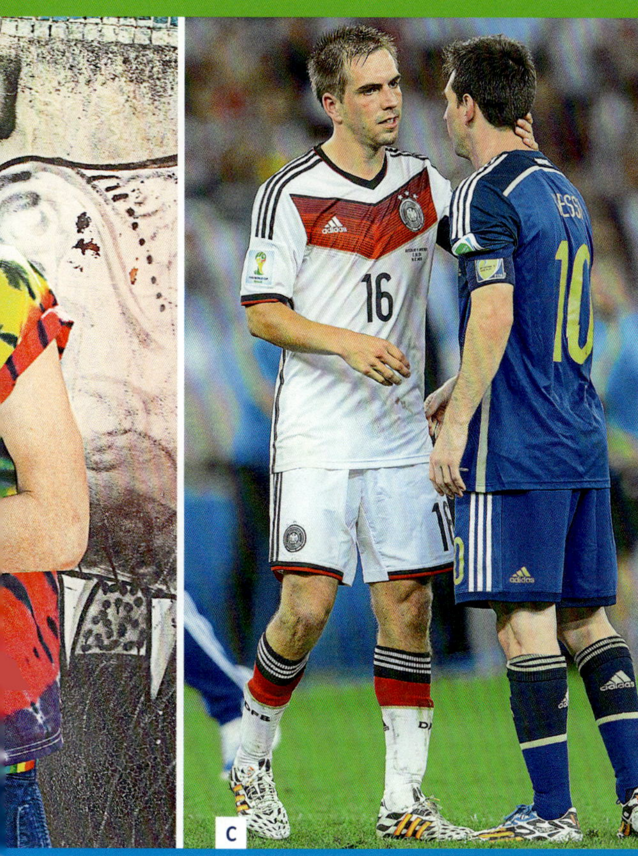

In Unit 2 you learn

… how to talk about what you and other people would do in different situations. You learn:

- vocabulary for talking about different interests and personalities
- conditional clauses type 2
- the language for agreeing, disagreeing and compromising

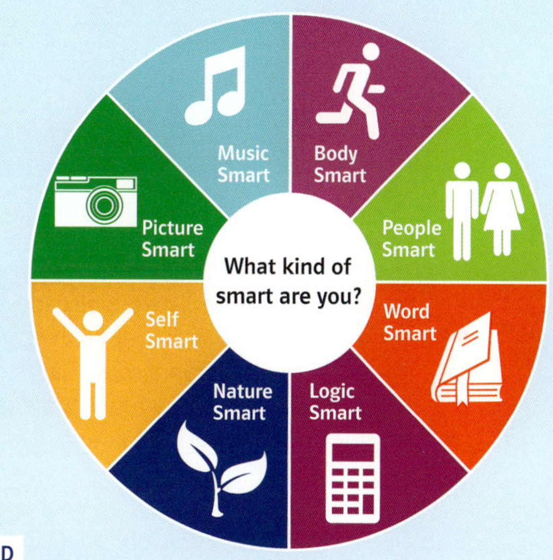

Folie 3/2: Vorentlastung des Hörverstehens
KV 22: A radio call-in
WB 14/1: Vocabulary (gapped text)

STENING  **2** **A radio call-in** → WB 14/1

a) *Before you listen, look at the diagram above. What do you think a 'body smart' person could be good at? And the other seven kinds of 'smart'? Talk about your ideas in class. The phrases in the box can help you.*

L 1/18–20

b) *Now listen to a radio call-in. What's the subject today? Who are the callers?*

→ S19–21
S19–21 Listening

c) *Listen again. What do the callers say about these things?*

their talents / what they're good at | their doubts about themselves | things they've learned about themselves

Useful phrases

Someone who is body smart / picture smart / music smart / logic smart / …
… is good with his / her hands / body / imagination / …
… is good at doing / showing / using / creating / explaining / teaching / …
… knows how to use … / play … / talk … / communicate / compete / …
… is creative / imaginative / confident / …
… likes to … / needs to … / feels … / understands … / …
A … smart person would probably be a good teacher / doctor / …

WB 14/2 Vocabulary (prepositions)

EAKING   **3** **Your turn: Your kind of 'smart'** → WB 14/2

ansfer

*With a partner, talk about what kind of smart **you** both are. Use the vocabulary on these pages for ideas.*

→ 115/1

ur turn:
d of 'smart'
p with …

G2 Revision: Conditional clauses type 1
G3 Conditional clauses type 2

L 1/21

They wouldn't worry if they didn't care!

Jay: Hey, look at this. A boy left school at 15 and became a millionaire!

Shahid: His family were already rich, right?

Jay: No, it says that he lived with his mother in a small flat.

Shahid: Well, only a few people get that kind of success so young. Everyone would be a millionaire if it was so easy. But it isn't.

Jay: Well, I wouldn't feel so stressed out if I had a million pounds.

Shahid: Why, what's the matter?

Jay: I got an e-mail today. I didn't get the lead part in that dance show. "You can be a backing dancer," they told me. But I want to be the *lead* dancer!

Shahid: Jay, relax. Your big chance will come. Anyway, you know you can't leave school until you're 18. If you just dropped out now, you wouldn't have any choices later.

Jay: But I want to be rich and famous.

Shahid: As what? Money doesn't just grow on trees. You have to *work* for it.

Jay: As a dancer or a singer! If Mum and Dad believed in my talent, they wouldn't tell me to do my homework all the time. But they don't believe in me. They always compare me with perfect Olivia, who gets perfect marks. Aarrgh!

Shahid: They're sure you'll get a good job one day if you get better marks now. They wouldn't worry if they didn't care. And you *are* a bit laid-back.

Jay: That's easy for you to say! Look, here's your picture on a magazine again! You make easy money as a model just because you look good. If I didn't have to go to school, I'd go to London and be a model too!

Shahid: But I do modelling just for fun! I'd be stupid if I just relied on my looks, so that's why I'm studying for a career in IT. If I make the right plans now, I'll have more choices later. And if *you* make the right choices, you'll find your place too.

READING

1 Jay and Shahid: Plans and dreams → WB 15/3

WB 15/3 Listening (multiple choice)

a) *What are Jay's plans for the future? And Shahid's?*

b) *Say what Jay's different problems are. The words on the right can help you with your answers.*

c) *What advice do you have for Jay? Discuss your ideas with a partner.*

- compares himself with …
- wants to be / have …
- can't wait to be / have …
- his parents always …

WB 15/3 Listening (multiple choice)
WB 15/4 Language (conditional clauses 1)

LANGUAGE

2 Revision: Conditional clauses type 1 → WB 15/3–4 → G2

→ △ 115/2

Maybe in the … how … After …

g: a) 2. … I'll have more … or my business ideas. … I'll go back to school. … won't know how young … 5. … live at home for … first years. 6. …, I'll win … 's and be rich. 7. … sell … business.

a) *Read the news report about David Karp. What were David's thoughts at the different times before and during his career? Finish his sentences and make* ***conditional clauses type 1****.*

Tumblr founder **David Karp** has just sold his New York business to Yahoo for $1.1 billion. He began learning HTML at the age of 11 and was soon designing websites for businesses. "I always used a deep voice when I was on the phone so people didn't know how young I was!" he says. Karp dropped out of school at the age of 15 and developed Tumblr, the social network company, in the bedroom of his mother's small flat. In 2009, the magazine BusinessWeek named Karp 'Best Young Tech Entrepreneur'.

Example: **1.** I'll be able to design websites for businesses if I **learn HTML**.

go back to school | not know how young I am | learn HTML ✔ | sell my business | have more time for my business ideas | live at home for the first years | win awards and be rich

1. I'll be able to design websites for businesses if I …
2. If I drop out of school, …
3. But if I don't succeed, …
4. If I use a deep voice on the phone, people …
5. I'll save money if I …
6. If my business is a big success, …
7. I'll have more than a billion dollars if I …

HA

b) *Give more information about David with* ***conditional clauses type 1****. Be creative!*

KV 23a+b: Working with language

LANGUAGE 

3 Find the rule: Conditional clauses type 2 → G3

a) *Now go back to the text about Jay and Shahid. Make sentences from the text.*

 a) 2a), 3b), 4e), 5f), 6c)

1. If you dropped out now,
2. If it was so easy,
3. I'd be a model too
4. If they didn't care,
5. I wouldn't be so stressed out
6. I'd be stupid

a) everyone would be a millionaire.
b) if I didn't have to go to school.
c) if I just relied on my looks.
d) you wouldn't have any choices later.
e) they wouldn't worry.
f) if I had a million pounds.

b) *Look at the sentences in a). What verb forms do you need in the* ***if-clause*** *and the* ***main clause****?*

c) *Now you know two types of* ***conditional clauses****. Look at the examples below. What's the difference in meaning between* ***conditional clauses type 1*** *and* ***type 2****?*

Type 1: If I **practise** a lot, I **will be** a better dancer. So come on, let's start now!
Type 2: If I **practised** more often, I **would get** better parts in dance shows. But I never find time to practise enough!

WB 15/5 Language (conditional clauses 1 or 2)
WB 16/6 Language (conditional clauses 1 or 2)

LANGUAGE

4 Chatroom posts: What would *you* do in Jay's shoes? → WB 15/5, 16/6

→ △ 115/3
→ ▲ 116/4

a) *In a chatroom, Jay has asked other young people for their advice about his problems. Read their advice for him. Put the verbs in the right form:* ***simple past*** *or* ***would / wouldn't*** *+* ***infinitive.***

calum13_leedsboy September 4, 20:05
If I **1** (be) you, I **2** (not be) sad about the backing part. I **3** (be) happy if I **4** (have) a backing part in a dance show, but I never get ANY parts!

koolkatie14_cardiff September 4, 20:08
You **5** (not feel) so stressed out if you **6** (not think) about your brother and his modelling job so much. But it sounds like you think about it A LOT!

jjm_uk14 September 4, 20:50
It sounds like you want to give up just because you didn't get the lead part this time. But you're only 13! If every dancer **7** (give up) so quickly, nobody **8** (ever become) a star!

skater4ever15 September 4, 21:14
It sounds like your parents don't know how good you are. If they **9** (know) about your talent, maybe they **10** (find) a way for you to have time for school AND for practising. So SHOW them!

→ △ 116/5

b) *In a group, think about different problems. Then think about what kind of advice you would give in a chatroom for the different problems. Use* ***conditional clauses type 2.***

Examples:
- If my best friend **told** others all my secrets, she **wouldn't be** a friend any more!
- If I **were** you, I **wouldn't worry** about how rich my friends are. Are they friends because you like them or because they have money?

115/3 Another chat comment for Jay
△→ After …
116/4 What would an adult say?
▲→ After …
116/5 Your friends need you!
△→ Help with …

Voc.: Continents, Countries, WB (Word bank), pp. 7–8

Lösung: a) *1. were 2. wouldn't be 3. would ('d) be 4. had 5. wouldn't feel 6. didn't think 7. gave up 8. would ever become 9. knew 10. would ('d) find*

WB 16/7 Writing (If I were …)
KV 24: What would you do if …?

LANGUAGE

5 A successful young fashion designer → WB 16/7

→ △ 116/6
→ ▲ 116/7

Ivy Francis is only 19 and has already become a rich and successful fashion designer. How would her life be different if she wasn't rich and successful? Make ***conditional clauses type 2.***

Example: **1.** If I **didn't get** so nervous before big shows, **I'd sleep** better.

116/6 A model who works for Ivy
△→ After …
116/7 What would you do if
▲→ After …

| not travel so often | know who liked me for me and not for my money | sleep better ✔ | not make a lot of money | not be famous | have more time for sports | not get to know lots of great places |

1. If I didn't get so nervous before big shows, …
2. My team and I would have more time for family and friends if …
3. But if I didn't travel so often, …
4. If I didn't work so hard, …
5. People wouldn't say hello to me if …
6. I couldn't buy what I wanted if …
7. If I didn't have a lot of money, …

Lösung: *2. … we didn't travel so often. 3. … I wouldn't get to know lots of great places. 4. … I would ('d) have more time for sports. 5. … I wasn't/weren'tfamous. 6. … I didn't make a lot of money. 7. … I would ('d) know who liked me for me and not for my money.*

EDIATION

6 A German talent show

→ △ 117/8
→ ▲ 117/9
→ S18

ediation
A German talent show
łelp with …
More helpful tips for
nglish friend
after …

You've made an English friend on a social network. She's going to take part in a talent show on German TV, but the information she's received for her audition is in German. You can help her: Send her a short message in English with the main points.

Sing dich zum Star!

- Wähle einen Song aus und bereite ihn gut vor. Achtung: Wenn du einen sehr bekannten Song auswählst, musst du auch sehr gut sein! Die Jurymitglieder hören solche Songs ständig. Du wirst einen besseren Eindruck machen, wenn du einen Song auswählst, der nicht in der aktuellen Hitparade ist.
- Wenn du viel übst, hast du schon viel gewonnen. Denn stell dir vor: Wenn du an deinem großen Tag auf der Bühne stehen und den Songtext vergessen würdest, würdest du dich ganz schön blamieren.
- Bitte denke auch an dein Äußeres. Du möchtest einen guten ersten Eindruck machen!
- Wenn du unter 18 bist, muss eine erwachsene Begleitperson dabei sein.

STENING

7 < A song: Holiday > Madonna

L1/23

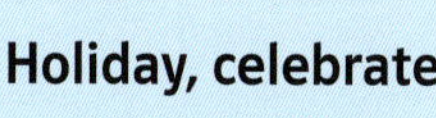

Holiday, celebrate

If we took a holiday
Took some time to celebrate
Just one day out of life
It would be, it would be so nice

Everybody spread the word
We're gonna have a celebration
All across the world
In every nation

It's time for the good times
Forget about the bad times
One day to come together,
to release the pressure
We need a holiday

If we took a holiday
Took some time to celebrate
(Come on, let's celebrate)
Just one day out of life
It would be, it would be so nice

ansfer
A

a) *How would Jay celebrate if he took a holiday for one day? Finish this sentence for him:*
Jay: If I took a holiday for one day, I'd …

b) *Your turn: What would be a special holiday for **you**? Finish the sentence in a) for yourself.*

WB 17/8 Vocabulary (crossword puzzle)
WB 17/9 Speaking (questions with if)

RITING 

8 Your turn: If I … → WB 17/8–9

ansfer

*Finish the sentences on the right and add information about how **you** would feel.*

If I were more competitive, … | If I were better at … | If everybody followed the crowd, … | If I had more time for … | If I knew how to … | If my friends were …

G4 Reflexive pronouns and each other

L1/24 ◎

You have to push yourself!

Folie 3/3: Bildbeschreibung, Vorentlastung des Hörverstehens

Olivia: Lucy, tidy your messy room!
Claire: Don't be so bossy, Olivia.
Lucy: I feel tired, Mum.
Olivia: You *always* feel tired. That's why you never tidy your room or do *anything*. When was the last time you practised your recorder?
Lucy: Er, I can't remember.
Olivia: Exactly! You never practise.
Claire: Olivia, relax. She's only seven – she needs to have some fun. You should do the same! You study so often and have so many activities. Do you ever really enjoy yourself? – Er, Olivia, are you listening to me? I'm talking to you but I feel like I'm talking to myself.
Olivia: Of course I'm listening, Claire. But isn't this about Lucy?
Lucy: I don't like the recorder any more and I can't decide on a new hobby.
Claire: Oh, you don't have to decide now.
Olivia: Well, I taught myself how to play the sax when I was five! Nobody taught me. If you want to be good at something, you have to push yourself!
Claire: (*doorbell*) Oh, saved by the bell! – Girls, go and see who it is.
Olivia: Oh, hi Shahid.
Shahid: Hey Olivia – er, are you feeling OK? Why are you and Lucy giving each other funny looks?
Claire: Hi Shahid, come in. I hope the girls can behave themselves for two minutes. At the moment, they fight whenever they see each other. If they saw themselves like that, they'd be embarrassed! – Anyway, you're here to see Desmond, right?
Shahid: Yeah. I need a web designer's opinion on a few things.
Claire: Girls, go and get your dad, OK?
Shahid: (*pause*) So, what's up with Olivia?
Claire: Well, I was just telling her that she's too serious. She needs to enjoy herself more.
Shahid: Wow! If Jay heard you say that, he'd be so jealous! Our parents would love it if Jay had Olivia's perfect marks. They always tell him, "Olivia will be a doctor one day!" But that's just not Jay. He can't wait to be a singer or dancer!
Claire: Yes … and Olivia has her own personality too. Hm, if she wasn't so busy and in charge of things, she wouldn't be Olivia, would she?

READING  **9**

Compare two families: the Azads and the Frasers

→ △ 117/10
→ S5–6

a) *Make a grid with columns for Olivia, Claire, Lucy, Jay and Jay's parents. Write down key words about the different people's personalities, opinions, problems. Then compare the two families. How are they the same? How are they different?*

→ △ 117/11

b) *What do you think about Olivia and her personality? How would you react in her shoes?*

HA
→ S11–14

c) *Imagine you're Olivia. Write a diary entry about how she feels about Claire and Lucy.*

S5–6 Reading **S11–14** Writing
117/10 The Azads and the Frasers △→ Help with …
117/11 If I were Olivia, I'd … △→ Help with …

WB 18/10 Listening (matching)
WB 18/11 Language (photo shoot)
KV 25: Working with language

LANGUAGE

10 Find the rule: Reflexive pronouns → WB 18/10–11 → G4

a) *Look at the pictures. Say why one sentence needs* **me** *and the other* **myself**. *Write the rule for object pronouns (me, him, them, etc.) and reflexive pronouns (myself, ourselves, themselves, etc.).*

A ✗ "Nobody taught **me** to play the sax."

B ✓ "I taught **myself**."

→ △ 118/12
→ △ 118/13

What Olivia told Holly
Help with …
Help! I can't do it myself!
After …
Reflexive pronouns, p. 179

Lösung: b) 1. me 2. you 3. yourself 4. ourselves 5. her 6. herself 7. her 8. herself 9. ourselves 10. him 11. himself 12. us 13. you

b) *Read what Olivia and Holly say. Decide if you need* **me / you / him / her / it / us / them** *or a reflexive form with* **-self** *or* **-selves** *(herself, themselves, etc.).*

Olivia: Claire was a bit hard on 1 today. But maybe I'm overreacting.
Holly: Why, what did she say to 2 ?
Olivia: Things like, "Don't be so bossy with Lucy" or "You never enjoy 3 ".
Holly: What?! You and I always enjoy 4 ! – But what about Lucy, what's the problem?
Olivia: I worry about 5 . She's got such a messy room and she'll hurt 6 with her stuff everywhere. And Claire never pushes 7 to be better, so Lucy will have to push 8 more.
Holly: Well, Olivia – not *everybody* is like you. People are different.
Olivia: I know, I know. So I *am* bossy?
Holly: No, you're my best friend. Stay the way you are! – But tell me more.
Olivia: Oh, what Claire said to Shahid was *really* embarrassing!
Holly: Why, what did she say?
Olivia: In Claire's opinion, Lucy and I don't behave 9 . That's what she told 10 ! I felt like a four-year-old in front of 'Mr Cool'! He was probably enjoying 11 and laughing at 12 .
Holly: No, Shahid is cool, he wouldn't laugh at 13 . You know how the Azads love you, Miss Perfect!
Olivia: Oh stop, you sound like Claire!

WB 19/12 Language (error spotting)
WB 19/13 Vocabulary (error spotting)
WB 20/14 Writing (dialogue)
WB 20/15 Mediation (dialogue)

LANGUAGE

11 *Themselves* or *each other*? → WB 19/12–13, 20/14–15 → G4

→ △ 118/14
→ ▲ 119/15

Themselves or each other …
After …
Each other? Themselves? What a difference!
After …

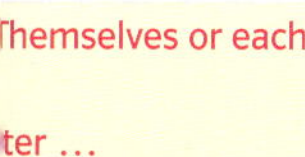

KV 4: Festigung von each other und themselves
Did you do it yourself?

a) *Look back at the sentences with* **each other** *and* **themselves** *in the text on p. 32 (lines 34–37). Now look at the pictures. Write a sentence for each picture with* **each other** *or* **themselves** *and with the verbs on the right.*

take
talk to
look at (2x)

1. The girls are …

2. The boys are …

3. They're …

4. The girls are …

b) *Now write your sentences in German. What's the rule?*

Lösung: a) 1. The girls are taking a picture of themselves. 2. The boys are looking at themselves. 3. They're talking to each other. 4. The girls are looking at themselves.

How to compromise

In the classroom, with friends, at home – it's normal to agree, to disagree and to try to find a compromise. This page can help you to practise typical discussion situations.

Yes, you've got a point. I've never thought about it like that. – OK, I've got an idea: Why don't we …

KV 27: Can we meet halfway?
WB 21/16 Skills (gapped conversation)
WB 21/17 Word smart (vocabulary grid)

1 The language of compromising → WB 21/16

Make a grid with the headings below. Then add the phrases in the box to your grid under the right heading:

Voc.: How to compromise, p. 180

- Asking for an opinion
- Making a suggestion
- Agreeing
- Disagreeing
- Finding a compromise

Useful phrases

Why don't we …? | I don't think that's a good idea. | Yes, we should do that. | Can we meet halfway? | How do you feel about …? | I've got an idea. Can we …? | You've got a point but … | No, I don't mind doing that. | What do you think about …? | I don't think we can do that. | If we did it this way, we could … | It would be better to …

2 Listening: Finding a compromise

KV 28 Listening: Finding a compromise

L1/26-27 → S19–21
S19–21 Listening

a) *Listen to this family as they try to agree about something. Then answer the questions:*

1. What does Matt want to do? 2. What problems do his parents have with the idea?
3. How does Matt feel misunderstood? 4. What compromise do they find?

b) *Listen again. Which phrases from Ex. 1 did they use? Make a list.*

c) *What do you think about the way the conversation ended? Who do you think is happiest about the decision?*

3 Role plays

KV 27: Can we meet halfway?

*In groups of three, choose **one** of the situations below. Write a discussion with phrases from Ex. 1 and decide which role each of you will play. Act out the conversation.*

→ △ 119/16
→ S17

1. You want a tattoo. Your parents disagree.
2. Your best friends don't agree with the guest list for *your* birthday party.
3. You have a great idea for a fun day with friends. But your friends have other ideas.
4. You've got a new hobby. Your friends think it's a bad idea.

119/16 Act it out!
△→ Help with …
S17 Mündliche Aufgaben und ihre Besonderheiten

Make a personality test!

You're going to design a personality test with ten questions to find out how competitive your classmates are. Before you start, look at the two example questions and the score below.

1. There's a cool new smartphone that everybody wants! If one of your friends got it first, would you
   a) ☐ not care? (1 point)
   b) ☐ be happy for him / her? (2 points)
   c) ☐ be angry because you didn't get it first? (3 points)

2. If your best friend won a swimming race (and you were second), would you
   a) ☐ give up swimming because now you know that it isn't the right thing for you? (1 point)
   b) ☐ say 'thanks' because he / she gave you the race of your life? (2 points)
   c) ☐ not talk to him / her any more? (3 points)

+++ **YOUR SCORE** +++

12 points or more: You seem to be competitive and like pushing yourself to be the best. That's a good thing, but it can take some of the fun out of life. Remember, if you always win, it means somebody else loses!

11 points or fewer: You always tell yourself, "It's only a game!" That's fine, but don't forget that it's sometimes good to compete and learn what your talents and limits are. Don't miss the chance to see what you're good at.

Step 1

WB 22/18 Mind maps

Collect ideas → WB 22/18

Get into groups of 3–4. Collect ideas about situations in which teenagers or young people are competitive. Think of the following topics:

family | gadgets | looks | school | sports / hobbies

Step 2

WB 22/19 Checklist and diary entry
WB 23/20 Answers to questions

Write and design your personality test → WB 22/19, 23/20

Look at the example questions again and the points for how competitive each answer is ('not very', 'a bit' or 'very'). Use your ideas from Step 1 to write ten questions for your questionnaire. If your group has different ideas, remember there are ways to find a compromise!
Maybe you can find good examples for personality tests in a magazine or on the internet to get ideas for the layout of your questionnaire.

→ if-clauses (pp. 28–31) → Compromising (p. 34)

Step 3

KV 29 Evaluate your group work
WB 23/21 Giving opinions

Take your personality test → WB 23/21

a) *Exchange tests with another group. Each of you takes the personality test. Compare your results in your group.*

b) *Should people take personality tests seriously? Discuss the question in your group.*

S1/11–17 L 1/28–34

Hang out with us instead!

KV 30: Hang out with us instead!

A Jay was bored and fed up. "Am I the only person in the world who just wants to have a bit of fun on a Saturday afternoon?" he thought to himself. He was feeling bad about an argument he had with Luke. They couldn't agree about anything these days, and now they weren't speaking at all. "What were we fighting about?" Jay couldn't even remember. "If Dave was here, he'd solve the problem in a moment," he thought. Dave was always able to find a compromise. But Dave now lived in Cornwall. For a moment, Jay thought about Holly, Olivia and Gwen. "Maybe we could do something together," he thought. But then he was sure he didn't need a 'girls day' today. Well, Jay wasn't allowed to go out anyway: He was in trouble with his parents for bad marks at school, and so he was grounded until next Friday. What a life!

"But I need to get out of this flat now!" he told himself. "My parents are out, so why not?" He felt a bit bad because they trusted him, but it made him crazy to stay at home all day. So he put on his trainers and left. "Freedom!" he shouted. He was already feeling much better.

B While Jay was walking towards the park, he thought about the next dance show – he was sure he could get the lead part next time. When Jay reached the park, he saw them.

Finn and Max. Two of the coolest boys at school. They were two years older and part of the in-crowd. They were sitting there on their skateboards, chilling out and looking cool and confident. They were laughing about something. "About me?" Jay hoped not. As he came closer, he felt a bit nervous, but he didn't need to: The boys were very friendly to him.

"Hey Jay!" said Finn, the blond boy. He was the in-crowd's 'boss'.

"He knows my name?!" Jay thought.

"Hey, what's going on?" asked Max.

Jay wasn't sure how to answer. *Nothing* was going on – that was the problem.

"We're going to go down to the high street for some coffee. Do you want to come with us and hang out?" Finn asked.

"Hanging out with the cool blokes. Luke will be so jealous!" he thought. But Jay tried to act cool and not show how excited he really felt. "Sure. I've got an hour before I need to be somewhere else," he told them.

C When they were all sitting down at the café, Jay started to relax a bit. Finn and Max were friendly and asked Jay a lot of questions. "I can't believe they're interested in me," he thought.

"Your brother is the model with the cool clothes, isn't he?" Finn asked.

"Yeah, that's him," Jay answered.

"All the girls think he looks great," Max added.

"I don't see it myself," Jay answered, and they all laughed. They chatted about films and video games and found they liked the same things. Soon Jay was telling them about his problems with Luke, and how he missed Dave. Finn and Max understood.

"Jay, you need some new friends," Finn said. "Your old friends are boring. Hang out with us instead!"

Stop and think:
What's going through Jay's head?

D "Your brother Shahid isn't just a model, he's a DJ too," Max said.

"Yeah," Finn added, "he's got some really cool mixes. We're planning a big party for next Saturday, for cool people."

"So," Max added, "would you be able to borrow Shahid's laptop? Just for the night?"

"He'll never lend it to me," Jay said.

"Hey Max, maybe you were right. Jay isn't cool enough for us," Finn said.

Not cool enough? Before he could stop himself, Jay said, "Wait! Er, Shahid is going to be away next Saturday. He's got an overnight modelling job in Manchester."

"Great! You can just borrow his laptop and he'll never know!" Max said.

"So come to our party with the laptop – but without your boring friends," Finn said.

"Well …," Jay didn't know what to say.

"Max wasn't sure about you, but I think you're cool. I'll give you my mobile number. Text me later if it's yes or no," Finn added.

Stop and think:

What would you do in Jay's shoes?

E Back home, Jay didn't know what to do. Were his old friends really so boring? Were his new friends really friends at all? And how could he go behind Shahid's back like that? Jay had to decide. Finally, he texted Finn these words: **cu on saturday. WITH the laptop.** ☺

F Jay had an awful week. Shahid knew Jay wasn't feeling so great, but he thought it was because of his bad marks. Shahid had more time for Jay than usual and told him about his conversation with Claire at Olivia's house. "It's funny. Now I know that not all families are the same." Shahid was talking to Jay as an adult – and all the time Jay was planning to take his music. He felt bad. But it was too late to change things now. Before he knew it, it was Saturday evening and Jay was at Finn's front door. Finn opened the door, smiled, and grabbed the laptop out of Jay's hands.

G At the party, Shahid's music sounded fantastic. His brother was a great DJ! Everyone was dancing, but nobody was paying attention to Jay. "And I'm wearing my coolest outfit!" he thought. Finn and Max were ignoring him too. But suddenly, three pretty girls were standing in front of Jay. He smiled at them.

"Ohh, poor baby. Have you lost your mummy, little boy?" one of them asked, and everyone laughed.

Jay felt so stupid. "Where's Luke when I really need him?" Jay asked himself. He really missed his friend.

Then, the music suddenly stopped. People started to leave. "What a stupid party!" some of them said. "No music, no party. Let's go!" others shouted. Jay then knew that something was very wrong.

"Hey Jay," Finn shouted. "Max dropped the laptop and now it's dead. So now we haven't got any music!"

"Yeah, thanks for nothing," Max added. "If your brother made real money as a model or DJ, he could buy something better than this piece of junk here!"

They didn't notice that Jay was white with anger. And they didn't care. Jay grabbed his brother's laptop, ran out the door, and ran all the way home.

Back in his room, he saw that Finn and Max were right: The laptop really was dead! It didn't work – at all. What would his brother do when he came home? Jay had one night to think about it. "And this is going to be one very long night," he knew.

SPEAKING

1 Your reaction

a) *What do you think about Jay's story? Share your ideas.*

b) *What kind of trouble have your brothers / sisters / cousins / friends got into before? Was it big trouble, or not so big? Maybe some of the phrases in the box can help you.*

Useful phrases

- One of my friends always gets into trouble for telling lies / making nasty comments / …
- My friend / cousin breaks the rules at home / at school / in our team / …
- There's always trouble when …
- I know somebody who always goes too far to be the best / to be popular / …
- He / She likes to start fights / tease people / …

READING

2 Understanding the story → WB 24/22–23

WB 24/22 Reading (matching pictures with paragraphs)
WB 24/23 Reading (true/false)

→ S5–6

S5 Schnelllesetechniken
S6 Wichtige Inhalte von Texten herausfinden

a) *Which of the themes on the right are important in the story? Say why.*

Example:
Jay really wants to be popular. That's important for the story because …
That's why he …

b) *With a partner, think of good headings for parts A–G of the story.*

Word bank

Nouns: the in-crowd | peer pressure | freedom | fun | excitement
Verbs: fit in | go behind somebody's back | lie to somebody
Adjectives: lonely | cool | popular | new | old | confused | boring | honest

SPEAKING

3 Role play: Turning points in the story

→ S7

S7 Wichtige Mermale von Erzähltexten, Gedichten und Theaterstücken erkennen

a) *First read the skills box. Then find the other turning points for Jay in the story.*

b) *Choose **one** of the turning points from a). Now imagine that Jay is having a video chat with Dave about what to do at one of the turning points. What advice would Dave give him? How would Jay react to Dave's advice? Write a short dialogue for them.*

c) *Now act out your dialogues in class with your partner.*

Lösung: a) *Turning points: lines 20–25; lines 68–70; lines 93–98*

Reading skills

A **turning point** is a part of a story where a character must make a decision about what to do next. The decision can be good – or bad – for the character and for others.

Example: In Part A you find the story's first turning point. Jay was grounded but decided to leave the house anyway. Good or bad idea?

WRITING

4 What happens next? → WB 24/24

WB 24/24 Writing/Reading/Speaking (optional tasks)

→ △ 119/17
→ S11–14

119/17 What happens next: Ideas for the ending
△→ Help with …
S11–14 Writing

a) *When Shahid comes back from his modelling job in Manchester, Jay needs to tell him about his laptop. How do you think Shahid will react? Collect ideas and write an ending to the story. Exchange texts with your partner and give each other feedback.*

b) *Now compare your texts with the two different endings on p. 267.*

When Sean came to visit
→ S22–23

S22–23 Film skills/Viewing
Folie 3/5 Bildbeschreibung, Vorentlastung/Sicherung des Hörsehverstehens

SPEAKING

1 Warm-up: How would you react?

Imagine this situation: You're doing something you aren't good at (e.g. a sport, singing). Other people can see you're having problems, and maybe they're teasing you about it.

How would you react? Would you …

laugh about it yourself? | feel really embarrassed? | just ignore it? | become angry?

Or do you have other ways to deal with situations like this?

VIEWING

2 Sean, the cousin from Northern Ireland
→ WB 25/25

WB 25/25 Vocabulary (internet phrases)
KV 31: Laura and Sean

DVD 3/1

a) *Watch the film. What do you think about Sean and Nathan?*

b) *Answer the questions. The words in the box can help you.*

Word bank

have a sense of humour | feel sorry for somebody | be optimistic | cheer somebody up | be a show-off | apologise | post / delete something on a wall | be careful with account settings | mean / not mean it

The basketball scene:
1. How did Nathan get on Sean's nerves?
2. How did Sean react?
3. How did Laura react?

The park bench scene:
1. What was so embarrassing for Nathan?
2. Was Sean able to help? How?

The ending:
1. How did things work out in the end?
2. What did you think of the ending?

VIEWING

3 Three different personalities
→ WB 25/26

WB 25/26 Writing (next film scene)
KV 32: Sinead – Sean's sister

escribing different alities, p. 183

a) *Look at the diagram on p. 27 again. What kind of 'smart' do you think Sean, Nathan and Laura are? Now watch the film again. In a grid, take notes about what each person is good at, and what adjectives could describe them. Then share your ideas.*

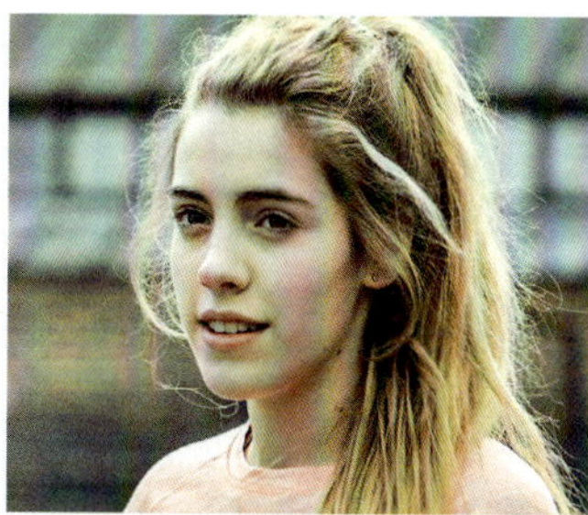

HA

b) *With a partner, think of how you could change the basketball scene so that it shows Nathan as more 'people smart'. Write a short dialogue between Nathan and Sean.*

KV 33: Working with vocabulary

KV 34–37 Test yourself
KV 38–40 Speaking cards
WB 27/1 Listening (true/false)

LISTENING

1 The saxophone lessons → WB 27/1

L 2/1

a) *Listen to the conversation between Helen and her mum. Then answer the questions.*

1. What's the problem between Helen and her mum?
2. Why does Helen's mum think that it's important to practise?
3. What compromise do they reach?

b) *What do you think is good or bad about the compromise between Helen and her mum? Give reasons for your opinion.*

c) *With a partner, act out a conversation with a different compromise. You can use one of these ideas or think of your own compromise:*

Helen will pay for part of the lessons. | Helen will do extra work around the house to help pay for the lessons. | Helen will continue with the lessons, but will do some extra practice for four weeks.

LANGUAGE

2 My success

a) *Put these signal words into the correct list:* ***simple past*** *or* ***present perfect****.*

last year | already | yesterday | two years ago | just | so far | in 1865 | (only) ever | five minutes ago | never | last night | (not) yet | when I was a child | three times | when I came home from school | in 2014

Lösung: b) *1. I've never been a show-off, but I've had a lot of success in life! 2. When I was 16, I was fed up with life in a small town. 3. I believed in my talents as a dancer and dropped out of school. 4. Five years ago, I moved to London. 5. And I've never looked back on my old life. 6. In London I started my career as a backing dancer. 7. At the beginning, I entered lots of auditions. 8. Two years later, I got my big chance. 9. I've danced in 20 different shows so far. 10. I haven't been in the big shows yet, but I've just received an interesting offer. Life is great!*

b) *Read what Ian, a successful dancer, says about his life. Use the words and phrases to make sentences in the* ***simple past*** *or the* ***present perfect****.*

1. I | never | be | a show-off, but | I | have | a lot of success in life! 2. When | I | be 16, I | be | fed up with life in a small town. 3. I | believe | in my talents as a dancer and | drop out | of school. 4. Five years ago | I | move | to London. 5. And | I | never | look back on my old life. 6. In London | I | start | my career as a backing dancer. 7. At the beginning | I | enter | lots of auditions. 8. Two years later | I | get | my big chance. 9. I | dance | in 20 different shows so far. 10. I | not be | in the big shows yet, but | I | just | receive | an interesting offer. Life is great!

WRITING

3 I'm sorry

You're staying with a family in Greenwich for six weeks. Yesterday you broke one of the family's rules. Write a short letter to the parents and apologise for what you did wrong. Which rule did you break? Here are some ideas:

you missed a family dinner | you got home late | you didn't do your jobs around the house

Start like this: Dear Jack and Diane, I'm sorry that I …

CABULARY

4 What's important?

a) *Make a pie chart[1] like the one on the right. Think of other things that parents love to say. Add them to your chart. Think of a good title for it.*

b) *Look at the example of a bar graph[2]. What things do you look for in a friend? Add them to your graph. Think of a good title for it.*

c) *Explain one of your graphs in 4–5 sentences. The phrases in the box can help you.*

d) *Choose one of the topics and take a survey in your class. Make a graph with the results.*

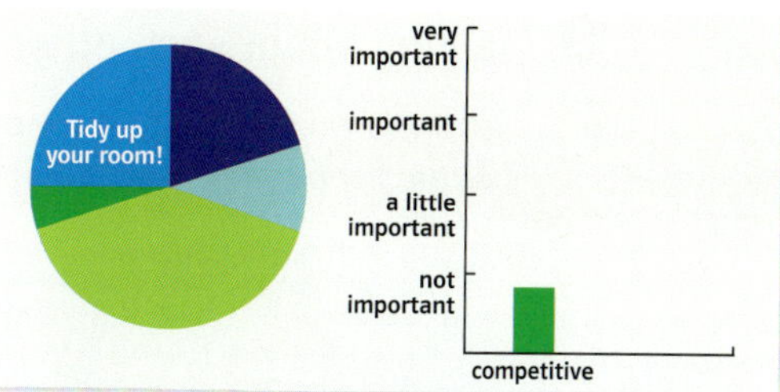

Word bank

a few | some | a lot of | most | nearly all | almost all | only a couple of | about half | … per cent[3] of …

NGUAGE

5 What will the future bring?

Use the prompts to make sentences with ***conditional clauses type 1****.*

Example: 1. If I practise a lot, I'll play in front of a big audience.

: 2. If I study a lot, … me a vet. 3. If I … ut of school, I'll never … d in life. 4. If I push … I'll play in a famous … team. 5. If I save … money, I'll open a … ant.

1 **pie chart** [ˈpaɪtʃɑːt] Kreisdiagramm | 2 **bar graph** [ˈbɑːɡrɑːf] Balkendiagramm | 3 **per cent** [pəˈsent] Prozent

WB 27/2 Language (conditional clauses 2)

LANGUAGE

6 Talking about each other → WB 27/2

*Read what two teenagers say about boys and girls. Decide if you need an **object pronoun** (me, him, her, etc.) or a **reflexive pronoun** (myself, himself, herself, etc.).*

Lösung: 1. *myself* 2. *themselves* 3. *themselves* 4. *them* 5. *me* 6. *her* 7. *herself* 8. *you* 9. *me* 10. *myself* 11. *them* 12. *themselves* 13. *myself* 14. *yourself* 15. *you* 16. *myself* 17. *me* 18. *him* 19. *me* 20. *herself* 21. *me* 22. *me*

A. What boys think about girls

"I look at 1 once in the morning and that's enough, but girls are always looking at 2 ! I guess they don't believe in 3 enough and always worry what other people think of 4 . And girls aren't good with secrets. For example, if my sister tells 5 a secret, I never tell anyone else. But if I tell 6 a secret, she can't keep it to 7 . So girls, well, I don't really trust 8 . And they think they know everything too. I don't need a girl to judge 9 because I can judge 10 . Boys know what they're good at and they don't need girls to tell 11 ."

B. What girls think about boys

"Boys don't know how to behave 12 ! I'd never forgive 13 if I acted like a boy. They just don't understand – if you say something mean, you aren't just hurting the other person, you're also hurting 14 because then people don't like 15 . Once I was in big trouble and I couldn't help 16 so I really needed someone to save 17 . A boy walked by but I couldn't even persuade 18 to help 19 . So a girl has to rely on 20 . But sometimes if I'm sad, my brother tells 21 jokes and that really cheers 22 up."

MEDIATION

7 Role play: Your place somewhere else

You're a scout[1] and want to take part in an international summer camp. The biggest one in Japan[2] is too expensive – more than €4,000! On the internet you've found another one in the Netherlands[3] which is only €335 (plus the train ticket), and you want to persuade your parents to let you go there. Read the text and look up new words in a dictionary. Then act out a role play in German. One of you is the child and one of you is the father / mother.

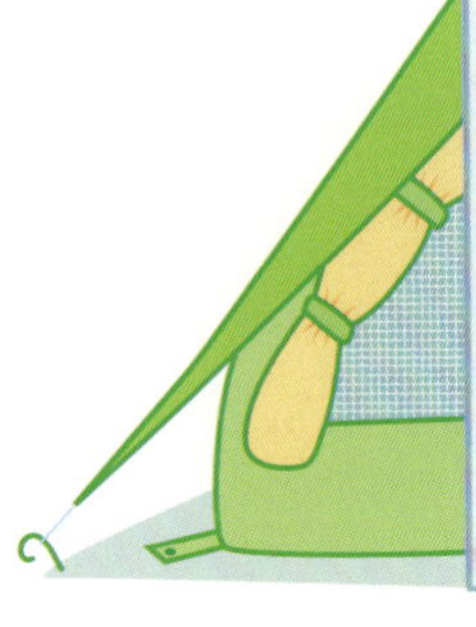

The 10-day Jamborette in the Netherlands is organised for scouts aged 10–17 years old and their leaders. There will be groups from all over Europe as well as India, Russia, Ghana, Egypt, Turkey, Israel, the USA and Canada.

The Jamborette is very much like a normal summer camp. Each group has its own campsite to set up its tents. You won't have to go shopping for food during the camp, because we'll give you the food and drink for every meal. However, you'll have to prepare it yourself, so don't forget to bring cooking gear like pots, pans and stoves!

The Jamborette is held in Recreatiegebied Spaarnwoude, a nature reserve located between Amsterdam, Haarlem and Velsen. This reserve has many hiking routes, a mountain bike track, swimming lakes and even a ski slope and a climbing wall. The Programme Team of the 2016 Haarlem Jamborette is working on organising a challenging, active and varied programme: Aqua (water), Trail, Hikes, Sports, Arts & Crafts and Jambotours (culture).

1 **scout** [skaʊt] Pfadfinder/-in | 2 **Japan** [dʒə'pæn] Japan | 3 **the Netherlands** ['neðələnz] die Niederlande

WB 27/2 Language (conditional clauses 2)

NGUAGE

8 Why I can't go to the school dance → WB 27/2

: 1. weren't
ln't be 3. paid – would
e 4. enjoyed – would
5. didn't have to –
d) enjoy –
– wouldn't have to
omised – would be
– would ('d) disagree

Jack is angry because he's been grounded and can't go to the school dance. Fill in the correct verb forms to make ***conditional clauses type 2****.*

1. If I ___ (not be) grounded, I'd go to the school dance. I love to dance. **2.** If I had better marks, I ___ (not be) grounded. It's so boring here at home. **3.** If I ___ (pay) attention at school, I ___ (have) better marks. I'd really like to succeed. **4.** If I ___ (enjoy) class more, I ___ (pay) attention. But it's so hard. **5.** If we ___ (not have to) learn so much grammar, I ___ (enjoy) class more. Cars would be an interesting topic for class. **6.** If English ___ (be) easier, we ___ (not have to) learn so much grammar. Who needs grammar? **7.** If we ___ (compromise) and made German and English the same, English ___ (be) so much easier. **8.** German isn't as hard as English. I bet if I ___ (ask) my teacher, she ___ (disagree) with me.

So you see – it's all because of English. That's why I can't go to the school dance!

BULARY

9 Different kinds of smart

a) *Kim and John spent the day together in Lonchester. Read what they say about their day.*

Kim:
The day in Lonchester was fantastic. It's a cool place. It was my first time here, but every underground in every city is almost the same. You just follow the colours and numbers! I found a great place for lunch – not where all the tourists go. I watched some kids our age and then we went where they went. I didn't go to Lonchester to hang out with tourists! John wanted to go to the harbour, but the first street looked like trouble so we took a different street, turned right, then left, then right and got there safely. I asked a few people and then we got a free tour of one of the ships!

John:
I really enjoyed our day in Lonchester. 625,000 people live there, but more than 1 million people work there. It's the home of a huge biscuit company. It took us 37 minutes to get there by underground. In the afternoon the trains leave every hour, always at half past. A famous architect designed the train station. We ate lunch at 12 o'clock and it only cost £3. The harbour was interesting because about 20 ships arrive and depart every day. It's the second biggest harbour in the south of England. You can't really take tours of the ships, but we got one! Kim just asked. I didn't know that was possible.

b) *What's the difference between 'street smart' and 'book smart'? Make a grid and put in examples from the text.*

c) *Are you more like Kim or John? Explain why you think so. Compare your ideas with a partner.*

LANGUAGE

10 Best friend?

Read about Sarah's problems with her friend Nina. Complete the text with the correct tenses: ***simple present***, ***simple past***, ***present perfect*** *or* ***will future***.

Lösung: 1. *behaves* 2. *will ('ll) give* 3. *felt* 4. *studied* 5. *told* 6. *don't push* 7. *will ('ll) never get* 8. *has ('s) ever got* 9. *will ('ll) meet* 10. *hung out* 11. *ignored* 12. *have ('ve) been stressed out* 13. *feel* 14. *listened* 15. *relies* 16. *doesn't need* 17. *is* 18. *will ('ll) chill out* 19. *will ('ll) enjoy*

I'm so fed up with Nina. She says she's my best friend, but she always **1** (behave) like she can do everything better. Wait – I **2** (give) you an example. Last week at school I **3** (feel) really optimistic about our Maths test. I **4** (study) a lot at the weekend, but then Nina **5** (tell) me, "If you **6** (not push) yourself more, you **7** (never get) marks as good as mine." I have to tell you this: The worst mark Nina **8** (ever get) was a B. After Maths Nina said, "I **9** (meet) you in the cafeteria for lunch!" But during lunch break she **10** (hang out) with Julia and **11** (ignore) me! I **12** (be) stressed out about Nina for three weeks! But I **13** (feel) a little better today because I **14** (listen) to a radio call-in last night. A caller said she always **15** (rely) on herself. She **16** (not need) other people to feel happy. So this **17** (be) my decision now: I **18** (chill out) about Nina and I **19** (enjoy) myself without her! I think it's time for some new friends!

WB 28/3 Writing (forum post)

WRITING

11 Follow or don't follow the crowd → WB 28/3

a) *Choose one of the cartoons and describe what you can see.*

Crying is cool now.

b) *What do you think the cartoon's message is? Do you agree with it? Explain why or why not. The phrases in the box can help you.*

c) *Write a comment about one of the cartoons.*

Start like this: I think you should always try to be … / Peer pressure can make you … / It doesn't matter if everybody else …

Useful phrases

In my opinion, the cartoon's message is … | I think the cartoon wants to show that … | The cartoonist wants us to think about … / wants to make fun of … | I agree / don't agree with the cartoon's message because …

LANGUAGE

12 Stay out of my bedroom!

a) *Talk about these situations with a partner. Put them into two lists:*

1. There is a real chance that it will happen. 2. It will probably never happen.

get my own bedroom | move to London | start an acting career | win an argument with my parents | start my own business | have more freedom | get a tattoo | become a millionaire

b) *Look at your lists from a) again and make* ***conditional clauses type 1 and 2.***

Example: If I get my own bedroom, I'll paint it purple.

c) *You want to convince your parents that a messy bedroom isn't so bad and you've found an article about this topic. Read the article and use the information to complete the sentences.*

g: c) 2. … would ('d) use agination more. 3. … I use ad to find different ways to a problem. 4. … we didn't so many arguments about lean a bedroom should … everyone could chill out. f I am in charge of my own 7. … I'll succeed in life. wouldn't behave so badly. can have a messy bedroom. you judge me too hard.

What's good about a messy bedroom?

Many parents think that their children's bedrooms are too messy. Maybe they're right, but a messy bedroom isn't always a bad thing. For example, people with messy bedrooms are usually very creative. Good marks at school in subjects like English, Art and even in Maths can be the result when children use their heads to find different ways to solve a problem. This doesn't mean that a bedroom should always be messy. Tidying up a bedroom once a month, for example, is usually enough and makes people use their imagination more. Children who have messy bedrooms often pay more attention to details.

Children – and parents! – are often stressed out because there are so many arguments about how clean a bedroom should be. It's a good idea for children and parents to compromise so that everyone can chill out. Children should be in charge of their own rooms because this is part of their job and then they learn to push themselves. It isn't always the parents pushing the children. Part of growing up is learning to rely on yourself and being your own boss. These children often succeed in life because they've learned to deal with freedom. Sometimes there are too many arguments about tidying up a room so then the children behave badly. It's important for children to form their own personality and a messy bedroom can be part of this. Some parents judge their children too hard and then lose their sense of humour. Instead they should cheer for their children and share their excitement when they find £20 under their bed or their saxophone behind their wardrobe.

Example: 1. If I have a messy room, I'll be more creative at school.

1. If I have a messy bedroom, …
2. If I tidied up my bedroom once a month, I …
3. I'll get good marks at school if …
4. We wouldn't be so stressed out if …
5. If we compromised, …
6. I'll learn to push myself if …
7. If I learn to deal with freedom, …
8. If we didn't have so many arguments, …
9. I'll have a strong personality if …
10. You'll lose your sense of humour if …

d) *Do you agree with what the author says about a messy bedroom? Explain why or why not. Discuss your ideas with your partner.*

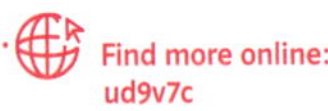

Text smart 1
Poems and songs

With the Text smart pages, you're going to learn how to deal with different text types and how to use them in your own work. Text smart 1 is about how poems and songs work in different ways.

Folie 3/6: Vorentlastung des Hörverstehens
KV 41: Poems

LISTENING

1 Warm-up: Thinking about the message

Outside a shop, somebody has written some interesting 'advice for life' statements on an old board.
Two friends, Jon and Mario, have just discovered it.

Jon: Hey look, some words with *real* meaning on a shopping street! The sign makes you stop and think, doesn't it? It reads like a poem.

Mario: Who needs real meaning on a shopping street?! I'm more into songs anyway.

a) *Read the text on the board out loud. Is Jon right?*

L2/3 → S19-21

S19-21 Listening

b) *Now listen to what Jon and Mario say.*

1. Explain why Jon likes poems.
2. Explain what Mario is more interested in.

c) *What do the lines on the board mean to **you**?*

Examples:
A: I'm into sports and fair play, so I think "Play like there are no winners" is a cool message.
B: I think *all* the statements are cool. When you read them, you think of how great things could be if everyone was happier, more generous or more creative.

WRITING

2 Your turn: Poems and songs in your life

a) *Where do **you** find poems and hear songs? Say which statements are true for you.*

I sometimes look up song lyrics on the internet. | I sing along to my favourite songs. | I know some poems by heart. | I'm good at rhyming words. | I often discover great songs / poems in TV adverts. | I write my own songs / poems.

→ △ 120/1

120/1 Your turn: Poems and songs in your life
△ → Help with …

b) *Go back to the statements on the board. How could you add a line or two of your own with the same verbs or with different verbs?*

Say it with a poem!

READING

3 Happy Poem by James Carter (b. 1959)

S1/19 L2/4

Happy as a rainbow
Happy as a bee
Happy as a dolphin
Splashing in the sea

Happy as bare feet
Running on the beach
Happy as a sunflower
Happy as a peach

Happy as a poppy
Happy as a spoon
Dripping with honey
Happy as June

Happy as a banjo
Plucking on a tune
Happy as a Sunday
Lazy afternoon

Happy as a memory
Shared by two
Happy as me …
When I'm with you!

Read the first verse (the first four lines) of the poem. Explain why you think things like a rainbow or a dolphin can be 'happy things'.

READING

4 The structure of poems: Some basics

→ S7, 15

…ntige Merkmale
…ähltexten, Gedich-
…d Theaterstücken
…en
…echen üben

Read the skills box and then read the rest of 'Happy Poem'. After that:

1. Say what the rhyme scheme is.
2. Copy the poem into your exercise book.
3. Read the poem out loud and mark the words or syllables you need to stress.

Lösung: 1. *rhyme scheme: ABCB; DEFE; GHIH; JKLK; MNON*

Reading skills

Poems which rhyme have a **rhyme scheme**. **AABB** and **ABAB** are very typical; so is **ABCB**:

Roses are red, (A)
Violets are blue. (B)
I like poems, (C)
What about you? (B)

But the rhyme scheme isn't everything! For the rhyme to work, a rhyming poem must have a **rhythm** with the same **stress** in each line:

Happy as a **rain**bow
Happy as a **bee**

WRITING

5 Your turn: What makes you happy? KV 41: Poems

…ansfer

→ S4

S4 Methoden

→ △ 120/2

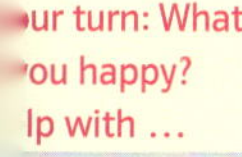
…ur turn: What
…ou happy?
…lp with …

a) *Do all the things in the poem mean happiness for you too? Discuss with your partner.*

b) *What makes **you** happy? Make a mind map with happy words. Your partner does the same. Then compare your mind maps. Are some things the same, or very different?*

c) *Now change the happy poem with your own happy words, e.g. from your mind map.*

d) *Recite your version of the poem to the class. Explain why you changed it the way you did.*

WB 29/1 Reading (poems)

READING

6 Understanding poems → WB 29/1

S 1/20 L 2/5

→ S7, 19–21

S7 Wichtige Merkmale von Erzähltexten, Gedichten und Theaterstücken erkennen
S19–21 Listening

a) *Your reaction: Close your eyes and just listen to the poem. Then answer questions 1 and 2. Tell the class what you think. (The phrases in the box can help you.)*

1. Describe how the poem makes you feel and why.
2. What could the poem be about?

The Arrow and the Song
by Henry Wadsworth Longfellow (1807–1882)

I shot an arrow into the air,
It fell to earth, I knew not where;
For, so swiftly it flew, the sight
Could not follow it in its flight.

I breathed a song into the air,
It fell to earth, I knew not where;
For who has sight so keen and strong,
That it can follow the flight of song?

Long, long afterward, in an oak
I found the arrow, still unbroke;
And the song, from beginning to end,
I found again in the heart of a friend.

Useful phrases

- The poem makes me feel …
- I'd describe the atmosphere as …
- The language in this poem is … while the other poem sounds …
- I think the poem is about …

Tip

When you read poems, don't forget to always **read them out loud** to yourself. This gives you a feeling for a poem's **rhythm** and **atmosphere**.

b) *Now divide yourselves up into pairs or small groups. Each pair/group looks at lines 1–4, 5–8 or 9–12. Decide together what your verse is about exactly. Then share your results with the class. Which groups have the same ideas?*

READING

7 Taking a second look

→ △ 120/3

120/3 Taking a second look
△ → Instead of …

a) *In the 'Arrow' poem, it would be possible to say some things in a more direct way. In your group, rewrite some of the sentences from the poem with simpler, more direct words to show that you understand what they mean.*

Example: I breathed a song into the air. → I sang a song out loud.
→ I sang a song so that others could hear it.

b) *What kind of lines do **you** like better: the simpler lines or the original ones? Does the original language make the poem special? If yes, how?*

WRITING

8 Your turn: Your idea of friendship

These are two key lines in the poem (lines 11–12):

And the song, from beginning to end,
I found again in the heart of a friend.

*Write 6–8 lines about what **you** would like to find in your friends' hearts. What do you think they'd like to find in your heart?*

Say it with a song!

LISTENING **9** **Count on me** by Bruno Mars (b. 1985)

L2/6 → S19–21 **S19–21** Listening

Read the skills box before you listen to the song.

Listening skills

- When you listen to a song, **focus on the words** and the **main message first.**
- Sometimes, **rhyme words** can help you to understand and remember the words better.
- When you think about the message, think also about how the **music** matches the message.

If you ever find yourself stuck in the middle of the sea,
I'll sail the world to find you
If you ever find yourself lost in the dark and you can't see,
I'll be the light to guide you

Find out what we're made of
When we are called to help our friends in need

Chorus:
You can count on me like one two three
I'll be there
And I know when I need it I can count on you like four three two
You'll be there
'Cause that's what friends are supposed to do, oh yeah

If you tossin' and you're turnin' and you just can't fall asleep
I'll sing a song beside you
And if you ever forget how much you really mean to me
Every day I will remind you

Find out what we're made of
When we are called to help our friends in need

(Repeat chorus)

You'll always have my shoulder when you cry
I'll never let go
Never say goodbye
You know you can …

(Repeat chorus)

READING

10 Understanding the song

a) *How do you like the song? Do you think the music matches the message? Why?*

b) *"You can count on me like one two three" (line 7): Which of the definitions below matches that line from the song the best? Or have you got other ideas?*

A. "Like one two three" means that friends are as basic and important as the most basic numbers.

B. It's just a play on words: The singer sings "Count on me" and then he really *counts* the numbers "one, two, three".

C. "Like one two three" means you'll be there to help your friend as fast as possible.

D. …

c) *Find the words / phrases in the song which have the same meanings as these definitions:*

1. If you feel you can't help yourself out of a difficult situation, you're ___.
2. In difficult situations, people learn their limits. After that they know ___.
3. If you'd do anything for someone, then you'd ___ for him / her.
4. If you need a strong person to go to with a problem, then you need a ___.

Lösung: c) *1. stuck in the middle of the sea 2. what they're made of 3. be there 4. light to guide you*

HA → △ 121/4

d) *Finish these lines with your own words and ideas about what **you** would do for a friend:*

1. If you ever find yourself stuck …
2. When you cry …
3. You can count on me when …
4. If you ever forget …

121/4 Trouble usually finds me …
△→ After …

KV 42: Present a song
WB 29/2 Reading/Speaking (poems and songs)

VOCABULARY

11 What makes a song catchy? → WB 29/2

a) *What makes a song catchy? Talk to your partner about the ideas on the right. Have you got more ideas?*

You can dance to it. | You can't keep your feet or hands still! | It's easy to sing along to. | You hear some of the words over and over again. | It makes you feel happy. | You can't get it out of your head for a long time because the melody is so great. | …

b) *How catchy is **your** favourite song? Say which statements in a) match your song.*

→ S3

c) *In the word bank you can see words which are typical for two popular themes in pop songs:*

1. Don't give up! / You can do it!
2. Happiness

With a partner, use these words (or your own) to write 2–4 lines for a song in one or both categories. Make sure the lines rhyme.

S3 Wörter im Zusammenhang

Word bank

1. 'Don't give up!' songs:
fight | win | lose | survive | fall down | stand up | die | champion

2. 'Happiness' songs:
fun | dream | sun | free | smile | laugh | party | friends | forever

WB 30/3 Vocabulary (crossword)
WB 30/4 Writing (poem or song)

12 Poem and song options → WB 30/3–4

→ △ 121/5

a) *Look at the following options. In class, talk about what could be difficult about each.*

b) *Now choose **one** of the options for yourself or for you and a partner.*

Poem
ong
ns
Help
…

S 1/21 L 2/7

Option A:

Read the poem below. Think of reasons why the friend went away. Write the story behind it.

Untitled poem
by Langston Hughes (1902–1967)

I loved my friend.
He went away from me.
There's nothing more to say.
The poem ends,
Soft as it began –
I loved my friend.

Reading skills

Poems which don't rhyme at all or have any clear structure like ABAB are called **free verse** poems. And sometimes, a poem can be somewhere in between, like the one you see on the left. The freer a poem is, the more important it is to **decide for yourself where the stress should be**, and where **a pause** could make it better or more interesting.

Option B:

First look at the photos that go with exercises 3, 8, 9 and 11. Explain how they match the different songs / poems / topics in those exercises. Now look at this photo. Find a song to go with it. Explain your choice.

Option C:

Find a song with an interesting story. Present it to your class: Talk about the lyrics, the music, the rhymes, the atmosphere. (If you like, you can also compare the original with a cover version.)

S 1/22 L 2/8

Option D:

Read this poem out loud over and over until you know it by heart. Then recite it to the class. Make sure you know which words you really want to stress to give more feeling.

A smile (author unknown)

A smile is quite a funny thing,
It wrinkles up your face.
And when it's gone,
You'll never find
Its secret hiding place.

But far more wonderful it is
To see what smiles can do.
You smile at one,
He smiles at you,
And the smile makes two.

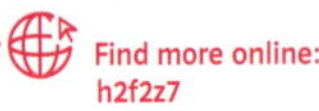
Find more online: h2f2z7

Reacting to a new situation

Folie 3/7: Bildbeschreibung, Reaktivierung von Vorwissen
WB 33/1 Vocabulary (odd one out)

VOCABULARY

1 Warm-up: Talking about food → WB 33/1

→ S3–4

S3–4 Vocabulary

Voc.: Crockery, Cutlery, Others, WB (Word bank), pp. 13–14

A

B

a) *Look at the film stills. Talk to your partner about what you can see. The word bank can help you.*

b) *Describe your typical breakfast. Compare it with your classmates' breakfasts. Say what's the same and what's different.*

c) *What other breakfast traditions do you know about?*

Word bank

bowl | plate | mug | cup | spoon | knife | fork | bread | bread rolls | toast | butter | jam | marmalade | honey | cereal | muesli | ham | bacon | tomatoes | baked beans | cheese | eggs | sausages | milk | tea | coffee | sugar

SPEAKING

2 Your turn: Your experiences

a) *Has anyone ever offered you food you didn't like? How did you feel? What did you say or do? Tell each other your experiences.*

b) *What do you think of how your partner reacted? Was he/she polite? Embarrassing? …*

Folie 3/8: Bildbeschreibung, Vorentlastung des Hörsehverstehens
KV 43: Reacting to a new situation

VIEWING

3 Breakfast with the host family (1)

DVD 3/2

→ S22–23

S22–23 Film skills/Viewing

a) *Watch the film and answer the questions about the two exchange students. Write down key words while you're watching.*

1. Who are Steffen and Brad?
2. Where are they and what are they doing?
3. What are they unfamiliar with? What's different to their own breakfast traditions?

b) *Why do you think there are two versions of the breakfast scene? Choose the correct answer.*

A. to show different types of English breakfast
B. to give more information about the same topic
C. to show different reactions to a new situation

Lösung: b) C. *to show different reactions to a new situation*

Folie 3/8: Bildbeschreibung, Vorentlastung des Hörsehverstehens
KV 43: Reacting to a new situation
WB 33/2 Speaking (dialogues)

VIEWING

4 Breakfast with the host family (2) → WB 33/2

a) *Watch the film again. Group A focuses on Reaction 1; Group B focuses on Reaction 2. Then answer the questions.*

1. Describe what's difficult for Steffen.
2. How does Steffen react?

b) *Think of possible headings for the two different reactions.*

Word bank

say sth nice | say the wrong thing | make somebody angry | upset somebody | make somebody feel better | try something new | show interest | show gratitude | feel embarrassed | be polite | be impolite | be rude

c) *Talk to a partner from the other group about the two reactions. Explain which one is more appropriate. What would you do in Steffen's situation?*

d) *Look at the two stills from the film. Match the phrases in the box below to each scene. Then sort them into more polite and less polite phrases. Make a grid.*

A

B

I usually drink milk but I'll try some tea. | Thank you. This looks interesting! | I'm sure English tea is nice too. | I don't eat hot food this early. | I can't eat that much in the morning. | I never drink tea. I'm not used to it. | I'm surprised. It's a very big plate of food. | What is it? I don't think I can drink it! | I'm not sure if I can eat it all but I'll try. | I don't want breakfast.

EAKING

5 Role play

KV 44: Food and eating customs

→ S17

In your group from Ex. 4, work with the film script and rehearse your scene. Learn your lines by heart and act out your scene to the class.

ıdliche Aufgaben
ː Besonderheiten

Unit 3
Let's go to Scotland!

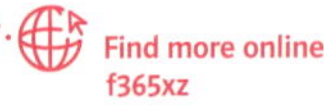
Find more online: f365xz

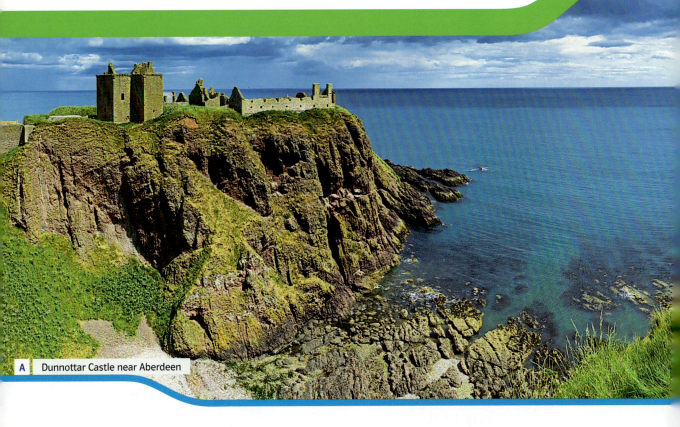

A Dunnottar Castle near Aberdeen

SPEAKING

1 Pictures from Scotland

Folie 3/9: Bildbeschreibung, Reaktivierung von Vorwissen

Voc.: Typically Scottish, p. 188

a) *Describe the photos above. Which one would most make you want to visit Scotland? Explain why. The words in the box can help you.*

b) *Imagine you're on holiday in Scotland. What do you think you can do there? Share your ideas in class.*

Word bank

beautiful landscape | an old castle | historic houses | busy places | modern buildings | traditional clothes | a popular festival | amazing coastline | go hiking / climbing / mountain biking | go sightseeing / shopping | visit museums

SPEAKING

2 Your turn: Present your country

KV 45a+b: Present your country

Transfer

a) *Your exchange partner would like to know more about Germany. You want to send him / her some photos to show what Germany is like. What kind of photos would you choose? Write down your ideas.*

b) *With your partner make a 'Top 5' list of photos about Germany. Present your results to the class. Give reasons for your choice.*

In Unit 3 you learn

... how to describe a place and the reasons for visiting it. You learn:

- vocabulary for talking about places and things to do
- how to talk about actions which started in the past and continue into the present
- how to use passive forms
- how to make a text more interesting

ern Glasgow

Ben Nevis (1,344 m)

D The Edinburgh Fringe Festival

E Going out in Edinburgh

KV 46: Listening: Ideas about Scotland
WB 34/1 Vocabulary (Scotland)
WB 34/2 Vocabulary (word puzzle)

STENING 

3 Ideas about Scotland → WB 34/1–2

a) *Think of what you've read or seen about Scotland before. What do you think is 'typically Scottish'?*

L 2/9–11 → S19–21 S19–21 Listening

b) *Listen to three Scottish teenagers – Jean, Stuart and Carol – talking about typical ideas about Scotland. Match the speakers with the ideas in the box.*

haggis | Scottish accents | tartan clothes / kilts | bagpipes | Scottish independence | the Loch Ness monster

Across cultures 

Scotland became part of the UK in 1707, but the **relationship between England and Scotland** has often been difficult. In September 2014, the people in Scotland had the chance to decide in a referendum if they wanted to become independent. 55 % voted against it, so Scotland is still part of the UK. Scotland has its own **national symbols**, like the flag and the thistle. Do you know any German national symbols?

c) *Listen again and note down what the speakers say about the different topics.*

er → △ 122/1

d) *Your turn: What are typical ideas about Germany? Do you think they're true? Explain why or why not. Share your ideas with a partner.*

L2/12

A new Holly?

Folie 3/10: Vorentlastung, Sicherung des Hörverstehens, Bildbeschreibung

Gwen and her parents are going to spend their next holiday in Scotland with Gwen's uncle and aunt and their son Ethan. Gwen has invited Holly and her sister Amber to come too.

Holly: Hi Gwen.

Gwen: Hi Holly. You're wearing orange and blue.

Holly: Yes. So?

Gwen: What happened to pink?

Holly: Pink is *old* Holly. New Holly isn't into pink any more.

Gwen: Your backpack is still pink.

Holly: Yes, I know. It isn't that old so I can't throw it away yet.

Gwen: Sounds good. Oh, I got your message. No problem with your mum, then.

Holly: No, she says it's fine if we go to Glasgow with you. But are you sure it's OK with your parents and your uncle and aunt?

Gwen: Yes, I'm sure. We've been planning things we can do together. It's going to be a fantastic holiday.

Holly: Yes, right.

Gwen: What's the matter? You haven't been talking about the trip much. Aren't you excited?

Holly: Yes, I am, but it's Amber. She hasn't been talking about anything else since you invited us.

Gwen: That's good, isn't it?

Holly: Yes, but she thinks she's going to be the boss of the whole trip, just because she's older than me.

Gwen: That's just a typical big-sister little-sister thing. And she's been telling you what to do for years, hasn't she? I didn't think it was a big problem for you.

Holly: I know, but it's been getting worse. I don't remember why we invited her.

Gwen: Yes, you do. She's the same age as my cousin Ethan. They'll be great friends, I'm sure.

Holly: Did you know she's been chatting with him online?

Gwen: No, I didn't. How long has she been doing that?

Holly: They've been sending each other messages since the weekend, and he's been sending her photos of himself and his band.

Gwen: Ooh … I think they really *are* going to be good friends! That means we can spend much more time alone. It'll be so much fun!

WB 35/3 Listening (Amber's friend)

READING → △ 122/2 → S5–6

Talking about Holly
…mber
…Help with …
…nellesetechniken
…htige Inhalte von
… herausfinden

1 Understanding the text → WB 35/3

a) *Answer the following questions about the text.*

1. How is 'new Holly' different from 'old Holly'?
2. What's Holly's problem with her older sister?

b) *Can you understand how Holly feels? Explain why or why not.*

KV 47a: Working with language
WB 35/4 Language (present perfect progressive)

…NGUAGE

→ △ 122/3 → ▲ 123/4

…He has been doing
…nce …
…fter …
…Scots and kilts
…fter …

2 What have people been doing? → WB 35/4 → G5

a) *Find sentences in the text that tell you what different people have or haven't been doing. Write them down and underline the verb forms.*

Examples: Gwen **has been planning** things they can do together.
You **haven't been talking** about the trip much.

b) *The new tense is the **present perfect progressive**. How do you make this tense? When do you use it?*

KV 47b: Working with language
WB 36/5 Language (for or since)

…NGUAGE

→ △ 123/5 → ▲ 123/6

…oint in time or
…of time?
…ter …
…cary castles
…ter …

3 Find the rule: *for* or *since*? → WB 36/5 → G5

a) *Look at the two sentences below. Compare the words and phrases that are used after **for** and **since**. Explain when you use each preposition.*

1. Gwen has been looking forward to the trip to Scotland **for a long time**. 2. Her uncle and aunt have been living in Scotland **since 1996**.

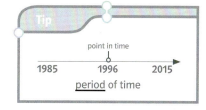

Tip
point in time
1985 1996 2015
period of time

b) *Write the sentences from a) in German. Explain what is different.*

…NGUAGE → △ 124/7 → ▲ 124/8

…t's dance!
…er …
…strange country
…er …

4 Did you know? KV 48: I've been waiting for you!

a) *Complete the sentences with the **present perfect progressive** and **for** or **since**.*

1. People ___ (look) for the Loch Ness monster ___ 1933. Loch Ness is now one of the most popular tourist attractions in Scotland.
2. Scotland ___ (produce) whisky ___ more than 500 years. It produces about 150 million litres per year.
3. Edinburgh ___ (organise) the Fringe Festival every year ___ 1947. It's the largest arts festival in the world.
4. The Scottish National Party ___ (campaign) for Scottish independence ___ more than 80 years. Today it's the biggest party in Scotland.
5. People in Scotland ___ (play) shinty ___ Celtic times. It's a team game which is similar to hockey.

b) *Your turn: Tell your partner interesting facts about yourself. Use the **present perfect progressive** and **for** or **since**.*

Example: I've been playing football since I was six years old / for eight years.

Lösung: a) *1. have been looking – since 2. has been producing – for 3. has been organising – since 4. has been campaigning – for 5. have been playing – since*

G5 The present perfect progressive

WB 37/6 Vocabulary (musical instruments)
WB 37/7 Writing (report)
WB 37/8 Speaking (planning a show)
WB 38/9 Pronunciation (syllables)

LANGUAGE

5 Chat with Ethan → WB 37/6–8, 38/9

Amber is having another smartphone chat with Ethan. Complete their chat with ***for, since*** *and the verbs in the* ***present perfect progressive****.*

Voc.: Musical instruments, WB (Word bank), p. 11

How long 1 (you live) in your new house?

Only 2 six months, but it's starting to feel like home.

What's the area like?

It's a nice quiet street. But not when my band is practising! We 3 (practise) a lot these last weeks because we've got some important gigs soon.

How long 4 (you play) together?

5 four years, but it feels much longer.

Amazing!

Did I tell you that I'm also in another band? It's a traditional Scottish band with just bagpipes and drums.

That's so cool! How long 6 (you play) the bagpipes?

7 I was about seven. They were bigger than me when I started! Oh, you know what? During your visit, there's going to be a festival at a castle near Glasgow, and both my bands are going to play. We 8 (plan) the festival 9 weeks now.

☺☺☺ I can't wait!

Lösung: 1. *have you been living* 2. *for* 3. *have ('ve) been practising* 4. *have you been playing* 5. *For* 6. *have you been playing* 7. *Since* 8. *have ('ve) been planning* 9. *for*

LISTENING

6 <A song: Flower of Scotland>

KV 49: <A song: Flower of Scotland>

L 2/15

O flower of Scotland
When will we see your like
again
That fought and died for
Your wee bit hill and glen
And stood against him
Proud Edward's army
And sent him homeward
Tae think again

The hills are bare now
And autumn leaves lie thick
and still
O'er land that is lost now
Which those so dearly held
And stood against him
Proud Edward's army
And sent him homeward
Tae think again

Those days are passed now
And in the past they must
remain
But we can still rise now
And be the nation again
That stood against him
Proud Edward's army
And sent him homeward
Tae think again

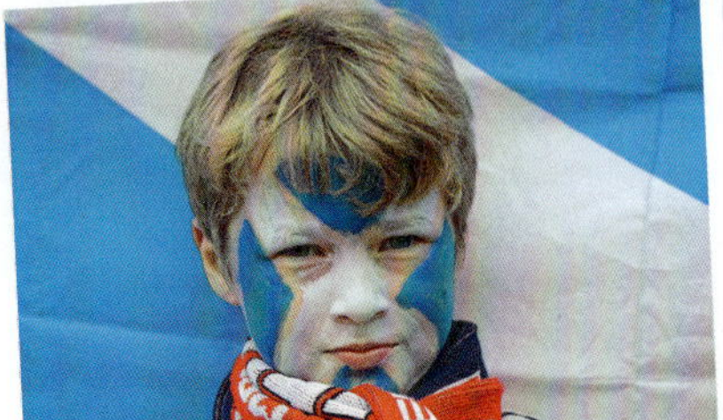

Across cultures

As part of the UK, Scotland's official **national anthem** is *God Save the Queen*. There are several unofficial anthems too, because Scotland has its own football and rugby teams. One of these anthems is the song *Flower of Scotland*. It's about Robert the Bruce who defeated the English King Edward and his soldiers in 1314.

L 2/16

Is that made with meat?

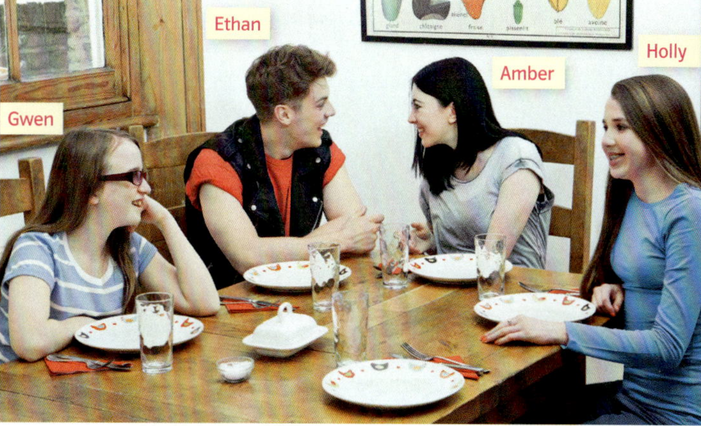

"I hope you're all hungry!" said Kirsty, Gwen's aunt. "We've prepared haggis for you!" It was the girls' first day in Glasgow. Kirsty brought a plate with a large brown object on it to the table. Then she brought some bowls of vegetables.

"Is that made with meat?" asked Holly as she saw the haggis.

"Yes," said Kirsty. "It's made with meat and …"

"I'm a vegetarian," said Holly. "Sorry, I forgot to mention it. I'll just have the vegetables."

"Holly has been a vegetarian since she was ten," said Amber. "She likes to be different."

Ethan laughed, and the others smiled. Holly started to feel embarrassed.

"That's why she always wears pink," Amber went on. "You can see her in her pink jacket with her little pink backpack from a mile away."

"I don't wear pink any more. Haven't you noticed?" said Holly in a cold, quiet voice.

"I like your new house," said Gwen as she tried to change the subject. "When was it built?"

"We think it was built about 150 years ago," said James, Gwen's uncle. "There are thousands of houses like this in Glasgow, but some of them have been pulled down."

"I love your Glasgow accent," said Amber and looked at Ethan. "It sounds so musical."

"I like your London accent too," said Ethan. "What's it like to live there?"

"It's great," said Holly. "I like …"

"She's got me to look after her," said Amber. "I tell her and her friends about all the cool places to go. I teach them how to be cool."

Ethan laughed again, but nobody else did. Holly stared at the table in front of her.

"Let's play a game," said James and gave Amber a strange look. "I'll tell you something about Glasgow, and our guests must say if it's right or wrong. OK, one: Most of the world's whisky is produced in Glasgow."

"Wrong!" said Holly. "Most of the world's whisky is produced in Scotland, but not in Glasgow."

"Correct!" said James. "Two: No ships have been built here since the 1990s."

"Wrong!" said Holly. "The shipbuilding industry isn't that important any more, but some ships are still built here."

"Correct again!" said James.

"I showed Holly how to find things out on the internet," said Amber quickly. "That's how she knows all this stuff."

Everybody looked at Amber. Then Kirsty said, "More haggis anyone?"

EADING

7 Big sister – little sister

a) *How does Amber react to what Holly says? Find examples in the text.*

elllese- n ige on eraus- → S5–6

Example: Amber says embarrassing things about Holly, e.g. lines 15–17: "Holly has been a vegetarian since she was ten. She likes to be different."

b) *Explain why Amber is behaving like this. What advice would you give her? Make notes and act out a dialogue between you and Amber.*

→ S17

dliche Aufgaben Besonderheiten

LANGUAGE

8 Find the rule: Passive forms → G6

KV 50: Working with language

*Look for **passive forms** in the text and collect them in a grid like this. Find the rule about how the passive is made in different tenses. What verb forms do you use?*

Simple present			Simple past			Present perfect		
Subject	'to be'	Past participle	Subject	...	...	Subject	...	...
Haggis	is	made	The house	was				

WB 38/10 Listening (festival plans)

LANGUAGE

9 Hogmanay → WB 38/10

*Write sentences in the **simple present passive**.*

Example: 1. In Scotland, the last day of the year is called Hogmanay.

1. In Scotland, people call the last day of the year Hogmanay.
2. They celebrate this event with street parties.
3. At midnight, they ring bells and set off fireworks.
4. Then people hold hands and sing 'Auld Lang Syne'.

Lösung: 1. *In Scotland, the last day of the year is called Hogmanay.* 2. *This event is celebrated with street parties.* 3. *At midnight, bells are rung and fireworks are set off.* 4. *Then hands are held and 'Auld Lang Syne' is sung.*

LANGUAGE

10 Famous Scots → WB 38/11

WB 38/11 Language (verb forms)

a) *A lot of important inventions and discoveries in the past were made by Scots. Use the words and phrases to make sentences in the **simple past passive**.*

Example:
first sheep | clone | Scottish scientists
→ The first sheep was cloned by Scottish scientists.

1. raincoat | invent | Charles Macintosh
2. Penicillin | discover | Alexander Fleming
3. first steam engine | build | James Watt
4. Sherlock Holmes | create | Sir Arthur Conan Doyle
5. first television station | start | John Logie Baird

Lösung: a) 1. *The raincoat was invented by Charles Macintosh.* 2. *Penicillin was discovered by Alexander Fleming.* 3. *The first steam engine was built by James Watt.* 4. *Sherlock Holmes was created by Sir Arthur Conan Doyle.* 5. *The first television station was started by John Logie Baird.*

Tip

In passive sentences you can use **by ...** if you want to say **who** did something.

b) *Find information about three other famous Scots. Make notes about them as in a). Then exchange your results and make sentences from your partner's notes.*

→ △ 124/9

124/9 Famous Scots
△→ Help with ...

LANGUAGE

11 Facts about haggis

KV 51: You weren't invited to the show!
KV 52: Mediation: Scottish dog breeds

*Complete the text with passive forms: **simple present**, **simple past** or **present perfect**.*

→ △ 125/10
→ ▲ 125/11

A traditional haggis 1 (make) from a sheep's stomach filled with sheep's heart and other parts of the animal, but there's vegetarian haggis too. It 2 (usually eat) with mashed potatoes and other vegetables, but you can also find it as a burger with chips, in a pasta sauce or as a pizza ingredient. Most of the world's haggis 3 (make) in Scotland, but it 4 (probably not invent) there. Some say that it 5 (bring) to Britain by the Romans. Others think it came from Scandinavia. Haggis 6 (sell) around the world, but some people say it isn't healthy. That's why it 7 (ban) in the USA since 1971.

Lösung: 1. *is made* 2. *is usually eaten* 3. *is made* 4. *probably wasn't invented* 5. *was brought* 6. *is sold* 7. *has ('s) been banned*

125/10 Scottish heroes and heroines
△→ After ...
125/11 The story of Greyfriar's Bobby
▲→ After ...

ANGUAGE

12 Active or passive?

a) *Look at the two sentences. Use the phrases on the right to explain why one sentence is* ***active*** *and the other is* ***passive****. Write down the rule.*

1. My mother makes the best haggis in Scotland.
2. Haggis is made from a sheep's stomach.

important who does the action

not important or clear who does the action

b) *Look at these examples. Say why the passive is or isn't used.*

1

POLICE REPORT
Expensive bagpipes were stolen at Glasgow station.

2

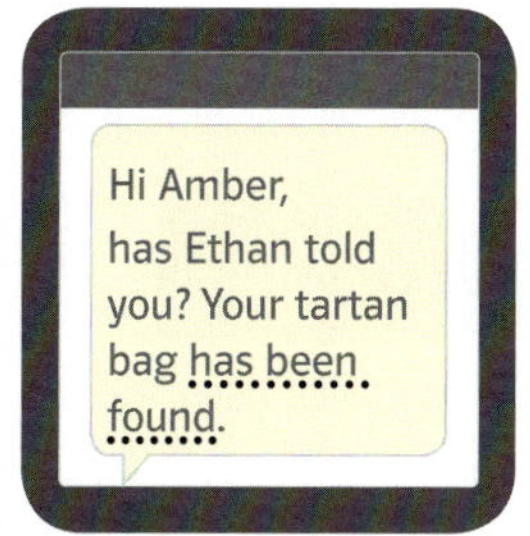

Hi Amber,
has Ethan told you? Your tartan bag has been found.

3

Hi Ethan,
I'll meet you after band practice.
Amber

4

Scottish tennis player
ANDY MURRAY
has been taken to
HOSPITAL!

WB 39/12 Language (passive verb forms)

NGUAGE

13 In Mary King's Close → WB 39/12

Holly and Gwen are planning their trips to different places in Scotland. They've found this information about a popular sight in Edinburgh. Put the active sentences into the passive, where possible. Decide if you need the by-agent.

Hundreds of years ago, people built very high houses in Edinburgh. They stood on dark and narrow streets or 'closes' which led off from the main street. Sometimes they named a close after a person who lived there, like Mary King. Over the centuries people have told many stories about Mary King's Close. One of the most famous is about a little girl called Annie, who died there in 1645. People have seen her ghost many times since. She isn't scary, but she always looks sad. That's why visitors leave so many toys behind for her.

Lösung: *… houses were built, … a close was named, … stories have been told, … ghost has been seen, … toys are left*

RITING

14 Glasgow is amazing!

a) *Look at the short text from a website about Glasgow. What kind of language does it use? How does it try to get the reader's attention?*

Do you know that Glasgow is famous for its shipbuilding industry? Titan Clydebank is a shipbuilding crane which has become one of the most amazing tourist attractions in Glasgow. Are you brave enough to climb up to the top? Fantastic views across Glasgow are waiting for you …

→ △ 125/12

b) *Find another Glasgow sight, attraction or event on the internet. Use your ideas from a) to write 2–3 sentences about it. Try to get the reader's attention.*

asgow is

with …

L 2/18–19

Holly's blog

Folie 3/11: Reaktivierung von Vorwissen, Sicherung des Hörverstehens

Hi folks! Time for a new update. We've been so busy these last days. Got lots of news for you. Hope you like my latest pics …

I thought the biggest lake in Scotland was Loch Ness, but it's actually Loch Lomond (in fact, it's the biggest lake in Britain). We went there for a boat trip. I know: typical tourists!

Just because Loch Ness was too far away to visit didn't mean we couldn't see the monster! Isn't she cute?

Voc.: Continents, Countries, WB (Word bank), pp. 7–11

On our second evening we went to a ceilidh, an event with traditional Gaelic music and dancing. At first I pronounced it 'kay-lid' but now I know it's actually 'kay-lee'. The dancing was easy to learn, and lots of fun. We really liked the band, but I think Ethan was a bit jealous. Oops!

You can't visit Balmoral Castle (unless you're a member of the Royal Family of course!) but we did see Will & Kate. Really – they came to visit Glasgow the day before yesterday! I tried to take a pic, but there were too many people. So here's a photo of Balmoral Castle from the internet. Not much bigger than Ethan's house!

Glasgow is in the Lowlands area, but we've taken a couple of trips north into the Highlands. Amazing landscape!

Gwen and I made some new friends. I don't think we have cows like this down south.

They really love dancing here! We saw this while we were walking around the shops. Nice kilts, gentlemen! Did you know that each clan has its own tartan? It's worn to weddings or ceilidhs, and some men wear it when they go out at night. I'd really like to know what they wear – or don't wear – under those kilts!

Yesterday we went to a living history show about a battle in 1314 when the Scots defeated the English. They were at war very often in those days! But in 1603, Scotland's King James also became King of England and in 1707, both countries formed Great Britain. It seems they can't live without each other …

Have you ever heard of the Highland Games? These are events which are held everywhere in Scotland (even in the Lowlands). I'd love to see them some time. I've just found some photos on the internet, and it looks amazing. What's this guy doing? I'm really curious.

Today we went to Edinburgh – finally! Glasgow is the biggest city, but of course Edinburgh is the capital and it's beautiful with all the historic houses. Personally, I like Glasgow – the 'ugly sister' – much more! Maybe it's because I know how it feels to be number two … 🙂

WB 39/13 Vocabulary (Scotland quiz)
WB 39/14 Writing (Germany quiz)
WB 40/15 Mediation (dialogue)
WB 40/16 Speaking (role play)

ADING

15 How much do you know about Scotland? → WB 39/13–14, 40/15–16

a) *Think of ten questions you can ask about Scotland. Use the information from Holly's blog and from what you've heard in this unit so far. Write down your questions on a piece of paper.*

Examples: What's the Scottish word for 'lake'?
How is 'ceilidh' pronounced?

b) *Now divide your class up into two groups. Take turns to ask each other your questions from a). For each correct answer your group gets one point. Make sure that nobody asks the same question twice!*

WB 40/16 Speaking (role play)

ITING

fer

16 Your turn: Write your own travel blog → WB 40/16

→ S11–14

S11–14 Writing

Write a travel blog about a holiday or a trip which was especially funny or interesting. Find pictures on the internet or draw the places / scenes. Think of interesting texts to go with the pictures.

How to write a persuasive text

When you write a text to persuade other people to do something, e.g. visit a particular place or attraction, it's important to make your text interesting and to grab your reader's attention.

1 Criteria for a good persuasive text

→ S5–6

Look at the ideas on the right. Find examples for these criteria in the text. Compare your results with a partner.

talking to the reader personally | local tips | longer sentences with linking words | humour | an interesting final sentence | strong adjectives

S5 Schnelllesetechniken
S6 Wichtige Inhalte von Texten herausfinden

Voc.: Describing nature and buildings, p. 191

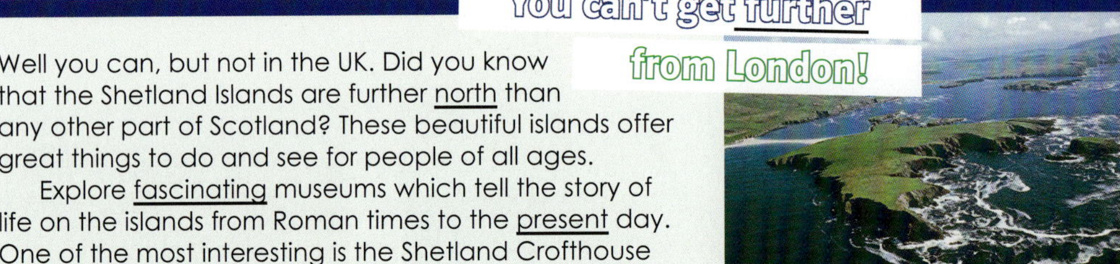

You can't get further from London!

Well you can, but not in the UK. Did you know that the Shetland Islands are further north than any other part of Scotland? These beautiful islands offer great things to do and see for people of all ages.

Explore fascinating museums which tell the story of life on the islands from Roman times to the present day. One of the most interesting is the Shetland Crofthouse Museum in Dunrossness. Here you can feel what it was like to live on the islands in the 1870s.

If history isn't your thing, our islands offer a lot of exciting outdoor activities. Take a boat trip along the amazing coastlines or improve your climbing skills at one of the spectacular cliffs. But please make sure you reach the top! After your personal adventure, you can relax and visit our tiny, world-famous Shetland ponies.

Probably the best reason to visit the Shetland Islands is to meet the people. Our islands may be small but we have big hearts! So come and see us – and leave everything behind …

WB 41/17 Skills (adjectives)

2 Strong adjectives → WB 41/17

a) *Strong adjectives can help you to make your text livelier and more interesting to read. Copy the grid. Then fill in the words on the right. Sometimes they fit in more than one category.*

small	good	nice	big
tiny			

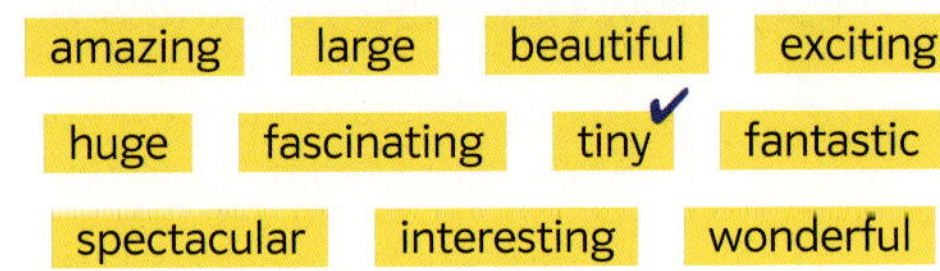

amazing | large | beautiful | exciting | huge | fascinating | tiny | fantastic | spectacular | interesting | wonderful

b) *Find more adjectives for each category and add them to your grid.*

WB 41/18 Writing/Speaking (options)

3 Write your own text → WB 41/18

HA → S11–14

S11–14 Writing

Choose one of these tasks. Write a short text and make it as interesting as possible. The criteria from Ex. 1 and the strong adjectives from Ex. 2 can help you. Then exchange your texts and give each other feedback.

- Write an advert to persuade tourists to visit your home town.
- Write a text for a flyer about a festival or other event which you enjoyed.

Visit Scotland!

A friend of your family has a house in Scotland and he wants to rent it out to families for their holidays. He asks you to help him with a travel brochure about the region where his house is.

Step 1

WB 42/19 Choose a place to visit (Visit Scotland)

Get organised

→ WB 42/19

Get into groups of 4–5. Choose a part of Scotland which you're interested in. This can be a city, an island or any other part of Scotland, but it should be a place people would want to visit for a holiday. (The map at the back of the book can help you.)

→ Introduction (pp. 54–55) → Holly's blog (pp. 62–63)

Step 2

WB 42/20 Find information (National Museum of Scotland)

Find information about your place

→ WB 42/20

HA

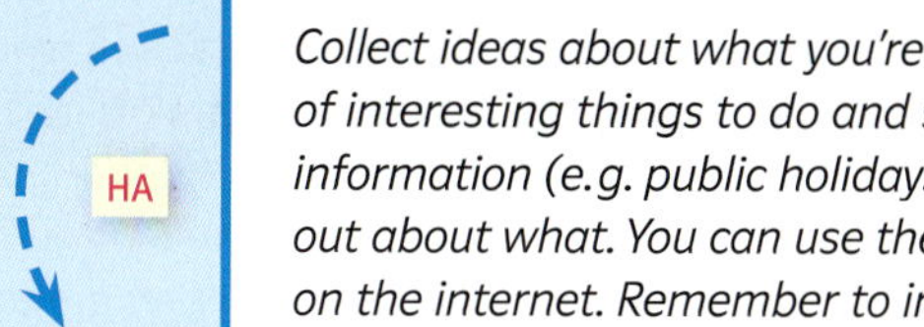

*Collect ideas about what you're going to put in the brochure. Include lots of interesting things to do and see in and around your place, and useful information (e.g. public holidays, transport, etc.). Agree on who's going to find out about what. You can use the information in this unit and do some research on the internet. Remember to include things to do for people of **all** ages.*

Step 3

WB 43/21 Organise information and design (Scottish National Gallery)

Organise the information

→ WB 43/21

a) *Now organise your information. What order should it be in? Does it cover all the important points? Have you found interesting pictures?*

b) *Try to find good examples for brochures in a travel agency or on the internet. How are texts and pictures arranged on the pages? Discuss your ideas of how you want to design your brochure.*

HA

Step 4

Write your brochure

KV 53: Visit Scotland!

Write your part of the brochure. When you've finished all your parts, put them together to make the brochure.

→ present perfect progressive (pp. 56–58) → passive forms (pp. 59–61) → Writing a persuasive text (p. 64)

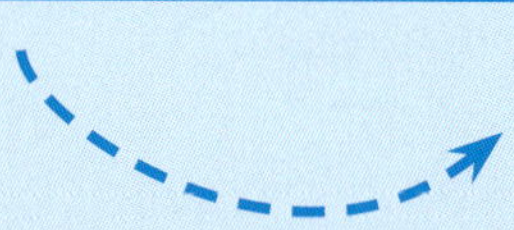

Step 5

Present your brochure

Put the brochures on tables around the classroom. Then have a look at the other groups' brochures. Decide which region you'd like to visit. Give reasons for your choice.

S1/26–29 L2/20–23

I don't believe in ghosts!

Folie 3/12: Vermutungen über Fortgang der Handlung anstellen

SPEAKING

1 Before you read

Have you ever been in a dangerous situation, or maybe someone you know? What happened? How did you or this other person feel? Share your experiences with a partner.

A "That last song from Ethan's band was really good," said Gwen. "I liked the part with the bagpipes. I've never heard that in a rock song." It was the end of the festival. The sky was getting dark and people were starting to go home. "Do you want to have a look round the castle? My parents won't be here for another hour."

"OK," said Holly. "If it's still open. I don't know when it closes."

They walked to the castle entrance. It was free to go in on the day of the festival, and there was nobody in the ticket office. They came through some big empty rooms with stone walls. Suddenly the lights went out.

"I can't see!" said Holly.

"Welcome to my world," said Gwen and laughed. "Don't worry, I'll get us back to the entrance."

Gwen took Holly's hand, led her back to the entrance hall and tried to open the door. It was locked.

"I'll call Amber," said Holly, and took her phone from her pocket. "Oh, there's no signal. Maybe because of the thick stone walls."

"Perhaps there's another way out. Let's find out."

Stop and think:

How do you think Holly and Gwen can get out of the castle?

B "We've been going round in circles," said Holly. "We're at the door for the museum again." She was using her mobile phone as a torch.

"Did you hear that?" said Gwen. There was a strange sound coming from another part of the castle. It sounded like a wounded animal.

"Yes, I heard it," Holly whispered. She was starting to feel scared. The noise came again, louder this time.

"Come on," said Gwen. "Let's find out what it is. I don't believe in ghosts!"

They went through some more rooms and then through a door into a tower. A little moonlight was coming through a small window.

"The sound is coming from above us," said Gwen.

The stairs going up the tower were very old, and some of them were missing. When they carefully climbed up the noise got louder. The stairs ended at an old wooden door.

"What do you think is in there?" Gwen asked in a nervous voice.

"There's only one way to find out," said Holly, and pushed open the door.

Stop and think:

Who or what do you think is behind the door?

C At first it was too dark inside the room, but then Holly saw something moving on the other side.

"Amber!" Holly shouted.

Amber stopped crying and looked up. "Holly! Is it really you?"

"What are *you* doing here?" Holly asked.

"I came up here to get a better view of Ethan's band. But look at the floor!"

There was no floor between the door and the other side of the tower, where Amber was sitting. "It started to fall down when I was walking across it," said Amber.

Then Holly noticed a sign on the door: DANGER! KEEP OUT!

A cracking sound came from where Amber was sitting.

"Oh no!" said Amber. "Now I think this part of the floor is going to fall too."

Holly realised they didn't have much time. "Got a knife?" she asked Gwen.

"I've got a little knife on my key ring." Holly took the knife from Gwen, and quickly took the pink backpack off her back. She cut the backpack into long pieces and tied them together to make a rope. "Here, catch!" Holly shouted and threw the rope across to Amber. "Hold onto the rope," she said. "I'll tie it to the door."

Amber caught the rope. Then there was a big crack, and the floor started to fall into the tower. Amber screamed and went down together with pieces of old wood. When she hit the side of the tower, she cried out in pain.

"Are you OK?" shouted Holly, as she held onto the rope as hard as she could.

"Yeah, I'm OK," came a very scared voice from below.

"I don't think we can pull her up," said Gwen. "She's too heavy."

Then they heard somebody shouting from below.

"It's Ethan!" said Gwen.

"I've been trying to find you since the end of the gig," he called up, as he climbed the stairs. "A man let me into the castle to look for you and …" He came through the door, and realised what was happening. "I think the three of us will be enough," he said, and took the end of the rope.

D "Nothing broken," said the doctor. "You can go home. And next time you see a sign that says KEEP OUT maybe you should do what it says."

Amber was sitting on a stone wall outside the castle. Holly, Gwen, Ethan and Gwen's parents were all looking at her.

"Thanks for saving my life," Amber said.

"You're welcome," Holly answered.

"I've been saying some stupid things, and I'm really sorry about it. I don't know why I've been doing it. Maybe it's just because I'm your big sister and I always think I have to show that. Please let's be friends again."

"Yes, let's be friends," Holly said with a smile. "You see, we love each other really," she said to the others.

"I'll buy you another backpack," said Amber. "But not pink."

"No, definitely not pink," said Holly.

EAKING

2 Your reaction

Which parts of the story did or didn't you like? Explain why.

KV 54: I don't believe in ghosts!
WB 44/22 Reading (true/false)
WB 44/23 Reading (sentence completion)

EADING

3 Understanding the story → WB 44/22–23

→ S5–6

ellesetechniken
tige Inhalte von
erausfinden

a) *Describe the picture. Which part of the story does it show? Sum up what happens before and after the scene in the picture.*

b) *For each part of the story, write down what the characters feel. How does this match what you talked about in Ex. 1?*

READING

4 The climax of the story

→ S7

S7 Wichtige Merkmale von Erzähltexten, Gedichten und Theaterstücken erkennen

a) *Read the information in the skills box. Explain where the climax in this story is.*

b) *Do you think the climax is realistic? Give reasons for your opinion.*

Start like this:
I think the climax is realistic because the castle is very old and dangerous. / I don't think it's realistic because …

Reading skills

The **climax** is the main turning point in a story, when the suspense is highest. At this point the main character usually gets in a difficult situation and changes in some way, e.g. becomes stronger and more confident.

c) *With a partner, think of ideas for a different climax. Then present them to the class. Give feedback about how realistic your classmates' ideas are.*

SPEAKING

5 Role play: An interview with Holly and Amber

→ △ 125/13
→ S17

125/13 An interview with Holly and Amber
△ → Help with …
S17 Mündliche Aufgaben und ihre Besonderheiten

a) *A reporter for the local newspaper wants to interview Holly and Amber about what happened. In groups of three, think of questions you'd like to ask the two girls and of possible answers they could give from their perspective.*

b) *Each of you takes the role of one of the characters – the reporter, Holly or Amber. Practise the interview. Then act it out in class.*

WB 44/24 Writing (conversation or review)

WRITING

6 Write an extra scene for the story → WB 44/24

HA → S11–14

S11–14 Writing

a) *Use your ideas from Ex. 5 to tell what happened to Amber* ***before*** *Holly and Gwen found her. Say why Amber went into the castle and climbed up the tower. Describe how she felt when she was trapped.*

Start like this: "Where on earth did all these people come from?" Amber tried hard to see Ethan and his band, but she soon gave up. Then she had an idea …

b) *Get into groups of 3–4. Read your extra scene to the other group members. Choose the version you like best. Try to improve it if you can. Then present your group's version to the class.*

MEDIATION

7 A Scottish legend: The spider

L 2/24

→ S18

S18 Mediation

a) *You're collecting interesting facts and stories about Scotland because you want to convince your parents to spend your next family holiday there. Listen to the legend about Robert the Bruce and make notes about what happens. The following words and phrases can help you:*

Robert the Bruce | fight the English | hide in a cave | spider's web | not give up

b) *Now sum up the legend in German for your parents, and say why it makes Scotland interesting for you.*

How times change → S22–23

Folie 3/13: Vorentlastung, Sicherung des Hörsehverstehens
S22–23 Film skills/Viewing

SPEAKING

1 Warm-up: Helping out in the neighbourhood

Have you ever helped out in your neighbourhood, e.g. done the shopping for someone, read books to an elderly person, etc.? Tell your partner about your experiences. Explain what it meant to the person you helped and what it meant to you.

KV 55: Viewing for detail
WB 45/25 Writing (e-mail)

VIEWING

2 Scotland is famous for its inventors → WB 45/25

DVD 3/3

a) *Watch the film. Look at the stills and find headings for the two parts. Sum up what happens in each part.*

A

B

b) *What Scottish inventors does Alva talk about? Choose from the list and match the inventors with the correct invention.*

1. Alexander Graham Bell
2. John Henry Holmes
3. Robert Hooke
4. John Logie Baird

a) tin can telephone
b) light switch
c) television
d) telephone

Lösung: b) *1d), 4c)*

EAKING

3 Old vs. new

KV 56: A famous Scottish inventor

a) *The film shows one example of how communication has changed over time (rotary phone vs. smartphone/internet). What other inventions (old vs. new) do you know about? Look at the categories below for ideas.*

uns and adjectives,

transport | free time | music | travel | media

Transfer
HA

b) *Your turn: "Scotland is famous for its inventors." What's your region/town famous for? Write 4–5 sentences.*

KV 58–61 Test yourself
KV 62–64 Speaking cards
WB 47/1 Listening (dialogues)

LISTENING

1 Landscapes → WB 47/1

L2/25

a) *Listen to the description of a landscape and draw it in your exercise book. Then compare your picture with those of a partner. Is anything missing?*

b) *Find a picture of a landscape or a city and describe it to your partner. Your partner must draw the picture. Compare it to the original picture.*

LANGUAGE

2 Berlin then and now

Use the words and phrases below to make sentences in the ***present*** *or* ***past passive***.

Lösung: 2. *In a survey, Berlin was voted the most 'fun' city in the world.* 3. *150 years ago, there were no cars so everything was pulled by horses.* 4. *In the 1800s, industry was growing and a lot of machines were produced in Berlin.* 5. *Berlin is very popular and every year its sights are visited by millions of tourists.* 6. *The 'curry-wurst', a popular street food dish, was invented by Herta Heuwer.* 7. *Today, to make extra money, many flats are rented out to tourists.* 8. *The fall of the Berlin wall is celebrated at the Brandenburg Gate each year.*

	+	+
1. The oldest church in Berlin 2. In a survey, Berlin 3. 150 years ago, there were no cars so everything 4. In the 1800s, industry was growing and a lot of machines 5. Berlin is very popular and every year its sights 6. The 'currywurst', a popular street food dish[1], 7. Today, to make extra money, many flats 8. The fall of the Berlin wall	pull visit invent celebrate rent out build vote produce	by Herta Heuwer. the most 'fun' city in the world. by horses. to tourists. in 1230. by millions of tourists. in Berlin. at the Brandenburg Gate each year.

Example: 1. The oldest church in Berlin was built in 1230.

VOCABULARY

3 Word puzzles

Lösung: 2. *mashed potatoes* 3. *backpack* 4. *bagpipes*

Find words and phrases in these word puzzles.

Example: 1. I understand

1 dish [dɪʃ] Gericht; Speise

ANGUAGE

4 Time for a change
→ WB 47/2

WB 47/2 Language (grammar)

ng: a) 1. have ('ve) been 2. for 3. haven't been ng 4. since 5. have ('ve) saving 6. since 7. haven't growing 8. since 9. has improving 10. haven't producing 11. for 12. have been renting out 13. have been thinking 14. have ('ve) doing 15. for

a) *Complete the text with* **for, since** *and the verbs in the* **present perfect progressive**.

Dear Mum and Dad,
You 1 (give) me the same pocket money 2 three years! Don't you think it's time for a change? Remember: I 3 (not wear) nappies[1] 4 I was about two. Think of all the money you 5 (save) 6 then. And I 7 (not grow) as much 8 I turned 15 so I don't need many new clothes. And you must agree: My behaviour[2] 9 (improve) these last few months. I 10 (not produce) whisky in the garage 11 six weeks now. Just joking! But I 12 (rent out) my tablet to friends to earn some extra money. And I 13 (think) about you too. It's unhealthy to stay the same. You 14 (do) the same thing 15 three years! So really I'm just trying to help you. We can both look forward to a change next month, right?
Love, Jack

b) *What have you been doing for a long time? Which things would you like to change in your life and why?*

EDIATION

5 Let's celebrate!

You're on an exchange in England and you've been trying to explain the German tradition of 'Karneval'. You've found this website and show it to your host brother. Tell him about it.

Fasching, Fastnacht, Karneval

In Süddeutschland, Bayern und Österreich wird diese besondere Zeit des Jahres „Fasching" oder „Fastnacht" genannt, in der Mitte und im Norden Deutschlands heißt es „Karneval". Die Traditionen und Bräuche[3] sind unterschiedlich, aber die Umzüge[4] und Feiern finden überall zur gleichen Zeit statt (vom 11. November bis einen Tag vor Aschermittwoch[5]). In Deutschland wird schon seit Jahrhunderten gefeiert, aber es heißt, dass auch die Römer schon Karneval kannten.
Manche Leute feiern Fasching, um den Winter zu beenden. Andere wollen viel feiern, bevor die Fastenzeit[6] vor Ostern beginnt. Und alle, die feiern, wollen ganz schön laut sein. Sie singen, machen Musik, lachen, laufen durch die Straßen und tanzen. In manchen Gegenden gibt es sogar Schulferien um diese Zeit!

1

„Seit Juni arbeiten wir an unserem Wagen für den Karnevalsumzug in Köln[7]."

2

„In meinem Dorf tragen wir seit 200 Jahren die gleichen Masken[8] und Kostüme."

3

„Meine Maske wurde schon von meinem Großvater und meinem Vater getragen!"

1 **nappy** ['næpi] Windel | 2 **behavior** [bɪ'heɪvjə] Verhalten | 3 **custom** ['kʌstəm] | 4 **parade** [pə'reɪd] | 5 **Ash Wednesday** [æʃ'wenzdeɪ] | 6 **Lent** [lent] | 7 **Cologne** [kə'ləʊn] | 8 **mask** [mɑ:sk]

VOCABULARY

6 Boring!

Lösung: a) Dear Sue, Edinburgh is amazing. I really feel at home here. […] I start walking and then I go round in circles. […] Sometimes you can still see people in traditional clothes, like the kilts. […] Edinburgh castle is world-famous and every August there's a huge festival here. The landscape is fascinating here too. If you go to the top of Calton Hill at night and look up, it feels like you're under a shower of stars. If you tell your friends about this, please try to whisper. I don't want billions of tourists here – just me! Best, Lilian

a) *Rewrite this e-mail to make it more interesting. Use the ideas on the right to replace the words and phrases in* blue.

at home here | whisper | a shower of stars | world-famous | huge | amazing | fascinating | billions of | go round in circles | traditional clothes

Dear Sue,
Edinburgh is so nice! I love it. I really feel like I've been living in this city forever. Well, sometimes I still get lost in the old part of the town. I start walking and then I come back to the same place that I started.
Edinburgh is a very old city. Sometimes you can still see people in clothes that are typical for Scotland, like the kilts. The city is full of fun things to do. Edinburgh Castle is known around the world and every August there's a very big arts festival here.
The landscape is nice here too. If you go to the top of Calton Hill at night and look up, it feels like you're under lots of stars which are falling down on you. If you tell your friends about this, please try to say it very quietly. I don't want too many tourists here – just me!
Best,
Lilian

b) *Use strong adjectives to answer one of these questions in 2–4 sentences.*

How was your day at school? | What did you have for lunch?

c) *Work in small groups. One person asks a 'boring' question like in b). The others take turns to give answers. Try to make your answers more and more interesting.*

LANGUAGE

7 Only in Scotland

Practise this dialogue with a partner. Where possible, change the active sentences to passive and the passive sentences to active to make the dialogue sound more natural.

Lösung: Alan: *Lots of people enjoyed the concert last night.*
David: *Most of us just ignored the storm.*
Alan: *Did the roof keep out the rain?*
David: *A lot of people put on raincoats.*
[…]
Alan: *A bagpipe contest has been planned by some people. And there's a new contest where people walk on thistles.*
David: *Well, now we can say thistle-walking was invented by the Scots!*
Alan: *The winners of the bagpipe contest judge the thistle-walking contest.*
David: *Yes, this can only be found in Scotland!*

Alan: The concert[1] last night was enjoyed by lots of people. But a storm interrupted[2] our gig. The weather really disappointed us.
David: Oh, that doesn't matter. The storm was just ignored by most of us.
Alan: Was the rain kept out by the roof?
David: Most of it! Raincoats were put on by a lot of people.
Alan: Were they rented out?
David: Yeah, they usually do that at concerts. What's going on at the Highland Games tomorrow?
Alan: Some people have planned a bagpipe contest. And there's a new contest where thistles are walked on. Sounds dangerous!
David: Well, now we can say the Scots invented thistle-walking!
Alan: And listen to this, this is great. The thistle-walking contest is judged by the winners of the bagpipe contest. Funny, isn't it?!
David: Yes, you only find that in Scotland!

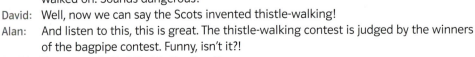

1 **concert** ['kɒnsət] Konzert | 2 **to interrupt** [ˌɪntəˈrʌpt] unterbrechen; stören

ANGUAGE

8 Scotland is the country which ...

a) *Complete these rules about **relative pronouns** and **relative clauses**.*

ng: a) 1. 'who' 2. things
nimals 3. 'that'
ect 5. subject
2h), 3j), 4a), 5d), 6g),
f), 9e), 10c)

1. The relative pronoun ... is used for people.
2. The relative pronoun 'which' is used for ...
3. The relative pronouns 'whose' and ... are used for people or things.
4. You don't need the relative pronoun if it's the ... of the sentence.
5. If the relative pronoun is the ..., it's always followed directly by a verb.

b) *Match the sentence parts and make sentences about Scotland with or without a relative pronoun.*

1. The Fringe is one of the many festivals	a) the Scots fought long and hard for in the 14th century.
2. Ewan McGregor is the Scottish actor	b) history goes back thousands of years.
3. Many people	c) discovery changed the world.
4. Independence from England is something	d) many people outside of Scotland have never played.
5. Shinty is a typical Scottish game	e) English and Scottish soldiers fought in 1314 was won by the Scots.
6. Haggis is a Scottish meal	f) they do at a ceilidh[1] is easy to learn.
7. Glasgow is a very old city	g) not everybody likes to eat.
8. The dancing	h) is best known for his role in *Star Wars*.
9. The battle[2]	i) are held[3] in Edinburgh each year.
10. Alexander Fleming was a Scottish scientist	j) are looking for an adventure go to Loch Ness.

Example: 1. The Fringe ist one of the many festivals which / that are held in Edinburgh each year.

ABULARY

9 How I've changed

a) *Complete the article with the missing words.*

vegetarian | definitely | discovery | independent | invent | realise | independence | worry | confident

: a) 1. invented
sed 3. discovery
itely 5. confident
tarian 7. independent
9. independence

When I look back at when I was little, I can't believe that I was like that. I played with toys and I wore any clothes that my mum chose for me. But since about last year I've **1** a new 'me'. That's when I **2** that I wanted to be my own person. It was a spectacular **3**! I babysit and earn some of my own money now so I don't need my parents as much. I've **4** become more **5**. That means I can buy my own clothes and I make more of my own decisions. I've become a **6** too. My dad has been calling me **7**. I like how that sounds. Sometimes they still **8** about me and I have to show them that they can trust me. So in some ways, **9** is like a job – you have to work for it and work at it. So at the moment, I feel more like an adult than a 14-year-old.

b) *Use the text in a) as an example and tell a partner how you've changed. Which of your hobbies / friends / interests have changed? Why? Because of age? peer pressure? parents? moved house?*

1 ceilidh ['keɪli] *schottisches Fest* | 2 battle ['bætl] Schlacht; Kampf | 3 to hold [həʊld] held, held abhalten

LANGUAGE

10 At Balmoral Castle

WB 48/3 Language (phrases)

a) *First change the **adjectives** into **adverbs**. Then make as many pairs with the verbs as possible.*

awful | happy | good | perfect | safe | thankful | cheap | fast

sing | run | act | smile | speak | arrive | answer | eat

b) *Adjective or adverb? Complete the text with the right forms.*

I just had to see William and Kate! I thought it would be very **1** (easy). In the news it said they'd be at Balmoral Castle at the weekend. I packed my backpack with **2** (warm) clothes, food and drinks. At 2:00 I arrived **3** (safe) at Balmoral Castle and **4** (confident) sat down in front of it. You can stay in **5** (little) houses at the castle, but it's very **6** (expensive), so I decided **7** (brave) to camp until the Royal Family arrived. I took everything out of my backpack. I had planned everything **8** (perfect). But then a guard came from behind and said to me **9** (rude), "What are you doing? You can't just sit here!" I answered very **10** (sweet), "I'm waiting for the Royal Family. I'd like to meet them **11** (personal)." He grabbed my arm **12** (rough[1]) and then **13** (quick) threw everything into my backpack. He walked me back to the road and that's when it happened. A car drove **14** (slow) towards the castle and then stopped **15** (quick). The guard greeted William and Kate and I could **16** (easy) see them through the open car windows. And they gave me a **17** (friendly) smile. So I was **18** (successful) after all!

Lösung: a) *sing awfully, happily, well, perfectly; run fast; act well, perfectly; smile happily, thankfully; speak well, fast; arrive happily, safely, fast; answer happily, well, thankfully, fast; eat cheaply, fast*
b) *1. easy 2. warm 3. safely 4. confidently 5. little 6. expensive 7. bravely 8. perfectly 9. rudely 10. sweetly 11. personally 12. roughly 13. quickly 14. slowly 15. quickly 16. easily 17. friendly 18. successful*

WRITING

11 Our school

WB 48/4 Speaking (role play)

In small groups, design a brochure or an internet page for your school in English. What makes your school different, spectacular, typical? What do you like most about it? These ideas can help you.

People
Our History teacher won a prize for ...
We have students from 15 different ...

Location
XYZ school is in the middle of ...
We are very close to ...

Activities
We have teams for ...
Every afternoon you can ...

Building
Our school is in a historic / modern ...
We have three buildings and a pool ...

Courses
Our school offers six different ...
The size of our classes is ...

1 rough [rʌf] grob

.ANGUAGE

12 New interests

*Make one sentence from two. Use **relative pronouns**.*

Example: 1. These are my new shoes (which / that) I bought last week.

1. These are my new shoes. I bought them last week. 2. Here are all my clothes. I don't like them any more. 3. I met a girl. Her sister is a model. 4. She gave me some new ideas. These will help me with my style. 5. She showed me her outfits. They all looked great. 6. Together we bought some new T-shirts. They were very expensive. 7. Before I met her, I had other hobbies. They were important for me. 8. Now I'm one of the fashionistas. They think of nothing else but[1] fashion.

Lösung: *2. Here are all my clothes (which / that) I don't like any more. 3. I met a girl whose sister is a model. 4. She gave me some new ideas which / that will help me with my style. 5. She showed me her outfits which / that all looked great. 6. Together we bought some new T-shirts which / that were very expensive. 7. Before I met her I had other hobbies which / that were important for me. 8. Now I'm one of the fashionistas who / that think of nothing else but fashion.*

ANGUAGE

13 At the ceilidh

a) *Which sentence matches which diagram?*

1. Ethan was playing the bagpipes when the phone rang.
2. Holly was looking at the landscape while Amber was looking at Ethan.
3. At 10:00 Gwen was talking to her mum on the phone.

A. 9:30 10:30

B. simple past / past progressive

C.

b) *Look at the pictures and make sentences. Use the **simple past** and the **past progressive**.*

Start like this: 1. They were having dinner when …

;: a) 1B, 2C, 3A
ey were having
when Holly's mobile
. At 20:00 they were
g at a ceilidh.
e the others were
g, Ethan and Amber
rting. 4. When
was singing, Amber
d. 5. When Ethan
ber were kissing,
ok photos of them.
Gwen was taking
, Holly was showing
photos.

1

have dinner

ring

2

20:00 dance at ceilidh

3

dance flirt

4

sing go red[2]

5

kiss[3] take photos

6

take a break show

1 **but** [bʌt] außer | 2 **to go red** rot werden | 3 **to kiss** [kɪs] küssen

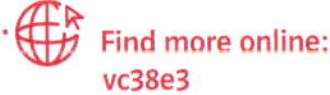
Find more online: vc38e3

Text smart 2
Factual texts

Text smart 2 is about factual texts: texts with useful facts and information. You're going to deal with different kinds of factual texts and learn what their features are, how to understand them and how you can write them yourself.

SPEAKING

1 Warm-up: Where to find information

a) *Read the boy and the girl's dialogue. How would **you** look for the same information?*

A: You're looking for cooking information for your mum? Here?
B: Well this is a library, and libraries have books!
A: Sure, but it's all on the internet, isn't it? Let's have a look …

b) *Your turn: Think of more situations when you need factual information on a topic. Where do you find it? What media do you use? Say why.*

VOCABULARY

2 Different kinds of factual texts

Match the situations on the left with the correct factual text on the right.

1. If you want to know the meaning of a word,
2. If you need basic information about something,
3. If you want to make a cake,
4. If you want to know about important news,
5. If you want to know how to do / make something,
6. If you need an answer to a question that lots of people have asked before,

a) you look for it in an FAQ.
b) you read / watch / listen to a news report.
c) you read a dictionary entry.
d) you follow a recipe for it.
e) you read a reference article.
f) you need to follow the instructions.

Losung: *1c), 2e), 3d), 4b), 5f), 6a)*

SPEAKING

3 Before you read

a) *Look at the next page. What do you expect from the text when you read the headline and look at the photos?*

b) *Say what you already know about hedgehogs. Have you ever seen one?*

Reading skills

A difficult text becomes easier once you **know something about the topic** before you read:

- First, think of your own experiences.
- Also think of questions on the topic that you'd like to ask, and try to collect useful vocabulary.
- And remember: You already know ways to deal with new words (→S10), so don't worry!

What do the instructions say?

S 2/1–4
L 2/30–33

Hedgehog over-wintering instructions

Before the winter months, many young hedgehogs try to eat a lot so they will survive hibernation. If you see a large hedgehog, you can help it by putting out some cat or dog food and water. If it is smaller, looking ill or behaving in an odd way, you should take it to your nearest wildlife hospital for a full examination.

If hedgehogs are too small to make it through the winter period alone, it is necessary to feed and clean them until their weight builds up and they are ready for release in the spring. This takes up a lot of the valuable space we need at the hospital to treat other wild animals. How YOU can help:

1. Take care of a small hedgehog until around mid-April, when the frosts are usually over.
2. Keep it in a warm area such as a shed or spare room. It will need an area where it can sleep and wander round a little bit without getting lost or stuck (they can fit into VERY small spaces). It is essential to keep it warm and active to avoid hibernation; it is too small and WILL NOT survive!
3. Give the hedgehog a container to sleep in. Leave it in the run area so that it can come out when it wants. This bed should contain shredded newspaper (NOT OFFICE PAPER – IT CUTS THEIR NOSE AND FEET), dry leaves or hay.
4. Line the run area with newspaper so you can clean it out daily. Just take up the top sheets of newspaper; that leaves it nice and clean underneath. Always make sure the layer of newspaper on the floor is thick enough to soak up any urine or water.
5. Hedgehogs must have fresh food daily and they MUST have fresh water at all times! The best food to give them is tinned cat or dog food.
6. We will give you a weight chart for each hedgehog. You MUST weigh it at least once a week to make sure it is gaining weight.
7. Only handle the hedgehog when you clean or weigh it. Hedgehogs are wild animals which MUST remain fearful of humans!

As soon as the hedgehog reaches the target weight of about 750g, you should contact us so we can release it back into the wild.

READING

4 Understanding the text

KV 65 Hedgehog over-wintering instructions
KV 66 More instructions

→ △ 126/1

126/1 What's that in English?
△→ Help with …

a) *Match these German words with English words in the text.*

Winterschlaf | überleben | vermeiden | Dosenfutter | Schicht aus Zeitungspapier | zunehmen | menschenscheu | aufsaugen | Auslauf | aktiv halten

→ S5–6

b) *Now say what the text is about and what the main parts are.*

S5 Schnelllesetechniken
S6 Wichtige Inhalte von Texten herausfinden

c) *In the text, find out the answers to these questions. Give line numbers.*

1. When should you take a hedgehog to the wildlife hospital?
2. Where can you keep a hedgehog?
3. What happens when small hedgehogs go into hibernation?
4. Why do you have to use a lot of paper?
5. What is the wrong kind of paper, and why?
6. What is the best food for hedgehogs?
7. When can you release the hedgehog back into the wild?

Lösung: a) Winterschlaf – *hibernation;* überleben – *survive;* vermeiden – *avoid;* Dosenfutter – *tinned food;* Schicht aus Zeitungspapier – *layer of newspaper;* zunehmen – *gain weight;* menschenscheu – *fearful of humans;* aufsaugen – *soak up;* Auslauf – *run area;* aktiv halten – *keep active* **c)** 1. *ll. 4–7,* 2. *ll. 16–17,* 3. *ll. 20–21,* 4. *ll. 27–32,* 5. *ll. 24-26,* 6. *ll. 34–35,* 7. *ll. 42–43*

READING

5 The language of instructions → WB 49/1

KV 65 Hedgehog over-wintering instructions **WB 49/1** Reading (hedgehog

→ △ 126/2
→ S12

126/2 Writing instructions
△→ Help with …
S12 Textsorten und ihre Besonderheiten

Read the skills box. Then make a grid with these two categories:

1. **Steps**
2. **Phrases**

Now go back to the hedgehog text and fill in your grid. (Write a heading for ***all seven*** *steps in the text.)*

Reading skills

Most **sets of instructions** have these typical features:

1. **Steps:** There are usually **clear steps** which you follow one after the other (Step 1, Step 2, etc.). Sometimes, these steps have **headings**.
2. **Phrases:** You often find **imperative** phrases like "Give the hedgehog …", "Keep it in …", etc.
For **very important information**, instructions often include words and phrases like "Make sure …", "You / It must …" or "Never …".

WRITING

6 Write a 'Hedgehog over-wintering FAQ'

→ △ 126/3
→ ▲ 126/4
→ S11–14

126/3 FAQs: Only important questions, please!
△→ After …
126/4 Time traveller with a smartphone
▲→ After …
S11–14 Writing

Internet FAQs ('Frequently Asked Questions') are popular for quick answers to popular questions. You can often find information more quickly in an FAQ than in a long text.

Use the information in the text to write an over-wintering FAQ for people who find a hedgehog in their garden and want to help it. Write 4–5 questions and answers for your FAQ.

Example from an FAQ about guinea pigs as pets:

Q: Can I feed my guinea pig treats?

A: Yes, but make sure they're special treats from the pet shop which are good for their teeth. Don't feed them sugar or honey; that's really bad for their teeth.

Tip

When people write FAQs about a special topic, they write questions for what **most people** will want to know. Then they write **helpful** answers with lots of facts and information.

Didn't you hear? It was in the news!

SPEAKING

7 Warm-up: Your news and where you get it

a) *What kind of news are you interested in: local / world / sports / celebrity / school news?*

Example: A: All I need is sports results and maybe some local news too.
B: I'm interested in celebrity news. I want to know all about my favourite stars!

b) *Where do you get your news from: the TV, the internet, your smartphone, …?*

READING

8 What makes a news report a news report?

→ S5–6, 12

nnelllesetechniken
chtige Inhalte von
n herausfinden
xtsorten und ihre
derheiten

a) *Read the two texts below and then answer these questions: 1. What are they about? 2. Which text is a news report and which is a blog post? Say why you think so.*

OMG, GET YOUR TISSUES OUT!

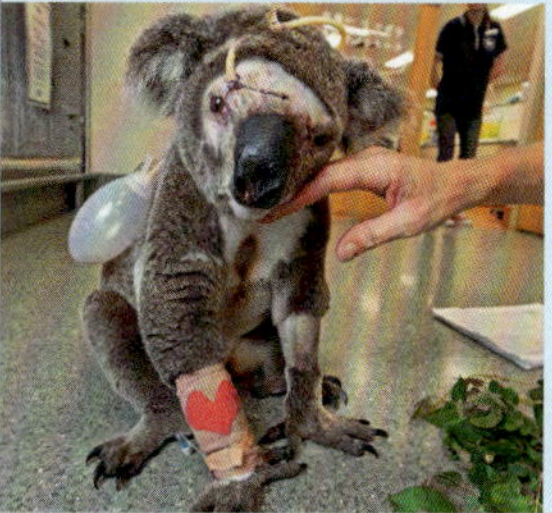

Have any of you heard about the poor koalas who are dying in the Australian bush fires?!?! OMG, I've never seen anything so sad! LOOK at this photo of a poor koala with injuries on its face and arms!!! 😟😟😟 The poor little guy just looks sooooo helpless and it BREAKS MY HEART! 💔💔💔 At least this one was saved. But I'm not sure people down there are doing enough to help the OTHERS! Time for me to cry AGAIN … 😭😭😭

Koalas: Cute but helpless in deadly bush fires

Moondarra State Park, Australia — by Dave Kovak, 10 February 2016

Every year, the extremely hot and dry summers in south-eastern Australia lead to deadly bush fires with loss of human life. But while most people are rescued before it's too late, thousands of animals aren't so lucky and die in the flames. But some animals are lucky, like this koala who was found by volunteer firefighters in Moondarra last week. The confused, helpless and thirsty koala was found on the roadside and taken to an animal shelter. His paws were badly burnt, but workers at the shelter are sure that he will soon be able to return to the bush.

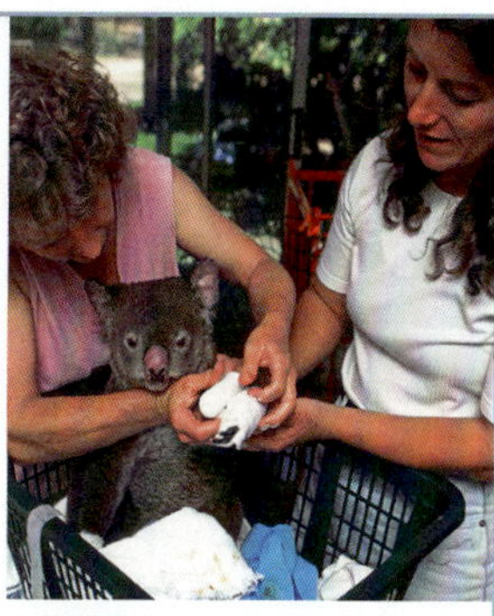

b) *Read the skills box. Write down examples of **facts** and **passive forms** you can find in the news report.*

c) *Go back to the blog post. Which statements are opinions and not facts? What are typical phrases for opinions?*

d) *Turn some of the **opinions** about the koalas in the blog post into **facts**. The skills box and the news report can help you.*

om blog to
port
lp with …

- A **headline** needs to give **important information** so the reader knows what the article is about straight away.
- News reports focus on **facts**. Writers' opinions don't belong in the news.
- News is **not** written in emotional language.
- News reports often use **passive forms**.

SPEAKING

9 Before you read

S 2/5–6
L 2/34–35

The news report below already has a headline. But the headlines in the box also match the report, as you will see. Which headline interests you the most? Which gives you the most information?

→ S12

S12 Textsorten und ihre Besonderheiten

A. Every nine hours a rhino is killed for its horn
B. Elephants and rhinos on the brink of extinction
C. The biggest ever global wildlife protest
D. We are the only hope for elephants and rhinos
E. Illegal poaching of elephants and rhinos still going on

When you read texts, always look for **useful phrases** to learn by heart. Use them again and again **for your own texts**.

No elephants in ten years?

by Ben Pulsford Friday, 3 October 2015

An elephant and two rhinos that still have their impressive tusks and horns

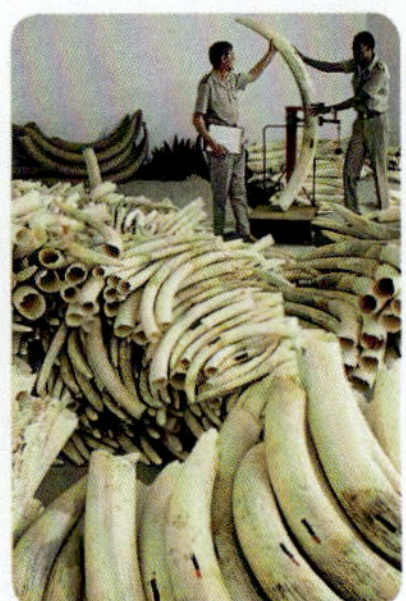

Illegal ivory

People all over the world will take to the streets tomorrow to march for the future of elephants and rhinos. The Global March for Elephants and Rhinos aims to bring attention to how many of the Earth's giants are killed by poachers for their tusks and horns.

Every nine hours a rhino is killed for its horn (that's around three every day), to be used in traditional Asian medicine. An elephant is killed for its ivory tusks every 15 minutes. This means that 100 elephants are killed every day. The ivory is used to make ornaments and objects such as piano keys. Although international trade in ivory was banned in 1989, illegal poaching is still going on.

If the killing goes on like this, there is a danger that both species will become extinct within ten years. Removing the animals' tusks or horns is also extremely violent and is sometimes done while the animals are still alive.

The march will be the biggest ever global wildlife protest; people in 100 cities across the world will take part. In the UK, official marches are taking place in London, Birmingham, Bristol, Liverpool and Edinburgh. Organisers hope that if enough people take part, those in power will do more to save elephants and rhinos before it's too late.

Jo from 'Action for Elephants UK' says: "Elephants and rhinos are on the brink of extinction because of poaching, and they have no voice of their own. We are their only hope."

Source: www.firstnews.co.uk

SPEAKING

10 Your reaction

After you read the report on p. 80, say what you think about the news report and how it makes you feel. The words in the box can help you.

Useful words and phrases

Phrases: I can't believe that people … | The article makes you think more about … | I hope more people will change … | Why do people …?

Adjectives: cruel | awful | sad | hopeful | …

READING

11 Understanding the text

→ WB 49/2

KV 67: On the brink of extinction
WB 49/2 Writing (post)

Understanding the text
nstead of …

a) *Go back to the different headlines in Ex. 9 and answer these questions:*

1. Now that you've read the article, which headline do you think matches the report best?
2. Why do you think the reporter chose a different heading?

→ △ 127/6

b) *All the phrases in the box on the right are from the news report. Can you write a sentence with each?*

→ △ 127/7
→ S18

c) ***Mediation:** Your little brother has seen the photos of the elephant and the rhinos and wants to know what the article is about. Give him the main ideas in German.*

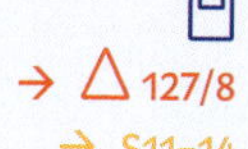

s that a text about
nts?
elp with …
diation

before it's too late (line 15) | on the brink of extinction (line 16) | there is a danger that … (line 9) | those in power (lines 14–15) | a / an … is killed for its … (lines 4–5)

READING

12 Comparing texts: Instructions and news reports

→ WB 50/3–4

WB 50/3 Vocabulary (synonyms)
WB 50/4 Reading/Language (text types)

How is the text about elephants and rhinos different from the text about hedgehogs on p.77? Make lists of what is the same and what is different. Share your ideas.

WRITING

13 Options: Write your own text

→ △ 127/8
→ S11–14

riting your own texts
lp with …
Writing

With a partner, choose option A or B and write your text together.

Option A: Write a set of instructions

a) *The hedgehog text is one example of a **set of instructions**. What other kinds (e.g. software manuals) have you read?*

b) *What kind of step-by-step instructions could you write? For what? Think of something useful. Here are some ideas to talk about:*

how to make a great breakfast for your family | how to plan a theme party | how to play a game

c) *Present your instructions to the class.*

Option B: Write a news report

a) *The elephant text is one example of a **news report**. What other kinds of news reports have you read in the last days / weeks?*

b) *What kind of news would you like to write about? Has something interesting happened? Here are some ideas:*

celebrity news (awards / love stories) | sports news (game results / big events) | school news | funny news

c) *Present your news report to the class.*

Making small talk

WB 53/1 Listening (small talk)

SPEAKING

1 What went wrong? → WB 53/1

→ S17

a) *Read the skills box about small talk.*

b) *Now talk about the cartoon with a partner. What went wrong?*

S17 Mündliche Aufgaben und ihre Besonderheiten

Speaking skills

Small talk is a friendly way to get to know someone or to talk to someone you don't know well. It's **light** conversation; no serious topics! Follow this pattern:

A asks a question.
B answers, then asks A another question.
A answers, then asks B another question. …

- Be a good talker **and** listener. (Don't hog the conversation!)
- Show interest in your partner: Ask questions.
- When you answer questions, offer more information than just 'yes' or 'no'. But not too much information!

"I just said how are you – I didn't think you'd get on the bus to tell me."

WB 53/2 Vocabulary (gapped dialogue)

SPEAKING

2 A game: Keep the ball bouncing → WB 53/2

a) *With your partner, choose one of these situations.*

There's a new girl at school. | It's your first day at the sports club. | A new boy has moved into the house next door.

→ S15–16

b) *Now make small talk with the person in the situation you've chosen. Each pair needs a small ball. Every time you ask a question, bounce the ball to your partner. Which pair can keep their ball bouncing the longest?*

S15 Sprechen üben
S16 Gesprochene Sprache

Useful phrases

Hi. You're new here at / in …, aren't you? | What do you think of …? | What's different about …? | Do you miss anything from …? | Are you enjoying …? | Have you ever …? | Why don't we …? | Have you tried …? | You should … | I've got a great tip: Check out the … I'm sure you'll like it. | Do you feel like hanging out? | If you have any questions / If there's anything you need, just let me know.

I'm … / My name is … | I feel (a bit) nervous / worried / excited / … | That's cool, cheers! | Can you tell me more about …? | I'd like to … | Do you have any favourite places to hang out? | What was that you mentioned about …? | Sorry, I didnt catch what you just said about …

Folie 3/14+15: Bildbeschreibung, Sicherung des Hörsehverstehens
KV 68: At a party
KV 69: Keep the ball bouncing

VIEWING

3 At a party

DVD 3/4

→ S22–23

3 Film skills/Viewing

a) *Watch the film. Read the conversations below and then decide which one matches each of the stills. Explain why.* **Lösung: a)** *1B, D; 2A, C*

1. Girl: It's interesting to compare different countries, isn't it?
   Steffen: Yes, you're right. Have you ever been on a student exchange?

2. Girl: Do you miss anything from home?
   Steffen: No, not really!

b) *Look at the skills box in Ex. 1 again. Then watch (00:38–01:24) and say what goes wrong in the conversation between Steffen, Julie and Nina.*

c) *Now watch the rest of the film. Discuss how Steffen improves his small talk skills.*

d) *Watch (02:18–03:09) again and take notes of the different phrases Steffen uses to keep the ball bouncing.*

WRITING

4 Writing a film script

a) *Work in groups of 3–4. Look at the situations in Ex. 2 again and choose one of them.*

b) *Read the skills box. Write the script for a short film scene about your situation.*

→ S11–14

S11–14 Writing

c) *Act out your scene to the class. Maybe you can also film each other's scenes.*

Writing skills

Stage directions: Only write what you can see or show in a film. You **can't** see a person's thoughts, but you can give hints at a person's feelings in the stage directions, e.g. when you give instructions for facial expressions.

Dialogues: Keep them short and to the point.

Unit 4
What was it like?

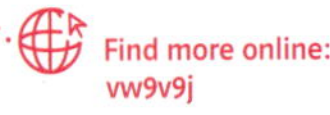

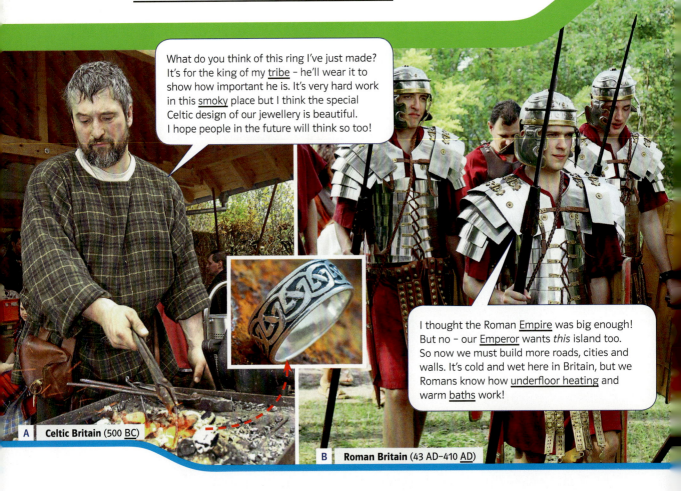

Find more online:
vw9v9j

What do you think of this ring I've just made? It's for the king of my tribe – he'll wear it to show how important he is. It's very hard work in this smoky place but I think the special Celtic design of our jewellery is beautiful. I hope people in the future will think so too!

A Celtic Britain (500 BC)

I thought the Roman Empire was big enough! But no – our Emperor wants *this* island too. So now we must build more roads, cities and walls. It's cold and wet here in Britain, but we Romans know how underfloor heating and warm baths work!

B Roman Britain (43 AD–410 AD)

SPEAKING

Voc.: Musical instruments, Tools, WB (Word bank), pp. 11–12

1 Warm-up: What was it like?

a) *Say what you know about your grandparents' lives when they were your age. What was different to your life?*

→ △ 128/1

b) *What's the oldest thing in your house? Describe it in a short text. Then tell the class about it.*

128/1 Look what I found in the attic! △→ Help with …

c) *With a partner, talk about what you think life was like a long time ago, e.g. 500 or 1,000 years ago. Think of places in your town or region which could give you ideas: castles, old walls, churches, …*

Useful phrases

- I can imagine it was … when my grandparents were young because …
- Back then, people had / didn't have / could / couldn't …
- So it was easier / more difficult / cheaper / more expensive / nicer / … for them.
- I can't imagine how they … because they didn't have … like we do!

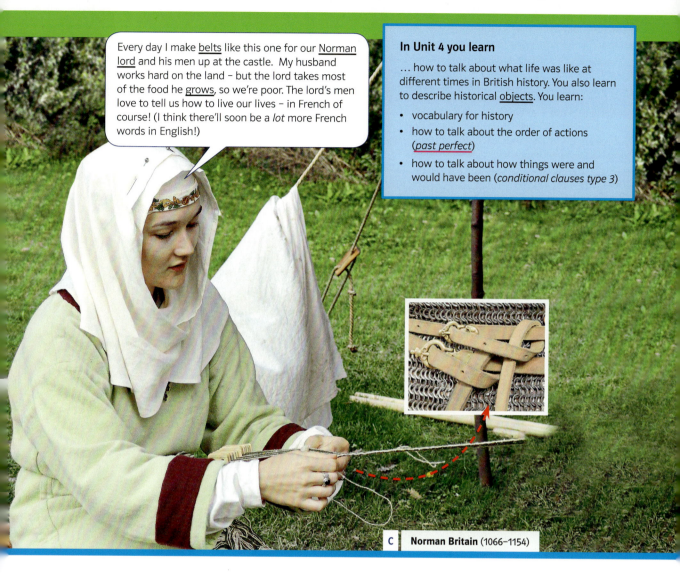

Every day I make belts like this one for our Norman lord and his men up at the castle. My husband works hard on the land – but the lord takes most of the food he grows, so we're poor. The lord's men love to tell us how to live our lives – in French of course! (I think there'll soon be a *lot* more French words in English!)

In Unit 4 you learn

... how to talk about what life was like at different times in British history. You also learn to describe historical objects. You learn:

- vocabulary for history
- how to talk about the order of actions (*past perfect*)
- how to talk about how things were and would have been (*conditional clauses type 3*)

C **Norman Britain** (1066–1154)

WB 54/1 Vocabulary/Reading (time line)

2 British history: Important periods → WB 54/1

a) *First, just look at the photos in A–E on pages 84–87. If you 'climbed into' these scenes, what do you think things would feel like or smell like? Explain why.*

Example:

A: I bet it wasn't so comfortable on that beach in all those clothes! Same thing in the Tudor period.

B: Who cares about clothes – what did people do without electricity?

Word bank

difficult | cold | wet | happy | exciting | boring | noisy | fun | scary | different | hot | (not) comfortable

b) *Look at the photos again and read the people's statements on pages 84–87. What do they say about the different periods they live in? Think of the main ideas behind each photo and write a caption for each.*

c) *In small groups, compare your captions and discuss which ones work best.*

Henry VIII, from the Tudor family, was a busy monarch: He founded the Church of England and the Navy, *and* he found time to marry six times! But his daughter, Queen Elizabeth, has been busy too! During her time as queen, we defeated the Spanish Armada in 1588 and now we're starting colonies in America. What an adventure! And while Elizabeth has been queen, it's been a golden age for our art, music and drama. Will William Shakespeare's plays live forever? I hope so!

D **The Tudor period** (1485–160

3 The community centre needs help: Claire's plan

L 3/1–3
→ S19–21
S19–21 Listening

a) *Olivia's step-mum Claire works at a community centre, and the centre needs help. Listen to Part 1 of the recording and answer these questions:*

1. How can Olivia and her friends help?
2. What do you think of the plan for the calendar?

b) *Now listen to Part 2. Then answer these questions:*

1. Say which students match the five different historical periods and photos on pages 84–87.
2. Say which different objects from the past the speakers talk about. The words on the right can help you.
3. Which historical period is Olivia's group going to do for the calendar?

boots map axe
coin ring mirror
necklace knife belt
sandals hairbrush

Lösung: b) 1.+2. *Boy 1: Norman era, photo C, axe people used to fight with in the batte of Hastings; Girl 1: Tudor period, photo D, map of Tudor England; Girl 2: Celtic era, photo A, her sister's Celtic necklace; Boy 2: Roman Britain, photo B, Roman sandals; Girl 3: Victorian period, photo E, her grandmother's Victorian mirror.* 3. *Olivia's group is going to do the Tudor group for the calendar.*

Our cities have become very noisy and smoky, with all the new factories. They're calling it 'the Industrial Revolution'. But the good news is that we have steam trains now, so we can travel more – and faster! This is our first time outside London – the sea air is wonderful! I hope we can soon travel to other countries in the British Empire too, like Canada and India. Life in Queen Victoria's time is very exciting!

As I was saying, after World War II, Britain's colonies became independent and Britain became less rich and powerful. But we still had a lot of tradition and history to look back on.

Britain isn't all about history and tradition, is it? What about the fun stuff? Think of all the music that has come out of this country – and is still coming out. We don't need to look back. In a world city like London, you can experience the past, present and future all at the same time!

KV 70: Milling around: Objects in your life
WB 54/2 Vocabulary (gapped conversation)

BULARY 

4 Your turn: Objects in your life → WB 54/2

ransfer

If you took a photo of yourself with two or three objects which are typical/important for ***your generation's lifestyle****, what objects would you show or wear? Say which objects you would choose, and why they're typical for you and people your age. Look at these two photos for ideas or think of these categories:*

story words, p. 198

clothes/jewellery | free time activities | gadgets

Across cultures 

The historical periods you've seen and heard about on these pages were all important in **British history**. What historical periods do you know which were important or very important for your country's history?

L3/4 He hadn't finished his game

KV 71: Tudor characters

Olivia: I'm *really* happy that we agreed to do the Tudor period for our calendar page. I'm going to be the perfect Queen Elizabeth!

Jay: Well, we didn't *all* agree. Anyway, who said *you* could be the queen?

Olivia: Well, she was strong and smart – just like me! Do you think she played the saxophone too?

Jay: Don't be silly! Life was boring back then because they hadn't invented all the fun things yet! That's why the Victorians were so much more interesting …

Gwen: Come on, Jay. There are lots of good Tudor characters.

Jay: Yes, but the star is the queen!

Olivia: Of course – it's all about girl power! Before Elizabeth, there had never been a really powerful queen.

Jay: But I'd like to be the star of something!

Holly: Look at this film still I've just found on my tablet. From the film *Elizabeth*. You could be Robert Dudley, the queen's favourite. He wanted to marry her …

Jay: No thanks!

Olivia: Don't panic – before Elizabeth became queen she had said, "I'll never marry!" And she never changed her mind!

Gwen: I know, Jay! You can be Walter Raleigh. He helped to found colonies in America, and then he made potatoes and tobacco popular back in England. The English hadn't tasted potatoes before so they were very excited. And as soon as they had tasted them, they couldn't get enough!

Jay: Yes, but who needed *tobacco*?

Holly: Well, what about William Shakespeare? He invented hundreds of famous phrases like "To be or not to be" or "All the world's a stage".

Jay: Stop! I'm a *dancer*, not a writer!

Gwen: OK. I've got the answer. You can be Francis Drake! There's a cool story about him: When the Spanish Armada came to invade England in 1588, Drake was playing bowls. He wasn't worried because he had fought in a lot of battles before. Anyway, he hadn't finished his game so his men had to wait for him. Then, when he was ready, they fought the Spanish – and won!

Jay: What a hero! … But no, I think I'll join the Victorian group. Then I can be the star. Maybe Sherlock Holmes! But wait, he wasn't a real person, was he?

Olivia: Well, do what you want. But let's talk about *my* dress and *my* crown now …

SPEAKING

1 Olivia, Jay and the calendar project

Compare Olivia and Jay's different thoughts and statements about the calendar project.

WB 55/3 Listening (conversations)

READING

2 Understanding the text: Match the sentence parts → WB 55/3

1. Before Elizabeth became queen,
2. Life was boring back then because
3. He hadn't finished his game, so
4. People hadn't eaten potatoes before so
5. Before Elizabeth,
6. After Drake had defeated the Armada,

a) his men had to wait for him.
b) she had said, "I'll never marry".
c) he was a hero!
d) there had never been such a powerful queen.
e) they were very excited about new food.
f) they hadn't invented all the fun things yet.

Lösung: *1b), 2f), 3a), 4e), 5d), 6c)*

3 The past perfect → G7

KV 72: Working with language

→ △ 128/2

The past perfect instead of ...

You use the **past perfect** to show that one event or action happened **before** another one:

This action (↓) happened before this one (↓) in the past.	
After Elizabeth had decided not to marry,	she never changed her mind.
past perfect (had + past participle)	**simple past**

When actions happened before other ones, sometimes you want to say **why**:

Why did Elizabeth never marry?	Elizabeth's father had had six wives, **so** that was probably one reason not to marry.
Why was life boring in the 16th century?	Life was boring back then **because** they hadn't invented all the fun things yet.

*Make a diagram to show which actions in each sentence happened **before** and which happened **after**.*

1. Before the Romans came, the Celts had already been in Britain for a long time.
2. Elizabeth's mother, Anne, had lived in France, so she spoke very good French.
3. After William of Normandy had become king of England in 1066, more and more people learned French.
4. People in Victorian Britain were able to see more and more of their own country after the steam trains had made it quicker and easier to travel.

WB 55/4 Language (past perfect)

LANGUAGE

4 The Tudor period: Everyday life in Queen Elizabeth's time → WB 55/4

→ △ 129/3
→ ▲ 129/4

Shakespeare's days ... er ... where was he? ... er ...

*Read the text about the Miller family and put the verbs into the correct form of the **past perfect**.*

Margaret Miller and her brother, Thomas, grew up in Tatley, where the Miller family **1** (have) a home for over a hundred years. Their father **2** (die) when they were very young and their mother **3** (have) five children before them, so life wasn't easy. Before the 1580s, only a few children **4** (be able) to get an education, so the Millers were lucky to go to school. But they were often late when they arrived because they **5** (help) their mother with lots of work at home first. And after they **6** (feed) all the animals and collected the wood, there was no more time for breakfast!

Lösung: 1. *had had* 2. *had died* 3. *had had* 4. *had been able* 5. *had helped* 6. *had fed*

KV 73: Talking about the order of past events
WB 56/5 Language (past perfect)
WB 56/6 Vocabulary (Victorian period)

LANGUAGE
ggf. HA
→ △ 129/5
→ ▲ 130/6

129/5
A boy who loved the stage
△→ After …
130/6 A superstar of the stage
▲→ After …

5 Simple past or past perfect? → WB 56/5–6

After Elizabeth **1** (become) queen, people **2** (have) big parties in the streets. Many (but not all) people in England **3** (be) happy that they **4** (have) a young and very smart queen. When she finally **5** (die) in 1603, she **6** (be) queen for 45 years. She **7** (be) the last of the Tudor monarchs. Most people **8** (feel) that Elizabeth's reign **9** (be) a 'golden age'. William Shakespeare **10** (be) also part of that golden age because he **11** (write) so many wonderful plays for England's theatres before he **12** (die) in 1616. 35 plays!

Lösung: 1. *had become* 2. *had* 3. *were* 4. *had* 5. *died* 6. *had been* 7. *had been* 8. *felt* 9. *had been* 10. *had also been* 11. *had written* 12. *died*

WB 57/7 Mediation (Osborne House)
WB 57/8 Writing (Bayeux Tapestry)

WRITING
→ △ 130/7

130/7 Tell the story
△→ Help with …

6 Write the story about Francis Drake → WB 57/7–8

*Start at picture D, and then find the right order for the rest of the story. Put the verbs in the right form (**simple past** or **past perfect**). Link the events with some of the words on the right.*

after | as soon as | but | because | when | then | so

Lösung: Correct order: *D, F, B, E, A, C*
Picture D: *After Francis Drake had seen so many ships as a boy, he wanted to have his own adventures at sea.* Picture F: *Then, on his first big adventure, he went to America and sold slaves he had captured in Africa before.* Picture B: *In America, the Spanish attacked his ships. He never forgot that because it had made him so angry.* Picture E: *The Spanish hated him because he had sailed around the world and had stolen gold and silver from Spanish ships in 1577.* Picture A: *After he had returned to England in 1580, he wasted no time and gave the queen his treasure, and so she was very happy.* Picture C: *After he had defeated the Spanish Armada in 1588, England felt safe again and Francis Drake was a national hero.*

A

in 1580 return to England | waste no time | give queen treasure | queen very happy

B

America | the Spanish attack his ships | make him angry | never forget that

C

in 1588 defeat Spanish Armada | England feel safe again | be a national hero

D

see so many ships as a boy | want to have his own adventures at sea

E

in 1577 sail around world | steal gold / silver | Spanish ships | Spanish hate him

F

on his first big adventure | go to America | sell slaves | capture in Africa before

Start like this: After Francis Drake **had seen** so many ships as a boy, he **wanted** to have his own adventures at sea. Then, on his first big …

WB 58/9 Speaking (presentation)

SPEAKING
Transfer
→ △ 130/8

130/8 Your turn: Funny or interesting things in your life
△→ Help with …

7 Your turn: Funny or interesting things in your life → WB 58/9

*Tell your partner about funny or interesting things that happened to **you** in the past. Say why they happened, what had happened before and what happened next.*

"Last January, I stayed with a friend in the mountains. I'd never had a holiday in the snow before and I really loved it. When I arrived, I could smell the wonderful hot meal his mum had cooked to welcome me! After the meal, we went out in the snow. But then …"

How to talk about history

Describing objects,

For the unit task you're going to present a historical object to your class and you need language to help you with this. This page will give you some useful phrases and help you with a prompt card.

KV 83a+b: Working with vocabulary
WB 58/10 Skills (error spotting)

1 Useful phrases for presenting facts and figures → WB 58/10

→ S3–4

a) *The text below is part of what a guide tells a tour group in London. Read what he says, and then put the phrases **in bold** under the headings in the grid.*

rter im Zusammenhang
thoden

"… Now, we're on Bankside and **in the 16th century** there were four theatres here along the river. In a moment, just around the corner, you'll see the famous Globe Theatre which **was built** in 1599. It **was used for** all kinds of entertainment – plays, musical events and animal fights. Of course, William Shakespeare wrote and acted here while Elizabeth I **reigned**. He **was born** in Stratford-upon-Avon **in 1564** but **moved to** London as a young man after he had married Anne Hathaway. I have in my hand a diary which perhaps belonged to Shakespeare himself! – But anyway, it's sad to say that the first Globe **was made of** wood, and when a fire started 400 years ago, the theatre burnt down in just two hours. That was in 1613. It was rebuilt the following year, put pulled down again in 1644–45. The modern Globe was opened in 1997 …"

Prepositions with times and dates	*Descriptions of places / objects*	*Biographical information*	*Typical history verbs*
in 1564	*… was used for …*	*… was born **in** 1878*	*reigned*
		*… was born **on** 15th April 1878*	

→ △ 131/9

seful phrases for
ing facts
stead of …

b) *Add these phrases to the right categories in your grid.*

for 200 years | at the beginning of | was worn by | it has | invented | was given to | moved to | from 1066 to 1154 | it looks | you can see a / an | at the end of | was brought from

KV 74: How to talk about history: A talking frame
WB 58/11 Picture/Word/People smart (pictures)

2 Preparing to speak about an object → WB 58/11

→ S12, 17

The prompts on this card are from the same categories as Ex. 1. Use the prompts to write a short speech for a tour guide.

tsorten und ihre
erheiten
ndliche Aufgaben
e Besonderheiten

- In this picture, you can see …
- Victorian student / 1890s / writing letter / using quill
- pens not yet invented / quills used for writing
- made from feathers / difficult to use

G8 Conditional clauses type 3

L 3/12–13

If I hadn't talked so much …

Folie 3/16: Bildbeschreibung, Sicherung des Hör-/Leseverstehens
KV 75: Listening: Where's Jay?
KV 76: If I hadn't talked so much …

LISTENING

8 Before you read: Where's Jay?

L 3/10–11

→ S19–21

S19–21 Listening

a) *Listen to the recording. What are the friends doing? Why?*

b) *What facts do they learn about the Globe Theatre? Make notes about:*

the building | the audience | the actors

c) *Now read how the story goes on and find out what happens to Jay.*

"The Globe sounds cool," Jay said to Holly and the others as they walked along a dark little road. "I'm sure it was great fun: People walked around and shouted during the plays back then! And there were *animals* there too! How funny." Jay talked and talked and talked. But then he noticed he was talking to – nobody. Where were the others?! He had turned into another dark little road and he could only hear the sound of water. "I'm close to the river," he thought. "But I'm really stupid! If I hadn't talked so much, I'd have noticed that the others had gone somewhere else." Jay tried to turn back but found himself in another dark road. Now he was scared. How could he get out of this place? "The others could have helped me if they hadn't turned off their phones," he thought.

Across cultures

The new **Globe Theatre** is one of London's most popular attractions. The theatre was rebuilt very much like the first Globe of Shakespeare's time, and audiences love the special atmosphere there: There's no roof, and you can get very close to the actors!

What special old buildings do you know about? What is special about their history?

Suddenly, he could hear a voice which was telling a scary story about a murder which had happened right here in this street! He moved towards the voice and found himself in a new tour group: the Victorian tour. What luck! The guide was talking about blood and crime and dirt and rats. He knew the Victorian period was interesting, but *this* interesting? Wow! He hadn't realised that people had lived like this – in London!

Of course, they would have lived in a better part of the city if they had had money. But there was probably much more action here. "I'd have missed these cool stories if I'd stayed with the others!" he thought. The guide suddenly said "Stop!" Everyone stopped and listened. Then, a man in Victorian clothes walked past them, slowly, like a ghost. He didn't make a sound. A moment later, a woman's voice came from one of the houses. She was screaming!

Then Jay saw that the 'ghost' had dropped something – his pipe? Jay ran forward and picked it up. "If I hadn't joined the wrong tour, I wouldn't have seen a man in Victorian clothes with a pipe," he thought. "And if I hadn't been so quick, I wouldn't have got a Victorian pipe for my calendar photo! Just wait till I tell the others – they'll never believe me!"

READING

9 What do you think?

a) *Why do you think Jay enjoyed the Victorian tour so much? What was so interesting?*

b) *Compare what you heard and read about the Globe/Tudor tour and the Victorian tour. Say which one sounds more interesting to you, and why.*

ANGUAGE

10 Find the rule: Conditional clauses type 3 → G8

KV 77: Working with language

English would have ifferent! fter … The world would een different! fter …

a) *Find six conditional clauses in the text and write them down.*

b) *Say what the verb forms for the* ***if-clause*** *and the* ***main clause*** *are.*

c) *The short text below has examples of* ***conditional clauses types 1, 2 and 3****. Compare them and explain why you need each type:*

Young tourist: Cool, there's a Roman walking tour today! **If I go** on that tour, **I'll learn** lots of interesting things! *(Two hours later …)* Oh no, the tour has already left! **If they had** a later tour today, **I would go** on that. But they don't have a later tour. Well, **if I had spent** less time in Oxford Street, **I wouldn't have been** late for the tour today. But there were so many cool shops and it took too long!

WB 59/12 Listening (murder story)
WB 59/13 Language (conditional clauses 3)

NGUAGE

A

11 Shakespeare's Globe → WB 59/12–13

Match the two parts to make correct sentences.

1. Men and boys **wouldn't have had** all the best roles
2. If the Globe hadn't been built with wood,
3. They could have used electric lights
4. The Globe wouldn't have been so popular
5. If the theatre had had a roof,
6. If they hadn't had pictures of the old Globe,

a) they couldn't have rebuilt it so well in the 1990s.
b) people could have stayed dry when it rained.
c) if girls and women **had been allowed** to act in plays.
d) it wouldn't have burnt down.
e) if they had had electricity.
f) if it hadn't been so cheap.

Lösung: *1c), 2d), 3e), 4f), 5b), 6a)*

KV 78: Talking about how things would have been
WB 60/14 Language (conditional clauses 3)
WB 60/15 Vocabulary (word building)

GUAGE

12 Imagine … → WB 60/14–15

→ △ 132/12

nagine … tead of …

Imagine how things would have been. Make new sentences with ***conditional clauses type 3****.*

Example:
1. If the Celts **hadn't worked** in dark and smoky places, it **would have been** easier for them.

1. The Celts worked in dark and smoky places, so it was very difficult for them.
2. A Celtic king always wore beautiful jewellery so it was clear to others how important he was.
3. The Romans built baths because they found Britain too cold for them.
4. The Normans spoke French so the English language changed.
5. Henry VIII married six times because he wanted a son to be the next monarch.
6. Elizabeth wanted to know more about the world so she sent sailors to America.
7. Queen Victoria reigned for 64 years so she saw a lot of changes.

SPEAKING
Transfer
HA
→ ▲ 132/13

132/13 A game: What would you have done? ▲→ After …

WB 61/16 Writing (short story)

13 Your turn: What would you have done? → WB 61/16

a) *Ask and answer these questions in pairs. What would you have done if …*

… you had got up late this morning?
… you had arrived at school and noticed your left and right shoes didn't match?
… your computer had crashed while you were doing your homework last night?
… you had found an expensive object (e.g. a gold bracelet) on your way to school this morning?
… you had found an old historical object on your last holiday?

b) *Think of some more questions like this to ask each other.*

MEDIATION
→ S18
S18 Mediation

WB 61/17 Speaking (interview)

14 A film about the Victorian period: Sherlock Holmes → WB 61/17

a) *A young exchange student is staying with your family for the week. You're online to look for a good film to watch in English together and you find* Sherlock Holmes *(2009). But before you download a film, you always look at viewer* ratings *first. Read the German comments below and then tell your guest what the viewers think, in English.*

Transfer

b) *Your turn: Discuss with your partner what you know about the film, and if it's a film for* ***you***.

Example:
A: One of the viewers thinks the film is too much like a James Bond film. Well, that's good news for me!
B: I like a good detective story. I want more Sherlock Holmes than James Bond! But what about the actors: Do you know any of them?

nils14_berlinboy September 4, 20:05
Rasend schnell geht's hier zu auf dieser Reise durch das alte viktorianische London. Super unterhaltsam. Besonders klasse: Echte Schauplätze wurden auf geschickte Weise mit CGI-Bildern vermischt, was in den Action-Szenen bombastisch wirkt!

koolkatie16_koeln September 10, 20:08
Ich habe den Film neulich mit meinem kleinen Bruder angeschaut, der gar keine Ahnung von den Detektiv-Geschichten über Sherlock Holmes und Dr. Watson hatte. Er fand es total spannend, in das London von vor über hundert Jahren einzutauchen. (Und die Action-Szenen mochten wir BEIDE!) Gut geeignet für Sherlock- Holmes-Einsteiger!

jcm_hh17 October 19, 19:55
Viel Action! Aber manchmal kam es mir schon ein bisschen albern vor. Man hat dem Hauptdarsteller wohl gesagt: „Spiele es wie James Bond, nicht wie der gute alte Sherlock Holmes aus der viktorianischen Zeit!" Etwas zu modern, nicht „alt-Englisch" genug für meinen Geschmack.

Our historical gallery walk

*Go for a walk through history! How? Each of you presents a historical object (or a picture of one) to the rest of the class. The best part: You **are** the historical person who presents the object. The best speech along the gallery walk wins! You can be young or old, rich or poor, famous or not famous. Here's an example of things to say in a **one- or two-minute presentation** about a famous ring:*

"My name is Elizabeth and this is my ring. As you can see, it's made of gold and jewels. When you open it, you can see two pictures: one of me and one of my mother, Anne Boleyn. If anyone had discovered the secret pictures in my ring, they'd have been surprised: I was only a little girl when she died and I never talked much about her. But I'm sure she'd have loved the ring if she'd had the chance to see it. My mother was the second of my father's six wives. He had wanted a son to become the next king. But if you close the ring, you'll see the letters 'ER' – Elizabeth Regina. Elizabeth, the Queen. That's me!"

HA

Step 1

WB 62/18 Pictures (matching)

Choose a period, character and object → WB 62/18

Find a photo of your object. Then make notes about what historical period it's from, what kind of object it is, and who it belonged to. This person is the character you'll play. In the grid you can find some example ideas to start with.

→ Introduction (pp. 84–87)

Historical period	Object	Character
Celtic Britain	clothes	a famous person
Roman Britain	weapon	a child
Norman Britain	jewellery	a rich / poor person
Tudor Britain	tool	a king / queen
Victorian Britain	...	...

Step 2

KV 74: How to talk about history: A talking frame
KV 79: Peer evaluation: A historical gallery walk
WB 63/19 Prompt cards

Write a prompt card → WB 63/19

For your card, remember to include these things:

prepositions with times and dates | a description of your object | biographical information | typical history words / phrases

→ Talking about history (p. 91)

Step 3

KV 79: Peer evaluation: A historical gallery walk
WB 63/20 Speech

Make your speech → WB 63/20

Now give your one- or two-minute speech about your object to your classmates. Answer any questions they ask you as a 'historical person'. Remember, you want to talk as if you were the person him- / herself.

→ Talking about history (p. 91) → conditional clauses type 3 (pp. 92–94)

S2/14-21
L3/15-22

It's a mystery!

KV 80: It's a mystery!

VOCABULARY

1 Before you read: What could go wrong?

Think about what happens at a photo shoot. In a few sentences, describe some things that could go wrong, and say why. Think of the people and things on the right.

models | photographer | other people / things on the set | props | equipment | accidents

A Jim slowly tried to open his eyes but he couldn't look into the lights; they really hurt his eyes. Where was he? In hospital? But why? What had happened to him? He closed his eyes again. He had a really bad headache. "Think!" Jim said to himself. "Try to focus." Slowly, pictures started to come back: Claire … the community centre … historical periods …"OK," he thought, "so I'd just taken some photos for a history calendar. I remember the Victorian picture and the boy – was his name Jay? – who had wanted to be the centre of attention." More memories were now coming back …

B "Quiet, please!" Claire had shouted. "I know you're excited but we need to get organised quickly!" Almost everyone had arrived at the community centre for the calendar photo shoot and everything was in chaos. "This is our photographer, Jim." said Claire. "Do you want to know how you can help him? Be in the right place at the right time and in the right costume! I see a mix of Roman and Norman clothes over there. The Romans and the Normans need to be in their own groups; don't mix up the historical periods!"

C "Where's Holly?" said Olivia. "She can't be late today. I need her now!"

"Well, she isn't your lady-in-waiting in real life!" Gwen said. "I'm sure you can put your dress on by yourself!"

"Yes, but I'll need her in the photo," said Olivia. "How can I look important if nobody is taking care of me? Let's hope she isn't too late or this photo will be a disaster!"

"Drama queen!" said Jay as he walked past the Tudor group. Olivia didn't even hear him; she was still in her own world as the queen. And then the door flew open.

"Sorry I'm late!!!" Holly shouted.

Everyone stopped what they were doing and stared at Holly. It was a shock for everyone. Then they all started talking at the same time. Chaos again. "Oh no!" – "Look at you!" – "What happened?!"

"I fell off my skates and broke my arm," Holly answered and showed them her plaster cast. A few boys and girls had already written their names on it. Olivia was the only quiet one; she didn't say a word.

"Great!" she finally said. "That's going to look really good in the photo! I mean, they didn't even have plaster casts back then!"

"Thanks a lot," said Holly. "My best friend doesn't even ask me if I'm OK!"

D Back in the Victorian room, Jay was having fun in front of the camera. He was a Victorian gentleman, and his partner in the photo was a fine Victorian lady. "Zoom in on me more," Jay shouted, as the girl rolled her eyes.

"Great!" said Jim finally, after he had taken lots of shots. "I think that's the one!"

They all wanted a look at the photos on the camera. "Hey, I look cool!" Jay said.

"You both look cool!" Jim added. "Now, I just need to go out to the car to get some more equipment before I start on the Tudor group. Back in two minutes …"

Stop and think:

What do you think is 'Victorian' about the photo of Jay with the girl on the next page? How do you know? Give examples from the unit or from your own sources.

E "… Would you like a glass of water?" asked the nurse, but Jim wasn't able to focus on anything.

"So, I'd gone down to the car and looked in the boot for my equipment … but after that I can't remember anything. Are they all still waiting for me? I should call Claire – but where's my phone? – Oh, my head! Nurse, could you call the community centre and tell Claire I'm in hospital?" And then he fell asleep again.

F Claire jumped in her car and drove off. The nurse had said that Jim would be OK and Claire was very happy about that. So her problem now was that the Tudor photo had been a disaster! "I just don't understand," she'd said at the time. "Where on earth is Jim? He went out half an hour ago – it's a mystery! I'll just have to try and take the photo myself. – Er, Olivia and Holly, stop fighting! Gwen, please stand still or the photo will be out of focus. And Jay, no photobombing – you're a Victorian!" Finally, everything was quiet and there was a FLASH. They had their photo, Claire hoped.

G "So," Claire finished telling her story to Jim, as he sat in his bed, "that's all I know."

"Show me your photo," he said.

"Oh no, it's awful," Claire answered.

Jim looked. "No, it's fine – maybe a bit dark but I've got some tricks to fix that," he said. "And I can easily edit out the mistakes and crop the photo a bit – it'll be perfect. But I'd still like to know why I'm in hospital."

Stop and think:
What do you think happened to Jim?

H In another part of the hospital, a girl with a broken leg was sitting on a bed. "I was on my bike," she told her parents, "when a man ran out of a building and opened his car boot. You could hear a lot of noise from inside the building so I looked up at the window to see what was happening. The next thing I knew, I had crashed into the man and I was in an ambulance. But who was the man and what happened to him?"

Stop and think:
How many mistakes do you think Jim will have to edit out of this Tudor photo?

VOCABULARY

Voc.: Monarchy words, p. 201

2 What belongs, what doesn't belong in the scene?

a) *Did any of the problems you mentioned in Ex. 1 come up in the story? Tell the class.*

b) *On the right you see Claire's photo* ***after*** *Jim has improved it. Say which mistakes he has edited out. How has Holly solved the problem with her arm? Explain why these changes were important for the Tudor photo. The word bank can help you.*

Example: Jay had photobombed the Tudor scene as a Victorian!

Word bank

out of focus | wrong period | modern objects | crop / lighten a photo | zoom in on | edit out | photobomb a scene

WB 64/21 Reading (error spotting)

READING

3 Flashbacks and the order of events → WB 64/21

→ S5–7

S5–7 Reading

a) *First read the skills box. Then find other examples of flashbacks in the story.*

b) *In groups of eight, each person chooses one of these moments from the story (A–H). Your group then lines up in the order you think they happened. Then compare with other groups. If there are differences, explain what's right and wrong.*

A. Jim opened his eyes in hospital.
B. Everyone arrived.
C. Holly broke her arm.
D. Jim went to his car.
E. The nurse called Claire.
F. Claire took the Tudor photo.
G. The girl crashed into Jim.
H. Jim took the Victorian photo.

Lösung: a) *Examples of flashbacks:*
– Parts A–D (ll. 7–68): Jim remembers what happened at the photo shoot.
– Part C, ll. 46–49: Holly tells about her accident.
– Part F, ll. 85–101: Claire remembers what happened at the photo shoot.
– Part H, ll. 112–120: The girl with the broken leg remembers the accident.
b) *C, B, H, D, G, F, A, E*

c) *Your turn: What books, films or TV shows do you know which use flashbacks? In a few sentences, describe a key scene.*

Transfer HA

Reading skills

A **flashback** is a part of a story when a character remembers things that had happened before another point in the story.

Example:
Part A: Jim was trying to remember what had happened earlier in the day. → His first flashback to some of the events at the photo shoot is described in Parts B–D.

Flashbacks are often used to make a story more interesting, like a puzzle for the reader.

WB 64/22 Writing (options)

SPEAKING

4 Key moments from the story: Freeze frames → WB 64/22

Your group chooses one of these two scenes from the story. Discuss how you can present your scene as a freeze frame. Talk about what each of the characters is thinking / feeling / doing?

A. Holly arrives with her arm in plaster.
B. Jay has fun in front of the camera for his Victorian photo.
C. Claire tries to organise the friends for the Tudor photo.

The girl from the past → S22–23

S22–23 Film skills/Viewing
Folie 3/17: Sicherung des Hörsehverstehens
Folie 3/18: Sicherung des Hörsehverstehens, Vorbereitung auf Schreibaufgabe

EAKING

1 School or work?

Many years ago, children from poorer families in Britain and Europe often had to work to earn money for their family. Lots of parents couldn't afford to send their children to school.

In the film you're going to watch, Marley says "I'd rather work than go to school and do this history homework." Can you identify with Marley's statement? Explain why or why not.

KV 81: The girl from the past
KV 82: Talking about the dream sequence
WB 65/23 Vocabulary (categories)

EWING

2 This is the year 1888? → WB 65/23

DVD 3/5 

a) *Watch the film. What happens? Think of Violet, her problem and how Marley can help her.*

Word bank

pawn shop | school fees | to travel through time | tea bag | pineapple | vitamins

b) *Read the skills box and look at the stills. How is the dream sequence shown in the film? And how does Marley travel through time? What other details in the film make you think of time travel?*

Film skills

A **dream sequence** is often used to show **time travel** in films. **Audio-visual effects** like music or blurred pictures mark the start and end of the sequence. The viewer (and the film character too) usually only realises at the end of the sequence that it's been a dream – when the character wakes up.

A

B

sfer

c) *Your turn: Talk about another film that you've seen with a dream sequence and/or time travel. Tell your partner how it's done in that film.*

RITING

3 Violet's diary

→ S12

Write a diary entry from Violet's point of view. How did she experience her trip to the 21st century? Remember to write about feelings too.

orten und ihre Besonderheiten

KV 84–87 Test yourself
WB 67/1 Listening (news report)

LISTENING

1 At the museum → WB 67/1

L 3/23–24

a) *Listen to the conversation between a teacher and a group of students at the British Museum. There are ten things the teacher tells the students to do. Make a list.*

Start like this: 1. pick up audio guide 2. …

b) *If you had been at the museum with this class, which group would you have chosen? Explain why.*

c) *Which kinds of museums are near where you live? In small groups, discuss which kinds of displays you'd like to add to them. Then present your ideas to the class.*

LANGUAGE

2 What's new?

a) *Olivia has to do a presentation for school. She's found this article about the history of different foods. Complete the text with the verbs in the* ***past perfect****.*

Voc.: Continents, Countries, WB (Word bank), pp. 7–11

There's a saying in English that goes like this: 'as American as apple pie'. But before 1625, people **1** (not grow) apples in America. Asians **2** (bring) them to Europe before they were taken to America. Did you know that the same thing happened with oranges and bananas? The people of South America **3** (never see) these fruits before the Spanish and Portuguese[1] explorers brought them along on their ships. And what about coffee? The people of South and North America didn't like coffee at first because they **4** (never taste) it before. Before it arrived in the Americas, coffee **5** (travel) from Yemen to Europe; the French brought it to South America and the British to North America.

Things travelled in the other direction too. Until the 1500s people in Europe **6** (never hear) of the drink that was so popular in South America – chocolate. After the Spanish **7** (defeat) the Aztecs[2], they started bringing chocolate as a drink to Spain with them. They made it sweeter with sugar and honey. By 1847 a British company **8** (produce) the first chocolate bar. Other food travelled too. Before the American turkey[3] arrived in Britain, Spanish explorers **9** (already take) it to the country of Turkey. After the Spanish **10** (see) the beautiful tomatoes in South America, they brought them to Europe. But even as late as 1800 most Europeans **11** (never taste) a tomato. They were only grown as decorations because for a long time people **12** (think) you could die if you ate them.

Lösung: a) *1. hadn't grown 2. had brought 3. had never seen 4. had ('d) never tasted 5. had travelled 6. had never heard 7. had defeated 8. had produced 9. had already taken 10. had seen 11. had never tasted 12. had thought*

b) *Find out about five other foods and drinks that you can buy in Germany. Where do they come from originally? How did they come here? Make notes and present your results to the class.*

1 **Portuguese** [ˌpɔːtʃəˈgiːz] Portugiese, Portugiesin | 2 **Aztec** [ˈæztek] Azteke, Aztekin | 3 **turkey** [ˈtɜːki] Truthahn

ABULARY

3 Which one doesn't belong?

a) *Find the word in each group that doesn't belong. Match each of these words to one of the other five groups. Write down the six new groups.*

g: a) 1. Roman, bath, or, heating 2. enter- ent, Globe, play, writer ttack, Spanish Armada, to defeat 4. Industrial tion, factory, British e, steam train 5. lady-in- g, dress, to take care of, 6. Norman, William the eror, belt, French

1	2	3
Roman bath emperor French	lady-in-waiting play Globe Theatre writer	to attack Spanish Armada battle Industrial Revolution

4	5	6
to defeat factory British Empire steam train	heating dress to take care of queen	Norman William the Conqueror belt entertainment

b) *For each group of words, write 1–3 sentences. Use all four words.*

c) *Give your sentences to a partner. Add one of these words to each of your partner's five sentences or write a new sentence with the word.*

everyday | mystery | lifestyle | back then | noisy | weapon

NGUAGE

4 TTS Visitor's Day

In June, students at TTS had to prepare for their Visitor's Day for family and friends. Read what happened before the event. Complete the sentences with the correct tense: ***past perfect*** *or* ***simple past****.*

Example: At the start of Visitor's Day, the students **were** very nervous because of all the things that **had gone** wrong before.

1. had asked – she – found – had bought ble 2. told – were – had – had found – were st finished – smelt – – had caught – had – realised – looked d 4. had just put aded 5. didn't know ver done 6. had left – – realised – had gone

1. After Mr Johnson ___ (ask) Julie to do a presentation on North America, she ___ (decide) to grow some tobacco in her garden. But then her cat ___ (find) it. Luckily, she ___ (buy) some extra seeds[1], so she ___ (be able) to grow a new crop[2].
2. When Mr Johnson ___ (tell) Tom and Rakesh about the noisy workshop in room 103, they ___ (be) upset at first because they ___ (plan) to stage their play in room 102. But after he ___ (find) a new room for them, they ___ (be) happy again.
3. Ayesha and Max ___ (just finish) their model of the Globe Theatre when they ___ (smell) something funny. Luke ___ (leave[3]) a candle on and part of the model ___ (catch) fire. But after they ___ (put out) the fire, they ___ (realise) that it ___ (look) even better because it ___ (show) the fire at the original Globe.
4. The students ___ (just put up) the last posters when the first visitors ___ (invade) the school.
5. They ___ (not know) if it would go well because they ___ (never do) an open house like this before.
6. After the last visitors ___ (leave), they finally ___ (relax). And then they ___ (realise) that everything ___ (go) well!

1 seed [si:d] Samen | 2 crop [krɒp] Ernte | 3 to leave on ['li:v‿ɒn] anlassen

LANGUAGE

5 History – right or wrong?

Are the verbs in the sentences right or wrong? Write down the correct verb form. Use the ***simple past*** *or the* ***present perfect****.*

Lösung: *1. wrong, correct verb form: Did he found 2. right 3. wrong, correct verb form: have invented 4. right 5. wrong, correct verb form: became 6. right 7. wrong, correct verb form: has become*

Example: Who has written the play *Romeo and Juliet*? – wrong, correct verb form: wrote

1. Henry VIII founded the Church of England. Has he founded the Navy too?
2. Has England ever defeated Spain?
3. The Industrial Revolution started in England. Since then people invented many more things.
4. Which British colonies have become independent so far?
5. India has become independent in 1947.
6. The British have made a lot of great music.
7. Air travel became more important than sea travel today.

VOCABULARY

6 Picture puzzle

a) *Find historic objects in the picture. Say which period in history you think they belong to.*

b) *Choose one or two of the objects from a) and think of a short scene in which they play a role. Practise your scene and act it out in class.*

ANGUAGE

7 The costume party

*Complete the dialogue with the correct verb forms for **conditional clauses type 1 or 2**. Then practise the dialogue with your partner.*

g: 1. will ('ll) have
ore 3. would you
4. were 5. will ('ll)
would ('d) win
't go 8. will ('ll)
wear 10. hides
't tell 12. won't have
ened 14. would ('d)

Lisa: Listen, if I go to the party, I **1** (have to) find a really cool costume.

Dylan: But you look good in everything. Even if you **2** (wear) an elephant costume, you'd look great.

Lisa: Well, I don't want to be an elephant. If you were in my shoes, what **3** (you choose)?

Dylan: It's a historical costume party so if I **4** (be) you, I'd get a royal costume.

Lisa: Oh, but everyone will have the same idea and if there are fourteen queens at the party, I **5** (feel) so stupid. I need something better!

Dylan: OK, historical doesn't have to be royal. If you had a really original costume, maybe you **6** (win) the prize for the best costume.

Lisa: So what else is historical? I **7** (not go) to the party if I can't find anything to wear.

Dylan: Historical, er, the Celts, the Roman Empire, the Tudors, the Industrial Revolution, the British Empire … If I say something that you like, you **8** (tell) me, right? Can I stop?

Lisa: The British Empire … I like that one. Here's my idea: If I **9** (wear) a mask, I'll be a mystery, right? And if the costume **10** (hide) my whole body, I'll be an even bigger mystery.

Dylan: And? I'm waiting. If you **11** (not tell) me your idea soon, I **12** (not have) any more time to help you.

Lisa: Think about the British Empire. Think about India. Think about the coolest costume. And what do you get? An elephant!

Dylan: Aarrgghh! You do this every time. If you just **13** (listen) to me sooner, we **14** (save) a lot of time!

DIATION

WB 67/2 Reading (newspaper article)

8 Who said it and why? → WB 67/2

a) *While you were on a class trip to England, you read these quotes in the brochure of a museum you visited. Back home, your grandparents have a look at the brochure and ask you about the quotes. Explain their meaning in German. Why did the people say it? What did they mean?*

1. "All the world's a stage."
   William Shakespeare, 1599, from the play *As You Like It*

2. "I came. I saw. I conquered."
   Julius Caesar, 46 BC

3. "Rome wasn't built in a day."
   Queen Elizabeth, 1563, in a speech in Cambridge

4. "The important thing is not what they think of me, but what I think of them."
   Queen Victoria

5. "History is written by the winners."
   Napoleon Bonaparte or Winston Churchill

6. "History is herstory too."
   Unknown

HA **b)** *Your exchange partner asks you about famous German quotes. Find quotes on the internet. Then explain their meaning in English.*

WB 68/4 Writing (report)

WRITING

9 Vellibia: A girl in Roman Britain → WB 68/4

a) *Use the pictures and the prompts to write a text about Vellibia. Use the **past perfect** and the **simple past**.*

Lösung: a) Picture A: *When I was 12 years old, my parents had already found a husband for me. I married Tiberius when I was 14 years old.* Picture B: *Before I married him, I'd never left my village and I'd always worked for my parents in the field.* Picture C: *My parents had never gone to school so I didn't go. Only rich boys went to school.* Picture D: *When I was 14 years old, I'd already learned from my mother how to cook and do the housework.* Picture E: *Life in my village was hard because the Romans hadn't brought all the new things yet.* Picture F: *My father had grown up in the countryside. Sometimes he shot rabbits or other animals for their meat.*

A

when 12 years | parents already find husband. marry Tiberius | when 14 years

B

before marry | never leave village. always work for parents in the field

C

parents never go to school | so I not go. only rich boys go to school

D

when 14 years | already learn to cook and to do the housework | from mother

E

life in my village hard | because Romans not yet bring all new things

F

father grow up in countryside | sometimes shoot rabbit or other meat

Start like this: When I was only 12 years old, my parents had already found a husband for me. I married …

b) *What do you think would be interesting about your everyday life for people in 2,000 years from now? Write a short report about your day.*

LANGUAGE

10 If Columbus had sailed east …

*Complete the sentences with the right tenses for **conditional clauses type 3**.*

Lösung: 1. *had sailed, he wouldn't have discovered,* 2. *had defeated, would have named,* 3. *had built, they'd have been ruined,* 4. *had married, she'd have been,* 5. *had been, he wouldn't have invaded,* 6. *had had guns, they'd have attacked*

1. If Christopher Columbus ___ (sail) east, he ___ (not discover) America.
2. If the Spanish ___ (defeat) the English, my parents ___ (name) me Juan and not John!
3. If the Romans ___ (build) their roads with wood, they ___ (be) ruined soon.
4. If Queen Elizabeth ___ (marry) Robert Dudley, she ___ (be) very unhappy.
5. If the Roman emperor ___ (be) happy with his empire, he ___ (not invade) Britain.
6. If the Africans ___ (have) guns, they ___ (attack) the British.

WB 68/3 Language (historical discoveries)

ANGUAGE

11 The Queen's favourite: Sir Walter Raleigh → WB 68/3

Read the text and choose the correct verb forms. Look out for signal words!

*g: 1. had already sailed
e been 2. had fought –
d – had been – became
received – founded –
succeed – were waiting
been 4. married – had
out – put 5. was
ing – had already died –
like*

1. By his early twenties, Sir Walter Raleigh (had already sailed | was already sailing) to America for the first time. Potatoes (were | have been) popular in England ever since Raleigh introduced them. And tobacco too.
2. After he (was fighting | had fought) some wars[1] in Ireland, Queen Elizabeth I (noticed | had noticed) him and gave him some land there. Because he (had been | has been) successful in the wars in 1579–1583, he (became | has become) one of the Queen's favourites.
3. After he (had received | received) permission[2] to rule any new lands he discovered, he (had founded | founded) a colony called Roanoke in North America – in 1584 and 1587. Both times the colony (hasn't succeeded | didn't succeed). While the people in the second colony (had waited | were waiting) for a ship from England with more food and tools, a disaster happened and all of the people in the colony disappeared[3]. It (was | has been) a mystery since 1590.

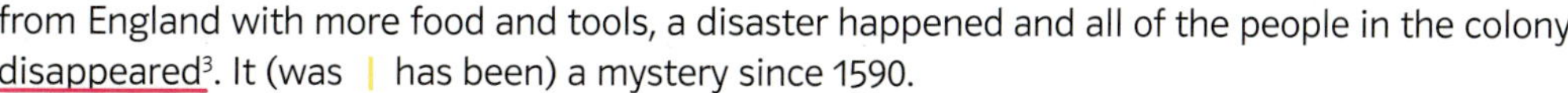

4. In 1591, Raleigh (married | has married) one of Queen Elizabeth's ladies-in-waiting in secret. After Elizabeth (has found out | had found out), she was very jealous and (has put | put) both of them in prison in the Tower of London for about three months.
5. Later, while Raleigh (was searching | had searched) for the 'City of Gold' in South America, he attacked some Spanish ships. This was against the rules. Queen Elizabeth (had already died | died) by this time and the new king, King James I, (didn't like | hadn't liked) Raleigh. So when Raleigh returned to England in 1618, he was executed[4].

NGUAGE

12 The great 'ifs' of history

a) *Match the sentence halves.*

*: a) 1f), 2d), 3b), 4g),
, 7c), 8e)*

1. If I grow up and found a new empire,	a) they'd have found Britain too cold for them.
2. If I had sailed with Drake to Africa,	b) will I become a queen?
3. If I marry a king,	c) I'd have found life very exciting.
4. If I captured an island,	d) I'd never have taken slaves.
5. If the Romans hadn't had underfloor heating,	e) we'll go to the British Museum!
6. If you invented a new machine,	f) maybe people will bring me lots of gold and silver.
7. If I'd lived during the Industrial Revolution,	g) then I could reign there all alone.
8. If we go to London next year,	h) they'd probably name it after you.

b) *What will the world be like in the year 2070? First collect ideas, then finish this sentence.*

If I'm still alive in the year 2070, I'll …

1 **war** [wɔ:] Krieg | 2 **permission** [pə'mɪʃn] Erlaubnis | 3 **to disappear** [ˌdɪsə'pɪə] verschwinden | 4 **to execute** ['eksɪkju:t] hinrichten

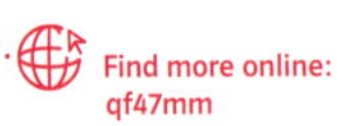

Text smart 3
Fictional texts

What are fictional texts? Why do people read them? In Text smart 3, you're going to read the opening lines of two different books which show you how fictional texts create suspense for the reader.

SPEAKING

1 Why you like to read

Read the statements about why teens read fiction. Which ones can you relate to? Why?

A: I want action and a great plot when I read, right away on the first page!
B: I love characters whose lives are really different to my own. Reading is my escape.
C: I don't like a good book to end, so I love books in a series.
D: I love scary stories – but only when they're fiction. Then I can tell myself, "It didn't really happen!"
E: I want to read about people just like me so I can identify with the characters.

VOCABULARY

2 Crime, horror, romance or …?

KV 88: Crime, horror, romance or …?

a) *The box on the right lists several genres of fiction. In groups of 3–4, talk about which features are typical of* ***two*** *of the genres. Make a grid and fill it in; the word bank can help you. Then share your results with the other groups. (And if your favourite genre is missing,* ***add it****! That can be* ***one*** *of the two genres for your grid.)*

crime | romance | mystery / detective | horror | science-fiction | travel adventure | animal stories | disaster | teen comedy | teen drama | fantasy | comics / graphic novels

Word bank

happy ending | adventure | death | murder | violence | puzzle / problem to solve | action | surviving (against all odds) | friendship | enemies | technology / gadgets | humour

→ △ 133/1

b) *Your turn: Think about your favourite genre. Tell your group why yours is 'the best'! Try to really 'sell' it to the others, with good reasons.*

Transfer
133/1 Your turn: Your favourite genre
△ → Help with …

LISTENING

3 What are you reading?

L 3/26–27
→ S19–21
S19–21 Listening

a) *Read what Tina and Rick say and then listen to the first part of their conversation. Then: 1. Say why each of them thinks that* ***their*** *book is the 'best ever'. 2. Whose arguments do you agree with? Say why.*

b) *Listen to the second part of their conversation. Who do you agree with now: Tina or Rick? Explain why.*

The best book ever!

Hey, what are you reading?

Oh no, not *that* book! Sorry, but I've got the best book ever.

KV 88: Crime, horror, romance or …?

Opening lines of a fictional text: Text 1

Among the Hidden: Chapter One

by Margaret Peterson Haddix (b. 1964)

He saw the first tree shudder and fall, far off in the distance. Then he heard his mother call out the kitchen window: "Luke! Inside. Now."

He had never disobeyed the order to hide. Even as a toddler, barely able to walk in the backyard's tall grass, he had somehow understood the fear in his mother's voice. But on this day, the day they began taking the woods away, he hesitated. He took one extra breath of the fresh air, scented with clover and honeysuckle and – coming from far away – pine smoke. He laid his hoe down gently, and enjoyed one last moment of feeling warm soil beneath his bare feet. He reminded himself, "I will never be allowed outside again. Maybe never again as long as I live."

He turned and walked into the house, as silently as a shadow.

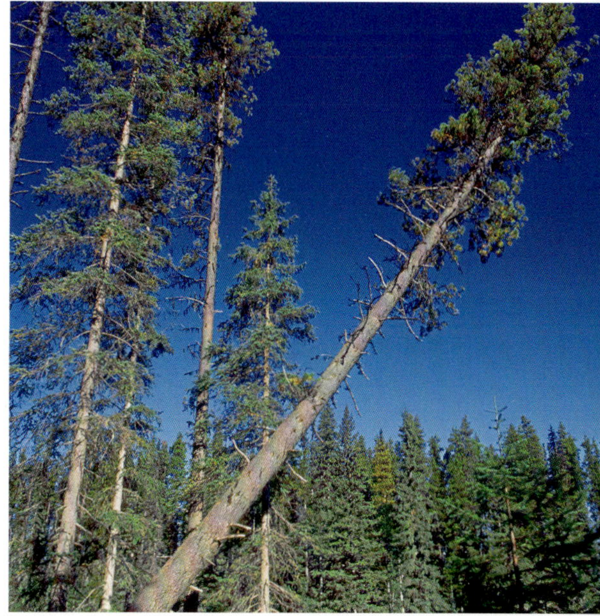

SPEAKING

4 Your reaction

The novel Among the Hidden *opens with the lines above. Read them and then answer these questions:*

1. Does the text make you want to read more? Or in other words: Does it 'hook' you? Explain why or why not.
2. The photos can help you to feel the atmosphere and understand more about the setting. Describe how.

Tip

Some words in the text are new and perhaps difficult for you. But they can often be important for atmosphere, e.g. 'shudder'. Don't worry: You already know ways to deal with new words! → S10 **S10** Umgang mit neuen Wörtern

WB 69/1 Reading (matching)

READING

5 Understanding the text → WB 69/1

→ △ 133/2
→ S5–6

Read the opening lines again and answer these questions:

1. What exactly do you learn about Luke? Work with a partner and note down what the text tells you.
2. What do you **want** to learn about Luke?

…ho is Luke?
…p with …
…elllesetechniken
…ige Inhalte von
…erausfinden

READING

6 Key lines from the text

133/3

133/3 Key lines from the text
△→ Instead of …

Below you see key lines from the text. Explain what they mean, and what they tell you about Luke's life.

- He had never disobeyed the order to hide.
- He had somehow understood the fear in his mother's voice.
- But on this day, he hesitated.
- I will never be allowed outside again. Maybe never again as long as I live.
- He turned and walked into the house, as silently as a shadow.

Useful phrases

- It feels like something scary / dangerous / … is happening. Words like … or … in line … tell me so.
- The lines … and … are both key lines because …

READING

7 The five senses

S7

S7 Wichtige Merkmale von Erzähltexten, Gedichten und Theaterstücken erkennen

First, read the skills box. Then go back to the text and say how the author uses the five senses there. What can Luke see, hear, feel? What do you think it feels like to be in his shoes?

Example:
A: Luke loves the way things smell outside.
B: Yes, everything outside seems better for him than what's inside. That's my feeling.

Reading skills

Every writer wants to **draw the reader into the story** with a great plot and interesting characters in a special setting. Many writers work with **the five senses** to do this. When you understand what the characters **see, hear, smell, taste** and **feel**, it's easier for you to understand what they do because you're 'in their shoes'.

WB 69/2 Writing (re-writing a text)

READING

8 Suspense in fictional texts → WB 69/2

S7

S7 Wichtige Merkmale von Erzähltexten, Gedichten und Theaterstücken erkennen

a) *Think – pair – share: Read the skills box on your own. Then go back to the text and note down words or lines that create suspense and reader interest. Share your ideas with each other and then with the class.*

Example:
Why was the mother so sharp with Luke? Why was there fear in her voice? For me, that's suspense!

Reading skills

An exciting book creates **suspense** and **reader interest**. This can happen in the first lines to draw the reader into the action. Or, the writer might build the suspense slowly.

Also, **strong** or **dramatic language** can draw the reader into the plot.

b) *Choose the line or lines in the text with the most suspense. Which words and ideas make you think so? Group your words / ideas around your line like a mind map.*

Example: 

It's happened before.
Today is somehow different.
He had never disobeyed.
Luke: good boy
mother: strict
Why does Luke have to hide?

c) *How could Luke's story go on?*

Opening lines of a fictional text: Text 2

Folie 3/19: Vorentlastung des Hör-/Leseverstehens, Reaktivierung von Adjektiven

S 2/23
L 3/28

Pig-Heart Boy by Malorie Blackman (b. 1962)

Chapter 1 – Dying

I am drowning in this roaring silence. I am drowning. I'm going to die.
I look up through the grey-white shimmer of the swimming pool water. High, high above I can see where the quality of the light changes. The surface. But it is metres above me. It might as well be kilometres. The chlorine stings my eyes. My lungs are on fire. Just one breath. Just one.
I have to take a breath, even though I know that I'll be breathing in water. But my lungs are burning and my blood is roaring and my whole body is screaming out for air. If I don't take a breath, I'll burst. If I do take a breath, I'll drown. Some choice. No choice.
I close my eyes, praying hard. And kick, kick, kick. I open my eyes. The surface of the water seems even further away. I'm going to drown. A fact. A fact as clear, as real as the silence around me. Part of me – a tiny, tiny part of me – laughs. I am going to drown. After everything I've been through in the last few months, this is how I'm going to bow out. One thought rises up in my mind. One thought.
Alex …
I stop kicking. I have no energy left.
I stop fighting. I'm so tired. I can feel my body begin to sink.

EAKING

9 Your reaction

→ △ 134/4

our reaction
elp with …

a) *What adjectives would you use to describe the situation and atmosphere above?*

b) *Is this the kind of book you'd like to read more of? Explain why or why not.*

WB 70/3 Reading (mixed tasks)
WB 70/4 Vocabulary (descriptions)

EADING

10 Key lines from the text → WB 70/3–4

→ △ 134/5
→ S5–7

In Ex. 6, you saw a collection of key lines from Text 1 to discuss. For Text 2, find the key lines yourself. Then explain why they're important. Think of ***suspense****,* ***characters*** *and* ***atmosphere****. Work with a partner.*

ey lines from the
tead of …
ading

WB 70/5 Vocabulary (grid)

READING

11 The five senses → WB 70/5

a) *How are the five senses featured in Text 2? Note down examples.*

b) *Now compare Texts 1 and 2. Describe in 5–6 sentences how the senses are featured similarly or differently. Is there is a bigger focus on some senses? Describe that too when you compare the texts.*

Examples:

- In Text 2, the focus is more on what the character in the water can feel. He's feeling pain, so that sense plays the biggest role here.
- In Text 1, the focus was more on …
- What the texts have in common is that the characters both feel / smell / …

READING

12 Another look at suspense

a) *In Text 2, what ways does the writer use to draw the reader into the story? (Look back at Ex. 8 for help and ideas, e.g. in the skills box.)*

b) *Now compare the suspense in Text 2 with Text 1. Which text 'hooks' you more?*

READING

13 Narrative perspectives

→ S7

a) *First, read the skills box. Then go back and reread the opening of Text 2.*

S7 Wichtige Mermale von Erzähltexten, Gedichten und Theaterstücken erkennen

Reading skills

The writer of a fictional text has a choice: "Who tells my story?" Or in other words:

"Who is my narrator?"

- **First-person narrator** (e.g. in *Pig-Heart Boy*): This kind of narrator tells the story from his / her own perspective. This person is often (but not always) the main character. The reader and a first-person narrator experience the story together, 'live'.
- **Third-person narrator** (e.g. in *Among the Hidden*): This kind of narrator tells the story from the outside. The perspective is *not* the main character's perspective.

b) *Now go back and re-read the opening of Text 1. Then answer these questions:*

1. When you compare Text 1 and Text 2, think of which features could be typical of a first-person narrator, a third-person narrator – or maybe both. Make a grid. Start with the ideas on the right.
2. How do you think Text 1 and Text 2 would feel differently if they were written from the **other** perspective?

The writer gives you time to think.

You jump into the action right away.

It's always clear what the main character is thinking.

You get close to the main character.

The writer gives you time to get to know the atmosphere, setting, characters.

KV 90: Working with vocabulary

EDIATION

14 < Finding out more about the books >

ediation

a) *Think: Which genre is each of these books? Find out more and see if you were right!*

→ S18

b) *Students at your school have been asked to send 'summer reading tips' to the school's website. Each tip should feature a short summary of the storyline, and each tip should be in German so that everyone can understand it. Find out more about one of the books and then write your tip.*

*g: **a)** Among the n: science fiction, ture; Pig-Heart Boy: rama*

WRITING

15 Writing options

KV 89: Creative writing

→ △ 134/6
→ S11–14

Writing options elp with … Writing

Now that you know more about the suspense, atmosphere and other ingredients of fictional texts, try out your new skills with one or more of the writing options below.

Option A: *Look at the pictures. They both show the opening scene of two different fictional texts. What could each book be about exactly? Decide for yourself and write 8–10 opening lines. Think of the points below:*

- How could the opening lines really draw the reader into the story?
- Who is telling the story: a first- or third-person narrator?
- Think of how you can include the different senses.

Option B: *If you have time, you can do **both** parts of Option B. Or, you can do just one:*

- *Rewrite Text 1 from Luke's perspective, as a **first-person narrator**.*
- *Rewrite Text 2 from a **third-person narrator's** perspective. For this you need to think of who could tell the story:*

  Could it be a character who is looking back after days / months / years?
  Could it be a character who is watching what is happening?

Option C: *Write **your own** opening lines (8–10) or opening page to a fictional text. Try to include **all five senses**, if you can. Be as creative as you want to be. Think of these points as you plan your text:*

- What genre of fiction would you like to write in?
- Do you want a first- or a third-person narrator? Why?
- Do you want to 'jump' into the story with your characters, as in *Pig-Heart Boy*? Or do you want to 'step' into the story more slowly, as in *Among the Hidden*?

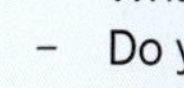

Legende

Diese Symbole und Erklärungen zeigen dir, wie du mit den Hilfen, Aufgaben und Aktivitäten auf den *Diff pool*-Seiten arbeiten kannst.

△ Hilfe zur Unit-Aufgabe | oder eine leichtere Variante der Unit-Aufgabe | oder eine zusätzliche Aufgabe

▲ eine zusätzliche Herausforderung

Unit 1

△ 1 Talking about places → Help with Check-In, p. 8/1

Where should these people go on holiday?

Start like this: Lou should go to Wales. She can visit …

1. Lou likes stories about the past and she likes to visit old castles.
2. Sandy loves horses and she likes to be outside every day.
3. Andrew is interested in music and traditions. He loves watching shows and listening to traditional songs.
4. Ellen is a good swimmer and loves the sea. She thinks it's great to walk along the beach and look for treasures.

△ 2 Frequently asked questions → After Station 1, p. 11/3

Work with a partner and fill in the gaps. Take turns to ask and answer the questions.

Lösung: 1. *Will it* 2. *will you* 3. *Will you* 4. *will you* 5. *will you* 6. *Will you* 7. *Will you* 8. *will you*

1. ___ rain today?
2. What ___ do ten years from now?
3. ___ meet friends after school?
4. Where ___ spend your holidays?
5. When ___ do your homework?
6. ___ watch a scary film with me?
7. ___ buy me some ice cream?
8. Where ___ live when you're 30?

▲ 3 Mediation: At a German station → After Station 1, p. 11/3

An English boy is trying to buy a ticket at a German station. He's talking to a man who doesn't speak English. Can you help the boy? Try to use the **will** *future where you can.*

Boy: Excuse me, I need to take the next train to Cologne. Will it wait a few more minutes?
Man: *Entschuldigung, ich spreche kein Englisch.*
You: *Dieser Junge muss …*
Man: *Ach so. Nein, der Zug wartet nicht. Aber ich bin sicher, der nächste Zug wird ihm besser gefallen. Es ist ein Express-Zug.*
You: Sorry, the train … But the man is sure …
Boy: Express train? Won't … expensive?
You: …
Man: *Warte kurz, ich schaue nach.*
You: …
Man: *Nein, es wird sogar günstiger! Und er wird früher in Köln ankommen als der frühere Zug!*
You: No, he says it'll … And, he says …
Boy: Cool! I … earlier and I … more money for my visit in Cologne! – Yes, I think I … buy that ticket.
You: Great, but I must go now or my train … leave without me!

△ 4 Buying train tickets on the internet → After Station 1, p. 12/5

Fill in the new travel words.

price | inward | arrive | one-way | return | change | fee | depart | outward

g: 1. return 2. price
-way 4. inward
ward 6. arrive
art 8. change 9. fee

First, Luke forgets to click on **1**, but he doesn't only need the **2** for a **3** ticket. So he has to fill in the dates for the **4** journey and then the **5** journey. He clicks on **6**, but then he remembers that he doesn't know how long the journey takes. So he chooses the time he wants to **7**. He learns that for St Agnes you have to **8** at London Bridge and Paddington. Then he wants to know how much the booking[1] **9** is.

△ 5 What will the weather be like? → Help with Station 1, p. 12/6

Here are weather pictures and words to help you with exercise 6 on page 12.

Start like this: Today the weather is still … | But tomorrow it'll be… | Temperatures[2] will … | There will be …

△ 6 Do we really need to leave Greenwich? → After Station 2, p. 15/9

*Read Dave and Mr Preston's dialogue and decide if you need **if** or **when**.*

: 1. when
3. if 4. if
when 7. if

Dad: Dave, your mum just doesn't feel at home in Greenwich any more. You'll understand **1** you're older.

Dave: But I'm *not* older, Dad. It's *now*, I'm young, and I know that **2** we leave Greenwich, I'll be really sad.

Dad: Yes, you're right. But **3** you don't try to change your point of view, things will never get better. Can you please try, for me and for your mum?

Dave: Well,… **4** I try to be happier, will you do something special for me?

Dad: **5** I say yes, will it cost a lot, Dave?

Dave: No, it won't. Don't worry about money. Anyway, three weeks from now, **6** we're in our new house, I know I'll be sad. But, **7** I have a party for my friends, I'll feel *much* better, I know it! May I? PLEASE …?

1 **booking** ['bʊkɪŋ] Reservierung | 2 **temperature** ['temprətʃə] Temperatur | 3 **degree** [dɪ'griː] Grad

▲ 7 German tourist attractions → After Station 2, p. 15/9

*Match the tourist attractions with the places or regions in Germany. Write tips for tourists, using **if + will / can / should** or the **imperative**. Add more information if you like. Remember: When you write your sentences, you can start with the **if-clause** or with the **main clause**!*

lots of Roman buildings fish market in the harbour a famous cake Germany's capital a very big cathedral (church) Germany's biggest island a boat trip to a famous rock a beautiful palace	+ go see visit like enjoy +	Berlin the Black Forest Cologne Hamburg Loreley Neuschwanstein Castle Rügen Trier

▲ 8 A poem about your home town → After Station 2, p. 16/14

Write a poem about your town or area. The word groups below rhyme[1]; they can help you with your poem. Maybe you can think of more words in English that rhyme?

city be sea me free

village language manage image

live give active

like bike hike

site bright night right light

run fun sun one

△ 9 Things to do in the country → Help with Film page, p. 21/1

Match these activities with phrases and words from the box.

1. feeding animals
2. milking cows
3. exploring a cave
4. swimming in a lake
5. playing in an adventure playground
6. reading ghost stories
7. walking
8. geocaching

Useful phrases

I think … is dangerous / scary / exciting / boring / fantastic / a lot of fun / …

I like farms, so … is the activity for me!

… is fantastic / great / … for small children, but I like more interesting / more exciting / … activities like …

I don't like sports, so I'm not into …

1 **to rhyme** [raɪm] sich reimen

Unit 2

△ 1 Your turn: Your kind of 'smart' → Help with Introduction, p. 27/3

Read what Julie says. Maybe some of her words can help you when you talk to your partner.

I think I'm body smart because I'm very good at sports. I like running, cycling and playing volleyball. And I never have problems when I learn new sports. Also, I'm self smart: I know what I'm good at, and I often think about what I want to do *before* I start something. People who are self smart often learn from their mistakes. That's what I do too.

△ 2 Maybe in the next show … → After Station 1, p. 29/2

*Find the right verb forms to make sentences with **if-clauses type 1**.*

g: 1. is 2. didn't get
tises 4. will ('ll) get
e sure 6. won't have
get 8. won't find
10. practise
't have

Right now, Jay **1** (be) sad because he **2** (not get) the lead part in the show. If he **3** (practise) hard enough, maybe he **4** (get) the lead part in the next show. But if his parents **5** (make sure) that he works harder for school, he **6** (not have) enough time to practise. "Don't be upset," Shahid tells Jay. "If you **7** (not get) good marks, you **8** (not find) a job later." "That's easy for you to say," Jay answers. "But if I **9** (work) hard *and* **10** (practise), I **11** (not have) time for my friends!"

△ 3 Another chat comment for Jay → After Station 1, p. 30/4a)

Read this advice for Jay. Put the verbs in the right form.

: 1. were 2. wouldn't
. would ('d) worry
. wouldn't earn
d put 7. didn't look
9. would ('d) make
would ('d) stop

mr_know_it_all_14 September 5, 19:27

If I **1** (be) you, I **2** (not worry) about dancing and singing. I **3** (worry) about SCHOOL! I mean, if your brother **4** (be) smarter, he **5** (not earn) his money as a model – what kind of a career is THAT?! No magazine **6** (put) his photo on the cover if he **7** (not look) good and young, but you can't stay young FOREVER. If I **8** (be) your father, I **9** (make sure) that you worked harder. And I **10** (stop) paying for your dancing lessons!

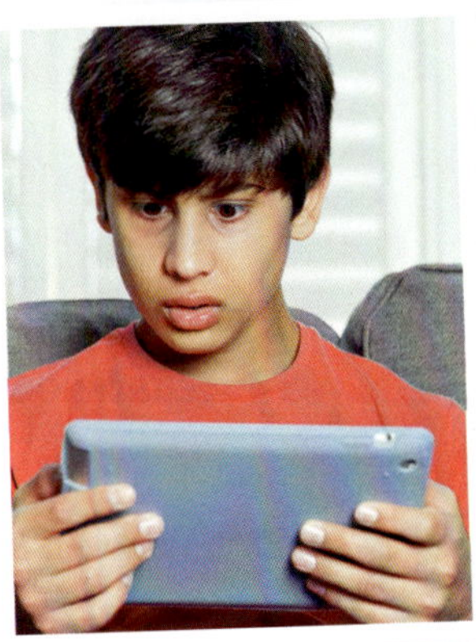

▲ 4 What would an adult say? → After Station 1, p. 30/4a)

*Read the chat room comments on p. 12 again. How do you think advice from an adult would be different? Write comments from the point of view of an adult, e.g. a sports star, a famous singer, a teacher, an uncle / aunt. Use **if-clauses type 2**.*

△ **5** **Your friends need you!** → Help with Station 1, p. 30/4b)

*Here are some problems to start with, and some ideas for the advice too. Use **if-clauses type 2**.*

Start like this: If I **were** you, I **would/wouldn't** …

My friend always wants to copy my homework!	My parents don't let me go out with my friends!	Everyone has a smartphone – but not me! It isn't fair.
tell him / her to do it himself / herself | ask to copy his / her homework next time | look for new friends	promise to take your phone and not turn it off | try to find a compromise | explain that friends are important	explain that smartphones are important to stay in touch | do jobs at home for extra money | babysit for friends

△ **6** **A model who works for Ivy** → After Station 1, p. 30/5

*Read what one of Ivy's models tells a fashion magazine and complete his sentences. Use **if-clauses type 2**.*

Lösung: 1. *didn't love* 2. *wouldn't be* 3. *would ('d) find* 4. *were* 5. *didn't like* 6. *wouldn't work* 7. *weren't* 8. *would ('d) have*

If I **1** (not love) fashion so much, I **2** (not be) a model. I'm lucky that there aren't so many boys and young men who work as models. I **3** (find) it a lot harder to get a job if I **4** (be) a girl! It's also great that I can choose who I work for. If I **5** (not like) Ivy's clothes, I **6** (not work) for her. We all love Ivy. If we **7** (not be) such a great team, we **8** (have) less success, I'm sure!

▲ **7** **What would you do if …** → After Station 1, p. 30/5

Think of a situation that could happen to you and your classmates.

Examples: you forgot about the Maths test | you miss the bus after school | your dad / mum cooks the worst dinner ever | you see a famous person

*Write down your situation on a piece of paper. Take turns to show each other what you wrote. Ask the others what they would do in this situation. Find at least three different ideas for each situation. Use **if-clauses type 2**.*

△ 8 A German talent show → Help with Station 1, p. 31/6

*Look at this list of things to do and **not** to do at an audition. The words can help you with your message.*

✔
- *prepare well*
- *practise a lot*
- *make sure you look great*
- *make a good impression*[1]

✘
- *choose a song that is popular at the moment*
- *come without an adult*
- *do embarrassing things on stage*[2]

▲ 9 More helpful tips for your English friend → After Station 1, p. 31/6

*Write some more helpful tips about what to do or **not** to do at an audition.*

△ 10 The Azads and the Frasers → Help with Station 2, p. 32/9a)

Copy the grid and complete it. Here are some ideas to help you:

Personality:	bossy | strong | serious | messy | clever | creative | is good at … | likes to get organised | likes to dream[3] (about the future) | likes to play … | likes to have fun
Opinions:	school is important | hobbies are good for you | find time to enjoy yourself | you must work hard and get good marks | no good job without good marks at school | you should teach yourself new things | you're too laid-back
Problems:	can't agree with parents | room is messy | gets bad marks | can't focus on important things | can only focus on important things like school

	Personality	Opinions	Problems
Olivia			
Claire			
…			

△ 11 If I were Olivia, I'd … → Help with Station 2, p. 32/9b)

You can use these phrases to talk about Olivia's reaction.

Useful phrases

She could also try to … | It would be a good idea if she … | It would be great for her if … | If that doesn't work, she can … | I'm sure her parents will … if …

1 **impression** [ɪm'preʃn] Eindruck | 2 **stage** [steɪdʒ] Bühne | 3 **to dream** [dri:m] träumen

△ 12 What Olivia told Holly → Help with Station 2, p. 33/10b)

Use the words on the right to do Ex. 10b).
*Be careful: You need **four** of the words **twice**!*

him | yourself | her | me | you
ourselves | himself | us | herself

△ 13 Help! I can't do it myself! → After Station 2, p. 33/10b)

Lucy is tidying up her room – but not alone. Complete the dialogue with the right forms.

Lösung: *1. me 2. yourself 3. her 4. myself 5. you 6. you 7. me 8. myself*

Lucy: I'm going to tidy up my room. Can you help 1, Olivia?
Olivia: No, I can't. Do it 2, Lucy.
Claire: Why can't you help 3?
Olivia: Why should I? When I was a little girl, I always had to tidy up my room 4.
Claire: Well, not exactly: I often helped 5, remember? I tidied up your wardrobe for 6!
Olivia: Well, maybe you're right. But it wasn't very often, believe me! And …
Lucy: Can you two please stop fighting now and show 7 where I can put my old clothes? I've already tidied up my wardrobe 8!

△ 14 *Themselves* or *each other*? → After Station 2, p. 33/11

*Sometimes people do things **themselves**, sometimes with **each other**. Read the situations A–D and decide if you need 'themselves' or 'each other'. The pictures can help you.*

Lösung: *1. themselves 2. each other 3. each other 4. themselves 5. themselves 6. themselves*

A. There are lots of things that very small children can't do 1 because they need their parents' help. These children are playing with 2. That's easy!
B. Friends like to talk to 3. But lonely people often talk to 4.
C. Some people like to take photos with no people in them. Other people like to take photos of 5.
D. Some people like the sound of their own voice. They like listening to 6.

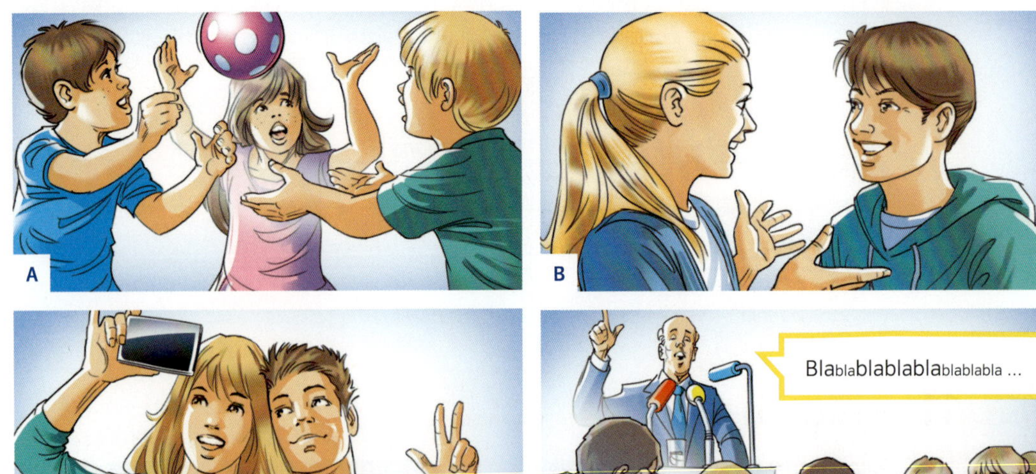

▲ 15 Each other? Themselves? There's a difference! → After Station 2, p. 33/11

ng: 1. … they were at home. / … they angry. 2. … she usy. / … when they to each other. play tennis. / … learn new grammar.

a) *Read these sentence pairs with* ***each other*** *and* ***themselves****.*
Can you complete them so that they make sense[1]?

1. The children hurt themselves when … / The children hurt each other when …
2. Claire told the children to look after themselves because … / Claire told the children to look at each other …
3. Some students teach themselves to … / Some students help each other to …

b) *Write more sentences like these and test your partner.*

△ 16 Act it out! → Help with Skills, p. 34/3

g: a) 1: disappointed; 2: happy / excited; 3: shocked; 4: angry; 5: not sure what

a) *Look at the words for feelings and match them with the photos, if possible. Then try to make the same face. Work with a partner. Can he / she guess which feeling you're acting?*

disappointed | angry | sad | not sure what to do | happy / excited | shocked[2]

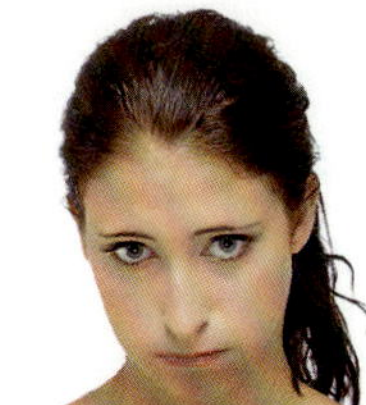
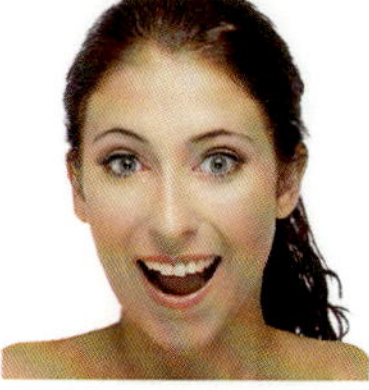

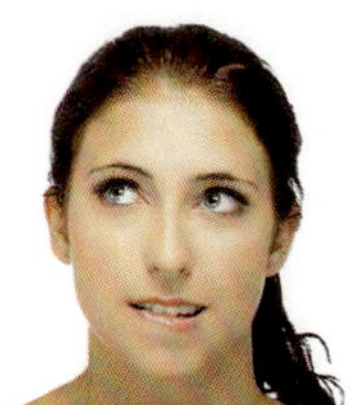

b) *Which words can you use in your dialogue on p. 16? Can you think of more?*

△ 17 What happens next: Ideas for the ending → Help with Story, p. 38/4

First choose an idea for the story's ending. Then follow the instructions.

1. Jay decides to get help from his friends. → Go to **A**!
2. Jay tells his parents. → Go to **B**!
3. Jay tells nobody – he helps himself. → Go to **C**!

A. Dave – can ask his new friends
OR Gwen – she's good with computers / she's clever and knows what to do
B. they tell Shahid
OR they're upset, but they promise to help
C. Jay finds help on the internet
OR Jay takes Shahid's laptop to an IT expert

Word bank

at first | then | suddenly | finally | feel awful / bad / sorry / scared / guilty[3] | be shocked / horrified | shout angrily / loudly | quickly need a lot of money / more information / a really good IT expert | explain / fix carefully | be thankful | relax

1 **to make sense** [meɪk ˈsens] einen Sinn ergeben | 2 **shocked** [ʃɒkt] geschockt | 3 **guilty** [ˈɡɪlti] schuldig

Text smart 1

△ 1 Your turn: Poems and songs in your life → Help with Introduction, p. 46/2b)

Here are some ideas to help you with your own lines:

Verbs from the photo:
live | love | laugh | sing | dance | dream | play | give | smile

Example: Smile
Till someone smiles back

Ideas for extra lines:
Like you had pockets full of money | As if you had no limits | As if you couldn't lose | As if you were a star | Until you cry | Until someone laughs with you | As if this was your last day | As if you had nothing to lose | Like you've found the greatest person in the world | As if you had the stage[1] to yourself

△ 2 Your turn: What makes you happy? → Help with Station 1, p. 47/5c) + d)

The rhyme words in the word bank can help you to write your own poem. Then you can use the phrases to talk about the changes you made.

Word bank

sun / fun / run | child / wild | day / play / way | tree / free / sea | pool / cool / rule | cake / break / make / take | grow / go / slow | hour / flower / power

Useful phrases

I changed the poem because for me, happiness is when … | … makes me happy because … | I feel good when … | I think … is great / wonderful / really cool.

Example: Happy as a child / Looking at the sun / Happy as friends / When they're having fun

△ 3 Taking a second look → Instead of Station 1, p. 48/7a)

Read the lines from the poem and the simpler, more direct versions[2] of them. Which of the two versions do you like best?

Line 2:
It fell to earth, I knew not where
1. I never found it.
2. I couldn't see where it landed.

Lines 7–8:
For who has sight so keen and strong,
That it can follow the flight of song?
1. Who has eyes good enough to see where a song goes?
2. Who has eyes to see how people react to a song?

Lines 3–4:
For, so swiftly it flew, the sight
Could not follow it in its flight.
1. I couldn't follow the flight of the arrow with my eyes.
2. I couldn't see where the arrow was going to land.

Lines 11–12:
And the song, from beginning to end,
I found again in the heart of a friend.
1. For me, finding a good friend was like singing that song again.
2. My friend liked the same song and sang it for me.

1 **stage** [steɪdʒ] Bühne | 2 **version** ['vɜːʃn] Version; Fassung

△ 4 Trouble usually finds me …

→ After Station 2, p. 50/10d)

*First, match the situations below with the expressions in the box. Sometimes more than one expression can be right. Which one do you think is best? Then use the situations and expressions to write **if-clauses**.*

be stuck in the middle of the sea | be the light to guide your friend | need a shoulder to cry on | be there for your friends | know what you are made of | be lost in the dark | count on me

1. A bully at school is making trouble for a classmate. You want to stop this and help.
2. You're on the bus to meet a friend. You fall asleep and when you wake up, you're in a part of the city you don't know at all. The neighbourhood doesn't look very nice, it's early evening, and now you're scared.
3. You're really trying to do better at History, but when you get your test back, you see that you got a really bad mark. The worst mark in the class!
4. A friend is going to have a big party for his birthday and needs a lot of help.
5. You go to an audition for a singing competition, but the people there tell you that you have no talent at all: "You'll *never* be a singer!"
6. Your best friend would like to become a member of the school's Drama Club, like you, but he / she doesn't know anything about acting.

Example: If I help my classmate with that bully, the bully will know what I'm made of!

△ 5 Poem and song options

→ Help with Options, p. 51/12

Here are some ideas and tips to help you with the option you choose on p. 51:

Option A:

Word bank

We were very close friends / always played together / often met at the weekends / … | One day something terrible / bad / strange happened … | We were at school / at my friend's house / at a party when I decided to … / when suddenly my friend … | I didn't mean to / didn't want to, but my friend … | When he left, I felt terrible, but I tried to call him / went to his house / talked to his parents / …

Option B:

Useful phrases

I think the photo goes well with the song / poem / topic because … | The song / poem is about …, and the photo shows … | The song / poem matches the atmosphere in the photo because … | The music of the song is … | In the photo you can see … | I often listen to songs like this when I'm …

Option C:

Useful phrases

The lyrics are about … / are interesting because … | The lines are catchy / easy / difficult to understand / … | The music is happy / sad / slow / fast / makes you want to dance / to tap your feet / to sing along. | The main instrument[1] is … | The atmosphere is … because of the music / the lyrics / …

Option D:

Tip

Practise your poem in front of a mirror[2] / to a friend or family. Write difficult parts on a piece of paper and put it where you can often see it. Try to match gestures with lines – this will help you remember more easily!

1 **instrument** ['ɪnstəmənt] Instrument | 2 **mirror** ['mɪrə] Spiegel

Unit 3

△ 1 Typically German? → Help with Introduction, p. 55/3d)

The picture and phrases can help you to talk about typical ideas people have about Germany.

Start like this: People from other countries believe / think that most / many Germans …

Word bank

good / great at football | like beer | love fast / good / expensive cars | drive fast | work hard / a lot | wear lederhosen and dirndl | always on time | make high quality products[1]

△ 2 Talking about Holly and Amber → Help with Station 1, p. 57/1

Complete these mind maps on Holly and Amber. Then use them to talk about the two girls.

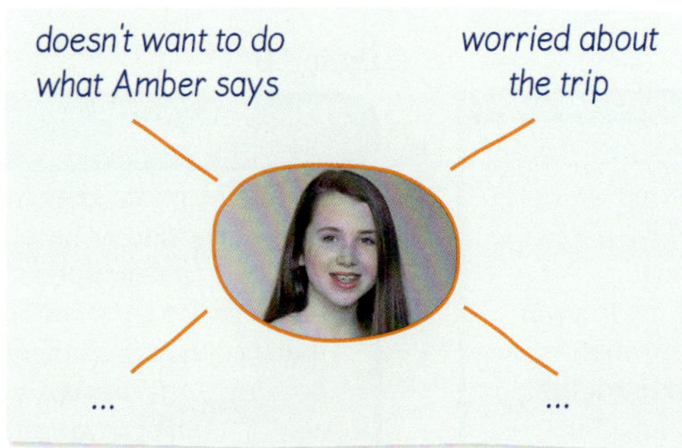

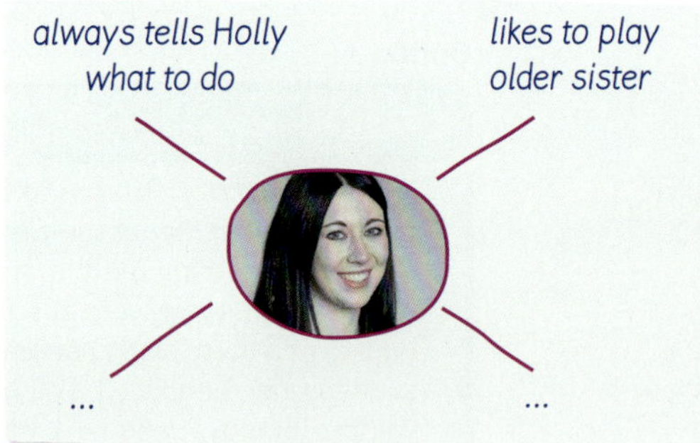

△ 3 He has been doing that since … → After Station 1, p. 57/2

Here are some famous Scots and information on what they've been doing since they were very young – but everything is mixed up. Work with a partner. Ask each other questions and find the right answers. One is not a Scot – who is it?

Example: 1. Has Ewan McGregor been playing tennis since he was very young? –
No, he hasn't been playing tennis. He's been acting in plays and in films.

1. Ewan McGregor – make music, play in a band 2. Andy Murray – sing, write her own songs 3. KT Tunstall – play football, train hard 4. David Beckham – act in plays[2] and in films, work hard to become an actor 5. Simple Minds – play tennis, do sports

1 **product** ['prɒdʌkt] Produkt | 2 **play** [pleɪ] Theaterstück

▲ 4 Scots and kilts → After Station 1, p. 57/2

Read the text and complete it with the ***present perfect simple*** *or the* ***present perfect progressive***.

g: 1. has been e been joking e been wear- has been ng 5. has had been telling bought

1. The kilt ▭ (be) a traditional piece of Scottish clothing[1] for hundreds of years, but it was only in the 19th century that kilts became part of the national costume. 2. Since then people ▭ (joke) about Scots in skirts. 3. For some years now, tourists ▭ (wear) kilts wherever they go in Scotland, but true Scotsmen only wear kilts to Scottish dances or weddings. 4. Ethan ▭ (wear) a kilt at gigs since he started to play in a traditional Scottish band. 5. He ▭ (have) his old kilt for some years, but the other band members ▭ (tell) him for months that he should get a new one. All the others ▭ (buy) new kilts with the same tartan pattern.

△ 5 Point in time or period of time? → After Station 1, p. 57/3

g: Point in time: e was a small boy; st ten; the 16th ; September 7th, ast July; November ar; last week; she was ergarten; he was ten; ay; his birthday last e break; of time: for ages; onths; a few days; d; as long as she can ber; centuries

Copy the grid and fill in the phrases. Remember: a point in time can be long too!

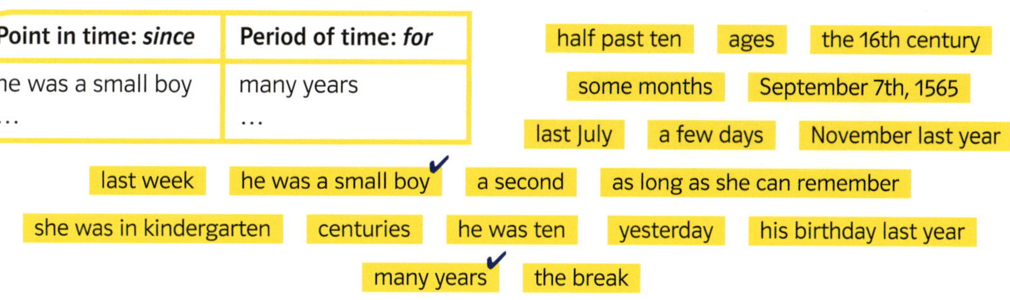

Point in time: *since*	Period of time: *for*
he was a small boy …	many years …

half past ten | ages | the 16th century | some months | September 7th, 1565 | last July | a few days | November last year | last week | he was a small boy ✔ | a second | as long as she can remember | she was in kindergarten | centuries | he was ten | yesterday | his birthday last year | many years ✔ | the break

▲ 6 Scary castles → After Station 1, p. 57/3

: a) Scottish clans en living in castles uries. Awful things ed there. In Ethie some men killed l Beaton in 1546. ous sounds have aring visitors since Duntrune Castle, ave been hearing of bagpipes since h of a bagpiper th century. In ie Castle, a white been kissing men leep for hundreds Her husband r and cut her in turies ago. The rt of the body walking upstairs lower been walking irs since that time.

a) *Write a short text about old Scottish castles. Use the correct tenses:* ***simple past, present perfect simple*** *and* ***present perfect progressive***.

Start like this: Scottish clans[2] have been living in castles for centuries. Awful things …

Scottish clans | live in castles | for centuries. Awful things | happen there. In Ethie Castle | some men | kill[3] Cardinal Beaton | in 1546. Mysterious sounds | scare[4] visitors | since then. In Duntrune Castle | people | hear sounds of bagpipes | since death of bagpiper | in 17th century. In Meggernie Castle | white lady | kiss[5] men in their sleep | for hundreds of years. Her husband | kill her and cut her in half | centuries ago. The upper part of body | walk upstairs | while lower part | walk downstairs | since that time.

b) *Find more Scottish ghost castles on the internet. Make notes about the stories and legends people tell about them. Present your castles in class.*

1 **piece of clothing** [ˌpiːs‿ɒv ˈkləʊðɪŋ] Kleidungsstück | 2 **clan** [klæn] Clan; Sippe | 3 **to kill** [kɪl] töten | 4 **to scare** [skeə] erschrecken | 5 **to kiss** [kɪs] küssen

△ 7 Let's dance! → After Station 1, p. 57/4

*Angus and Ian are talking about their plans for the weekend. Read their conversation and fill in **for** or **since**.*

Lösung: *1. for 2. since 3. since 4. since 5. since 6. for 7. since*

Angus: Hey, Ian. Do you want to come to the ceilidh[1] with us on Saturday? I haven't been to one **1** ages[2]!

Ian: Well, I haven't been to one **2** last year, and I'm not even sure if I still know what to do!

Angus: I'm sure you'll remember. Just come with us on Saturday.

Ian: OK, but let's ask Fiona too.

Angus: Fiona? I haven't seen her **3** she moved to Glasgow last year.

Ian: She's staying in Edinburgh with her aunt and uncle for the summer holidays. She's loved Scottish music and ceilidhs **4** she was in kindergarten, and I guess she still knows the right steps. She's been dancing at festivals with a group of dancers **5** she went to Glasgow.

Angus: Oh, I didn't know that. I haven't heard from her **6** a very long time. How long has she been back?

Ian: She's been back **7** last Saturday. I'll text her – it'll be great to see her again!

▲ 8 A strange country → After Station 1, p. 57/4

In this unit you've learned that in Scotland some men wear kilts, that even young people like traditional Scottish music, and that lots of people enjoy a strange meal called haggis. Write a short text about a country that you've made up[3] and think of things people have been doing there for a very long time. Present your text to the class.

Start like this: In the strange country of Galumphia, men have been …
All the people there have …

△ 9 Famous Scots → Help with Station 2, p. 60/10b)

Here are some ideas to help you with the exercise:

Lösung: *The radar was invented by Robert Wattson-Watt. Tunnels, canals and roads were built by Thomas Telford. Scottish castles were designed by Robert Adams. James Bond was played by Sean Connery. Lots of money was given to charity by Andrew Carnegie. Treasure Island was written by Robert Louis Stevenson.*

- radar[4] – invent – Robert Wattson-Watt
- tunnels, canals[5] and roads – build – Thomas Telford
- Scottish castles – design – Robert Adams
- James Bond – play – Sean Connery
- lots of money – give to charity – Andrew Carnegie
- *Treasure Island* – write – Robert Louis Stevenson

1 **ceilidh** ['keɪli] *schottisches Fest* | 2 **ages** [eɪdʒɪz] eine Ewigkeit | 3 **to make up** [ˌmeɪk_ˈʌp] sich ausdenken | 4 **radar** ['reɪdɑː] Radar | 5 **canal** [kə'næl] Kanal

△ 10 Scottish heroes and heroines → After Station 2, p. 60/11

*Complete the text with passive forms: **simple present**, **simple past** or **present perfect simple**.*

g: 1. have been was put up 3. was ped 4. was brought told 6. is always ed 7. was defeated hidden

Stories about heroes and heroines **1** (tell) in Scotland for centuries. There are stories about men and women, and even a dog. In 1872, a statue[1] of Greyfriar's Bobby **2** (put up) in a park in Edinburgh. Bobby, a Skye terrier, was so sad about his owner's[2] death[3] that he sat on his grave[4] for fourteen years. Another Scottish heroine is Flora Macdonald. Her father died when she was a child, and her mother **3** (kidnap[5]) – so Flora **4** (bring) to her father's cousin, the chief[6] of the Macdonald clan. Later, Flora **5** (tell) to move to the island of Benbecula. Today Flora **6** (always describe) in stories as a very brave young woman. And so she was! When Bonnie Prince Charlie, who wanted to become King of Scotland, **7** (defeat) by British soldiers, he escaped to Benbecula and **8** (hide) by Flora.

▲ 11 The story of Greyfriar's Bobby → After Station 2, p. 60/11

Read this short text about Greyfriar's Bobby. Present it in your own words. Explain why you think he was a hero or not.

John Gray worked for the City Police in Edinburgh more than a hundred years ago. He had a small dog: a Skye terrier called Bobby. When John Gray died, Bobby was so sad that he didn't want to leave John's grave. He sat there for fourteen years, and the people of Edinburgh brought him food and drink. He became one of the most famous dogs in the world. His story has been told in a number of books and films. When you go to Edinburgh, you can see his statue in the Old Town or have a drink in a bar that has his name.

△ 12 Glasgow is amazing! → Help with Station 2, p. 61/14b)

Here are some notes on famous Glasgow sights that can help you with your answer:

The Tall Ship | built in 1896 | explore every corner | sit in captain's chair | read the log book | learn about ship's history	The Willow[7] Tearooms | order a traditional afternoon tea | enjoy Scottish cakes and scones[8] | relax in rooms designed over 100 years ago	Escape[9] Glasgow | play team game for groups of 2–6 | work together as a team | find clues | solve problems | escape the room | have fun

△ 13 An interview with Holly and Amber → Help with Story, p. 68/5

Reporters are interested in the main facts of a story, but also in feelings and thoughts, because these make their reports more interesting. Here are some useful phrases for your interview.

Useful phrases

What happened? | When / Where did it happen? | Who was there? | Why did it happen? | What did you feel when … | Were you scared / upset / worried / …? | Did you think about … / think of … | What did you think when … | What has changed for you?

1 **statue** ['stætʃu:] Statue | 2 **owner** ['əʊnə] Besitzer/-in | 3 **death** [deθ] Tod | 4 **grave** [greɪv] Grab | 5 **to kidnap** ['kɪdnæp] entführen | 6 **chief** [tʃi:f] Anführer; Oberhaupt | 7 **willow** ['wɪləʊ] Weide | 8 **scone** [skɒn] brötchenartiges Gebäck | 9 **to escape** [ɪ'skeɪp] fliehen; flüchten

Text smart 2

△ 1 What's that in English? → Help with Station 1, p. 78/4a)

Lösung: Winterschlaf – *hibernation;* überleben – *survive;* vermeiden – *avoid;* Dosenfutter – *tinned food;* Schicht aus Zeitungspapier – *layer of newspaper;* zunehmen – *gain weight;* menschenscheu – *fearful of humans;* aufsaugen – *soak up;* Auslauf – *run area;* aktiv halten – *keep active*

Match the German words on the left with the English words on the right. Then find sentences with the English words in the hedgehog text.

Winterschlaf | überleben | vermeiden | Dosenfutter | Schicht aus Zeitungspapier | zunehmen | menschenscheu | aufsaugen | Auslauf | aktiv halten

layer of newspaper | fearful of humans | gain weight | tinned food | hibernation | run area | avoid | survive | soak up | keep active

△ 2 Writing instructions → Help with Station 1, p. 78/5

These words and phrases can help you to start your grid:

Steps:
1. The right time to help
2. A warm area for your hedgehog
3. Your hedgehog's bed
4. …

Phrases:
- Take care …
- Keep it …
- It is essential to …
- Give the hedgehog …
- …

△ 3 FAQs: Only important questions, please! → After Station 1, p. 78/6

Which of the questions below are important enough to show in an FAQ about a new smartphone model[1]? Choose the important questions and write answers for them.

1. Are there lots of new apps for the new model?
2. Does its screen[2] break easily?
3. Why is the new model better than the old one?
4. Has the design changed a lot?
5. Is the new phone waterproof[3]?
6. Are there new games on it now?
7. Does the new model have a better camera?

▲ 4 Time traveller with a smartphone → After Station 1, p. 78/6

You've travelled back in time to 1960. The people you meet see your smartphone and have lots of questions: How do you answer them? Use strong adjectives!

1 **model** [ˈmɒdl] Modell | 2 **screen** [skriːn] Bildschirm | 3 **waterproof** [ˈwɔːtəpruːf] wasserdicht

△ 5 From blog to news report → Help with Station 2, p. 79/8d)

Here are some expressions that can help you to write down facts. Don't forget to read the tip too!

Many animals are burnt / killed / saved / rescued / … | When the animals are found, they are often confused / helpless / thirsty / … | Photos of koalas with burns / with injuries make people think about …

Tip

In the blog post, expressions like "It breaks my heart" or "I'm not sure …" are part of the writer's **opinion**, not the facts. So don't use sentences with '**I**' or '**me**' for your facts.

△ 6 Understanding the text → Instead of Station 2, p. 81/11b)

Match the parts to make sentences.

- Elephants and rhinos in Africa are …
- There is a danger that …
- Those in power …
- We must do something about poaching …
- An elephant is … / A rhino is …
- All the wild animals in Africa are …

… killed for its tusk. / for its horn.
… on the brink of extinction.
… soon nobody will care about elephants any more.
… must learn about the situation in Africa.
… before it's too late.

: – Elephants …nos in Africa are on the … – There's a danger …n nobody will care … in power must learn …he … – We must do …ing about poaching be- too late. – An elephant for its tusk. / A rhino is …r its horn. – All the wild … in Africa are on …k of …

△ 7 Is that a text about elephants? → Help with Station 2, p. 81/11c)

Here are some words and phrases that can help you to explain the main ideas of the text in German:

Stoßzähne | auf die Straße gehen | Klaviertasten und Dekoartikel aus Elfenbein | verbotene Wilderei | vom Aussterben bedroht | weltweite Protestmärsche

△ 8 Writing your own texts → Help with Options, p. 81/13

Here are some ideas to help you with your options:

Option A:
*Start with very **basic** information / tips first before you write about lots of details.*

Your family will *really* like the breakfast you make if you make their favourite things. So always think about what each person likes first. Then, follow these steps …

Option B:
*If your introduction is interesting, your reader will want to read the **whole** report!*

Beautiful actor Jennifer Ashton was seen … She came to present her wonderful new …, but the people were much more interested in …

Before you start writing, go through your text in your head and make notes. What do you want to focus on? Sometimes pictures give you ideas. Find some on the internet!

Unit 4

△ 1 Look what I found in the attic! → Help with Introduction, p. 84/1b)

Here are pictures of some old things that people have found in their attic. Below you can also find a list of more things. Perhaps these things / words can give you ideas for your text.

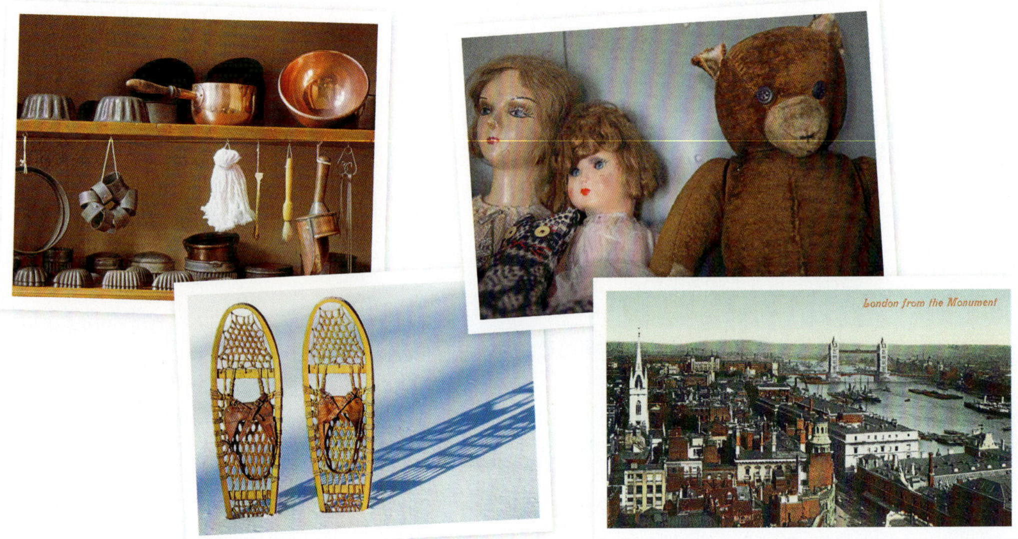

Word bank

baking moulds[1] / pots[2] / pans[3] | old toys (china doll[4] / soft toy[5]) | a pair of snowshoes[6] | old photos / letters / postcards | a telescope | keys | jewellery | chair / table / wardrobe / …

Useful phrases

I found this in … | It belonged to my grandad / grandma / … | He / She used it to … | It was very important to my …, so he / she didn't throw it away. | Today we use … instead.

△ 2 The past perfect → Instead of Station 1, p. 89/3

a) *Read these sentences. Find the* ***simple past*** *and* ***past perfect*** *forms. Make a list.*

Lösung: *Simple past forms: came, spoke, learned, were able to; Past perfect forms: had been, had lived, had become, had made*

1. Before the Romans came, the Celts had already been in Britain for a long time.
2. Elizabeth's mother, Anne, had lived in France, so she spoke very good French.
3. After William of Normandy had become king of England in 1066, more and more people learned French.
4. People in Victorian Britain were able to see more and more of their own country after the steam trains had made it quicker and easier to travel.

b) *Make a diagram to show which actions in each sentence happend* ***before*** *and which happened* ***after****.*

1 **baking mould** ['beɪkɪŋ ˌməʊld] Backform | 2 **pot** [pɒt] Topf | 3 **pan** [pæn] Pfanne | 4 **china doll** [ˌtʃaɪnə 'dɒl] Porzellanpuppe | 5 **soft toy** [ˌsɒft‿'tɔɪ] Plüsch- / Stofftier | 6 **snowshoes** ['snəʊʃuːz] Schneeschuhe

△ 3 Shakespeare's school days → After Station 1, p. 89/4

Read the text below and complete it with the correct forms of the ***past perfect****.*

g: 1. *had lived* n't *learned* *understood* *sat* 5. *had* d

Before William Shakespeare moved to London, he 1 (live) in the small town of Stratford-upon-Avon. His father John Shakespeare 2 (not learn) to read and write himself, but he 3 (understand) how important a good education was, so he sent his son to the local grammar school. Back then, the school days were very long – the students could only go home after they 4 (sit) at their desks from 6 a.m. to 5 p.m.! When Shakespeare finally left school, he 5 (learn) enough Latin to read any Latin book that interested him.

▲ 4 Where was he? → After Station 1, p. 89/4

Shakespeare had left Stratford-upon-Avon some years before he became a famous writer in London – but nobody knows where he was or what he did exactly. Look at the three ideas below and choose ***one*** *you'd like to write about. Then add some more details and explain why you think it's right. Use a dictionary if you need more words.*

Start like this: I think that before Shakespeare came to London, he had …

a) join a group of actors and travel across England | act in lots of different plays | see many different cities
b) work as a teacher for a rich man and read a lot of books | meet a lot of famous and important people | become a friend to some of them
c) travel to Italy and get the idea for his play *Romeo and Juliet* there | learn more about Roman history | visit a lot of Italian cities

△ 5 A boy who loved the stage → After Station 1, p. 90/5

Complete the text about a young actor. Use the correct tenses: ***simple past*** *or* ***past perfect****.*

: 1. *was*, 2. *were*, *'led*, 4. *performed*, 5. *didn't trust*, 7. *n talked*, 8. *died*, *t seemed*, 10. *had* . *began*, 12. *had just* 13. *joined*, 14. *was*, *me*, 16. *had already* 7. *had become*

When Nathan Field 1 (be) born in 1587, there 2 (be) only a few theatres. Most actors 3 (travel) around the country and 4 (perform) their plays outside pubs. Back then, actors 5 (have) a bad reputation[1] and people 6 (not trust) them. Nathan's own father, a priest[2], 7 (often talk) angrily about them too before he 8 (die) in 1588. So, for Nathan, a career in acting 9 (not seem) possible at first. But in the later years of the 16th century, after the Elizabethans 10 (build) a lot of theatres, opinions about acting and actors finally 11 (begin) to change. And in 1600, after he 12 (just turn) 13, Nathan 13 (join) a group of boy actors. Soon he 14 (be) one of their best players and 15 (become) very famous. By the age of 26, he 16 (already act) in front of the Queen and 17 (become) one of the superstars of his time.

1 **reputation** [ˌrepjəˈteɪʃn] Ruf | 2 **priest** [priːst] Priester

▲ 6 A superstar of the stage → After Station 1, p. 90/5

Use the key words below to write a text about Nathan Field, an actor from the time of Queen Elizabeth and a superstar of the stage. Use the ***simple past*** *and the* ***past perfect****. (Look at p. 129 for the meaning of the new words here.)*

When Nathan Field | born in 1587 | only a few theatres. Most actors | travel around country | perform plays outside pubs. Back then | actors | have bad reputation | people | not trust them. | Nathan's own father | a priest | talk angrily about them too | before | die | in 1588. So, for Nathan, | career in acting | not seem possible | at first. But | later years of 16th century | after | Elizabethans | build | a lot of theatres | opinions about acting and actors | finally | begin to change. And in 1600 | after just turn 13 | Nathan | join | group of boy actors. Soon | be | one of their best players | become very famous. By the age of 26 | already act | in front of Queen | become one of the superstars | of his time.

△ 7 Tell the story → Help with Station 1, p. 90/6

These phrases can help you to write your story:

Lösung: *Correct order: D, F, B, E, A, C*

Then, on his first big adventure, he went to America to … | When he was in America … | This made him angry … | He never forgot … | In 1577, Drake sailed … | After he had stolen … the Spanish really hated … | As soon as Drake had returned to … | he wasted … | He gave the queen … | She was … and couldn't believe her … | After Drake had defeated the …, England felt … | Drake was now a …

△ 8 Your turn: Funny or interesting things in your life → Help with Station 1, p. 90/7

Here are some ideas for Ex. 7. Maybe things like this have happened to you?

Before: take wrong bag | hurry to meet friends | ask mum for money | **At pool:** people having fun | open bag | find tennis clothes | wrong bag! | **After:** go home | get right bag

Before: go to first concert[1] | take phone | tell parents not to worry | **At concert:** enjoy the show | loud music | not hear phone | **After:** lots of calls | angry texts from parents

Before: excited about party | not sure what to wear | not read the whole invitation | **At party:** only one in colourful clothes | feel stupid | **After:** look at invitation again | see 'dress code'[2]

1 **concert** ['kɒnsət] Konzert | 2 **dress code** ['dres kəʊd] Kleiderordnung (z. B. für Mottoparty)

△ 9 Useful phrases for presenting facts → Instead of Skills, p. 91/1b)

Copy the grid and complete it with the list of phrases under the grid. The tip box on the right can help you to remember what kind of words you need.

Tip

- **Prepositions** are words like 'for', 'from' or 'at'.
- **Common history verbs** often tell us what people did, e.g. 'travel' or 'fight'.
- **Biographical information** tells you about important events in a person's life, e.g. when he / she was born or died.

Prepositions with times and dates	Descriptions of places / objects	Biographical information	Typical history verbs
in 1564	... was used for ...	was born **in** 1878	reigned
		was born **on** 15th April 1878	

for 200 years | at the beginning of | was worn by | it has | invented | was given to | moved to | from 1066 to 1154 | it looks | you can see a / an | at the end of | was brought from

△ 10 English would have been different! → After Station 2, p. 93/10

Finish these sentences to say how English would have been different.

: 1. hadn't come – 't have given 't stayed – wouldn't fluenced 3. wouldn't me – hadn't d 4. wouldn't have o – hadn't become 't loved – wouldn't itten 6. wouldn't vented – hadn't 7. hadn't explored – 't have brought

1. If the Romans ___ (not come) to England, they ___ (not give) a new name to this country – Britain.
2. If the Romans ___ (not stay) for such a long time, their language ___ (not influence) the English language so much.
3. The Normans ___ (not come) to England if William the Conqueror ___ (not believe) he had a right[1] to be king of England.
4. The people in England ___ (not give up) so many of their English words if French ___ (not become) so popular after the Normans had arrived.
5. If the people in the 16th century ___ (not love) the theatre so much, Shakespeare ___ (not write) so many plays.
6. Shakespeare ___ (not invent) so many new words if he ___ (not write) so many plays and poems.
7. If English sailors ___ (not explore) so many countries, they ___ (not bring) new things and words for them back to England.

Some French words in English:

This **restaurant** looks **brilliant**[1]! I hope they have a **table**.
The Georgian
The Georgian
Menu
Let's look at the **menu**[2] first …

1 **brilliant** ['brɪliənt] hervorragend | 2 **menu** ['menju:] Speisekarte

▲ 11 The world would have been different! → After Station 2, p. 93/10

*Work with a partner. One of you thinks of an important event in history and imagines what would have happened – or **wouldn't** have happened – without this event. Your partner then continues. How long can you take turns?*

Example: A: If Christopher Columbus[1] hadn't sailed west, he wouldn't have discovered America and the New World.
B: If Columbus hadn't discovered the New World, Francis Drake wouldn't have travelled there.
A: If Francis Drake …

△ 12 Imagine … → Instead of Station 2, p. 93/12

*Imagine how things would have been. Put the verbs into the correct tenses to make sentences with **if-clauses type 3**.*

Lösung: *1. hadn't always worn, it wouldn't have been, 2. hadn't built, they would have found, 3. hadn't spoken, wouldn't have changed, 4. hadn't wanted, he wouldn't have married, 5. hadn't wanted to know, she wouldn't have sent, 6. hadn't reigned, she wouldn't have seen*

1. If a Celtic king ___ (not always wear) beautiful jewellery, it ___ (not be) clear to others how important he was.
2. If the Romans ___ (not build) baths, they ___ (find) Britain too cold for them.
3. If the Normans ___ (not speak) French, the English language ___ (not change).
4. If Henry VIII ___ (not want) a son to be the next monarch, he ___ (not marry) six times.
5. If Elizabeth ___ (not want) to know more about the world, she ___ (not send) sailors to America.
6. If Queen Victoria ___ (not reign) for 64 years, she ___ (not see) so many changes in the time she lived.

▲ 13 A game: What would you have done? → After Station 2, p. 94/13

*In this activity, write sentences with **if-clauses type 3**. Do it with a partner.*

First, work alone. Write the if-clause of a sentence on a card. Then turn your card over and finish your sentence with the main clause. Do this with five different cards. Your sentences can be about history, or about anything you like. Be creative!

Example 1: First part: If I **had taken** an embarrassing photo of a really famous person on my last holiday, …
Second part: I **would have sold** it to a magazine!

Example 2: First part: If I **had lived** in the time of Queen Elizabeth I, …
Second part: I **would have been** an important person for the queen!

*Now read the first part of your if-clause to your partner, and ask him/her to finish it. If your partner can finish the sentence correctly, he/she keeps the card. If not, **you** can keep it. Take turns to read your cards. The partner with the most cards at the end wins!*

1 Christopher Columbus [ˌkrɪstefəˌkəˈlʌmbəs]

Text smart 3

△ 1 Your turn: Your favourite genre → Help with Introduction, p. 106/2b)

These phrases can help you to talk about your favourite genre:

I think the best books are …
I love … / really enjoy …
I can never put[1] … books down. They're real page-turners[2].
My absolutely favourite genre is …
I only read …
… are fantastic because …
You must read … because …
… books open up[3] new worlds to you / allow you to travel in your mind[4].

△ 2 Who is Luke? → Help with Station 1, p. 107/5

a) *Read the text on p. 107 again. Decide which parts of the sentences below make the most sense[5].*

…: a) 1. in the woods …nough to work in …den 3. is afraid …e's outside 4. is …ld to go inside …tside 6. are taking …he trees

1. Luke and his family live in the woods | in a city | near the sea.
2. Luke is a toddler | a teenager | old enough to work in the garden.
3. Luke's mother likes Luke to be outside | is afraid when he's outside | is always scared.
4. Luke often works in the garden | is often told to go inside | often plays outside.
5. Luke might not be allowed to go barefoot | go outside | go into the woods again.
6. This has something to do with the people who are working on the farm | are taking down the trees | are living nearby[6].

b) *These categories can help you to find questions to ask about Luke:*

Luke: Age? Activities? Link to the title of the book?

Family: Brothers / sisters? Parents? Parents' jobs?

Home: Farm? Flat? Big house? Neighbours?

Friends: School? Neighbourhood? Internet? Lonely?

△ 3 Key lines from the text → Instead of Station 1, p. 108/6

Match these key lines from the text with the explanations on the right.

1e), 2d), 3a), 4b), 5c)

1. He had never disobeyed the order to hide.
2. He had somehow understood the fear in his mother's voice.
3. But on this day, he hesitated.
4. I will never be allowed outside again. Maybe never again as long as I live.
5. He turned and walked into the house, as silently as a shadow.

a) This day is different from all the other days, so Luke doesn't obey immediately.
b) Something has changed in Luke's life that will stop him from going outside.
c) Nobody should see or hear Luke.
d) His mother is afraid of something outside that might hurt Luke.
e) It's extremely important that Luke hides when he's told to do so.

1 **to put down** [ˌpʊt‿ˈdaʊn] weglegen | 2 **page-turner** [ˈpeɪdʒˌtɜːnə] fesselndes Buch | 3 **to open up** [ˌəʊpn‿ˈʌp] eröffnen | 4 **mind** [maɪnd] Geist; Verstand | 5 **to make sense** [meɪk ˈsens] Sinn ergeben | 6 **nearby** [ˌnɪəˈbaɪ] in der Nähe

△ 4 First reactions → Help with Station 2, p. 109/9a)

Choose five adjectives that you think best describe the atmosphere and situation. Then discuss your words with a partner. Together, decide on the three best adjectives.

scary | challenging | calm | strange | bad | relaxed | sunny | cheerful[1] | terrible | depressing[2] | frightening[3] | exciting | dark | confusing | sad | fantastic | friendly

△ 5 Key lines from the text → Instead of Station 2, p. 109/10

*Which of these lines are key lines from the text, which ones are **not**? Why? Discuss with a partner. The useful phrases on p. 108, Ex. 6 can help you.*

1. I'm going to die.
2. I look up through the grey-white shimmer of the swimming pool water.
3. My lungs are on fire.
4. Just one breath. Just one.
5. I have to take a breath, even though I know that I'll be breathing in water.
6. I close my eyes, praying hard.
7. Part of me – a tiny, tiny part of me – laughs.
8. After everything I've been through in the last few months, this is how I'm going to bow out.
9. Alex …
10. I stop fighting. I'm so tired. I can feel my body begin to sink.

△ 6 Writing options → Help with Options, p. 111/15

Here are some ideas to help you with your options:

Option A:
Choose from one of these first lines. Then take your story from there.

"Run!" Mike shouted, but Laura … | I had never wanted to go on a camping trip – it was … | Sam entered his office on the 25th floor with a smile. How could he know what … | I could hear their footsteps. They were coming closer …

Option B:
Choose one of these two perspectives for Text 2. (Cameron is the main character in Pig-Heart-Boy*). Use the key phrases below to start your story.*

Marlon, Cameron's friend
often go to the pool together | parents don't know | Cameron too sick | always look out for Cameron | can't see him | panic | …

Cathy, Cameron's mum
always worried about Cameron | thinks he is at Marlon's home, doing homework | at the pool instead | call from the hospital | …

1 cheerful [ˈtʃɪəfl] fröhlich | 2 depressing [dɪˈpresɪŋ] deprimierend | 3 frightening [ˈfraɪtnɪŋ] Furcht erregend; beängstigend

Vocabulary

S1 Vokabelheft

Lege ein dreispaltiges Vokabelheft an, in dem du auch neue Vokabeln notierst, die nicht in der Wortliste stehen (1. Spalte: englische Vokabel; 2. Spalte: Übersetzung; 3. Spalte: Beispielsätze oder alles, was dir hilft, dir die Bedeutung zu merken, z. B. *mind maps*).

S2 Vokabelkartei

Lerne neue Vokabeln mit einer Vokabelkartei. Sie besteht aus Karteikarten für die Vokabeln und einem Karton mit fünf Fächern für die Karten. (Vorderseite: englische Vokabel, Rückseite: Übersetzung sowie weitere Merkhilfen)
Stelle alle Karten ins erste Fach. Übe jeden Tag fünf bis zehn Minuten. Wenn du die Übersetzung weißt, stellst du die Karten ins zweite Fach. Mache weiter, bis das erste Fach leer ist. Das zweite Fach bearbeitest du dann einmal in der Woche, das dritte Fach alle zwei Wochen, usw.

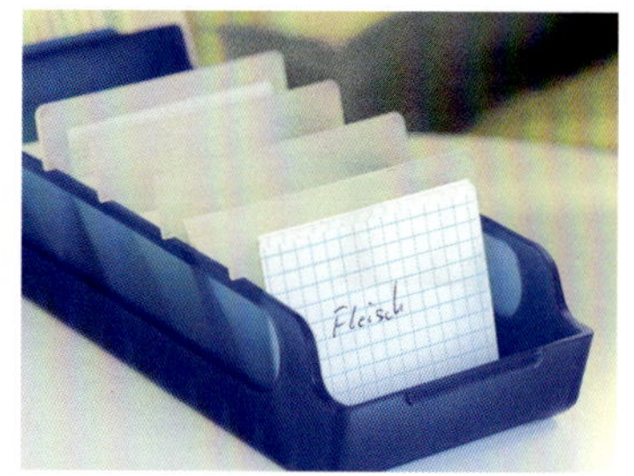

S3 Wörter im Zusammenhang

Wörter sind die Bausteine der Sprache. Du musst sie natürlich lernen und jedes für sich verstehen. Zur Beherrschung einer Sprache gehört aber auch zu wissen, welche Kombinationen dieser Bausteine möglich sind. Deshalb ist es wichtig, mit den Wörtern die richtigen Kombinationen mitzulernen. Schreibe deshalb Wörter möglichst immer in typischen Zusammenhängen auf.

Lerne bei Verben passende Ergänzungen mit, z. B.:

to ***read*** *a book, a magazine, a comic, a manga*
to ***write*** *a letter, an e-mail, an invitation, a blog*
to ***go*** *swimming, shopping, home, away, to the cinema*

Schreibe auf, welche bestimmten grammatischen Formen auf bestimmte Wörter folgen, z. B.:

I ***would like*** ***to*** *swim,* ***to*** *read,* ***to*** *go shopping*
I ***like*** *swimm**ing**, read**ing**, go**ing** shopping*

Notiere dir Beispiele bei Wörtern mit Präpositionen:

The party is ***on Friday****,* ***at seven****,* ***at the weekend****.*
My house is ***in Dover Street****. We're* ***on the road to London****.*
London is ***on the Thames****.*

Achte beim Lesen unterschiedlicher Textsorten auf hilfreiche Formulierungen (*useful phrases*). Diese kannst du später in eigenen Texten immer wieder verwenden.

1. Take care of a small hedgehog until around mid-April, when the frosts are usually over.
2. Keep it in a warm area such as a shed or spare room. It will need an area where it can sleep and wander round a little bit without getting lost or stuck (they can fit into VERY small spaces). It is essential to keep it warm and active to avoid hibernation; it is too small and WILL NOT survive!
3. Give the hedgehog a container to sleep under/in. Leave it in the run area so that it can come out when it wants. This bed should contain shredded newspaper (NOT OFFICE PAPER – IT CUTS THEIR NOSE AND FEET), dry leaves or hay.
4. Line the run area with newspaper so you can clean it out daily. Just take up the top sheets of newspaper; that leaves it nice and clean

S4 Methoden

Du hast schon mehrere Methoden gelernt, wie du dir Vokabeln besser einprägen kannst:

- Klebezettel mit englischen Wörtern an die entsprechenden Gegenstände in deinem Zimmer kleben
- Wörter als Bildwörter oder mit passenden Bildern aufmalen
- Wörter mit anderen Begriffen, die zu einem Thema gehören, anhand von Überbegriffen in *mind maps* oder Tabellen strukturieren
- Wörter pantomimisch darstellen und gegenseitig erraten lassen
- Wörter aussprechen, zusammen mit ihrer Übersetzung und vielleicht einem Beispielsatz aufnehmen und immer wieder anhören
- Wörter mit ähnlichen Wörtern in anderen Sprachen notieren
- Wörter, die miteinander in Beziehung stehen, zusammen notieren, z. B. verwandte Wörter, Gegensatzpaare, zusammengehörige Paare

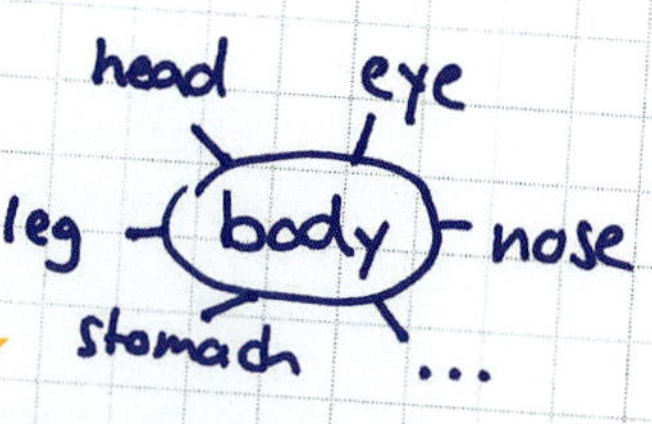

to compete with
- konkurrieren mit
-> Lat. competere

to exaggerate
- übertreiben
-> Fr. exagérer

Reading

S5 Schnelllesetechniken

Wenn du eine Aufgabe zu einem Text bekommst oder eine bestimmte Information suchst, liest du den Text ganz gezielt. Diese Techniken helfen dir, wenn die Zeit begrenzt ist.

Skimming („den Rahm abschöpfen“)	**Scanning („maschinell durchsuchen“)**
Wenn du danach gefragt wirst, worum es in einem Text geht, sollst du ihn nicht einfach nacherzählen, sondern nur das Wichtigste (*gist*) zusammenfassen. Dazu kannst du den ganzen Text überfliegen und darauf achten, ob bestimmte Wörter (*key words*) oder Personen häufiger vorkommen. Auch die Überschrift oder Bilder können dir helfen einzuschätzen, was wichtig ist und was nicht. Diese Art des Schnelllesens nennt man *skimming*.	Wenn du nach bestimmten Einzelheiten (*details*) in einem Text gefragt wirst, musst du ihn überfliegen und die Stellen mit der wichtigen Information finden. Dazu suchst du gezielt nach passenden Stichwörtern (*key words*). Sie zeigen an, welche Teile du genauer lesen solltest, um die gesuchte Information zu bekommen. Diese Art des Überfliegens nennt man auch *scanning*.

S6 Wichtige Inhalte von Texten herausfinden

Wenn du einen Text liest, solltest du danach immer folgende Fragen beantworten können:

Who ...? Wer ist beteiligt?	What ...? Was geschieht?	When ...? Wann?	Where ...? Wo?

Wende hierzu Schnelllesetechniken an, markiere Textstellen und notiere Fragen und Anmerkungen (→ S9). Wenn du Informationen aus einer bestimmten Textstelle entnimmst, notiere die Quelle (Seitenzahl, Zeilennummer). So kannst du deine Ergebnisse anhand des Texts belegen und findest die Textstelle später leicht wieder. Wenn du den Text noch genauer liest, kannst du weitere Fragen beantworten, z. B. Für wen wurde der Text geschrieben? Wer erzählt die Geschichte? Warum geschieht etwas? (→ S7)

S7 Wichtige Merkmale von Erzähltexten, Gedichten und Theaterstücken erkennen

1. Story

Wenn du eine Geschichte genauer liest oder analysierst, solltest du nicht nur über die Handlung (*plot*) selbst nachdenken, sondern auch darüber, wie die Geschichte erzählt wird. Zu den wichtigsten Erzähltechniken (*narrative techniques*) gehören:

Atmosphere/ Mood	Bestimmte Wörter und Beschreibungen schaffen in einer Geschichte eine gewisse Stimmung (*atmosphere* oder *mood*). Stimmung entsteht z. B. dadurch, dass die fünf Sinne (*five senses*) angesprochen werden: Wenn man liest, was die Figuren sehen, hören, riechen, schmecken und fühlen, ist es leichter, sich in sie hineinzuversetzen.
Climax	Der Höhepunkt (*climax*) ist der Hauptwendepunkt in einer Geschichte. Die Spannung ist hier am höchsten. Die Hauptfigur befindet sich oft in einer schwierigen Situation und macht Veränderungen durch, sie wird z. B. stärker oder selbstbewusster. (Siehe auch *turning point*)
Flashback	Eine Rückblende (*flashback*) erzählt Ereignisse, die vor einem bestimmten Zeitpunkt in der Geschichte stattgefunden haben, z. B. wird die Erinnerung einer Figur an etwas Vergangenes beschrieben.
Narrative perspective	Die Wirkung, die eine Geschichte auf den Leser hat, wird stark von der Erzählperspektive (*narrative perspective*) beeinflusst. Wer ist der Erzähler und wie ist seine Einstellung zu den Figuren der Geschichte? Was erzählt er und wann? Die häufigsten Erzählperspektiven sind: **1. Ich-Erzähler (*first-person narrator*)** Der Ich-Erzähler erzählt die Geschichte aus seiner Perspektive. Oft (aber nicht immer) ist der Ich-Erzähler die Hauptfigur der Geschichte. Der Leser und der Ich-Erzähler erleben die Geschichte sozusagen „gemeinsam". **2. Er / Sie-Erzähler (*third-person narrator*)** Dieser Erzähler erzählt die Geschichte „von außen". Die Perspektive ist nicht die der Hauptfigur.

Suspense	Spannung (*suspense*) ist eine wichtige Erzähltechnik, um den Leser in die Geschichte hineinzuziehen. Spannung kann direkt in den ersten Zeilen der Geschichte aufgebaut werden oder aber langsam im Verlauf der Geschichte. Sie wird z. B. durch starke, dramatische Sprache erzeugt oder durch das Zurückhalten von Informationen.
Turning point	Ein Wendepunkt ist der Teil einer Geschichte, in dem eine Figur eine wichtige Entscheidung treffen muss. Diese Entscheidung beeinflusst den weiteren Verlauf der Geschichte. Sie kann für die Hauptfigur und die anderen Figuren gut oder schlecht sein. (Siehe auch *climax*)

2. Poetry

Ein Gedicht ist wie eine Zeichnung oder ein Gemälde, das mit Wörtern „gemalt“ wurde. In einem Gedicht ist jedes einzelne Wort wichtig. Denke daran: Beim Verständnis von Gedichten geht es nicht darum, die „richtige“ Bedeutung zu finden – das gleiche Gedicht kann von verschiedenen Menschen ganz unterschiedlich verstanden werden. Wichtig ist aber, dass du deine Deutung am Text belegen kannst. Dazu ist es hilfreich, auch formale Merkmale zu untersuchen und mit dem Inhalt in Verbindung zu bringen. Zu den wichtigsten Merkmalen von Gedichten gehören:

Rhyme scheme	Gedichte, die sich reimen, folgen immer einem bestimmten Reimschema (*rhyme scheme*). Typische Reimschemata sind: **AABB** und **ABAB** sowie **ABCB**. Es gibt aber auch Gedichte, die sich nicht reimen, sogenannte *free verse poems*.
Rhythm / Stress	Ein Gedicht funktioniert nur mit dem richtigen Rhythmus (*rhythm*). Er bestimmt, welche Stelle in jeder Zeile betont wird. Die Betonung (*stress*) liegt dann immer an der gleichen Stelle. Bei Gedichten, die sich nicht reimen (*free verse poems*), ist es wichtig, dass du selbst entscheidest, wo die Betonung liegt oder wo eine Pause gemacht werden sollte.
Symbol / Simile / Metaphor	In Gedichten spielen Symbole eine wichtige Rolle. Ein **Symbol** (*symbol*) steht stellvertretend für etwas anderes, z. B. für ein Gefühl, eine Idee oder eine Handlung. So ist das Herz ein Symbol für die Liebe. Bei einem **Vergleich** (*simile*) werden Dinge oder Personen mit etwas anderem verglichen, um auszudrücken, dass sie die gleichen Eigenschaften besitzen. Dabei wird *like* oder *as* verwendet: *Happy as a rainbow.* Eine **Metapher** (*metaphor*) ist ein verkürzter Vergleich ohne *like* oder *as*: *I'll be the light to guide you.*

3. Drama

Theaterstücke sind in Akte (*act*) und Szenen (*scene*) unterteilt. Sie sind dafür vorgesehen, von Schauspielerinnen und Schauspielern auf der Bühne aufgeführt zu werden. Es gibt in der Regel keinen Erzähler, der die Figuren genauer beschreibt. Stattdessen wird die Handlung direkt durch die gesprochene Sprache und durch die Darstellung der Figuren vermittelt. Deshalb ist es bei der Interpretation von Theaterstücken besonders wichtig, neben dem Text auch auf die Sprechweise, Gestik und Mimik zu achten. So kannst du Rückschlüsse auf Charaktereigenschaften, Gedanken und Gefühle der Figuren ziehen.

Characters	Die Figuren (*characters*) stellen oft klassische Typen (oder Rollen) dar. Auf der einen Seite gibt es einen Helden / eine Heldin (*good guy*), auf der anderen Seite einen Bösewicht (*bad guy*). Das Handeln dieser Figuren wird von guten oder bösen Motiven angetrieben.
Language	In Theaterstücken wird die Handlung durch gesprochene Sprache vermittelt. Die Figuren sprechen in Dialogen miteinander.
Stage directions	Alles, was nicht durch gesprochene Sprache vermittelt werden kann, wird in Regieanweisungen (*stage directions*) vorgegeben. Sie beschreiben, wie die Schauspieler ihre Figur spielen sollen und wie sie sprechen. Sie machen auch Angaben zu Requisiten (*props*), Bühnenbild, Licht, usw. Wenn man ein Theaterstück liest, können die Regieanweisungen wichtige Hinweise auf z. B. die Stimmung der Szene und die Gefühle der Figuren geben. Sieht man das Theaterstück auf der Bühne, wird die Handlung und Stimmung des Stückes auch von Körpersprache, Bewegungen, Bühnenbild, Licht, usw. getragen.

S8 Gliederung als Hilfe

Um einen Text besser zu verstehen, kann es dir helfen, ihn in mehrere Abschnitte zu gliedern. Orientiere dich dabei z. B. an Absätzen und inhaltlichen Punkten, die du dir markiert hast. Überlege anschließend, was in den einzelnen Teilen jeweils das Wichtigste ist und formuliere passende Überschriften. Dies erleichtert es dir, Texte zusammenzufassen oder *Mediation*-Aufgaben zu lösen.

A Henry hopes to play the lead
B Henry is disappointed
C Henry sees the positive side of things

S9 Textbearbeitung mit Markierungen und Notizen

Im geliehenen Buch darfst du das zwar nicht, aber auf Kopien oder in Arbeitsheften solltest du dir angewöhnen, wichtige Stellen in Texten zu markieren und Randnotizen zu machen (z. B. Fragen oder Anmerkungen). Verwende am besten verschiedene Farben:

Markiere z. B. wichtige inhaltliche Punkte grün und Informationen zu den Figuren / Charakteren blau. Wörter, die du nachschlagen musst, solltest du auch hervorheben. Unterstreiche sie beispielsweise und notiere die richtige Übersetzung am Rand. So fällt dir das erneute Lesen leichter.

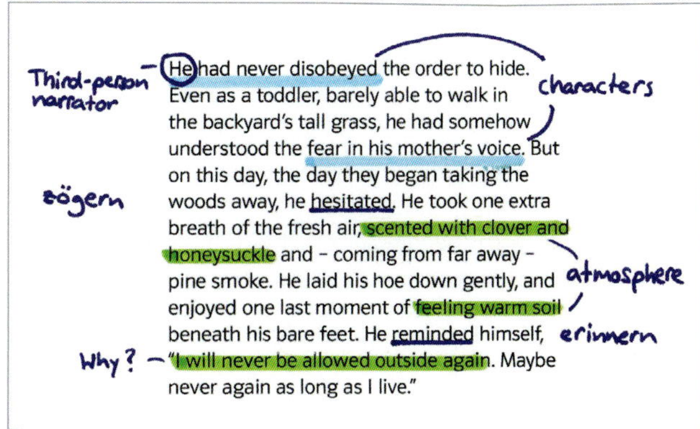
He had never disobeyed the order to hide. Even as a toddler, barely able to walk in the backyard's tall grass, he had somehow understood the fear in his mother's voice. But on this day, the day they began taking the woods away, he hesitated. He took one extra breath of the fresh air, scented with clover and honeysuckle and – coming from far away – pine smoke. He laid his hoe down gently, and enjoyed one last moment of feeling warm soil beneath his bare feet. He reminded himself, "I will never be allowed outside again. Maybe never again as long as I live."

S10 Umgang mit neuen Wörtern

Viele Wörter kannst du schon verstehen, obwohl du sie noch nicht gelernt hast.

1. **Ähnlichkeit mit Wörtern, die du schon kennst**
   Oft haben verwandte Wörter den gleichen Stamm, aber andere Präfixe oder Suffixe. Wenn du z. B. *usual* schon kennst, wirst du *unusual* sicher verstehen. Englische Wörter haben oft keine Suffixe, aber es gibt sie in verschiedenen Wortarten. Wenn du also das Wort *guide* als Nomen kennst, kannst du dir bestimmt denken, was das Verb *to guide* oder die Zusammensetzung *travel guide bedeutet*.

2. **Ähnlichkeit mit Wörtern, die du aus einer anderen Sprache kennst**
   Viele englische Wörter gibt es genauso oder ähnlich auch im Deutschen, z. B. *computer* oder *hobby*. Manchmal hilft dir auch ein Wort, das du aus einer anderen Sprache kennst (Französisch, Latein, …) ein englisches Wort zu verstehen, z. B. weil es ähnlich geschrieben wird oder ähnlich klingt.

3. **Verstehen der Wörter im Zusammenhang**
   Manchmal kannst du dir anhand eines Bildes oder einer Überschrift denken, was ein Wort in einem Text bedeutet. Und wenn du alle Wörter in einem Satz verstehst außer einem, kann dieses oft nur eine bestimmte Bedeutung haben. Was bedeutet z. B. *ridiculous* in folgendem Satz: *That's the silliest thing I've ever heard. It's **ridiculous**!*

   Auf den Zusammenhang musst du auch achten, wenn du Wörter im Wörterbuch nachschlägst, denn dort findest du meist mehrere Bedeutungen für ein Wort:
   *Take the second street on the **right**. That's the **right** way for the station.*
   *I haven't got **time** to sit and chat today. We can chat when I come next **time**.*
   *This is a very small **room**. There's **room** for only one bed.*

Writing

S11 Planung deines Textes

Überlege, für wen dein Text bestimmt ist (Adressat) und welchen Zweck er erfüllen soll. Vor dem Schreiben machst du dir am besten einen Plan: Notiere in Stichwörtern, was in der Einleitung, dem Hauptteil und dem Schluss deines Textes stehen soll. So vergisst du nichts Wichtiges und findest auch leichter eine schöne Einleitung und einen guten Schluss.

S12 Textsorten und ihre Besonderheiten

Du kennst schon einige wichtige Textsorten und ihre Haupteigenschaften:

Blog	Ein Blog ist eine Art Online-Tagebuch, in dem regelmäßig Beiträge veröffentlicht werden. Es gibt unterschiedliche Arten von Blogs, z. B. Reiseblogs, Nachrichtenblogs oder Musikblogs. Meist sind Blog-Posts in der Ich-Perspektive geschrieben und sind von dem persönlichen Standpunkt des Bloggers / der Bloggerin geprägt.
Dialogue / Film script	Wenn du einen Dialog, z. B. für eine Filmszene, schreibst, denke daran, dass du ihn kurz hältst und echte mündliche Sprache verwendest, also z. B. *short forms*, *question tags*, verstärkende Ausdrücke usw. Beachte bei den *stage directions* für ein Filmskript, dass du nur das angibst, was man auch sehen oder darstellen kann. Gedanken kann man nicht sehen. Aber du kannst in den *stage directions* Hinweise auf die Gefühle einer Person geben, z. B. durch Anweisungen für Gesichtsausdrücke.
Diary entry	Ein Tagebucheintrag erzählt und kommentiert vergangene und erwartete Ereignisse aus der ganz persönlichen Sicht einer Person und ist normalerweise nicht für andere Leser bestimmt. Verwende ausdrucksstarke Adjektive und Adverbien, um Gedanken und Gefühle zu beschreiben.
E-mail / Letter Postcard / Invitation	Achte auf die richtige Anrede für den Adressaten, z. B. *Dear …*, Grußformeln am Schluss, z. B. *Yours / Love / Best wishes*, und beachte die Höflichkeitsregeln. Bei formellen E-Mails oder Briefen verwendet man eher die Langformen, z. B. *I am* statt *I'm*. Denke bei einem Brief an die Angabe der Empfänger- und Absenderadresse und an das Datum.
Flyer	Ein Flyer sollte gut lesbar sein (Schriftart- und größe) und alle wichtigen Informationen enthalten: *Who? What? When? Where? Why?* Formuliere außerdem einen ansprechenden Slogan.
Instructions	Anweisungen sind meist in mehrere, klare Schritte gegliedert. Diese Schritte können von Überschriften eingeleitet werden. Sprachlich werden vor allem Imperative und *phrases* wie *Make sure …*, *You / It must …* oder *Never …* verwendet.
News report	Konzentriere dich bei einem Tatsachenbericht auf die Fakten und spare deine persönliche Meinung aus. Achte außerdem auf eine sachliche Sprache und vermeide emotionale Ausdrücke. Die Schlagzeile sollte direkt auf das Thema des Artikels hinweisen und außerdem das Interesse des Lesers wecken. In Zeitungsberichten werden häufig Passivformen verwendet.
Persuasive text	Ein Werbetext soll den Leser direkt ansprechen und überzeugen. Dies gelingt z. B. mit rhetorischen Fragen, persönlichen Formulierungen und etwas Humor. Verbinde deine Sätze mit Konjunktionen und mache sie mit ausdrucksstarken Adjektiven interessant. Überlege dir für den Schluss einen besonders überzeugenden Satz, der dem Leser im Gedächtnis bleibt.

Prompt cards	Wenn du dich auf eine Präsentation vorbereitest, notiere auf Karteikarten nur Stichwörter, die dich an die einzelnen Punkte des Vortrags erinnern. Schreibe z. B. wichtige Namen, Ereignisse, Orte und Daten unter die Überschriften *Who? What? Where? When?*
Report	Bei einem Bericht ist die Vollständigkeit und Verständlichkeit der sachlichen Informationen das Wichtigste. Er wird im *simple past* geschrieben.
Review	Eine Rezension bzw. Kritik bietet dem Leser eine Entscheidungshilfe, ob es sich lohnt, z. B. eine bestimmte Veranstaltung zu besuchen oder ein Buch zu lesen. Zuerst werden kurz die wichtigsten Details beschrieben, dann wird eine mit Argumenten belegte Bewertung abgegeben.
Story	Wenn du Geschichten oder Bildergeschichten schreibst, schmücke sie aus und gestalte sie sprachlich abwechslungsreich. Meistens sind Geschichten im *simple past* geschrieben. Wenn du eine Geschichte vervollständigen sollst, muss dein Teil zum vorgegebenen Text passen. Vermeide also inhaltliche Widersprüche. Außerdem sollten die Erzählperspektive und die Erzählzeit nicht wechseln.

S13 Überarbeitung deines Textes

Wenn du einen Entwurf erstellt hast, liest du ihn am besten noch einmal gründlich durch. Meistens entdeckst du so noch einige Fehler und kannst holprige Formulierungen verbessern. Nimm dabei eine Checkliste zur Hilfe (siehe rechts), damit du nichts Wichtiges vergisst. Es ist auch hilfreich, die Texte mit einem Partner zu tauschen.

Checkliste

Rechtschreibung:
- Wörter richtig geschrieben?
- Am Satzanfang groß?
- Getrennt oder zusammen?

Grammatik:
- Richtige Zeitformen?
- Richtige Formenbildung?

Inhalt:
- Alle wesentlichen Punkte enthalten?
- Keine inhaltlichen Fehler?
- Zusammenhänge erkennbar und logisch?

S14 Sprachliche Verbesserungen

Je größer dein Wortschatz wird, desto mehr Möglichkeiten eröffnen sich dir beim Schreiben von Texten.
Gestalte Sätze interessanter, indem du z. B. Nomen durch Adjektive oder durch weitere Nomen näher beschreibst. Verben kannst du durch adverbiale Bestimmungen ergänzen. Vergleiche die folgenden beiden Sätze:

A *I went to the shop.*

B *I went to the big pet shop in Greenwich with my sister last Saturday.*

Ein Text liest sich leichter, wenn die Sätze darin miteinander verknüpft sind. Mit Hilfe von Konjunktionen (*linking words*) werden logische Zusammenhänge hergestellt.
Vergleiche die beiden folgenden Textausschnitte. Der erste wirkt durch die unverbundenen Hauptsätze abgehackt. Der zweite liest sich durch Satzgefüge aus Haupt- und Nebensätzen und durch Konjunktionen flüssiger. Außerdem geben die vielen Adjektive und Adverbien genauere Informationen und machen den Text interessanter.

A *I went to the shop. I wanted a guinea pig. We looked at all the guinea pigs. I didn't like them. We wanted to leave. A girl came in with a box. She brought back a guinea pig. It was cute! I bought it. I'm happy.*

B *I went to the big pet shop in Greenwich with my sister last Saturday* ***because*** *I wanted to buy a nice guinea pig. We looked at all the guinea pigs,* ***but*** *I didn't like them.* ***Just when*** *I wanted to leave, a girl came in with a box. She brought back a guinea pig* ***which*** *was really cute.* ***So*** *I bought it* ***and*** *I'm very happy now.*

Speaking

S15 Sprechen üben

Sprechen lernt man nur durch Sprechen. Du solltest dir angewöhnen, im Englischunterricht immer Englisch zu sprechen, ob mit deiner Lehrerin / deinem Lehrer oder in der Partner- und Gruppenarbeit. Auch zu Hause kannst du Englisch sprechen – vielleicht üben deine Freunde, Eltern oder Geschwister mit dir?

Wichtig ist, dass du englische Wörter richtig aussprichst. Im Buch kann dir die Lautschrift dabei helfen. Sage sie dir immer wieder laut vor. Einfacher und einprägsamer ist es, die Vokabeln anzuhören und nachzusprechen. Hilfsmittel dafür sind Audio-CDs mit den Schülerbuchtexten, Lernsoftware, Online-Wörterbücher oder Vokabel-Apps, in denen du jedes Wort anklicken und anhören kannst.

Übe Laute, die anders sind als im Deutschen, z. B. das stimmhafte oder stimmlose *th*, das *w* im Kontrast zum *v* oder ein stimmhaftes *d* oder *g* am Wortende. Dazu kannst du (lustige) Sätze erfinden, sie dir immer wieder vorsprechen und dabei das Tempo steigern, bis die Aussprache zuverlässig klappt.

Wenn du ganze Texte hörst, bekommst du ein Gefühl dafür, wie die Wörter im Textzusammenhang ausgesprochen werden. Die Aussprache unterscheidet sich manchmal stark von der Aussprache der Einzelwörter. Aufeinander treffende Laute werden z. B. häufig miteinander verbunden.

They **th**ought of **th**e **th**ree **th**ousand **th**ankful **th**ieves.

Why **w**ork **w**ith **v**ocabulary **w**hen you can **v**isit a **w**onderful **v**illage **w**orld?

She wante**d** her ba**g** back and sai**d** what a nice hat she ha**d**.

This is th**e e**n**d of t**he story. They know ove**r a** hundred different stories.

Du kannst auch üben, wie die Betonung die Aussprache beeinflusst, wenn jemand besonders starke Gefühle ausdrücken will.

It's **so** unfair! Why doesn't anyone **ever** ask **me** what I'm feeling?

S16 Gesprochene Sprache

Beim Sprechen kommt es auf die Situation und deinen Gesprächspartner an, wie du dich ausdrückst. Denke z. B. auch an Höflichkeitsregeln (siehe Beispiele rechts). In der gesprochenen Sprache ist es normal, dass Pausen, unvollständige Sätze, Wiederholungen oder Füllwörter vorkommen:

***Well, I – I** really don't know. It's – **er**, maybe you want to …?*

- Während bei Gleichaltrigen ein *Hi!* als Begrüßung ausreicht, ist Lehrpersonen oder fremden Erwachsenen gegenüber ein *Good morning!* / *Good afternoon* / … eher angemessen.
- Statt *I want* … sagst du höflicher *I would like* … oder *Could I please have* …?
- Entscheidungsfragen beantwortest du mit Kurzantworten, nicht einfach mit *Yes* oder *No*: *Yes, I do.* / *No, I'm not.*

Es ist wichtig, einem Dialogpartner immer das Gefühl zu geben, dass er einbezogen wird. Dazu dienen *feedback phrases*, Nachfragen und *question tags*.

*Then we went to the new shoe shop in the city centre, **you know**. And there were these amazing trainers – **I showed you a photo, didn't I? Guess what Linda said when she saw them!***

S17 Mündliche Aufgaben und ihre Besonderheiten

Beim Sprechen gibt es ganz unterschiedliche Situationen. Wenn du dich mit einem Gesprächspartner abwechselst, nennt man das dialogisches Sprechen. Beim monologischen Sprechen hingegen sprichst du längere Zeit am Stück allein. Hier sind einige Beispiele:

1. Dialogisches Sprechen

Dialogue / Role play	Gib deinem **Dialogpartner** immer das Gefühl, dass er einbezogen wird. Dazu dienen *feedback phrases*, Nachfragen und *question tags* (*… you know.* / *… didn't you?* / *Guess what …!*) Wenn du ***Small talk*** führst, vermeide sehr persönliche Themen und achte darauf, dass die Konversation nicht abrupt abbricht. Bei **Rollenspielen** musst du versuchen nachzufühlen, was die Person weiß, denkt und fühlt. Unterstütze deine Worte mit Mimik und Gestik.

Interview	Sei höflich, aber scheue dich nicht nachzufragen, wenn du etwas nicht sofort verstehst. Achte bei den Fragen und Antworten auf die richtige Zeitform und das richtige Hilfsverb.
Asking / Showing the way	Auch hier ist Höflichkeit wichtig, ebenso wie bestimmte *phrases*, z. B. *go down X Street, go straight on, go past / turn left / right into Y Lane, it's on the left / right / opposite Z.*

2. Monologisches Sprechen

Presentation	Bereite deine Präsentation gut vor. Recherchiere die Fakten gründlich und konzentriere dich auf das Wichtige. Besorge Material, das du zeigen willst, und bereite es so auf, dass es gut aussieht und verständlich ist. Mache dir einen Ablaufplan. Schreibe dir Notizen auf *prompt cards*. Sprich langsam und deutlich und möglichst ohne abzulesen. Übe deine Präsentation vorher und stoppe die Zeit, die du brauchst.

Mediation

S18 Bearbeitung von Mediation-Aufgaben

Mediation ist die Übertragung wichtiger Informationen aus einem gesprochenen oder geschriebenen Text in eine andere Sprache, z. B. aus dem Englischen ins Deutsche oder umgekehrt. Das machst du, wenn du einen Text für jemanden zusammenfassen sollst, der die Sprache des Ausgangstexts nicht versteht. Gelegentlich kann es auch sein, dass du dolmetschen musst, also zwischen Gesprächspartnern vermittelst, die nicht dieselbe Sprache sprechen. Ganz wichtig: Es geht bei der *Mediation* niemals um eine wörtliche Übersetzung (*translation*)!

Lies dir die *Mediation*-Aufgabe gut durch und beachte besonders folgende Dinge:

Adressat:
Für wen ist die Information bestimmt?
--> Je nachdem, wer die Person ist und wie viel sie schon weiß, sprichst du sie unterschiedlich an.

Zweck:
Wozu benötigt die Person die Information?
--> Du musst nur die Informationen wiedergeben, die für den Adressaten in der jeweiligen Situation wichtig sind. Alles andere kannst du weglassen. Es kann aber auch vorkommen, dass du Dinge zusätzlich erklären musst.

Beispiel: Dein Ausgangstext ist die Infobroschüre eines Museums, die alle Öffnungszeiten und Eintrittspreise enthält. Wenn dein Gegenüber dich fragt, ob das Museum heute geöffnet ist, musst du nicht unbedingt sagen, wann es sonst noch geöffnet oder geschlossen ist. Will die Person den Eintrittspreis wissen, kommt es auf ihr Alter an und darauf, ob sie allein oder mit einer Gruppe unterwegs ist.

Einen schriftlichen Ausgangstext kannst du in Ruhe durchlesen und die wichtigen Informationen auswählen. Dabei helfen dir alle Techniken, die unter *Reading* (→ S5–S10) beschrieben sind. Formuliere die entsprechenden Inhalte so, dass der Adressat sie gut verstehen kann.
Bei einer Dolmetschaufgabe wird eine echte mündliche Gesprächssituation simuliert. Deshalb musst du schneller reagieren, um möglichst viel von dem sinngemäß wiederzugeben, was die Gesprächspartner zueinander sagen.

Wenn dir ein Wort in der Zielsprache nicht einfällt, umschreibe es mit anderen Worten (*paraphrasing*). Beachte bei der schriftlichen und mündlichen Bearbeitung von *Mediation*-Aufgaben außerdem die Tipps unter *Writing* (→ S11–S14) und *Speaking* (→ S15–S17).

Listening

S19 Hörverstehen üben

Grundsätzlich ist es zur Übung immer sinnvoll, viele echte englische Texte anzuhören, z. B. Nachrichten in Radio und Fernsehen oder Hörbücher. Dabei ist es nicht schlimm, wenn du nicht jedes Wort verstehst. Dir wird außerdem auffallen, wie unterschiedlich die Aussprache des Englischen je nach Herkunft des Sprechers sein kann. So gibt es neben Unterschieden zwischen britischem und amerikanischem Englisch auch innerhalb Großbritanniens verschiedene Dialekte oder regionale Akzente. Auch dann ist es nicht schlimm, wenn du nicht alles verstehst. Selbst ein Engländer aus London könnte Schwierigkeiten haben, einen Schotten aus Glasgow auf Anhieb zu verstehen.

S20 Techniken des Hörverstehens

Analog zum Lesen helfen dir auch beim Hörverstehen unterschiedliche Techniken.

Listening for gist	**Listening for detail**
Versuche, das Wichtigste in einem Hörtext zu erkennen und zusammenzufassen. Achte dabei besonders auf Wörter und Themen, die mehrmals vorkommen und vermutlich eine wichtige Rolle spielen.	Versuche gezielt, dem Text bestimmte Einzelinformationen zu entnehmen. Achte dabei besonders auf Wörter, die du in der Antwort erwartest, und die Informationen dazu.

Auch beim Hörverstehen kann dier wie beim Leseverstehen eine Tabelle mit den nachfolgenden Fragenhelfen. In der Tabelle kannst du dir während des Hörens Notizen machen.

Who ...?	What ...?	When ...?	Where ...?

S21 Typische Hörverstehenssituationen

Manchmal hilft dir beim Hörverstehen auch die Kenntnis von typischen Textsorten und Situationen. Wenn du die Textsorte des Hörtextes kennst, überlege dir, worauf es beim Telefonieren, beim Dolmetschen, bei Präsentationen, Durchsagen, Radio- oder Fernsehsendungen ankommt und welche Themen jeweils zu erwarten sind. Gelegentlich geben dir auch Bilder Hinweise zur entsprechenden Situation: Wenn z. B. bestimmte Personen oder Orte dargestellt sind, kannst du leichter einschätzen, worum es in dem Hörtext geht. Achte beim Hören auf Geräusche sowie Stimme und Tonfall des Sprechers. In echten Gesprächssituationen oder Filmen können dir auch Gestik und Mimik das Verständnis erleichtern.

Film skills / Viewing

S22 Inhalt und Gliederung

Ein Film ist auch eine Art Text. Deshalb lassen sich viele ähnliche Fragen dazu stellen:

- Worum geht es?
- Wird eine Geschichte erzählt?
- Welche Personen spielen mit?
- Welches sind die Hauptpersonen?
- Was passiert in welcher Reihenfolge?
- Wann und wo passiert es?
- Welche Gliederung und welche Themen sind zu erkennen?
- Aus wessen Sicht wird die Geschichte erzählt?
- Wer hat den Film gemacht, für welches Publikum und wozu?

Das Anschauen und Verstehen eines Films verlangt dir jedoch nicht nur das Verständnis der Sprache ab, sondern du musst auch auf viele weitere Dinge achten.

S23 Wichtige filmische Mittel

Wie stellen die Schauspieler den Charakter der Personen dar, die sie verkörpern? Wie drücken sie Gefühle aus?

--➤ Achte vor allem auf Sprache, Mimik und Gestik. Aber auch Kleidung oder Frisuren können eine Rolle spielen.

Wie werden Handlungsort und -zeit dargestellt (*setting*)?
--➤ Achte auf Landschaften, Gebäude und Innenräume, Kleidung und Gegenstände.

Wie wird eine bestimmte Atmosphäre geschaffen (*atmosphere*)?
--➤ Achte auf Bilder, Licht, Farben, Musik, Geräusche.

Wie unterstützt die Musik den Inhalt des Films?
--➤ Achte darauf, wann welche Musik ertönt und wann sie wechselt.

Wie helfen bestimmte Kameraeinstellungen den Inhalt deutlicher darzustellen (*shot*)?
--➤ Achte z. B. auf Nahaufnahmen (*close-ups*).

Wie wird Spannung erzeugt (*suspense*)?
--➤ Achte auf Vorandeutungen, Musik, Licht, Geräusche und natürlich die Gestik und Mimik der Schauspieler.

Mit der Zeit wirst du weitere filmische Mittel kennen lernen, die bestimmte Wirkungen auf den Zuschauer erzeugen.

S24 Filmgenres

Es gibt viele unterschiedliche Arten von Filmen, man nennt sie auch Genres. Du erkennst Filme eines Genres normalerweise daran, dass sie ähnliche Hauptmerkmale aufweisen.

Hier sind einige Beispiele:

Action	In Actionfilmen geht es meist um einen Helden oder eine Heldin im Kampf gegen das Böse. Dabei kommen häufig spektakuläre Stunts, Verfolgungsjagden und Gewaltszenen vor.
Crime	Im Mittelpunkt eines Kriminalfilms steht ein Verbrechen, das häufig im Laufe des Films aufgeklärt wird. Dabei gibt es viele spannende Szenen und überraschende Wendungen.

Action
Crime

Comedy	Komödien haben eine humorvolle Handlung, die zum Lachen anregt. Häufig werden die Charaktere übertrieben dargestellt und Sprachwitz spielt eine wichtige Rolle.
Fantasy	Fantasyfilme handeln von magischen oder übernatürlichen Kräften. Häufig steht ein Held oder eine Heldin im Mittelpunkt der Handlung.
Historical	Historienfilme spielen in einer bestimmten geschichtlichen Epoche. Häufig basieren sie auf wahren Begebenheiten. Die Kostüme und Requisiten sind meist aufwändig gestaltet.
Romance	In Liebesfilmen steht die Beziehung zwischen zwei Figuren im Mittelpunkt. Das Ende dieser Filme fällt meist positiv aus.
Science Fiction	Science-Fiction-Filme handeln z.B. von Erfindungen in Wissenschaft und Technik, von Zeitreisen oder Außerirdischen. Sie spielen häufig in der Zukunft und wirken unrealistisch.

Kooperative Lernformen

Hier findest du die Erklärung für einige ausgewählte Methoden der kooperativen Arbeit.

S25 Think – Pair – Share

1. *Think*: Du sammelst still mögliche Lösungen zu der Aufgabe. Du kannst deine Ideen in Stichpunkten notieren.
2. *Pair*: Zusammen mit deinem Partner besprichst du leise deine gesammelten Ideen.
3. *Share*: Im Klassengespräch meldet ihr euch und teilt euren Mitschülern die Ergebnisse eurer Partnergespräche mit.

Variante: *Placemat* in Vierergruppen

S26 Milling around (Marktplatz)

Du gehst durch das Klassenzimmer, erfragst von deinen Mitschülern bestimmte Informationen und gibst auch selbst Auskunft. Versuche mit möglichst vielen Mitschülern zu sprechen und verschiedene Informationen zu sammeln. Ihr könnt auch ein Signal vereinbaren, zu dem ihr eure Gesprächspartner wechselt.

S27 Inside outside circle (Kugellager)

1. Bildet zwei Stuhlkreise, einen inneren und einen äußeren.
2. Setzt euch in den Stuhlkreisen so hin, dass immer ein Schüler des äußeren und des inneren Stuhlkreises sich gegenüber sitzen.
3. Stellt euch gegenseitig eure Fragen und beantwortet diese.
4. Rutscht im inneren oder äußeren Kreis nach dem Ende der Gesprächsrunde einen Platz weiter und beginnt ein Gespräch mit einem neuen Mitschüler.

S28 Bus stop (Lerntempoduett)

Sobald du deine Aufgabe fertig bearbeitet hast, gehst du zu einem vereinbarten Treffpunkt, dem *bus stop*. Dort wartest du auf den nächsten Mitschüler, der fertig ist, und zusammen besprecht und vergleicht ihr eure Lösungen. Anschließend verlasst ihr den *bus stop* und bearbeitet die nächste Aufgabe.

S29 Gallery walk (Museumsgang)

1. *Group work*: In der Gruppe erarbeitet ihr ein Thema und haltet euer Ergebnis, z. B. auf einem Poster, fest.
2. *Gallery walk*: Es werden neue Gruppen gebildet. In jeder Gruppe ist ein Schüler jeder Ausgangsgruppe. Jede Gruppe betrachtet die verschiedenen Ergebnisse der Gruppenarbeiten. Jeder präsentiert nun in der neuen Gruppe das Ergebnis seiner Ausgangsgruppe.

Grammar

Liebe Schülerin, lieber Schüler,
in diesem Grammatik-Anhang findest du ausführliche Erklärungen zu allen grammatischen Themen, die in den *Units* in Green Line 3 behandelt werden. Die Grammatikkapitel (**G**) helfen dir, die Grammatik zu verstehen, einzelne Punkte nachzuholen, wenn du ein paar Stunden gefehlt hast, oder bestimmte Regeln für Hausaufgaben und die Vorbereitung von Tests und Klassenarbeiten nachzuschlagen.

Regeln sind mit einem blauen Punkt (⊙) gekennzeichnet. Ein Ausrufezeichen (!) bedeutet, dass du hier besonders aufpassen musst. In der **English summary** sind die wichtigsten Regeln auf Englisch zusammengefasst. Jedes Kapitel endet mit einer Aufgabe (**Test yourself**), mit der du überprüfen kannst, ob du alles verstanden hast. Die Lösungen findest du ab Seite 266.

Grammatical terms

English term		Example	*Deutsche Bezeichnung*
conditional clause type 1	G2	**If** I **become** a famous singer, I'**ll earn** a lot of money.	*Bedingungssatz Typ 1*
conditional clause type 2	G3	**If** I **had** the choice, I **would drop out of** school.	*Bedingungssatz Typ 2*
conditional clause type 3	G8	**If** we **hadn't been** in such a hurry, we **wouldn't have left** our mobiles at home.	*Bedingungssatz Typ 3*
passive	G6	Haggis **is made** with meat.	*Passiv*
past perfect simple	G7	In 43 AD the Romans arrived in Britain. But, of course, they **had been** here before.	*Plusquamperfekt*
present perfect progressive	G5	Tell us what you'**ve been doing**.	*Verlaufsform des Perfekts*
reflexive pronouns and *each other*	G4	Come to northwest Scotland – and enjoy **yourself**!	*Reflexivpronomen*
will future	G1	We'**ll** miss you, Dave!	*Futur mit* will

Unit 1

G1 I'll miss you so much!

Seiten 10–12

Das Futur mit will
Will future

But the house looks fantastic! I'm sure your mum **will be** happy there with all the farm animals to work with.
I'**ll miss** you so much!

Du verwendest das Futur mit will für spontane Entscheidungen, Versprechen, Hoffnungen und Vorhersagen, die die Zukunft betreffen.

- *Mit dem* will future …
  a) *drückst du spontane Entscheidungen oder Versprechen aus.*

I'**ll text** you.
Holly and I **will visit** you in Cornwall.

  b) *machst du Vorhersagen über zukünftige Ereignisse. (Der Sprecher kann diese nicht beeinflussen.)*

Gwen:	We'**ll miss** you, Dave.
Assistant:	The trip to St Agnes **will take** about seven hours.

  c) *sagst du, was jemand über ein zukünftiges Ereignis denkt, hofft oder vermutet. Diese Sätze beginnen häufig mit* I hope, I think *oder* I'm sure.

Jay:	I think you'**ll make** lots of new friends quickly.
Dave:	I'm sure Sid **will hate** his new home.

- *Signalwörter für das* will future *sind:* tomorrow, next week / month / year, in a year, probably, perhaps, maybe.

1 **weeds** [wiːdz] Unkraut

- *Das* will future *bildest du für alle Personen aus dem Hilfsverb* **will (not) + *Grundform des Verbs.*** *Die Kurzform lautet* 'll *bzw. bei verneinten Sätzen* won't.

Aussage:	Dave hopes that his friends **will visit** him in St Agnes.
Verneinung:	Aunt Frances **won't come** to Cornwall with them.
Ergänzungsfrage:	What do you think Dave's new school **will be** like?
Entscheidungsfrage mit Kurzantwort:	**Will** your dad **find** work there? – Yes, he **will**. / No, he **won't**.

! Um die Zukunftsform der Modalverben zu bilden, brauchst du ihre Ersatzformen (→G15):

can, can't → (not) be able to:	Dave hopes his friends **will be able to** find enough money to visit him in St Agnes. *… werden in der Lage sein …*
can, can't, may, mustn't → (not) be allowed to:	The friends **won't be allowed to** go to Cornwall without an adult. *… werden nicht … dürfen*
must, needn't → (not) have to:	Holly **will have to** ask her mum for money. *… wird … müssen*

! *Mit dem* going-to *und dem* will future *kennst du zwei Zeitformen der Zukunft. Möchtest du* über *Zukünftiges sprechen, musst du abwägen:*
Für feststehende ***Pläne*** *oder* ***Absichten*** → going-to future (→G8):
The Prestons **are going to move** to Cornwall in summer.
Für ***spontane Entscheidungen*** → will future:
"I need to put all my things into boxes." – "Don't worry. **I'll help** you."
Für ***Vermutungen, Hoffnungen*** *oder* ***Vorhersagen*** → will future:
I think Dave **will be** OK in Cornwall.

! *Verwechsle nicht „Ich will …"* (= I want to …) *und* "I will …" (= Ich werde …).

English summary

- You form the will future with ***will / 'll*** and the **infinitive** of a verb: *I'll text you.*
- The **negative** form of will is ***won't***: *Aunt Frances won't come to Cornwall.*
- You **use** the will future
  - for **spontaneous decisions**: *The phone is ringing - I'll get it.*
  - for **predictions**: *Dave will be happy in Cornwall.*
  - to talk about the **weather**: *It'll be cool in the morning and warm in the afternoon.*

Test yourself *What do the friends say when Dave isn't with them? Complete the sentences.*

1. Olivia: I hope Dave … his new school. (love)
2. Holly: I'm sure the Prestons … Granny Rose and Aunt Frances in London soon. (visit)
3. Luke: I don't think the new home … a problem for Sid. There are lots of fields and he …. He … new cat friends quickly. He … ! (be / be able to run around / make / not get bored)
4. Gwen: I hope Dave … us. (not forget)

G2 If you look at a map of Great Britain, you'll find Cornwall in the far west.

Seiten 14–15

Bedingungssätze Typ 1
Conditional clauses type 1

If you **like** beaches and fishing harbours, you'**ll find** that Cornwall is just the right place for you.

Well, you **can** go fishing **if** we **go** to Cornwall. What do you think?

Mit dem Bedingungssatz Typ 1 drückst du aus, was unter einer bestimmten Bedingung passieren wird. Der Sprecher hält die Bedingung für erfüllbar. Es ist also wahrscheinlich, dass die Folge eintritt.

- *Der Bedingungssatz Typ 1 besteht aus einem* **if-*Satz*** *(Nebensatz) und einem Hauptsatz. Im* **if-*Satz*** *drückst du die Bedingung aus, im Hauptsatz sagst du, was passiert oder passieren kann, falls diese Bedingung erfüllt wird.*
- *Im* **if-*Satz*** *verwendest du das* **simple present**, *im* ***Hauptsatz*** *das* **will future**.

Bedingung im if-*Satz:* simple present	*Folge im Hauptsatz:* will future
If you **look** at a map,	you'**ll see** that Cornwall is on the Atlantic Ocean.
If the friends **visit** Dave in Cornwall,	they **won't get** bored.

- *Neben dem* **will future** *kannst du im* ***Hauptsatz*** *häufig auch die* ***Modalverben*** (can, must, should + infinitive) *oder den* **Imperativ** *verwenden.*

if-*Satz:* simple present	*Hauptsatz:* *Modalverb* + infinitive *oder Imperativ*
If you **aren't** into sports,	you **can** go to a museum. (Möglichkeit)
If you **want** to learn about the environment,	you **should** visit the Eden Project. (Ratschlag)
If you **go** to Cornwall,	**try** real Cornish food. (Ratschlag / Aufforderung)

❗ *Bedingungssätze können entweder mit dem* **if-*Satz*** *oder mit dem* ***Hauptsatz*** *beginnen:*
If you look at a map of Great Britain, you'**ll** find Cornwall in the far west.
You'**ll** find Cornwall in the far west **if** you look at a map of Great Britain. (*kein Komma vor* **if***!*)

Verwechsle nicht **if** *(wenn / falls = Bedingung) mit* **when** *(wenn = zeitlicher Zusammenhang)!*
If we go on a beach holiday, I'll try surfing.
Wenn / Falls wir einen Strandurlaub machen, versuche ich zu surfen.
We'll see Dave **when** he visits his granny in London.
Wir werden Dave treffen, wenn er seine Großmutter in London besucht.

Test yourself *There's a teacher from Scotland at your school. In the next holidays he wants to travel around Germany. Tell him what he can and should do.*

Example: If you go to Berlin, you can visit the Brandenburg Gate.
If you go to Leipzig, you should try "Leipziger Lerche".
If you visit Frankfurt, you'll see lots of tall buildings.

Unit 2

G3 They wouldn't worry if they didn't care.

→ Seiten 28–31

Bedingungssätze Typ 2
Conditional clauses type 2

I know you want to become a famous singer. But **if** you **didn't think about** singing and dancing all the time, you **would have** better marks. **If** you **had** better marks, Mum and Dad **would support** you. So **if** I **were** you, I **would listen** to them and try harder at school.
If I **had** the choice, I **would drop out of** school.

Mit dem Bedingungssatz Typ 2 drückst du aus, was unter einer bestimmten Bedingung passieren könnte. Der Sprecher hält diese Bedingung für nicht oder nicht so einfach erfüllbar. Es ist also (zur Zeit) eher unwahrscheinlich, dass die Folge eintritt.

- *Für die Bedingung im* ***if-Satz*** *verwendest du das* **simple past**, *für die Folge im* ***Hauptsatz*** **would(n't) / could(n't) + infinitive.**
  Die entsprechende Kurzform von would *lautet* **'d** (I'd, you'd, he'd …)

Bedingung im if-*Satz:* simple present	*Folge im Hauptsatz:* conditional (would / could + infinitive)
If Jay **had** the choice,	he **would** / he**'d drop out of** school.
Wenn Jay die Wahl hätte, würde er die Schule abbrechen.	
If Jay **didn't have to** go to school,	he **could sing and dance** all day.
Wenn Jay nicht zur Schule gehen müsste, könnte er den ganzen Tag singen und tanzen.	
If I **looked** as good as Shahid,	I**'d work** as a model too.
Wenn ich so gut aussehen würde wie Shahid, würde ich auch als Model arbeiten.	
If I **were** Jay,	I**'d take** Shahid's advice.
Wenn ich Jay wäre, würde ich Shahids Rat annehmen.	

- *Nach* I / he / she / it *kannst du* **was** *oder* **were** *verwenden.*
  If I were / was rich, I'd …
  If he / she / it were / was famous, he'd …

! *Achte darauf, dass du* **would** *nur für die* ***Folge im Hauptsatz*** *verwendest! Die* **Bedingung** *im* **if-*Satz*** *steht immer im* **simple past***.*
If Shahid **didn't work** as a model, he **wouldn't** have so much money.
*Wenn Shahid **nicht** als Model **arbeiten würde**, **würde** er nicht so viel Geld haben.*

English summary

A conditional sentence has two parts: an **if-clause** and a **main clause**.

- You use **type 1** when the **action in the if-clause** is **possible** and **probable**.
  The verb in the **if-clause** is in the **simple present**; the verb in the **main clause** is in the **will future**: *If you make the right decisions now, you'll have more choices later.*
- You use **type 2** when the **action in the if-clause** is **possible** but **not probable**.
  The verb in the **if-clause** is in the **simple past**; the verb in the **main clause** is in the **conditional** tense: *If I had a million pounds, I'd travel the world.*

Test yourself *Jay has had another fight with his parents. He is talking to Shahid about his problems with them now. Complete this part of their conversation.*

Jay: If Mum and Dad (try) to understand me, we (not fight) so often.
Shahid: They're just worried about you, Jay. You (not have) so many fights if you (work) harder for school and (get) better marks.
Jay: The problem is that they don't believe in me, Shahid. If they (believe) in me, they (not worry) about my marks.
Shahid: They only worry because they care about you, Jay. Maybe if you (not be) so laid-back, they (not have to) worry so much.

G4 You have to push yourself.

→ Seiten 32–33

Reflexivpronomen
Reflexive pronouns and each other

Wow! Olivia plays the sax really well. Did **you** teach **her**?
No, I didn't. **She** taught **herself**. And **she** even wrote the music **herself**.

Im Englischen verwendest du die Reflexivpronomen (Pronomen auf -self / -selves*), wenn das* ***Objekt*** *sich auf das* ***Subjekt*** *im Satz zurückbezieht. Subjekt und Objekt sind dabei* ***dieselbe Person.***
Du verwendest die Reflexivpronomen auch, wenn du eine Person oder Sache im Satz hervorheben willst.

- *Die Singularformen der Reflexivpronomen enden auf* -self (herself)*; die Pluralformen auf* -selves (themselves).

	1. Person	*2. Person*	*3. Person*
Singular:	(I) … myself	(you) … yourself	(he, she, it) … himself, herself, itself
Plural:	(we) … ourselves	(you) … yourselves	(they) … themselves

- *Die* -self-*Pronomen kommen im Englischen als Reflexivpronomen (rückbezügliche Pronomen) und als verstärkende Pronomen vor.*

a) *Reflexiver Gebrauch*

- *Im Englischen verwendest du die Pronomen auf* -self / -selves, *wenn das* ***Objekt dieselbe Person*** *bezeichnet wie das* ***Subjekt****. In diesem Fall entsprechen sie den deutschen Pronomen mich / mir, dich / dir, sich (selbst), usw. Vergleiche:*

Did **you** teach **her**.	her = *andere Person (Objektpronomen)*
She taught **herself**.	herself = *dieselbe Person (Reflexivpronomen).*

	Subjekt	*Verb*	*Objekt / Reflexivpronomen*	*Deutsch*
I'm so angry	**I**	could hit	**myself**.	ich – mich
Did	**you**	hurt	**yourself**?	du – dich / du – dir
Jay wants to become a famous singer.	**He**	really pushes	**himself** with singing and dancing.	er – sich
Claire often feels like	**she**'s	talking to	**herself**.	sie – (mit) sich (selbst)
	We	always enjoy	**ourselves.**	wir – uns
Why can't	**you**	behave	**yourselves?**	ihr – euch
Don't worry about the boys.	**They**	can look after	**themselves.**	sie – sich

❗ *Die Reflexivpronomen werden im Englischen wesentlich seltener gebraucht als im Deutschen. Viele Verben, die **im Deutschen reflexiv** sind, werden **im Englischen ohne** **-self** oder **-selves** gebildet.*
How do you feel today? – *Wie fühlst du **dich** heute?*
I'm looking forward to the weekend. – *Ich freue **mich** auf das Wochenende.*

change	*sich (ver)ändern*	look forward to	*sich freuen auf*
decide	*sich entscheiden*	meet	*sich treffen*
feel	*sich fühlen*	relax	*sich entspannen*
hide	*sich verstecken*	remember	*sich erinnern*
hurry	*sich beeilen*	sit down	*sich hinsetzen*
imagine	*sich vorstellen*	worry	*sich Sorgen machen*

b) ***Verstärkender Gebrauch***

- *Mit den Reflexivpronomen kannst du auch eine Person oder eine Sache im Satz besonders hervorheben. In diesem Fall entspricht* myself, yourself, himself … *dem deutschen **selbst / allein**:*
  Wow, that's a cool song. – Thanks, **I** wrote it **myself**. *(selbst)*
  You don't have to help us. **We** can do it **ourselves**. *(allein, ohne fremde Hilfe)*

c) **Themselves *oder* each other?**

- *Wenn du ausdrücken möchtest, dass zwischen Personen etwas wechselseitig geschieht oder es um Gegenseitigkeit geht, verwendest du* **each other**. *Im Deutschen wird* each other *meist mit **sich**, **einander** oder **gegenseitig** wiedergegeben.*

They're looking at **themselves**.

They're looking at **each other**.

❗ *Achte darauf, dass du die Reflexivpronomen nicht mit* each other *verwechselst.*

English summary

- The singular forms of the reflexive pronouns end in **-self** (myself); the plural forms end in **-selves** (ourselves).
- You use the reflexive pronoun
  a) when subject and object of the sentence are the same person: *He hurt himself.*
  b) as an emphasizing (*hervorhebendes*) pronoun: *Nobody helped me. I did it myself.*
- You use 'each other' to talk about an interaction between people: *We talk to each other every day.*

Test yourself *Olivia and Lucy are fighting again. Complete these sentences. Decide whether you need an object pronoun, a reflexive pronoun or 'each other'.*

Olivia: Claire, I'm hungry. Can I make … a sandwich?
Lucy: That's a good idea, Olivia. Can you make … one too?
Olivia: No, I can't. You can do that …
Claire: Hey you two, please behave … You know I hate it when you fight with …

Unit 3

G5 How long have they been chatting?

→ Seiten 56–58

Die Verlaufsform des Perfekts
The present perfect progressive

Did you know that Ethan and Amber **have been chatting** with each other online?
Really? Ooh, that's interesting. How long **have** they **been doing** that?
Oh, just for a few days. They**'ve been sending** each other messages since the weekend, I think.

Das **present perfect progressive** *ist die Verlaufsform des* present perfect. *Mit dieser Zeitform drückst du aus, dass eine Handlung in der Vergangenheit begann, bis zum Zeitpunkt des Sprechens (also in die Gegenwart) hineinreicht und möglicherweise auch in der Zukunft noch andauern wird.*

- *Das* **present perfect progressive** *bildest du aus* **have / has + been + present participle** (verb + ing).

Aussage:	Amber **has been chatting** with Ethan online.
Verneinung:	She **hasn't been doing** her homework.
Ergänzungsfrage:	How long **has** she **been doing** that?
Entscheidungsfrage mit Kurzantwort:	**Have** they **been talking** to each other on the phone too? Yes, they **have**. / No, they **haven't**.

- *Mit dem* **present perfect** *verbindest du die Vergangenheit mit der Gegenwart.*
Wie du schon weißt, verwendest du das **present perfect simple** (I have done), *um das* ***Ergebnis*** *einer vergangenen Handlung zu betonen.*
Das **present perfect progressive** (I have been doing) *verwendest du hingegen, um den* ***Verlauf*** *oder die* ***Dauer*** *der Handlung in den Vordergrund zu stellen.*

Vergleiche:

Gwen **has invited** Holly and Amber to Scotland.	*Diese Handlung ist beendet; das Ergebnis steht im Vordergrund.*
Gwen and her family **have been planning** things they can do together.	*Diese Handlung dauert bis zum Zeitpunkt des Sprechens und möglicherweise darüber hinaus an; im Vordergrund steht die Handlung selbst.*

- *Oft verwendest du mit dem* present perfect progressive *eine Zeitangabe, die angibt, seit wann* (**since**) *oder wie lange* (**for**) *die Handlung schon andauert.*

Mit **since** *(seit, seitdem) gibst du den* ***Zeitpunkt*** *an, an dem eine Handlung begann.*	*z. B.* since 1996; since 10 o'clock; since Monday; since last week; since August; since he moved to Scotland.
Mit **for** *(seit) gibst du den* ***Zeitraum*** *an, den eine Handlung bereits andauert.*	*z. B.* for hours; for days; for weeks; for months; for years; for a long time.

I have been ...ing since ...	
Gwen's uncle and aunt **have been living** in Scotland **since 1996**.	
	... wohnen schon seit 1996 in Schottland.
Amber **has been talking about** their trip to Scotland **since Gwen invited them**.	
	spricht schon davon, seitdem Gwen sie eingeladen hat.

I have been ...ing for ...	
Amber and Ethan **have been chatting** online **for a few days now**.	
	... unterhalten sich (jetzt schon) seit ein paar Tagen.
Amber **has been telling** Holly what to do **for years**.	
	... erzählt ... schon seit Jahren / jahrelang ...

❗ *Denke daran, dass es diese Zeitform im Deutschen nicht gibt. Wir benutzen stattdessen das* ***Präsens*** *und betonen die Dauer des Vorgangs mit* ***„schon“****.*

∘ *Weitere Signalwörter für das* present perfect progressive *sind:* how long; recently *(in letzter Zeit)*; all day / week / year *(den ganzen Tag …) sowie* all the time *(die ganze Zeit).*

❗ *Beachte, dass du das* present perfect progressive *wie alle Verlaufsformen* ***nur bei Tätigkeitsverben*** *verwenden kannst, (z. B.* work, play, live*). Bei Verben, die keine Tätigkeit, sondern einen Zustand bezeichnen (z. B.* be, know, believe, see*) benutzt du das* present perfect simple, *z. B.* Gwen and Holly **have known** each other for a long time now.

❗ *Beachte, dass die unterschiedlichen* progressive-*Formen auch unterschiedlich verwendet werden.*

Present progressive:	Gwen is running.	*Dies tut sie gerade.*
Past progressive:	Gwen was running when …	*Dies tat sie gerade, als …*
Present perfect progressive:	Gwen has been running since / for …	*Dies tut sie seit …*

English summary

You use the present perfect progressive **(have / has + been + present participle)**

1. for an activity which began in the past, is still happening in the present and may still go on in the future. — *Amber and Holly have been fighting with each other again.*
2. to say how long an action has been happening. — *Ethan has been sending Amber messages since the weekend / for a few days now.*
   You use **since** with a **point in time** (since 1996; since yesterday) and **for** with a **period of time** (for years; for a long time).

Test yourself *Read this information about the Wilsons. Then ask a question and give an answer for each situation. Start your question with how long and use* **since** *or* **for** *in your answer.*

Example: The Wilsons live in Aberdeen.
→ They moved there in 2008.
How long **have** the Wilsons **been living** in Aberdeen?
→ They **have been living** there **since** 2008.

1. Mr Wilson works in a hotel. He started his job there in 2012.
2. Mrs Wilson teaches English. She started five years ago.
3. Their children Sam and Jack both go to school. Sam started three years ago and Jack started last year.

G6 Is Haggis made with meat?

→ Seiten 59–61

Das Passiv
The passive

Active:
They build ships in Scotland.

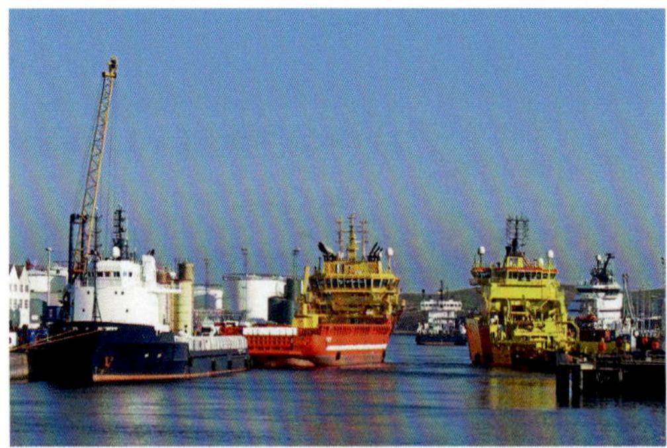

Passive:
Ships **are built** in Scotland.

Du benutzt das Passiv, wenn der Ausführende einer Handlung unwichtig oder nicht bekannt ist. Damit rückt die Handlung selbst in den Vordergrund. Das Passiv wird häufig in Zeitungsberichten, Sachtexten und technischen Beschreibungen verwendet.

- *Das Passiv bildest du mit einer Form von* **be** *in der jeweiligen Zeitform und dem* **past participle** *des Vollverbs* (infinitive + ed *oder unregelmäßige Form).*

Zeitform	*Form von* be + past participle	*Beispiel*
simple present	am / is / are + past participle	Haggis **is made** with meat. *… wird … gemacht.*
simple past	was / were + past participle	The house **was built** 20 years ago. *… wurde … gebaut.*
present perfect	have / has been + past participle	Whisky **has been produced** in Scotland for 500 years. *… ist … hergestellt worden.*

❗ *Im Deutschen verwendest du für das Passiv eine Form von „werden".*

- *Wenn du in einem Passivsatz sagen möchtest, von wem die Handlung ausgeführt wird, verwendest du die Präposition* **by** *(auf Deutsch: von). Du entscheidest im Einzelfall, ob diese Zusatzinformation wichtig ist oder nicht:*
  Gaelic **is only spoken by** a few people today.
  Gälisch ***wird*** heute nur ***von*** wenigen Menschen ***gesprochen***.
  Der Verursacher der Handlung wird **by-agent** *genannt.*

- *Wenn du einen Aktivsatz in einen Passivsatz umwandelst, musst du Folgendes beachten:*
  1. *Das Objekt des Aktivsatzes wird zum Subjekt im Passivsatz. Aus* ***Objektpronomen*** (me, you, him, her, it, us, you, them) *werden* ***Subjektpronomen*** (I, you, he, she, it, we, you, they).

Aktiv:	Passiv:
We **build** **ships** in Scotland.	**Ships** **are built** in Scotland.
We **build** **them** in Glasgow.	**They** **are built** in Glasgow.

  2. *Ist der Ausführende einer Handlung* ***eine unbestimmte Person*** *wie* somebody, we, you, they … ***lässt*** *du ihn im Passivsatz* ***weg****. Ist der Ausführende aber* ***eine bestimmte Person*** *oder Sache wird er im Passivsatz mit* **by** *(von) angehängt.*

Aktiv:	Passiv:
They **have built** some famous ships in Glasgow.	Some famous ships **have been built** in Glasgow.
The Scots **have built** some famous ships.	Some famous ships **have been built** **by the Scots**.

! *Die Zeitform im Aktivsatz und im Passivsatz bleibt gleich.*

English summary

You form the passive voice with a form of **be** and the **past participle**.

1. You use the active to stress what the subject does.
2. You use the passive to stress what is done. Often you don't know who has done the action, or you think this is not important.
3. If you want to say who does the action, you use the **by-agent**.

   The electric clock ***was invented by*** *the Scotsman Alexander Bain.*

Test yourself *Complete this short text about the Scottish game of Shinty. Use passive forms of the verbs in brackets and be careful with the tenses.*

Shinty is one of the oldest games in the world. Some people think that it (invent) in Ireland 2000 years ago and that it (bring) to Scotland by the Irish in the 6th century. Others say that it (play) in Scotland since Celtic times. Shinty is similar to field hockey but faster and more dangerous. In the past, whole villages played against each other. Today, Shinty is a club sport which (play) between two teams of 12 players.

Unit 4

G7 He hadn't finished his game

→ Seiten 88–90

Das Plusquamperfekt
The past perfect simple

Mit dem past perfect simple *betonst du, dass etwas* ***vor einem Zeitpunkt in der Vergangenheit*** *stattgefunden hat und abgeschlossen ist.*

Drake **wasn't** worried when he **heard** about the Spanish Armada …	because he **had fought** a lot of battles before.
Drake war nicht beunruhigt, als er von der spanischen Armada erfuhr,	*weil er (zuvor) schon viele Schlachten geschlagen hatte.*

- *Das* **past perfect simple** *bildest du aus* **had + past participle** *(3. Verbform)*

Aussage:	Drake **had seen** the Spanish Armada.
Verneinung:	But he **hadn't finished** his game of bowls.
Ergänzungsfrage:	Why **had** they **come**?
Entscheidungsfrage mit Kurzantwort:	**Had** they **come** to destroy his ships? Yes, they **had**.

- *Das* past perfect simple *spielt vor allem in literarischen Texten, Erzählungen und Berichten eine Rolle. Es steht meist in Verbindung mit dem* simple past.
  Mit dem **simple past** *drückst du aus, was sich in der* ***Vergangenheit*** *ereignet hat. Für Handlungen oder Zustände, die noch* ***vor diesem Zeitpunkt der Vergangenheit*** *stattgefunden haben, verwendest du das* **past perfect simple**.

simple past *(Vergangenheit)*	past perfect simple *(Vorvergangenheit)*
Before Elizabeth I **became** queen,	she **had said**: "I'll never marry."
When she **died** in 1603,	she **had been** queen for 45 years.

❗ *Das Ereignis/die Handlung im* **past perfect simple** *kann auch am* ***Satzanfang*** *stehen.*

past perfect simple *(Vorvergangenheit)*	simple past *(Vergangenheit)*
People in England **had** never **tasted** potatoes	before Walter Raleigh **brought** them back from America.
After Drake **had defeated** the Spanish,	he **became** a national hero.

❗ *Wenn du in einer Erzählung oder in einem Bericht die Ereignisse der Reihe nach erzählst, benutzt du das* **simple past**:
Elizabeth I **was** born in 1533 and **became** Queen of England in 1588 when she **was** 25 years old.
Blickst du bei deiner Erzählung jedoch auf ein Ereignis zurück, das zuvor stattgefunden hat und abgeschlossen ist, verwendest du das **past perfect**:
She **was** the daughter of Henry VIII and his second wife Anne Boleyn. But Elizabeth I never really **knew** her mother because she **had died** in 1536.

English summary

You use the **past perfect simple (had + past participle)** to show that one event happened before another in the past.

Shakespeare took many of the ideas for his plays from stories which he ***had read*** *at school.*

Test yourself **Henry VIII and the Church of England**

Read the text and put the verbs into the correct form of the simple past or past perfect simple.

In 1509, seven weeks after Henry VIII (become) the new king of England, he (marry) Catherine of Aragon. She had been the wife of his older brother Arthur, who (die) in 1502. Together, Henry and Catherine (have) a daughter, Mary. But Henry (need) a boy who could become the next king.
So, in 1533, after Catherine (become) too old to have any more children, Henry (decide) to marry Anne Boleyn, who he (meet) and (fall in love) with in about 1525. When the Pope (say) "no", Henry (break) with Rome and (found) his own Church – the Church of England.

G8 If I hadn't talked so much

→ Seiten 92–94

Bedingungssätze Typ 3
Conditional clauses type 3

Oh no! I'm really stupid! **If** I **hadn't talked** so much, I **wouldn't have lost** the others. But why have they turned their phones off? **If** they **hadn't done** that, I **could have rung** them.

Mit dem Bedingungssatz Typ 3 drückst du aus, was passiert wäre (oder hätte passieren können), wenn eine bestimmte Bedingung in der Vergangenheit eingetreten wäre.

- *Im Gegensatz zu den Bedingungssätzen Typ 1 (→ G1) und Typ 2 (→ G2) beschreibst du mit Typ 3 eine Situation, die sich nicht mehr verwirklichen lässt. Da die Bedingung in der Vergangenheit liegt, bleibt sie* ***unerfüllbar****.*
- *Für die Bedingung im* **if-*Satz*** *verwendest du das* **past perfect***, für die Folge im* ***Hauptsatz*** **would/n't / could(n't) have + past participle**.

Nicht mehr erfüllbare Bedingung im if-*Satz* (had + past participle):	*Folge im Hauptsatz* (would / could / should have + past participle):
If Jay **had stayed** with his friends,	he **wouldn't have found out** so much about life in Victorian Britain.
If he **hadn't got lost**,	he **would / he'd have missed** all the cool stories.
If Jay's friends **hadn't turned off** their mobile phones,	they **could have helped** him.

English summary

You use a conditional sentence **type 3** when the **action in the if-clause** is **no longer possible** because the situation took place in the past and you cannot change what has already happened.
The verb in the **if-clause** is in the **past perfect**; the verb in the **main clause** is in the conditional perfect (**would have + past participle**): *If Jay hadn't joined the Victorian tour, he wouldn't have found a pipe for his calendar.*

Test yourself **And all because of a problem with the hot water**

Read the story of how Gwen's mother met her father.
What would or wouldn't have happened if things had been different?

Start like this: If there hadn't been a problem with the hot water, she wouldn't have left the house late.

In 1995, Gwen's mother wanted to spend the day in London. She planned to take the train at 8:20, but she left the house late because there was a problem with the hot water. Because of that, she didn't arrive at the station on time and missed her train. She hadn't had time for breakfast that morning, so she went to the café for a cup of tea and a sandwich while she was waiting for the next train. She was sitting at a table for two when a nice young man sat down opposite her and they started to chat. That nice young man is now Gwen's father.

Vocabulary

Im ***Vocabulary*** findest du alle wichtigen englischen Wörter und Redewendungen aus *Green Line* 3. Sie stehen in der Reihenfolge, in der sie im Buch vorkommen. Diese Wörter solltest du lernen und anwenden können. Andere nützliche Wörter und Begriffe (z. B. Arbeitsanweisungen), die du **nicht** auswendig lernen musst, findest du ab S. 260.
Auf das *Vocabulary* folgt das ***Dictionary (English - German, German - English)***. Falls du ein Wort vergessen hast, kannst du in diesen alphabetischen Wortlisten nachsehen.

Englische Begriffe wie *e-mail*, *cool* oder *cornflakes*, die du auch im Deutschen verwendest, stehen nicht im *Vocabulary*. Du kannst ihre Aussprache und Übersetzung aber im *Dictionary* nachschlagen. Das gleiche gilt für Wörter, die auf Englisch und Deutsch fast gleich geschrieben und ausgesprochen werden, wie z. B. *park* oder *partner*.

In den vier Teilen von ***Text smart*** musst du nicht alle neuen Vokabeln auswendig lernen. Die Wörter und Ausdrücke, die im *Vocabulary* aufgelistet sind, sind die wichtigsten und sie solltest du lernen und anwenden können. Alle anderen neuen Wörter aus Text smart kannst du ebenfalls hinten im *Dictionary* ab S. 206 nachschlagen.

Abkürzungen und Zeichen

pl	Mehrzahl (Plural)	↔	ist das Gegenteil von
sg	Einzahl (Singular)	→	ist verwandt mit
coll/ugs	umgangssprachlich	=	entspricht
5	In dieser Übung kommen die Wörter vor.	≠	entspricht nicht
!	Achtung!	*Fr./Lat.*	verwandte Wörter in anderen Fremdsprachen

Englische Laute

Konsonanten

[b]	**b**ed	[p]	**p**icture
[d]	**d**ay	[r]	**r**ed
[ð]	**th**e	[s]	**s**ix
[f]	**f**amily	[ʃ]	**sh**e
[g]	**g**o	[t]	**t**en
[ŋ]	morni**ng**	[tʃ]	**ch**air
[h]	**h**ouse	[v]	**v**ideo
[j]	**y**ou	[w]	**w**e, **o**ne
[k]	**c**an, mil**k**	[z]	ea**s**y
[l]	**l**etter	[ʒ]	revi**s**ion
[m]	**m**an	[dʒ]	pa**ge**
[n]	**n**o	[θ]	**th**ank you

Vokale

[ɑː]	c**ar**	[i]	happ**y**
[æ]	**a**pple	[iː]	t**ea**cher
[e]	p**e**n	[ɒ]	d**o**g
[ə]	**a**gain	[ɔː]	b**a**ll
[ɜː]	g**ir**l	[ʊ]	b**oo**k
[ʌ]	b**u**t	[u]	Jan**u**ary
[ɪ]	**i**t	[uː]	t**oo**, tw**o**

Doppellaute

[aɪ]	**I**, m**y**
[aʊ]	n**ow**, m**ou**se
[eɪ]	n**a**me, th**ey**
[eə]	th**ere**, p**air**
[ɪə]	h**ere**, id**ea**
[əʊ]	hell**o**
[ɔɪ]	b**oy**
[ʊə]	s**ure**

[ː]	der vorangehende Laut ist lang, z. B. *you* [juː]
[‿]	der Bindebogen zeigt, dass zwei Wörter in der Aussprache verbunden werden
[ˈ]	die folgende Silbe trägt den Hauptakzent
[ˌ]	die folgende Silbe trägt den Nebenakzent

Unit 1 Goodbye Greenwich

Introduction

	journey ['dʒɜ:ni]	Reise; Fahrt	On our *journey* through England we met a lot of nice people.
	future ['fju:tʃə]	Zukunft	What will the *future* be like? ***Fr.*** future *(m)*
	to **will** [wɪl]	werden *(futurisch)*	
	medieval [ˌmedi'i:vl]	mittelalterlich	Is every castle *medieval*? – No, of course not. ***Fr.*** médiéval/-e
	living history show [ˌlɪvɪŋ 'hɪstəri ˌʃəʊ]	*Show, in der historischer Alltag nachgespielt wird*	
	pony trekking ['pəʊni ˌtrekɪŋ]	Ponyreiten im Gelände	You go *pony trekking* in the country.
	Scottish ['skɒtɪʃ]	schottisch	Edinburgh is the *Scottish* capital.
1	to **include** [ɪn'klu:d]	einschließen; beinhalten	The trip will be expensive, but the price *includes* all our meals. ***Lat.*** includere
2	**negative** ['negətɪv]	negativ; verneint	*negative* ↔ positive ***Fr.*** négatif/négative
	landscape ['lændskeɪp]	Landschaft	
3	**sandy** ['sændi]	sandig; Sand-	
	rocky ['rɒki]	felsig; steinig	Not every beach is sandy. Many are *rocky*.
	wide [waɪd]	breit; weit; ausgedehnt	This table is too *wide*, we can't get it through the door.
	deep [di:p]	tief	You mustn't go into *deep* water if you can't swim.
	island ['aɪlənd]	Insel	The British Isles are a group of *islands*.
	harbour ['hɑ:bə]	Hafen	The weather is bad, so the boats are staying in the *harbour*.
	hiking ['haɪkɪŋ]	Wandern	Wales is great for *hiking*.
	mountain biking ['maʊntɪn ˌbaɪkɪŋ]	Mountainbikefahren	
	(wind)surfing ['(wɪnd)sɜ:fɪŋ]	(Wind-)Surfen	! Beachte: Surfen und Windsurfen sind verschiedene Sportarten.
	palm tree ['pɑ:m ˌtri:]	Palme	
	to **grow** [grəʊ], **grew** [gru:], **grown** [grəʊn]	wachsen	All kinds of flowers *grow* in our garden.

Places and what you can do there

Places		Activities	
in a city / town	in einer Stadt	to visit a museum / castle to go to a festival to get to know the capital of …	ein Museum / Schloss besichtigen ein Festival besuchen die Hauptstadt von … kennen lernen
in the fields in the forest	auf den Wiesen und Feldern im Wald	to go hiking / mountain biking / pony trekking to go for a walk	wandern / Mountainbike fahren / wanderreiten gehen spazieren gehen
in the mountains	in den Bergen	to go climbing / hiking / mountain biking / pony trekking to go for a walk to climb a mountain	klettern / … einen Berg besteigen
on an island at the seaside, by the sea, on the coast on the beach, on the shore on the river bank, on the shore	auf einer Insel am Meer, an der Küste am Strand, am Meeresufer am Flussufer	to go climbing / hiking / mountain biking / pony trekking to go for a walk to climb a mountain to go fishing	klettern/ … angeln gehen
in the sea in a river in a lake	im Meer in einem Fluss in einem See	to go swimming / surfing / windsurfing	schwimmen / surfen / windsurfen gehen

Station 1: Moving to the middle of nowhere

to **move (house)** [mu:v (haʊs)]	umziehen	When you *move house*, you leave your old home and go to live in a new one. ***Lat.*** movere
nowhere [ˈnəʊweə]	nirgendwo; nirgendwohin	*nowhere* → somewhere → everywhere

	Cornish ['kɔ:nɪʃ]	aus/in Cornwall	Dave and his parents are going to move to a *Cornish* town.
	countryside ['kʌntrisaɪd]	Land	in the *countryside* = auf dem Land
	to **miss** [mɪs]	vermissen	I *miss* you. = Du fehlst mir.
	to **stay** [steɪ]	übernachten	We *stayed* at a really nice hotel.
	(not) any longer [nɒt‿eni 'lɒŋgə]	(nicht) mehr; (nicht) länger	I don't like it here; I don't want to stay here *any longer*.
	all of us ['ɔ:l‿əv ˌʌs]	wir alle	
1	**transport** ['trænspɔ:t]	Verkehrsmittel; Transport	*Transport* can be expensive. ***Lat.*** transportare
3	**travel agent's** ['trævl‿eɪdʒnts]	Reisebüro	You can buy holidays at the *travel agent's*.
	ticket ['tɪkɪt]	Fahrschein	***Fr.*** ticket *(m)*
	to **depend (on)** [dɪ'pend‿(ɒn)]	abhängen von	The price of the ticket *depends on* the date. ***Fr.*** dépendre (de)
	per [pɜ:; pə]	pro	The price for the tickets is £5 *per* person.
	to **promise** ['prɒmɪs]	versprechen	Can his parents *promise* that Dave will like Cornwall?
5	to **book** [bʊk]	buchen; reservieren	You can *book* a ticket for a journey, a holiday, a table at a restaurant.
	to **return** [rɪ'tɜ:n]	zurückkehren; zurückfahren	*to return* = to go or come back ***Fr.*** retourner
	form [fɔ:m]	Formular	You often have to fill in *forms* on the internet.
	to **click on** ['klɪk‿ɒn]	anklicken	*Click on* 'SEND' to send your e-mail.
	connection [kə'nekʃn]	Verbindung	What *connections* are there from Greenwich to St Agnes today?
	one-way ticket ['wʌnweɪ ˌtɪkɪt]	einfache Fahrkarte	
	single ticket ['sɪŋgl ˌtɪkɪt]	einfache Fahrkarte	*single ticket* = one-way ticket
	return ticket [rɪ'tɜ:n ˌtɪkɪt]	Hin- und Rückfahrkarte	*return ticket* ↔ one-way ticket
	fee [fi:]	Gebühr	Is there an extra *fee* on the ticket?
	to **depart** [dɪ'pɑ:t]	abfahren	When does the train *depart*?
	to **arrive** [ə'raɪv]	ankommen	And when does the next train *arrive*? ***Fr.*** arriver
	outward ['aʊtwəd]	abfahrend	*Outward* trains leave the station.
	inward ['ɪnwəd]	ankommend	*Inward* trains arrive at the station.
	fare [feə]	Fahrpreis	Is there a special *fare* for groups?
	platform ['plætfɔ:m]	Plattform; Bahnsteig	
	to **get on (the bus)** [ˌget‿'ɒn]	einsteigen (in den Bus)	*to get on* ↔ to get off
	starting place ['stɑ:tɪŋ pleɪs]	Startpunkt	

Travel words

to travel	reisen
travel agent's	Reisebüro
to take a journey / trip	eine Reise machen
transport	Transport
by train / coach / car / Underground	mit dem Zug / Bus / Auto / mit der-U-Bahn
station	Bahnhof, Station
airport	Flughafen
on the road	auf der Straße; unterwegs
one way; single / return	einfach / hin und zurück
outward / inward journey	Hinfahrt / Rückfahrt
to depart / arrive	abfahren / ankommen
to change	umsteigen

Tell your partner about a trip you took last summer / last year / …

6	**weather forecast** [ˈweðə ˌfɔːkɑːst]	Wettervorhersage	It tells you what the weather will be like.

Weather words

It's / The weather is	cold warm cloudy sunny	kalt warm wolkig; bewölkt sonnig
There is / are	clouds sun rain wind storm thunder lightning	Wolken Sonne Regen Wind Sturm Donner Blitz
It's raining. The sun is shining.		Es regnet. Die Sonne scheint.

Say what the weather is like today and what it will be like tomorrow.

Skills: How to get information

1	**tourist board** ['tʊərɪst bɔːd]	Touristeninformation	At a *tourist board* you can get information about a country or region.
2	**Dear Sir or Madam** [dɪə ˌsɜːr‿ɔː 'mædəm]	Sehr geehrte Dame, sehr geehrter Herr	You begin a formal letter like this.
	grammar school ['græmə ˌskuːl]	Gymnasium	A school (in Britain) that is similar to the German 'Gymnasium'.
	Best wishes [ˌbest 'wɪʃɪz]	Viele Grüße; Herzliche Grüße	You can finish a formal letter like this.
	to **send off** [send‿'ɒf]	abschicken	Before you *send off* your e-mail, read it again.
	yourselves [jɔː'selvz]	ihr/euch/Sie/sich (selbst); selber	Did you enjoy *yourselves*? – Oh yes, the party was really great.

Station 2: Visit Cornwall – You'll love it!

in the far west [ɪn ðə fɑː 'west]	im äußersten Westen	Cornwall is *in the far west* of Great Britain.
coastline ['kəʊstlaɪn]	Küste; Küstenverlauf	Cornwall's *coastline* is almost 300 miles long.
fishing ['fɪʃɪŋ]	Angeln; Fischen; Fischerei	*fishing* → a fish
to **get to know** [ˌget tə 'nəʊ]	kennenlernen	I would like to *get to know* your friends.
wild [waɪld]	wild	pets – farm animals – *wild* animals
prehistoric [ˌpriːhɪ'stɒrɪk]	vorgeschichtlich	
monument ['mɒnjəmənt]	Monument; Denkmal	In Cornwall you can visit lots of prehistoric *monuments*. ***Lat.*** monumentum *(nt)*
walking trail ['wɔːkɪŋ treɪl]	Wanderweg	On *walking trails* you can only go on foot.
plant [plɑːnt]	Pflanze	 A tree is a *plant*.
from around the world [frɒm əˌraʊnd ðə 'wɜːld]	aus aller Welt	In our town there are people *from around the world*.
environment [ɪn'vaɪrnmənt]	Umwelt; Umgebung	Our *environment* is the world (or area) we live in. ***Fr.*** environnement *(m)*
mining ['maɪnɪŋ]	Bergbau	Cornwall has a long *mining* history.
Bronze Age ['brɒnz eɪdʒ]	Bronzezeit *(ca. 2200–800 v. Chr.)*	
cross [krɒs]	Kreuz	***Fr.*** croix *(f)*; ***Lat.*** crux *(f)*
Irish ['aɪrɪʃ]	irisch; Irisch	There are lots of nice *Irish* songs.

	Gaelic ['geɪlɪk]	gälisch; Gälisch	*Gaelic* is a Celtic language.
	besides [bɪ'saɪdz]	neben	Do you speak any languages *besides* German?
7	**geography** [dʒi'ɒgrəfi]	Geografie; Erdkunde	What do you know about the *geography* of Cornwall?
	tourism ['tʊərɪzm]	Tourismus	*tourism* → tour → tourist
11	**local** ['ləʊkl]	örtlich; lokal	The schools in your area are your *local* schools.
	dialect ['daɪəlekt]	Dialekt	Do people speak a *dialect* where you live?
	accent ['æksnt]	Akzent	My granny has a strong German accent when she speaks English.
12	**announcement** [ə'naʊnsmənt]	Ankündigung; Durchsage	I never understand the *announcements* at the station. ***Lat.*** annuntiare
13	**couple** ['kʌpl]	Paar	 ***Fr.*** couple *(m)*
	customer ['kʌstəmə]	Kunde/Kundin	A *customer* buys things in a shop. *customer* ↔ assistant
14	to **supply** [sə'plaɪ]	versorgen	Shops *supply* people with the things they need.
	to **rule** [ru:l]	herrschen; regieren	Elizabeth II *rules* the UK.

Story: Things will get better

to **get** [get], **got** [gɒt], **got** [gɒt]	werden	If you learn more words, your English will *get* better.
to **come in** [ˌkʌm‿'ɪn]	hereinkommen	Mrs Preston invites the friends to *come in*.
hall [hɔ:l]	Flur; Diele; Korridor	
electricity [ˌelɪk'trɪsəti]	Elektrizität; Strom	If there's no *electricity*, you can't make tea. ***Fr.*** électricité *(f)*
What's the matter? [ˌwɒts ðə 'mætə]	Was ist los?; Was hast du?	
Oh dear! [ˌəʊ 'dɪə]	Oje!	I've hurt my leg. – *Oh dear!*
to **go out** [ˌgəʊ‿'aʊt]	ausgehen; hinausgehen	Let's *go out*!
coastal path [ˌkəʊstl 'pɑ:θ]	Küstenweg	
mine [maɪn]	Mine	*mine* → mining
plumber ['plʌmə]	Installateur/-in; Klempner/-in	A *plumber* can fix your water pipes.
hill [hɪl]	Berg; Hügel	Our house is on a *hill* and we've got a fantastic view.
by [baɪ]	bei; neben; an	*by* = next to

chimney ['tʃɪmni]	Kamin; Schornstein	
roof [ruːf]	Dach	a *roof* with a chimney
cloud [klaʊd]	Wolke	
tin [tɪn]	Zinn	There's an old *tin* mine near Dave's house.
to **go right back to** [ˌgəʊ raɪt 'bæk tə]	zurückgehen auf	Cornwall's mining history *goes right back to* Celtic times.
geocaching ['dʒiːəʊkæʃɪŋ]	Geocaching	
to **solve** [sɒlv]	lösen	Dave and his friends want to *solve* the puzzle. ***Lat.*** solvere
to **boom** [buːm]	dröhnen	A loud voice *booms*.
to **keep away from** [ˌkiːp‿ə'weɪ frəm]	(sich) fernhalten von	*Keep away from* my chocolate!
skirt [skɜːt]	Rock	
trousers *(pl)* ['traʊzəz]	Hose	! *trousers* steht immer im Plural: You've got cool *trousers*.
spear [spɪə]	Speer	The *spear* is broken.
to **move in/into** [ˌmuːv‿'ɪn/'ɪntə]	einziehen in	Dave and his parents *moved into* a new house in Cornwall.
warrior ['wɒriə]	Krieger	
society [sə'saɪəti]	Verein; Gesellschaft	Bob is a member of a local history *society*. ***Fr.*** société *(f)*
twin [twɪn]	Zwilling; Zwillings-	
tool [tuːl]	Werkzeug; Gerät	A plumber needs special *tools*.
electrician [ˌelɪk'trɪʃn]	Elektriker/-in	*electrician* → electricity
plumbing ['plʌmɪŋ]	Sanitärarbeit	*plumbing* → plumber
electrics [ɪ'lektrɪks]	Elektrik	An electrician can fix the *electrics* in your house.
change [tʃeɪndʒ]	Änderung; Veränderung; Wechsel	*change* → to change
to **turn to** ['tɜːn tə]	sich wenden an; sich zuwenden	I *turned to* him to say something but he wasn't there any more.

More jobs

Who?		What and where?
mechanic	Mechaniker/-in	to fix, car, tools
pilot	Pilot/-in	to travel, journey, airport
plumber	Klempner/-in, Sanitärinstallateur/-in	to fix, plumbing, tools
electrician	Elektriker/-in	to fix, electrics, electricity

3	**diary entry** ['daɪəri entri]	Tagebucheintrag	A *diary entry* is a personal text in which you write about what happened and what you felt.
	nobody else ['nəʊbədi els]	niemand anderes	Only you and *nobody else* should read your diary entries.
	postcard ['pəʊstkɑ:d]	Postkarte	I love it when I get a real *postcard* and not just photos in an e-mail!
	sailboat ['seɪlbəʊt]	Segelboot	
	to **camp** [kæmp]	campen; zelten	*to camp* → camping

Action UK! The caves

	cave [keɪv]	Höhle	***Fr.*** caverne *(f)*
1	to **feed** [fi:d], **fed** [fed], **fed** [fed]	füttern; ernähren	Did you *feed* the dog this morning? People must work to *feed* their families.
	to **milk** [mɪlk]	melken	
	cow [kaʊ]	Kuh	
2	**love** [lʌv]	Liebe	*love* → to love
3	to **get lost** [ˌget 'lɒst]	verloren gehen; sich verirren	In a big city, it's easy to *get lost*.
	darkness ['dɑ:knəs]	Dunkelheit	*darkness* → dark

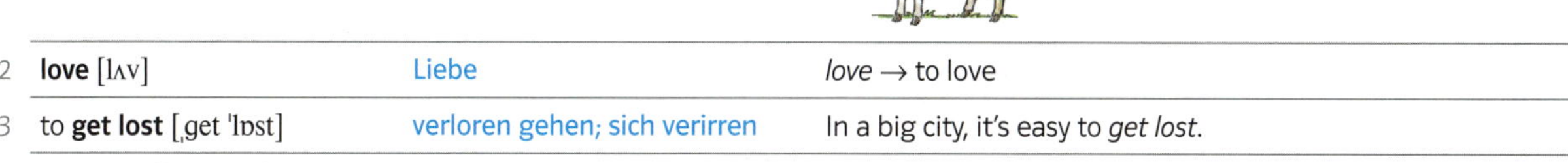

Across cultures 1 British stories and legends

	legend ['ledʒənd]	Legende; Sage	An old story – maybe true in parts.
2	**ingredient** [ɪn'gri:diənt]	Zutat	Something is missing in this cake; hm, what *ingredient* did I forget?

	completely [kəm'pli:tli]	völlig	What your saying isn't *completely* true! Some of it's wrong, sorry.
	cruel ['kru:əl]	grausam	People are sometimes *cruel* to each other. ***Fr.*** cruel/-le
	magical ['mædʒɪkəl]	magisch; Zauber-	The world of Harry Potter is a *magical* world.
	wizard ['wɪzəd]	Zauberer	
	hero, heroes *(pl)* ['hɪərəʊ, 'hɪərəʊz]	Held	The most important character in a book or film, usually good and brave.
	heroine ['herəʊɪn]	Heldin	Who is your favourite *heroine*?
	villain ['vɪlən]	Bösewicht	*villain* ↔ hero
	knight [naɪt]	Ritter	
	criminal ['krɪmɪnəl]	Kriminelle/-r; Verbrecher/-in	*criminal* = villain ***Lat.*** criminalis
	powerful ['paʊəfl]	stark; mächtig	Who's the most *powerful* person in the world?
	power [paʊə]	Kraft; Macht; Stärke	*power* → powerful
	private detective [ˌpraɪvət dɪ'tektɪv]	Privatdetektiv/-in	There are lots of books and films about Sherlock Holmes, the famous *private detective*.
	mysterious [mɪ'stɪəriəs]	mysteriös; geheimnisvoll	
	crime [kraɪm]	Verbrechen; Kriminalität	*crime* → criminal ***Lat.*** crimen *(nt)*
	robber ['rɒbə]	Räuber/-in	A *robber* is a criminal.
	outlaw ['aʊtlɔ:]	Geächtete/-r; Gesetzlose/-r	Robin Hood was a famous *outlaw*.
	to **hide** [haɪd], **hid** [hɪd], **hidden** ['hɪdn]	(sich) verstecken	My sister sometimes *hides* my things. She thinks it's funny.
3	**the Round Table** [ðə ˌraʊnd 'teɪbl]	die Tafelrunde	King Arthur and his knights met at the *Round Table*.
	the rich [ðə rɪtʃ]	die Reichen	Robin Hood was famous because he stole money from *the rich*.
	the poor [ðə pʊə]	die Armen	*the poor* ↔ the rich
4	**prop** [prɒp]	Requisite	You need lots of *props* for a film.
	set [set]	Umgebung; Rahmen	A film's *set* shows where the people live, work, etc.
	to **carry** ['kæri]	tragen	Can you *carry* this box for me, please?

Unit 2 Find your place

Introduction

	would [wʊd]	würde/-st/-n/-t	What *would* you do in this situation?
	personality [ˌpɜːsn'æləti]	Persönlichkeit	*personality* → person
	to **disagree** [ˌdɪsə'griː]	anderer Meinung sein; nicht einverstanden sein	*to disagree* ↔ to agree
	to **compromise** ['kɒmprəmaɪz]	Kompromisse eingehen	It isn't always easy to *compromise*.
	smart [smɑːt]	schlau; klug; intelligent	*smart* ↔ stupid
	logic ['lɒdʒɪk]	Logik	
	self [self], **selves** [selvz] *(pl)*	das Selbst	
	body ['bɒdi]	Körper	Are you logic smart, self smart or *body* smart? Or anything else?
1	**saying** ['seɪɪŋ]	Redensart; Sprichwort	'When the cat's away, the mice will play' is an English *saying*.
	to **judge** [dʒʌdʒ]	beurteilen; bewerten	Never *judge* people by their clothes.
	cover ['kʌvə]	Cover; Titelblatt	I like the *cover* of this book – it's crazy!
	practice ['præktɪs]	Training; Übung	*practice* = training *practice* → to practise
	It doesn't matter. [ɪt ˌdʌznt 'mætə]	Es ist egal.	*It doesn't matter* if you win or lose!
2	**call-in** ['kɔːlɪn]	*Sendung, bei der sich das Publikum telefonisch beteiligen kann*	
	imagination [ɪˌmædʒɪ'neɪʃn]	Fantasie; Vorstellungskraft	***Fr.*** imagination *(f)*
	to **compete (with)** [kəm'piːt]	konkurrieren (mit); sich messen (mit); in Wettbewerb treten (mit)	*to compete with* → competition ***Lat.*** competere
	imaginative [ɪ'mædʒɪnətɪv]	einfallsreich; fantasievoll	*imaginative* → imagination, to imagine
	subject ['sʌbdʒɪkt]	Thema	What are you talking about? What's the *subject* of the conversation?
	doubt [daʊt]	Zweifel	Claire isn't sure if she has made the right decision. She has *doubts*.
	to **learn about** ['lɜːn‿əˌbaʊt]	erfahren über	What did they *learn about* themselves?

Station 1: They wouldn't worry if they didn't care!

millionaire [ˌmɪljə'neə]	Millionär/-in	*millionaire* → million
rich [rɪtʃ]	reich	= to have lots of money ***Fr.*** riche
success [sək'ses]	Erfolg	If you work hard for school, you will probably have *success*.

	to **be stressed out** [bi ˌstrest‿ ˈaʊt]	völlig gestresst sein	Why are you so *stressed out*? Just relax.
	lead part [ˌliːd ˈpɑːt]	Hauptrolle	My favourite actor has had the *lead part* in lots of films.
	dance [dɑːns]	Tanz; Tanzveranstaltung	*dance* → to dance *Fr.* danse *(f)*
	backing dancer [ˈbækɪŋ ˌdɑːnsə]	Backgroundtänzer/-in	*backing dancer* ↔ lead dancer
	to **drop out (of)** [ˌdrɒp ˈaʊt‿ əv]	abbrechen	She *dropped out of* school when she was 14. = She didn't finish school.
	mark [mɑːk]	Note	What was your worst *mark* in English?
	laid-back [ˌleɪdˈbæk]	entspannt; locker	= very relaxed
	modelling [ˈmɒdəlɪŋ]	Modeln	Shahid does *modelling* just for fun. ***Fr.*** modèle *(m)*
	to **rely (on)** [rɪˈlaɪ‿ɒn]	sich verlassen (auf); vertrauen (auf)	Can I *rely on* you?
	looks *(pl)* [lʊks]	Aussehen	If you want to be a model you need good *looks*.
	to **study** [ˈstʌdi]	studieren; lernen	If you *study* a subject, you learn a lot about it.
	career [kəˈrɪə]	Beruf; Laufbahn; Karriere	***Fr.*** carrière *(f)*
	IT *(= Information Technology)* [ˌaɪˈtiː]	Informatik; Informationstech-nik	In *IT* you work a lot with computers.
2	**business** [ˈbɪznɪs]	Geschäft; Business	My mum has got her own *business*.
	billion [ˈbɪliən]	Milliarde	*billion* = 1,000,000,000
	age [eɪdʒ]	Alter	at the *age* of 15 = when he was 15
	company [ˈkʌmpəni]	Gesellschaft; Firma; Unterneh-men	My dad works for an American *company*.
	to **succeed (in)** [səkˈsiːd‿ɪn]	Erfolg haben (in/bei/mit)	*to succeed* → success
	to **save** [seɪv]	sparen	! to *save* time or money = sparen to *save* a person's life = retten
4	**in Jay's shoes** [ɪn dʒeɪz ˈʃuːz]	an Jays Stelle	What would you do *in Jay's shoes*?
	to **give up** [ˌɡɪv‿ˈʌp]	aufgeben	I can't play this game. I *give up*.
5	**successful** [səkˈsesfl]	erfolgreich	*successful* → to succeed → success
6	**audition** [ɔːˈdɪʃn]	Vorsprechen; Vorsingen; Vor-tanzen	He didn't get the lead part in the dance show because his *audition* didn't go well.
8	**competitive** [kəmˈpetɪtɪv]	leistungsorientiert; konkurrie-rend	*competitive* → competition → to compete

Station 2: You have to push yourself!

to **push oneself** [ˈpʊʃ wʌnˌself]	sich alles abverlangen; sich Mühe geben	Olivia's parents don't push her. She *pushes herself*.
messy [ˈmesi]	unordentlich	Lucy must tidy up her room because it's *messy*.

bossy ['bɒsi]	herrisch; rechthaberisch	*bossy* → boss
recorder [rɪ'kɔ:də]	Flöte	
to **enjoy oneself** [ɪn'dʒɔɪ]	Spaß haben; sich amüsieren	= to have a good time
doorbell ['dɔ:bel]	Türklingel	I rang the *doorbell* three times but nobody heard me.
saved by the bell [ˌseɪvd baɪ ðə 'bel]	noch mal Glück gehabt	
funny ['fʌni]	merkwürdig; komisch	*funny* = strange
to **give sb funny looks** [ˌgɪv fʌni 'lʊks]	jmdn. schief/komisch anschauen	Olivia and Lucy are *giving* each other *funny looks.*
to **behave** [bɪ'heɪv]	sich benehmen; sich verhalten	You're silly! You *behave* like a little child.
pause [pɔ:z]	Pause	
What's up? [ˌwɒts‿'ʌp]	Was ist los?	Why are you shouting at each other? *What's up?*
to **be in charge (of)** [bi‿ɪn 'tʃɑ:dʒ‿əv]	die Verantwortung tragen (für); zuständig sein (für)	Who *is in charge of* the food for the party?

Reflexive pronouns

Many words are used with a reflexive pronoun in German, but not in English.

to **behave**	sich benehmen	to **look forward to**	sich freuen auf
to **change**	sich (ver)ändern	to **meet**	sich treffen
to **decide**	sich entscheiden	to **move**	sich bewegen
to **feel**	sich fühlen	to **relax**	sich entspannen
to **hide**	sich verstecken	to **remember**	sich erinnern
to **hurry**	sich beeilen	to **sit down**	sich hinsetzen
to **imagine**	sich vorstellen	to **worry**	sich Sorgen machen

Write sentences with five of these verbs and translate them.

10 to **be hard on sb** [bi 'hɑ:d‿ɒn]	streng mit jmdm. sein	Don't *be* so *hard on* him.
Stay the way you are. [ˌsteɪ ðə weɪ ju 'ɑ:]	Bleib wie du bist.	
Miss [mɪs]	Fräulein *(Anrede)*	*Miss* Perfect – Mr Perfect

Skills: How to compromise

to **have a point** [ˌhæv‿ə 'pɔɪnt]	nicht ganz unrecht haben	Yes, you*'ve got a point.* I've never thought about it like that.

1	to **meet halfway** [ˌmiːt hɑːˈfweɪ]	sich auf halbem Weg treffen	I don't agree! But I don't want to fight, so let's *meet halfway*.
	I don't mind … *(+ -ing)* [ˌaɪ dəʊnt ˈmaɪnd]	Ich habe nichts dagegen (zu) …; Mir macht es nichts aus (zu) …	*I don't mind* doing that.
2	**misunderstood** [ˌmɪsʌndəˈstʊd]	missverstanden	Every time I talk to my parents I feel *misunderstood*.
3	**guest** [gest]	Gast	a person you invite to your house or to a party, or who stays at your house for a time

How to compromise

Asking for/Giving an opinion:
What do you think about …?
How do you feel about …?
What's your opinion about …?
I think …
In my opinion …

Making a suggestion:
Why don't we …?
If we did it this way, we could …
I've got an idea. Can we …?
It would be better to …

Agreeing:
Yes, we should do that.
No, I don't mind doing that.
I agree with you.
Yes, you're right.

Disagreeing:
I don't think that's a good idea.
You've got a point but …
I don't think we can do that.
I disagree.
I think you're wrong here.
I don't think you're right.

Finding a compromise:
Can we meet halfway?
The compromise (between the two suggestions) is …

Nach einer Meinung fragen/seine Meinung sagen:
Was denkst du über …?
Was hältst du von …?
Wie ist deine Meinung zu …?
Ich glaube/denke …
Meiner Meinung nach …

Einen Vorschlag machen:
Warum machen/… wir nicht …?
Wenn wir es so machen würden, dann könnten wir …
Ich habe eine Idee. Können wir …?
Es wäre besser, wenn wir …

Zustimmen:
Ja, das sollten wir tun.
Nein, es macht mir nichts aus, das zu tun.
Ich stimme dir zu.
Ja, du hast recht.

Nicht zustimmen:
Ich halte das für keine gute Idee.
Da hast du recht, aber …
Ich glaube nicht, dass wir das machen können.
Da bin ich anderer Meinung.
Ich glaube, du liegst hier falsch.
Ich glaube nicht, dass du recht hast.

Einen Kompromiss finden:
Können wir uns in der Mitte treffen?
Der Kompromiss (zwischen den beiden Vorschlägen) lautet …

You want to go to the cinema and the film ends at nine in the evening. Your parents think that's too late. Discuss and find a compromise.

Unit task: Make a personality test!

to **seem** [si:m]	scheinen	The dog *seemed* friendly at first, but then he suddenly became aggressive.
else [els]	andere/-r/-s; sonst noch	We've got everything on Mum's list now. I don't think we need anything *else*.
limit ['lɪmɪt]	Limit; Grenze	Find out what your talents and *limits* are. *Fr.* limite *(f)*
gadget ['gædʒɪt]	Gerät; technische Spielerei	Smartphones and play stations are *gadgets*.

Story: Hang out with us instead!

to **hang out (with)** [ˌhæŋ‿'aʊt wɪð], **hung out (with)** [ˌhʌŋ‿'aʊt wɪð], **hung out (with)** [ˌhʌŋ‿'aʊt wɪð] *(infml)*	sich herumtreiben (mit); rumhängen (mit); sich treffen (mit)	When you *hang out* with friends, you meet them and spend time with them.
instead [ɪn'sted]	stattdessen	If the weather is too cold for swimming, we could go for a walk *instead*.
to **be fed up (with)** [bi fed‿'ʌp wɪð]	sauer sein (auf); die Nase voll haben (von)	Jay *was fed up* with his friends.
argument ['ɑ:gjəmənt]	Auseinandersetzung; Streit	The boys didn't agree with each other. They had a big *argument*.
could [kʊd]	konnte/-n	My best friend *couldn't* come to my party because she was on holiday. *could* = was able to
these days [ˌði:z 'deɪz]	zurzeit	*these days* ↔ in the past
to **be grounded** [bi 'graʊndɪd]	Hausarrest haben	Jay *was grounded* for five days.
to **trust** [trʌst]	vertrauen	I know what I'm doing. Please *trust* me.
to **put on** [ˌpʊt‿'ɒn]	anziehen	We're going out now. *Put* your shoes *on*, please.
trainer ['treɪnə]	Turnschuh	*Trainers* are special shoes that people wear for running.
freedom *(no pl)* ['fri:dəm]	Freiheit; Unabhängigkeit	*freedom* → free
in-crowd ['ɪnkraʊd]	Szene; die Angesagten; die Beliebten	Finn and Max are part of the *in-crowd*.
to **chill out** [tʃɪl‿'aʊt]	chillen	
blond [blɒnd]	blond	
What's going on? [wɒts ˌgəʊɪŋ‿'ɒn]	Was ist los?; Was geht ab?	*What's going on?* What are you doing?
the high street [ðə 'haɪ ˌstri:t]	die Haupteinkaufsstraße	Let's go to *the high street* for some burgers. ! In größeren Städten wie London gibt es in jedem Viertel eine *high street*.
bloke *(fam)* [bləʊk]	Typ *(ugs.)*	

	to **lend** [lend], **lent** [lent], **lent** [lent] **(to)**	leihen; verleihen	*to lend* ↔ to borrow
	overnight [ˌəʊvə'naɪt]	über Nacht	Shahid won't be back until tomorrow. He's got an *overnight* modelling job.
	usual ['ju:ʒl]	üblich	*usual* → usually
	to **pay attention to sb/sth** [ˌpeɪ‿ə'tenʃn tʊ]	seine Aufmerksamkeit auf jmdn./etw. richten	Nobody was *paying attention* to Jay.
	to **ignore** [ɪg'nɔ:]	ignorieren; außer Acht lassen	If you don't look at sth and don't listen to it, even if you know it's there, you *ignore* it.
	pretty ['prɪti]	hübsch	*pretty* eyes
	poor [pɔ:; pʊə]	arm	*poor* ↔ rich
	mummy ['mʌmi]	Mama; Mami; Mutti	
	piece of junk [ˌpi:s‿əv 'dʒʌŋk]	Stück Schrott	After the party Shahid's laptop was a *piece of junk*.
	anger *(no pl)* ['æŋgə]	Zorn; Wut	Jay was white with *anger*! *anger* → angry
1	**lie** [laɪ]	Lüge	*lie* → to lie
	to **tease sb** [ti:z]	jmdn. aufziehen; jmdn. hänseln; jmdn. ärgern	Olivia sometimes *teases* Lucy.
2	**peer pressure** ['pɪə ˌpreʃe]	Gruppenzwang	
	excitement *(no pl)* [ɪk'saɪtmənt]	Aufregung	*excitement* → excited → exciting
	confused [kən'fju:zd]	verwirrt; wirr; konfus	What happened? Why is Jay so *confused*?
	honest ['ɒnɪst]	ehrlich	Don't lie. Be *honest*! ***Lat.*** honestus

Action UK! When Sean came to visit

1	to **react** [ri'ækt]	reagieren	*to react* → reaction
2	**sense of humour** *(no pl)* [ˌsens‿əv 'hju:mə]	Sinn für Humor	Do your teachers have a *sense of humour*?
	to **feel sorry for** [ˌfi:l 'sɒri fɔ:]	Mitleid haben mit; bedauern	I *felt sorry for* him. = Er hat mir leid getan.
	optimistic [ˌɒptɪ'mɪstɪk]	optimistisch	Everything will be fine, let's be *optimistic*!
	to **cheer sb up** [ˌtʃɪər‿'ʌp]	jmdn. aufheitern	Are you sad? What can I do to *cheer you up*?
	show-off ['ʃəʊ‿ɒf]	Angeber/-in	*show-off* → to show off
	to **apologise** [ə'pɒlədʒaɪz]	sich entschuldigen	= to say sorry
	to **delete** [dɪ'li:t]	löschen	They *deleted* all the music on Shahid's laptop.
	wall [wɔ:l]	Online-Pinnwand	
	account settings [ə'kaʊnt ˌsetɪŋz]	Profileinstellungen	Check your *account settings* for your social network carefully.

bench [benʃ]	Bank; Sitzbank	Let's sit down on this *bench*.
to **work out** [ˌwɜːk‿ˈaʊt]	funktionieren; klappen	How did things *work out* in the end?

Describing different personalities

to **have a sense of humour**	(einen Sinn für) Humor haben
to **be a show-off**	angeberisch sein
to **be creative/confident/ competitive/honest/funny/ bossy/messy/laid-back/ optimistic/smart**	kreativ/selbstsicher/selbstbewusst/ konkurrierend/ehrlich/lustig/ rechthaberisch/unordentlich/ locker/optimistisch/klug sein
to **never give up**	nie aufgeben
to **always get into trouble**	immer in Schwierigkeiten geraten
to **start fights**	Streit anfangen
to **push oneself to**	sich zwingen zu
to **follow the crowd**	der Masse folgen
to **compare oneself with**	sich vergleichen mit
to **be good with/at**	gut sein bei/in
…	…

Describe your friend's personality.

Text smart 1 Poems and songs

Introduction

1	**board** [bɔːd]	Brett; Tafel	You can make a box with *boards*.
	fair play [feə ˈpleɪ]	Fairplay	*Fair play* in sports is very important.
	generous [ˈdʒenrəs]	großzügig	A *generous* person likes to give things to others. *Fr.* généreux/généreuse
2	**(song) lyrics** *(pl)* [sɒŋ ˈlɪrɪks]	Liedtext	Are the *lyrics* of songs important to you, or just the music?
	to **sing along** [ˌsɪŋ‿əˈlɒŋ]	mitsingen	
	to **rhyme** [raɪm]	(sich) reimen	'Bee' *rhymes* with 'sea'.
	advert [ˈædvɜːt]	Anzeige; Werbespot	I saw a really funny *advert* for dog food on TV yesterday.

Station 1: Say it with a poem!

3	**rainbow** ['reɪnbəʊ]	Regenbogen	
	dolphin ['dɒlfɪn]	Delfin	
	bare [beə]	nackt; bloß	His legs/arms/feet/hands were *bare*.
	sunflower ['sʌnflaʊə]	Sonnenblume	
	peach [pi:tʃ]	Pfirsich	*Fr.* pêche *(f)*
	spoon [spu:n]	Löffel	I like eating pasta with a *spoon*.
	honey ['hʌni]	Honig	We get *honey* from bees.
	tune [tju:n]	Melodie	If you don't know the lyrics of the song, you can just hum along to the *tune*.
	lazy ['leɪzi]	faul	*lazy* ↔ busy
4	to **read/sing out loud** [ˌri:d/sɪŋ‿aʊt 'laʊd]	laut vorlesen/vorsingen	*Read* the poem *out loud*.
6	**arrow** ['ærəʊ]	Pfeil	
	to **shoot** [ʃu:t], **shot** [ʃɒt], **shot** [ʃɒt] **(at)**	schießen (auf)	He *shot* an arrow into the air.
	air [eə]	Luft	Let's go for a walk and get some fresh *air*.
	to **fly** [flaɪ], **flew** [flu:], **flown** [fləʊn]	fliegen	The bird *flew* up to the top of the church.
	sight [saɪt]	*hier:* Blick	*sight* → to see
	flight [flaɪt]	Flug	*flight* → to fly
	oak [əʊk]	Eiche	= a tree that you find in the forest
7	**direct** [dɪ'rekt]	direkt	Being too *direct* in conversations is not always a good thing.
	simple ['sɪmpl]	einfach; simpel	*simple* ↔ difficult *Fr.* simple

Station 2: Say it with a song!

9	**stuck in the middle of …** [ˌstʌk ɪn ðə ˈmɪdl‿əv]	mitten in … stecken; feststecken in …	Whenever I'm *stuck in the middle of* my homework, the phone rings.
	to **sail** [seɪl]	segeln; umsegeln	*to sail* → sailor
	to **guide** [gaɪd]	führen; leiten	*to guide* → guide *Fr.* guider
	to **be made of** [bi ˈmeɪd‿əv]	bestehen aus	Windows *are made of* glass.
	to **be called to do sth** [bi ˈkɔːld tə duː]	auserwählt sein, etw. zu tun	
	to **remind (sb of sth/sb)** [rɪˈmaɪnd əv]	(jmdn. an etw./jmdn.) erinnern	**!** I didn't remember Dad's birthday. Mum had to remind me.
	to **cry** [kraɪ]	weinen	*to cry* ↔ to laugh
10	**play on words** [ˌpleɪ‿ɒn ˈwɜːdz]	Wortspiel	
11	**catchy** [ˈkætʃi]	eingängig; einprägsam	If a song has a *catchy* tune, it's easy to remember.
	to **dance to** [ˈdɑːns tə]	tanzen auf	The song is great – let's *dance to* it. ***Fr.*** danser
	to **keep one's feet or hands still** [ˌkiːp wʌnzː ˈfiːt‿ɔː ˈhændz stɪl]	die Beine und Hände ruhig halten	My brother can't *keep his feet and hands still*!
	over and over again [ˌəʊvər‿ən‿ˌəʊvər‿əˈgen]	immer wieder	I could watch that film *over and over again*.
	to **get sth out of one's head** [get ˌaʊt‿əv wʌnz ˈhed]	etw. aus dem Kopf bekommen	They can't *get the pictures* of the accident *out of their heads*.
	melody [ˈmelədi]	Melodie	*Fr.* mélodie *(f)*
	You can do it! [juː kən ˈduː ɪt]	Du schaffst es!	It's not difficult. I'm sure *you can do it*!
	to **survive** [səˈvaɪv]	überleben	
	to **fall down** [ˌfɔːl‿ˈdaʊn]	stürzen; hinunterfallen	I *fell down* the stairs and hurt my leg.
	to **die** [daɪ]	sterben	Robert has only got one grandma. His other grandma *died* four years ago.
	champion [ˈtʃæmpiən]	Gewinner/-in; Sieger/-in; Champion	We are the *champions*!

Across cultures 2 Reacting to a new situation

1	**plate** [pleɪt]	Teller	There's too much food on the *plate*.
	mug [mʌg]	Becher	
	cup [kʌp]	Tasse	Put the *cups* into the cupboard please.
	knife [naɪf], **knives** [naɪvz] *(pl)*	Messer	! Achtung Aussprache: Das ***k*** wird nicht gesprochen.
	fork [fɔ:k]	Gabel	*fork* and knife
	bread roll ['bred rəʊl]	Brötchen	
	butter ['bʌtə]	Butter	
	jam [dʒæm]	Marmelade; Konfitüre	I love my bread rolls with butter and *jam*.
	marmalade ['mɑ:məleɪd]	Marmelade aus Zitrusfrüchten	! Achte auf die Schreibung: *marm**a**lade*
	muesli ['mju:zli]	Müsli	
	ham [hæm]	Schinken	I'd like a sandwich. – With cheese and tomato? Or *ham*?
	sausage ['sɒsɪdʒ]	Wurst; Bratwurst	
	sugar ['ʃʊgə]	Zucker	Do you like your tea with *sugar* or honey?
3	**host family** ['həʊst ˌfæmli]	Gastfamilie	While I'm in Greenwich, I'll be at the Jacksons' house. The Jacksons are my *host family*.
	exchange student [ɪks'tʃeɪndʒ ˌstju:dnt]	Austauschschüler/-in	Our *exchange student* comes from England and wants to learn German.
	unfamiliar [ˌʌnfə'mɪliə]	nicht vertraut; unbekannt	Staying with a host family is an *unfamiliar* situation for Brad.
4	to **make angry** [meɪk 'æŋgri]	wütend machen; verärgern	Don't *make* me *angry*!
	to **upset** [ʌp'set], **upset** [ʌp'set], **upset** [ʌp'set]	aus der Fassung bringen; aufregen	The fights between Jay and Luke *upset* Olivia.
	gratitude ['grætɪtju:d]	Dankbarkeit	If you want to say thank you to somebody, you can show your *gratitude* in different ways.
	impolite [ˌɪmp'laɪt]	unhöflich	*impolite* ↔ polite ***Fr.*** impoli/e
	this early ['ðɪs ˌɜ:li]	so früh	Do you really have to go home *this early*?
	that much [ðæt 'mʌtʃ]	so viel	Sorry, I can't eat *that much* in the morning.
	to **be used to** *(+ -ing)* [bi 'ju:s_tə]	gewöhnt sein an; gewohnt sein	I'm not *used to* drinking coffee.
	I'm (not) sure ... [ˌaɪm nɒt 'ʃʊə]	Ich bin mir (nicht) sicher ...	*I'm not sure* if I can help you with your homework, but I'll try.

Unit 3 Let's go to Scotland!

Introduction

	fringe [frɪndʒ]	Rand-; Alternativ-	The Edinburgh *Fringe* Festival takes place every year.
1	**historic** [hɪ'stɒrɪk]	historisch	*historic* → history
	traditional [trə'dɪʃnl]	traditionell	*traditional* → tradition *Fr.* traditionnel/le
2	to **be like** [bi 'laɪk]	sein	Please tell me more about your school. What *is* it *like*?
3	**typically** ['tɪpɪkli]	typisch	What's *typically* German?
	haggis ['hægɪs]	Haggis *(schottisches Gericht aus in einem Schafsmagen gekochten Schafsinnereien und Haferschrot)*	
	tartan ['tɑ:tn]	Schottenkaro *(bestimmtes Muster eines Clans)*; karierter Schottenstoff	Different families have *tartans* of different colours, e. g. with a red, blue or green background.
	kilt [kɪlt]	Kilt; Schottenrock	
	bagpipes *(pl)* ['bægpaɪps]	Dudelsack	
	independence *(no pl)* [ˌɪndɪ'pendəns]	Unabhängigkeit	*Fr.* indépendance *(f)*; ***Lat.*** de + pendere
	loch [lɒx; lɒk]	See *(in Schottland)*	! Achtung Aussprache: In Schottland wird das „ch" in *loch* wie ein deutsches „ch" ausgesprochen.
	referendum [ˌrefr'endəm]	Referendum; Volksentscheid	In 2014, the Scottish people voted in a *referendum* on independence.
	independent [ˌɪndɪ'pendənt]	unabhängig	*independent* → independence *Fr.* indépendant/e
	flag [flæg]	Flagge; Fahne	The colours of the German *flag* are black, red and gold.
	thistle ['θɪsl]	Distel	A *thistle* is a plant with beautiful pink flowers.

Typically Scottish

the **Scottish flag**

bagpipes

a **thistle**

a **kilt**

tartan

haggis

Station 1: A new Holly?

	son [sʌn]	Sohn	Ethan is the *son* of Gwen's uncle and aunt.
	backpack ['bækpæk]	Rucksack	a bag that you carry on your back
	since *(+ Zeitpunkt)* [sɪns]	seit; seitdem	They have been living in Scotland *since* 1996.
	for *(+ Zeitraum)* [fɔ:; fə]	seit	We've been learning English *for* three years. = We started to learn English three years ago.
3	**period** ['pɪəriəd]	Periode; Zeitspanne	An hour is a short *period* of time. ! Achtung Aussprache.
4	to **produce** [prə'dju:s]	herstellen; produzieren	What does your company *produce*?
	litre (l) ['li:tə]	Liter	*Fr.* litre *(m)*
	party ['pɑ:ti]	Partei	Which *party* does Mrs Merkel belong to?
	to **campaign (for)** [kæm'peɪn fɔ:]	demonstrieren (für); aufmerksam machen (auf); sich engagieren (für)	The Scottish National Party *campaigns for* Scotland's independence.
	shinty ['ʃɪnti]	Shinty *(eine Art Hockey)*	= a popular sport in Scotland
5	**gig** [gɪg]	Auftritt; Gig	Ethan and his band play *gigs* every weekend.

	drums *(pl)* [drʌmz]	Schlagzeug	
6	**official** [ə'fɪʃl]	offiziell	
	anthem ['ænθəm]	Hymne	Can you sing Germany's national *anthem*?
	inofficial [ˌɪnə'fɪʃl]	inoffiziell	*inofficial* ↔ official
	to **defeat** [dɪ'fi:t]	besiegen	*to defeat* = to beat
	soldier ['səʊldʒə]	Soldat/-in	a person whose job is to fight, usually for his or her country

Station 2: Is that made with meat?

	meat *(no pl)* [mi:t]	Fleisch	
	vegetable ['vedʒtəbl]	Gemüse	Carrots are *vegetables*.
	vegetarian [ˌvedʒɪ'teəriən]	Vegetarier/-in	*Vegetarians* don't eat meat.
	jacket ['dʒækɪt]	Jacke	In summer you don't need a *jacket*.
	to **pull down** [ˌpʊl‿'daʊn]	abreißen	They *pulled down* the house to build a new one.
	musical ['mju:zɪkl]	musikalisch; Musik-	*musical* → music
	shipbuilding ['ʃɪpbɪldɪŋ]	Schiffsbau	
	industry ['ɪndəstri]	Industrie; Branche; Gewerbe	Scotland still has a shipbuilding *industry*.
9	**midnight** ['mɪdnaɪt]	Mitternacht	= twelve o'clock at night
	to **set off** [ˌset‿'ɒf], **set off** [ˌset'ɒf], **set off** [ˌset'ɒf]	*hier:* ein Feuerwerk zünden	
10	**Scot** [skɒt]	Schotte/Schottin	*Scot* → Scotland, Scottish
	invention [ɪn'venʃn]	Erfindung	***Fr.*** invention *(f)*; ***Lat.*** inventio *(f)*
	discovery [dɪ'skʌvri]	Entdeckung	*discovery* → to discover
	by [baɪ]	von	a CD *by* Beyoncé
	to **clone** [kləʊn]	klonen	It's possible to *clone* animals.
	scientist ['saɪəntɪst]	Wissenschaftler/-in	*scientist* → science
	raincoat ['reɪnkəʊt]	Regenmantel	
	to **invent** [ɪn'vent]	erfinden	*to invent* → invention ***Fr.*** inventer
	penicillin [ˌpenɪ'sɪlɪn]	Penicillin	
	steam engine ['sti:m‿endʒɪn]	Dampfmaschine	The *steam engine* was the most important invention of the 18th century.
	to **start** [stɑ:t]	*hier:* gründen	John Logie Baird *started* the first television station.
11	to **fill** [fɪl]	(sich) füllen	She *filled* her glass with water.
	vegetarian [ˌvedʒɪ'teəriən]	vegetarisch	Today you can even buy *vegetarian* sausages.

	mashed potatoes *(pl)* [ˌmæʃt pəˈteɪtəʊz]	Kartoffelpüree	Haggis is often eaten with *mashed potatoes*.
	sauce [sɔːs]	Soße	I love ice cream with chocolate *sauce*.
	to **ban** [bæn]	bannen; verbieten; sperren	If you *ban* something, it's not allowed any more.
13	**close** [kləʊs]	schmaler Durchgang	The people in Edinburgh call the narrow streets *'closes'*.
	hundreds of [ˈhʌndrədz‿əv]	Hunderte (von)	*Hundreds of* people listened to Ethan's band last weekend.
	narrow [ˈnærəʊ]	eng; schmal	a *narrow* street, a *narrow* bridge
	to **lead off** [liːd‿ˈɒf]	wegführen	Closes *lead off* from the main streets.
	to **lead** [liːd], **led** [led], **led** [led]	führen; anführen	Where does this way *lead*?
	to **leave behind** [ˌliːv‿bɪˈhaɪnd]	zurücklassen	Never *leave* your rubbish *behind* after a picnic.
14	**crane** [kreɪn]	Kran	If you want to fix the roof of a tall building, you'll need a *crane*.

Skills: How to write a persuasive text

1	**humour** *(no pl)* [ˈhjuːmə]	Humor; Stimmung	My grandad's sense of *humour* is very special.
	final [ˈfaɪnl]	letzte/-r/-s	*final* = last
	further [ˈfɜːðə]	weiter (weg)	*further* → far
	north [nɔːθ]	nördlich; im Norden	Which is further *north*: Scotland or Ireland?
	fascinating [ˈfæsɪneɪtɪŋ]	faszinierend	= very, very interesting
	present [ˈpreznt]	heutig; Gegenwarts-	The museum shows the life on the islands from Roman times to the *present* day.
	spectacular [spekˈtækjələ]	spektakulär	*Fr.* spectaculaire
	cliff [klɪf]	Klippe; Kliff	The views from the *cliffs* are spectacular.
	tiny [ˈtaɪni]	klein; winzig	A mouse looks *tiny* next to a horse.

Describing nature and buildings

nature	cliff, mountain, hill, park, island, coastline, …	beautiful, amazing, fascinating, wonderful, fantastic, spectacular, …	
buildings	castle, museum, church, tower, …	old, modern, big, huge, nice, tiny, interesting, fascinating, made of stone/wood, stairs, wall, …	

Describe your school building. Write 3–5 sentences.

Unit task: Visit Scotland!

to **rent (out)** [ˌrent‿ˈaʊt]	(ver)mieten	Last year our friends *rented* their house in England *out* to us.
travel agency [ˈtrævl‿ˌeɪdʒnsi]	Reisebüro	You can book a holiday at the *travel agency*.

Story: I don't believe in ghosts!

sky [skaɪ]	Himmel	At the end of the festival the *sky* was getting dark.
entrance [ˈentrəns]	Eingang; Eintritt	Where is the *entrance* to the castle? *entrance* → to enter
ticket office [ˈtɪkɪt ˌɒfɪs]	Kartenschalter	The *ticket office* is at the entrance.
empty [ˈemti]	leer	*empty* ↔ full
stone [stəʊn]	Stein; Stein-	The castle has a *stone* floor and *stone* walls.
pocket [ˈpɒkɪt]	Tasche; Hosentasche	He put his smartphone into his trouser *pocket*.
signal [ˈsɪgnl]	Signal; Empfang	I can't use my phone because there's no *signal*.
thick [θɪk]	dick *(nicht für Personen)*	The stone walls of the castle are very *thick*.
perhaps [pəˈhæps]	vielleicht	*perhaps* = maybe
to **go round in circles** [gəʊ ˌraʊnd ɪn ˈsɜːklz]	sich im Kreis drehen	
wounded [ˈwuːndɪd]	verwundet; verletzt	We found a small bird in the garden. It was *wounded*, so we took it to the vet.
tower [taʊə]	Turm	

moonlight ['mu:nlaɪt]	Mondlicht	There's no *moonlight* tonight because the sky is cloudy.
stairs *(pl)* [steəz]	Treppe	! The stair**s** go up. = Die Treppe führ**t** nach oben. *stairs* → downstairs → upstairs
wooden ['wʊdn]	hölzern; aus Holz	Our house has *wooden* stairs.
danger ['deɪndʒə]	Gefahr	*danger* → dangerous *Fr.* danger *(m)*
to **keep out (of)** [ˌki:p‿'aʊt əv]	draußen bleiben; draußen halten	Parents must *keep out* of my room!
cracking ['krækɪŋ]	knackend; brechend	
to **realise** ['rɪəlaɪz]	erkennen; realisieren	Holly *realised* they didn't have much time.
key ring ['ki: ˌrɪŋ]	Schlüsselbund; Schlüsselanhänger	
to **tie (to)** ['taɪ tə]	binden (an); fesseln (an)	If you *tie* a dog to something, it can't run away.
rope [rəʊp]	Seil	
to **hold onto** [ˌhəʊld‿'ɒntə]	(sich) festhalten an	Amber caught the rope and *held onto* it.
crack [kræk]	Knacken; Krachen	*crack* → cracking
wood [wʊd]	Holz	*wood* → wooden
heavy ['hevi]	schwer; stark	I can't carry this box – it's too *heavy*.
definitely ['defɪnətli]	bestimmt; definitiv; eindeutig	Do you want a pink backpack? – No, *definitely* not.
7 **spider** ['spaɪdə]	Spinne	
web [web]	Netz; Spinnennetz	Spiders make *webs*.

Action UK! How times change

1 to **help out** [ˌhelp‿'aʊt]	aushelfen	Our neighbour wasn't able to go shopping, so I *helped* her *out*.
neighbourhood ['neɪbəhʊd]	Nachbarschaft	*neighbourhood* → neighbour
to **do the shopping** [ˌdu: ðə 'ʃɒpɪŋ]	Einkäufe machen; Besorgungen machen	
elderly ['eldəli]	älter	= a more polite word for 'old' (when you speak about people)
2 **inventor** [ɪn'ventə]	Erfinder/-in	*inventor* → to invent, invention

	tin can ['tɪn kæn]	Blechdose	You can buy most drinks in *tin cans*.
	switch [swɪtʃ]	Schalter	I can't see anything. Where's the light *switch*?
3	**versus (vs.)** ['vɜːsəs]	gegen	old *vs.* new old *vs.* young
	rotary phone ['rəʊtri fəʊn]	Telefon mit Wählscheibe	

Nouns and adjectives

adjectives with -y	
anger	angry
cloud	cloudy
day	daily
friend	friendly
fun	funny
health	healthy
mud	muddy
adjectives with -al	
centre	central
history	historical
music	musical
person	personal
tradition	traditional
adjectives with -ing	
excitement	exciting
interest	interesting
surprise	surprising

adjectives with -ful/-less	
colour	colourful
help	helpful, helpless
hope	hopeful, hopeless
power	powerful
success	successful
other adjectives	
competition	competitive
crowd	crowded
danger	dangerous
difference	different
freedom	free
independence	independent
possibility	possible
vegetarian	vegetarian
wood	wooden

Text smart 2 Factual texts

Introduction

1	**library** ['laɪbri]	Bibliothek; Bücherei	You can borrow books from the *library*.
2	**news report** ['njuːz rɪˌpɔːt]	Tatsachenbericht; Nachrichtenbeitrag; Meldung	What did the *news report* say about the car accident?

	entry ['entri]	Eintrag	a diary *entry*, a dictionary *entry*
	recipe ['resɪpi]	Rezept	! Achtung Aussprache.
	reference article ['refrns ˌɑ:tɪkl]	Referenzartikel	If you need basic information about something, look for a *reference article*.
3	**headline** ['hedlaɪn]	Schlagzeile	= the title of a news report
	hedgehog ['hedʒhɒg]	Igel	

Station 1: What do the instructions say?

	winter ['wɪntə]	Winter	= the months of December, January and February
	hibernation [ˌhaɪbə'neɪʃn]	Winterschlaf	During *hibernation* the animals sleep and don't eat.
	food [fu:d]	Futter	Hedgehogs eat cat and dog *food*.
	ill [ɪl]	krank	If you're *ill*, it's best to go to bed.
	weight [weɪt]	Gewicht	You should only feed small hedgehogs that don't have enough *weight* to survive the winter.
	spring [sprɪŋ]	Frühling	= the months of March, April and May
	warm [wɔ:m]	warm	*warm* ↔ cold
	to **avoid** [ə'vɔɪd]	vermeiden; meiden; aus dem Weg gehen	Try to *avoid* spelling mistakes in your texts.
	run area ['rʌn ˌeəriə]	Gehege; Auslauf	My rabbits live in a *run area* in our garden. *run* → to run → runner
	newspaper ['nju:sˌpeɪpə]	Zeitung	My dad reads the *newspaper* every morning while he's having breakfast. *newspaper* → news
	dry [draɪ]	trocken	*dry* ↔ wet
	clean [kli:n]	sauber	If you clean something, it becomes *clean*.
	layer (of) ['leɪər‿əv]	Schicht (aus); Lage (aus)	On the floor of the run area is a *layer* of newspaper.
	to **soak up** [səʊk‿'ʌp]	aufsaugen	The layer of newspaper *soaks up* water.
	to **weigh** [weɪ]	wiegen	*to weigh* → weight
	fearful ['fɪəfl]	ängstlich	*fearful* → fear
6	**treat** [tri:t]	*hier:* Leckerli; Belohnung	A *treat* is often something good to eat.

Station 2: Didn't you hear? It was in the news!

7	**celebrity** [sə'lebrəti]	Prominente/-r; berühmte Person	*Celebrities* are famous people you often see on TV or read about in magazines.
8	**Australian** [ɒs'treɪliən]	australisch; Australier/-in	
	bush [bʊʃ]	Busch *(Buschlandschaft)*; Wildnis	*Bush* is the word you use to describe open country, e. g. in Australia or Africa.
	fire [faɪə]	Feuer	Did you hear about the bush *fire* in Australia?

hot [hɒt]	heiß	The sun is *hot*.
to **rescue** ['reskju:]	retten	*to rescue* → rescue
flame [fleɪm]	Flamme	
thirsty ['θɜ:sti]	durstig	I'm *thirsty*. Can I have a glass of water, please?
animal shelter ['ænɪml ˌʃeltə]	Tierheim	I sometimes walk the dogs from the *animal shelter*.
9 **rhino** ['raɪnəʊ]	Rhinozeros; Nashorn	
to **kill** [kɪl]	töten; umbringen	People *kill* rhinos for their horns.
elephant ['elɪfənt]	Elefant	
on the brink of [ˌɒn ðə 'brɪŋk‿əv]	am Rande von; kurz vor	
extinction *(no pl)* [ɪks'tɪŋkʃn]	Aussterben	A lot of animals are on the brink of *extinction*.
protest ['prəʊtest]	Protest	! Achtung Aussprache.
illegal [ɪ'li:gl]	illegal; unrechtmäßig; rechtswidrig	
poaching *(no pl)* ['pəʊtʃɪŋ]	Wilderei	*Poaching* is illegal.
tusk [tʌsk]	Stoßzahn	People kill elephants for their *tusks*.
ivory *(no pl)* ['aɪvri]	Elfenbein	Elephant tusks are made of *ivory*.
to **march** [mɑ:tʃ]	marschieren	The people *marched* together in a protest against illegal poaching. *Fr.* marcher
medicine *(no pl)* ['medsn]	Medizin; Medikamente	If you don't feel well, you should ask the doctor for some *medicine*.
to **become extinct** [bɪˌkʌm‿ɪk'stɪŋkt]	aussterben	There is a danger that elephants and rhinos will *become extinct*. *to become extinct* → extinction
violent ['vaɪələnt]	gewaltsam; gewalttätig; brutal	*Violent* criminals often carry knives.
those in power [ˌðəʊz ɪn 'paʊə]	die Regierenden; die Herrschenden	

Across cultures 3 Making small talk

1	**light** [laɪt]	leicht	Small talk is *light* conversation.
	talker ['tɔːkə]	Sprecher/-in	*talker* → to talk
	to **hog a conversation** [ˌhɒg‿ə kɒnvə'seɪʃn]	ein Gespräch für sich in Beschlag nehmen; ein Gespräch dominieren	You shouldn't *hog a conversation*, you should also listen to your partner.
2	to **keep the ball bouncing** [ˌkiːp ðə bɔːl 'baʊntsɪŋ]	*hier:* das Gespräch am Laufen halten	= to keep the conversation going
	to **bounce** [baʊnts]	springen; hüpfen	The ball *bounced* away and broke the window.
	next door [ˌnekst 'dɔː]	(von) nebenan	Your neighbours live *next door*.
	to **check out** *(coll)* [ˌtʃek‿'aʊt]	prüfen; abchecken; auschecken	I've got a great tip. *Check out* the new swimming pool in Greenwich.
	worried ['wʌrid]	beunruhigt; besorgt	I feel a bit *worried* about the Maths test next week.
	Cheers! [tʃɪəz]	Danke!	Young people in Britain often say "*Cheers*!" when they want to say "Thanks!" today.
	to **catch** [kætʃ], **caught** [kɔːt], **caught** [kɔːt]	mitbekommen *(ugs.)*; mitkriegen *(ugs.)*	*to catch* = to understand
3	**student exchange** ['stjuːdnt ɪksˌtʃeɪndʒ]	Schüleraustausch	
4	**script** [skrɪpt]	Drehbuch; Skript	The actor didn't want to act in the film because he didn't like the *script*.
	stage direction ['steɪdʒ dɪˌrekʃn]	Regieanweisung	A *stage direction* is an instruction in the script of a play that tells the actors what to do.
	hint [hɪnt]	Hinweis; Andeutung; Tipp	Can't you give me just a little *hint* about my birthday present? Please!
	facial expression [ˌfeɪʃl ɪk'spreʃn]	Gesichtsausdruck	The *facial expression* of people sometimes tells you more than what they say. ***Lat.*** expressio *(f)*
	to the point [tə ðə 'pɔɪnt]	prägnant; treffend	Keep your dialogues short and *to the point*.

Unit 4 What was it like?

Introduction

object ['ɒbdʒɪkt]	Gegenstand	Describe a historical *object*.
What was it like? [ˌwɒt wɒz‿ɪt 'laɪk]	Wie war es?	*What was life like* in the 18th century?
tribe [traɪb]	Stamm; Volksstamm	2,000 years ago, people lived in *tribes*. ***Fr.*** tribu *(f)*

smoky ['sməʊki]	verraucht	This room is very *smoky*. Let's open the window.
BC (= before Christ) [ˌbiːˈsiː]	vor Christus	
empire ['empaɪə]	Reich; Kaiserreich	the Roman *Empire*, the British *Empire*
emperor ['emprə]	Kaiser	*Fr.* empereur *(m)*
underfloor heating *(no pl)* [ˌʌndəflɔː 'hiːtɪŋ]	Fußbodenheizung	The Romans used *underfloor heating* to keep their houses warm.
baths *(pl)* [bɑːθs]	Badehaus; Therme	
AD (= Anno Domini) [ˌeɪ'diː]	nach Christus	*AD* ↔ BC
belt [belt]	Gürtel	
Norman ['nɔːmən]	Normanne/Normannin; normannisch	The *Normans* came to Britain in the 11th century.
lord [lɔːd]	Lord; Herr	
to **grow** [grəʊ], **grew** [gruː], **grown** [grəʊn]	anbauen; züchten	We *grow* vegetables in our garden.
Tudor ['tjuːdə]	Tudor-	
monarch ['mɒnək]	Monarch/-in	*monarchs* = kings and queens
to **found** [faʊnd]	gründen	! to find, found, found (finden) *to found*, *founded*, *founded* (gründen)
to **marry** ['mæri]	heiraten	Henry VIII *married* six times.
daughter ['dɔːtə]	Tochter	How many *daughters* did Henry VIII have? – Two: Mary I and Elizabeth I.
Spanish ['spænɪʃ]	spanisch; Spanisch; die Spanier	During Elizabeth's time as queen, the English defeated the *Spanish* Armada.
golden age [ˌgəʊldn 'eɪdʒ]	goldenes Zeitalter	Queen Elizabeth's time was a *golden age* for art, music and drama.
play [pleɪ]	Theaterstück	William Shakespeare wrote lots of *plays*.
Victorian [vɪk'tɔːriən]	viktorianisch; Viktorianer/-in	The *Victorian* period was in the 19th century.
noisy ['nɔɪzi]	laut	*noisy* → noise
factory ['fæktri]	Fabrik; Werk	Cars, washing machines and cookers are all made in *factories*.
less [les]	weniger	*less* ↔ more
to **experience** [ɪk'spɪəriəns]	erfahren; erleben	*to experience* → experience

History words

Celts	Kelten	people who had come to the British Isles from Europe a long time before the Romans arrived
Roman Empire	Römisches Reich	Rome and the area the Romans had invaded from the 8th century BC to the 7th century AD
Romans	Römer	people who were born in the Roman Empire
Normans	Normannen	people who lived in France and fought against the English in 1066
Church of England		official Christian church in England whose head is the British king or queen
Spanish Armada	spanische Armada	the Spanish navy that attacked England in the 16th century
Henry VIII	(1491–1547)	King of England from 1509 to 1547, King of Ireland from 1541 to 1547
Anne Boleyn	(1501/1507–1536)	second wife of Henry VIII, mother of Elizabeth I
Elizabeth I	(1533–1603)	Queen of England from 1558 to 1603
Elizabethan	elisabethanisch	the time when Elizabeth I ruled
Tudors		family of kings and queens that ruled England and Wales
William Shakespeare	(1564–1616)	famous English writer
Anne Hathaway	(1556–1623)	wife of William Shakespeare
Robert Dudley	(1532–1588)	favourite of Queen Elizabeth I.
Walter Raleigh	(1552/1554–1618)	favourite of Queen Elizabeth I.
Francis Drake	(1540–1596)	English sailor who fought against the Spanish Armada
Queen Victoria	(1819–1901)	Queen of Great Britain from 1837 to 1901
Victorian Age	viktorianisches Zeitalter	the time when Queen Victoria reigned
Industrial Revolution	Industrielle Revolution	the period between 1750 and 1914 when important inventions (e.g. the steam engine) were made

1	**back then** [bæk 'ðen]	damals	My grandparents didn't have smartphones *back then*.
2	to **smell** [smel], **smelt** [smelt], **smelt** [smelt]	riechen; duften	The flowers *smell* beautiful.
3	**calendar** ['kæləndə]	Kalender	You can find all the dates in a *calendar*.
	boot [buːt]	Stiefel	You wear *boots* in winter because they're warmer than shoes.
	axe [æks]	Axt	
	mirror ['mɪrə]	Spiegel	If you look in a *mirror*, you see yourself.
	necklace ['nekləs]	Halskette	A *necklace* is a piece of jewellery.
	sandal ['sændl]	Sandale	*Sandals* are shoes that you wear when it's hot.

	hairbrush ['heəbrʌʃ]	Haarbürste	
4	**generation** [ˌdʒenə'reɪʃn]	Generation	Your parents come from a different *generation*.
	lifestyle ['laɪfstaɪl]	Lebensstil; Lifestyle	

Station 1: He hadn't finished his game

	favourite ['feɪvrɪt]	Favorit/-in; Günstling	Robert Dudley was the queen's *favourite*.
	to **change one's mind** [ˌtʃeɪndʒ wʌnz 'maɪnd]	seine Meinung ändern	I hated the film at first, but now I like it. I've *changed my mind* about it.
	tobacco *(no pl)* [tə'bækəʊ]	Tabak	
	to **taste** [teɪst]	schmecken; probieren	Mmm! This cake *tastes* fantastic!
	stage [steɪdʒ]	Bühne	In Shakespeare's time, only men and boys were allowed to act on *stage*.
	writer ['raɪtə]	Autor/-in; Verfasser/-in	William Shakespeare was a very famous *writer*.
	to **invade** [ɪn'veɪd]	einmarschieren (in); eindringen (in); überfallen	The Spanish tried to *invade* England.
	to **play bowls** [ˌpleɪ 'bəʊlz]	Bowling spielen	
	battle ['bætl]	Schlacht; Kampf	Armies fight in *battles*.
	dress [dres]	Kleid	My sister hates *dresses*. She only wears jeans.
	crown [kraʊn]	Krone	
3	**Celt** [kelt]	Kelte/Keltin	*Celt* → Celtic
4	**everyday** ['evrideɪ]	alltäglich	An *everyday* situation is the kind of thing that happens every day.
	to **grow up** [ˌgrəʊ‿'ʌp]	aufwachsen; erwachsen werden	Shakespeare *grew up* in Stratford-upon-Avon and later moved to London.
	education *(no pl)* [ˌedʒʊ'keɪʃn]	Erziehung; Bildung	*Education* steht immer im Singular. It's important to go to school and get a good *education*.
5	**reign** [reɪn]	Herrschaft; Regierungszeit	Queen Elizabeth I's *reign* was from 1558 to 1603.
6	to **attack** [ə'tæk]	angreifen	Yesterday a cat *attacked* my dog but he wasn't hurt badly.
	slave [sleɪv]	Sklave/Sklavin	
	to **capture** ['kæptʃə]	ergreifen; einfangen	Drake *captured* people in Africa and sold them in America as slaves.

7	**snow** [snəʊ]	Schnee	

Skills: How to talk about history

1	**entertainment** *(no pl)* [ˌentəˈteɪnmənt]	Unterhaltung	The Globe Theatre was used for all kinds of *entertainment*.
	to **reign** [reɪn]	herrschen; regieren	*to reign* → reign
	to **be born** [bi ˈbɔːn]	geboren werden	*to be born* ↔ to die
	to **burn down** [ˌbɜːn ˈdaʊn]	abbrennen; niederbrennen	The first Globe Theatre *burnt down* in 1613.
	to **burn** [bɜːn], **burnt** [bɜːnt], **burnt** [bɜːnt]	brennen; verbrennen	Dry wood *burns* very well.
	to **rebuild** [ˌriːˈbɪld], **rebuilt** [ˌriːˈbɪlt], **rebuilt** [ˌriːˈbɪlt]	wieder aufbauen	The Globe Theatre was *rebuilt* in the 20th century. *to rebuild* → building → to build
	biographical [ˌbaɪəʊˈgræfɪkl]	biografisch	What do we know about his life? How much *biographical* information do we have?
2	**quill** [kwɪl]	Federkiel	In Victorian times people wrote with *quills*.
	feather [ˈfeðə]	Feder	

Describing objects

It's **(very) old/big/small/expensive** …	Es ist (sehr) alt/groß/klein/teuer/…
It **has** …	Es hat …
It's **made of gold/wood** …	Es ist aus Gold/Holz/… (gemacht).
It **looks like** …	Es sieht aus wie …
It **dates back to the year/period** …	Es stammt aus dem Jahr/der Zeit …
People **used it for** …	Man verwendete es für …
We got it from …	Wir haben es von/vom … (bekommen).

Describe a family object you like.

Station 2: If I hadn't talked so much ...

8	**murder** ['mɜ:də]	Mord	The guide told a scary story about a *murder*.
	What luck! [wɒt 'lʌk]	Was für ein Glück!	I lost my mobile but my brother found it. *What luck*!
	blood [blʌd]	Blut	There's *blood* on your T-shirt. Did you hurt yourself?
	dirt [dɜ:t]	Schmutz; Dreck	*dirt* → dirty
	forward ['fɔ:wəd]	vorwärts	Don't turn around. Move *forward*.
	to **pick up** [ˌpɪk‿'ʌp]	aufheben; mitnehmen; abholen	There's a pen on the floor, please *pick* it *up*.
11	**electric** [ɪ'lektrɪk]	elektrisch	*electric* → electricity → electrician
14	**rating** ['reɪtɪŋ]	Kritik	I always look at the *ratings* before I book a hotel.
	detective [dɪ'tektɪv]	Detektiv/-in	! Achtung Betonung.

Unit task: Our historical gallery walk

jewel ['dʒu:əl]	Juwel; Edelstein	*jewel* → jewellery
secret ['si:krət]	geheim	It's *secret*. = It's a secret.
weapon ['wepən]	Waffe	What kind of *weapons* did the Romans fight with?

Story: It's a mystery!

	mystery ['mɪstri]	Mysterium; Rätsel; Geheimnis	
1	**photo shoot** ['fəʊtəʊ ˌʃu:t]	Fotoshooting ; Fotoaufnahmen	
	photographer [fə'tɒgrəfə]	Fotograf/-in	! Achtung Betonung.
	set [set]	Aufnahmeort; Drehort	The *set* is the place where a photo shoot takes place.
	chaos ['keɪɒs]	Chaos; Durcheinander	When everything goes wrong at the same time, there's *chaos*.
	to **mix (up)** [mɪks‿'ʌp]	mischen; vermischen	Don't *mix up* the historical periods.
	lady-in-waiting [ˌleɪdiɪn'weɪtɪŋ]	Hofdame	Queens usually have *ladies-in-waiting*.

Monarchy words

empire	(Kaiser-)Reich
emperor	Kaiser
lord	Adeliger
monarch	Monarch/Monarchin
king/queen	König/Königin
crown	Krone
to reign	regieren; herrschen
lady-in-waiting	Hofdame

Write five sentences about Queen Elizabeth I of England.

1	to **take care of sb** [ˌteɪk‿ˈkeər‿əv]	sich um jmdn. kümmern; für jmdn. sorgen	While my neighbours were on holiday, I *took care* of their cats.
	plaster cast [ˈplɑːstə kɑːst]	Gipsverband	If you break your leg or arm, it has to be put in a *plaster cast*.
	to **zoom in (on)** [ˌzuːm‿ˈɪn ɒn]	heranzoomen (auf)	If the camera *zooms in on* somebody, you get a close-up picture of that person.
	to **roll one's eyes** [ˌrəʊl wʌnz‿ˈaɪz]	die Augen verdrehen	
	shot [ʃɒt]	Aufnahme	*shot* → photo shoot
	nurse [nɜːs]	Krankenschwester; Krankenpfleger	
	boot [buːt]	Kofferraum	I've put all the bags into the *boot* of the car. We're ready to leave now.
	to **drive off** [draɪv‿ˈɒf]	wegfahren	She jumped into the car and *drove off*.
	to **drive** [draɪv], **drove** [drəʊv], **driven** [ˈdrɪvn]	fahren	Who usually *drives* the family car?
	half an hour [ˌhɑːf‿ən‿ˈaʊər]	eine halbe Stunde	*half an hour* = 30 minutes
	out of focus [ˌaʊt‿əv ˈfəʊkəs]	unscharf	The photo was *out of focus* because Gwen didn't stand still.
	to **photobomb** [ˈfəʊtəʊbɒm]	ins Foto laufen	No *photobombing*!
	flash [flæʃ]	Blitz; Lichtblitz	
	to **edit out** [ˌedɪt‿ˈaʊt]	herausschneiden	Jim was able to *edit out* the mistakes in the photo.
	to **crop (a photo)** [krɒp]	(ein Foto) zurechtschneiden	The photo doesn't fit, we'll have to *crop* it.
	to **crash** [kræʃ]	zusammenstoßen	
	ambulance [ˈæmbjələns]	Krankenwagen	! Achtung Betonung.
2	to **lighten** [ˈlaɪtn]	aufhellen	*to lighten* → light
3	**flashback** [ˈflæʃbæk]	Rückblende; Flashback	*Flashbacks* are often used in films and books to show an event that happened in the past.

Action UK! The girl from the past

1	to **afford** [əˈfɔːd]	sich leisten	My grandparents didn't have much money so they could never *afford* to go on holiday.
	I'd rather [aɪd ˈrɑːðə]	ich würde lieber	I don't want to watch the film on TV. *I'd rather* watch it at the cinema.
2	**pawn shop** [ˈpɔːn ʃɒp]	Pfandhaus; Pfandleihe	People who need money sometimes take their jewellery or other expensive things to the *pawn shop*.

school fees ['sku:l fi:z]	Schulgeld; Schulgebühren	In the past, parents had to pay *school fees* to send their children to school. Today most schools are free.
tea bag ['ti: bæg]	Teebeutel	***Fr.*** thé *(m)*
pineapple ['paɪnæpl]	Ananas	
vitamin ['vɪtəmɪn]	Vitamin	
blurred [blɜ:d]	verschwommen; verwischt	In dream sequences, the pictures are often *blurred*.
start [stɑ:t]	Anfang; Start	*start* → to start
to **wake up** [ˌweɪk‿'ʌp], **woke up** [ˌwəʊk‿'ʌp], **woken up** [ˌwəʊkn‿'ʌp]	aufwachen; aufwecken	It's 7:30 and he has just *woken up*.

Text smart 3 Fictional texts

Introduction

1	**teen** [ti:n]	Teenager; Jugendliche/-r	*teen* = teenager
	fiction *(no pl)* ['fɪkʃn]	Erzählliteratur; Prosa	I'd rather read *fiction* than stories about real people.
	plot [plɒt]	Handlung	What happens in the film? What's the *plot*?
	escape [ɪ'skeɪp]	Flucht	Reading is my *escape*.
	series ['sɪəri:z], **series** ['sɪəri:z] *(pl)*	Serie	"Harry Potter" is a *series* of seven books.
	fiction *(no pl)* ['fɪkʃn]	Erfindung; Fiktion	I don't like real stories. I only read *fiction*.
	to **identify with** [aɪ'dentɪfaɪ wɪð]	sich identifizieren mit	I love the book because it's easy to *identify with* the characters.
2	**horror** ['hɒrə]	Horrorgeschichte; Horrorfilm; Horror	
	romance [rə'mæns]	Liebesgeschichte; Liebesfilm	
	genre ['ʒɑ̃:nrə]	Gattung	This film belongs to the horror *genre*.
	detective [dɪ'tektɪv]	Detektivgeschichte; Kriminalroman; Kriminalfilm; Krimi	! Achtung Betonung.
	comedy ['kɒmədi]	Komödie	= a play or film that is written to make the audience laugh
	graphic novel [ˌgræfɪk 'nɒvl]	Bildergeschichte; Comic	

	happy ending [ˌhæpi ˈendɪŋ]	Happy End	My sister only watches films with *happy endings*.
	death [deθ]	Tod	*death* → dead
	violence *(no pl)* [ˈvaɪəlns]	Gewalt	*violence* → violent *Fr.* violence *(f)*
	against all odds [əˌgenst‿ɔːl‿ ˈɒdz]	entgegen allen Erwartungen	The main character survived *against all odds*.
	enemy [ˈenəmi]	Feind/-in	*enemy* ↔ friend
3	**the best ... ever** [ˈbest ˌevə]	der/die/das beste ... überhaupt	It's a fantastic film. For me, it's *the best* film *ever*.

Station 1: Opening lines of a fictional text: Text 1

	among [əˈmʌŋ]	unter; inmitten	! *among ≠ under* He stood *among* his friends. He stood under a tree.
	to **disobey** [ˌdɪsəˈbeɪ]	nicht gehorchen; ungehorsam sein	
	order [ˈɔːdə]	Befehl	I've never disobeyed my parents' *orders*.
	backyard [ˌbækˈjɑːd]	Garten; Hinterhof	My friend's parents have a pond in the *backyard*.
	wood [wʊd]	Wald; Wäldchen	= a small forest
	to **hesitate** [ˈhezɪteɪt]	zögern	She *hesitated* for a few seconds, then she entered the room.
	smoke [sməʊk]	Rauch	*smoke* → smoky
	to **turn** [tɜːn]	drehen; (sich) umdrehen	I *turned* to look for my dog.
	silent [ˈsaɪlənt]	still; ruhig; schweigsam; stumm	If you say nothing, you stay *silent*.
	shadow [ˈʃædəʊ]	Schatten	
4	to **hook** [hʊk]	*hier:* fesseln	Did the story *hook* you?
7	**sense** [sens]	Sinn	With your five *senses* you see, hear, smell, taste and feel.
	to **be in somebody's shoes** [ˌbiː ɪn sʌmbɒdɪz ˈʃuːz]	an jemandes Stelle sein; in jemandes Haut stecken	If I *were in your shoes*, I wouldn't do it. = If I were you, I wouldn't do it.
8	**sharp** [ʃɑːp]	scharf; schneidend	Be careful. This knife is very *sharp*.
	strict [strɪkt]	streng; strikt	The rules at our school are very *strict*.

Station 2: Opening lines of a fictional text: Text 2

	to **drown** [draʊn]	ertrinken; ertränken	The child fell into the pond and nearly *drowned*.
	roaring [ˈrɔːrɪŋ]	dröhnend; tosend; donnernd	There was a *roaring* sound in the air.
	silence *(no pl)* [ˈsaɪləns]	Stille; Schweigen; Ruhe	*silence* → silent *Fr.* silence *(f)*

	It might as well be … [ˌɪt maɪt əs ˈwel biː □]	Es könnte/-n auch … sein.	It's only a few metres away but *it might as well be* kilometres.
	to **sting** [stɪŋ], **stung** [stʌŋ], **stung** [stʌŋ]	stechen	Bees can *sting*.
	the lungs *(pl)* [ðə ˈlʌŋz]	die Lunge	If there's water in your *lungs*, you can't breathe.
	to **be on fire** [ˌbiː‿ɒn ˈfaɪə]	brennen	*to be on fire* = to burn
	to **take a breath** [ˌteɪk‿ə ˈbreθ]	Luft holen; Atem holen	*Take a* deep *breath* and relax.
	to **roar** [rɔː]	dröhnen; brüllen; rauschen; tosen	A lion *roars*. *to roar* → roaring
	to **pray** [preɪ]	beten	A lot of people *pray* before they go to bed.
	to **rise up in one's mind** [raɪz‿ˌʌp ɪn wʌnz ˈmaɪnd]	jmdm. in den Sinn kommen	The thought of my next exam suddenly *rose up in my mind*.
	to **rise** [raɪz], **rose** [rəʊz], **risen** [ˈrɪzn]	steigen; sich erheben	*to rise* = to go up
	mind [maɪnd]	Geist; Verstand	I don't know what he's thinking. I don't know what's going on in his *mind*.
	energy [ˈenədʒi]	Energie; Kraft	*Fr.* énergie *(f)*
	to **sink** [sɪŋk], **sank** [sæŋk], **sunk** [sʌŋk]	untergehen; sinken	
11	**focus** [ˈfəʊkəs]	Blickpunkt; Schwerpunkt; Fokus	*focus* → to focus (on)
	to **have in common** [ˌhæv‿ɪn ˈkɒmən]	gemeinsam haben	Friends usually *have* a lot *in common*.

Options

15	to **step into a story slowly** [step‿ˌɪntʊ ə ˌstɔːri ˈsləʊli]	eine Geschichte langsam entwickeln	I'd rather *step into a story slowly* than jump into it.

Dictionary

In dieser alphabetischen Wortliste findest du das gesamte Vokabular von *Green Line* 1, 2 und 3.
Namen stehen in einer extra Liste am Ende des *Dictionary*.
Einträge, die aus mehreren Wörtern bestehen, kannst du meist unter verschiedenen Stichwörtern nachschlagen. So ist z.B. *after all* unter *after* und unter *all* eingetragen.
Die Fundstellen stehen immer hinter dem jeweiligen Wort und zeigen dir an, wo es zum ersten Mal vorkommt, z.B.:
anger ['æŋgə] Zorn; Wut **III U2**, 37 kommt zum ersten Mal vor in Band 3, Unit 2, Seite 37
air [eə] Luft **III TS1**, 48 kommt zum ersten Mal vor in Band 3, Text smart 2, Seite 48
U = Unit, AC = Across cultures, TS = Text smart
Die mit * gekennzeichneten Verben sind unregelmäßig.
Die mit ° gekennzeichneten Vokabeln sind rezeptiv.
Die mit <> gekennzeichneten Vokabeln sind fakultativ.

A

a [ə] ein/-e **I**
a bit [ə 'bɪt] ein bisschen; ein wenig **II**
a couple of [ə 'kʌpl‿əv] ein paar **I**
a few [ə 'fju:] ein paar; wenige; einige **I**
a girl from Germany [ə ˌgɜ:l frəm 'dʒɜ:məni] ein Mädchen aus Deutschland **I**
a group of three [ə ˌgru:p‿əv 'θri:] eine Dreiergruppe **I**
a little [ə 'lɪtl] ein wenig; etwas **I**
a lot [ə 'lɒt] viel **I**
a lot of [ə 'lɒt‿əv] viel/-e; eine Menge **I**
a lot to learn [ə ˌlɒt tə 'lɜ:n] viel zu lernen **I**
a.m. [ˌeɪ'em] vormittags *(Uhrzeit)* **I**
*to be **able** to (do sth) [bi‿'eɪbl tə] fähig sein zu; können; dürfen **II**
aboard [ə'bɔ:d] an Bord **I**
about [ə'baʊt] ungefähr; circa; etwa **I**
out and **about** [ˌaʊt‿ən‿ə'baʊt] unterwegs **II**
about [ə'baʊt] über; von **I**
What **about** …? ['wɒt‿əbaʊt] Wie wär's mit …?; Was ist mit …? **I**
What is … **about**? [ˌwɒt‿ɪz …‿ə'baʊt] Worum geht es in/im …? **I**
above [ə'bʌv] oben **II**
absolutely [ˌæbsə'lu:tli] absolut; völlig **II**
accent ['æksnt] Akzent **III U1**, 15
accident ['æksɪdnt] Unfall **II**
account settings [ə'kaʊnt ˌsetɪŋz] Profileinstellungen **III U2**, 39
across [ə'krɒs] auf der anderen Seite von; über; hinüber; herüber; quer durch **I**
Across cultures [əˌkrɒs 'kʌltʃəz] Interkulturelles **I**
to **act** [ækt] spielen *(Theater)* **I**
to **act** like ['ækt laɪk] tun als ob **II**
to **act** out [ækt 'aʊt] nachspielen **II**
acting a scene [ˌæktɪŋ‿ə 'si:n] eine Theaterszene spielen **I**
acting ['æktɪŋ] Schauspielen °**III U1**, 21
action ['ækʃn] Handlung; Action; Aktion **I**
active ['æktɪv] aktiv °**III U3**, 61
activity [æk'tɪvəti] Aktivität **I**
actor ['æktə] Schauspieler/-in **II**
actually ['æktʃuəli] tatsächlich; wirklich; eigentlich ⟨**III U3**, 62⟩
AD (= Anno Domini) [ˌeɪ'di:] nach Christus **III U4**, 84
to **add** [æd] hinzufügen; ergänzen **I**
additional [ə'dɪʃnl] zusätzlich **II**
address [ə'dres] Adresse **I**
adjective ['ædʒɪktɪv] Adjektiv; Eigenschaftswort **II**
adult ['ædʌlt] Erwachsene/-r **II**
adventure [əd'ventʃə] Abenteuer **II**
adverb ['ædvɜ:b] Adverb **II**
advert ['ædvɜ:t] Anzeige; Werbespot **III TS1**, 46
advice [əd'vaɪs] Rat; Ratschlag **II**
to **afford** [ə'fɔ:d] sich leisten **III U4**, 99
after ['ɑ:ftə] nach *(zeitlich)* **I**
after all [ˌɑ:ftər‿'ɔ:l] doch; schließlich; immerhin **I**
after that [ˌɑ:ftə 'ðæt] danach **I**
afternoon [ˌɑ:ftə'nu:n] Nachmittag **I**
this **afternoon** [ðɪs 'ɑ:ftənu:n] heute Nachmittag **II**
afterward ['ɑ:ftəwəd] danach; hinterher ⟨**III TS1**, 48⟩
again [ə'gen] wieder; noch einmal; noch mal **I**
over and over **again** [ˌəʊvər‿ən‿ˌəʊvər‿ə'gen] immer wieder **III TS1**, 50
against [ə'genst] gegen **II**
against all odds [əˌgenst‿ɔ:l‿'ɒdz] entgegen allen Erwartungen **III TS3**, 106
age [eɪdʒ] Alter **III U2**, 29
Bronze **Age** ['brɒnz eɪdʒ] Bronzezeit *(ca. 2200–800 v. Chr.)* **III U1**, 14
golden **age** [ˌgəʊldn 'eɪdʒ] goldenes Zeitalter **III U4**, 86
travel **agency** ['trævl‿ˌeɪdʒnsi] Reisebüro **III U3**, 65
travel **agent's** ['trævl‿ˌeɪdʒnts] Reisebüro **III U1**, 11
aggressive [ə'gresɪv] aggressiv **II**
ago [ə'gəʊ] vor *(zeitlich)* **II**
agony aunt ['ægəni‿ˌɑ:nt] Kummerkastentante **II**
to **agree** (on) [ə'gri:] sich einigen (auf) °**III U1**, 17
to **agree** (with) [ə'gri:] einer Meinung sein (mit); zustimmen **II**
to **aim** [eɪm] anstreben; abzielen auf ⟨**III TS2**, 80⟩
air [eə] Luft **III TS1**, 48
airport ['eəpɔ:t] Flughafen **II**
alarm clock [ə'lɑ:m ˌklɒk] Wecker **II**
alien ['eɪliən] Außerirdische/-r; außerirdisches Wesen **I**
alive [ə'laɪv] lebend; am Leben; lebendig ⟨**III TS2**, 80⟩
all [ɔ:l] alle/-s; ganz **I**
after **all** [ˌɑ:ftər‿'ɔ:l] doch; schließlich; immerhin **I**
all day [ˌɔ:l 'deɪ] den ganzen Tag **II**
all night [ˌɔ:l 'naɪt] die ganze Nacht **I**
all over [ˌɔ:l‿'əʊvə] überall (in) **I**
all the time [ˌɔ:l ðə 'taɪm] die ganze Zeit **II**
at **all** [ət‿'ɔ:l] überhaupt **I**
all of them ['ɔ:l‿əv ˌðem] alle **I**
all of us ['ɔ:l‿əv ˌʌs] wir alle **III U1**, 10
bowling **alley** ['bəʊlɪŋ‿ˌæli] Bowlingbahn **I**
*to be **allowed** to (do sth) [bi‿ə'laʊd tə] dürfen **II**
almost ['ɔ:lməʊst] fast; beinahe **II**
alone [ə'ləʊn] allein; ohne fremde Hilfe **I**
along [ə'lɒŋ] entlang **I**
*to sing **along** [ˌsɪŋ‿ə'lɒŋ] mitsingen **III TS1**, 46
alphabet ['ælfəbet] Alphabet **I**
alphabetical [ˌælfə'betɪkl] alphabetisch **II**
already [ɔ:l'redi] schon; bereits **I**
also ['ɔ:lsəʊ] auch **II**
although [ɔ:l'ðəʊ] obwohl ⟨**III TS2**, 80⟩
always ['ɔ:lweɪz] immer; ständig **I**

amazing [ə'meɪzɪŋ] unglaublich; toll; erstaunlich **II**
ambulance ['æmbjələns] Krankenwagen **III U4**, 97
American [ə'merɪkən] Amerikanisch; amerikanisch; aus Amerika; Amerikaner/-in **II**
among [ə'mʌŋ] unter; inmitten **III TS3**, 107
an [ən] ein/-e **I**
and [ænd; ənd] und **I**
anger *(no pl)* ['æŋgə] Zorn; Wut **III U2**, 37
angry ['æŋgri] wütend; zornig; verärgert; böse **I**
*to make sb **angry** [meɪk 'æŋgri] jmdn. wütend machen; jmdn. verärgern **III AC2**, 53
animal ['ænɪməl] Tier **I**
animal shelter ['ænɪml ˌʃeltə] Tierheim **III TS2**, 79
ankle ['æŋkl] Fußgelenk; Fußknöchel **II**
to twist your **ankle** [ˌtwɪst jɔ:r‿'æŋkl] sich den Knöchel verrenken **II**
announcement [ə'naʊnsmənt] Ankündigung; Durchsage **III U1**, 15
anonymous [ən'ɒnɪməs] anonym **II**
another [ə'nʌðə] ein/-e andere/-r/-s; noch ein/-e; ein/-e andere/-r/-s **I**
answer ['ɑ:nsə] Antwort **I**
short **answer** [ˌʃɔ:t‿'ɑ:nsə] Kurzantwort **I**
to **answer** ['ɑ:nsə] antworten; beantworten **I**
to **answer** the phone [ˌɑ:nsə ðə 'fəʊn] einen Anruf entgegennehmen **I**
answering machine ['ɑ:nsrɪŋ məˌʃi:n] Anrufbeantworter **I**
anthem ['ænθəm] Hymne **III U3**, 58
any ['eni] irgendein/-e/-er; irgendwelche **I**
not **any** more [ˌnɒt‿eni 'mɔ:] nicht mehr **I**
not … **any** [nɒt … eni] kein/-e/-en **I**
anyone else [ˌeniwʌn 'els] jemand anderes **II**
Anything else? [ˌeniθɪŋ‿'els] Sonst noch etwas? **I**
not … **anything** [ˌnɒt 'eniθɪŋ] nichts **I**
anyway ['eniweɪ] trotzdem; jedenfalls; sowieso **II**
anywhere ['eniweə] irgendwo; überall (egal, wo) **II**
to **apologise** [ə'pɒlədʒaɪz] sich entschuldigen **III U2**, 39
app [æp] App **II**
apple ['æpl] Apfel **I**
appropriate [ə'prəʊpriət] angemessen °**III AC2**, 53
April ['eɪprəl] April **I**
architect ['ɑ:kɪtekt] Architekt/-in **II**
How **are** you? [ˌhaʊ‿'ɑ: jə] Wie geht es dir?; Wie geht es euch?; Wie geht es Ihnen? **I**
area ['eəriə] Areal; Gebiet; Fläche **II**
run **area** ['rʌn ˌeəriə] Gehege; Auslauf **III TS2**, 77
argument ['ɑ:gjəmənt] Auseinandersetzung; Streit **III U2**, 36; Argument °**III TS3**, 106
arm [ɑ:m] Arm **II**
army ['ɑ:mi] Armee ⟨**III U3**, 58⟩
around [ə'raʊnd] um … herum; umher **I**
to turn **around** [ˌtɜ:n‿(ə)'raʊnd] (sich) umdrehen; wenden **II**
around [ə'raʊnd] ungefähr; gegen ⟨**III TS2**, 80⟩
to **arrange** [ə'reɪndʒ] arrangieren; anordnen °**III U3**, 65
to **arrest** [ə'rest] festnehmen; verhaften **II**
to **arrive** [ə'raɪv] ankommen **III U1**, 12
arrow ['ærəʊ] Pfeil **III TS1**, 48
Art [ɑ:t] Kunstunterricht **I**
art [ɑ:t] Kunst **II**
article ['ɑ:tɪkl] Artikel; Bericht *(in einer Zeitschrift, Zeitung)* **II**
reference **article** ['refrns ˌɑ:tɪkl] Referenzartikel **III TS2**, 76
as [æz; əz] als **II**
as if [əz‿'ɪf] als ob ⟨**III TS1**, 46⟩⌀ °**III U4**, 95
as … **as** [əz … əz] so … wie **I**
as [æz] während; indem **I**; wie **II**
as soon **as** [əz 'su:n‿əz] sobald **II**
Asian ['eɪʒn] asiatisch ⟨**III TS2**, 80⟩
to **ask** [ɑ:sk] fragen; bitten **I**
Ask about … ['ɑ:sk‿əˌbaʊt] Frage/Fragt nach … **I**
to **ask** for ['ɑ:sk fə] fragen nach; bitten um **I**
*to be **asleep** [ˌbi ə'sli:p] schlafen **II**
*to fall **asleep** [ˌfɔ:l‿ə'sli:p] einschlafen **I**
assembly [ə'sembli] Versammlung; Morgenappell **II**
assistant [ə'sɪstnt] Assistent/-in; Verkäufer/-in **II**
at [æt; ət] in; auf; bei; an; um *(bei Uhrzeitangaben)* **I**
at 7:30 [ət ˌsevn‿'θɜ:ti] um halb acht **I**
at all [ət‿'ɔ:l] überhaupt **I**
at first [ət 'fɜ:st] zuerst; zunächst **II**
at home [ət 'həʊm] zu Hause **I**
at last [ət 'lɑ:st] endlich; schließlich **I**
at least [ət 'li:st] mindestens; wenigstens **II**
at the back of [ət ðə 'bæk‿əv] hinten; am Ende; im hinteren Teil **II**
at the moment [ət ðə 'məʊmənt] im Moment; gerade **I**
at the same time [ət ðə ˌseɪm 'taɪm] zur selben Zeit; gleichzeitig **I**
at the weekend [ət ðə ˌwi:k'end] am Wochenende **I**
atlas ['ætləs] Atlas **II**
atmosphere ['ætməsfɪə] Atmosphäre; Stimmung **II**
to **attack** [ə'tæk] angreifen **III U4**, 90
attention [ə'tenʃn] Aufmerksamkeit; Beachtung **II**
*to pay **attention** to sb/sth [ˌpeɪ‿ə'tenʃn tʊ] jmdn./etw. beachten **III U2**, 37
attic ['ætɪk] Dachboden **II**
attraction [ə'trækʃn] Attraktion; Sehenswürdigkeit **II**
audience ['ɔ:diəns] Publikum **II**
audio ['ɔ:diəʊ] Audio-; Hör- **I**
audio tour ['ɔ:diəʊ ˌtʊə] Audioführung **II**
audio-visual effect [ˌɔ:diəʊvɪʒuəl ɪ'fekt] audiovisueller Effekt **II**
audition [ɔ:'dɪʃn] Vorsprechen; Vorsingen; Vortanzen **III U2**, 31
August ['ɔ:gəst] August **I**
aunt [ɑ:nt] Tante **I**
agony **aunt** ['ægəni‿ɑ:nt] Kummerkastentante **II**
Australian [ɒs'treɪliən] australisch; Australier/-in **III TS2**, 79
author ['ɔ:θə] Autor/-in °**III TS1**, 51
autumn ['ɔ:təm] Herbst ⟨**III U3**, 58⟩
to **avoid** [ə'vɔɪd] vermeiden; meiden; aus dem Weg gehen **III TS2**, 77
award [ə'wɔ:d] Auszeichnung; Preis **II**
away [ə'weɪ] weg **I**
right **away** [ˌraɪt‿ə'weɪ] sofort; gleich **I**
*to run **away** [ˌrʌn‿ə'weɪ] wegrennen **I**
straight **away** [ˌstreɪt‿ə'weɪ] sofort; gleich °**III TS2**, 79
*to throw **away** [ˌθrəʊ‿ə'weɪ] wegwerfen **I**
awful ['ɔ:fl] schrecklich; furchtbar **I**
axe [æks] Axt **III U4**, 86

B

baby ['beɪbi] Baby; Säugling **I**
back [bæk] Rückseite; Rücken °**III U1**, 17
at the **back** of [ət ðə 'bæk‿əv] hinten; am Ende; im hinteren Teil **II**
back to **back** [ˌbæk tʊ 'bæk] Rücken an Rücken **I**
back [bæk] zurück **I**
back then [bæk 'ðen] damals **III U4**, 84
*to go right **back** to [ˌgəʊ raɪt 'bæk tə] zurückgehen auf **III U1**, 18
to turn **back** [tɜ:n 'bæk] umkehren; zurückgehen **II**
backache ['bækeɪk] Rückenschmerzen; Rückenweh **II**
background ['bækgraʊnd] Hintergrund **I**
backing ['bækɪŋ] Hintergrund-; Background- **III U2**, 28
backing dancer ['bækɪŋ ˌdɑ:nsə] Backgroundtänzer/-in **III U2**, 28
backpack ['bækpæk] Rucksack **III U3**, 56
backyard [bæk'jɑ:d] Garten; Hinterhof **III TS3**, 107
bacon ['beɪkn] Schinkenspeck; Speck **I**
bad [bæd] schlecht; böse; schlimm *(ugs.)* **I**
Too **bad**! [ˌtu: 'bæd] Zu dumm!; Schade! **I**
badminton ['bædmɪntən] Badminton **I**

bag [bæg] Tasche; Tüte **I**
tea **bag** ['ti: bæg] Teebeutel **III U4**, 99
bagpipes *(pl)* ['bægpaɪps] Dudelsack **III U3**, 55
baked beans *(pl)* [ˌbeɪkt 'bi:nz] weiße Bohnen in Tomatensoße **I**
ball [bɔ:l] Ball **I**
*to keep the **ball** bouncing [ˌki:p ðə bɔ:l 'baʊntsɪŋ] *hier:* das Gespräch am Laufen halten **III AC3**, 82
to **ban** [bæn] bannen; verbieten; sperren **III U3**, 60
banana [bə'nɑ:nə] Banane **I**
band [bænd] Band; Musikgruppe **III U3**, 56
Bang! [bæŋ] Peng! **II**
banjo ['bændʒəʊ] Banjo ⟨**III TS1**, 47⟩
bank [bæŋk] Ufer **II**
word **bank** ['wɜ:d ˌbæŋk] Wortsammlung °**III TS1**, 50
snack **bar** ['snæk ˌbɑ:] Café; Imbissstube **I**
bare [beə] nackt; bloß **III TS1**, 47
barely ['beəli] kaum ⟨**III TS3**, 107⟩
bargain ['bɑ:gɪn] Schnäppchen **I**
to **bark** [bɑ:k] bellen **I**
basic ['beɪsɪk] grundlegend; Grund- **II**
basics *(pl)* ['beɪsɪks] Grundlagen °**III TS1**, 47
basketball ['bɑ:skɪtbɔ:l] Basketball **I**
bath [bɑ:θ] Bad; Badewanne **I**
baths *(pl)* [bɑ:θs] Badehaus; Therme **III U4**, 84
bathroom ['bɑ:θrʊm] Bad; Badezimmer **I**
battery ['bætri] Batterie; Akku **II**
battle ['bætl] Schlacht; Kampf **III U4**, 88
BC (= before Christ) [ˌbi:'si:] vor Christus **III U4**, 84
*to **be** [bi:] sein **I**
*to **be** able to (do sth) [bi‿'eɪbl tə] fähig sein zu; können; dürfen **II**
*to **be** about [bi:‿ə'baʊt] sich handeln um **I**
*to **be** allowed to (do sth) [bi‿ə'laʊd tə] dürfen **II**
*to **be** asleep [ˌbi ə'sli:p] schlafen **II**
*to **be** born [bi 'bɔ:n] geboren werden **III U4**, 91
*to **be** called [bi 'kɔ:ld] heißen; genannt werden °**III TS1**, 51
*to **be** called to do sth [bi 'kɔ:ld tə du:] auserwählt sein, etw. zu tun **III TS1**, 49
*to **be** connected [bi kə'nektɪd] zusammenhängen; in Zusammenhang stehen **II**
*to **be** fed up (with) [bi fed‿'ʌp wɪð] sauer sein (auf); die Nase voll haben (von) **III U2**, 36
*to **be** gone [bi: 'gɒn] verschwunden sein; weg sein **II**
*to **be** good at [bi: 'gʊd‿ət] gut sein in **I**
*to **be** grounded [bi 'graʊndɪd] Hausarrest haben **III U2**, 36
*to **be** hard on sb [bi 'hɑ:d‿ɒn] streng mit jmdm. sein **III U2**, 33
*to **be** in [bi‿'ɪn] dabei sein; mitmachen **II**
*to **be** in charge (of) [bi‿ɪn 'tʃɑ:dʒ‿əv] die Verantwortung tragen (für); zuständig sein (für) **III U2**, 32
*to **be** in sb's shoes [ˌbi: ɪn sʌmbɒdɪz 'ʃu:z] an jmds. Stelle sein; in jmds. Haut stecken **III TS3**, 108
*to **be** in the way [bi:‿ɪn ðə 'weɪ] im Weg sein/stehen **I**
*to **be** interested in [bi‿'ɪntrəstɪd‿ɪn] interessiert sein an; sich interessieren für **II**
*to **be** into [bi:‿'ɪntə] mögen; stehen auf **I**
*to **be** jealous (of) [bi: 'dʒeləs] eifersüchtig sein (auf); neidisch sein (auf) **I**
*to **be** late [bi: 'leɪt] zu spät dran sein; zu spät kommen **I**
*to **be** like [bi 'laɪk] sein **III U3**, 54
*to **be** lucky [bi‿'lʌki] Glück haben **II**
*to **be** made of [bi 'meɪd‿əv] bestehen aus **III TS1**, 49
*to **be** on [bi‿'ɒn] an sein; laufen **II**
*to **be** on fire [ˌbi:‿ɒn 'faɪə] brennen **III TS3**, 109
*to **be** right [bi 'raɪt] recht haben **I**
*to **be** scared (of) [bi: 'skeəd‿əv] Angst haben (vor) **I**
*to **be** sorry [bi: 'sɒri] leid tun **I**
*to **be** stressed out [bi ˌstrest‿'aʊt] völlig gestresst sein **III U2**, 28
*to **be** supposed to (do) [bi sə'pəʊzd tə] (tun) sollen ⟨**III TS1**, 49⟩
*to **be** surprised [bi sə'praɪzd] überrascht sein **II**
*to **be** trapped [bi 'træpt] eingeschlossen sein; in der Falle sitzen °**III U3**, 68
*to **be** unlucky [bi:‿ʌn'lʌki] Pech haben **I**
*to **be** up to [bi‿'ʌp tə] vorhaben **II**
*to **be** used to *(+ -ing)* [bi 'ju:s‿tə] gewöhnt sein an; gewohnt sein **III AC2**, 53
*to **be** worried [bi 'wʌrid] beunruhigt sein; besorgt sein **II**
*to **be** worth [bi: 'wɜ:θ] wert sein **I**
*to **be** wrong [bi: 'rɒŋ] unrecht haben; sich irren **I**
Be careful! [bi: 'keəfl] Vorsicht!; Pass/Passt auf! **I**
Be polite. [bi: pə'laɪt] Sei/Seid höflich. **I**
Here you **are**. [ˌhɪə ju‿'ɑ:] Bitte schön. **I**
How **are** you? [ˌhaʊ‿'ɑ: jə] Wie geht es dir?; Wie geht es euch?; Wie geht es Ihnen? **I**
How much **is/are** …? [ˌhaʊ 'mʌtʃ‿ɪz/ɑ:] Wie viel (kostet/kosten) …? **I**
I'**m** from … [ˌaɪm frɒm] Ich bin aus … **I**
Is this how you (do) …? [ɪz 'ðɪs haʊ jʊ ˌdu:] Machst du so …? **I**
beach [bi:tʃ] Strand **II**
baked **beans** *(pl)* [ˌbeɪkt 'bi:nz] weiße Bohnen in Tomatensoße **I**
bear [beə] Bär **II**
*to **beat** [bi:t] schlagen; besiegen **II**
beautiful ['bju:tɪfl] schön; hübsch; wunderbar **II**
because [bɪ'kɒz] weil; da **I**
because of [bɪ'kɒz‿əv] wegen **II**
*to **become** [bɪ'kʌm] werden **II**
*to **become** extinct [bɪˌkʌm‿ɪk'stɪŋkt] aussterben **III TS2**, 80
bed [bed] Bett **I**
*to go to **bed** [ˌgəʊ tə 'bed] ins Bett gehen **I**
bedroom ['bedrʊm] Schlafzimmer **I**
bee [bi:] Biene **II**
Beefeater ['bi:fˌi:tə] königlicher Leibgardist **II**
before [bɪ'fɔ:] schon einmal; vorher; zuvor **II**
before [bɪ'fɔ:] vor *(zeitlich)*; bevor **I**
*to **begin** [bɪ'gɪn] beginnen; anfangen **II**
beginning [bɪ'gɪnɪŋ] Anfang; Beginn **II**
to **behave** [bɪ'heɪv] sich benehmen; sich verhalten **III U2**, 32
behind [bɪ'haɪnd] hinter **I**
*to leave **behind** [ˌli:v‿bɪ'haɪnd] zurücklassen **III U3**, 61
to **believe** [bɪ'li:v] glauben **I**
He couldn't **believe** his eyes. [hi ˌkʊdnt bɪˌli:v hɪz‿'aɪz] Er traute seinen Augen nicht. **II**
bell [bel] Glocke **II**
saved by the **bell** [ˌseɪvd baɪ ðə 'bel] noch mal Glück gehabt **III U2**, 32
to **belong** (to) [bɪ'lɒŋ (tə)] gehören (zu) **II**
below [bɪ'ləʊ] unterhalb; unten **I**
belt [belt] Gürtel **III U4**, 85
bench [benʃ] Bank; Sitzbank **III U2**, 39
beneath [bɪ'ni:θ] unter; unterhalb ⟨**III TS3**, 107⟩
beside [bɪ'saɪd] neben ⟨**III TS1**, 49⟩
besides [bɪ'saɪdz] neben **III U1**, 14
(the) **best** [best] (der/die/das) Beste **II**
best [best] beste/-r/-s; am besten **I**
Best wishes [ˌbest 'wɪʃɪz] Viele Grüße; Herzliche Grüße **III U1**, 13
the **best** … ever ['best … ˌevə] der/die/das beste … überhaupt **III TS3**, 106
I **bet** [aɪ 'bet] ich wette **II**
better ['betə] besser; lieber **I**
between [bɪ'twi:n] zwischen **I**
in **between** [ˌɪn bɪ'twi:n] dazwischen °**III TS1**, 51
bicycle motocross [ˌbaɪsɪkl 'məʊtəʊkrɒs] Fahrradmotocross **II**
big [bɪg] groß **I**
bike [baɪk] Fahrrad **I**
mountain **biking** ['maʊntɪn ˌbaɪkɪŋ] Mountainbikefahren **III U1**, 9
bilingual [baɪ'lɪŋgwl] zweisprachig **II**

billion ['bɪliən] Milliarde **III U2**, 29
biographical [ˌbaɪəʊ'græfɪkl] biografisch **III U4**, 91
bird [bɜ:d] Vogel **II**
birdwatching ['bɜ:dˌwɒtʃɪŋ] Vogelbeobachtung **II**
birthday ['bɜ:θdeɪ] Geburtstag **I**
Happy **Birthday**! [ˌhæpi 'bɜ:θdeɪ] Alles Gute zum Geburtstag!; Herzlichen Glückwunsch zum Geburtstag! **I**
biscuit ['bɪskɪt] Keks **I**
wee **bit** ['wi: bɪt] klitzeklein ⟨**III U3**, 58⟩
a **bit** [ə 'bɪt] ein bisschen; ein wenig **II**
*to **bite** [baɪt] beißen **II**
black [blæk] schwarz **I**
*to go **black** [ˌgəʊ 'blæk] schwarz werden **II**
building **block** ['bɪldɪŋ blɒk] Baustein **II**
to **block** [blɒk] blockieren; abblocken **II**
blog [blɒg] Blog; Internettagebuch **III TS2**, 79
bloke *(fam)* [bləʊk] Typ *(ugs.)* **III U2**, 36
blond [blɒnd] blond **III U2**, 36
blood [blʌd] Blut **III U4**, 92
*to **blow** out [ˌbləʊ‿'aʊt] ausblasen; auspusten **I**
blue [blu:] blau **I**
blurred [blɜ:d] verschwommen; verwischt **III U4**, 99
BMX [ˌbi:em'eks] BMX **II**
board [bɔ:d] Brett; Tafel **III TS1**, 46
tourist **board** ['tʊərɪst bɔ:d] Touristeninformation **III U1**, 13
boat [bəʊt] Boot **I**
boating lake ['bəʊtɪŋ ˌleɪk] See zum Rudern **I**
body ['bɒdi] Körper **III U2**, 27
human **body** [ˌhju:mən 'bɒdi] menschlicher Körper **II**
bold [bəʊld] fett gedruckt °**III U4**, 91
bonfire ['bɒnfaɪə] Lagerfeuer; Freudenfeuer **I**
book [bʊk] Buch **I**
exercise **book** ['eksəsaɪz ˌbʊk] Übungsheft **I**
to **book** [bʊk] buchen; reservieren **III U1**, 12
to **boom** [bu:m] dröhnen **III U1**, 18
boot [bu:t] Stiefel **III U4**, 86; Kofferraum **III U4**, 97
bored [bɔ:d] gelangweilt **I**
boring ['bɔ:rɪŋ] langweilig **I**
*to be **born** [bi 'bɔ:n] geboren werden **III U4**, 91
to **borrow** ['bɒrəʊ] (sich) ausleihen **II**
boss [bɒs] Boss; Chef **III U2**, 36
bossy ['bɒsi] herrisch; rechthaberisch **III U2**, 32
both [bəʊθ] beide **II**
bottle ['bɒtl] Flasche **I**
to **bounce** [baʊnts] springen; hüpfen **III AC3**, 82
*to keep the ball **bouncing** [ˌki:p ðə bɔ:l 'baʊntsɪŋ] *hier:* das Gespräch am Laufen halten **III AC3**, 82
to **bow** out [bəʊ‿'aʊt] sich verabschieden ⟨**III TS3**, 109⟩
bowl [bəʊl] Schale; Schälchen; Schüssel **I**
to play **bowls** [ˌpleɪ 'bəʊlz] Bowling spielen **III U4**, 88
bowling alley ['bəʊlɪŋ‿ˌæli] Bowlingbahn **I**
box [bɒks] Box; Kasten; Schachtel; Kiste **I**
boxing ['bɒksɪŋ] Boxen **II**
round of **boxing** [ˌraʊnd‿əv 'bɒksɪŋ] Boxrunde **II**
boy [bɔɪ] Junge **I**
cabin **boy** ['kæbɪn ˌbɔɪ] Schiffsjunge **I**
bracelet ['breɪslət] Armband **I**
bracket ['brækɪt] Klammer °**III U1**, 15
brave [breɪv] mutig; tapfer **I**
bread [bred] Brot **I**
bread roll ['bred rəʊl] Brötchen **III AC2**, 52
break [breɪk] Pause **II**
half-term **break** [ˌhɑ:ftɜ:m 'breɪk] Halbjahresferien **I**
lunch **break** ['lʌnʃbreɪk] Mittagspause **I**
*to **break** [breɪk] brechen; zerbrechen **I**
broken ['brəʊkn] gebrochen; kaputt **I**
breakfast ['brekfəst] Frühstück **I**
*to have **breakfast** [ˌhæv 'brekfəst] frühstücken **I**
breath [breθ] Atem; Atemzug **III TS3**, 109
*to take a **breath** [ˌteɪk‿ə 'breθ] Luft holen; Atem holen **III TS3**, 109
Take a deep **breath**. [ˌteɪk‿ə ˌdi:p 'breθ] Atme(t) tief ein. **II**
to **breathe** [bri:ð] atmen **II**
bridge [brɪdʒ] Brücke **II**
*to **bring** [brɪŋ] bringen; mitbringen **I**
on the **brink** of [ˌɒn ðə 'brɪŋk‿əv] am Rande von; kurz vor **III TS2**, 80
British ['brɪtɪʃ] britisch; Brite/Britin **I**
brochure ['brəʊʃə] Broschüre; Prospekt **I**
broken ['brəʊkn] gebrochen; kaputt **I**
Bronze Age ['brɒnz eɪdʒ] Bronzezeit *(ca. 2200–800 v. Chr.)* **III U1**, 14
brother ['brʌðə] Bruder **I**
brown [braʊn] braun **I**
bucket ['bʌkɪt] Eimer **II**
*to **build** [bɪld] bauen **II**; aufbauen °**III TS3**, 108
*to **build** up [ˌbɪld‿'ʌp] aufbauen; *hier:* zunehmen ⟨**III TS2**, 77⟩
building ['bɪldɪŋ] Gebäude **I**
building block ['bɪldɪŋ blɒk] Baustein **II**
cyber **bully** [ˌsaɪbə 'bʊli] *jemand, der andere in sozialen Netzwerken belästigt oder mobbed* **II**
*to give the **bumps** [ˌgɪv ðə 'bʌmps] hochleben lassen **I**
burger ['bɜ:gə] Hamburger **I**
*to **burn** [bɜ:n] brennen; verbrennen **III U4**, 91
*to **burn** down [ˌbɜ:n 'daʊn] abbrennen; niederbrennen **III U4**, 91
burnt [bɜ:nt] verbrannt ⟨**III TS2**, 79⟩
*to **burst** [bɜ:st] bersten; platzen ⟨**III TS3**, 109⟩
bus [bʌs] Bus **I**
bus station ['bʌs ˌsteɪʃn] Busbahnhof **I**
bush [bʊʃ] Busch *(Buschlandschaft)*; Wildnis **III TS2**, 79
business ['bɪznɪs] Geschäft; Business **III U2**, 29
busy ['bɪzi] belebt; beschäftigt **I**
but [bʌt] aber **I**
butter ['bʌtə] Butter **III AC2**, 52
*to **buy** [baɪ] kaufen **I**
buyer ['baɪə] Käufer/-in **I**
by [baɪ] bei; neben; an **III U1**, 18; von **III U3**, 60
by *(bike)* [baɪ] mit *(dem Fahrrad)* **I**
by the river [baɪ ðə 'rɪvə] am Fluss **II**
Bye! [baɪ] Tschüss! **II**

C

cabin boy ['kæbɪn ˌbɔɪ] Schiffsjunge **I**
cache [kæʃ] Cache **III U1**, 18
café ['kæfeɪ] Café **I**
cafeteria [ˌkæfə'tɪəriə] Cafeteria **I**
cake [keɪk] Kuchen; Torte **I**
calendar ['kæləndə] Kalender **III U4**, 86
(phone) **call** ['fəʊn ˌkɔ:l] Anruf; Telefonanruf **I**
to **call** [kɔ:l] nennen; anrufen; rufen **I**
*to be **called** [bi 'kɔ:ld] heißen; genannt werden °**III TS1**, 51
*to be **called** to do sth [bi 'kɔ:ld tə du:] auserwählt sein, etw. zu tun **III TS1**, 49
caller ['kɔ:lə] Anrufer/-in **I**
call-in ['kɔ:lɪn] *Sendung, bei der sich das Publikum telefonisch beteiligen kann* **III U2**, 27
to **calm** down [ˌkɑ:m 'daʊn] sich beruhigen **II**
camel racing ['kæml ˌreɪsɪŋ] Kamelrennen **II**
camera ['kæmrə] Fotoapparat; Kamera **II**
caught on **camera** [ˌkɔ:t‿ɒn 'kæmrə] ertappt; mit der Kamera festgehalten **II**
summer **camp** ['sʌmə kæmp] Sommerferienlager **II**
to **camp** [kæmp] campen; zelten **III U1**, 20
to **campaign** (for) [kæm'peɪn fɔ:] demonstrieren (für); aufmerksam machen (auf); sich engagieren (für) **III U3**, 57
camping ['kæmpɪŋ] Camping; Zelten **II**
can [kæn] Dose; Büchse **I**
tin **can** ['tɪn kæn] Blechdose **III U3**, 69
can [kæn; kən] können; dürfen **I**
can't [kɑ:nt] kann nicht; können nicht **I**
Can you name …? ['kæn jʊ ˌneɪm] Kannst du … nennen? **I**
candle ['kændl] Kerze **I**

candlelight *(no pl)* ['kændlaɪt] Kerzenlicht **II**
cannot ['kænɒt] kann nicht; können nicht **II**
capital ['kæpɪtl] Hauptstadt **II**
capital letter [ˌkæpɪtl 'letə] Großbuchstabe **I**
captain ['kæptɪn] Kapitän/-in; Mannschaftsführer/-in **I**
caption ['kæpʃn] Bildunterschrift; Untertitel °**III U4**, 85
to capture ['kæptʃə] ergreifen; einfangen **III U4**, 90
car [kɑ:] Auto **I**
card [kɑ:d] Karte; Spielkarte **I**
prompt **card** ['prɒmpt kɑ:d] Stichwortkarte; Rollenkarte **II**
*to take care of sb [ˌteɪk‿'keər‿əv] sich um jmdn. kümmern; für jmdn. sorgen **III U4**, 96
to care (about) ['keər‿əˌbaʊt] wichtig nehmen; sich kümmern (um); sich interessieren (für) **II**
career [kə'rɪə] Beruf; Laufbahn; Karriere **III U2**, 28
careful ['keəfl] vorsichtig; sorgfältig **II**
Be **careful**! [bi: 'keəfl] Vorsicht!; Pass/Passt auf! **I**
carnival ['kɑ:nɪvl] Karneval **II**
carpet ['kɑ:pɪt] Teppich **II**
carrot ['kærət] Karotte; Möhre **I**
to carry ['kæri] tragen **III AC1**, 25
cartoon [kɑ:'tu:n] Cartoon; Zeichentrickfilm **III AC3**, 82
plaster cast ['plɑ:stə kɑ:st] Gipsverband **III U4**, 96
castle ['kɑ:sl] Schloss; Burg **II**
cat [kæt] Katze **I**
*to catch [kætʃ] fangen **II**; mitbekommen *(ugs.)*; mitkriegen *(ugs.)* **III AC3**, 82
catchy ['kætʃi] eingängig; einprägsam **III TS1**, 50
category ['kætəgri] Kategorie; Klasse **II**
caught on camera [ˌkɔ:t‿ɒn 'kæmrə] ertappt; mit der Kamera festgehalten **II**
to cause [kɔ:z] verursachen **II**
'cause [kɒz] weil; da ⟨**III TS1**, 49⟩
cave [keɪv] Höhle **III U1**, 21
ceilidh ['keɪli] *schottisches Fest, bei dem getanzt und musiziert wird* ⟨**III U3**, 62⟩
to celebrate ['seləbreɪt] feiern **I**
celebration [ˌselə'breɪʃn] Feier ⟨**III U2**, 31⟩
celebrity [sə'lebrəti] Prominente/-r; berühmte Person **III TS2**, 79
Celt [kelt] Kelte/Keltin **III U4**, 89
Celtic ['keltɪk; 'seltɪk] keltisch **II**
cent [sent] Cent *(Währung)* **I**
central ['sentrl] zentral; Zentral- **II**
centre ['sentə] Zentrum; Center **I**
community **centre** [kə'mju:nəti ˌsentə] Gemeindezentrum **I**
leisure **centre** ['leʒə ˌsentə] Freizeitzentrum **I**
tourist information **centre** [ˌtʊərɪst ɪnfə'meɪʃn ˌsentə] Touristeninformation **I**
century ['senʃri] Jahrhundert **II**
cereal *(no pl)* ['sɪəriəl] Frühstückszerealie; Getreideprodukt *(z. B. Cornflakes oder Müsli)* **I**
chair [tʃeə] Stuhl; Sessel **I**
challenge ['tʃælɪndʒ] Herausforderung **II**
champion ['tʃæmpiən] Gewinner/-in; Sieger/-in; Champion **III TS1**, 50
chance [tʃɑ:ns] Chance; Gelegenheit; Möglichkeit **II**
change [tʃeɪndʒ] Änderung; Veränderung; Wechsel **III U1**, 19
to change [tʃeɪndʒ] wechseln; (sich) ändern **II**
to **change** one's mind [ˌtʃeɪndʒ wʌnz 'maɪnd] seine Meinung ändern **III U4**, 88
to change (onto) [tʃeɪndʒ ('ɒntʊ)] umsteigen (in) **II**
chant [tʃɑ:nt] Sprechgesang **II**
chaos ['keɪɒs] Chaos; Durcheinander **III U4**, 96
chapter ['tʃæptə] Kapitel °**III TS3**, 107
character ['kærəktə] Charakter; Figur **I**
*to be in charge (of) [bi‿ɪn 'tʃɑ:dʒ‿əv] die Verantwortung tragen (für); zuständig sein (für) **III U2**, 32
charity ['tʃærɪti] Wohltätigkeitsverein; wohltätige Zwecke; Wohlfahrt **I**
charity shop ['tʃærɪti ʃɒp] Second-Hand-Laden **I**
lucky charm [ˌlʌki 'tʃɑ:m] Glücksbringer; Talisman **I**
chart [tʃɑ:t] Tabelle ⟨**III TS2**, 77⟩
to chase [tʃeɪs] jagen; nachjagen **I**
chat [ˌtʃæt] Chat **III U3**, 58
chat room ['tʃæt rʊm] Chatroom **II**
video **chat** ['vɪdiəʊ ˌtʃæt] Videochat **II**
to chat [tʃæt] plaudern; chatten *(sich online unterhalten)* **I**
cheap [tʃi:p] billig; preiswert **I**
to check [tʃek] überprüfen; prüfen; kontrollieren **I**
to **check** out *(coll)* [ˌtʃek‿'aʊt] prüfen; abchecken; auschecken **III AC3**, 82
Check-in ['tʃekɪn] Einchecken **I**
checklist ['tʃeklɪst] Checkliste **II**
Check-out ['tʃekaʊt] Auschecken **I**
to cheer [tʃɪə] anfeuern; jubeln; zujubeln **II**
to **cheer** sb up [ˌtʃɪər‿'ʌp] jmdn. aufheitern **III U2**, 39
Cheers! [tʃɪəz] Danke! **III AC3**, 82
cheese [tʃi:z] Käse **I**
to cherish ['tʃerɪʃ] schätzen ⟨**III TS1**, 46⟩
chess [tʃes] Schach **II**
chicken ['tʃɪkɪn] Huhn; Hähnchen **I**
chicken tikka masala [ˌtʃɪkɪn ˌtɪkə mə'sɑ:lə] *indisches Hühnchengericht* **I**
child, children *(pl)* ['tʃaɪld; 'tʃɪldrən] Kind **I**
only **child** ['əʊnli ˌtʃaɪld] Einzelkind **I**
to chill out [tʃɪl‿'aʊt] chillen **III U2**, 36
chimney ['tʃɪmni] Kamin; Schornstein **III U1**, 18
chips *(pl) (BE)* [tʃɪps] Pommes frites **I**
chlorine *(no pl)* ['klɔ:ri:n] Chlor ⟨**III TS3**, 109⟩
chocolate ['tʃɒklət] Schokolade **I**
choice [tʃɔɪs] Wahl; Auswahl **II**
*to choose [tʃu:z] auswählen; wählen **II**
chorus ['kɔ:rəs] Refrain °**III TS1**, 49
Christmas ['krɪsməs] Weihnachten **I**
church [θʃʔ:tʃ] Kirche **I**
cinema ['sɪnəmə] Kino **I**
circle ['sɜ:kl] Kreis; Ring **I**
*to go round in **circles** [gəʊ ˌraʊnd ɪn 'sɜ:klz] sich im Kreis drehen **III U3**, 66
city ['sɪti] Stadt; Großstadt **I**
clan [klæn] Clan; Sippe; Stamm ⟨**III U3**, 63⟩
to clap [klæp] klatschen **I**
Clap your hands. [ˌklæp jɔ: 'hændz] Klatsch/Klatscht in die Hände. **I**
class [klɑ:s] Klasse; Schulklasse **I**; *hier:* Unterricht **II**
class display ['klɑ:s dɪˌspleɪ] Ausstellung in der Klasse **I**
class poster ['klɑ:s ˌpəʊstə] Klassenposter **I**
classmate ['klɑ:smeɪt] Klassenkamerad/-in; Mitschüler/-in **I**
classroom ['klɑ:srʊm] Klassenzimmer **I**
contact clause ['kɒntækt ˌklɔ:z] *Relativsatz ohne Relativpronomen* **II**
defining relative **clause** [dɪˌfaɪnɪŋ 'relətɪv ˌklɔ:z] notwendiger Relativsatz **II**
if-**clause** ['ɪfˌklɔ:z] if-Satz °**III U1**, 14
main **clause** ['meɪn ˌklɔ:z] Hauptsatz °**III U1**, 14
clay pipe ['kleɪ paɪp] Tonpfeife **II**
to clean [kli:n] säubern; reinigen **I**
clean [kli:n] sauber **III TS2**, 77
to clear out [ˌklɪər‿'aʊt] ausräumen; entrümpeln **I**
clear [klɪə] klar; deutlich **I**
clever ['klevə] schlau; klug **II**
click [klɪk] Klicken; Klick **II**
to click on ['klɪk‿ɒn] anklicken **III U1**, 12
cliff [klɪf] Klippe; Kliff **III U3**, 64
climax ['klaɪmæks] Höhepunkt °**III U3**, 68
to climb [klaɪm] klettern; besteigen; steigen **I**
climbing ['klaɪmɪŋ] Klettern **II**
clock [klɒk] Uhr **I**
alarm **clock** [ə'lɑ:m ˌklɒk] Wecker **II**
o'**clock** [ə'klɒk] Uhr *(Zeitangabe bei vollen Stunden)* **I**
to clone [kləʊn] klonen **III U3**, 60
close [kləʊs] schmaler Durchgang **III U3**, 61
to close [kləʊz] schließen; zumachen **I**

close [kləʊs] eng; knapp **I**; nahe **II**
Look **closely** … [ˌlʊk 'kləʊsli] Schau(t) genau … **II**
That was **close**! [ˌðæt wɒz 'kləʊs] Das war knapp! **I**
close-up ['kləʊsʌp] Nahaufnahme **II**
clothes *(pl)* [kləʊðz] Kleider; Kleidung **I**
cloud [klaʊd] Wolke **III U1**, 18
word **cloud** ['wɜ:d ˌklaʊd] Wörterwolke **II**
cloudy ['klaʊdi] bedeckt; bewölkt **II**
clover *(no pl)* ['kləʊvə] Klee ⟨**III TS3**, 107⟩
clown [klaʊn] Clown **II**
club [klʌb] Klub; Verein; AG **I**
Cooking **Club** ['kʊkɪŋ ˌklʌb] Koch-AG **I**
clue [klu:] Hinweis; Spur **II**
coach [kəʊtʃ] Trainer/-in **I**; Reisebus **II**
coastal path [ˌkəʊstl 'pɑ:θ] Küstenweg **III U1**, 18
coastline ['kəʊstlaɪn] Küste; Küstenverlauf **III U1**, 14
coconut ['kəʊkənʌt] Kokosnuss **II**
coffee ['kɒfi] Kaffee **I**
coin [kɔɪn] Münze **I**
coke ['kəʊk] Cola **I**
cold [kəʊld] Erkältung **II**
cold [kəʊld] kalt **II**
to **collect** [kə'lekt] sammeln **I**
collection [kə'lekʃn] Kollektion; Sammlung **II**
collocation [ˌkɒlə'keɪʃn] Wortverbindung **II**
colony ['kɒləni] Kolonie **II**
colour ['kʌlə] Farbe **I**
What **colour** is …? [ˌwɒt 'kʌlər‿ɪz] Welche Farbe hat …? **I**
colourful ['kʌləfl] farbenfroh; bunt **I**
column ['kɒləm] Spalte °**III U2**, 32
*to **come** [kʌm] kommen **I**
*to **come** down [ˌkʌm 'daʊn] herunterkommen **I**
*to **come** in [ˌkʌm‿'ɪn] hereinkommen **III U1**, 18
*to **come** up [ˌkʌm‿'ʌp] vorkommen °**III U4**, 98
Come on! [ˌkʌm‿'ɒn] Komm schon!; Komm jetzt! **I**
comedian [kə'mi:diən] Komiker/-in; Comedian **II**
comedy ['kɒmədi] Komödie **III TS3**, 106
comedy show ['kɒmədi ˌʃəʊ] Comedy Show **II**
comfortable ['kʌmftəbl] komfortabel; bequem **II**
comic ['kɒmɪk] Comicheft **II**
comment ['kɒment] Kommentar **II**
to **comment** (on) ['kɒment‿(ɒn)] kommentieren **II**
*to have in **common** [ˌhæv‿ɪn 'kɒmən] gemeinsam haben **III TS3**, 110
to **communicate** [kə'mju:nɪkeɪt] kommunizieren; sich verständigen **II**
communication [kəˌmju:nɪ'keɪʃn] Kommunikation **II**

community centre [kə'mju:nəti ˌsentə] Gemeindezentrum **I**
company ['kʌmpəni] Gesellschaft; Firma; Unternehmen **III U2**, 29
comparative [kəm'pærətɪv] Komparativ **II**
to **compare** (with/to) [kəm'peə] vergleichen (mit) **I**
comparison [kəm'pærɪsn] Vergleich **II**
to **compete** (with) [kəm'pi:t] konkurrieren (mit); sich messen (mit); in Wettbewerb treten (mit) **III U2**, 27
competition [ˌkɒmpə'tɪʃn] Wettbewerb; Turnier **II**
competitive [kəm'petɪtɪv] leistungsorientiert; konkurrierend **III U2**, 31
Complete … [kəm'pli:t] Vervollständige/Vervollständigt … **I**
completely [kəm'pli:tli] völlig **III AC1**, 24
compound word ['kɒmpaʊnd wɜ:d] Kompositum *(zusammengesetztes Wort)* **II**
compromise ['kɒmprəmaɪz] Kompromiss **II**
to **compromise** ['kɒmprəmaɪz] Kompromisse eingehen **III U2**, 27
computer [ˌkəm'pju:tə] Computer **I**
con [kɒn] Argument dagegen **II**
conditional sentence [kənˌdɪʃnl 'sentəns] Bedingungssatz °**III U1**, 9
confident ['kɒnfɪdnt] selbstsicher; selbstbewusst **II**
confused [kən'fju:zd] verwirrt; wirr; konfus **III U2**, 38
*to be **connected** [bi kə'nektɪd] zusammenhängen; in Zusammenhang stehen **II**
connection [kə'nekʃn] Verbindung **III U1**, 12
contact ['kɒntækt] Kontakt **II**
contact clause ['kɒntækt ˌklɔ:z] *Relativsatz ohne Relativpronomen* **II**
to **contact** ['kɒntækt] sich in Verbindung setzen; kontaktieren ⟨**III TS2**, 77⟩
to **contain** [kən'teɪn] enthalten ⟨**III TS2**, 77⟩
container [kən'teɪnə] Container; Behälter; Behältnis ⟨**III TS2**, 77⟩
contest ['kɒntest] Wettkampf; Wettbewerb **I**
to **continue** [kən'tɪnju:] fortfahren; andauern; weitermachen °**III U3**, 55
conversation [ˌkɒnvə'seɪʃn] Konversation; Gespräch; Unterhaltung **I**
to hog a **conversation** [ˌhɒg‿ə kɒnvə'seɪʃn] ein Gespräch für sich in Beschlag nehmen; ein Gespräch dominieren **III AC3**, 82
to **convince** [kən'vɪns] überzeugen **II**
to **cook** [kʊk] kochen **II**
cooker ['kʊkə] Herd **I**
cooking ['kʊkɪŋ] Kochen **I**
Cooking Club ['kʊkɪŋ ˌklʌb] Koch-AG **I**
*to leave it to **cool** [ˌli:v‿ɪt tə 'ku:l] kalt stellen **I**
cool [ku:l] cool; super **I**

to **copy** ['kɒpi] abschreiben; kopieren **I**
corner ['kɔ:nə] Ecke **II**
Cornish ['kɔ:nɪʃ] in Cornwall **III U1**, 10
Correct … [kə'rekt] Korrigiere/Korrigiert … **I**
correct [kə'rekt] richtig; korrekt **I**
*to **cost** [kɒst] kosten **I**
costume ['kɒstju:m] Kostüm **I**
cough [kɒf] Husten **II**
could [kʊd] könnte/-n **II**; konnte/-n **III U2**, 36
to **count** (on) ['kaʊnt‿ɒn] zählen (auf) **I**
country, **countries** *(pl)* ['kʌntri; 'kʌntriz] Land **I**
countryside ['kʌntrisaɪd] Land **III U1**, 10
couple ['kʌpl] Paar **III U1**, 16
a **couple** of [ə 'kʌpl‿əv] ein paar **I**
course [kɔ:s] Kurs **II**
of **course** [əv 'kɔ:s] natürlich; selbstverständlich **I**
court [kɔ:t] Spielfeld **II**
cousin ['kʌzn] Cousin/Cousine **I**
cover ['kʌvə] Cover; Titelblatt **III U2**, 26
cover version ['kʌvə ˌvɜ:ʃn] Coverversion °**III TS1**, 51
to **cover** ['kʌvə] abdecken; bedecken; zudecken °**III U3**, 65
cow [kaʊ] Kuh **III U1**, 21
crack [kræk] Knacken; Krachen **III U3**, 67
cracking ['krækɪŋ] knackend; brechend **III U3**, 66
cramp [kræmp] Krampf **II**
crane [kreɪn] Kran **III U3**, 61
to **crash** [kræʃ] abstürzen **II**; zusammenstoßen **III U4**, 97
crazy ['kreɪzi] verrückt **I**
*to go **crazy** [ˌgəʊ 'kreɪzi] ausflippen; durchdrehen; verrückt werden **II**
cream [kri:m] Creme; Sahne **I**
ice **cream** [ˌaɪs 'kri:m] Eis; Eiscreme **I**
to **create** [kri'eɪt] schaffen; erschaffen; erfinden **I**
creative [kri'eɪtɪv] kreativ **I**
credit ['kredɪt] Guthaben **II**
cricket ['krɪkɪt] Cricket **II**
crime [kraɪm] Verbrechen; Kriminalität **III AC1**, 24
criminal ['krɪmɪnəl] Kriminelle/-r; Verbrecher/-in **III AC1**, 24
crisp *(BE)* [krɪsp] Kartoffelchip **I**
criterion [kraɪ'tɪəriən], **criteria** [kraɪ'tɪəriə] *(pl)* Kriterium; Argument °**III U3**, 64
to **crop** (a photo) [krɒp] (ein Foto) zurechtschneiden **III U4**, 97
cross [krɒs] Kreuz **III U1**, 14
to **cross** [krɒs] überqueren; kreuzen **II**
*to keep your fingers **crossed** [ˌki:p jɔ: ˌfɪŋgəz 'krɒst] die Daumen drücken **I**
crowd [kraʊd] Menschenmenge **II**
crown [kraʊn] Krone **III U4**, 88
crown jewels [ˌkraʊn 'dʒu:əlz] Kronjuwelen **II**

cruel ['kru:əl] grausam **III AC1**, 24
to **cry** [kraɪ] schreien; rufen **II**; weinen **III TS1**, 49
CU *(= See you)* ['si: ju] Bis dann!; Bis ... **I**
culture ['kʌltʃə] Kultur **I**
Across **cultures** [əˌkrɒs 'kʌltʃəz] Interkulturelles **I**
cup [kʌp] Tasse **III AC2**, 52
cupboard ['kʌbəd] Küchenschrank; Schrank **I**
curious ['kjʊəriəs] neugierig ⟨**III U3**, 63⟩
curry ['kʌri] Curry *(Gewürz oder Gericht)* **I**
custard ['kʌstəd] Vanillesoße; Vanillepudding **I**
customer ['kʌstəmə] Kunde/Kundin **III U1**, 16
*to **cut** (off) [kʌt (ɒf)] schneiden; abschneiden **II**
cute [kju:t] niedlich; süß **I**
cyber bully [ˌsaɪbə 'bʊli] *jemand, der andere in sozialen Netzwerken belästigt oder mobbed* **II**
cycling ['saɪklɪŋ] Radfahren **I**

D

dad [dæd] Papa **I**
daily ['deɪli] täglich ⟨**III TS2**, 77⟩
dance [dɑ:ns] Tanz; Tanzveranstaltung **III U2**, 28
to **dance** [dɑ:ns] tanzen **I**
to **dance** to ['dɑ:ns tə] tanzen zu **III TS1**, 50
I like singing and **dancing**. [ˌaɪ laɪk ˌsɪŋɪŋ‿ənd 'dɑ:nsɪŋ] Ich singe und tanze gern. **I**
dancer ['dɑ:nsə] Tänzer/-in **II**
backing **dancer** ['bækɪŋ ˌdɑ:nsə] Backgroundtänzer/-in **III U2**, 28
dancing ['dɑ:nsɪŋ] Tanz ⟨**III U3**, 62⟩
danger ['deɪndʒə] Gefahr **III U3**, 66
dangerous ['deɪndʒrəs] gefährlich **I**
the **dark** [ðə 'dɑ:k] Dunkelheit **II**
dark [dɑ:k] dunkel **II**
darkness ['dɑ:knəs] Dunkelheit **III U1**, 21
date [deɪt] Datum **I**
daughter ['dɔ:tə] Tochter **III U4**, 86
day [deɪ] Tag **I**
all **day** [ˌɔ:l 'deɪ] den ganzen Tag **II**
one **day** [wʌn 'deɪ] eines Tages **II**
these **days** [ˌði:z 'deɪz] zurzeit **III U2**, 36
a **day** out in ... [ə ˌdeɪ‿'aʊt ɪn] ein Tag in ... **II**
in those **days** [ˌɪn ðəʊz 'deɪz] damals ⟨**III U3**, 63⟩
the next **day** [ðə ˌnekst 'deɪ] am nächsten Tag **II**
dead [ded] tot **II**
deadly ['dedli] tödlich ⟨**III TS2**, 79⟩
*to **deal** (with) [di:l] sich befassen mit; umgehen mit **II**
Oh **dear**! [ˌəʊ 'dɪə] Oje! **III U1**, 18

Dear ... [dɪə] Lieber ...; Liebe ... *(Anrede in Briefen)* **I**
Dear Sir or Madam [dɪə ˌsɜ:r‿ɔ: 'mædəm] Sehr geehrte Dame, sehr geehrter Herr **III U1**, 13
dearly ['dɪəli] lieb ⟨**III U3**, 58⟩
death [deθ] Tod **III TS3**, 106
December [dɪ'sembə] Dezember **I**
to **decide** [dɪ'saɪd] (sich) entscheiden **I**
decision [dɪ'sɪʒn] Entscheidung °**III U1**, 11
*to make a **decision** [ˌmeɪk‿ə dɪ'sɪʒn] eine Entscheidung treffen **II**
deck [dek] Deck **I**
to **decorate** ['dekəreɪt] dekorieren; verzieren; schmücken **I**
decorations *(pl)* [ˌdekə'reɪʃnz] Dekoration; Schmuck **I**
deep [di:p] tief **III U1**, 9
to **defeat** [dɪ'fi:t] besiegen **III U3**, 58
defining relative clause [dɪˌfaɪnɪŋ 'relətɪv ˌklɔ:z] notwendiger Relativsatz **II**
definitely ['defɪnətli] bestimmt; definitiv; eindeutig **III U3**, 67
definition [ˌdefɪ'nɪʃn] Definition °**III U1**, 12
to **delete** [dɪ'li:t] löschen **III U2**, 39
to **depart** [dɪ'pɑ:t] abfahren **III U1**, 12
to **depend** (on) [dɪ'pend‿(ɒn)] abhängen von **III U1**, 11
to **describe** [dɪ'skraɪb] beschreiben **I**
description [dɪ'skrɪpʃn] Beschreibung **II**
to **deserve** [dɪ'zɜ:v] verdienen **II**
design [dɪ'zaɪn] Design; Gestaltung; Entwurf **II**
to **design** [dɪ'zaɪn] entwerfen; gestalten **II**
designer [dɪ'zaɪnə] Designer/-in **III U2**, 30
web **designer** ['web dɪˌzaɪnə] Webdesigner **III U2**, 32
detail ['di:teɪl] Detail; Einzelheit **II**
detective [dɪ'tektɪv] Detektiv/-in **III U4**, 94; Detektivgeschichte; Kriminalroman; Kriminalfilm; Krimi **III TS3**, 106
private **detective** [ˌpraɪvət dɪ'tektɪv] Privatdetektiv/-in **III AC1**, 24
to **develop** [dɪ'veləp] (sich) entwickeln ⟨**III U2**, 29⟩
diagram ['daɪəgræm] Diagramm **I**
dialect ['daɪəlekt] Dialekt **III U1**, 15
dialogue ['daɪəlɒg] Dialog; Gespräch **I**
diary ['daɪəri] Tagebuch **III U1**, 20
diary entry ['daɪəri entri] Tagebucheintrag **III U1**, 20
dice [daɪs] Würfel **II**
Roll two **dice**. [ˌrəʊl ˌtu: 'daɪs] Würfle/Würfelt mit zwei Würfeln. **I**
throw the **dice** twice [ˌθrəʊ ðə daɪs 'twaɪs] würfle zweimal **II**
dictionary ['dɪkʃnri] Wörterbuch **I**
to **die** [daɪ] sterben **III TS1**, 50
difference ['dɪfrəns] Unterschied **I**
different ['dɪfrnt] anders; unterschiedlich; verschieden **I**
difficult ['dɪfɪklt] schwierig **II**

*to **dig** [dɪg] graben **II**
dinner ['dɪnə] Abendessen **I**
dinosaur ['daɪnəsɔ:] Dinosaurier **II**
direct [dɪ'rekt] direkt **III TS1**, 48
direction [dɪ'rekʃn] Richtung **I**
stage **direction** ['steɪdʒ dɪˌrekʃn] Regieanweisung **III AC3**, 83
dirt [dɜ:t] Schmutz; Dreck **III U4**, 92
dirty ['dɜ:ti] dreckig; schmutzig **II**
to **disagree** [ˌdɪsə'gri:] anderer Meinung sein; nicht einverstanden sein **III U2**, 27
disappointed [ˌdɪsə'pɔɪntɪd] enttäuscht **I**
disaster [dɪ'zɑ:stə] Desaster; Katastrophe; Unglück **II**
to **discover** [dɪ'skʌvə] entdecken **II**
discovery [dɪ'skʌvri] Entdeckung **III U3**, 60
to **discuss** [dɪ'skʌs] diskutieren **I**
discussion [dɪ'skʌʃn] Diskussion **II**
to **disobey** [ˌdɪsə'beɪ] nicht gehorchen; ungehorsam sein **III TS3**, 107
display [dɪ'spleɪ] Ausstellung **II**
class **display** ['klɑ:s dɪˌspleɪ] Ausstellung in der Klasse **I**
distance ['dɪstns] Distanz; Entfernung **II**
to **divide** (up) [dɪ'vaɪd] aufteilen °**III TS1**, 48
DJ [ˌdi:'dʒeɪ] DJ; Discjockey **III U2**, 37
*to **do** [du:] machen; tun **I**
*to **do** about ['du:‿əˌbaʊt] unternehmen wegen **II**
*to **do** our hair [ˌdu:‿aʊə 'heə] uns frisieren; unsere Haare machen **I**
*to **do** the shopping [ˌdu: ðə 'ʃɒpɪŋ] Einkäufe machen; Besorgungen machen **III U3**, 69
Don't translate ... [ˌdəʊnt trænz'leɪt] Übersetze/Übersetzt nicht ... **I**
Don't worry! [ˌdəʊnt 'wʌri] Keine Sorge! **I**
We **did** it! [ˌwi: 'dɪd‿ɪt] Wir haben es geschafft! **II**
You can **do** it! [ˌju: kən 'du: ɪt] Du schaffst es! **III TS1**, 50
doctor ['dɒktə] Arzt/Ärztin **II**
dog [dɒg] Hund **I**
to walk the **dog** [ˌwɔ:k ðə 'dɒg] den Hund ausführen; mit dem Hund spazieren gehen **I**
I'm **dog-tired**. [ˌaɪm ˌdɒg'taɪəd] Ich bin hundemüde. **I**
dollar ['dɒlə] Dollar *(Währung)* **III U2**, 29
dolphin ['dɒlfɪn] Delfin **III TS1**, 47
door [dɔ:] Tür **I**
front **door** [ˌfrʌnt 'dɔ:] Haustür **II**
next **door** [ˌnekst 'dɔ:] (von) nebenan **III AC3**, 82
doorbell ['dɔ:bel] Türklingel **III U2**, 32
doubt [daʊt] Zweifel **III U2**, 27
down [daʊn] nach unten; herunter; hinunter **II**
*to come **down** [ˌkʌm 'daʊn] herunterkommen **I**

*to go **down** [ˌgəʊ 'daʊn] hinuntergehen; nach unten gehen; entlanggehen **I**
to note **down** [ˌnəʊt 'daʊn] notieren; aufschreiben **II**
to pull **down** [ˌpʊl‿'daʊn] abreißen **III U3**, 59
*to sit **down** [ˌsɪt 'daʊn] sich hinsetzen; sich setzen **I**
*to write **down** [ˌraɪt 'daʊn] aufschreiben **I**

to **download** [ˌdaʊn'ləʊd] herunterladen *(aus dem Internet)* **II**
downstairs [ˌdaʊn'steəz] nach unten; im Untergeschoss; unten **II**
draft [drɑ:ft] Entwurf; Konzept **I**
drama ['drɑ:mə] Theater; Drama **II**
dramatic [drə'mætɪk] dramatisch **II**
*to **draw** [drɔ:] zeichnen **I**; ziehen °**III U1**, 17
*to **draw** the reader into the story/action [ˌdrɔ: ðə ˌri:də ɪntə ðə 'stɔ:ri/'ækʃn] den Leser/die Leserin in die Geschichte/Handlung hineinziehen °**III TS3**, 108
drawing ['drɔ:ɪŋ] Zeichnung **I**
dream [dri:m] Traum **II**
*to **dream** [dri:m; dremt; dremt] träumen ⟨**III TS1**, 46⟩
dress [dres] Kleid **III U4**, 88
fancy **dress** ['fænsi dres] Verkleidung; Kostüm **II**
drink [drɪŋk] Getränk **I**
*to **drink** [drɪŋk] trinken **I**
to **drip** [drɪp] tropfen ⟨**III TS1**, 47⟩
*to **drive** [draɪv] fahren **III U4**, 97
*to **drive** off [draɪv‿'ɒf] wegfahren **III U4**, 97
driver ['draɪvə] Fahrer/-in **II**
to **drop** [drɒp] fallen (lassen) **II**
to **drop** out (of) [ˌdrɒp 'aʊt‿əv] abbrechen **III U2**, 28
to **drown** [draʊn] ertrinken; ertränken **III TS3**, 109
drums *(pl)* [drʌmz] Schlagzeug **III U3**, 58
dry [draɪ] trocken **III TS2**, 77
during *(+ noun)* ['djʊərɪŋ] während *(+ Nomen)* **II**
DVD [ˌdi:vi:'di:] DVD **I**

E

e.g. *(= for example)* [ˌi:'dʒi:] z.B. *(= zum Beispiel)* **I**
each [i:tʃ] jede/-r/-s **I**
each other [ˌi:tʃ‿'ʌðə] einander; sich; sich gegenseitig **I**
each [i:tʃ] pro Person; pro Stück **I**
early ['ɜ:li] früh **I**
this **early** ['ðɪs ˌɜ:li] so früh **III AC2**, 53
to **earn** [ɜ:n] verdienen **I**
earth [ɜ:θ] Erdboden; Erde; die Erde **II**
What on **earth** ...? [ˌwɒt‿ɒn‿'ɜ:θ] Was um alles in der Welt ...? **II**
east [i:st] Osten; Ost- **I**
Easter ['i:stə] Ostern **I**
easy ['i:zi] einfach; leicht **I**
*to **eat** [i:t] essen; fressen **I**
Eco ['i:kəʊ] Öko- **II**
to **edit** out [ˌedɪt‿'aʊt] herausschneiden **III U4**, 97
education *(no pl)* [ˌedʒʊ'keɪʃn] Erziehung; Bildung **III U4**, 89
audio-visual **effect** [ˌɔ:diəʊvɪʒuəl ɪ'fekt] audiovisueller Effekt **II**
egg [eg] Ei **I**
eight [eɪt] acht **I**
elderly ['eldəli] älter **III U3**, 69
electric [ɪ'lektrɪk] elektrisch **III U4**, 93
electrician [ˌelɪk'trɪʃn] Elektriker/-in **III U1**, 19
electricity [ˌelɪk'trɪsəti] Elektrizität; Strom **III U1**, 18
electrics [ɪ'lektrɪks] Elektrik **III U1**, 19
electronic [ˌelek'trɒnɪk] elektronisch **II**
element ['elɪmənt] Element °**III U1**, 21
elephant ['elɪfənt] Elefant **III TS2**, 80
eleven [ɪ'levn] elf **I**
else [els] andere/-r/-s; sonst noch **III U2**, 35
nobody **else** ['nəʊbədi els] niemand anderes **III U1**, 20
what **else** [ˌwɒt‿'els] was sonst; was noch **I**
e-mail ['i:meɪl] E-Mail **I**
to **e-mail** ['i:meɪl] mailen; per E-Mail schicken **II**
embarrassed [ɪm'bærəst] verlegen **II**
embarrassing [ɪm'bærəsɪŋ] peinlich **II**
emotional [ɪ'məʊʃnl] emotional; Gefühls- °**III TS2**, 79
emperor ['emprə] Kaiser **III U4**, 84
empire ['empaɪə] Reich; Kaiserreich **III U4**, 84
empty ['emti] leer **III U3**, 66
end [end] Ende; Schluss **I**
in the **end** [ˌɪn ði‿'end] schließlich; zum Schluss **II**
to **end** [end] enden; beenden **II**
to **end** up [ˌend‿'ʌp] enden; landen **II**
ending ['endɪŋ] Ende; Schluss *(einer Geschichte)* **I**
happy **ending** [ˌhæpi 'endɪŋ] Happy End **III TS3**, 106
enemy ['enəmi] Feind/-in **III TS3**, 106
energy ['enədʒi] Energie; Kraft **III TS3**, 109
steam **engine** ['sti:m‿ˌendʒɪn] Dampfmaschine **III U3**, 60
English ['ɪŋglɪʃ] englisch; Englisch; aus England; Engländer/-in **I**
English-speaking ['ɪŋglɪʃˌspi:kɪŋ] englischsprachig **I**
I'm **English**. [aɪm‿'ɪŋglɪʃ] Ich bin Engländer/-in. **I**
to **enjoy** [ɪn'dʒɔɪ] genießen; sich freuen an **II**
to **enjoy** oneself [ɪn'dʒɔɪ] Spaß haben; sich amüsieren **III U2**, 32
enough [ɪ'nʌf] genug; genügend **I**
to **enter** ['entə] hineingehen; betreten; eintreten; *hier:* mitmachen **II**
entertainment *(no pl)* [ˌentə'teɪnmənt] Unterhaltung **III U4**, 91
entrance ['entrəns] Eingang; Eintritt **III U3**, 66
entrepreneur [ˌɒntrəprə'nɜ:] Unternehmer/-in ⟨**III U2**, 29⟩
entry ['entri] Eintrag **III TS2**, 76
diary **entry** ['daɪəri entri] Tagebucheintrag **III U1**, 20
environment [ɪn'vaɪrnmənt] Umwelt; Umgebung **III U1**, 14
equipment [ɪ'kwɪpmənt] Ausstattung; Ausrüstung **II**
er [ɜ:] äh **I**
escalator ['eskəleɪtə] Rolltreppe **I**
escape [ɪ'skeɪp] Flucht **III TS3**, 106
especially [ɪ'speʃli] besonders; vor allem ⟨**III U3**, 63⟩
essential [ɪ'senʃl] essenziell; entscheidend ⟨**III TS2**, 77⟩
etc. *(= et cetera)* [ɪt'setrə] usw. *(= und so weiter)* **II**
euro ['jʊərəʊ] Euro *(Währung)* **I**
even ['i:vn] sogar; selbst **I**
even though [ˌi:vn 'ðəʊ] auch wenn; obwohl ⟨**III TS3**, 109⟩
evening ['i:vnɪŋ] Abend **I**
in the **evenings** [ɪn ði‿'i:vnɪŋz] abends **I**
event [ɪ'vent] Ereignis; Veranstaltung **I**
ever ['evə] jemals **II**
the best ... **ever** ['best ... ˌevə] der/die/das beste ... überhaupt **III TS3**, 106
every ['evri] jede/-r/-s **I**
everybody ['evribɒdi] jeder; alle **II**
everyday ['evrideɪ] alltäglich **III U4**, 89
everyone ['evriwʌn] jeder; alle **I**
everything ['evriθɪŋ] alles **I**
everywhere ['evriweə] überall **I**
exactly [ɪg'zæktli] genau **II**
exam [ɪg'zæm] Examen; Prüfung **II**
examination [ɪgˌzæmɪ'neɪʃn] Untersuchung; Prüfung ⟨**III TS2**, 77⟩
example [ɪg'zɑ:mpl] Beispiel **I**
for **example** [fər‿ɪg'zɑ:mpl] zum Beispiel **II**
exchange [ɪks'tʃeɪndʒ] Austausch; Austausch- **III AC2**, 52
exchange student [ɪks'tʃeɪndʒ ˌstju:dnt] Austauschschüler/-in **III AC2**, 52
student **exchange** ['stju:dnt ɪksˌtʃeɪndʒ] Schüleraustausch **III AC3**, 83
to **exchange** [ɪks'tʃeɪndʒ] austauschen **II**
excited [ɪk'saɪtɪd] aufgeregt; begeistert **I**
excitement *(no pl)* [ɪk'saɪtmənt] Aufregung **III U2**, 38
exciting [ɪk'saɪtɪŋ] spannend; aufregend **I**

Excuse me ... [ɪk'skju:z mi] Entschuldigung!; Entschuldigen Sie! **I**
exercise ['eksəsaɪz] Übung; Aufgabe **I**
exercise book ['eksəsaɪz ˌbʊk] Übungsheft **I**
to **expect** [ɪk'spekt] erwarten °**III TS2**, 76
expensive [ɪk'spensɪv] teuer **I**
experience [ɪk'spɪəriəns] Erfahrung **II**
to **experience** [ɪk'spɪəriəns] erfahren; erleben **III U4**, 87
expert ['ekspɜ:t] Experte/Expertin **II**
to **explain** [ɪk'spleɪn] erklären **I**
to **explore** [ɪk'splɔ:] auf Entdeckungsreise gehen; sich umschauen; erkunden; erforschen **I**
to **express** [ɪk'spres] ausdrücken **II**
expression [ɪk'spreʃn] Ausdruck; Wendung; Äußerung **II**
facial **expression** [ˌfeɪʃl ɪk'spreʃn] Gesichtsausdruck **III AC3**, 83
*to become **extinct** [bɪˌkʌm‿ɪk'stɪŋkt] aussterben **III TS2**, 80
extinction *(no pl)* [ɪks'tɪŋkʃn] Aussterben **III TS2**, 80
extra ['ekstrə] extra; zusätzlich **I**
extremely [ɪk'stri:mli] äußerst; sehr ⟨**III TS2**, 79⟩
eye [aɪ] Auge **II**
to roll one's **eyes** [ˌrəʊl wʌnz‿'aɪz] die Augen verdrehen **III U4**, 96
He couldn't believe his **eyes**. [hi ˌkʊdnt bɪˌli:v hɪz‿'aɪz] Er traute seinen Augen nicht. **II**
eyewitness ['aɪwɪtnəs] Augenzeuge/Augenzeugin **II**

F

face [feɪs] Gesicht **I**
Put ... **face** down. [pʊt ˌfeɪs 'daʊn] Lege/Legt ... umgedreht hin. **I**
face-to-face [ˌfeɪstə'feɪs] *hier:* persönlich; von Angesicht zu Angesicht **II**
facial expression [ˌfeɪʃl ɪk'spreʃn] Gesichtsausdruck **III AC3**, 83
fact [fækt] Fakt; Tatsache **II**
in **fact** [ɪn 'fækt] tatsächlich; eigentlich; genau genommen ⟨**III U3**, 62⟩
factory ['fæktri] Fabrik; Werk **III U4**, 87
factual ['fæktʃʊəl] sachlich °**III TS2**, 76
factual text [ˌfæktʃʊəl 'tekst] Sachtext °**III TS2**, 76
fair [feə] gerecht; fair **I**
fair play [feə 'pleɪ] Fairplay **III TS1**, 46
to **fake** [feɪk] vortäuschen; fälschen **II**
*to **fall** [fɔ:l] fallen; hinfallen **I**
*to **fall** asleep [ˌfɔ:l‿ə'sli:p] einschlafen **I**
*to **fall** down [ˌfɔ:l‿'daʊn] stürzen; hinunterfallen **III TS1**, 50
*to **fall** off [ˌfɔ:l‿'ɒf] herunterfallen; hinunterfallen **II**
*to **fall** over [ˌfɔ:l‿'əʊvə] hinfallen; umkippen **I**
family ['fæmli] Familie **I**
family tree ['fæmli ˌtri:] Stammbaum **I**
host **family** ['həʊst ˌfæmli] Gastfamilie **III AC2**, 52
famous ['feɪməs] berühmt **I**
fan [fæn] Fan; Anhänger/-in **II**
fancy dress ['fænsi dres] Verkleidung; Kostüm **II**
fantastic [fæn'tæstɪk] fantastisch; großartig **II**
fantasy ['fæntəsi] Fantasie; Traum- **I**; Fantasy **III TS3**, 106
fanzine [fæn'zi:n] Fanzeitschrift **II**
FAQ [ˌefeɪ'kju:] Liste mit häufig gestellten Fragen °**III TS2**, 76
in the **far** west [ɪn ðə fɑ: 'west] im äußersten Westen **III U1**, 14
far [fɑ:] weit **II**
far more ['fɑ: mɔ:] weitaus ⟨**III TS1**, 51⟩
so **far** [ˌsəʊ 'fɑ:] bis jetzt **II**
fare [feə] Fahrpreis **III U1**, 12
farm [fɑ:m] Farm; Bauernhof **I**
farmer ['fɑ:mə] Farmer/-in; Landwirt/-in **II**
fascinating ['fæsɪneɪtɪŋ] faszinierend **III U3**, 64
fashion ['fæʃn] Mode **II**
fast [fɑ:st] schnell **I**
father ['fɑ:ðə] Vater **I**
favourite ['feɪvrɪt] Favorit/-in; Günstling **III U4**, 88
favourite ['feɪvrɪt] Lieblings- **I**
My **favourite** ... [maɪ 'feɪvrɪt] Mein/e Lieblings ... **I**
What's your **favourite** ...? ['wɒts jə ˌfeɪvrɪt] Was ist dein/-e Lieblings...? **I**
fear [fɪə] Angst; Furcht; Befürchtung **II**
fearful ['fɪəfl] ängstlich **III TS2**, 77
feather ['feðə] Feder **III U4**, 91
feature ['fi:tʃə] Eigenschaft; Merkmal °**III TS2**, 76
to **feature** ['fi:tʃə] zeigen; aufweisen °**III TS3**, 106
February ['februri] Februar **I**
*to be **fed up (with)** [bi fed‿'ʌp wɪð] sauer sein (auf); die Nase voll haben (von) **III U2**, 36
fee [fi:] Gebühr **III U1**, 12
school **fees** *(pl)* ['sku:l fi:z] Schulgeld; Schulgebühren **III U4**, 99
*to **feed** [fi:d] füttern; ernähren **III U1**, 21
feedback ['fi:dbæk] Feedback; Rückmeldung **II**
*to **feel** [fi:l] fühlen; sich fühlen **I**
*to **feel** left out [ˌfi:l left‿'aʊt] sich ausgeschlossen fühlen **II**
*to **feel** sick [ˌfi:l 'sɪk] Übelkeit verspüren; sich schlecht fühlen **II**
*to **feel** sorry for [ˌfi:l 'sɒri fɔ:] Mitleid haben mit; bedauern **III U2**, 39
feeling ['fi:lɪŋ] Gefühl **II**
festival ['festɪvl] Festival; Fest **I**
fever ['fi:və] Fieber **II**
few [fju:] wenige **II**
a **few** [ə 'fju:] ein paar; wenige; einige **I**
fiction *(no pl)* ['fɪkʃn] Erzählliteratur; Erfindung; Prosa; Fiktion **III TS3**, 106
science **fiction** [ˌsaɪəns 'fɪkʃn] Science-Fiction *(Zukunftsdichtung)* **II**
fictional ['fɪkʃnl] fiktional; fiktiv; erdichtet °**III TS3**, 106
field [fi:ld] Feld; Spielfeld; Wiese; Weide; Acker **II**
fifteen [ˌfɪf'ti:n] fünfzehn **I**
fight [faɪt] Kampf; Streit **II**
*to **fight** [faɪt] kämpfen; (sich) streiten **II**
figure ['fɪgə] Figur; Gestalt **II**; Ziffer; Zahl °**III U4**, 91
wax **figure** ['wæks ˌfɪgə] Wachsfigur **II**
to **fill** [fɪl] (sich) füllen **III U3**, 60
to **fill** in [ˌfɪl‿'ɪn] ausfüllen **II**
film [fɪlm] Film **I**
to **film** [fɪlm] filmen; drehen °**III U1**, 21
filmmaker ['fɪlmˌmeɪkə] Filmemacher/-in **II**
final ['faɪnl] endgültig **II**; letzte/-r/-s **III U3**, 64
finally ['faɪnli] schließlich; endlich; zum Schluss; letztlich **II**
*to **find** [faɪnd] finden; herausfinden **I**
*to **find** out [ˌfaɪnd‿'aʊt] herausfinden **I**

fine [faɪn] gut; in Ordnung; schön **I**
I'm **fine**. [ˌaɪm 'faɪn] Mir geht's gut. **I**
finger ['fɪŋgə] Finger **I**
*to keep your **fingers** crossed [ˌki:p jɔ: ˌfɪŋgəz 'krɒst] die Daumen drücken **I**
finish line ['fɪnɪʃ ˌlaɪn] Ziellinie **II**
to **finish** ['fɪnɪʃ] beenden; enden; fertigstellen; aufhören **I**
finished ['fɪnɪʃt] fertig **II**
fire [faɪə] Feuer **III TS2**, 79
*to be on **fire** [ˌbi:‿ɒn 'faɪə] brennen **III TS3**, 109
firefighter ['faɪəˌfaɪtə] Feuerwehrmann/-frau ⟨**III TS2**, 79⟩
fireworks *(pl)* ['faɪəwɜ:ks] Feuerwerk **I**
first [fɜ:st] zuerst; als Erstes; erste/-r/-s **I**
at **first** [ət 'fɜ:st] zuerst; zunächst **II**
first language [ˌfɜ:st 'læŋgwɪdʒ] Muttersprache **II**
first person narrator [ˌfɜ:st ˌpɜ:sn nə'reɪtə] Ich-Erzähler/-in °**III TS3**, 109
fish, fish *(pl)* [fɪʃ] Fisch **I**
fishing ['fɪʃɪŋ] Angeln; Fischen; Fischerei **III U1**, 14
to **fit** [fɪt] passen **II**
*to get **fit** [ˌget 'fɪt] in Form kommen; fit werden **I**
five [faɪv] fünf **I**
to **fix** [fɪks] reparieren; befestigen **II**
flag [flæg] Flagge; Fahne **III U3**, 55
flair [fleə] Flair; Atmosphäre **II**

flame [fleɪm] Flamme **III TS2**, 79
flash [flæʃ] Blitz; Lichtblitz **III U4**, 97
flashback ['flæʃbæk] Rückblende; Flashback **III U4**, 98
flat [flæt] Wohnung **I**
flea market ['fli: ˌmɑ:kɪt] Flohmarkt **I**
flight [flaɪt] Flug **III TS1**, 48
floor [flɔ:] Fußboden **I**
to **flow** out [fləʊ‿'aʊt] hinausfließen **II**
flower ['flaʊə] Blume **II**
*to **fly** [flaɪ] fliegen **III TS1**, 48
flyer ['flaɪə] Flyer **I**
focus ['fəʊkəs] Blickpunkt; Schwerpunkt; Fokus **III TS3**, 110
out of **focus** [ˌaʊt‿əv 'fəʊkəs] unscharf **III U4**, 97
to **focus** (on) ['fəʊkəs‿ɒn] sich konzentrieren (auf) **II**
folder ['fəʊldə] Ordner; Mappe **I**
folks *(infml) (pl)* [fəʊks] Leute ⟨**III U3**, 62⟩
to **follow** ['fɒləʊ] folgen; hinterhergehen; befolgen **II**
the **following** [ðə 'fɒləʊɪŋ] folgende/-r/-s °**III U1**, 9
food [fu:d] Essen; Lebensmittel **I**; Futter **III TS2**, 77
foot, feet *(pl)* [fʊt; fi:t] Fuß **I**
*to keep one's **feet** or hands still [ˌki:p wʌnz: 'fi:t‿ɔ: 'hændz stɪl] die Beine und Hände ruhig halten **III TS1**, 50
on **foot** [ɒn 'fʊt] zu Fuß **II**
football ['fʊtbɔ:l] Fußball **I**
for [fɔ:; fə] für **I**; wegen **II**
for *(+ Zeitraum)* [fɔ:; fə] seit **III U3**, 56
for example [fər‿ɪg'zɑ:mpl] zum Beispiel **II**
for … [fɔ:; fə] … lang **II**
for [fɔ:; fə] denn ⟨**III TS1**, 48⟩
weather **forecast** ['weðə ˌfɔ:kɑ:st] Wettervorhersage **III U1**, 12
foreign language [ˌfɒrɪn 'læŋgwɪdʒ] Fremdsprache **II**
forest ['fɒrɪst] Wald **II**
forever [fə'revə] für immer; ewig **II**
*to **forget** [fə'get] vergessen **I**
*to **forgive** [fə'gɪv] vergeben; verzeihen **II**
fork [fɔ:k] Gabel **III AC2**, 52
form [fɔ:m] Form **I**; Formular **III U1**, 12
negative **form** ['negətɪv ˌfɔ:m] verneinte Form **I**
past **form** ['pɑ:st fɔ:m] Vergangenheitsform **II**
possessive **form** [pəˌsesɪv 'fɔ:m] Possessivform **I**
short **form** ['ʃɔ:t fɔ:m] Kurzform **I**
to **form** [fɔ:m] formen; bilden **II**
formal ['fɔ:ml] formal; formell; förmlich **II**
forum ['fɔ:rəm] Forum **II**
forward ['fɔ:wəd] vorwärts **III U4**, 92
to look **forward** to [ˌlʊk 'fɔ:wəd tə] sich freuen auf **II**
to **found** [faʊnd] gründen **III U4**, 86
founder ['faʊndə] Gründer/-in ⟨**III U2**, 29⟩
four [fɔ:] vier **I**
Four and six is ten. [ˌfɔ:r‿ənd ˌsɪks‿ɪz 'ten] Vier plus sechs ist zehn. **I**
fox [fɒks] Fuchs **II**
freeze frame ['fri:z ˌfreɪm] Standbild °**III U4**, 98
free [fri:] frei; kostenlos **I**
free time [ˌfri: 'taɪm] Freizeit **I**
freedom *(no pl)* ['fri:dəm] Freiheit; Unabhängigkeit **III U2**, 36
freeze frame ['fri:z ˌfreɪm] Standbild °**III U4**, 98
French [frenʃ] französisch; Französisch **II**
frequently asked [ˌfri:kwəntli‿'ɑ:skt] häufig gefragt **I**
fresh [freʃ] frisch **I**
Friday ['fraɪdeɪ] Freitag **I**
fridge [frɪdʒ] Kühlschrank **I**
friend [frend] Freund/-in **I**
*to make **friends** [ˌmeɪk 'frendz] Freundschaft schließen **II**
That's what **friends** are for. [ˌðæts wɒt 'frendz‿ɑ: ˌfɔ:] Dafür sind Freunde da. **I**
friendly ['frendli] freundlich; nett **II**
friendship ['frendʃɪp] Freundschaft **II**
fringe [frɪndʒ] Rand-; Alternativ- **III U3**, 55
from [frɒm; frəm] aus; von **I**
from … to [frəm … tə] von … bis **I**
Where … **from**? [ˌweə … 'frɒm] Woher …? **I**
from around the world [frɒm əˌraʊnd ðə 'wɜ:ld] aus aller Welt **III U1**, 14
front [frʌnt] Vorderseite; Front-; Vorder- °**III U1**, 17
front door [ˌfrʌnt 'dɔ:] Haustür **II**
in **front** of [ɪn 'frʌnt‿əv] vor **I**
frost [frɒst] Frost ⟨**III TS2**, 77⟩
fruit [fru:t] Frucht; Obst **I**
full (of) [fʊl‿əv] voll (von) **I**
fun [fʌn] Freude; Spaß **I**
*to have **fun** [ˌhæv 'fʌn] Spaß haben; sich amüsieren **I**
It's **fun**. [ɪts 'fʌn] Es macht Spaß. **I**
fun [fʌn] lustig; witzig; fröhlich **I**
funny ['fʌni] lustig; witzig **I**; merkwürdig; komisch **III U2**, 32
further ['fɜ:ðə] weiter (weg) **III U3**, 64
future ['fju:tʃə] Zukunft **III U1**, 9

G

gadget ['gædʒɪt] Gerät; technische Spielerei **III U2**, 35
Gaelic ['geɪlɪk] gälisch; Gälisch **III U1**, 14
to **gain** weight [ˌgeɪn 'weɪt] zunehmen ⟨**III TS2**, 77⟩
gallery walk ['gælri ˌwɔ:k] Museumsrundgang; Vernissage **I**
game [geɪm] Spiel **I**
guessing **game** ['gesɪŋ ˌgeɪm] Ratespiel **II**
gap [gæp] Lücke; Spalt; Abstand **I**
garage ['gærɑ:ʒ] Garage **I**
garden ['gɑ:dn] Garten **I**
generation [ˌdʒenə'reɪʃn] Generation **III U4**, 87
generous ['dʒenrəs] großzügig **III TS1**, 46
genius ['dʒi:niəs] Genie **II**
genre ['ʒɑ̃:nrə] Gattung **III TS3**, 106
gentle ['dʒentl] behutsam; sanft ⟨**III TS3**, 107⟩
gentleman ['dʒentlmən], **gentlemen** ['dʒentlmen] *(pl)* Gentleman; feiner Herr **III U4**, 96
geocaching ['dʒi:əʊkæʃɪŋ] Geocaching **III U1**, 18
geography [dʒi'ɒgrəfi] Geografie; Erdkunde **III U1**, 14
German ['dʒɜ:mən] deutsch; Deutsch; aus Deutschland; Deutsche/-r **I**
*to **get** [get] holen; bringen; bekommen; besorgen; kaufen **I**; werden **III U1**, 18
*to **get** around [ˌget‿ə'raʊnd] *hier:* sich fortbewegen **II**
*to **get** away with [ˌget‿ə'weɪ wɪð] davonkommen mit **II**
*to **get** fit [ˌget 'fɪt] in Form kommen; fit werden **I**
*to **get** in the way [ˌget‿ɪn ðə 'weɪ] stören; im Weg stehen **II**
*to **get** into [ˌget‿'ɪntə] einsteigen; hineingelangen **I**
*to **get** lost [ˌget 'lɒst] verloren gehen; sich verirren **III U1**, 21
*to **get** off (a bus/train) [ˌget‿'ɒf] aussteigen (aus einem Bus/Zug) **II**
*to **get** on (the bus) [ˌget‿'ɒn] einsteigen (in den Bus) **III U1**, 12
*to **get** on people's nerves [ˌget‿ɒn sʌmbɒdiz 'nɜ:vz] jemandem auf die Nerven gehen **I**
*to **get** organised [get 'ɔ:gənaɪzd] sich organisieren °**III U1**, 17
*to **get** out of [get ˌaʊt‿əv] aussteigen **II**
*to **get** right [get 'raɪt] richtig beantworten °**III U1**, 17
*to **get** started [ˌget 'stɑ:tɪd] anfangen **II**
*to **get** sth out of one's head [get ˌaʊt‿əv wʌnz 'hed] etw. aus dem Kopf bekommen **III TS1**, 50
*to **get** stuck [ˌget 'stʌk] stecken bleiben ⟨**III TS2**, 77⟩
*to **get** there ['get ðeə] hinkommen **I**
*to **get** to ['get tə] kommen zu; kommen nach; erreichen **I**
*to **get** to know [ˌget tə 'nəʊ] kennenlernen **III U1**, 14
*to **get** up [ˌget‿'ʌp] aufstehen *(aus dem Bett)* **I**
Time to **get** up! [ˌtaɪm tə ˌget‿'ʌp] Es ist Zeit aufzustehen! **I**
ghost [gəʊst] Geist **II**
giant [dʒaɪənt] Riese; Gigant ⟨**III TS2**, 80⟩

gig [gɪg] Auftritt; Gig **III U3**, 58
girl [gɜːl] Mädchen **I**
a **girl** from Germany [ə ˌgɜːl frəm ˈdʒɜːməni] ein Mädchen aus Deutschland **I**
girlfriend [ˈgɜːlfrend] Freundin *(in einer Paarbeziehung)* **II**
gist [dʒɪst] das Wesentliche **II**
*to **give** [gɪv] geben; schenken **I**
*to **give** sb funny looks [ˌgɪv fʌni ˈlʊks] jmdn. schief anschauen **III U2**, 32
*to **give** the bumps [ˌgɪv ðə ˈbʌmps] hochleben lassen **I**
*to **give** up [ˌgɪv‿ˈʌp] aufgeben **III U2**, 30
glass [glɑːs] Glas **I**
glasses *(pl)* [ˈglɑːsɪz] Brille **II**
glen [glen] Schlucht ⟨**III U3**, 58⟩
global [ˈgləʊbl] global; weltweit ⟨**III TS2**, 80⟩
glove [glʌv] Handschuh **I**
*to **go** [gəʊ] gehen; fahren **I**
*to **go** black [ˌgəʊ ˈblæk] schwarz werden **II**
*to **go** crazy [ˌgəʊ ˈkreɪzi] ausflippen; durchdrehen; verrückt werden **II**
*to **go** down [ˌgəʊ ˈdaʊn] hinuntergehen; nach unten gehen; entlanggehen **I**
*to **go** for a walk [ˌgəʊ fər‿ə ˈwɔːk] spazieren gehen **II**
*to **go** on [ˌgəʊ‿ˈɒn] weitergehen; weitermachen; weiterführen; fortfahren **I**
*to **go** out [ˌgəʊ‿ˈaʊt] ausgehen; hinausgehen **III U1**, 18
*to **go** over to [ˌgəʊ ˈəʊvə tə] hinübergehen zu; zu jmdm. nach Hause gehen **II**
*to **go** right back to [ˌgəʊ raɪt ˈbæk tə] zurückgehen auf **III U1**, 18
*to **go** round in circles [gəʊ ˌraʊnd ɪn ˈsɜːklz] sich im Kreis drehen **III U3**, 66
*to **go** shopping [ˌgəʊ ˈʃɒpɪŋ] einkaufen gehen **I**
*to **go** swimming [ˌgəʊ ˈswɪmɪŋ] Schwimmen gehen **I**
*to **go** to bed [ˌgəʊ tə ˈbed] ins Bett gehen **I**
*to **go** together [ˌgəʊ təˈgeðə] zueinander passen; zueinander gehören **I**
*to **go** with [ˈgəʊ wɪð] passen zu; gehören zu **I**
*to **go** wrong [ˌgəʊ ˈrɒŋ] schiefgehen **I**
*to let **go** (of) [ˌlet ˈgəʊ (əv)] loslassen **II**
It's **gone**. [ɪts ˈgɒn] Es ist weg. **II**
What's **going** on? [wɒts ˌgəʊɪŋ‿ˈɒn] Was ist los?; Was geht ab? **III U2**, 36
goal [gəʊl] Tor; Ziel **I**
gold [gəʊld] Gold **III U4**, 90
golden age [ˌgəʊldn ˈeɪdʒ] goldenes Zeitalter **III U4**, 86
golf [gɒlf] Golf **III U1**, 14
*to be **gone** [biː ˈgɒn] verschwunden sein; weg sein **II**
gonna (= going to) *(coll)* [ˈgɒnə] wird/werden ⟨**III U2**, 31⟩
good [gʊd] gut **I**
*to be **good** at [biː ˈgʊd‿ət] gut sein in **I**
Good morning. [ˌgʊd ˈmɔːnɪŋ] Guten Morgen. **I**
goodbye [gʊdˈbaɪ] auf Wiedersehen **I**
gorge scrambling [ˈgɔːdʒ ˌskræmblɪŋ] Schluchtenklettern **II**
to **grab** [græb] greifen; ergreifen; schnappen **II**
grammar [ˈgræmə] Grammatik **II**
grammar school [ˈgræmə ˌskuːl] Gymnasium **III U1**, 13
grandad [ˈgrændæd] Opa **I**
grandma [ˈgrænmɑː] Oma **I**
grandparents *(pl)* [ˈgrænˌpeərənts] Großeltern **I**
granny [ˈgræni] Oma **I**
graphic novel [ˌgræfɪk ˈnɒvl] Bildergeschichte; Comic **III TS3**, 106
grass [grɑːs] Gras ⟨**III TS3**, 107⟩
gratitude [ˈgrætɪtjuːd] Dankbarkeit **III AC2**, 53
great [greɪt] großartig; toll; super **I**
It's **great** for … [ɪts ˈgreɪt fə] Es ist super zum/für … **I**
… is a **great** sport. [ɪz‿ə ˈgreɪt ˌspɔːt] … ist ein toller Sport. **I**
green [griːn] grün **I**
Greenwich Mean Time *(= GMT)* [ˌgrenɪdʒ ˈmiːn ˌtaɪm] westeuropäische Zeit **I**
greeting [ˈgriːtɪŋ] Gruß **I**
grey [greɪ] grau **I**
grid [grɪd] Gitter; Tabelle; Raster **I**
*to be **grounded** [bi ˈgraʊndɪd] Hausarrest haben **III U2**, 36
group [gruːp] Gruppe; Klasse **I**
a **group** of three [ə ˌgruːp‿əv ˈθriː] eine Dreiergruppe **I**
tutor **group** [ˈtjuːtə ˌgruːp] Klasse *(in einer englischen Schule)* **I**
to **group** (around) [gruːp (əˈraʊnd)] gruppieren (um) °**III TS3**, 108
*to **grow** [grəʊ] wachsen **III U1**, 9; anbauen; züchten **III U4**, 85
*to **grow** up [ˌgrəʊ‿ˈʌp] aufwachsen; erwachsen werden **III U4**, 89
guard [gɑːd] Wache; Wächter/-in **II**
to **guess** [ges] raten; erraten; vermuten **I**
guessing game [ˈgesɪŋ ˌgeɪm] Ratespiel **II**
guest [gest] Gast **III U2**, 34
guide [gaɪd] Führer/-in; Reiseführer **II**
to **guide** [gaɪd] führen; leiten **III TS1**, 49
guinea pig [ˈgɪniː ˌpɪg] Meerschweinchen **I**
guy [gaɪ] Typ; Kerl; *(Pl.)* Leute **II**

H

haggis [ˈhægɪs] Haggis *(schottisches Gericht aus in einem Schafsmagen gekochten Schafsinnereien und Haferschrot)* **III U3**, 55
hair [ˌduː‿aʊə ˈheə] Haar(e) **I**
*to do our **hair** [ˌduː‿aʊə ˈheə] uns frisieren; unsere Haare machen **I**
hairbrush [ˈheəbrʌʃ] Haarbürste **III U4**, 86
half, halves *(pl)* (of) [hɑːf; hɑːvz] die Hälfte **I**
half an hour [ˌhɑːf‿ən‿ˈaʊər] eine halbe Stunde **III U4**, 97
half [hɑːf] halb **I**
half past [ˌhɑːf ˈpɑːst] halb *(bei Uhrzeitangaben)* **I**
half-sister [ˈhɑːfˌsɪstə] Halbschwester **I**
half-term break [ˌhɑːftɜːm ˈbreɪk] Halbjahresferien **I**
*to meet **halfway** [ˌmiːt hɑːfˈweɪ] sich auf halbem Weg treffen **III U2**, 34
hall [hɔːl] Halle; Saal **II**; Flur; Diele; Korridor **III U1**, 18
ham [hæm] Schinken **III AC2**, 52
hammer [ˈhæmə] Hammer **II**
hand [hænd] Hand **I**
Clap your **hands**. [ˌklæp jɔː ˈhændz] Klatsch/Klatscht in die Hände. **I**
On the one **hand** …, (but) on the other **hand** … [ɒn ðə‿ˈwʌn ˌhænd … (bʌt) ɒn ði‿ˈʌðə ˌhænd …] Einerseits …, (aber) andererseits … **II**
to **handle** [ˈhændl] umgehen mit; *hier:* anfassen ⟨**III TS2**, 77⟩
*to **hang** up [ˌhæŋ‿ˈʌp] aufhängen **II**
*to **hang** out (with) *(infml)* [ˌhæŋ‿ˈaʊt wɪð] sich herumtreiben (mit); rumhängen (mit); sich treffen (mit) **III U2**, 36
to **happen** [ˈhæpn] geschehen; passieren **I**
happiness [ˈhæpɪnəs] Glück; Zufriedenheit; Fröhlichkeit ⟨**III TS1**, 47⟩
happy [ˈhæpi] glücklich; froh; fröhlich **I**
happy ending [ˌhæpi ˈendɪŋ] Happy End **III TS3**, 106
Happy Birthday! [ˌhæpi ˈbɜːθdeɪ] Alles Gute zum Geburtstag!; Herzlichen Glückwunsch zum Geburtstag! **I**
harbour [ˈhɑːbə] Hafen **III U1**, 9
hard [hɑːd] hart; schwer; schwierig; *hier:* stark **II**
*to be **hard** on sb [bi ˈhɑːd‿ɒn] streng mit jmdm. sein **III U2**, 33
hat [hæt] Hut **I**
to **hate** [heɪt] hassen; nicht mögen **II**
*to **have** [hæv] haben **I**
*to **have** a look (at) [ˌhæv‿ə ˈlʊk] anschauen **II**
*to **have** a point [ˌhæv‿ə ˈpɔɪnt] nicht ganz unrecht haben **III U2**, 34
*to **have** breakfast [ˌhæv ˈbrekfəst] frühstücken **I**

*to **have** fun [ˌhæv ˈfʌn] Spaß haben; sich amüsieren **I**
*to **have** got [hæv ˈgɒt] besitzen; haben **I**
*to **have** in common [ˌhæv‿ɪn ˈkɒmən] gemeinsam haben **III TS3**, 110
*to **have** to [ˈhæv tə] müssen **II**
***to have** *(a sweet)* [hæv] *(ein Bonbon)* nehmen; *(ein Bonbon)* essen **I**
hay [heɪ] Heu ⟨**III TS2**, 77⟩
he [hiː] er **I**
head [hed] Kopf **I**
*to get sth out of one's **head** [get ˌaʊt‿əv wʌnz ˈhed] etw. aus dem Kopf bekommen **III TS1**, 50
head of state [ˌhed‿əv ˈsteɪt] Staatsoberhaupt **II**
With a very big **head**! [ˌwɪð ə ˌveri bɪg ˈhed] Und ein Angeber! **II**
headache *(no pl)* [ˈhedeɪk] Kopfschmerzen; Kopfweh **II**
heading [ˈhedɪŋ] Überschrift; Titel **I**
headline [ˈhedlaɪn] Schlagzeile **III TS2**, 76
headphones *(pl)* [ˈhedfəʊnz] Kopfhörer **II**
health [helθ] Gesundheit **II**
healthy [ˈhelθi] gesund **I**
***to hear** [hɪə] hören **I**
I **hear** … [aɪ ˈhɪə] Ich habe gehört, dass … **I**
heart [hɑːt] Herz; *hier:* Zentrum **II**
*to learn … by **heart** [ˌlɜːn baɪ ˈhɑːt] auswendig lernen **I**
heating [ˈhiːtɪŋ] Heizung **III U4**, 84
underfloor **heating** *(no pl)* [ˌʌndəflɔː ˈhiːtɪŋ] Fußbodenheizung **III U4**, 84
heaven [ˈhevn] Himmel ⟨**III TS1**, 46⟩
heavy [ˈhevi] schwer; stark **III U3**, 67
hedgehog [ˈhedʒhɒg] Igel **III TS2**, 76
Hello. [helˈəʊ] Hallo. **I**
*to say **hello** (to) [ˌseɪ helˈəʊ tə] grüßen; Grüße ausrichten (an) **I**
help [help] Hilfe **I**
to help [help] helfen **I**
to **help** out [ˌhelp‿ˈaʊt] aushelfen **III U3**, 69
helpful [ˈhelpfl] hilfsbereit; hilfreich **I**
helpless [ˈhelpləs] hilflos **I**
her [hɜː] ihr/-e; sie **I**
here [hɪə] hier **I**
right **here** [ˌraɪt ˈhɪə] genau hier **II**
Here you are. [ˌhɪə ju‿ˈɑː] Bitte schön. **I**
Here's … [hɪəz] Hier ist … **I**
hero, heroes *(pl)* [ˈhɪərəʊ, ˈhɪərəʊz] Held **III AC1**, 24
heroine [ˈherəʊɪn] Heldin **III AC1**, 24
to hesitate [ˈhezɪteɪt] zögern **III TS3**, 107
Hey! [heɪ] Hi.; He!; Hallo. **I**
Hi. [haɪ] Hi.; Hallo. **I**
hibernation [ˌhaɪbəˈneɪʃn] Winterschlaf **III TS2**, 77
hidden [ˈhɪdn] versteckt ⟨**III TS3**, 107⟩
***to hide** [haɪd] (sich) verstecken **III AC1**, 24
hiding place [ˈhaɪdɪŋ ˌpleɪs] Versteck ⟨**III TS1**, 51⟩
high [haɪ] hoch; groß **II**
high tide [ˈhaɪ ˌtaɪd] Flut **II**
the **high** street [ðə ˈhaɪ ˌstriːt] die Haupteinkaufsstraße **III U2**, 36
highlight [ˈhaɪlaɪt] Highlight; Höhepunkt **II**
hiking [ˈhaɪkɪŋ] Wandern **III U1**, 9
hill [hɪl] Berg; Hügel **III U1**, 18
him [hɪm] ihn; ihm **I**
himself [hɪmˈself] er/sich (selbst); selber **II**
hint [hɪnt] Hinweis; Andeutung; Tipp **III AC3**, 83
his [hɪz] sein/-e **I**
historic [hɪˈstɒrɪk] historisch **III U3**, 54
historical [hɪˈstɒrɪkl] historisch; geschichtlich **I**
history [ˈhɪstri] Geschichte **II**
living **history** show [ˌlɪvɪŋ ˈhɪstəri ˌʃəʊ] *Show, in der historischer Alltag nachgespielt wird* **III U1**, 8
***to hit** [hɪt] schlagen; treffen **I**
hobby, hobbies *(pl)* [ˈhɒbi; ˈhɒbiz] Hobby **I**
hockey [hɒki] Hockey **II**
hoe [həʊ] Hacke ⟨**III TS3**, 107⟩
to hog a conversation [ˌhɒg‿ə kɒnvəˈseɪʃn] ein Gespräch für sich in Beschlag nehmen; ein Gespräch dominieren **III AC3**, 82
***to hold** [həʊld] halten; festhalten **I**; abhalten ⟨**III U3**, 63⟩
*to **hold** onto [ˌhəʊld‿ˈɒntə] (sich) festhalten an **III U3**, 67
hole [həʊl] Loch **II**
holiday [ˈhɒlədeɪ] Urlaub; Feiertag **I**
holidays *(pl)* [ˈhɒlədeɪz] Ferien **I**
home [həʊm] Zuhause; Heim **I**
at **home** [ət ˈhəʊm] zu Hause **I**
home [həʊm] nach Hause **I**
homepage [ˈhəʊmpeɪdʒ] Homepage **I**
homeward [ˈhəʊmwəd] heimwärts ⟨**III U3**, 58⟩
homework [ˈhəʊmwɜːk] Hausaufgabe(n) **I**
honest [ˈɒnɪst] ehrlich **III U2**, 38
honey [ˈhʌni] Honig **III TS1**, 47
honeysuckle [ˈhʌnisʌkl] Geißblatt ⟨**III TS3**, 107⟩
to hook [hʊk] *hier:* fesseln **III TS3**, 107
hope [həʊp] Hoffnung **II**
to hope [həʊp] hoffen **I**
hopeful [ˈhəʊpfl] hoffnungsvoll **I**
horn [hɔːn] Horn **III TS2**, 80
horrified [ˈhɒrɪfaɪd] entsetzt **I**
horror [ˈhɒrə] Horrorgeschichte; Horrorfilm; Horror **III TS3**, 106
horse [hɔːs] Pferd **I**
hospital [ˈhɒspɪtl] Hospital; Krankenhaus **II**
host family [ˈhəʊst ˌfæmli] Gastfamilie **III AC2**, 52
hot [hɒt] heiß **III TS2**, 79
hotel [həʊˈtel] Hotel **II**
hour [aʊə] Stunde **II**
half an **hour** [ˌhɑːf‿ən‿ˈaʊər] eine halbe Stunde **III U4**, 97
house [haʊs] Haus **I**
to move (house) [muːv (haʊs)] umziehen **III U1**, 10
how [haʊ] wie **I**
How many …? [ˌhaʊ ˈmeni] Wie viele …? **I**
How are you? [ˌhaʊ‿ˈɑː jə] Wie geht es dir?; Wie geht es euch?; Wie geht es Ihnen? **I**
How much (is/are) …? [ˌhaʊ ˈmʌtʃ‿ɪz/ɑː] Wie viel (kostet/kosten) …? **I**
How old are you? [haʊ‿ˈəʊld‿ə juː] Wie alt bist du?; Wie alt sind Sie? **I**
How to … [ˈhaʊ tə] Wie man … **I**
Is this **how** you (do) …? [ɪz ˈðɪs haʊ jʊ ˌduː] Machst du so …? **I**
that's **how** [ðæts ˈhaʊ] so **II**
to hug [hʌg] umarmen **I**
huge [hjuːdʒ] riesig; riesengroß; gewaltig **II**
to hum [hʌm] summen **II**
human [ˈhjuːmən] Mensch ⟨**III TS2**, 77⟩
human [ˈhjuːmən] menschlich; Menschen- ⟨**III TS2**, 79⟩
human body [ˌhjuːmən ˈbɒdi] menschlicher Körper **II**
Humanities *(pl)* [hjuːˈmænətiz] Sozialwissenschaften **II**
humour *(no pl)* [ˈhjuːmə] Humor; Stimmung **III U3**, 64
sense of **humour** *(no pl)* [ˌsens‿əv ˈhjuːmə] Sinn für Humor **III U2**, 39
hundreds of [ˈhʌndrədz‿əv] Hunderte (von) **III U3**, 61
hungry [ˈhʌŋgri] hungrig **I**
to hurry [ˈhʌri] eilen; sich beeilen **I**
***to hurt** [hɜːt] verletzen; weh tun **II**
you have never been **hurt** [ju hæv ˌnevə biːn ˈhɜːt] du bist noch nie verletzt worden ⟨**III TS1**, 46⟩
hurt [hɜːt] verletzt **II**
husband [ˈhʌzbənd] Ehemann **II**

I

I [aɪ] ich **I**
I don't know! [ˌaɪ ˌdəʊnt ˈnəʊ] Ich weiß (es) nicht! **I**
I don't like … [aɪ ˈdəʊnt laɪk] Ich mag … nicht.; Ich mache … nicht gern. **I**
I hear … [aɪ ˈhɪə] Ich habe gehört, dass … **I**
I like … [aɪ ˈlaɪk] Mir gefällt …; Ich mag … **I**
I love you. [aɪ ˈlʌv ju] Ich liebe dich.; Ich mag dich. **I**
I love … [aɪ ˈlʌv] Ich liebe …; Ich mag … total gern. **I**
I'd like to … *(= I would like to)* [aɪd ˈlaɪk tə] Ich möchte …; Ich würde gern … **I**

I'd rather [aɪd 'rɑːðə] ich würde lieber **III U4**, 99
I'm (not) scared of ... [ˌaɪm (nɒt) 'skeəd‿əv] Ich habe (keine) Angst vor ... **I**
I'm dog-tired. [ˌaɪm ˌdɒg'taɪəd] Ich bin hundemüde. **I**
I'm English. [aɪm‿'ɪŋglɪʃ] Ich bin Engländer/-in. **I**
I'm fine. [ˌaɪm 'faɪn] Mir geht's gut. **I**
I'm from ... [ˌaɪm frɒm] Ich bin aus ... **I**
I'm sorry! [ˌaɪm 'sɒri] Tut mir leid! **I**
I'm ... [aɪm] Ich bin ... **I**
ice [aɪs] Eis **I**
ice cream [ˌaɪs 'kriːm] Eis; Eiscreme **I**
ice rink ['aɪs ˌrɪŋk] Eisbahn; Schlittschuhbahn **I**
idea [aɪ'dɪə] Idee; Einfall **I**
no **idea** [ˌnəʊ‿aɪ'dɪə] keine Ahnung **II**
to **identify** with [aɪ'dentɪfaɪ wɪð] sich identifizieren mit **III TS3**, 106
identity [aɪ'dentəti] Identität **II**
idiot ['ɪdiət] Idiot/-in **II**
if [ɪf] wenn; falls; ob **I**
as **if** [əz‿'ɪf] als ob ⟨**III TS1**, 46⟩∅ °**III U4**, 95
if-clause ['ɪf‿klɔːz] if-Satz °**III U1**, 14
to **ignore** [ɪg'nɔː] ignorieren; außer Acht lassen **III U2**, 37
ill [ɪl] krank **III TS2**, 77
illegal [ɪ'liːgl] illegal; unrechtmäßig; rechtswidrig **III TS2**, 80
imagination [ɪˌmædʒɪ'neɪʃn] Fantasie; Vorstellungskraft **III U2**, 27
imaginative [ɪ'mædʒɪnətɪv] einfallsreich; fantasievoll **III U2**, 27
to **imagine** [ɪ'mædʒɪn] sich (etwas) vorstellen **I**
imperative [ɪm'perətɪv] Imperativ; Befehlsform °**III TS2**, 78
impolite [ˌɪmp'laɪt] unhöflich **III AC2**, 53
important [ɪm'pɔːtnt] wichtig **I**
impossibility [ɪmˌpɒsə'bɪləti] (Ding der) Unmöglichkeit ⟨**III TS1**, 46⟩
impressed [ɪm'prest] beeindruckt **II**
impressive [ɪm'presɪv] beeindruckend ⟨**III TS2**, 80⟩
to **improve** [ɪm'pruːv] sich verbessern; verbessern **I**
in [ɪn] in; im; rein; herein **I**
in between [ˌɪn bɪ'twiːn] dazwischen °**III TS1**, 51
in fact [ɪn 'fækt] tatsächlich; eigentlich; genau genommen ⟨**III U3**, 62⟩
in front of [ɪn 'frʌnt‿əv] vor **I**
in need [ɪn 'niːd] bedürftig; in Not **II**
in secret [ɪn 'siːkrət] heimlich **II**
in the end [ˌɪn ði‿'end] schließlich; zum Schluss **II**
in the evenings [ɪn ði‿'iːvnɪŋz] abends **I**
in the mornings [ˌɪn ðə 'mɔːnɪŋz] morgens; vormittags **I**
in the photo(s) [ˌɪn ðə 'fəʊtəʊ(z)] auf dem Foto/den Fotos **I**
in the street [ˌɪn ðə 'striːt] in der Straße; auf der Straße **I**
in those days [ˌɪn ðəʊz 'deɪz] damals ⟨**III U3**, 63⟩
to **include** [ɪn'kluːd] einschließen; beinhalten **III U1**, 8; aufnehmen; einbeziehen °**III U3**, 65
in-crowd ['ɪnkraʊd] Szene; die Angesagten; die Beliebten **III U2**, 36
independence *(no pl)* [ˌɪndɪ'pendəns] Unabhängigkeit **III U3**, 55
independent [ˌɪndɪ'pendənt] unabhängig **III U3**, 55
Indian ['ɪndiən] Inder/-in; indisch **I**
individual [ˌɪndɪ'vɪdʒuəl] individuell; einzeln **II**
industry ['ɪndəstri] Industrie; Branche; Gewerbe **III U3**, 59
infinitive [ɪn'fɪnətɪv] Infinitiv **I**
to **influence** ['ɪnfluəns] beeinflussen **II**
information *(no pl)* [ˌɪnfə'meɪʃn] Information; Informationen **I**
ingredient [ɪn'griːdiənt] Zutat **III AC1**, 24
injury ['ɪndʒəri] Verletzung **II**
inline skating ['ɪnlaɪn ˌskeɪtɪŋ] Inlineskatefahren **I**
inside [ˌɪn'saɪd] innen; im Innern; hinein; nach drinnen; in; drin **I**
instead [ɪn'sted] stattdessen **III U2**, 36
instruction [ɪn'strʌkʃn] Instruktion; Anweisung **I**
instructor [ɪn'strʌktə] Lehrer/-in; Betreuer/-in **II**
interest ['ɪntrəst] Interesse **II**
to **interest** ['ɪntrəst] (sich) interessieren **II**
*to be **interested** in [bi‿'ɪntrəstɪd‿ɪn] interessiert sein an; sich interessieren für **II**
interesting ['ɪntrəstɪŋ] interessant **I**
international [ˌɪntə'næʃnl] international **I**
internet ['ɪntənet] Internet **I**
interview ['ɪntəvjuː] Interview; Befragung **I**
to **interview** ['ɪntəvjuː] interviewen; befragen **I**
into ['ɪntə] in; in ... hinein **I**
*to be **into** [biː‿'ɪntə] mögen; stehen auf **I**
You're **into** ... ['jɔːr‿ɪntə] Du magst ...; Du stehst auf ... **I**
Introduce ... [ˌɪntrə'djuːs] Stelle/Stellt ... vor. **I**
introduction [ˌɪntrə'dʌkʃn] Einführung; Einleitung; Vorstellung **II**
to **invade** [ɪn'veɪd] einmarschieren (in); eindringen (in); überfallen **III U4**, 88
to **invent** [ɪn'vent] erfinden **III U3**, 60
invention [ɪn'venʃn] Erfindung **III U3**, 60
inventor [ɪn'ventə] Erfinder/-in **III U3**, 69
invitation [ˌɪnvɪ'teɪʃn] Einladung **I**
to **invite** [ɪn'vaɪt] einladen **I**
inward ['ɪnwəd] ankommend **III U1**, 12
Irish ['aɪrɪʃ] irisch; Irisch **III U1**, 14
irregular [ɪ'regjələ] unregelmäßig **I**
Is this how you (do) ...? [ɪz 'ðɪs haʊ jʊ ˌduː] Machst du so ...? **I**
island ['aɪlənd] Insel **III U1**, 9
it [ɪt] es **I**
*to make **it** ['meɪk‿ɪt] es schaffen ⟨**III TS2**, 77⟩
It's fun. [ɪts 'fʌn] Es macht Spaß. **I**
It's great for ... [ɪts 'greɪt fə] Es ist super zum/für ... **I**
It's your turn. [ˌɪts 'jɔː tɜːn] Du bist dran. **I**
It's .../They're ... [ɪts/ðeə] Es kostet .../Sie kosten ... **I**
IT *(= Information Technology)* [ˌaɪ'tiː] Informatik; Informationstechnik **III U2**, 28
its [ɪts] sein/-e; ihr/-e **I**
ivory *(no pl)* ['aɪvri] Elfenbein **III TS2**, 80

J

jacket ['dʒækɪt] Jacke **III U3**, 59
jam [dʒæm] Marmelade; Konfitüre **III AC2**, 52
January ['dʒænjuri] Januar **I**
*to be **jealous** (of) [bi: 'dʒeləs] eifersüchtig sein (auf); neidisch sein (auf) **I**
jelly ['dʒeli] Tortenguss; Götterspeise; Wackelpudding; Gelee **I**
jewel ['dʒuːəl] Juwel; Edelstein **III U4**, 95
crown **jewels** [ˌkraʊn 'dʒuːəlz] Kronjuwelen **II**
jewellery ['dʒuːəlri] Schmuck **I**
job [dʒɒb] Arbeit; Aufgabe; Job **I**
mouth **jogging** ['maʊθ ˌdʒɒgɪŋ] Training für den Mund **I**
to **join** [dʒɔɪn] beitreten; sich anschließen; verbinden **II**
joke [dʒəʊk] Witz **I**
to **joke** [dʒəʊk] scherzen **II**
journey ['dʒɜːni] Reise; Fahrt **III U1**, 9
to **judge** [dʒʌdʒ] beurteilen; bewerten **III U2**, 26
juggling ['dʒʌglɪŋ] Jonglieren **II**
juice [dʒuːs] Saft **I**
July [dʒʊ'laɪ] Juli **I**
to **jump** [dʒʌmp] springen **I**
to **jump** back [ˌdʒʌmp‿'bæk] zurückspringen; *hier:* zurückschrecken **II**
to **jump** the queue [ˌdʒʌmp ðə 'kjuː] sich vordrängeln **I**
June [dʒuːn] Juni **I**
piece of **junk** [ˌpiːs‿əv 'dʒʌŋk] Stück Schrott **III U2**, 37
just [dʒʌst] gerade; nur; einfach **I**

K

keen [kiːn] scharf; fein ⟨**III TS1**, 48⟩
*to **keep** [kiːp] behalten; aufbewahren; halten **I**
*to **keep** away from [ˌkiːp‿ə'weɪ frəm] (sich) fernhalten von **III U1**, 18

*to **keep** going [ˌkiːp ˈɡəʊɪŋ] aufrechterhalten **II**
*to **keep** one's feet or hands still [ˌkiːp wʌnz: ˈfiːt‿ɔː ˈhændz stɪl] die Beine und Hände ruhig halten **III TS1**, 50
*to **keep** out (of) [ˌkiːp‿ˈaʊt əv] draußen bleiben; draußen halten **III U3**, 66
*to **keep** the ball bouncing [ˌkiːp ðə bɔːl ˈbaʊntsɪŋ] *hier:* das Gespräch am Laufen halten **III AC3**, 82
*to **keep** up (with) [ˌkiːp‿ˈʌp (wɪð)] mithalten (mit); Schritt halten (mit) **II**
*to **keep** your fingers crossed [ˌkiːp jɔː ˌfɪŋɡəz ˈkrɒst] die Daumen drücken **I**
key [kiː] Schlüssel **II**
key ring [ˈkiː ˌrɪŋ] Schlüsselbund; Schlüsselanhänger **III U3**, 67
key word [ˈkiː wɜːd] Stichwort; Schlüsselbegriff **I**
piano **key** [piˈænəʊ ˌkiː] Klaviertaste ⟨**III TS2**, 80⟩
to **kick** [kɪk] schießen; treten **II**
to **kill** [kɪl] töten; umbringen **III TS2**, 80
killing [ˈkɪlɪŋ] Töten ⟨**III TS2**, 80⟩
kilometre (km) [ˈkɪləˌmiːtə; kɪˈlɒmɪtə] Kilometer **III TS3**, 109
kilt [kɪlt] Kilt; Schottenrock **III U3**, 55
kind [kaɪnd] Art; Sorte **I**
king [kɪŋ] König **I**
kitchen [ˈkɪtʃɪn] Küche **I**
knife [naɪf], **knives** [naɪvz] *(pl)* Messer **III AC2**, 52
knight [naɪt] Ritter **III AC1**, 24
knob [nɒb] Griff **II**
*to **know** [nəʊ] kennen; wissen **I**
*to get to **know** [ˌɡet tə ˈnəʊ] kennenlernen **III U1**, 14
I don't **know**! [ˌaɪ ˌdəʊnt ˈnəʊ] Ich weiß (es) nicht! **I**
You **know** how to … [juː ˈnəʊ ˌhaʊ tə] Du weißt, wie man …; Ihr wisst, wie man … **I**
koala [kəʊˈɑːlə] Koala **III TS2**, 79
Korean [kəˈriːən] koreanisch; Koreanisch; Koreaner/-in **II**
South **Korean** [ˌsaʊθ kəˈriːən] Südkoreaner/-in; südkoreanisch; Südkoreanisch **II**

L

ladder [ˈlædə] Leiter **II**
lady [ˈleɪdi] Lady; Dame **III U4**, 96
lady-in-waiting [ˌleɪdiɪnˈweɪtɪŋ] Hofdame **III U4**, 96
laid-back [ˌleɪdˈbæk] entspannt; locker **III U2**, 28
lake [leɪk] See **I**
boating **lake** [ˈbəʊtɪŋ ˌleɪk] See zum Rudern **I**
lamb [læm] Lamm; Lämmchen **I**
land [lænd] Land **I**
to **land** [lænd] landen **II**
landscape [ˈlændskeɪp] Landschaft **III U1**, 8
language [ˈlæŋɡwɪdʒ] Sprache **I**
first **language** [ˌfɜːst ˈlæŋɡwɪdʒ] Muttersprache **II**
foreign **language** [ˌfɒrɪn ˈlæŋɡwɪdʒ] Fremdsprache **II**
official **language** [əˌfɪʃl ˈlæŋɡwɪdʒ] Amtssprache **II**
laptop [ˈlæptɒp] Laptop **II**
large [lɑːdʒ] groß; riesig **II**
lassi [ˈlʌsi] Lassi **I**
last [lɑːst] letzte/-r/-s **I**
at **last** [ət ˈlɑːst] endlich; schließlich **I**
late [leɪt] spät; zu spät **I**
*to be **late** [biː ˈleɪt] zu spät dran sein; zu spät kommen **I**
later [ˈleɪtə] später **I**
latest [ˈleɪtɪst] neueste/-r/-s ⟨**III U3**, 62⟩
to **laugh** [lɑːf] lachen **I**
*to **lay** down [ˌleɪ ˈdaʊn] hinlegen ⟨**III TS3**, 107⟩
layer (of) [ˈleɪər‿əv] Schicht (aus); Lage (aus) **III TS2**, 77
layout [ˈleɪaʊt] Layout; Anordnung **III U2**, 35
lazy [ˈleɪzi] faul **III TS1**, 47
lead part [ˌliːd ˈpɑːt] Hauptrolle **III U2**, 28
*to **lead** [liːd] führen; anführen **III U3**, 61
*to **lead** off [liːd‿ˈɒf] wegführen **III U3**, 61
lead [liːd] Haupt- **III U2**, 28
leaf [liːf], **leaves** [liːvz] *(pl)* Blatt ⟨**III U3**, 58⟩
*to **learn** [lɜːn] lernen **I**
*to **learn** about [ˈlɜːn‿əˌbaʊt] erfahren über **III U2**, 27
*to **learn** … by heart [ˌlɜːn baɪ ˈhɑːt] auswendig lernen **I**
a lot to **learn** [ə ˌlɒt tə ˈlɜːn] viel zu lernen **I**
at **least** [ət ˈliːst] mindestens; wenigstens **II**
*to **leave** [liːv] verlassen; lassen; abfahren; losgehen **II**
*to **leave** a message [ˌliːv‿ə ˈmesɪdʒ] eine Nachricht hinterlassen **I**
*to **leave** behind [ˌliːv‿bɪˈhaɪnd] zurücklassen **III U3**, 61
*to **leave** it to cool [ˌliːv‿ɪt tə ˈkuːl] kalt stellen **I**
*to **leave** space [liːv ˈspeɪs] Platz lassen **I**
left [left] linke/-r/-s; links **I**
on the **left** [ɒn ðə ˈleft] auf der linken Seite; links **I**
left [left] übrig **I**
leg [leɡ] Bein **II**
legend [ˈledʒənd] Legende; Sage **III AC1**, 24
leisure [ˈleʒə] Freizeit; Freizeit- **I**
leisure centre [ˈleʒə ˌsentə] Freizeitzentrum **I**
lemon [ˈlemən] Zitrone **II**
lemonade [ˌleməˈneɪd] Limonade **I**
*to **lend** [ˈlend tə] leihen; verleihen **III U2**, 37
less [les] weniger **III U4**, 87
lesson [ˈlesn] Unterrichtsstunde; Schulstunde; Unterricht **I**
*to **let** [let] lassen **I**
*to **let** go (of) [ˌlet ˈɡəʊ (əv)] loslassen **II**
Let's … [lets] Lass/Lasst uns … **I**
letter [ˈletə] Buchstabe **I**; Brief **II**
capital **letter** [ˌkæpɪtl ˈletə] Großbuchstabe **I**
library [ˈlaɪbri] Bibliothek; Bücherei **III TS2**, 76
lie [laɪ] Lüge **III U2**, 38
to **lie** [laɪ] lügen **II**
*to **lie** [laɪ] liegen **II**
life, **lives** *(pl)* [laɪf, laɪvz] Leben **II**
lifeboat [ˈlaɪfbəʊt] Rettungsboot **I**
lifebuoy [ˈlaɪfbɔɪ] Rettungsring **I**
lifestyle [ˈlaɪfstaɪl] Lebensstil; Lifestyle **III U4**, 87
light [laɪt] Licht; Lampe **II**
light [laɪt] leicht **III AC3**, 82
to **lighten** [ˈlaɪtn] aufhellen **III U4**, 98
lightning *(no pl)* [ˈlaɪtnɪŋ] Blitz **II**
your **like** [jɔː ˈlaɪk] jemanden wie dich ⟨**III U3**, 58⟩
to **like** [laɪk] mögen; gern haben **I**
would **like** [wʊd ˈlaɪk] würde/-st/-n/-t gern; hätte/-st/-n/-t gern **I**
I don't **like** … [aɪ ˈdəʊnt laɪk] Ich mag … nicht.; Ich mache … nicht gern. **I**
I **like** singing and dancing. [ˌaɪ laɪk ˌsɪŋɪŋ‿ənd ˈdɑːnsɪŋ] Ich singe und tanze gern. **I**
I **like** … [aɪ ˈlaɪk] Mir gefällt …; Ich mag … **I**
I'd **like** to … *(= I would like to)* [aɪd ˈlaɪk tə] Ich möchte …; Ich würde gern … **I**
Would you **like** …? [ˌwʊd jʊ ˈlaɪk] Möchtest du …?; Möchten Sie …?; Möchtet ihr …? **II**
like [laɪk] wie **I**
*to be **like** [bi ˈlaɪk] sein **III U3**, 54
like that [laɪk ˈðæt] so **I**
like this [laɪk ˈðɪs] so **I**
What was it **like**? [ˌwɒt wɒz‿ɪt ˈlaɪk] Wie war es? **III U4**, 84
limit [ˈlɪmɪt] Limit; Grenze **III U2**, 35
line [laɪn] Zeile; Linie **I**
finish **line** [ˈfɪnɪʃ ˌlaɪn] Ziellinie **II**
opening **line** [ˈəʊpnɪŋ‿ˌlaɪn] der erste Satz °**III TS3**, 106
time **line** [ˈtaɪm ˌlaɪn] Zeitstrahl **I**
to **line** [laɪn] auslegen ⟨**III TS2**, 77⟩
to **line** up [laɪn‿ˈʌp] (sich) aufstellen °**III U4**, 98
link [lɪŋk] Link; Verbindung **II**
to **link** [lɪŋk] verbinden **II**
linking word [ˈlɪŋkɪŋ ˌwɜːd] Bindewort **I**
lion [laɪən] Löwe **II**
list [lɪst] Liste **I**

to **listen** (to) ['lɪsn] zuhören; anhören **I**
Listen again. [ˌlɪsn‿ə'gen] Hör/Hört noch einmal zu. **I**
to **listen** for ['lɪsn fə] horchen auf **I**
listener ['lɪsənə] Zuhörer/-in **II**
listening ['lɪsnɪŋ] Hören **I**
litre (l) ['li:tə] Liter **III U3**, 57
little ['lɪtl] klein **I**
a **little** [ə 'lɪtl] ein wenig; etwas **I**
to **live** [lɪv] wohnen; leben **I**
live [laɪv] live **III TS3**, 110
lively ['laɪvli] lebendig **II**
living room ['lɪvɪŋ rʊm] Wohnzimmer **I**
living history show [ˌlɪvɪŋ 'hɪstəri ˌʃəʊ] *Show, in der historischer Alltag nachgespielt wird* **III U1**, 8
local ['ləʊkl] örtlich; lokal **III U1**, 15
location [ləʊ'keɪʃn] Handlungsort; Lage; Standort **II**
loch [lɒx; lɒk] See *(in Schottland)* **III U3**, 55
locked [lɒkt] abgeschlossen **II**
locker ['lɒkə] Schließfach; Spind **I**
loft [lɒft] Dachboden **I**
logic ['lɒdʒɪk] Logik **III U2**, 27
LOL (= laughing out loud) [lɒl] LOL **II**
Londoner ['lʌndənə] Londoner/-in **I**
lonely ['ləʊnli] einsam **I**
long [lɒŋ] lang **I**
(not) any **longer** [nɒt‿eni 'lɒŋgə] (nicht) mehr; (nicht) länger **III U1**, 10
look [lʊk] Blick **I**
*to give sb funny **looks** [ˌgɪv fʌni 'lʊks] jmdn. schief anschauen **III U2**, 32
*to have a **look** (at) [ˌhæv‿ə 'lʊk] anschauen **II**
*to take a **look** at [ˌteɪk‿ə 'lʊk‿æt] einen Blick werfen auf **II**
to **look** [lʊk] schauen; sehen; aussehen **I**
Look! [lʊk] Schau/Schaut mal! **I**
to **look** after [ˌlʊk‿'ɑ:ftə] aufpassen auf; hüten; sich kümmern um **I**
to **look** at ['lʊk‿ət] anschauen; ansehen **I**
to **look** for ['lʊk fɔ:] suchen nach **I**
to **look** forward to [ˌlʊk 'fɔ:wəd tə] sich freuen auf **II**
to **look** out [ˌlʊk‿'aʊt] aufpassen **II**
to **look** up [ˌlʊk‿'ʌp] nachschlagen; nachschauen **I**
Look closely … [ˌlʊk 'kləʊsli] Schau(t) genau … **II**
what the man **looked** like [ˌwɒt ðə mæn 'lʊkt laɪk] wie der Mann aussah **II**
looks *(pl)* [lʊks] Aussehen **III U2**, 28
lord [lɔ:d] Lord; Herr **III U4**, 85
*to **lose** [lu:z] verlieren **II**
loss [lɒs] Verlust ⟨**III TS2**, 79⟩
*to get **lost** [ˌget 'lɒst] verloren gehen; sich verirren **III U1**, 21
a **lot** [ə 'lɒt] viel **I**
a **lot** of [ə 'lɒt‿əv] viel/-e; eine Menge **I**
lots (of) ['lɒts‿əv] viel/-e; jede Menge **I**
loud [laʊd] laut **I**
*to read/sing out **loud** [ˌri:d/sɪŋ‿aʊt 'laʊd] laut vorsingen **III TS1**, 47
love [lʌv] Liebe **III U1**, 21
Love … [lʌv] Liebe Grüße *(am Briefende)*; Herzliche Grüße *(am Briefende)* **I**
to **love** [lʌv] lieben; gern mögen **I**
would **love** [wʊd 'lʌv] würde/-st/-n/-t sehr gern; hätte/-st/-n/-t sehr gern **I**
I **love** you. [aɪ 'lʌv ju] Ich liebe dich.; Ich mag dich. **I**
I **love** … [aɪ 'lʌv] Ich liebe …; Ich mag … total gern. **I**
lovebirds *(pl)* ['lʌvˌbɜ:dz] Turteltauben **II**
low [ləʊ] niedrig **II**
low tide ['ləʊ ˌtaɪd] Ebbe **II**
What **luck**! [wɒt 'lʌk] Was für ein Glück! **III U4**, 92
lucky … ['lʌki] … der/die Glückliche **I**
*to be **lucky** [bi‿'lʌki] Glück haben **II**
lucky charm [ˌlʌki 'tʃɑ:m] Glücksbringer; Talisman **I**
… is/are **lucky**. [ɪz/ɑ: 'lʌki] … hat/haben Glück. **I**
lunch [lʌnʃ] Mittagessen **I**
lunch break ['lʌnʃbreɪk] Mittagspause **I**
the **lungs** *(pl)* [ðə 'lʌŋz] die Lunge **III TS3**, 109
(song) **lyrics** *(pl)* [sɒŋ 'lɪrɪks] Liedtext **III TS1**, 46

M

machine [mə'ʃi:n] Automat; Maschine; Apparat; Gerät **I**
answering **machine** ['ɑ:nsrɪŋ məˌʃi:n] Anrufbeantworter **I**
washing **machine** ['wɒʃɪŋ məˌʃi:n] Waschmaschine **II**
mad [mæd] verrückt **II**
Dear Sir or **Madam** [dɪə ˌsɜ:r‿ɔ: 'mædəm] Sehr geehrte Dame, sehr geehrter Herr **III U1**, 13
magazine [ˌmægə'zi:n] Zeitschrift **I**
magical ['mædʒɪkəl] magisch; Zauber- **III AC1**, 24
to **mail** ['i:meɪl] mailen; per E-Mail schicken **II**
main [meɪn] Haupt- **I**
main clause ['meɪn ˌklɔ:z] Hauptsatz °**III U1**, 14
*to **make** [meɪk] machen; tun; bilden; *hier:* ergeben **I**
*to be **made** of [bi 'meɪd‿əv] bestehen aus **III TS1**, 49
*to **make** a decision [ˌmeɪk‿ə dɪ'sɪʒn] eine Entscheidung treffen **II**
*to **make** a wish [ˌmeɪk‿ə 'wɪʃ] sich etwas wünschen **I**
*to **make** friends [ˌmeɪk 'frendz] Freundschaft schließen **II**
*to **make** it ['meɪk‿ɪt] es schaffen ⟨**III TS2**, 77⟩
*to **make** money [ˌmeɪk 'mʌni] Geld verdienen **I**
*to **make** notes [ˌmeɪk 'nəʊts] Notizen machen **I**
*to **make** sb angry [meɪk 'æŋgri] jmdn. wütend machen; jmdn. verärgern **III AC2**, 53
*to **make** somebody do something [meɪk] jmdn. dazu bringen, etw. zu tun **II**
*to **make** sure [ˌmeɪk 'ʃɔ:] sich versichern **I**
*to **make** trouble [ˌmeɪk 'trʌbl] Ärger machen; in Schwierigkeiten bringen **I**
man, **men** *(pl)* [mæn; men] Mann **I**
what the **man** looked like [ˌwɒt ðə mæn 'lʊkt laɪk] wie der Mann aussah **II**
manga ['mæŋgə] Manga *(japanischer Comic)* **II**
mango ['mæŋgəʊ] Mango **I**
software **manual** ['sɒftweə ˌmænjuəl] Softwarehandbuch °**III TS2**, 81
many ['meni] viele **I**
How **many** …? [ˌhaʊ 'meni] Wie viele …? **I**
map [mæp] Stadtplan; Landkarte **I**
mind **map** ['maɪnd mæp] Wörternetz *(eine Art Schaubild)* **I**
marathon ['mærəθn] Marathon **II**
March [mɑ:tʃ] März **I**
march [mɑ:tʃ] Marsch; Kundgebung ⟨**III TS2**, 80⟩
to **march** [mɑ:tʃ] marschieren **III TS2**, 80
mark [mɑ:k] Note **III U2**, 28
market ['mɑ:kɪt] Markt **I**
flea **market** ['fli: ˌmɑ:kɪt] Flohmarkt **I**
marmalade ['mɑ:məleɪd] Marmelade aus Zitrusfrüchten **III AC2**, 52
to **marry** ['mæri] heiraten **III U4**, 86
mashed potatoes *(pl)* [ˌmæʃt pə'teɪtəʊz] Kartoffelpüree **III U3**, 60
raven **master** ['reɪvn ˌmɑ:stə] Herr der Raben **II**
match [mætʃ] Spiel; Match **II**
to **match** [mætʃ] zuordnen; passen zu; entsprechen **I**
mate [meɪt] Schiffsoffizier; Maat **I**
material [mə'tɪəriəl] Material **II**
Maths [mæθs] Mathematik; Mathe **II**
What's the **matter**? [ˌwɒts ðə 'mætə] Was ist los?; Was hast du? **III U1**, 18
It doesn't **matter**. [ɪt ˌdʌznt 'mætə] Es ist egal. **III U2**, 26
May [meɪ] Mai **I**
may [meɪ] (vielleicht) können; dürfen **II**
maybe ['meɪbi] vielleicht **I**
me [mi:] ich; mich; mir **I**
meal [mi:l] Mahlzeit; Essen **II**
ready **meal** [ˌredi 'mi:l] Fertiggericht **I**
*to **mean** [mi:n] bedeuten; meinen **II**

meaning ['mi:nɪŋ] Bedeutung; Sinn **II**
meat *(no pl)* [mi:t] Fleisch **III U3**, 59
mechanic [mə'kænɪk] Mechaniker/-in; Kfz-Mechaniker/-in **II**
media ['mi:diə] Medien **II**
mediation [ˌmi:di'eɪʃn] Sprachmittlung **I**
medicine *(no pl)* ['medsn] Medizin; Medikamente **III TS2**, 80
medieval [ˌmedi'i:vl] mittelalterlich **III U1**, 8
*to **meet** [mi:t] treffen; sich treffen **I**
*to **meet** halfway [ˌmi:t hɑ:f'weɪ] sich auf halbem Weg treffen **III U2**, 34
melody ['melədi] Melodie **III TS1**, 50
member ['membə] Mitglied **II**
memory ['memri] Erinnerung; Gedächtnis **II**
to **mention** ['menʃn] erwähnen **II**
merchant ['mɜ:tʃənt] Kaufmann; Händler **II**
message ['mesɪdʒ] Botschaft; Nachricht **I**
*to leave a **message** [ˌli:v‿ə 'mesɪdʒ] eine Nachricht hinterlassen **I**
*to take a **message** [ˌteɪk‿ə 'mesɪdʒ] eine Nachricht entgegennehmen; jmdm. etw. ausrichten **I**
text (**message**) ['tekst ˌmesɪdʒ] SMS; Kurznachricht **I**
messy ['mesi] unordentlich **III U2**, 32
metre ['mi:tə] Meter **II**
mid- [mɪd] Mitte ⟨**III TS2**, 77⟩
middle ['mɪdl] Mitte **I**
midnight ['mɪdnaɪt] Mitternacht **III U3**, 60
It **might** as well be … [ˌɪt maɪt əs 'wel bi: …] Es könnte/-n auch … sein. **III TS3**, 109
mile [maɪl] Meile *(brit. Längenmaß)* **II**
milk [mɪlk] Milch **I**
to **milk** [mɪlk] melken **III U1**, 21
million ['mɪljən] Million **II**
I've done this a **million** times before. [ˌaɪv dʌn ðɪs ə ˌmɪljən taɪmz bɪ'fɔ:] Ich habe das schon eine Million Mal gemacht. **II**
millionaire [ˌmɪljə'neə] Millionär/-in **III U2**, 28
mind [maɪnd] Geist; Verstand **III TS3**, 109
to change one's **mind** [ˌtʃeɪndʒ wʌnz 'maɪnd] seine Meinung ändern **III U4**, 88
mind map ['maɪnd mæp] Wörternetz *(eine Art Schaubild)* **I**
*to rise up in one's **mind** [raɪz‿ʌp ɪn wʌnz 'maɪnd] jmdm. in den Sinn kommen **III TS3**, 109
I don't **mind** … *(+ -ing)* [ˌaɪ dəʊnt 'maɪnd] Ich habe nichts dagegen (zu) …; Mir macht es nichts aus (zu) … **III U2**, 34
mine [maɪn] Mine **III U1**, 18
mine [maɪn] mein/-er/-e/-es **II**
mini [mɪni] Mini- **II**
mining ['maɪnɪŋ] Bergbau **III U1**, 14
minute ['mɪnɪt] Minute **I**
mirror ['mɪrə] Spiegel **III U4**, 86
Miss [mɪs] Fräulein *(Anrede)* **III U2**, 33
to **miss** [mɪs] verpassen; versäumen **II**; vermissen **III U1**, 10
missing ['mɪsɪŋ] fehlend; verschwunden **II**
What is **missing**? [ˌwɒt‿ɪz 'mɪsɪŋ] Was fehlt? **I**
mistake [mɪ'steɪk] Fehler **I**
misunderstood [ˌmɪsʌndə'stʊd] missverstanden **III U2**, 34
mix [mɪks] Mix **III U2**, 37
to **mix** (up) [mɪks‿'ʌp] mischen; vermischen **III U4**, 96
mobile ['məʊbaɪl] Handy; Mobiltelefon **II**
modal ['məʊdl] Modalverb **II**
model ['mɒdl] Modell; Tonmodell; Model **I**
modelling ['mɒdəlɪŋ] Modeln **III U2**, 28
modern ['mɒdn] modern **II**
moment ['məʊmənt] Moment; Augenblick **II**
at the **moment** [ət ðə 'məʊmənt] im Moment; gerade **I**
monarch ['mɒnək] Monarch/-in **III U4**, 86
Monday ['mʌndeɪ] Montag **I**
on **Mondays** [ɒn 'mʌndeɪz] montags **I**
money ['mʌni] Geld **I**
*to make **money** [ˌmeɪk 'mʌni] Geld verdienen **I**
pocket **money** ['pɒkɪt ˌmʌni] Taschengeld **I**
to raise **money** [ˌreɪz 'mʌni] Geld sammeln **II**
monster ['mɒnstə] Monster; Ungeheuer **I**
month [mʌnθ] Monat **II**
monument ['mɒnjəmənt] Monument; Denkmal **III U1**, 14
mood [mu:d] Stimmung; Laune **II**
moonlight ['mu:nlaɪt] Mondlicht **III U3**, 66
more [mɔ:] mehr; weitere **I**
not any **more** [ˌnɒt‿eni 'mɔ:] nicht mehr **I**
more … than ['mɔ: ðən] mehr … als **I**
morning ['mɔ:nɪŋ] Morgen; Vormittag **I**
in the **mornings** [ˌɪn ðə 'mɔ:nɪŋz] morgens; vormittags **I**
Good **morning**. [ˌgʊd 'mɔ:nɪŋ] Guten Morgen. **I**
(the) **most** [ðə 'məʊst] der/die/das meiste; die meisten **I**
mother ['mʌðə] Mutter **I**
to **motivate** ['məʊtɪveɪt] motivieren **I**
bicycle **motocross** [ˌbaɪsɪkl 'məʊtəʊkrɒs] Fahrradmotocross **II**
mountain ['maʊntɪn] Berg **II**
mountain biking ['maʊntɪn ˌbaɪkɪŋ] Mountainbikefahren **III U1**, 9
mouse *(sg)*, **mice** *(pl)* [maʊs; maɪs] Maus/Mäuse **I**
mouth [maʊθ] Mund **I**
mouth jogging ['maʊθ ˌdʒɒgɪŋ] Training für den Mund **I**
move [mu:v] Bewegung **I**
to **move** [mu:v] (sich) bewegen **I**
to **move** in/into [ˌmu:v‿'ɪn/'ɪntə] einziehen in **III U1**, 18
to **move** (house) [mu:v (haʊs)] umziehen **III U1**, 10
Mr ['mɪstə] Herr *(Anrede)* **I**
Mrs ['mɪsɪz] Frau *(Anrede)* **I**
much [mʌtʃ] viel **I**
that **much** [ðæt 'mʌtʃ] so viel **III AC2**, 53
mud [mʌd] Schlamm **II**
muddy ['mʌdi] schlammig **II**
mudlark ['mʌdlɑ:k] *jemand, der im Schlamm nach Sachen sucht, die er dann verkaufen kann* **II**
muesli ['mju:zli] Müsli **III AC2**, 52
mug [mʌg] Becher **III AC2**, 52
multi-ethnic [ˌmʌlti'eθnɪk] Vielvölker-; international **II**
mum [mʌm] Mama **I**
mummy ['mʌmi] Mama; Mami; Mutti **III U2**, 37
murder ['mɜ:də] Mord **III U4**, 92
museum [mju:'zi:əm] Museum **I**
music ['mju:zɪk] Musik **I**
musical ['mju:zɪkl] musikalisch; Musik- **III U3**, 59
musician [mju:'zɪʃn] Musiker/-in **II**
must [mʌst] müssen **I**
mustn't ['mʌsnt] nicht dürfen **I**
my [maɪ] mein/-e **I**
My favourite … [maɪ 'feɪvrɪt] Mein/e Lieblings … **I**
My name is … [maɪ 'neɪm‿ɪz] Ich heiße … **I**
myself [maɪ'self] ich/mir/mich (selbst); selber **II**
mysterious [mɪ'stɪəriəs] mysteriös; geheimnisvoll **III AC1**, 24
mystery ['mɪstri] Mysterium; Rätsel; Geheimnis **III U4**, 96

N

name [neɪm] Name **I**
name day ['neɪm ˌdeɪ] Namenstag **I**
My **name** is … [maɪ 'neɪm‿ɪz] Ich heiße … **I**
What's your **name**? [ˌwɒts jə 'neɪm] Wie heißt du?; Wie heißen Sie? **I**
to **name** [neɪm] nennen; benennen **I**
Can you **name** …? ['kæn jʊ ˌneɪm] Kannst du … nennen? **I**
narrative perspective [ˌnærətɪv pə'spektɪv] Erzählperspektive °**III TS3**, 110
narrator [nə'reɪtə] Erzähler/-in °**III TS3**, 107
first person **narrator** [ˌfɜ:st ˌpɜ:sn nə'reɪtə] Ich-Erzähler/-in °**III TS3**, 109
third person **narrator** [ˌθɜ:d ˌpɜ:sn nə'reɪtə] Er/Sie-Erzähler/-in °**III TS3**, 107
narrow ['nærəʊ] eng; schmal **III U3**, 61
nasty ['nɑ:sti] garstig; gemein **II**
nation ['neɪʃn] Nation ⟨**III U2**, 31⟩
national ['næʃnl] national; landesweit **I**

nature ['neɪtʃə] Natur **II**
near [nɪə] nahe; in der Nähe von **I**
nearly ['nɪəli] fast; annähernd **II**
necessary ['nesəsri] nötig; notwendig; erforderlich ⟨**III TS2**, 77⟩
necklace ['nekləs] Halskette **III U4**, 86
with special **needs** [wɪð ˌspeʃl 'ni:dz] behindert **II**
in **need** [ɪn 'ni:d] bedürftig; in Not **II**
to **need** (to do) [ni:d] (tun) müssen **I**
needn't ['ni:dnt] nicht brauchen; nicht müssen **I**
to **need** (to) [ni:d] brauchen; benötigen **I**
negative ['negətɪv] negativ; verneint **III U1**, 8
negative form ['negətɪv ˌfɔ:m] verneinte Form **I**
neighbour *(BE)* ['neɪbə] Nachbar/-in **I**
neighbourhood ['neɪbəhʊd] Nachbarschaft **III U3**, 69
*to get on people's **nerves** [ˌget‿ɒn sʌmbɒdiz 'nɜ:vz] jemandem auf die Nerven gehen **I**
nervous ['nɜ:vəs] nervös; aufgeregt **II**
net [net] Netz **II**
netball ['netbɔ:l] Korbball **I**
social **network** [ˌsəʊʃl 'netwɜ:k] soziales Netzwerk **II**
never ['nevə] nie; niemals **I**
new [nju:] neu **I**
news *(sg)* [nju:z] Nachrichten; Neuigkeiten **II**
news report ['nju:z rɪˌpɔ:t] Tatsachenbericht; Nachrichtenbeitrag; Meldung **III TS2**, 76
newspaper ['nju:sˌpeɪpə] Zeitung **III TS2**, 77
next [nekst] nächste/-r/-s; der/die Nächste(n) **I**
next door [ˌnekst 'dɔ:] (von) nebenan **III AC3**, 82
next to ['nekst tə] neben **I**
the **next** day [ðə ˌnekst 'deɪ] am nächsten Tag **II**
next [nekst] als Nächstes **I**
nice [naɪs] nett; schön; lieb **I**
night [naɪt] Nacht **I**
all **night** [ɔ:l 'naɪt] die ganze Nacht **I**
night walk ['naɪt wɔ:k] Nachtwanderung **II**
nine [naɪn] neun **I**
2nite *(= tonight)* [tə'naɪt] heute Abend **I**
no [nəʊ] kein/-e **I**
no idea [ˌnəʊ‿aɪ'dɪə] keine Ahnung **II**
no [nəʊ] nein **I**
nobody ['nəʊbədi] niemand **II**
nobody else ['nəʊbədi els] niemand anderes **III U1**, 20
noise [nɔɪz] Lärm; Geräusch **II**
noisy ['nɔɪzi] laut **III U4**, 87
non- [nɒn] nicht- **II**
normal ['nɔ:ml] normal **II**
Norman ['nɔ:mən] Normanne/Normannin; normannisch **III U4**, 85
north [nɔ:θ] Norden; Nord- **II**
north [nɔ:θ] nördlich; im Norden **III U3**, 64
nose [nəʊz] Nase **II**
not [nɒt] nicht **I**
not any more [ˌnɒt‿eni 'mɔ:] nicht mehr **I**
not ... any [nɒt eni] kein/-e/-en **I**
not ... anything [ˌnɒt 'eniθɪŋ] nichts **I**
not ... yet [nɒt 'jet] noch nicht **II**
note [nəʊt] Notiz; Anmerkung **I**
*to make **notes** [ˌmeɪk 'nəʊts] Notizen machen **I**
*to take **notes** [ˌteɪk 'nəʊts] sich Notizen machen **I**
to **note** down [ˌnəʊt 'daʊn] notieren; aufschreiben **II**
nothing ['nʌθɪŋ] nichts **I**
to **notice** ['nəʊtɪs] bemerken; wahrnehmen **II**
noticeboard ['nəʊtɪsbɔ:d] schwarzes Brett **II**
noun [naʊn] Nomen; Hauptwort **I**
novel ['nɒvl] Roman °**III TS3**, 107
graphic **novel** [ˌgræfɪk 'nɒvl] Bildergeschichte; Comic **III TS3**, 106
November [nə'vembə] November **I**
now [naʊ] jetzt; nun **I**
right **now** [ˌraɪt 'naʊ] jetzt gleich; sofort; gerade **II**
nowhere ['nəʊweə] nirgendwo; nirgendwohin **III U1**, 10
number ['nʌmbə] Zahl; Nummer **I**
nurse [nɜ:s] Krankenschwester; Krankenpfleger **III U4**, 97
nut [nʌt] Nuss **I**

O

o'clock [ə'klɒk] Uhr *(Zeitangabe bei vollen Stunden)* **I**
o'er ['əʊə] über ⟨**III U3**, 58⟩
oak [əʊk] Eiche **III TS1**, 48
object ['ɒbdʒɪkt] Objekt **II**; Gegenstand **III U4**, 85
object pronoun [ˌɒbdʒɪkt 'prəʊnaʊn] Objektpronomen °**III U2**, 33
October [ɒk'təʊbə] Oktober **I**
against all **odds** [əˌgenst‿ɔ:l‿'ɒdz] entgegen allen Erwartungen **III TS3**, 106
odd [ɒd] seltsam; komisch ⟨**III TS2**, 77⟩
of [ɒv; əv] von **I**
of course [əv 'kɔ:s] natürlich; selbstverständlich **I**
of one's own [ˌəv wʌnz‿'əʊn] eigen °**III TS1**, 46
off [ɒf] von ... weg/ab/herunter ⟨**III TS3**, 107⟩
*to take **off** [ˌteɪk‿'ɒf] abnehmen; herunternehmen; ausziehen **I**
to turn **off** [ˌtɜ:n‿'ɒf] abschalten; ausschalten **II**
special **offer** [ˌspeʃl‿'ɒfə] Sonderangebot **I**
to **offer** ['ɒfə] anbieten **II**
office ['ɒfɪs] Büro **I**
ticket **office** ['tɪkɪt ˌɒfɪs] Kartenschalter **III U3**, 66
police **officer** [pə'li:s‿ɒfɪsə] Polizeibeamter; Polizist/-in **II**
official [ə'fɪʃl] Schiedsrichter/-in **II**
official [ə'fɪʃl] offiziell **III U3**, 58
official language [əˌfɪʃl 'læŋgwɪdʒ] Amtssprache **II**
offline ['ɒflaɪn] offline **II**
often ['ɒfn] oft; häufig **I**
oh [əʊ] null *(bei Telefonnummern und Uhrzeitangaben)* **I**
Oh! [əʊ] O! **I**
Oh dear! [ˌəʊ 'dɪə] Oje! **III U1**, 18
ointment ['ɔɪntmənt] Salbe **II**
OK [əʊ'keɪ] o.k.; in Ordnung **I**
old [əʊld] alt **I**
How **old** are you? [haʊ‿'əʊld‿ə ju:] Wie alt bist du?; Wie alt sind Sie? **I**
11-year-**old** [ɪˌlevn'jɪərəʊld] 11-Jährige/-r **II**
OMG! (Oh my god!) [ˌəʊ maɪ 'gɒd] OMG! (Oh mein Gott!) ⟨**III TS2**, 79⟩
*to put **on** [ˌpʊt‿'ɒn] anziehen **III U2**, 36
on [ɒn] auf; an; am; in; im **I**
*to be **on** [bi‿'ɒn] an sein; laufen **II**
on Mondays [ɒn 'mʌndeɪz] montags **I**
on my own [ˌɒn maɪ‿'əʊn] allein; für mich **II**
on the brink of [ˌɒn ðə 'brɪŋk‿əv] am Rande von; kurz vor **III TS2**, 80
on the left [ɒn ðə 'left] auf der linken Seite; links **I**
on the right [ɒn ðə 'raɪt] auf der rechten Seite; rechts **I**
on time [ɒn 'taɪm] pünktlich **II**
on top [ɒn 'tɒp] oben; obendrauf **I**
Come **on**! [ˌkʌm‿'ɒn] Komm schon!; Komm jetzt! **I**
once [wʌns] einmal; einst **I**
one [wʌn] eins **I**
one *(sg)*/**ones** *(pl)* [wʌn/wʌnz] eine/-r/-s **II**
one-way ticket ['wʌnweɪ ˌtɪkɪt] einfache Fahrkarte **III U1**, 12
online [ˌɒn'laɪn] online **II**
only ['əʊnli] einzige/-r/-s **II**
only ['əʊnli] erst; bloß; nur **I**
only child ['əʊnli ˌtʃaɪld] Einzelkind **I**
Oops! [u:ps] Hoppla!; Huch! **I**
to **open** ['əʊpn] öffnen; aufmachen **I**; *hier:* beginnen °**III TS3**, 107
open ['əʊpn] offen; geöffnet; aufgeschlagen **I**
opening ['əʊpnɪŋ] Öffnung; Beginn °**III TS3**, 110
opening line ['əʊpnɪŋ‿laɪn] der erste Satz °**III TS3**, 106
opinion [ə'pɪnjən] Meinung **II**

opposite ['ɒpəzɪt] gegenüber; auf der anderen Seite von **I**
optimistic [ˌɒptɪ'mɪstɪk] optimistisch **III U2**, 39
option ['ɒpʃn] Möglichkeit; Wahl; Option °**III TS1**, 51
or [ɔ:] oder **I**
orange ['ɒrɪndʒ] Orange **I**
orange ['ɒrɪndʒ] orange **I**
order ['ɔ:də] Reihenfolge; Ordnung **I**; Befehl **III TS3**, 107
word **order** ['wɜ:dˌɔ:də] Wortstellung; Satzstellung **I**
organisation [ˌɔ:gnaɪ'zeɪʃn] Organisation °**III U1**, 13
to **organise** ['ɔ:gənaɪz] organisieren **I**
*to get **organised** [get 'ɔ:gənaɪzd] sich organisieren °**III U1**, 17
organiser ['ɔ:gənaɪzə] Organisator/-in ⟨**III TS2**, 80⟩
original [ə'rɪdʒnl] Original °**III TS1**, 51
original [ə'rɪdʒnl] original; ursprünglich °**III TS1**, 48
originally [ə'rɪdʒnli] ursprünglich **II**
ornament ['ɔ:nəmənt] Schmuckstück ⟨**III TS2**, 80⟩
other ['ʌðə] anders; andere/-r/-s; weitere **I**
each **other** [i:tʃˌ'ʌðə] einander; sich; sich gegenseitig **I**
the **others** [ðiˌ'ʌðəz] die anderen **I**
Ouch! [aʊtʃ] Aua! **II**
our [aʊə; ɑ:] unser/-e **I**
out [aʊt] außerhalb; heraus; hinaus; nach draußen **I**
to clear **out** [klɪərˌ'aʊt] ausräumen; entrümpeln **I**
to drop **out** (of) [drɒp 'aʊtˌəv] abbrechen **III U2**, 28
*to hang **out** (with) *(infml)* [ˌhæŋˌ'aʊt wɪð] sich herumtreiben (mit); rumhängen (mit); sich treffen (mit) **III U2**, 36
out and about [ˌaʊtˌənˌə'baʊt] unterwegs **II**
out of focus [ˌaʊtˌəv 'fəʊkəs] unscharf **III U4**, 97
a day **out** in ... [ə ˌdeɪˌ'aʊt ɪn] ein Tag in ... **II**
outdoor [ˌaʊt'dɔ:] Freiluft-; Outdoor- **II**
outfit ['aʊtfɪt] Outfit; Kleidung **II**
outlaw ['aʊtlɔ:] Geächtete/-r; Gesetzlose/-r **III AC1**, 24
outside [aʊt'saɪd] nach draußen; draußen; außerhalb **I**
outward ['aʊtwəd] abfahrend **III U1**, 12
over ['əʊvə] hinüber; über **I**; vorüber; vorbei **II**
*to go **over** to [ˌgəʊ 'əʊvə tə] hinübergehen zu; zu jmdm. nach Hause gehen **II**
over and **over** again [ˌəʊvərˌənˌəʊvərˌə'gen] immer wieder **III TS1**, 50
overnight [ˌəʊvə'naɪt] über Nacht **III U2**, 37
to **overreact** [ˌəʊvəri'ækt] überreagieren **II**
over-wintering [ˌəʊvə'wɪntrɪŋ] Überwintern ⟨**III TS2**, 77⟩
own [əʊn] eigene/-r/-s **I**
of one's **own** [ˌəv wʌnzˌ'əʊn] eigen °**III TS1**, 46
on my **own** [ɒn maɪˌ'əʊn] allein; für mich **II**

P

p.m. [ˌpi:'em] nachmittags *(Uhrzeit)*; abends *(Uhrzeit)* **I**
packet ['pækɪt] Päckchen; Paket; Packung **I**
page [peɪdʒ] Seite **I**
pain [peɪn] Schmerz **II**
to **paint** [peɪnt] anmalen; malen **I**
painting ['peɪntɪŋ] Malerei; Gemälde **II**
pair [peə] Paar **I**
pair work ['peə wɜ:k] Partnerarbeit **II**
to **pair** [peə] Paare bilden °**III TS3**, 108
palm tree ['pɑ:m ˌtri:] Palme **III U1**, 9
to **panic** ['pænɪk] panisch werden **II**
piece of **paper** [ˌpi:sˌəv 'peɪpə] Stück Papier **I**
paper ['peɪpə] Papier **I**
paradise ['pærədaɪs] Paradies **II**
parcel ['pɑ:sl] Paket; Päckchen **I**
parents *(pl)* ['peərənts] Eltern **I**
park [pɑ:k] Park **I**
part [pɑ:t] Teil; Stadtteil **I**; Rolle **III U2**, 28
lead **part** [ˌli:d 'pɑ:t] Hauptrolle **III U2**, 28
*to take **part** (in) [ˌteɪk 'pɑ:t (ɪn)] teilnehmen (an) **II**
partially sighted [ˌpɑ:ʃəli 'saɪtɪd] sehbehindert **II**
to **participate** [pɑ:'tɪsɪpeɪt] teilnehmen **II**
past **participle** [ˌpɑ:st pɑ:'tɪsɪpl] Partizip **II**
particular [pə'tɪkjələ] bestimmte/-r/-s °**III U3**, 64
partner ['pɑ:tnə] Partner/-in **I**
party ['pɑ:ti] Party; Feier **I**; Partei **III U3**, 57
to **pass** [pɑ:s] zupassen; zuspielen **II**
to **pass** (on) [ˌpɑ:sˌ'ɒn] weitergeben **I**
passed [pɑ:st] vorüber ⟨**III U3**, 58⟩
passive ['pæsɪv] Passiv °**III U3**, 55
passive ['pæsɪv] passiv °**III U3**, 59
past [pɑ:st] Vergangenheit **II**
past form ['pɑ:st fɔ:m] Vergangenheitsform **II**
past participle [ˌpɑ:st pɑ:'tɪsɪpl] Partizip **II**
past perfect [ˌpɑ:st 'pɜ:fɪkt] Plusquamperfekt °**III U4**, 85
past progressive [ˌpɑ:st prə'gresɪv] Verlaufsform der Vergangenheit **II**
simple **past** [ˌsɪmpl 'pɑ:st] Vergangenheitsform **II**
past [pɑ:st] nach *(bei Uhrzeitangaben)*; vorbei (an); vorüber (an) **I**
half **past** [ˌhɑ:f 'pɑ:st] halb *(bei Uhrzeitangaben)* **I**
quarter **past**/to ['kwɔ:tə pɑ:st/tə] Viertel nach/vor **I**
pasta ['pæstə] Pasta; Nudeln **I**
coastal **path** [ˌkəʊstl 'pɑ:θ] Küstenweg **III U1**, 18
pattern ['pætn] Muster °**III U1**, 14
pause [pɔ:z] Pause **III U2**, 32
paw [pɔ:] Pfote ⟨**III TS2**, 79⟩
pawn shop ['pɔ:n ʃɒp] Pfandhaus; Pfandleihe **III U4**, 99
*to **pay (for)** [peɪ] bezahlen **I**
*to **pay** attention to sb/sth [ˌpeɪˌə'tenʃn tʊ] jmdn./etw. beachten **III U2**, 37
PC *(= Personal Computer)* [pi:'si:] PC **II**
PE *(= Physical Education)* [ˌpi:'i:; ˌfɪzɪklˌedʒʊ'keɪʃn] Sportunterricht **II**
peach [pi:tʃ] Pfirsich **III TS1**, 47
peer pressure ['pɪə ˌpreʃe] Gruppenzwang **III U2**, 38
to **peer-edit** ['pɪərˌedɪt] gegenseitig kontrollieren **II**
pen [pen] Füller **I**
penny, pence *(pl)* ['peni; pens] Penny *(brit. Währungseinheit)*; Pence *(brit. Währungseinheit)* **I**
pencil ['pensl] Bleistift; Buntstift **I**
pencil-case ['pensl ˌkeɪs] Federmäppchen; Mäppchen **I**
penicillin [ˌpenɪ'sɪlɪn] Penicillin **III U3**, 60
penny, pence *(pl)* ['peni; pens] Penny *(brit. Währungseinheit)*; Pence *(brit. Währungseinheit)* **I**
people *(pl)* ['pi:pl] Leute; Menschen **I**
per [pɜ:; pə] pro **III U1**, 11
past **perfect** [ˌpɑ:st 'pɜ:fɪkt] Plusquamperfekt °**III U4**, 85
present **perfect** [ˌpreznt 'pɜ:fɪkt] das Perfekt **II**
present **perfect** progressive [ˌpreznt ˌpɜ:fɪkt prə'gresɪv] Verlaufsform des Perfekts °**III U3**, 57
perfect ['pɜ:fɪkt] perfekt; vollkommen **I**
perhaps [pə'hæps] vielleicht **III U3**, 66
period ['pɪəriəd] Periode; Zeitspanne **III U3**, 57
person, people *(pl)* ['pɜ:sn; 'pi:pl] Person; Mensch **I**
first **person** narrator [ˌfɜ:st ˌpɜ:sn nə'reɪtə] Ich-Erzähler/-in °**III TS3**, 109
third **person** narrator [ˌθɜ:d ˌpɜ:sn nə'reɪtə] Er/Sie-Erzähler/-in °**III TS3**, 107
personal ['pɜ:snl] persönlich **I**
personality [ˌpɜ:sn'æləti] Persönlichkeit **III U2**, 27
Personally, ... ['pɜ:snli] Ich persönlich ... ⟨**III U3**, 63⟩
perspective [pə'spektɪv] Perspektive; Blickwinkel **II**
narrative **perspective** [ˌnærətɪv pə'spektɪv] Erzählperspektive °**III TS3**, 110
to **persuade** [pə'sweɪd] überreden **II**

persuasive [pə'sweɪsɪv] überzeugend °**III U3**, 64
pet [pet] Haustier **I**
phone [fəʊn] Telefon; Handy **I**
to answer the **phone** [ˌɑ:nsə ðə 'fəʊn] einen Anruf entgegennehmen **I**
phone call ['fəʊn ˌkɔ:l] Anruf; Telefonanruf **I**
rotary **phone** ['rəʊtri fəʊn] Telefon mit Wählscheibe **III U3**, 69
photo ['fəʊtəʊ] Foto; Fotografie **I**
in the **photo**(s) [ˌɪn ðə 'fəʊtəʊ(z)] auf dem Foto/den Fotos **I**
photo shoot ['fəʊtəʊ ˌʃu:t] Fotoshooting; Fotoaufnahmen **III U4**, 96
photo story ['fəʊtəʊ ˌstɔ:ri] Fotostory; Bildgeschichte **I**
*to take **photos** [ˌteɪk 'fəʊtəʊz] fotografieren; Fotos machen **I**
to **photobomb** ['fəʊtəʊbɒm] ins Foto laufen **III U4**, 97
photographer [fə'tɒgrəfə] Fotograf/-in **III U4**, 96
phrase [freɪz] Redewendung; Ausdruck; Satz **I**
Useful **phrases** [ˌju:sfl 'freɪsɪz] nützliche Ausdrücke **I**
piano key [pi'ænəʊ ˌki:] Klaviertaste ⟨**III TS2**, 80⟩
pic (= picture) [pɪk] Foto ⟨**III U3**, 62⟩
to **pick** [pɪk] auswählen; aussuchen **II**
to **pick** up [ˌpɪk‿'ʌp] aufheben; mitnehmen; abholen **III U4**, 92
pick-up ['pɪkʌp] Pick-up; Wiederaufnehmen **I**
picnic ['pɪknɪk] Picknick **I**
picture ['pɪktʃə] Bild; Foto **I**
pie [paɪ] Kuchen; Pastete **I**
piece [pi:s] Stück **I**
piece of junk [ˌpi:s‿əv 'dʒʌŋk] Stück Schrott **III U2**, 37
piece of paper [ˌpi:s‿əv 'peɪpə] Stück Papier **I**
pier [pɪə] Pier; Hafendamm **I**
pig [pɪg] Schwein **I**
guinea **pig** ['gɪni: ˌpɪg] Meerschweinchen **I**
pill [pɪl] Pille; Tablette **II**
pilot ['paɪlət] Pilot/-in **II**
pine [paɪn] Kiefer ⟨**III TS3**, 107⟩
pineapple ['paɪnæpl] Ananas **III U4**, 99
pink [pɪŋk] pink; rosa **I**
pipe [paɪp] Rohr; Rohrleitung; Pfeife **II**
clay **pipe** ['kleɪ paɪp] Tonpfeife **II**
pitch [pɪtʃ] Spielfeld; Platz **II**
pizza ['pi:tsə] Pizza **I**
place [pleɪs] Ort; Stelle; Platz **I**
hiding **place** ['haɪdɪŋ ˌpleɪs] Versteck ⟨**III TS1**, 51⟩
starting **place** ['stɑ:tɪŋ pleɪs] Startpunkt **III U1**, 12
*to take **place** [ˌteɪk 'pleɪs] stattfinden **I**
to **place** [pleɪs] legen °**III U1**, 17
placemat ['pleɪsmæt] Placemat; Platzdeckchen **I**
plan [plæn] Plan; Entwurf **I**
to **plan** [plæn] planen **I**
planet ['plænɪt] Planet **II**
planner ['plænə] Handbuch; Kalender **I**
plant [plɑ:nt] Pflanze **III U1**, 14
to **plant** [plɑ:nt] pflanzen; anpflanzen **II**
plaster cast ['plɑ:stə kɑ:st] Gipsverband **III U4**, 96
plate [pleɪt] Teller **III AC2**, 52
platform ['plætfɔ:m] Plattform; Bahnsteig **III U1**, 12
play [pleɪ] Theaterstück **III U4**, 86
fair **play** [feə 'pleɪ] Fairplay **III TS1**, 46
play on words [ˌpleɪ‿ɒn 'wɜ:dz] Wortspiel **III TS1**, 50
role **play** ['rəʊl ˌpleɪ] Rollenspiel **I**
to **play** [pleɪ] spielen **I**
to **play** a trick (on) [ˌpleɪ‿ə 'trɪk‿ɒn] einen Streich spielen **I**
to **play** bowls [ˌpleɪ 'bəʊlz] Bowling spielen **III U4**, 88
player ['pleɪə] Spieler/-in; Mitspieler/-in **II**
Please. [pli:z] Bitte. **I**
plot [plɒt] Handlung **III TS3**, 106
to **pluck** [plʌk] zupfen ⟨**III TS1**, 47⟩
plumber ['plʌmə] Installateur/-in; Klempner/-in **III U1**, 18
plumbing ['plʌmɪŋ] Sanitärarbeit **III U1**, 19
plural ['plʊərəl] Plural; Mehrzahl **I**
poacher ['pəʊtʃə] Wilderer ⟨**III TS2**, 80⟩
poaching *(no pl)* ['pəʊtʃɪŋ] Wilderei **III TS2**, 80
pocket ['pɒkɪt] Tasche; Hosentasche **III U3**, 66
pocket money ['pɒkɪt ˌmʌni] Taschengeld **I**
poem ['pəʊɪm] Gedicht **I**
point [pɔɪnt] Punkt; Zeitpunkt **II**
*to have a **point** [ˌhæv‿ə 'pɔɪnt] nicht ganz unrecht haben **III U2**, 34
point of view [ˌpɔɪnt‿əv 'vju:] Standpunkt; Ansicht; Perspektive **II**
to the **point** [tə ðə 'pɔɪnt] prägnant; treffend **III AC3**, 83
turning **point** ['tɜ:nɪŋ ˌpɔɪnt] Wendepunkt °**III U2**, 38
Point to … ['pɔɪnt tə] Zeige/Zeigt auf … **I**
Point. [pɔɪnt] Zeige/Zeigt darauf. **I**
police [pə'li:s] Polizei **II**
police officer [pə'li:s‿ɒfɪsə] Polizeibeamter; Polizist/-in **II**
polite [pə'laɪt] höflich **I**
Be **polite.** [bi: pə'laɪt] Sei/Seid höflich. **I**
pollution [pə'lu:ʃn] Verschmutzung **II**
pond [pɒnd] Teich **II**
pony ['pəʊni] Pony **I**
pony trekking ['pəʊni ˌtrekɪŋ] Ponyreiten im Gelände **III U1**, 9
swimming **pool** ['swɪmɪŋ ˌpu:l] Swimmingpool; Schwimmbecken **III TS3**, 109
the **poor** [ðə pʊə] die Armen **III AC1**, 25
poor [pɔ:; pʊə] arm **III U2**, 37
poppy ['pɒpi] Mohnblume ⟨**III TS1**, 47⟩
popular ['pɒpjələ] beliebt; populär **I**
positive ['pɒzətɪv] positiv **II**
possessive form [pəˌsesɪv 'fɔ:m] Possessivform **I**
possibility [ˌpɒsə'bɪləti] Möglichkeit °**III U1**, 14
possible ['pɒsəbl] möglich **I**
post [pəʊst] Post *(Eintrag im Internet)* **I**
to **post** [pəʊst] online stellen; posten **II**
postcard ['pəʊstkɑ:d] Postkarte **III U1**, 20
poster ['pəʊstə] Poster **I**
class **poster** ['klɑ:s ˌpəʊstə] Klassenposter **I**
postman ['pəʊstmən] Briefträger **II**
potato [pə'teɪtəʊ], **potatoes** [pə'teɪtəʊz] *(pl)* Kartoffel **III U3**, 60
mashed **potatoes** *(pl)* [ˌmæʃt pə'teɪtəʊz] Kartoffelpüree **III U3**, 60
pound (£) [paʊnd] Pfund *(brit. Währungseinheit)* **I**
to **pour** [pɔ:] einschenken; eingießen; schütten **I**
power [paʊə] Kraft; Macht; Stärke **III AC1**, 24
power cut ['paʊə ˌkʌt] Stromausfall **II**
Word **power** ['wɜ:d ˌpaʊə] die Kraft der Wörter *(Wortschatzübung)* **I**
those in **power** [ˌðəʊz ɪn 'paʊə] die Regierenden; die Herrschenden **III TS2**, 80
powerful ['paʊəfl] stark; mächtig **III AC1**, 24
practical ['præktɪkl] praktisch **II**
practice ['præktɪs] Training; Übung **III U2**, 26
to **practise** ['præktɪs] üben; trainieren **I**
practising ['præktɪsɪŋ] Üben **I**
to **pray** [preɪ] beten **III TS3**, 109
prediction [prɪ'dɪkʃn] Vorhersage; Voraussage °**III U1**, 11
prehistoric [ˌpri:hɪ'stɒrɪk] vorgeschichtlich **III U1**, 14
to **prepare** [prɪ'peə] vorbereiten; zubereiten **I**
preposition [ˌprepə'zɪʃn] Präposition **I**
pre-reading [ˌpri:'ri:dɪŋ] vor dem Lesen **I**
prescription [prɪ'skrɪpʃn] Rezept *(für Arzneimittel)* **II**
present ['preznt] Geschenk **I**; Gegenwart; Präsens **II**
present perfect [ˌpreznt 'pɜ:fɪkt] das Perfekt **II**
present progressive [ˌpreznt prə'gresɪv] Verlaufsform des Präsens/der Gegenwart **I**
present perfect progressive [ˌpreznt ˌpɜ:fɪkt prə'gresɪv] Verlaufsform des Perfekts °**III U3**, 57

simple **present** [ˌsɪmpl ˈpreznt] Gegenwart; Präsens **I**
to **present** [prɪˈzent] präsentieren; vorstellen **I**
present [ˈpreznt] heutig; Gegenwarts- **III U3**, 64
presentation [ˌpreznˈteɪʃn] Präsentation; Vortrag **I**
presenter [prɪˈzentə] Moderator/-in **I**
to **press** [pres] drücken; pressen **II**
pressure [ˈpreʃə] Druck ⟨**III U2**, 31⟩
peer **pressure** [ˈpɪə ˌpreʃe] Gruppenzwang **III U2**, 38
pretty [ˈprɪti] hübsch **III U2**, 37
price [praɪs] Preis **I**
primary school [ˈpraɪmri ˌskuːl] Grundschule **I**
print [prɪnt] gedruckt; Druck- **II**
prison [ˈprɪzn] Gefängnis **II**
private detective [ˌpraɪvət dɪˈtektɪv] Privatdetektiv/-in **III AC1**, 24
prize [praɪz] Preis; Gewinn **I**
pro [prəʊ] Argument dafür **II**
probably [ˈprɒbəbli] möglicherweise; wahrscheinlich **II**
problem [ˈprɒbləm] Problem; Schwierigkeit **I**
to **produce** [prəˈdjuːs] herstellen; produzieren **III U3**, 57
profile [ˈprəʊfaɪl] Profil; Porträt **I**
programme [ˈprəʊgræm] Programm; Sendung **II**
progress [ˈprəʊgres] Fortschritt **II**
past **progressive** [ˌpɑːst prəˈgresɪv] Verlaufsform der Vergangenheit **II**
present perfect **progressive** [ˌpreznt ˌpɜːfɪkt prəˈgresɪv] Verlaufsform des Perfekts °**III U3**, 57
present **progressive** [ˌpreznt prəˈgresɪv] Verlaufsform des Präsens/der Gegenwart **I**
project [ˈprɒdʒekt] Projekt **I**
to **promise** [ˈprɒmɪs] versprechen **III U1**, 11
prompt [prɒmpt] Stichwort °**III U4**, 91
prompt card [ˈprɒmpt kɑːd] Stichwortkarte; Rollenkarte **II**
object **pronoun** [ˌɒbdʒɪkt ˈprəʊnaʊn] Objektpronomen °**III U2**, 33
reflexive **pronoun** [rɪˌfleksɪv ˈprəʊnaʊn] Reflexivpronomen °**III U2**, 32
relative **pronoun** [ˌrelətɪv ˈprəʊnaʊn] Relativpronomen **II**
to **pronounce** [prəˈnaʊns] aussprechen ⟨**III U3**, 62⟩
pronunciation [prəˌnʌnsiˈeɪʃn] Aussprache **I**
prop [prɒp] Requisite **III AC1**, 25
protest [ˈprəʊtest] Protest **III TS2**, 80
proud (of) [ˈpraʊd‿əv] stolz (auf) **II**
public [ˈpʌblɪk] öffentlich **II**
public transport *(no pl)* [ˌpʌblɪk ˈtrænspɔːt] öffentliche Verkehrsmittel **II**
pudding [ˈpʊdɪŋ] Pudding; Nachtisch **I**
to **pull** [pʊl] ziehen **I**
to **pull** down [ˌpʊl‿ˈdaʊn] abreißen **III U3**, 59
purple [ˈpɜːpl] violett; lila **I**
to **push** [pʊʃ] stoßen; schieben; schubsen **II**
to **push** oneself [ˈpʊʃ wʌnˌself] sich alles abverlangen; sich Mühe geben **III U2**, 32
*to **put** [pʊt] setzen; stellen; legen **I**
Put in … [pʊt‿ˈɪn] Setze/Setzt ein … **I**
Put it in … [ˌpʊt‿ɪt‿ˈɪn] Lege/Legt es in …; Stelle/Stellt es in … **I**
*to **put** on [ˌpʊt‿ˈɒn] anziehen **III U2**, 36
*to **put** through [ˌpʊt‿ˈθruː] verbinden **I**
*to **put** up [ˌpʊt‿ˈʌp] aufstellen; errichten; aufhängen **II**
Put … face down. [pʊt ˌfeɪs ˈdaʊn] Lege/Legt … umgedreht hin. **I**
puzzle [ˈpʌzl] Rätsel; Puzzle **I**
pyjamas *(pl)* [pɪˈdʒɑːməz] Schlafanzug; Pyjama **II**

Q

quality [ˈkwɒləti] Qualität **I**
quarter past/to [ˈkwɔːtə pɑːst/tə] Viertel nach/vor **I**
queen [kwiːn] Königin **II**
question [ˈkwestʃən] Frage **I**
question tag [ˈkwestʃən ˌtæg] Frageanhängsel; Bestätigungsfrage **II**
questionnaire [ˌkwestʃəˈneə] Fragebogen °**III U2**, 35
queue [kjuː] Schlange; Warteschlange **I**
to jump the **queue** [ˌdʒʌmp ðə ˈkjuː] sich vordrängeln **I**
quick [kwɪk] schnell **I**
quickly [ˈkwɪkli] schnell **II**
quiet [kwaɪət] still; ruhig; leise **I**
quill [kwɪl] Federkiel **III U4**, 91
quite a [ˈkwaɪt‿ə] ein/-e wirkliche/-r/-s; ein/-e ziemliche/-r/-s ⟨**III TS1**, 51⟩
quiz [kwɪz] Quiz; Rätsel **I**
quote [kwəʊt] Zitat **II**

R

rabbit [ˈræbɪt] Kaninchen **I**
race [reɪs] Wettlauf; Rennen **II**
camel **racing** [ˈkæml ˌreɪsɪŋ] Kamelrennen **II**
racquet [ˈrækɪt] Schläger **II**
radio [ˈreɪdiəʊ] Radio **II**
raffle [ˈræfl] Tombola **I**
to **rain** [reɪn] regnen **II**
rainbow [ˈreɪnbəʊ] Regenbogen **III TS1**, 47
raincoat [ˈreɪnkəʊt] Regenmantel **III U3**, 60
to **raise** money [ˌreɪz ˈmʌni] Geld sammeln **II**
rap [ræp] Rap **I**
to **rap** [ræp] rappen **I**
rat [ræt] Ratte **I**
I'd **rather** [aɪd ˈrɑːðə] ich würde lieber **III U4**, 99
rating [ˈreɪtɪŋ] Kritik **III U4**, 94
raven [ˈreɪvn] Rabe **II**
raven master [ˈreɪvn ˌmɑːstə] Herr der Raben **II**
RE *(= Religious Education)* [ˌɑːrˈiː; rɪˌlɪdʒəs‿edʒʊˈkeɪʃn] Religion *(Schulfach)* **II**
to **reach** [riːtʃ] erreichen; dran kommen **II**
to **react** [riˈækt] reagieren **III U2**, 39
reaction [riˈækʃn] Reaktion **II**
*to **read** [riːd] lesen **I**
*to **read** out loud [ˌriːd/sɪŋ‿aʊt ˈlaʊd] laut vorsingen **III TS1**, 47
reader [ˈriːdə] Leser/-in **I**
*to draw the **reader** into the story/action [ˌdrɔː ðə ˌriːdə ɪntə ðə ˈstɔːri/ˈækʃn] den Leser/die Leserin in die Geschichte/Handlung hineinziehen °**III TS3**, 108
reading [ˈriːdɪŋ] Lesen **I**
ready [ˈredi] fertig; bereit **II**
ready meal [ˌredi ˈmiːl] Fertiggericht **I**
real [rɪəl] echt; richtig; wirklich **II**
to **realise** [ˈrɪəlaɪz] erkennen; realisieren **III U3**, 66
realistic [ˌrɪəˈlɪstɪk] realistisch **II**
really [ˈrɪəli] wirklich **I**
reason [ˈriːzn] Grund **II**
*to **rebuild** [ˌriːˈbɪld] wieder aufbauen **III U4**, 91
to **receive** [rɪˈsiːv] empfangen; erhalten; bekommen **II**
recipe [ˈresɪpi] Rezept **III TS2**, 76
to **recite** [rɪˈsaɪt] vortragen; rezitieren °**III TS1**, 47
to **record** [rɪˈkɔːd] aufnehmen; aufzeichnen **II**
recorder [rɪˈkɔːdə] Flöte **III U2**, 32
recording [rɪˈkɔːdɪŋ] Aufnahme; Aufzeichnung **I**
recording studio [rɪˈkɔːdɪŋ ˌstjuːdiəʊ] Aufnahmestudio; Tonstudio **I**
recycling [ˌriːˈsaɪklɪŋ] Recycling; Wiederaufbereitung **II**
red [red] rot **I**
to **reef** the sails [ˌriːf ðə ˈseɪlz] die Segel einholen **I**
reference article [ˈrefrns ˌɑːtɪkl] Referenzartikel **III TS2**, 76
referendum [ˌrefrˈendəm] Referendum; Volksentscheid **III U3**, 55
reflexive [rɪˈfleksɪv] reflexiv; Reflexiv- °**III U2**, 33
reflexive pronoun [rɪˌfleksɪv ˈprəʊnaʊn] Reflexivpronomen °**III U2**, 32
region [ˈriːdʒn] Region; Gegend **II**
registration [ˌredʒɪsˈtreɪʃn] Anwesenheitskontrolle **II**
regular [ˈregjələ] regelmäßig; gleichmäßig **I**

to **rehearse** [rɪ'hɜ:s] proben °**III AC2**, 53
reign [reɪn] Herrschaft; Regierungszeit **III U4**, 90
to **reign** [reɪn] herrschen; regieren **III U4**, 91
to **relate** to [rɪ'leɪt tə] Zugang finden zu °**III TS3**, 106
relationship [rɪ'leɪʃnʃɪp] Beziehung **II**
defining **relative** clause [dɪˌfaɪnɪŋ 'relətɪv ˌklɔ:z] notwendiger Relativsatz **II**
relative pronoun [ˌrelətɪv 'prəʊnaʊn] Relativpronomen **II**
to **relax** [rɪ'læks] sich entspannen; sich ausruhen; sich beruhigen **II**
release [rɪ'li:s] Freigabe; Freisetzung; *hier:* Aussetzen ⟨**III TS2**, 77⟩
to **release** [rɪ'li:s] loslassen ⟨**III U2**, 31⟩ø *hier:* freilassen ⟨**III TS2**, 77⟩
religious [rɪ'lɪdʒəs] religiös; gläubig **I**
to **rely** (on) [rɪ'laɪ‿ɒn] sich verlassen (auf); vertrauen (auf) **III U2**, 28
to **remain** [rɪ'meɪn] bleiben ⟨**III U3**, 58⟩
to **remember** [rɪ'membə] sich erinnern (an); sich merken; denken an **I**
Remember? [rɪ'membə] Erinnerst du dich?; Erinnert ihr euch? **I**
to **remind** (sb of sth/sb) [rɪ'maɪnd əv] (jmdn. an etw./jmdn.) erinnern **III TS1**, 49
to **remove** [rɪ'mu:v] entfernen ⟨**III TS2**, 80⟩
to **rent** (out) [ˌrent‿'aʊt] mieten **III U3**, 65
to **repeat** [rɪ'pi:t] wiederholen **II**
reply [rɪ'plaɪ] Antwort; Erwiderung; Entgegnung **I**
to **reply** [rɪ'plaɪ] antworten; erwidern; entgegnen **I**
report [rɪ'pɔ:t] Bericht; Meldung **II**
news **report** ['nju:z rɪˌpɔ:t] Tatsachenbericht; Nachrichtenbeitrag; Meldung **III TS2**, 76
travel **report** [ˌtrævl rɪ'pɔ:t] Reisebericht **II**
reporter [rɪ'pɔ:tə] Reporter/-in **II**
*to **reread** ['ri:ri:d] noch einmal lesen °**III TS3**, 110
rescue ['reskju:] Rettung **II**
to **rescue** ['reskju:] retten **III TS2**, 79
research *(no pl)* [rɪ'sɜ:tʃ] Recherche; Forschung; Untersuchung °**III U3**, 65
the **rest** [rest] der Rest **I**
restaurant ['restrɒnt] Restaurant; Gaststätte **I**
result [rɪ'zʌlt] Ergebnis; Resultat **II**
*to **retell** [ˌri:'tel] nacherzählen; nochmals erzählen **I**
return ticket [rɪ'tɜ:n ˌtɪkɪt] Hin- und Rückfahrkarte **III U1**, 12
to **return** [rɪ'tɜ:n] zurückkehren; zurückfahren **III U1**, 12
revision [rɪ'vɪʒn] Wiederholung **II**
*to **rewrite** [ˌri:'raɪt] umschreiben; neu schreiben °**III TS1**, 48

rhino ['raɪnəʊ] Rhinozeros; Nashorn **III TS2**, 80
rhyme [raɪm] Reim **I**
rhyme scheme ['raɪm ski:m] Reimschema °**III TS1**, 47
to **rhyme** [raɪm] (sich) reimen **III TS1**, 46
rhyming ['raɪmɪŋ] sich reimend °**III TS1**, 47
rhythm ['rɪðm] Rhythmus **I**
the **rich** [ðə rɪtʃ] die Reichen **III AC1**, 25
rich [rɪtʃ] reich **III U2**, 28
rigging ['rɪgɪŋ] Takelage **I**
right [raɪt] richtig; korrekt; rechts; rechte/-r/-s **I**
*to be **right** [bi 'raɪt] recht haben **I**
*to get **right** [get 'raɪt] richtig beantworten °**III U1**, 17
on the **right** [ɒn ðə 'raɪt] auf der rechten Seite; rechts **I**
right away [ˌraɪt‿ə'weɪ] sofort; gleich **I**
right here [ˌraɪt 'hɪə] genau hier **II**
right now [ˌraɪt 'naʊ] jetzt gleich; sofort; gerade **II**
ring [rɪŋ] Ring **III U4**, 84
key **ring** ['ki: ˌrɪŋ] Schlüsselbund; Schlüsselanhänger **III U3**, 67
*to **ring** [rɪŋ] klingeln; läuten **I**
ice **rink** ['aɪs ˌrɪŋk] Eisbahn; Schlittschuhbahn **I**
*to **rise** [raɪz] sich erheben; aufstehen ⟨**III U3**, 58⟩ø steigen **III TS3**, 109
*to **rise** up in one's mind [raɪz‿ʌp ɪn wʌnz 'maɪnd] jmdm. in den Sinn kommen **III TS3**, 109
river ['rɪvə] Fluss **I**
by the **river** [baɪ ðə 'rɪvə] am Fluss **II**
road [rəʊd] Straße **II**
on the **roadside** [ˌɒn ðə 'rəʊdsaɪd] am Straßenrand ⟨**III TS2**, 79⟩
to **roar** [rɔ:] dröhnen; brüllen; rauschen **III TS3**, 109
roaring ['rɔ:rɪŋ] dröhnend; tosend; donnernd **III TS3**, 109
robber ['rɒbə] Räuber/-in **III AC1**, 24
rock [rɒk] Rock *(Musik)* **III U3**, 66
rock 'n' roll [ˌrɒk‿ən 'rəʊl] Rock 'n' Roll **II**
rocky ['rɒki] felsig; steinig **III U1**, 9
role [rəʊl] Rolle **I**
role play ['rəʊl ˌpleɪ] Rollenspiel **I**
to swap **roles** [ˌswɒp 'rəʊlz] Rollen tauschen **I**
bread **roll** ['bred rəʊl] Brötchen **III AC2**, 52
rock 'n' **roll** [ˌrɒk‿ən 'rəʊl] Rock 'n' Roll **II**
to **roll** off [rəʊl] hinunterrollen; herunterrollen **II**
to **roll** one's eyes [ˌrəʊl wʌnz‿'aɪz] die Augen verdrehen **III U4**, 96
Roll two dice. [ˌrəʊl ˌtu: 'daɪs] Würfle/Würfelt mit zwei Würfeln. **I**
Roman ['rəʊmən] Römer/-in; römisch **II**
romance [rə'mæns] Liebesgeschichte; Liebesfilm **III TS3**, 106

Romanian [rʊ'meɪniən] Rumäne/Rumänin; rumänisch; Rumänisch **II**
roof [ru:f] Dach **III U1**, 18
room [ru:m; rʊm] Zimmer; Raum **I**
chat **room** ['tʃæt rʊm] Chatroom **II**
living **room** ['lɪvɪŋ rʊm] Wohnzimmer **I**
spare **room** [ˌspeə 'rʊm] Gästezimmer ⟨**III TS2**, 77⟩
roommate ['ru:mmeɪt] Zimmergenosse/Zimmergenossin **I**
rope [rəʊp] Seil **III U3**, 67
rose [rəʊz] Rose ⟨**III TS1**, 47⟩
rotary phone ['rəʊtri fəʊn] Telefon mit Wählscheibe **III U3**, 69
round [raʊnd] Runde **II**
round of boxing [ˌraʊnd‿əv 'bɒksɪŋ] Boxrunde **II**
the **Round** Table [ðə ˌraʊnd 'teɪbl] die Tafelrunde **III AC1**, 25
*to go **round** in circles [gəʊ ˌraʊnd ɪn 'sɜ:klz] sich im Kreis drehen **III U3**, 66
to turn **round** [ˌtɜ:n‿(ə)'raʊnd] (sich) umdrehen; wenden **II**
round [raʊnd] um … herum **II**
route [ru:t] Strecke; Route **II**
royal ['rɔɪəl] königlich **I**
rubber ['rʌbə] Radiergummi **I**
rubbish ['rʌbɪʃ] Müll; Gerümpel **I**
rude [ru:d] unhöflich; unverschämt **I**
rugby ['rʌgbi] Rugby **II**
to **ruin** ['ru:ɪn] ruinieren; zerstören **II**
rule [ru:l] Regel **I**
What's the **rule** for …? [ˌwɒts ðə 'ru:l fə] Was ist die Regel für …? **I**
to **rule** [ru:l] herrschen; regieren **III U1**, 16
ruler ['ru:lə] Lineal **I**
run [rʌn] Rennen; Lauf **II**
run area ['rʌn ˌeəriə] Gehege; Auslauf **III TS2**, 77
*to **run** [rʌn] rennen; laufen **I**
*to **run** away [ˌrʌn‿ə'weɪ] wegrennen **I**
runner ['rʌnə] Läufer/-in **II**
running ['rʌnɪŋ] Laufen; Rennen **II**

S

sad [sæd] traurig **I**
safe [seɪf] sicher; ungefährlich **II**
to reef the **sails** [ˌri:f ðə 'seɪlz] die Segel einholen **I**
to **sail** [seɪl] segeln; umsegeln **III TS1**, 49
sailboat ['seɪlbəʊt] Segelboot **III U1**, 20
sailor ['seɪlə] Seemann; Matrose **I**
salad ['sæləd] Salat **I**
sale [seɪl] Verkauf **II**
the **same** way as [ˌðə seɪm 'weɪ æz] genauso wie **II**
the **same** [ðə 'seɪm] der-/die-/dasselbe; der/die/das gleiche **I**
sandal ['sændl] Sandale **III U4**, 86
sandwich ['sænwɪdʒ] Sandwich; belegtes Brot **I**

sandy ['sændi] sandig; Sand- **III U1**, 9
Saturday ['sætədeɪ] Samstag **I**
sauce [sɔ:s] Soße **III U3**, 60
sausage ['sɒsɪdʒ] Wurst; Bratwurst **III AC2**, 52
to save [seɪv] retten; bergen **I**; sparen **III U2**, 29
saved by the bell [ˌseɪvd baɪ ðə 'bel] noch mal Glück gehabt **III U2**, 32
sax ['sæks] Saxofon **I**
saxophone ['sæksəfəʊn] Saxofon **I**
*to say [seɪ] sagen; aufsagen; sprechen **I**
*to **say** hello (to) [ˌseɪ hel'əʊ tə] grüßen; Grüße ausrichten (an) **I**
saying ['seɪɪŋ] Redensart; Sprichwort **III U2**, 26
to scan [skæn] scannen; nach Details durchsuchen **II**
*to be scared (of) [bi: 'skeəd‿əv] Angst haben (vor) **I**
I'm (not) **scared** of ... [ˌaɪm (nɒt) 'skeəd‿əv] Ich habe (keine) Angst vor ... **I**
scary ['skeəri] unheimlich; gruselig; beängstigend **II**
scene [si:n] Szene **I**; Schauplatz **II**
acting a **scene** [ˌæktɪŋ‿ə 'si:n] eine Theaterszene spielen **I**
scented ['sentɪd] duftend; parfümiert ⟨**III TS3**, 107⟩
rhyme scheme ['raɪm ski:m] Reimschema °**III TS1**, 47
school [sku:l] Schule **I**
grammar **school** ['græmə ˌsku:l] Gymnasium **III U1**, 13
primary **school** ['praɪmri ˌsku:l] Grundschule **I**
school fees *(pl)* ['sku:l fi:z] Schulgeld; Schulgebühren **III U4**, 99
schoolbag ['sku:lbæg] Schultasche **I**
Science [saɪəns] Naturwissenschaften **II**
science fiction [ˌsaɪəns 'fɪkʃn] Science-Fiction *(Zukunftsdichtung)* **II**
scientist ['saɪəntɪst] Wissenschaftler/-in **III U3**, 60
score [skɔ:] Punktestand; Spielstand **II**
Scot [skɒt] Schotte/Schottin **III U3**, 60
Scottish ['skɒtɪʃ] schottisch **III U1**, 9
gorge scrambling ['gɔ:dʒ ˌskræmblɪŋ] Schluchtenklettern **II**
to scream [skri:m] schreien; kreischen **II**
script [skrɪpt] Drehbuch; Skript **III AC3**, 83
sea [si:] Meer **I**
search [sɜ:tʃ] Suche; Such- **II**
second ['seknd] zweite/-r/-s **I**
secret ['si:krət] Geheimnis **II**
in **secret** [ɪn 'si:krət] heimlich **II**
secret ['si:krət] geheim **III U4**, 95
section ['sekʃn] Abschnitt; Paragraf **II**
*to see [si:] sehen **I**
See you! ['si: jə] Bis dann!; Bis ... **I**
Wait and **see**! [ˌweɪt‿ənd 'si:] Warte ab! **I**
to seem [si:m] scheinen **III U2**, 35

self [self], selves [selvz] *(pl)* das Selbst **III U2**, 27
self-critical ['selfˌkrɪtɪkl] selbstkritisch **II**
self-evaluation [ˌselfɪˌvælju'eɪʃn] Selbsteinschätzung **I**
selfie ['selfi] Selfie **II**
*to sell [sel] verkaufen **I**
seller ['selə] Verkäufer/-in *(auf einem Flohmarkt)* **I**
*to send [send] schicken; senden **I**
*to **send** off [send‿'ɒf] abschicken **III U1**, 13
sense [sens] Sinn **III TS3**, 108
sense of humour *(no pl)* [ˌsens‿əv 'hju:mə] Sinn für Humor **III U2**, 39
sentence ['sentəns] Satz **I**
conditional **sentence** [kənˌdɪʃnl 'sentəns] Bedingungssatz °**III U1**, 9
separate ['seprət] separat; getrennt; verschieden **II**
September [sep'tembə] September **I**
sequence ['si:kwəns] Sequenz; Szene °**III U4**, 99
series ['sɪəri:z], series ['sɪəri:z] *(pl)* Serie **III TS3**, 106
serious ['sɪəriəs] ernsthaft; ernst **I**
set [set] Umgebung; Rahmen **III AC1**, 25; Aufnahmeort; Drehort **III U4**, 96
a **set** of [ə 'set‿əv] eine Liste von °**III TS2**, 78
*to set off [ˌset‿'ɒf] *hier:* ein Feuerwerk zünden **III U3**, 60
*to **set** up [ˌset‿'ʌp] einrichten; aufbauen **I**
setting ['setɪŋ] Schauplatz; Rahmen **II**
account **settings** [ə'kaʊnt ˌsetɪŋz] Profileinstellungen **III U2**, 39
seven ['sevn] sieben **I**
several ['sevrl] einige; mehrere; verschiedene **II**
shadow ['ʃædəʊ] Schatten **III TS3**, 107
to share [ʃeə] teilen **II**
sharp [ʃɑ:p] scharf; schneidend **III TS3**, 108
she [ʃi:] sie **I**
shed [ʃed] Schuppen; Stall; Gartenhäuschen ⟨**III TS2**, 77⟩
sheep, sheep *(pl)* [ʃi:p] Schaf **II**
sheet [ʃi:t] Blatt ⟨**III TS2**, 77⟩
animal shelter ['ænɪml ˌʃeltə] Tierheim **III TS2**, 79
shimmer ['ʃɪmə] Schimmer; Schimmern ⟨**III TS3**, 109⟩
*to shine [ʃaɪn] scheinen; glänzen **II**
shinty ['ʃɪnti] Shinty *(eine Art Hockey)* **III U3**, 57
ship [ʃɪp] Schiff **I**
shipbuilding ['ʃɪpbɪldɪŋ] Schiffsbau **III U3**, 59
shock [ʃɒk] Schock **II**
shoe [ʃu:] Schuh **I**

*to be in sb's **shoes** [ˌbi: ɪn sʌmbɒdɪz 'ʃu:z] an jmds. Stelle sein; in jmds. Haut stecken **III TS3**, 108
in Jay's **shoes** [ɪn dʒeɪz 'ʃu:z] an Jays Stelle **III U2**, 30
photo shoot ['fəʊtəʊ ˌʃu:t] Fotoshooting; Fotoaufnahmen **III U4**, 96
*to shoot [ʃu:t‿(ət)] schießen (auf) **III TS1**, 48
shop [ʃɒp] Geschäft; Laden **I**
charity **shop** ['tʃærɪti ʃɒp] Second-Hand-Laden **I**
pawn **shop** ['pɔ:n ʃɒp] Pfandhaus; Pfandleihe **III U4**, 99
shopping ['ʃɒpɪŋ] Einkaufen; Einkäufe **I**
*to do the **shopping** [ˌdu: ðə 'ʃɒpɪŋ] Einkäufe machen; Besorgungen machen **III U3**, 69
*to go **shopping** [ˌgəʊ 'ʃɒpɪŋ] einkaufen gehen **I**
shore [ʃɔ:] Ufer; Küste **II**
short [ʃɔ:t] kurz **I**
short answer [ˌʃɔ:t‿'ɑ:nsə] Kurzantwort **I**
short form ['ʃɔ:t fɔ:m] Kurzform **I**
shorts *(pl)* [ʃɔ:ts] Shorts; kurze Hose **II**
shot [ʃɒt] Einstellung; Kameraeinstellung **II**; Aufnahme **III U4**, 96
should [ʃʊd] sollte; solltest; sollten; solltet **II**
shouldn't ['ʃʊdnt] sollte(n) nicht **II**
shoulder ['ʃəʊldə] Schulter **II**
to shout [ʃaʊt] schreien; rufen **I**
show [ʃəʊ] Show; Schau; Aufführung **II**
comedy **show** ['kɒmədi ˌʃəʊ] Comedy Show **II**
living history **show** [ˌlɪvɪŋ 'hɪstəri ˌʃəʊ] *Show, in der historischer Alltag nachgespielt wird* **III U1**, 8
talent **show** ['tælənt ˌʃəʊ] Talentwettbewerb **I**
to show [ʃəʊ] zeigen **I**
to **show** off [ʃəʊ‿'ɒf] angeben **II**
shower ['ʃaʊə] Dusche **I**
show-off ['ʃəʊ‿ɒf] Angeber/-in **III U2**, 39
shredded ['ʃredɪd] zerrissen ⟨**III TS2**, 77⟩
to shudder ['ʃʌdə] zittern; beben ⟨**III TS3**, 107⟩
to shuffle ['ʃʌfl] mischen °**III U1**, 9
shy [ʃaɪ] schüchtern **II**
sick [sɪk] krank; unwohl **II**
*to feel **sick** [ˌfi:l 'sɪk] Übelkeit verspüren; sich schlecht fühlen **II**
side [saɪd] Seite **II**
sight [saɪt] Sehenswürdigkeit; Anblick **II**; *hier:* Blick **III TS1**, 48
sightseeing ['saɪtsi:ɪŋ] Sightseeing-; Besichtigungs- **II**
sign [saɪn] Zeichen; Schild **II**
signal ['sɪgnl] Signal; Empfang **III U3**, 66
signal word ['sɪgnəl ˌwɜ:d] Signalwort **I**
silence *(no pl)* ['saɪləns] Stille; Schweigen; Ruhe **III TS3**, 109

silent ['saɪlənt] still; ruhig; schweigsam; stumm **III TS3**, 107
silly ['sɪli] Dummkopf **II**
silly ['sɪli] dumm; doof; albern **I**
silver ['sɪlvə] Silber **II**
similar ['sɪmɪlə] ähnlich **II**
simple ['sɪmpl] einfach; simpel **III TS1**, 48
simple past [ˌsɪmpl 'pɑ:st] Vergangenheitsform **II**
simple present [ˌsɪmpl 'preznt] Gegenwart; Präsens **I**
since *(+ Zeitpunkt)* [sɪns] seit; seitdem **III U3**, 56
*to sing [sɪŋ] singen **I**
*to **sing** along [ˌsɪŋ‿ə'lɒŋ] mitsingen **III TS1**, 46
*to **sing** out loud [ˌri:d/sɪŋ‿aʊt 'laʊd] laut vorsingen **III TS1**, 47
I like **singing** and dancing. [ˌaɪ laɪk ˌsɪŋɪŋ‿ənd 'dɑ:nsɪŋ] Ich singe und tanze gern. **I**
singer ['sɪŋə] Sänger/-in **II**
single ticket ['sɪŋgl ˌtɪkɪt] einfache Fahrkarte **III U1**, 12
*to sink [sɪŋk] untergehen; sinken **III TS3**, 109
Dear Sir or Madam [dɪə ˌsɜ:r‿ɔ: 'mædəm] Sehr geehrte Dame, sehr geehrter Herr **III U1**, 13
sister ['sɪstə] Schwester **I**
half-**sister** ['hɑ:fˌsɪstə] Halbschwester **I**
*to sit [sɪt] sitzen **I**
Sit! [sɪt] Sitz! *(Befehl für Hunde)*; Platz! *(Befehl für Hunde)* **I**
*to **sit** down [ˌsɪt 'daʊn] sich hinsetzen; sich setzen **I**
*to **sit** face to face [ˌsɪt feɪs tə ˌfeɪs] sich gegenüber sitzen **I**
site [saɪt] Webseite **II**
situation [ˌsɪtju'eɪʃn] Situation **I**
six [sɪks] sechs **I**
Four and **six** is ten. [ˌfɔ:r‿ənd ˌsɪks‿ɪz 'ten] Vier plus sechs ist zehn. **I**
size [saɪz] Größe; Kleidergröße **I**
to skate [skeɪt] Inlineskates fahren; Schlittschuh laufen **I**
skateboard ['skeɪtbɔ:d] Skateboard **II**
skateboarding ['skeɪtbɔ:dɪŋ] Skateboardfahren **I**
skates *(pl)* [skeɪts] Inlineskates; Rollschuhe; Schlittschuhe **I**
(inline) skating ['ɪnlaɪn ˌskeɪtɪŋ] Inlineskatefahren **I**
skill [skɪl] Fertigkeit; Geschick **I**
to skim [skɪm] überfliegen **II**
skirt [skɜ:t] Rock **III U1**, 18
sky [skaɪ] Himmel **III U3**, 66
slave [sleɪv] Sklave/Sklavin **III U4**, 90
*to sleep [sli:p] schlafen **I**
sleepover ['sli:pˌəʊvə] Übernachtung **I**
to slice [slaɪs] in Scheiben schneiden **I**
slide [slaɪd] Rutschbahn **I**
water **slide** ['wɔ:tə ˌslaɪd] Wasserrutsche **I**
slogan ['sləʊgən] Slogan; Werbespruch **II**
time slot ['taɪm slɒt] Zeitfenster **II**
slow [sləʊ] langsam **I**
to step into a story **slowly** [stepˌ‿ɪntʊ ə ˌstɔ:ri 'sləʊli] eine Geschichte langsam entwickeln **III TS3**, 111
small [smɔ:l] klein **I**
small talk ['smɔ:l ˌtɔ:k] Smalltalk **III AC3**, 82
smart [smɑ:t] schlau; klug; intelligent **III U2**, 27
smartcard ['smɑ:tkɑ:d] Chipkarte **II**
smartphone ['smɑ:tfəʊn] Smartphone **II**
*to smell [smel] riechen; duften **III U4**, 85
smile [smaɪl] Lächeln **I**
to smile [smaɪl] lächeln **I**
smoke [sməʊk] Rauch **III TS3**, 107
smoky ['sməʊki] verraucht **III U4**, 84
snack [snæk] Snack; Imbiss **I**
snack bar ['snæk ˌbɑ:] Café; Imbissstube **I**
word snake ['wɜ:d ˌsneɪk] Wortschlange **I**
to sneak around [ˌsni:k‿ə'raʊnd] herumschleichen **II**
to snore [snɔ:] schnarchen **I**
snow [snəʊ] Schnee **III U4**, 90
so [səʊ] so; also **I**
so far [ˌsəʊ 'fɑ:] bis jetzt **II**
so is ['səʊ ɪz] ebenso wie °**III TS1**, 47
to soak up [səʊk‿'ʌp] aufsaugen **III TS2**, 77
social network [ˌsəʊʃl 'netwɜ:k] soziales Netzwerk **II**
society [sə'saɪəti] Verein; Gesellschaft **III U1**, 19
sofa ['səʊfə] Sofa; Couch **I**
soft [sɒft] weich; sanft ⟨**III TS1**, 51⟩
software manual ['sɒftweə ˌmænjuəl] Softwarehandbuch °**III TS2**, 81
soil [sɔɪl] Erde; Boden ⟨**III TS3**, 107⟩
soldier ['səʊldʒə] Soldat/-in **III U3**, 58
solution [sə'lu:ʃn] Lösung **II**
to solve [sɒlv] lösen **III U1**, 18
some [sʌm; səm] einige; ein paar; etwas **I**
somebody ['sʌmbədi] jemand **I**
somehow ['sʌmhaʊ] irgendwie ⟨**III TS3**, 107⟩
someone ['sʌmwʌn] jemand **II**
something ['sʌmθɪŋ] etwas **I**
sometimes ['sʌmtaɪmz] manchmal **I**
somewhere ['sʌmweə] irgendwo **II**
son [sʌn] Sohn **III U3**, 56
song [sɒŋ] Song; Lied **I**
soon [su:n] bald **II**
as **soon** as [əz 'su:n‿əz] sobald **II**
Sorry! ['sɒri] Entschuldigung!; Tut mir leid! **I**
*to be **sorry** [bi: 'sɒri] leid tun **I**
*to feel **sorry** for [ˌfi:l 'sɒri fɔ:] Mitleid haben mit; bedauern **III U2**, 39
I'm **sorry**! [ˌaɪm 'sɒri] Tut mir leid! **I**
to sort into [sɔ:t 'ɪntʊ] einsortieren; sortieren nach °**III AC2**, 53
sound [saʊnd] Ton; Geräusch; Klang **I**
to sound [saʊnd] klingen **I**
source [sɔ:s] Quelle °**III U1**, 17
south [saʊθ] Süden; Süd- **II**
South Korean [ˌsaʊθ kə'ri:ən] Südkoreaner/-in; südkoreanisch; Südkoreanisch **II**
south [saʊθ] südlich; im Süden ⟨**III U3**, 62⟩
south-eastern [ˌsaʊθ'i:stn] südöstlich ⟨**III TS2**, 79⟩
souvenir [ˌsu:vn'ɪə] Souvenir; Andenken **II**
space [speɪs] Raum; Fläche; Platz; Ort **II**
*to leave **space** [li:v 'speɪs] Platz lassen **I**
spaceship ['speɪsʃɪp] Raumschiff **II**
Spanish ['spænɪʃ] spanisch; Spanisch; die Spanier **III U4**, 86
spare room [ˌspeə 'rʊm] Gästezimmer ⟨**III TS2**, 77⟩
*to speak [spi:k] sprechen **I**
speaker ['spi:kə] Redner/-in; Sprecher/-in **I**
speaking ['spi:kɪŋ] Sprechen **I**
spear [spɪə] Speer **III U1**, 18
special ['speʃl] besonders; speziell **I**
special offer [ˌspeʃl‿'ɒfə] Sonderangebot **I**
with **special** needs [wɪð ˌspeʃl 'ni:dz] behindert **II**
species ['spi:ʃi:z], species ['spi:ʃi:z] *(pl)* Art; Spezies ⟨**III TS2**, 80⟩
spectacular [spek'tækjələ] spektakulär **III U3**, 64
speech [spi:tʃ] Rede °**III U4**, 91
speech bubble ['spi:tʃ ˌbʌbl] Sprechblase **I**
*to spell [spel] buchstabieren **I**
spelling ['spelɪŋ] Rechtschreibung **I**
*to spend [spend] ausgeben *(Geld)* **I**; verbringen *(Zeit)* **II**
spider ['spaɪdə] Spinne **III U3**, 68
to splash [splæʃ] spritzen; planschen ⟨**III TS1**, 47⟩
spoken ['spəʊkn] gesprochen **II**
sponge [spʌndʒ] Rühr-; Biskuit- **I**
spontaneous [spɒn'teɪniəs] spontan °**III U1**, 11
spoon [spu:n] Löffel **III TS1**, 47
sport [spɔ:t] Sport; Sportart **I**
… is a great **sport**. [ɪz‿ə 'greɪt ˌspɔ:t] … ist ein toller Sport. **I**
*to spread [spred] (sich) verbreiten ⟨**III U2**, 31⟩
spring [sprɪŋ] Frühling **III TS2**, 77
squirrel ['skwɪrəl] Eichhörnchen **I**
stadium ['steɪdiəm] Stadion **II**
stage [steɪdʒ] Bühne **III U4**, 88
stage direction ['steɪdʒ dɪˌrekʃn] Regieanweisung **III AC3**, 83
stairs *(pl)* [steəz] Treppe **III U3**, 66
*to stand [stænd] stehen **I**

*to **stand** up [ˌstænd‿'ʌp] aufstehen *(von einer Sitzgelegenheit)* **I**
star [stɑː] Star; Stern **I**
to **stare** [steə] starren; anstarren **I**
start [stɑːt] Anfang; Start **III U4**, 99
to **start** [stɑːt] anfangen; beginnen; starten **I**; *hier:* gründen **III U3**, 60
*to get **started** [ˌget 'stɑːtɪd] anfangen **II**
starting place ['stɑːtɪŋ pleɪs] Startpunkt **III U1**, 12
head of **state** [ˌhed‿əv 'steɪt] Staatsoberhaupt **II**
statement ['steɪtmənt] Aussage; Behauptung; Erklärung **II**
station ['steɪʃn] Haltestelle; Bahnhof; Station **I**; Sender **II**
bus **station** ['bʌs ˌsteɪʃn] Busbahnhof **I**
to **stay** [steɪ] bleiben **I**; übernachten **III U1**, 10
to **stay** away from [ˌsteɪ‿ə'weɪ frəm] fernbleiben von; meiden **II**
to **stay** in touch (with) [ˌsteɪ ɪn 'tʌtʃ (wɪð)] in Kontakt bleiben (mit) **II**
to **stay** with ['steɪ wɪð] wohnen bei **II**
Stay the way you are. [ˌsteɪ ðə weɪ ju 'ɑː] Bleib wie du bist. **III U2**, 33
steak [steɪk] Steak **I**
*to **steal** [stiːl] stehlen **II**
steam [stiːm] Dampf **III U3**, 60
steam engine ['stiːm‿endʒɪn] Dampfmaschine **III U3**, 60
step [step] Stufe; Schritt **I**
step-by-**step** [ˌstepbaɪ'step] Schritt-für-Schritt- **II**
to **step** into a story slowly [step‿ɪntʊ ə ˌstɔːri 'sləʊli] eine Geschichte langsam entwickeln **III TS3**, 111
stepmum ['stepmʌm] Stiefmutter **I**
still [stɪl] Standbild **II**
still [stɪl] still **I**
still [stɪl] noch; immer noch **I**; dennoch **II**
*to keep one's feet or hands **still** [ˌkiːp wʌnz‿'fiːt‿ɔː 'hændz stɪl] die Beine und Hände ruhig halten **III TS1**, 50
*to **sting** [stɪŋ] stechen **III TS3**, 109
stomach ['stʌmək] Magen; Bauch **II**
stomachache ['stʌməkeɪk] Bauchschmerzen; Bauchweh **II**
stone [stəʊn] Stein; Stein- **III U3**, 66
stop [stɒp] Haltestelle; Halt **II**
to **stop** [stɒp] aufhören (mit); anhalten; stoppen **I**
Stop and think [ˌstɒp‿ənd 'θɪŋk] Warte/Wartet und denk/denkt nach. **I**
Stop it! ['stɒp‿ɪt] Mach/Macht das aus!; Hör/Hört auf! **I**
storm [stɔːm] Sturm **I**
story, **stories** *(pl)* ['stɔːri; 'stɔːriz] Story; Geschichte; Erzählung **I**
photo **story** ['fəʊtəʊ ˌstɔːri] Fotostory; Bildgeschichte **I**
to step into a **story** slowly [step‿ɪntʊ ə ˌstɔːri 'sləʊli] eine Geschichte langsam entwickeln **III TS3**, 111
storyline ['stɔːrilaɪn] Handlung ⟨**III TS3**, 111⟩
straight on [streɪt‿'ɒn] geradeaus **I**
straight away [ˌstreɪt‿ə'weɪ] sofort; gleich °**III TS2**, 79
strange [streɪndʒ] fremd; seltsam; merkwürdig **I**
street [striːt] Straße *(in der Stadt)* **I**
in the **street** [ˌɪn ðə 'striːt] in der Straße; auf der Straße **I**
*to take to the **streets** [ˌteɪk tu ðə 'striːts] auf die Straße gehen ⟨**III TS2**, 80⟩
the high **street** [ðə 'haɪ ˌstriːt] die Haupteinkaufsstraße **III U2**, 36
stress [stres] Betonung °**III TS1**, 47
to **stress** [stres] betonen; hervorheben °**III TS1**, 47
*to be **stressed** out [bi ˌstrest‿'aʊt] völlig gestresst sein **III U2**, 28
strict [strɪkt] streng; strikt **III TS3**, 108
strong [strɒŋ] stark **II**
structure ['strʌktʃə] Struktur; Aufbau; Gliederung °**III TS1**, 47
*to get **stuck** [ˌget 'stʌk] stecken bleiben ⟨**III TS2**, 77⟩
stuck in the middle of … [ˌstʌk ɪn ðə 'mɪdl‿əv] mitten in … stecken; feststecken in … **III TS1**, 49
student ['stjuːdnt] Schüler/-in; Student/-in **I**
exchange **student** [ɪks'tʃeɪndʒ ˌstjuːdnt] Austauschschüler/-in **III AC2**, 52
student exchange ['stjuːdnt ɪksˌtʃeɪndʒ] Schüleraustausch **III AC3**, 83
studies *(pl)* ['stʌdiz] Studium; Lernen; Arbeit für die Schule **II**
recording **studio** [rɪ'kɔːdɪŋ ˌstjuːdiəʊ] Aufnahmestudio; Tonstudio **I**
to **study** ['stʌdi] studieren; lernen **III U2**, 28
stuff [stʌf] Zeug **I**
stupid ['stjuːpɪd] dumm; blöd **II**
subject ['sʌbdʒɪkt] Schulfach; Subjekt; Satzgegenstand **II**; Thema **III U2**, 27
substitute ['sʌbstɪtjuːt] Ersatz; Ersatz- **II**
to **succeed** (in) [sək'siːd‿ɪn] Erfolg haben (in/bei/mit) **III U2**, 29
success [sək'ses] Erfolg **III U2**, 28
successful [sək'sesfl] erfolgreich **III U2**, 30
such [sʌtʃ] solch; solche/-r/-s **II**
such as ['sʌtʃ‿əz] (solche) wie; wie (zum Beispiel) ⟨**III TS2**, 77⟩
suddenly ['sʌdnli] plötzlich; auf einmal **I**
sugar ['ʃʊgə] Zucker **III AC2**, 52
suggestion [sə'dʒestʃn] Vorschlag; Anregung **I**
to **sum** up [ˌsʌm‿'ʌp] zusammenfassen **II**
summary ['sʌmri] Zusammenfassung ⟨**III TS3**, 111⟩
summer ['sʌmə] Sommer **II**
summer camp ['sʌmə kæmp] Sommerferienlager **II**
sun [sʌn] Sonne **II**
Sunday ['sʌndeɪ] Sonntag **I**
sunflower ['sʌnflaʊə] Sonnenblume **III TS1**, 47
superlative [suː'pɜːlətɪv] Superlativ **II**
supermarket ['suːpəˌmɑːkɪt] Supermarkt **I**
superpower ['suːpəˌpaʊə] Supermacht **II**
to **supply** [sə'plaɪ] versorgen **III U1**, 16
*to be **supposed** to (do) [bi sə'pəʊzd tə] (tun) sollen ⟨**III TS1**, 49⟩
sure [ʃʊə; ʃɔː] sicher **I**
*to make **sure** [ˌmeɪk 'ʃɔː] sich versichern **I**
I'm (not) **sure** … [ˌaɪm nɒt 'ʃʊə] Ich bin mir (nicht) sicher … **III AC2**, 53
surface ['sɜːfɪs] Oberfläche ⟨**III TS3**, 109⟩
surfing ['sɜːfɪŋ] Surfen **III U1**, 9
surgery ['sɜːdʒəri] Arztpraxis; Praxis; Praxisräume **I**
surprise [sə'praɪz] Überraschung **I**
to **surprise** [sə'praɪz] überraschen **II**
*to be **surprised** [bi sə'praɪzd] überrascht sein **II**
surprising [sə'praɪzɪŋ] überraschend **II**
survey ['sɜːveɪ] Umfrage; Studie **I**
to **survive** [sə'vaɪv] überleben **III TS1**, 50
suspense [sə'spens] Spannung °**III U1**, 21
to **swap** roles [ˌswɒp 'rəʊlz] Rollen tauschen **I**
sweet [swiːt] süß **I**
sweets *(pl)* [swiːts] Süßigkeiten; Bonbons **I**
swift [swɪft] schnell ⟨**III TS1**, 48⟩
*to **swim** [swɪm] schwimmen **I**
swimming ['swɪmɪŋ] Schwimmen **I**
*to go **swimming** [ˌgəʊ 'swɪmɪŋ] Schwimmen gehen **I**
swimming pool ['swɪmɪŋ ˌpuːl] Swimmingpool; Schwimmbecken **III TS3**, 109
switch [swɪtʃ] Schalter **III U3**, 69
syllable ['sɪləbl] Silbe °**III TS1**, 47
symbol ['sɪmbl] Symbol **II**

T

table ['teɪbl] Tisch **I**
the Round **Table** [ðə ˌraʊnd 'teɪbl] die Tafelrunde **III AC1**, 25
tablet ['tæblət] Tablet **II**
tae [tə] um zu ⟨**III U3**, 58⟩
taekwondo [ˌtækwʌn'duː] Taekwondo **II**
question **tag** ['kwestʃən ˌtæg] Frageanhängsel; Bestätigungsfrage **II**
tail [teɪl] Schwanz; Schweif **I**
*to **take** [teɪk] nehmen; mitnehmen; wegnehmen; bringen; mitbringen **I**; dauern; (Zeit) brauchen **II**
*to **take** a breath [ˌteɪk‿ə 'breθ] Luft holen; Atem holen **III TS3**, 109
*to **take** a look at [ˌteɪk‿ə 'lʊk‿æt] einen Blick werfen auf **II**

*to **take** a message [ˌteɪk‿ə 'mesɪdʒ] eine Nachricht entgegennehmen; jmdm. etw. ausrichten **I**
*to **take** a test [ˌteɪk‿ə 'test] einen Test machen **II**
*to **take** a vote [ˌteɪk‿ə 'vəʊt] abstimmen **I**
*to **take** care of sb [ˌteɪk‿'keər‿əv] sich um jmdn. kümmern; für jmdn. sorgen **III U4**, 96
*to **take** notes [ˌteɪk 'nəʊts] sich Notizen machen **I**
*to **take** off [ˌteɪk‿'ɒf] abnehmen; herunternehmen; ausziehen **I**
*to **take** part (in) [ˌteɪk 'pɑ:t (ɪn)] teilnehmen (an) **II**
*to **take** photos [ˌteɪk 'fəʊtəʊz] fotografieren; Fotos machen **I**
*to **take** place [ˌteɪk 'pleɪs] stattfinden **I**
*to **take** to the streets [ˌteɪk tu ðə 'stri:ts] auf die Straße gehen ⟨**III TS2**, 80⟩
Take turns. [ˌteɪk 'tɜ:nz] Wechselt euch ab. **I**
*to **take** up [ˌteɪk‿'ʌp] beanspruchen ⟨**III TS2**, 77⟩
Take a deep breath. [ˌteɪk‿ə ˌdi:p 'breθ] Atme(t) tief ein. **II**
talent ['tælənt] Talent **I**
talent show ['tælənt ˌʃəʊ] Talentwettbewerb **I**
small **talk** ['smɔ:l ˌtɔ:k] Smalltalk **III AC3**, 82
to **talk** [tɔ:k] sprechen; reden **I**
to **talk** about … ['tɔ:k‿əbaʊt] sprechen über; erzählen von **I**
to **talk** to ['tɔ:k tə] reden mit **I**
talker ['tɔ:kə] Sprecher/-in **III AC3**, 82
talking ['tɔ:kɪŋ] Sprechen **I**
tall [tɔ:l] groß; hoch **II**
to **tap** [tæp] antippen **II**
target ['tɑ:gɪt] Ziel; Ziel- ⟨**III TS2**, 77⟩
tartan ['tɑ:tn] Schottenkaro *(bestimmtes Muster eines Clans)*; karierter Schottenstoff **III U3**, 55
task [tɑ:sk] Aufgabe; Auftrag **I**
to **taste** [teɪst] schmecken; probieren **III U4**, 88
tattoo [tæt'u:] Tattoe; Tätowierung **III U2**, 34
taxi ['tæksi] Taxi **II**
tea [ti:] Tee **I**
tea bag ['ti: bæg] Teebeutel **III U4**, 99
*to **teach** [ti:tʃ] unterrichten; lehren; beibringen **II**
*to **teach** somebody a lesson [ˌti:tʃ‿ə 'lesn] jmdm. eine Lehre/Lektion erteilen **II**
teacher ['ti:tʃə] Lehrer/-in **I**
team [ti:m] Team; Gruppe **II**
to **tease** sb [ti:z] jmdn. aufziehen; jmdn. hänseln; jmdn. ärgern **III U2**, 38

Technology [tek'nɒlədʒi] Technik; Computerunterricht **II**
technology [tek'nɒlədʒi] Technologie **II**
teen [ti:n] Jugend- **II**; Teenager; Jugendliche/-r **III TS3**, 106
teenager ['ti:nˌeɪdʒə] Teenager; Jugendliche/-r **I**
telephone ['telɪfəʊn] Telefon **I**
*to **tell** [tel] erzählen; sagen; mitteilen **I**
Tell me about … ['tel mi:‿əˌbaʊt] Erzähle mir von … **I**
ten [ten] zehn **I**
ten times [ten 'taɪmz] zehnmal **I**
Four and six is **ten.** [ˌfɔ:r‿ənd ˌsɪks‿ɪz 'ten] Vier plus sechs ist zehn. **I**
tennis ['tenɪs] Tennis **I**
tense [tens] Zeit; Zeitform *(grammatisch)* **II**
test [test] Test; Klassenarbeit; Prüfung **I**
*to take a **test** [ˌteɪk‿ə 'test] einen Test machen **II**
to **test** [test] testen; prüfen °**III U1**, 17
text [tekst] Text **I**
factual **text** [ˌfæktʃʊəl 'tekst] Sachtext °**III TS2**, 76
text (message) ['tekst ˌmesɪdʒ] SMS; Kurznachricht **I**
to **text** [tekst] eine SMS schicken **II**
than [ðæn] als *(bei Vergleichen)* **II**
more … **than** ['mɔ: ðən] mehr … als **I**
to **thank** [θæŋk] danken **II**
Thank you. ['θæŋk ju] Danke. **I**
thankful ['θæŋkfl] dankbar **I**
Thanks. [θæŋks] Danke. **I**
that [ðæt] so *(Betonung)* **III AC2**, 53
that much [ðæt 'mʌtʃ] so viel **III AC2**, 53
that [ðæt; ðət] dass **I**
that [ðæt] das; jenes **I**
after **that** [ˌɑ:ftə 'ðæt] danach **I**
like **that** [laɪk 'ðæt] so **I**
That was close! [ˌðæt wəz 'kləʊs] Das war knapp! **I**
that's how [ðæts 'haʊ] so **II**
That's what friends are for. [ˌðæts wɒt 'frendz‿ɑ: ˌfɔ:] Dafür sind Freunde da. **I**
that's why [ðæts 'waɪ] deshalb **II**
That's … [ðæts] Das macht … **I**
that [ðæt] der; dem; den; die; das *(Relativpronomen)* **II**
the [ðə; ði] der; die *(auch Pl.)*; das **I**
the others [ði‿'ʌðəz] die anderen **I**
the same [ðə 'seɪm] der-/die-/dasselbe; der/die/das gleiche **I**
the … **the** [ðə … ðə] je … desto **II**
theatre ['θɪətə] Theater **I**
their [ðeə] ihr/-e *(Pl.)* **I**
them [ðem] sie *(Pl.)*; ihnen **I**
theme [θi:m] Thema; Motto **I**
then [ðen] dann; danach **I**
back **then** [bæk 'ðen] damals **III U4**, 84
there [ðeə] da; dort; dahin; dorthin **I**

there is/are [ðər‿'ɪz/'ɑ:] da ist/sind; es gibt **I**
these [ði:z] diese (hier) **I**
these days [ˌði:z 'deɪz] zurzeit **III U2**, 36
they [ðeɪ] sie *(Pl.)* **I**
It's …/**They**'re … [ɪts/ðeə] Es kostet …/ Sie kosten … **I**
thick [θɪk] dick *(nicht für Personen)* **III U3**, 66
thing [θɪŋ] Ding; Sache **I**
*to **think** [θɪŋk] denken; nachdenken; glauben **I**
Stop and **think** [ˌstɒp‿ənd 'θɪŋk] Warte/ Wartet und denk/denkt nach. **I**
*to **think** of ['θɪŋk‿əv] halten von; denken über **I**
*to **think** of ['θɪŋk‿əv] (sich) ausdenken; sich etwas einfallen lassen **II**
Think of … ['θɪŋk‿əv] Denke/Denkt an … **I**
third [θɜ:d] dritte/-r/-s **I**
third person narrator [ˌθɜ:d ˌpɜ:sn nə'reɪtə] Er/Sie-Erzähler/-in °**III TS3**, 107
thirsty ['θɜ:sti] durstig **III TS2**, 79
thirteen [ˌθɜ:'ti:n] dreizehn **I**
this [ðɪs] dies; diese/-r/-s **I**
this afternoon [ðɪs 'ɑ:ftənu:n] heute Nachmittag **II**
this early ['ðɪs ˌɜ:li] so früh **III AC2**, 53
This is … ['ðɪs‿ɪz] Das (hier) ist … **I**
thistle ['θɪsl] Distel **III U3**, 55
those [ðəʊz] diese dort; jene **I**
those in power [ˌðəʊz ɪn 'paʊə] die Regierenden; die Herrschenden **III TS2**, 80
even **though** [ˌi:vn 'ðəʊ] auch wenn; obwohl ⟨**III TS3**, 109⟩
thought [θɔ:t] Gedanke **II**
thousands of ['θaʊzndz‿əv] tausende (von) **I**
three [θri:] drei **I**
through [θru:] durch **I**
*to **throw** (at) [θrəʊ] werfen (nach) **I**
*to **throw** away [ˌθrəʊ‿ə'weɪ] wegwerfen **I**
throw the dice twice [ˌθrəʊ ðə daɪs 'twaɪs] würfle zweimal **II**
thumb [θʌm] Daumen **II**
thunder *(no pl)* ['θʌndə] Donner **II**
Thursday ['θɜ:zdeɪ] Donnerstag **I**
to **tick** [tɪk] abhaken **II**
ticket ['tɪkɪt] Los; Ticket; Eintrittskarte **I**; Fahrschein **III U1**, 11
one-way **ticket** ['wʌnweɪ ˌtɪkɪt] einfache Fahrkarte **III U1**, 12
return **ticket** [rɪ'tɜ:n ˌtɪkɪt] Hin- und Rückfahrkarte **III U1**, 12
single **ticket** ['sɪŋgl ˌtɪkɪt] einfache Fahrkarte **III U1**, 12
ticket office ['tɪkɪt ˌɒfɪs] Kartenschalter **III U3**, 66
high **tide** ['haɪ ˌtaɪd] Flut **II**
low **tide** ['ləʊ ˌtaɪd] Ebbe **II**

to **tidy** *(a room)* ['taɪdi] aufräumen; in Ordnung bringen **I**
to **tie** (to) ['taɪ tə] binden (an); fesseln (an) **III U3**, 67
till [tɪl] bis **I**
time [taɪm] Zeit **I**; Mal **II**
all the **time** [ˌɔ:l ðə 'taɪm] die ganze Zeit **II**
at the same **time** [ət ðə ˌseɪm 'taɪm] zur selben Zeit; gleichzeitig **I**
free **time** [ˌfri: 'taɪm] Freizeit **I**
on **time** [ɒn 'taɪm] pünktlich **II**
ten **times** [ten 'taɪmz] zehnmal **I**
time line ['taɪm ˌlaɪn] Zeitstrahl **I**
time slot ['taɪm slɒt] Zeitfenster **II**
I can't wait till next **time**. [aɪ kɑ:nt ˌweɪt tɪl nekst 'taɪm] Ich kann es bis zum nächsten Mal kaum erwarten. **II**
Time to get up! [ˌtaɪm tə ˌget‿'ʌp] Es ist Zeit aufzustehen! **I**
What **time**? [ˌwɒt 'taɪm] Um wie viel Uhr? **I**
What's the **time**? [ˌwɒts ðə 'taɪm] Wie spät ist es?; Wie viel Uhr ist es? **I**
timetable ['taɪmˌteɪbl] Stundenplan; Fahrplan **I**
tin [tɪn] Zinn **III U1**, 18
tin can ['tɪn kæn] Blechdose **III U3**, 69
tinned [tɪnd] Dosen-; aus der Dose **I**
tiny ['taɪni] klein; winzig **III U3**, 64
tip [tɪp] Tipp; Ratschlag **I**
to **tiptoe** ['tɪptəʊ] auf Zehenspitzen gehen **II**
tired [taɪəd] müde **I**
Get your **tissues** out! [ˌget jɔ: 'tɪsju:z aʊt] Das ist so unglaublich traurig! ⟨**III TS2**, 79⟩
title ['taɪtl] Titel; Überschrift **II**
to [tʊ; tə] zu; nach; auf; in; vor *(bei Uhrzeitangaben)* **I**
from … **to** [frəm … tə] von … bis **I**
quarter past/**to** ['kwɔ:tə pɑ:st/tə] Viertel nach/vor **I**
to the point [tə ðə 'pɔɪnt] prägnant; treffend **III AC3**, 83
toast [təʊst] Toast **I**
tobacco *(no pl)* [tə'bækəʊ] Tabak **III U4**, 88
today [tə'deɪ] heute **I**
toddler ['tɒdlə] Kleinkind ⟨**III TS3**, 107⟩
together [tə'geðə] zusammen; miteinander; gemeinsam **I**
toilet ['tɔɪlət] Toilette **I**
tomato, **tomatoes** *(pl)* [tə'mɑ:təʊ; tə'mɑ:təʊz] Tomate **I**
tomorrow [tə'mɒrəʊ] morgen **I**
too [tu:] auch; zu **I**
Too bad! [ˌtu: 'bæd] Zu dumm!; Schade! **I**
You **too**? [ju: 'tu:] Du auch? **I**
tool [tu:l] Werkzeug; Gerät **III U1**, 19
top [tɒp] Spitze; oberer Teil; oberes Ende **I**
on **top** [ɒn 'tɒp] oben; obendrauf **I**
to **top** up [tɒp‿'ʌp] aufladen **II**
topic ['tɒpɪk] Thema **II**
torch [tɔ:tʃ] Fackel; Taschenlampe **II**
to **toss** and turn (in bed) ['tɒs ənd ˌtɜ:n] sich (im Bett) hin und her wälzen ⟨**III TS1**, 49⟩
to stay in **touch** (with) [ˌsteɪ ɪn 'tʌtʃ (wɪð)] in Kontakt bleiben (mit) **II**
tour [tʊə] Tour; Fahrt; Rundgang **II**
audio **tour** ['ɔ:diəʊ ˌtʊə] Audioführung **II**
tourism ['tʊərɪzm] Tourismus **III U1**, 14
tourist ['tʊərɪst] Tourist/-in **I**
tourist board ['tʊərɪst bɔ:d] Touristeninformation **III U1**, 13
tourist information centre [ˌtʊərɪst ɪnfə'meɪʃn ˌsentə] Touristeninformation **I**
towards [tə'wɔ:dz] in Richtung; auf … zu; darauf zu **II**
tower [taʊə] Turm **III U3**, 66
town [taʊn] Stadt **I**
toy [tɔɪ] Spielzeug **I**
to **trace** [treɪs] verfolgen; nachspüren **I**
trade [treɪd] Handel ⟨**III TS2**, 80⟩
to **trade** [treɪd] austauschen **II**
tradition [trə'dɪʃn] Tradition **I**
traditional [trə'dɪʃnl] traditionell **III U3**, 54
walking **trail** ['wɔ:kɪŋ treɪl] Wanderweg **III U1**, 14
train [treɪn] Zug **I**
to **train** [treɪn] trainieren **II**
trainer ['treɪnə] Turnschuh **III U2**, 36
training ['treɪnɪŋ] Training **II**
to **translate** [trænz'leɪt] übersetzen **I**
Don't **translate** … [ˌdəʊnt trænz'leɪt] Übersetze/Übersetzt nicht … **I**
translation [trænz'leɪʃn] Übersetzung **I**
transport ['trænspɔ:t] Verkehrsmittel; Transport **III U1**, 10
public **transport** *(no pl)* [ˌpʌblɪk 'trænspɔ:t] öffentliche Verkehrsmittel **II**
*to be **trapped** [bi 'træpt] eingeschlossen sein; in der Falle sitzen °**III U3**, 68
travel ['trævl] (das) Reisen; Reise **II**
travel agency ['trævl‿eɪdʒənsi] Reisebüro **III U3**, 65
travel agent's ['trævl‿eɪdʒənts] Reisebüro **III U1**, 11
travel report [ˌtrævl rɪ'pɔ:t] Reisebericht **II**
to **travel** ['trævl] fahren; reisen **II**
treasure ['treʒə] Schatz **II**
treat [tri:t] *hier:* Leckerli; Belohnung **III TS2**, 78
to **treat** [tri:t] behandeln ⟨**III TS2**, 77⟩
tree [tri:] Baum **I**
family **tree** ['fæmli ˌtri:] Stammbaum **I**
palm **tree** ['pɑ:m ˌtri:] Palme **III U1**, 9
pony **trekking** ['pəʊni ˌtrekɪŋ] Ponyreiten im Gelände **III U1**, 9
trial [traɪəl] Qualifikation **II**
tribe [traɪb] Stamm; Volksstamm **III U4**, 84
trick [trɪk] Trick; Streich **I**
to play a **trick** (on) [ˌpleɪ‿ə 'trɪk‿ɒn] einen Streich spielen **I**
trifle ['traɪfl] Trifle *(englischer Nachtisch)* **I**
trip [trɪp] Trip; Reise; Ausflug; Fahrt **II**
trouble ['trʌbl] Ärger; Probleme; Schwierigkeiten **II**
*to make **trouble** [ˌmeɪk 'trʌbl] Ärger machen; in Schwierigkeiten bringen **I**
trousers *(pl)* ['traʊzəz] Hose **III U1**, 18
trowel ['traʊəl] kleiner Spaten **II**
true [tru:] wahr **II**
to **trust** [trʌst] vertrauen **III U2**, 36
to **try** [traɪ] versuchen; probieren **I**
to **try** on [ˌtraɪ‿'ɒn] anprobieren **II**
to **try** out [ˌtraɪ‿'aʊt] ausprobieren °**III TS3**, 111
Try … [traɪ] Versuch es mal mit …; Probier mal … **I**
T-shirt ['ti:ʃɜ:t] T-Shirt **I**
the **Tube** [ðə 'tju:b] die Londoner U-Bahn **II**
Tudor ['tju:də] Tudor- **III U4**, 86
Tuesday ['tju:zdeɪ] Dienstag **I**
tune [tju:n] Melodie **III TS1**, 47
tunnel ['tʌnl] Tunnel **I**
It's your **turn**. [ˌɪts 'jɔ: tɜ:n] Du bist dran. **I**
Take **turns**. [ˌteɪk 'tɜ:nz] Wechselt euch ab. **I**
Your **turn**. ['jɔ: tɜ:n] Du bist dran. **I**
to **turn** [tɜ:n] einbiegen; abbiegen **I**
to toss and **turn** (in bed) ['tɒs ənd ˌtɜ:n] sich (im Bett) hin und her wälzen ⟨**III TS1**, 49⟩
to **turn** (a)round [ˌtɜ:n‿(ə)'raʊnd] (sich) umdrehen; wenden **II**
to **turn** back [tɜ:n 'bæk] umkehren; zurückgehen **II**
to **turn** off [ˌtɜ:n‿'ɒf] abschalten; ausschalten **II**
to **turn** to ['tɜ:n tə] sich wenden an; sich zuwenden **III U1**, 19
turning point ['tɜ:nɪŋ ˌpɔɪnt] Wendepunkt °**III U2**, 38
to **turn** [tɜ:n] drehen; (sich) umdrehen **III TS3**, 107
tusk [tʌsk] Stoßzahn **III TS2**, 80
tutor ['tju:tə] Klassenlehrer/-in **I**
tutor group ['tju:tə ˌgru:p] Klasse *(in einer englischen Schule)* **I**
TV [ˌti:'vi:] Fernsehen; Fernseher **I**
to watch **TV** [ˌwɒtʃ ti:'vi:] fernsehen **I**
twelve [twelv] zwölf **I**
twice [twaɪs] zweimal ⟨**III U3**, 63⟩
twin [twɪn] Zwilling; Zwillings- **III U1**, 19
to **twist** your ankle [ˌtwɪst jɔ:r‿'æŋkl] sich den Knöchel verrenken **II**
two [tu:] zwei **I**
the **two** of them [ðə 'tu:‿əv ðəm] beide **II**
two of which ['tu:‿əv wɪtʃ] zwei von ihnen °**III U1**, 17
type [taɪp] Typ; Art; Sorte °**III U2**, 27

typical ['tɪpɪkl] typisch **I**
typically ['tɪpɪkli] typisch **III U3**, 55

U

u *(= you)* [juː; jə] du; Sie; ihr **I**
UFO [ˌjuːef'əʊ] UFO **II**
ugly ['ʌgli] hässlich ⟨**III U3**, 63⟩
unbroke [ʌn'brəʊk] unbeschädigt ⟨**III TS1**, 48⟩
uncle ['ʌŋkl] Onkel **I**
under ['ʌndə] unter **I**
underfloor heating *(no pl)* [ˌʌndəflɔː 'hiːtɪŋ] Fußbodenheizung **III U4**, 84
underground ['ʌndəgraʊnd] U-Bahn **II**
to **underline** [ˌʌndə'laɪn] unterstreichen °**III U3**, 57
underneath [ˌʌndə'niːθ] unterhalb; unten ⟨**III TS2**, 77⟩
*to **understand** [ˌʌndə'stænd] verstehen **I**
understanding [ˌʌndə'stændɪŋ] Verständnis **II**
unfair [ʌn'feə] unfair **II**
unfamiliar [ˌʌnfə'mɪliə] nicht vertraut; unbekannt **III AC2**, 52
unfriendly [ʌn'frendli] unfreundlich **II**
uniform ['juːnɪfɔːm] Uniform **I**
unit ['juːnɪt] Lektion; Kapitel; Einheit **I**
unknown [ˌʌn'nəʊn] unbekannt ⟨**III TS1**, 51⟩
unless [ən'les] wenn nicht; es sei denn, (dass) … ⟨**III U3**, 62⟩
*to be **unlucky** [biː‿ʌn'lʌki] Pech haben **I**
unofficial [ˌʌnə'fɪʃl] inoffiziell **III U3**, 58
until [ʌn'tɪl] bis; erst wenn **II**
untitled [ʌn'taɪtld] ohne Titel ⟨**III TS1**, 51⟩
to **unwrap** [ʌn'ræp] auswickeln; auspacken **I**
up [ʌp] hinauf; nach oben **II**
to end **up** [ˌend‿'ʌp] enden; landen **II**
*to get **up** [ˌget‿'ʌp] aufstehen *(aus dem Bett)* **I**
*to give **up** [ˌgɪv‿'ʌp] aufgeben **III U2**, 30
to look **up** [ˌlʊk‿'ʌp] nachschlagen; nachschauen **I**
What's **up**? [ˌwɒts‿'ʌp] Was ist los? **III U2**, 32
to **update** [ʌp'deɪt] aktualisieren; auf den neuesten Stand bringen ⟨**III U3**, 62⟩
*to **upset** [ʌp'set] aus der Fassung bringen **III AC2**, 53
upset [ʌp'set] aufgebracht; bestürzt **II**
upstairs [ʌp'steəz] nach oben; im Obergeschoss; oben **II**
urine ['jʊərɪn] Urin ⟨**III TS2**, 77⟩
us [ʌs] uns **I**
to **use** [juːz] benutzen; verwenden; gebrauchen **I**
*to be **used** to *(+ -ing)* [bi 'juːs‿tə] gewöhnt sein an; gewohnt sein **III AC2**, 53
useful ['juːsfl] nützlich; hilfreich **I**
Useful phrases [ˌjuːsfl 'freɪsɪz] nützliche Ausdrücke **I**
usual ['juːʒl] üblich **III U2**, 37
usually ['juːʒli] normalerweise; gewöhnlich; meistens **I**

V

valuable ['væljuəbl] wertvoll ⟨**III TS2**, 77⟩
vegetable ['vedʒtəbl] Gemüse **III U3**, 59
vegetarian [ˌvedʒɪ'teəriən] Vegetarier/-in **III U3**, 59
vegetarian [ˌvedʒɪ'teəriən] vegetarisch **III U3**, 60
verb [vɜːb] Verb **I**
verse [vɜːs] Vers; Strophe °**III TS1**, 47
version ['vɜːʃn] Version °**III TS1**, 47
cover **version** ['kʌvə ˌvɜːʃn] Coverversion °**III TS1**, 51
versus (vs.) ['vɜːsəs] gegen **III U3**, 69
very ['veri] sehr **I**
very much [ˌveri 'mʌtʃ] sehr **I**
vet [vet] Tierarzt/Tierärztin **I**
Victorian [vɪk'tɔːriən] viktorianisch; Viktorianer/-in **III U4**, 87
video ['vɪdiəʊ] Video **II**
video chat ['vɪdiəʊ ˌtʃæt] Videochat **II**
view [vjuː] Aussicht; Sicht; Ausblick; Blick **II**
point of **view** [ˌpɔɪnt‿əv 'vjuː] Standpunkt; Ansicht; Perspektive **II**
viewer ['vjuːə] Zuschauer/-in **II**
viewing ['vjuːɪŋ] Hör-/Sehverstehen **I**
village ['vɪlɪdʒ] Dorf **I**
villain ['vɪlən] Bösewicht **III AC1**, 24
violence *(no pl)* ['vaɪəlns] Gewalt **III TS3**, 106
violent ['vaɪəlnt] gewaltsam; gewalttätig; brutal **III TS2**, 80
violet ['vaɪələt] Veilchen ⟨**III TS1**, 47⟩
visit ['vɪzɪt] Besuch **I**
to **visit** ['vɪzɪt] besichtigen; besuchen **I**
visitor ['vɪzɪtə] Besucher/-in **I**
vitamin ['vɪtəmɪn] Vitamin **III U4**, 99
vocabulary [və'kæbjələri] Vokabular; Wortschatz **I**
voice [vɔɪs] Stimme **I**
volleyball ['vɒlibɔːl] Volleyball **I**
volunteer [ˌvɒlən'tɪə] freiwillig; ehrenamtlich ⟨**III TS2**, 79⟩
*to take a **vote** [ˌteɪk‿ə 'vəʊt] abstimmen **I**
to **vote** [vəʊt] abstimmen; wählen **I**

W

to **wait** (for) [weɪt] warten (auf) **I**
I can't **wait** till next time. [aɪ kɑːnt ˌweɪt tɪl nekst 'taɪm] Ich kann es bis zum nächsten Mal kaum erwarten. **II**
Wait and see! [ˌweɪt‿ənd 'siː] Warte ab! **I**
*to **wake** up [weɪk‿'ʌp] aufwachen; aufwecken **III U4**, 99
*to go for a **walk** [ˌgəʊ fər‿ə 'wɔːk] spazieren gehen **II**
gallery **walk** ['gælri ˌwɔːk] Museumsrundgang; Vernissage **I**
night **walk** ['naɪt wɔːk] Nachtwanderung **II**
to **walk** [wɔːk] gehen; laufen **I**
to **walk** the dog [ˌwɔːk ðə 'dɒg] den Hund ausführen; mit dem Hund spazieren gehen **I**
walking ['wɔːkɪŋ] Wandern **II**
walking trail ['wɔːkɪŋ treɪl] Wanderweg **III U1**, 14
wall [wɔːl] Wand; Mauer **I**; Online-Pinnwand **III U2**, 39
to **wander** round [ˌwɒndə 'raʊnd] herumlaufen ⟨**III TS2**, 77⟩
to **want** (to) ['wɒnt tə] wollen; mögen **I**
war [wɔː] Krieg ⟨**III U3**, 63⟩
wardrobe ['wɔːdrəʊb] Kleiderschrank **I**
to **warm** up [ˌwɔːm‿'ʌp] aufwärmen; sich aufwärmen **I**
warm [wɔːm] warm **III TS2**, 77
warm-up ['wɔːm‿ʌp] Aufwärmübung **I**
warrior ['wɒriə] Krieger **III U1**, 18
to **wash** [wɒʃ] waschen; sich waschen **I**
to **wash** up [ˌwɒʃ‿'ʌp] angespült werden **II**
washing machine ['wɒʃɪŋ məˌʃiːn] Waschmaschine **II**
to **waste** [weɪst] verschwenden **II**
to **watch** [wɒtʃ] beobachten; (sich) ansehen; zuschauen **I**
to **watch** TV [ˌwɒtʃ tiː'viː] fernsehen **I**
water ['wɔːtə] Wasser **I**
water slide ['wɔːtə ˌslaɪd] Wasserrutsche **I**
wave [weɪv] Welle **I**
wax [wæks] Wachs **II**
wax figure ['wæks ˌfɪgə] Wachsfigur **II**
way [weɪ] Weg; Art und Weise **I**
*to be in the **way** [biː‿ɪn ðə 'weɪ] im Weg sein/stehen **I**
*to get in the **way** [ˌget‿ɪn ðə 'weɪ] stören; im Weg stehen **II**
in other **ways** [ɪn‿'ʌðə weɪz] auf andere Weise **II**
the same **way** as [ˌðə seɪm 'weɪ æz] genauso wie **II**
we [wiː; wi] wir **I**
We're from … ['wɪə frəm] Wir sind aus … **I**
weapon ['wepən] Waffe **III U4**, 95
*to **wear** [weə] anhaben; tragen *(Kleidung)* **I**
weather ['weðə] Wetter **I**
weather forecast ['weðə ˌfɔːkɑːst] Wettervorhersage **III U1**, 12
web [web] Netz; Spinnennetz **III U3**, 68
web designer ['web dɪˌzaɪnə] Webdesigner **III U2**, 32
website ['websaɪt] Website; Internetauftritt **I**

wedding [ˈwedɪŋ] Hochzeit **I**
Wednesday [ˈwenzdeɪ] Mittwoch **I**
wee bit [ˈwiː bɪt] klitzeklein ⟨**III U3**, 58⟩
week [wiːk] Woche **I**
weekday [ˈwiːkdeɪ] Wochentag **II**
weekend [ˌwiːkˈend] Wochenende **I**
at the **weekend** [ət ðə ˌwiːkˈend] am Wochenende **I**
to **weigh** [weɪ] wiegen **III TS2**, 77
weight [weɪt] Gewicht **III TS2**, 77
to gain **weight** [ˌgeɪn ˈweɪt] zunehmen ⟨**III TS2**, 77⟩
weird [wɪəd] merkwürdig; seltsam; sonderbar **II**
Welcome! [ˈwelkəm] Willkommen! **II**
to **welcome** [ˈwelkəm] willkommen heißen **II**
You're **welcome**. [jɔː ˈwelkəm] Bitte schön.; Nichts zu danken.; Gern geschehen. **I**
well [wel] tja; nun **I**
Welsh [welʃ] walisisch; Walisisch; Waliser/-in **II**
west [west] Westen; West- **I**
in the far **west** [ɪn ðə fɑː ˈwest] im äußersten Westen **III U1**, 14
wet [wet] nass **II**
what [wɒt] was; welche/-r/-s; was für ein **I**
What about ... ? [ˈwɒt‿əbaʊt] Wie wär's mit ...?; Was ist mit ...? **I**
What are ...? [ˈwɒt‿ɑː] Welche ... sind es? **I**
What colour is ...? [ˌwɒt ˈkʌlər‿ɪz] Welche Farbe hat ...? **I**
what else [ˌwɒt‿ˈels] was sonst; was noch **I**
What is missing? [ˌwɒt‿ɪz ˈmɪsɪŋ] Was fehlt? **I**
What is ... about? [ˌwɒt‿ɪz ...‿əˈbaʊt] Worum geht es in/im ...? **I**
what it's like [ˌwɒt‿ɪts ˈlaɪk] wie das ist **II**
What luck! [wɒt ˈlʌk] Was für ein Glück! **III U4**, 92
What on earth ...? [ˌwɒtː‿ɒn‿ˈɜːθ] Was um alles in der Welt ...? **II**
What time? [wɒt ˈtaɪm] Um wie viel Uhr? **I**
what to ... [ˈwɒt tə] was man ... **I**
What was it like? [ˌwɒt wɒz‿ɪt ˈlaɪk] Wie war es? **III U4**, 84
What's that? [wɒts ˈðæt] Was ist das? **I**
What's the rule for ...? [ˌwɒts ðə ˈruːl fə] Was ist die Regel für ...? **I**
What's up? [ˌwɒts‿ˈʌp] Was ist los? **III U2**, 32
What's your favourite ...? [ˈwɒts jə ˌfeɪvrɪt] Was ist dein/-e Lieblings...? **I**
What's your name? [ˌwɒts jə ˈneɪm] Wie heißt du?; Wie heißen Sie? **I**
What's going on? [wɒts ˌgəʊɪŋ‿ˈɒn] Was ist los?; Was geht ab? **III U2**, 36
What's the matter? [ˌwɒts ðə ˈmætə] Was ist los?; Was hast du? **III U1**, 18
What's the time? [ˌwɒts ðə ˈtaɪm] Wie spät ist es?; Wie viel Uhr ist es? **I**
... **what** to do. [ˈwɒt tə duː] ... was ich tun soll. **II**
what the man looked like [ˌwɒt ðə mæn ˈlʊkt laɪk] wie der Mann aussah **II**
wheel [wiːl] Rad; Steuerrad; Steuer **I**
wheelchair [ˈwiːltʃeə] Rollstuhl **II**
when [wen] wenn; wann; als **I**
whenever [wenˈevə] wann immer; jedes Mal, wenn; so oft **II**
where [weə] wo; wohin **I**
Where ... from? [ˌweə ... ˈfrɒm] Woher ...? **I**
... **where** to go. [ˌweə tə ˈgəʊ] ... wohin ich gehen kann. **II**
which [wɪtʃ] welche/-r/-s **I**
which [wɪtʃ] der *(Relativpronomen)*; die *(Relativpronomen)*; das *(Relativpronomen)*; dem *(Relativpronomen)*; den *(Relativpronomen)* **II**
a **while** [ə ˈwaɪl] eine Weile **II**
while [waɪl] während **I**
to **whip** [wɪp] schlagen **I**
whisky [ˈwɪski] Whisky **III U3**, 57
to **whisper** [ˈwɪspə] flüstern **I**
white [waɪt] weiß **I**
who [huː] wer; wem; wen **I**
Who ... for? [ˌhuː ˈfɔː] Für wen ...? **I**
Who is it? [ˌhuː‿ˈɪz‿ɪt] Wer ist es? **I**
Who's in? [huːz‿ˈɪn] Wer macht mit?; Wer ist dabei? **II**
who [huː] der *(Relativpronomen)*; dem *(Relativpronomen)*; den *(Relativpronomen)*; die *(Relativpronomen)* **II**
whole [həʊl] ganz **I**
whoosh [wʊʃ] wusch **I**
whose [huːz] dessen *(Relativpronomen)*; deren *(Relativpronomen)* **II**
why [waɪ] warum **I**
that's **why** [ðæts ˈwaɪ] deshalb **II**
wide [waɪd] breit; weit; ausgedehnt **III U1**, 9
wife, **wives** *(pl)* [waɪf, waɪvz] Ehefrau **II**
the **wild** [ðə ˈwaɪld] Wildnis; freie Wildbahn ⟨**III TS2**, 77⟩
wild [waɪld] wild **III U1**, 14
wildlife [ˈwaɪldlaɪf] Tierwelt *(in freier Wildbahn)* **II**
will [wɪl] werden *(futurisch)* **III U1**, 9
*to **win** [wɪn] gewinnen; siegen **I**
wind [wɪnd] Wind **III U1**, 18
window [ˈwɪndəʊ] Fenster **I**
windsurfing [ˈwɪndsɜːfɪŋ] Windsurfen **III U1**, 9
wine [waɪn] Wein **I**
winner [ˈwɪnə] Gewinner/-in; Sieger/-in **I**
winter [ˈwɪntə] Winter **III TS2**, 77
wish [wɪʃ] Wunsch **I**
*to make a **wish** [ˌmeɪk‿ə ˈwɪʃ] sich etwas wünschen **I**
Best **wishes** [ˌbest ˈwɪʃɪz] Viele Grüße; Herzliche Grüße **III U1**, 13
with [wɪð] mit; bei **I**
within [wɪˈðɪn] innerhalb ⟨**III TS2**, 80⟩
without [wɪˈðaʊt] ohne **I**
witness [ˈwɪtnəs] Zeuge/Zeugin **II**
wizard [ˈwɪzəd] Zauberer **III AC1**, 24
wobbly [ˈwɒbli] wackelig **II**
woman, **women** *(pl)* [ˈwʊmən; ˈwɪmɪn] Frau **I**
wonderful [ˈwʌndəfl] wunderbar **II**
wood [wʊd] Wald; Wäldchen **III TS3**, 107
wood [wʊd] Holz **III U3**, 67
wooden [ˈwʊdn] hölzern; aus Holz **III U3**, 66
Woof! [wʊf] Wau! **I**
word [wɜːd] Wort **I**
compound **word** [ˈkɒmpaʊnd wɜːd] Kompositum *(zusammengesetztes Wort)* **II**
key **word** [ˈkiː wɜːd] Stichwort; Schlüsselbegriff **I**
linking **word** [ˈlɪŋkɪŋ ˌwɜːd] Bindewort **I**
play on **words** [ˌpleɪ‿ɒn ˈwɜːdz] Wortspiel **III TS1**, 50
signal **word** [ˈsɪgnəl ˌwɜːd] Signalwort **I**
word bank [ˈwɜːd ˌbæŋk] Wortsammlung °**III TS1**, 50
word cloud [ˈwɜːd ˌklaʊd] Wörterwolke **II**
word order [ˈwɜːd‿ˌɔːdə] Wortstellung; Satzstellung **I**
Word power [ˈwɜːd ˌpaʊə] die Kraft der Wörter *(Wortschatzübung)* **I**
word snake [ˈwɜːd ˌsneɪk] Wortschlange **I**
word-building [ˈwɜːdˌbɪldɪŋ] Wortbildung **II**
work [wɜːk] Arbeit **I**
pair **work** [ˈpeə wɜːk] Partnerarbeit **II**
to **work** [wɜːk] arbeiten **I**; funktionieren **II**
to **work** out [ˌwɜːk‿ˈaʊt] herausfinden; ausarbeiten **II**; funktionieren; klappen **III U2**, 39
worker [ˈwɜːkə] *hier:* Mitarbeiter/-in ⟨**III TS2**, 79⟩
workshop [ˈwɜːkʃɒp] Workshop **I**
world [wɜːld] Erde; Welt **I**
from around the **world** [frɒm əˌraʊnd ðə ˈwɜːld] aus aller Welt **III U1**, 14
worm [wɜːm] Wurm **I**
worried [ˈwʌrid] beunruhigt; besorgt **III AC3**, 82
*to be **worried** [bi ˈwʌrid] beunruhigt sein; besorgt sein **II**
to **worry** [ˈwʌri] sich Sorgen machen **II**
Don't **worry**! [ˌdəʊnt ˈwʌri] Keine Sorge! **I**
the **worst** [ðə ˈwɜːst] der/die/das schlimmste; der/die/das schlechteste **II**

*to be **worth** [bi: 'wɜ:θ] wert sein **I**
would [wʊd] würde/-st/-n/-t **III U2**, 27
would like [wʊd 'laɪk] würde/-st/-n/-t gern; hätte/-st/-n/-t gern **I**
would love [wʊd 'lʌv] würde/-st/-n/-t sehr gern; hätte/-st-/-n/-t sehr gern **I**
Would you like ...? [ˌwʊd jʊ 'laɪk] Möchtest du ...?; Möchten Sie ...?; Möchtet ihr ...? **II**
wounded ['wu:ndɪd] verwundet; verletzt **III U3**, 66
Wow! [waʊ] Wow! **I**
to **wrap** [ræp] einwickeln; einpacken **I**
wrapping ['ræpɪŋ] Verpackung; Hülle **I**
to **wrinkle** ['rɪŋkl] zerknittern ⟨**III TS1**, 51⟩
wrist [rɪst] Handgelenk **II**
*to **write** [raɪt] schreiben **I**
*to **write** down [ˌraɪt 'daʊn] aufschreiben **I**
writer ['raɪtə] Autor/-in; Verfasser/-in **III U4**, 88
writing ['raɪtɪŋ] Schreiben **I**
wrong [rɒŋ] falsch **I**
*to be **wrong** [bi: 'rɒŋ] unrecht haben; sich irren **I**
*to go **wrong** [ˌgəʊ 'rɒŋ] schiefgehen **I**

X

XOXO [ˌhʌgz‿ən 'kɪsɪz] Umarmungen und Küsse *(am Ende von E-Mails und SMS)* **I**

Y

yeah *(infml)* [jeə] ja **I**
year [jɪə] Jahr; Schuljahr **I**
11-**year**-old [ɪˌlevn'jɪərəʊld] 11-Jährige/-r **II**
18-**year**-old [ˌeɪti:n 'jɪər‿əʊld] 18-jährig **II**
yearbook ['jɪəbʊk] Jahrbuch **II**
yellow ['jeləʊ] gelb **I**
yes [jes] ja **I**
yesterday ['jestədeɪ] gestern **II**
yet [jet] schon; noch **II**
not ... **yet** [nɒt 'jet] noch nicht **II**
yoghurt ['jɒgət] Joghurt **I**
you [ju:; jə] du; ihr; Sie **I**
You know how to ... [ju: 'nəʊ ˌhaʊ tə] Du weißt, wie man ...; Ihr wisst, wie man ... **I**
You too? [ju: 'tu:] Du auch? **I**
You're into ... ['jɔ:r‿ɪntə] Du magst ...; Du stehst auf ... **I**
You're welcome. [ˌjɔ: 'welkəm] Bitte schön.; Nichts zu danken.; Gern geschehen. **I**
You're ... [jɔ:r] Sie sind ...; Du bist ... **I**
young [jʌŋ] jung **I**
your [jɔ:; jə] dein/-e; euer/eure; Ihr/-e **I**
What's **your** name? [ˌwɒts jə 'neɪm] Wie heißt du?; Wie heißen Sie? **I**
Your turn. ['jɔ: tɜ:n] Du bist dran. **I**
yours [jɔ:z] dein/-er/-e/-es; eure/-r/-s; Ihr/-e **II**
Yours ... [jɔ:z] Viele Grüße ... *(am Ende von Briefen und Mails)* **II**
yourself [jɔ:'self] du/dir/dich/Sie/sich (selbst); selber **I**
yourselves [jɔ:'selvz] ihr/euch/Sie/sich (selbst); selber **III U1**, 13

Z

zero ['zɪərəʊ] null **I**
zoo [zu:] Zoo; Tierpark **II**
to **zoom** in (on) [zu:m‿'ɪn ɒn] heranzoomen (auf) **III U4**, 96

Boys' names

Amir [ˌɑ:'mi:r] **II**
Ben [ben] **I**
Bob [bɒb] **I**
Brad [bræd] **III AC2**, 52
Damian ['deɪmiən] **I**
Dave [deɪv] **I**
David ['deɪvɪd] **I**
Desmond ['dezmənd] **I**
Ed [ed] **II**
Ethan ['i:θn] **III U3**, 56
Filip ['fɪlɪp] **I**
Finn [fɪn] **III U2**, 36
Frank [fræŋk] **II**
Henry ['henri] **I**
Jack [dʒæk] **I**
Jahangir [dʒə'hʌŋgɪə] **I**
James [dʒeɪmz] **II**
Jamie ['dʒeɪmi] **I**
Jay [dʒeɪ] **I**
Jim [dʒɪm] **III U4**, 96
Jinsoo ['dʒɪnzu:] **II**
John [dʒɒn] **II**
Jon [dʒɒn] **II**
Luke [lu:k] **I**
Mario ['mæriəʊ] **III TS1**, 46
Marley ['mɑ:li] **II**
Matt [mæt] **III U2**, 34
Max [mæks] **III U2**, 36
Mick [mɪk] **II**
Mike [maɪk] **II**
Nathan ['neɪθn] **II**
Nick [nɪk] **II**
Peter ['pi:tə] **II**
Rick [rɪk] **III TS3**, 106
Sean [ʃɔ:n] **III U2**, 39
Shahid [ʃɑ:'hi:d] **I**
Steve [sti:v] **I**
Stuart ['stu:ət] **III U3**, 55
Thomas ['tɒməs] **III U4**, 89
Tony ['təʊni] **I**
Tyler ['taɪlə] **I**
Will [wɪl] **II**

Girls' names

Alice ['ælɪs] **II**
Alicia [ə'lɪsiə; ə'lɪʃə] **I**
Alva ['ælvə] **III U3**, 69
Amber ['æmbə] **I**
Anna ['ænə] **I**
Anne [æn] **I**
Annie ['æni] **III U3**, 61
Ayla ['eɪlə] **II**
Beata [bi'ɑ:tə] **I**
Bunko ['bʌŋkəʊ] **II**
Carol ['kærəl] **I**
Ceri ['keri] **II**
Claire ['kleə] **I**
Emily ['emɪli] **I**
Frances ['frɑ:nsɪs] **I**
Gwen [gwen] **II**
Helen ['helɪn] **III U1**, 19
Holly ['hɒli] **I**
Irina [ɪ'ri:nə] **I**
Ivy ['aɪvi] **III U2**, 30
Jean [dʒi:n] **III U3**, 55
Judith ['dʒu:dɪθ] **III U1**, 16
Julie ['dʒu:li] **I**
Kate [keɪt] **II**
Kirsty ['kɜ:sti] **III U3**, 59
Laura ['lɔ:rə] **I**
Lauren ['lɔ:rən] **II**
Lou [lu:] **I**
Lucy ['lu:si] **I**
Maisie ['meɪzi] **II**
Margaret ['mɑ:grət] **III U4**, 89
Mary ['meəri] **II**
Megan ['megən] **III U1**, 20
Mila ['mi:lə] **I**
Mina ['mi:nə] **II**
Olivia [ɒl'ɪviə] **I**
Pia ['pi:ə] **I**
Polly ['pɒli] **II**
Rose [rəʊz] **I**
Ruby ['ru:bi] **II**
Sally ['sæli] **I**
Seeta ['si:tə] **I**
Tamara [tə'mɑ:rə] **III U1**, 19
Tina ['ti:nə] **III TS3**, 106
Tomoko [tə'mɒkəʊ] **II**
Violet ['vaɪələt] **III U4**, 99
Vivien ['vɪvjən] **III AC1**, 25

Surnames

Ashton ['æʃtən] **II**
Azad [ə'zɑ:d] **I**
Bayram ['beɪrəm] **II**
Elliot ['eliət] **I**
Francis ['frɑ:nsɪs] **III U2**, 30
Fraser ['freɪzə] **I**
Green [gri:n] **I**
Karp [kɑ:p] **III U2**, 29
King [kɪŋ] **III U3**, 61
Miller ['mɪlə] **III U4**, 89

Nicholls ['nɪkəlz] **III U1**, 16
Parker ['pɑ:kə] **II**
Preston ['prestən] **I**
Pulsford ['pʌlsfɔ:d] **III TS2**, 80
Richardson ['rɪtʃədsn] **I**
Swindon ['swɪndən] **I**
Thompson ['tɒmsən] **II**
Walker ['wɔ:kə] **I**
Wright [raɪt] **II**
Zajac ['zeɪdʒæk] **I**

Place names

Aberdeen [ˌæbə'di:n] *Stadt in Schottland* **III U3**, 54
Baker Street ['beɪkə ˌstri:t] **III AC1**, 25
Bankside ['bæŋksaɪd] *Stadtteil von London* **III U4**, 91
Begbie Road [ˌbegbi 'rəʊd] **II**
Birmingham ['bɜ:mɪŋəm] **III TS2**, 80
Bradford ['brædfəd] **II**
Brick Lane [ˌbrɪk 'leɪn] **II**
Bristol ['brɪstl] **III TS2**, 80
Brook Lane [ˌbrʊk 'leɪn] **I**
Caerphilly [keə'fɪli] *walisische Stadt* **III U1**, 8
Camden Market ['kæmdən ˌmɑ:kɪt] **II**
College Way [ˌkɒlɪdʒ 'weɪ] **I**
Cologne [kə'ləʊn] Köln **I**
Covent Garden [ˌkɒvnt 'gɑ:dn] **II**
Cracow ['krækɒv; 'krɑ:kaʊ] Krakau **I**
Dunrossness **III U3**, 64
Edinburgh ['edɪnbrə] **III U1**, 9
Enfield [en'fi:ld] **I**
Glasgow ['glɑ:zgəʊ] *Stadt in Schottland* **III U3**, 55
Greenwich Park [ˌgrenɪdʒ 'pɑ:k] **I**
Greenwich Pier [ˌgrenɪdʒ 'pɪə] **I**
Hollywood ['hɒliwʊd] **II**
Hyde Park [ˌhaɪd 'pɑ:k] **II**
Isle of Man [ˌaɪl‿əv 'mæn] **III U1**, 15
Kidbrooke Gardens [ˌkɪdbrʊk 'gɑ:dnz] **I**
King William Walk [ˌkɪŋ 'wɪljəm ˌwɔ:k] **I**
Leicester Square [ˌlestə 'skweə] **II**
Liverpool ['lɪvəpu:l] **III TS2**, 80
London ['lʌndən] **I**
Moondarra ['mu:ndrə] *Ort in Australien* **III TS2**, 79
Nelson Road [ˌnelsn 'rəʊd] **I**
New York [ˌnju: 'jɔ:k] **III U2**, 29
Nottingham ['nɒtɪŋəm] **III AC1**, 25
Oxford Street ['ɒksfəd ˌstri:t] **II**
Paddington ['pædɪŋtən] **III U1**, 11
South Street ['saʊθ ˌstri:t] **I**
Southend [saʊθ'end] **II**
St Agnes [ˌseɪnt 'ægnəs] **III U1**, 10
St Austell [ˌseɪnt 'ɔstel] **III U1**, 14
Stratford-upon-Avon [ˌstrætfədəpɒn'eɪvn] *Geburtsort Shakespeares* **III U4**, 91
Tatley ['tætli] **III U4**, 89
Tintagel [tɪn'tædʒl] **III AC1**, 25
Tower Hill [ˌtaʊə 'hɪl] **II**
Ty'n y Berth [ti:n‿ə 'bɜ:θ] **II**
Victoria Park [ˌvɪktɔ:riə 'pɑ:k] **I**
Village Way ['vɪlɪdʒ ˌweɪ] **I**
Wimbledon ['wɪmbldən] **I**

Geographical names

Africa ['æfrɪkə] Afrika **III U4**, 90
America [ə'merɪkə] **II**
Atlantic Ocean [ətˌlæntɪk 'əʊʃn] Atlantischer Ozean **III U1**, 14
Australia [ɒs'treɪliə] Australien **II**
Austria ['ɔ:striə] Österreich **II**
Ben Nevis [ˌben 'nevɪs] *Berg in Schottland* **III U3**, 55
Britain ['brɪtn] Großbritannien **I**
British Empire [ˌbrɪtɪʃ‿'empaɪə] britisches Königreich **II**
British Isles [ˌbrɪtɪʃ‿'aɪlz] Britische Inseln **III U1**, 9
Canada ['kænədə] Kanada **I**
China ['tʃaɪnə] China **I**
Cornwall ['kɔ:nwɔ:l] **III U1**, 8
England ['ɪŋglənd] England **I**
European Union (EU) [ˌjʊərəpiən 'ju:njən (i:ju:)] Europäische Union **II**
France [frɑ:ns] Frankreich **II**
Germany ['dʒɜ:məni] Deutschland **I**
Great Britain (GB) [ˌgreɪt 'brɪtn] Großbritannien **III U1**, 8
India ['ɪndiə] Indien **II**
Isle of Dogs [ˌaɪl‿əv 'dɒgz] **I**
Italy ['ɪtəli] Italien **II**
Kent [kent] *Grafschaft im Südosten Englands* **II**
Loch Lomond [ˌlɒx 'ləʊmənd] *See in Schottland* 〈**III U3**, 62〉
Loch Ness [ˌlɒx 'nes; ˌlɒk 'nes] *See in Schottland* **III U3**, 55
the Lowlands [ðə 'ləʊləndz] *schottische Landschaft* 〈**III U3**, 62〉
Normandy ['nɔ:məndi] die Normandie **II**
North Sea [ˌnɔ:θ 'si:] Nordsee **III U1**, 9
Northern Ireland [ˌnɔ:ðn‿'aɪələnd] Nordirland **III U1**, 8
Pakistan [ˌpɑ:kɪ'stɑ:n] **I**
Poland ['pəʊlənd] Polen **I**
Republic of Ireland [rɪˌpʌblɪk‿əv‿'aɪələnd] Republik Irland **III U1**, 8
Scandinavia [ˌskændɪ'neɪviə] Skandinavien **III U3**, 60
Scotland ['skɒtlənd] Schottland **III U1**, 13
Sherwood Forest [ˌʃɜ:wʊd 'fɒrɪst] **III AC1**, 25
the Shetland Islands [ðə 'ʃetlənd ˌaɪləndz] die Shetlandinseln **III U3**, 64
Snowdonia National Park [snəʊˌdəʊniə ˌnæʃnl 'pɑ:k] **II**
South Africa [ˌsaʊθ‿'æfrɪkə] Südafrika **II**
Spain [speɪn] Spanien **II**
Thames [temz] **I**
United Kingdom (UK) [ju:'keɪ] Vereinigtes Königreich von Großbritannien und Nordirland **I**
USA (United States of America) [ˌju:es'eɪ (ju:ˌnaɪtɪd ˌsteɪts‿əv‿ə'merɪkə)] USA (Vereinigte Staaten von Amerika) **II**
Wales [weɪlz] **II**

Other names

Arches Leisure Centre [ˌɑ:tʃɪz 'leʒə ˌsentə] **I**
Auld Lang Syne [ˌɔ:ld læŋ 'saɪn] *schottisches Volkslied* **III U3**, 60
Balmoral Castle [bælˌmɒrəl 'kɑ:sl] *schottische Residenz der britischen Königsfamilie* 〈**III U3**, 62〉
Ben Briggs [ˌben 'brɪgz] **I**
Best Young Tech Entrepreneur [ˌbest jʌŋ ˌtek ɒntrəprə'nɜ:] **III U2**, 29
Big Ben [ˌbɪg 'ben] **II**
British Museum [ˌbrɪtɪʃ mju:'zi:əm] **II**
Buckingham Palace [ˌbʌkɪŋəm 'pælɪs] **II**
Business Week ['bɪznɪs wi:k] *Wirtschaftszeitung* **III U2**, 29
Changing of the Guards [ˌtʃeɪndʒɪŋ əv ðə 'gɑ:dz] *Wachwechsel vor dem Buckingham Palace* **II**
Church of England [ˌθʃ?:tʃ‿əv 'ɪŋglənd] **III U4**, 86
Comic Relief [ˌkɒmɪk rɪ'li:f] *wohltätige Organisation* **II**
2Cool Performing Academy [ˌtu:ku:l pəˌfɔ:mɪŋ ə'kædəmi] **I**
Croeso i Gymru [ˌkrɔɪsəʊ‿i: 'gʌmri] **II**
Crossharbour ['krɒsˌhɑ:bə] **II**
Cutty Sark [ˌkʌti 'sɑ:k] **I**
Diwali [dɪ'wɑ:li] **I**
Docklands Light Railway *(DLR)* [ˌdɒklændz ˌlaɪt 'reɪlweɪ] *Regionalbahn im Osten Londons* **I**
Dunnottar Castle **III U3**, 54
Edinburgh Fringe Festival [ˌedɪnbrə 'frɪndʒ ˌfestɪvl] **III U3**, 55
Eid [i:d] **I**
Elephant & Castle ['elɪfənt ənd kɑ:sl] **II**
Fan Museum [ˌfæn mju:'zi:əm] **I**
For he's a jolly good fellow [fə ˌhi:z‿ə ˌdʒɒli gʊd 'feləʊ] *Volkslied* **I**
the Globe Theatre [ðə ˌgləʊb 'θɪətə] **III U4**, 91
God Save the Queen ['gɒd seɪv ðə ˌkwi:n] Gott schütze die Königin *(britische Nationalhymne)* **III U3**, 58
Greenwich Foot Tunnel [ˌgrenɪdʒ 'fʊt ˌtʌnl] **I**
Guy Fawkes Night ['gaɪ fɔ:ks ˌnaɪt] **I**
Halloween [ˌhæləʊ'i:n] *Tag vor Allerheiligen* **I**
Hanukkah ['hɑ:nəkə] **I**
the Highland Games ['haɪlənd geɪmz] 〈**III U3**, 63〉

Hogmanay ['hɒgməneɪ] *traditionelles schottisches Neujahrsfest* **III U3**, 60
Honey ['hʌni] **I**
the **Houses of Parliament** [ðə ˌhaʊzɪz‿əv 'pɑːləmənt] *britisches Parlamentsgebäude* **II**
HTML [ˌeɪdʒtiːem'el] **III U2**, 29
Industrial Revolution [ɪnˌdʌstriəl revl'uːʃn] die industrielle Revolution **III U4**, 87
London Eye [ˌlʌndən‿'aɪ] **II**
London Wall [ˌlʌndən 'wɔːl] **II**
London Zoo [ˌlʌndən 'zuː] **II**
Madame Tussauds [ˌmædəm tʊ'sɔːdz] **II**
Manchester City [ˌmæntʃɪstə 'sɪti] *englischer Fußballclub* **II**
Meridian Line [məˌrɪdiən 'laɪn] Nullmeridian **I**
Mickey Mouse [ˌmɪki 'maʊs] **I**
Millennium Footbridge [mɪˌleniəm 'fʊtbrɪdʒ] **II**
Mother's Day ['mʌðəz ˌdeɪ] **I**
Mousebook ['maʊsbʊk] **II**
Mr Fluff [ˌmɪstə 'flʌf] **I**
Mudchute Farm [ˌmʌdʃuːt 'fɑːm] **I**
Natural History Museum [ˌnætʃrl 'hɪstri mjuːˌziːəm] **II**
Navy ['neɪvi] Marine **III U4**, 86
Notting Hill Carnival [ˌnɒtɪŋ hɪl 'kɑːnɪvl] **I**
Oyster card ['ɔɪstə ˌkɑːd] **II**
Pancake Day ['pænkeɪk ˌdeɪ] **I**
Pets Corner [ˌpets 'kɔːnə] **I**
Red Nose Day [ˌred nəʊz 'deɪ] **II**
Regina [rɪ'dʒaɪnə] **III U4**, 95
Rocky ['rɒki] **II**
Roman Empire [ˌrəʊmən 'empaɪə] Römisches Reich **III U4**, 84
Royal Observatory [ˌrɔɪəl‿əb'zɜːvətri] **I**
Rugby Football Club (RFC) [ˌrʌgbi ˌfʊtbɔːl 'klʌb (ɑːr‿ef 'siː)] **II**
Sherlock ['ʃɜːlɒk] **I**
Shetland Crofthouse Museum **III U3**, 64
Shrove Tuesday [ˌʃrəʊv 'tjuːzdeɪ] Fastnachtsdienstag **I**
Sid [sɪd] **I**
Spanish Armada [ˌspænɪʃ ɑː'mɑːdə] *Spanische Flotte* **III U4**, 86
star4ever [ˌstɑːfə'revə] **I**
Tandoori [tæn'dʊəri] **I**
Thomas Tallis School *(= TTS)* [ˌtɒməs 'tælɪs ˌskuːl] **I**
Titan Clydebank **III U3**, 61
the **Tower of London** [ðə ˌtaʊər‿əv 'lʌndən] **II**
Transport Museum [ˌtrænspɔːt mjuː'ziːəm] **II**
TTS planner [ˌtiːtiːˌes 'plænə] Handbuch für TTS-Schülerinnen und -Schüler **I**
Tumblr ['tʌmblə] **III U2**, 29
Valentine's Day ['væləntaɪnz ˌdeɪ] **I**
Victoria [vɪk'tɔːriə] **II**
Whitehall ['waɪthɔːl] *Straße in London* **II**
World War II [ˌwɜːld ˌwɔː 'tuː] Zweiter Weltkrieg **II**
Yahoo [jə'huː] **III U2**, 29

Famous names

Agatha Christie [ˌægəθə 'krɪsti] **III AC1**, 25
Alexander Fleming [ˌælɪgzɑːndə 'flemɪŋ] **III U3**, 60
Alexander Graham Bell [ˌælɪgzɑːndə ˌgreɪəm 'bel] **III U3**, 69
Andy Murray [ˌændi 'mʌri] *schottischer Tennisspieler* **III U3**, 61
Anne Boleyn [ˌæn 'bʊlɪn] *Mutter von Elizabeth I.* **III U4**, 95
Anne Hathaway [ˌæn 'hæðəweɪ] *Shakespeares Frau* **III U4**, 91
Bruno Mars **III TS1**, 49
Charles Macintosh **III U3**, 60
Christopher Wren [ˌkrɪstəfə 'ren] **II**
Daniel Craig [ˌdænjəl 'kreɪg] **II**
Dr Watson [ˌdɒktə 'wɒtsən] **III AC1**, 25
Elizabeth I [ɪˌlɪzəbəθ ðə 'fɜːst] **II**
Francis Drake [ˌfrɑːnsɪs 'dreɪk] **III U4**, 88
Henry VIII [ˌhenri ði 'eɪtθ] Heinrich VIII. **III U4**, 86
Henry Wadsworth Longfellow **III TS1**, 48
James Bond [ˌdʒeɪmz 'bɒnd] **II**
James Carter [ˌdʒeɪmz 'kɑːtə] **III TS1**, 47
James Watt [ˌdʒeɪmz 'wɒt] **III U3**, 60
John Henry Holmes [ˌdʒɒn ˌhenri 'həʊmz] **III U3**, 69
John Logie Baird **III U3**, 60
King Arthur [ˌkɪŋ‿'ɑːθə] König Artus **III AC1**, 25
King Edward [kɪŋ 'edwəd] **III U3**, 58
Langston Hughes [ˌlæŋstən 'hjuːs] **III TS1**, 51
Lenny Harry [ˌleni 'hæri] *britischer Comedian* **II**
Louis Armstrong [ˌluːi 'ɑːmstrɒŋ] **II**
Maid Marian [ˌmeɪd 'mæriən] **III AC1**, 25
Malorie Blackman **III TS3**, 109
Margaret Peterson Haddix [ˌmɑːgrət ˌpiːtəsən 'hædɪks] **III TS3**, 107
Miss Marple [mɪs 'mɑːpl] **III AC1**, 25
Prince Albert [ˌprɪns 'ælbət] **II**
Queen Victoria [ˌkwiːn vɪk'tɔːriə] **II**
Robert Dudley [ˌrɒbət 'dʌdli] **III U4**, 88
Robert Hooke [ˌrɒbət 'hʊk] **III U3**, 69
Robert the Bruce [ˌrɒbət ðə 'bruːs] **III U3**, 58
Robin Hood [ˌrɒbɪn 'hʊd] **III AC1**, 25
Sherlock Holmes [ˌʃɜːlɒk 'həʊmz] **III AC1**, 24
Walter Raleigh [ˌwɔːltə 'rɔːli] **III U4**, 88
William Shakespeare [ˌwɪljəm 'ʃeɪkspɪə] *englischer Dramatiker (1564–1616)* **III U4**, 86
William the Conqueror [ˌwɪljəm ðə 'kɒŋkrə] **II**

A

abbiegen to turn I
abblocken to block II
abbrechen to drop out (of) III U2, 28
abbrennen *to burn down III U4, 91
abchecken to check out *(coll)* III AC3, 82
Abend evening I
  heute **Abend** 2nite *(= tonight)* I
Abendessen dinner I
abends in the evenings I
abends *(Uhrzeit)* p.m. I
Abenteuer adventure II
aber but I
abfahren *to leave II; to depart III U1, 12
abfahrend outward III U1, 12
abgeschlossen locked II
abhaken to tick II
abhängen von to depend (on) III U1, 11
abholen to pick up III U4, 92
abnehmen *to take off I
abreißen to pull down III U3, 59
abschalten to turn off II
abschicken *to send off III U1, 13
abschneiden *to cut (off) II
Abschnitt section II
abschreiben to copy I
absolut absolutely II
Abstand gap I
abstimmen *to take a vote; to vote I
abstürzen to crash II
sich alles **abverlangen** to push oneself III U2, 32
außer **Acht** lassen to ignore III U2, 37
acht eight I
Acker field II
Action action I
Adjektiv adjective II
Adresse address I
Adverb adverb II
AG club I
aggressiv aggressive II
äh er I
ähnlich similar II
keine **Ahnung** no idea II
Akku battery II
Aktion action I
Aktivität activity I
Akzent accent III U1, 15
albern silly I
alle all of them; everyone I; everybody II
alle/-s all I
  wir **alle** all of us III U1, 10
allein alone I; on my own II
alles everything I
alltäglich everyday III U4, 89
Alphabet alphabet I
alphabetisch alphabetical II
als as II
als *(bei Vergleichen)* than II
als when I
also so I
alt old I
  Wie **alt** bist du? How old are you? I
  Wie **alt** sind Sie? How old are you? I
Alter age III U2, 29
älter elderly III U3, 69
Alternativ- fringe III U3, 55
am on I
  am besten best I
  am Fluss by the river II
  am Wochenende at the weekend I
aus **Amerika** American II
Amerikaner/-in American II
amerikanisch American II
Amtssprache official language II
sich **amüsieren** *to have fun I; to enjoy oneself III U2, 32
an on; at I; by III U1, 18
  an Bord aboard I
  an sein *to be on II
Ananas pineapple III U4, 99
anbauen *to grow III U4, 85
anbieten to offer II
Anblick sight II
Andenken souvenir II
die **anderen** the others I
andere/-r/-s other I; else III U2, 35
  ein/-e **andere**/-r/-s another I
Einerseits …, (aber) **andererseits** … On the one hand …, (but) on the other hand … II
seine Meinung **ändern** to change one's mind III U4, 88
  (sich) **ändern** to change II
anders different; other I
Änderung change III U1, 19
Andeutung hint III AC3, 83
Anfang beginning II; start III U4, 99
anfangen to start I; *to get started; *to begin II
anfeuern to cheer II
anführen *to lead III U3, 61
angeben to show off II
Angeber/-in show-off III U2, 39
  Und ein **Angeber**! With a very big head! II
Angeln fishing III U1, 14
die **Angesagten** in-crowd III U2, 36
von **Angesicht** zu **Angesicht** face-to-face II
angespült werden to wash up II
angreifen to attack III U4, 90
Angst fear II
  Angst haben (vor) *to be scared (of) I
  Ich habe (keine) **Angst** vor … I'm (not) scared of … I
ängstlich fearful III TS2, 77
anhaben *to wear I
anhalten to stop I
Anhänger/-in fan II
anhören to listen (to) I
anklicken to click on III U1, 12
ankommen to arrive III U1, 12
ankommend inward III U1, 12
Ankündigung announcement III U1, 15
anmalen to paint I
Anmerkung note I
annähernd nearly II
anonym anonymous II
Anordnung layout III U2, 35
anpflanzen to plant II
anprobieren to try on II
Anregung suggestion I
Anruf phone call I
  einen **Anruf** entgegennehmen to answer the phone I
Anrufbeantworter answering machine I
anrufen to call I
Anrufer/-in caller I
anschauen to look at I; *to have a look (at) II
  jmdn. schief/komisch **anschauen** *to give sb funny looks III U2, 32
sich **anschließen** to join II
ansehen to look at I
(sich) **ansehen** to watch I
Ansicht point of view II
anstarren to stare I
antippen to tap II
Antwort answer; reply I
antworten to answer; to reply I
Anweisung instruction I
Anwesenheitskontrolle registration II
Anzeige advert III TS1, 46
anziehen *to put on III U2, 36
Apfel apple I
App app II
Apparat machine I
April April I
Arbeit job; work I
Arbeit für die Schule studies *(pl)* II
arbeiten to work I
Architekt/-in architect II
Areal area II
Ärger trouble II
  Ärger machen *to make trouble I
jmdn. **ärgern** to tease sb III U2, 38
Argument dafür pro II
  Argument dagegen con II
Arm arm II
arm poor III U2, 37
die **Armen** the poor III AC1, 25
Art und Weise way I
Artikel article II
Arzt/**Ärztin** doctor II
Arztpraxis surgery I
Assistent/-in assistant II
Atem breath III TS3, 109
  Atem holen *to take a breath III TS3, 109
Atemzug breath III TS3, 109
Atlantischer Ozean Atlantic Ocean III U1, 14

Atlas atlas **I**
atmen to breathe **II**
Atmosphäre flair; atmosphere **II**
Attraktion attraction **II**
Aua! Ouch! **II**
auch too **I**; also **II**
Du **auch**? You too? **I**
Audio- audio **I**
Audioführung audio tour **II**
audiovisueller Effekt audio-visual effect **II**
auf on; at; to **I**
auf dem Foto/den Fotos in the photo(s) **I**
auf der anderen Seite von across; opposite **I**
auf der Straße in the street **I**
auf einmal suddenly **I**
auf Wiedersehen goodbye **I**
auf ... zu towards **II**
wieder **aufbauen** *to rebuild **III U4**, 91
aufbewahren *to keep **I**
Aufführung show **II**
Aufgabe task; exercise; job **I**
aufgeben *to give up **III U2**, 30
aufgebracht upset **II**
aufgeregt excited **I**; nervous **II**
aufgeschlagen open **I**
aufhängen *to put up; *to hang up **II**
aufheben to pick up **III U4**, 92
jmdn. **aufheitern** to cheer sb up **III U2**, 39
aufhellen to lighten **III U4**, 98
aufhören to finish **I**
aufhören (mit) to stop **I**
Hör/**Hört auf**! Stop it!
aufladen to top up **II**
aufmachen to open **I**
aufmerksam machen (auf) to campaign (for) **III U3**, 57
Aufmerksamkeit attention **II**
Aufnahme recording **I**; shot **III U4**, 96
Aufnahmeort set **III U4**, 96
Aufnahmestudio recording studio **I**
aufnehmen to record **II**
aufpassen to look out **II**
aufpassen auf to look after **I**
Pass/**Passt auf**! Be careful! **I**
aufräumen to tidy *(a room)* **I**
aufrechterhalten *to keep going **II**
aufregend exciting **I**
Aufregung excitement *(no pl)* **III U2**, 38
aufsagen *to say **I**
aufsaugen to soak up **III TS2**, 77
aufschreiben *to write down **I**; to note down **II**
aufstehen *(aus dem Bett)* *to get up **I**
Es ist Zeit **aufzustehen**! Time to get up! **I**
aufstehen *(von einer Sitzgelegenheit)* *to stand up **I**
aufstellen *to put up **II**
Auftrag task **I**
Auftritt gig **III U3**, 58
aufwachen *to wake up **III U4**, 99
aufwachsen *to grow up **III U4**, 89
aufwärmen to warm up **I**
sich **aufwärmen** to warm up **I**
Aufwärmübung warm-up **I**
aufwecken *to wake up **III U4**, 99
aufzeichnen to record **II**
Aufzeichnung recording **I**
jmdn. **aufziehen** to tease sb **III U2**, 38
Auge eye **II**
die **Augen** verdrehen to roll one's eyes **III U4**, 96
Er traute seinen **Augen** nicht. He couldn't believe his eyes. **II**
Augenblick moment **II**
Augenzeuge/**Augenzeugin** eyewitness **II**
August August **I**
aus from **I**
aus Cornwall Cornish **III U1**, 10
aus aller Welt from around the world **III U1**, 14
ausarbeiten to work out **II**
ausblasen *to blow out **I**
Ausblick view **II**
Auschecken Check-out **I**
auschecken to check out *(coll)* **III AC3**, 82
(sich) **ausdenken** *to think of **II**
Ausdruck phrase **I**; expression **II**
nützliche **Ausdrücke** Useful phrases **I**
ausdrücken to express **II**
Auseinandersetzung argument **III U2**, 36
auserwählt sein, etw. zu tun *to be called to do sth **III TS1**, 49
ausflippen *to go crazy **II**
Ausflug trip **II**
den Hund **ausführen** to walk the dog **I**
ausfüllen to fill in **II**
ausgeben *(Geld)* *to spend **I**
ausgedehnt wide **III U1**, 9
ausgehen *to go out **III U1**, 18
sich **ausgeschlossen** fühlen *to feel left out **II**
aushelfen to help out **III U3**, 69
Auslauf run area **III TS2**, 77
(sich) **ausleihen** to borrow **II**
auspacken to unwrap **I**
auspusten *to blow out **I**
ausräumen to clear out **I**
jmdm. etw. **ausrichten** *to take a message **I**
sich **ausruhen** to relax **II**
Ausrüstung equipment **II**
Aussage statement **II**
ausschalten to turn off **II**
aussehen to look **I**
wie der Mann **aussah** what the man looked like **II**
Aussehen looks *(pl)* **III U2**, 28
außer Acht lassen to ignore **III U2**, 37
im **äußersten** Westen in the far west **III U1**, 14
außerhalb outside; out **I**
Außerirdische/-r alien **I**
Äußerung expression **II**
Aussicht view **II**
Aussprache pronunciation **I**
Ausstattung equipment **II**
aussteigen *to get out of **II**
aussteigen (aus einem Bus/Zug) *to get off (a bus/train) **II**
Ausstellung display **II**
Ausstellung in der Klasse class display **I**
Aussterben extinction *(no pl)* **III TS2**, 80
aussterben *to become extinct **III TS2**, 80
aussuchen to pick **II**
Austausch exchange **III AC2**, 52
Austausch- exchange **III AC2**, 52
austauschen to exchange; to trade **II**
Austauschschüler/-in exchange student **III AC2**, 52
Australier/-in Australian **III TS2**, 79
australisch Australian **III TS2**, 79
Auswahl choice **II**
auswählen *to choose; to pick **II**
auswendig lernen *to learn ... by heart **I**
auswickeln to unwrap **I**
Auszeichnung award **II**
ausziehen *to take off **I**
Auto car **I**
Automat machine **I**
Autor/-in writer **III U4**, 88
Axt axe **III U4**, 86

B

Baby baby **I**
Background- backing **III U2**, 28
Backgroundtänzer/-in backing dancer **III U2**, 28
Bad bath **I**
Badehaus baths *(pl)* **III U4**, 84
Badewanne bath **I**
Badezimmer bathroom **I**
Badminton badminton **I**
Bahnhof station **I**
Bahnsteig platform **III U1**, 12
bald soon **II**
Ball ball **I**
Banane banana **I**
Band band **III U3**, 56
Bank bench **III U2**, 39
bannen to ban **III U3**, 60
Bär bear **II**
Basketball basketball **I**
Batterie battery **II**
Bauch stomach **II**
Bauchschmerzen stomachache **II**
Bauchweh stomachache **II**
bauen *to build **II**

Bauernhof farm **I**
Baum tree **I**
Baustein building block **II**
jmdn./etw. **beachten** *to pay attention to sb/sth **III U2**, 37
Beachtung attention **II**
beängstigend scary **II**
beantworten to answer **I**
Becher mug **III AC2**, 52
bedauern *to feel sorry for **III U2**, 39
bedeckt cloudy **II**
bedeuten *to mean **II**
Bedeutung meaning **II**
bedürftig in need **II**
sich **beeilen** to hurry **I**
beeindruckt impressed **II**
beeinflussen to influence **II**
beenden to finish **I**; to end **II**
sich **befassen** mit *to deal (with) **II**
Befehl order **III TS3**, 107
befestigen to fix **II**
befolgen to follow **II**
befragen to interview **I**
Befragung interview **I**
Befürchtung fear **II**
begeistert excited **I**
Beginn beginning **II**
beginnen to start **I**; *to begin **II**
behalten *to keep **I**
Behauptung statement **II**
behindert with special needs **II**
bei with; at **I**; by **III U1**, 18
beibringen *to teach **II**
beide both **II**
beide the two of them **II**
Bein leg **II**
die **Beine** und Hände ruhig halten *to keep one's feet or hands still **III TS1**, 50
beinahe almost **II**
beinhalten to include **III U1**, 8
Beispiel example **I**
zum **Beispiel** for example **II**
beißen *to bite **II**
beitreten to join **II**
bekommen *to get **I**; to receive **II**
etw. aus dem Kopf **bekommen** *to get sth out of one's head **III TS1**, 50
belebt busy **I**
beliebt popular **I**
die **Beliebten** in-crowd **III U2**, 36
bellen to bark **I**
Belohnung treat **III TS2**, 78
bemerken to notice **II**
sich **benehmen** to behave **III U2**, 32
benötigen to need (to) **I**
benutzen to use **I**
beobachten to watch **I**
bequem comfortable **II**
bereit ready **II**
bereits already **I**
Berg mountain **II**; hill **III U1**, 18
Bergbau mining **III U1**, 14
bergen to save **I**
Bericht report **II**
Bericht *(in einer Zeitschrift, Zeitung)* article **II**
Beruf career **III U2**, 28
sich **beruhigen** to relax; to calm down **II**
berühmt famous **I**
berühmte Person celebrity **III TS2**, 79
beschäftigt busy **I**
beschreiben to describe **I**
Beschreibung description **II**
besichtigen to visit **I**
Besichtigungs- sightseeing **II**
besiegen *to beat **II**; to defeat **III U3**, 58
besitzen *to have got **I**
besonders special **I**
besorgen *to get **I**
besorgt worried **III AC3**, 82
besorgt sein *to be worried **II**
Besorgungen machen *to do the shopping **III U3**, 69
besser better **I**
Bestätigungsfrage question tag **II**
(der/die/das) **Beste** (the) best **II**
bestehen aus *to be made of **III TS1**, 49
besteigen to climb **I**
beste/-r/-s best **I**
am **besten** best **I**
der/die/das **beste** … überhaupt the best … ever **III TS3**, 106
bestimmt definitely **III U3**, 67
bestürzt upset **II**
Besuch visit **I**
besuchen to visit **I**
Besucher/-in visitor **I**
beten to pray **III TS3**, 109
betreten to enter **II**
Betreuer/-in instructor **II**
Bett bed **I**
ins **Bett** gehen *to go to bed **I**
beunruhigt worried **III AC3**, 82
beunruhigt sein *to be worried **II**
beurteilen to judge **III U2**, 26
bevor before **I**
(sich) **bewegen** to move **I**
Bewegung move **I**
bewerten to judge **III U2**, 26
bewölkt cloudy **II**
bezahlen *to pay (for) **I**
Beziehung relationship **II**
Bibliothek library **III TS2**, 76
Biene bee **II**
Bild picture **I**
bilden *to make **I**; to form **II**
Bildergeschichte graphic novel **III TS3**, 106
Bildgeschichte photo story **I**
Bildung education *(no pl)* **III U4**, 89
billig cheap **I**
binden (an) to tie (to) **III U3**, 67
Bindewort linking word **I**
biografisch biographical **III U4**, 91
Bis … CU *(= See you)*; See you! **I**
Bis dann! CU *(= See you)*; See you! **I**
bis jetzt so far **II**
von … **bis** from … to **I**
bis till **I**; until **II**
Biskuit- sponge **I**
ein **bisschen** a bit **II**
Bitte. Please. **I**
Bitte schön. Here you are.; You're welcome. **I**
bitten to ask **I**
bitten um to ask for **I**
blau blue **I**
Blechdose tin can **III U3**, 69
bleiben to stay **I**
draußen **bleiben** *to keep out (of) **III U3**, 66
Bleib wie du bist. Stay the way you are. **III U2**, 33
Bleistift pencil **I**
Blick look **I**; view **II**
hier: **Blick** sight **III TS1**, 48
einen **Blick** werfen auf *to take a look at **II**
Blickpunkt focus **III TS3**, 110
Blickwinkel perspective **II**
Blitz lightning *(no pl)* **II**; flash **III U4**, 97
blockieren to block **II**
blöd stupid **II**
Blog blog **III TS2**, 79
blond blond **III U2**, 36
bloß bare **III TS1**, 47
bloß only **I**
Blume flower **II**
Blut blood **III U4**, 92
BMX BMX **II**
weiße **Bohnen** in Tomatensoße baked beans *(pl)* **I**
Bonbons sweets *(pl)* **I**
Boot boat **I**
an **Bord** aboard **I**
böse angry; bad **I**
Bösewicht villain **III AC1**, 24
Boss boss **III U2**, 36
Botschaft message **I**
Bowling spielen to play bowls **III U4**, 88
Bowlingbahn bowling alley **I**
Box box **I**
Boxen boxing **II**
Boxrunde round of boxing **II**
Branche industry **III U3**, 59
Bratwurst sausage **III AC2**, 52
brauchen to need (to) **I**
nicht **brauchen** needn't **I**
(Zeit) **brauchen** *to take **II**
braun brown **I**
brechen *to break **I**
brechend cracking **III U3**, 66
breit wide **III U1**, 9

brennen *to burn **III U4**, 91; *to be on fire **III TS3**, 109
Brett board **III TS1**, 46
schwarzes **Brett** noticeboard **II**
Brief letter **II**
Briefträger postman **II**
Brille glasses *(pl)* **II**
bringen *to bring; *to get; *to take **I**
in Schwierigkeiten **bringen** *to make trouble **I**
jmdn. dazu **bringen**, etw. zu tun *to make somebody do something **II**
Brite/Britin British **I**
britisch British **I**
Bronzezeit *(ca. 2200–800 v. Chr.)* Bronze Age **III U1**, 14
Broschüre brochure **I**
Brot bread **I**
belegtes **Brot** sandwich **I**
Brötchen bread roll **III AC2**, 52
Brücke bridge **II**
Bruder brother **I**
brüllen to roar **III TS3**, 109
brutal violent **III TS2**, 80
Buch book **I**
buchen to book **III U1**, 12
Bücherei library **III TS2**, 76
Büchse can **I**
Buchstabe letter **I**
buchstabieren *to spell **I**
Bühne stage **III U4**, 88
bunt colourful **I**
Buntstift pencil **I**
Burg castle **II**
Büro office **I**
Bus bus **I**
Busbahnhof bus station **I**
Busch *(Buschlandschaft)* bush **III TS2**, 79
Business business **III U2**, 29
Butter butter **III AC2**, 52

C

Cache cache **III U1**, 18
Café café; snack bar **I**
Cafeteria cafeteria **I**
campen to camp **III U1**, 20
Camping camping **II**
Cartoon cartoon **III AC3**, 82
Cent *(Währung)* cent **I**
Center centre **I**
Champion champion **III TS1**, 50
Chance chance **II**
Chaos chaos **III U4**, 96
Charakter character **I**
Chat chat **III U3**, 58
Chatroom chat room **II**
chatten *(sich online unterhalten)* to chat **I**
Checkliste checklist **II**
Chef boss **III U2**, 36
chillen to chill out **III U2**, 36
China China **I**
Chipkarte smartcard **II**
nach **Christus** AD (= Anno Domini) **III U4**, 84
vor **Christus** BC (= before Christ) **III U4**, 84
circa about **I**
Clown clown **II**
Cola coke **I**
Comedian comedian **II**
Comedy Show comedy show **II**
Comic comic **II**; graphic novel **III TS3**, 106
Comicheft comic **II**
Computer computer **I**
Computerunterricht Technology **II**
cool cool **I**
aus **Cornwall** Cornish **III U1**, 10
Couch sofa **I**
Cousin/Cousine cousin **I**
Cover cover **III U2**, 26
Creme cream **I**
Cricket cricket **II**
Curry *(Gewürz oder Gericht)* curry **I**

D

da because **I**
da there **I**
da ist/sind there is/are **I**
dabei sein *to be in **II**
Dach roof **III U1**, 18
Dachboden loft **I**; attic **II**
Ich habe nichts **dagegen** (zu) ... I don't mind ... *(+ -ing)* **III U2**, 34
dahin there **I**
damals back than **III U4**, 84
Dame lady **III U4**, 96
Sehr geehrte **Dame**, sehr geehrter Herr Dear Sir or Madam **III U1**, 13
Dampf steam **III U3**, 60
Dampfmaschine steam engine **III U3**, 60
danach then; after that **I**
dankbar thankful **I**
Dankbarkeit gratitude **III AC2**, 53
Danke! Cheers! **III AC3**, 82
Danke. Thank you.; Thanks. **I**
danken to thank **II**
Nichts zu **danken**. You're welcome. **I**
dann then **I**
darauf zu towards **II**
das the **I**
das that **I**
Das (hier) ist ... This is ... **I**
Das macht ... That's ... **I**
Das war knapp! That was close! **I**
das *(Relativpronomen)* which **II**
dass that **I**
Datum date **I**
dauern *to take **II**
Daumen thumb **II**
die **Daumen** drücken *to keep your fingers crossed **I**
davonkommen mit *to get away with **II**
Deck deck **I**
definitiv definitely **III U3**, 67
dein/-e your **I**
dein/-er/-e/-es yours **II**
Dekoration decorations *(pl)* **I**
dekorieren to decorate **I**
Delfin dolphin **III TS1**, 47
dem *(Relativpronomen)* who; which **II**
demonstrieren (für) to campaign (for) **III U3**, 57
den *(Relativpronomen)* who; which **II**
denken *to think **I**
Denke/Denkt an ... Think of ... **I**
denken an to remember **I**
denken über *to think of **I**
Denkmal monument **III U1**, 14
dennoch still **II**
der the **I**
der; **dem**; **den**; **die**; **das** *(Relativpronomen)* that **II**
der *(Relativpronomen)* who; which **II**
deren *(Relativpronomen)* whose **II**
der-/die-/dasselbe the same **I**
Desaster disaster **II**
deshalb that's why **II**
Design design **II**
Designer/-in designer **III U2**, 30
dessen *(Relativpronomen)* whose **II**
Detail detail **II**
nach **Details** durchsuchen to scan **II**
Detektiv/-in detective **III U4**, 94
Detektivgeschichte detective **III TS3**, 106
deutlich clear **I**
Deutsch German **I**
deutsch German **I**
Deutsche/-r German **I**
aus **Deutschland** German **I**
Dezember December **I**
Diagramm diagram **I**
Dialekt dialect **III U1**, 15
Dialog dialogue **I**
dick *(nicht für Personen)* thick **III U3**, 66
die *(auch Pl.)* the **I**
die *(Relativpronomen)* who; which **II**
Diele hall **III U1**, 18
Dienstag Tuesday **I**
dies this **I**
diese (hier) these **I**
diese dort those **I**
diese/-r/-s this **I**
Ding thing **I**
Dinosaurier dinosaur **II**
direkt direct **III TS1**, 48
Discjockey DJ **III U2**, 37
Diskussion discussion **II**
diskutieren to discuss **I**
Distanz distance **II**
Distel thistle **III U3**, 55

DJ DJ III U2, 37
doch after all I
Dollar (Währung) dollar III U2, 29
ein Gespräch dominieren to hog a conversation III AC3, 82
Donner thunder (no pl) II
donnernd roaring III TS3, 109
Donnerstag Thursday I
doof silly I
Dorf village I
dort there I
dorthin there I
Dose can I
aus der Dose tinned I
Dosen- tinned I
Drama drama II
dramatisch dramatic II
dran kommen to reach II
Du bist dran. Your turn.; It's your turn. I
draußen outside I
draußen bleiben *to keep out (of) III U3, 66
draußen halten *to keep out (of) III U3, 66
nach draußen out I
Dreck dirt III U4, 92
dreckig dirty II
Drehbuch script III AC3, 83
drehen to turn III TS3, 107
sich im Kreis drehen *to go round in circles III U3, 66
Drehort set III U4, 96
drei three I
eine Dreiergruppe a group of three I
dreizehn thirteen I
drin inside I
dritte/-r/-s third I
dröhnen to boom III U1, 18; to roar III TS3, 109
dröhnend roaring III TS3, 109
Druck- print II
drücken to press II
die Daumen drücken *to keep your fingers crossed I
du you; u (= you) I
Du auch? You too? I
Du bist dran. Your turn.; It's your turn. I
Du bist … You're … I
Du weißt, wie man … You know how to … I
du/dir/dich/Sie/sich (selbst) yourself I
Dudelsack bagpipes (pl) III U3, 55
duften *to smell III U4, 85
dumm silly I; stupid II
Zu dumm! Too bad! I
Dummkopf silly II
dunkel dark II
Dunkelheit the dark II; darkness III U1, 21
durch through I
durchdrehen *to go crazy II
Durcheinander chaos III U4, 96
schmaler Durchgang close III U3, 61
Durchsage announcement III U1, 15
nach Details durchsuchen to scan II
dürfen can I; *to be allowed to (do sth); *to be able to (do sth); may II
nicht dürfen mustn't I
durstig thirsty III TS2, 79
Dusche shower I
DVD DVD I

E

Ebbe low tide II
echt real II
Ecke corner II
Edelstein jewel III U4, 95
(der Garten) Eden Eden III U1, 14
audiovisueller Effekt audio-visual effect II
Es ist egal. It doesn't matter. III U2, 26
Ehefrau wife, wives (pl) II
Ehemann husband II
ehrlich honest III U2, 38
Ei egg I
Eiche oak III TS1, 48
Eichhörnchen squirrel I
eifersüchtig sein (auf) *to be jealous (of) I
eigene/-r/-s own I
Eigenschaftswort adjective II
eilen to hurry I
Eimer bucket II
ein/-e a; an I
ein paar a couple of I
ein wenig a little I
ein/-e andere/-r/-s another I
noch ein/-e another I
einander each other I
Atme(t) tief ein. Take a deep breath. II
einbiegen to turn I
Einchecken Check-in I
eindeutig definitely III U3, 67
eindringen (in) to invade III U4, 88
eine/-r/-s one (sg)/ones (pl) II
Einerseits …, (aber) andererseits … On the one hand …, (but) on the other hand … II
einfach easy I; simple III TS1, 48
einfache Fahrkarte one-way ticket; single ticket III U1, 12
einfach just I
Einfall idea I
sich etwas einfallen lassen *to think of II
einfallsreich imaginative III U2, 27
einfangen to capture III U4, 90
Einführung introduction II
Eingang entrance III U3, 66
eingängig catchy III TS1, 50
eingießen to pour I
Einheit unit I
die Segel einholen to reef the sails I
einige some; a few I; several II
Einkäufe machen *to do the shopping III U3, 69
Einkäufe shopping I
Einkaufen shopping I
einkaufen gehen *to go shopping I
einladen to invite I
Einladung invitation I
Einleitung introduction II
einmal once I
einmarschieren (in) to invade III U4, 88
einpacken to wrap I
einprägsam catchy III TS1, 50
einrichten *to set up I
eins one I
einsam lonely I
einschenken to pour I
einschlafen *to fall asleep I
einschließen to include III U1, 8
einst once I
einsteigen *to get into I
einsteigen (in den Bus) *to get on (the bus) III U1, 12
Einstellung shot II
Eintrag entry III TS2, 76
eintreten to enter II
Eintritt entrance III U3, 66
Eintrittskarte ticket I
nicht einverstanden sein to disagree III U2, 27
einwickeln to wrap I
Einzelheit detail II
Einzelkind only child I
einzeln individual II
einziehen in to move in/into III U1, 18
einzige/-r/-s only II
Eis ice; ice cream I
Eisbahn ice rink I
Eiscreme ice cream I
Elefant elephant III TS2, 80
Elektrik electrics III U1, 19
Elektriker/-in electrician III U1, 19
elektrisch electric III U4, 93
Elektrizität electricity III U1, 18
elektronisch electronic II
elf eleven I
Elfenbein ivory (no pl) III TS2, 80
Eltern parents (pl) I
E-Mail e-mail I
per E-Mail schicken to mail II
Empfang signal III U3, 66
empfangen to receive II
Ende ending; end I
am Ende at the back of II
enden to finish I; to end up; to end II
endgültig final II
endlich at last I; finally II
Energie energy III TS3, 109
eng close I; narrow III U3, 61
sich engagieren (für) to campaign (for) III U3, 57
aus England English I

Engländer/-in English **I**
Ich bin **Engländer**/-in. I'm English. **I**
Englisch English **I**
englisch English **I**
englischsprachig English-speaking **I**
entdecken to discover **II**
Entdeckung discovery **III U3**, 60
auf **Entdeckungsreise** gehen to explore **I**
Entfernung distance **II**
entgegen allen Erwartungen against all odds **III TS3**, 106
eine Nachricht **entgegennehmen** *to take a message **I**
einen Anruf **entgegennehmen** to answer the phone **I**
entgegnen to reply **I**
Entgegnung reply **I**
entlang along **I**
entlanggehen *to go down **I**
entrümpeln to clear out **I**
(sich) **entscheiden** to decide **I**
eine **Entscheidung** treffen *to make a decision **II**
Entschuldigen Sie! Excuse me … **I**
sich **entschuldigen** to apologise **III U2**, 39
Entschuldigung! Sorry!; Excuse me … **I**
entsetzt horrified **I**
sich **entspannen** to relax **II**
entspannt laid-back **III U2**, 28
entsprechen to match **I**
enttäuscht disappointed **I**
entwerfen to design **II**
eine Geschichte langsam **entwickeln** to step into a story slowly **III TS3**, 111
Entwurf plan; draft **I**; design **II**
er he **I**
Erdboden earth **II**
Erde world **I**; earth **II**
die **Erde** earth **II**
Erdkunde geography **III U1**, 14
Ereignis event **I**
erfahren to experience **III U4**, 87
erfahren über *to learn about **III U2**, 27
Erfahrung experience **II**
erfinden to create **I**; to invent **III U3**, 60
Erfinder/-in inventor **III U3**, 69
Erfindung invention **III U3**, 60; fiction *(no pl)* **III TS3**, 106
Erfolg success **III U2**, 28
Erfolg haben (in/bei/mit) to succeed (in) **III U2**, 29
erfolgreich successful **III U2**, 30
erforschen to explore **I**
ergänzen to add **I**
Ergebnis result **II**
ergreifen to grab **II**; to capture **III U4**, 90
erhalten to receive **II**
sich **erheben** *to rise **III TS3**, 109
(jmdn. an etw./jmdn.) **erinnern** to remind (sb of sth/sb) **III TS1**, 49
sich **erinnern** (an) to remember **I**
Erinnerst du dich? Remember? **I**
Erinnert ihr euch? Remember? **I**
Erinnerung memory **II**
Erkältung cold **II**
erkennen to realise **III U3**, 66
erklären to explain **I**
Erklärung statement **II**
erkunden to explore **I**
erleben to experience **III U4**, 87
ernähren *to feed **III U1**, 21
ernst serious **I**
ernsthaft serious **I**
erraten to guess **I**
erreichen *to get to **I**; to reach **II**
errichten *to put up **II**
Ersatz substitute **II**
Ersatz- substitute **II**
erschaffen to create **I**
erst only **I**
erst wenn until **II**
erstaunlich amazing **II**
erste/-r/-s first **I**
als **Erstes** first **I**
ertappt caught on camera **II**
ertränken to drown **III TS3**, 109
ertrinken to drown **III TS3**, 109
erwachsen werden *to grow up **III U4**, 89
Erwachsene/-r adult **II**
erwähnen to mention **II**
entgegen allen **Erwartungen** against all odds **III TS3**, 106
erwidern to reply **I**
Erwiderung reply **I**
erzählen *to tell **I**
erzählen von to talk about … **I**
nochmals **erzählen** *to retell **I**
Erzähle mir von … Tell me about … **I**
Erzählliteratur fiction *(no pl)* **III TS3**, 106
Erzählung story, stories *(pl)* **I**
Erziehung education *(no pl)* **III U4**, 89
es it **I**
Es ist super zum/für … It's great for … **I**
Essen food **I**; meal **II**
(ein Bonbon) **essen** *to have *(a sweet)* **I**
essen *to eat **I**
etwa about **I**
etwas some; something; a little **I**
euer/**eure** your **I**
eure/-r/-s yours **II**
Euro *(Währung)* euro **I**
Europäische Union European Union (EU) **II**
ewig forever **II**
Examen exam **II**
Experte/**Expertin** expert **II**
extra extra **I**

F

Fabrik factory **III U4**, 87
Fackel torch **II**
fähig sein zu *to be able to (do sth) **II**
Fahne flag **III U3**, 55
fahren *to go **I**; to travel **II**; *to drive **III U4**, 97
Fahrer/-in driver **II**
einfache **Fahrkarte** one-way ticket; single ticket **III U1**, 12
Fahrplan timetable **I**
Fahrpreis fare **III U1**, 12
Fahrrad bike **I**
Fahrradmotocross bicycle motocross **II**
Fahrschein ticket **III U1**, 11
Fahrt trip; tour **II**; journey **III U1**, 9
fair fair **I**
Fairplay fair play **III TS1**, 46
Fakt fact **II**
fallen *to fall **I**
fallen (lassen) to drop **II**
falls if **I**
falsch wrong **I**
fälschen to fake **II**
Familie family **I**
Fan fan **II**
fangen *to catch **II**
Fantasie fantasy **I**; imagination **III U2**, 27
fantasievoll imaginative **III U2**, 27
fantastisch fantastic **II**
Fantasy fantasy **III TS3**, 106
Fanzeitschrift fanzine **II**
Farbe colour **I**
Welche **Farbe** hat …? What colour is …? **I**
farbenfroh colourful **I**
Farm farm **I**
Farmer/-in farmer **II**
aus der **Fassung** bringen *to upset **III AC2**, 53
fast nearly; almost **II**
Fastnachtsdienstag Shrove Tuesday **I**
faszinierend fascinating **III U3**, 64
faul lazy **III TS1**, 47
Favorit/-in favourite **III U4**, 88
Februar February **I**
Feder feather **III U4**, 91
Federkiel quill **III U4**, 91
Federmäppchen pencil-case **I**
Feedback feedback **II**
Was **fehlt**? What is missing? **I**
fehlend missing **II**
Fehler mistake **I**
Feier party **I**
feiern to celebrate **I**
Feiertag holiday **I**
Feind/-in enemy **III TS3**, 106
Feld field **II**
felsig rocky **III U1**, 9
Fenster window **I**

Ferien holidays *(pl)* **I**
fernbleiben von to stay away from **II**
(sich) fernhalten von *to keep away from **III U1**, 18
Fernsehen TV **I**
fernsehen to watch TV **I**
Fernseher TV **I**
fertig ready; finished **II**
Fertiggericht ready meal **I**
Fertigkeit skill **I**
fertigstellen to finish **I**
fesseln (an) to tie (to) **III U3**, 67
hier: **fesseln** to hook **III TS3**, 107
Fest festival **I**
festhalten *to hold **I**
(sich) **festhalten** an *to hold onto **III U3**, 67
Festival festival **I**
festnehmen to arrest **II**
feststecken in … stuck in the middle of … **III TS1**, 49
Feuer fire **III TS2**, 79
Feuerwerk fireworks *(pl)* **I**
hier: ein **Feuerwerk** zünden *to set off **III U3**, 60
Fieber fever **II**
Figur character **I**; figure **II**
Fiktion fiction *(no pl)* **III TS3**, 106
Film film **I**
Filmemacher/-in filmmaker **II**
finden *to find **I**
Finger finger **I**
Firma company **III U2**, 29
Fisch fish, fish *(pl)* **I**
Fischen fishing **III U1**, 14
Fischerei fishing **III U1**, 14
fit werden *to get fit **I**
Fläche space; area **II**
Flagge flag **III U3**, 55
Flair flair **II**
Flamme flame **III TS2**, 79
Flasche bottle **I**
Flashback flashback **III U4**, 98
Fleisch meat *(no pl)* **III U3**, 59
fliegen *to fly **III TS1**, 48
Flohmarkt flea market **I**
Flöte recorder **III U2**, 32
Flucht escape **III TS3**, 106
Flug flight **III TS1**, 48
Flughafen airport **II**
Flur hall **III U1**, 18
Fluss river **I**
am **Fluss** by the river **II**
flüstern to whisper **I**
Flut high tide **II**
Flyer flyer **I**
Fokus focus **III TS3**, 110
folgen to follow **II**
Form form **I**
in **Form** kommen *to get fit **I**
verneinte **Form** negative form **I**
formal formal **II**
formell formal **II**
formen to form **II**
förmlich formal **II**
Formular form **III U1**, 12
hier: sich fortbewegen *to get around **II**
fortfahren *to go on **I**
Fortschritt progress **II**
Forum forum **II**
Foto photo; picture **I**
auf dem **Foto**/den **Fotos** in the photo(s) **I**
Fotos machen *to take photos **I**
ins **Foto** laufen to photobomb **III U4**, 97
Fotoapparat camera **II**
Fotoaufnahmen photo shoot **III U4**, 96
Fotograf/-in photographer **III U4**, 96
Fotografie photo **I**
fotografieren *to take photos **I**
Fotoshooting photo shoot **III U4**, 96
Fotostory photo story **I**
Frage question **I**
Frageanhängsel question tag **II**
fragen to ask **I**
Frage/Fragt nach … Ask about … **I**
fragen nach to ask for **I**
Französisch French **II**
französisch French **II**
Frau woman, women *(pl)* **I**
Frau *(Anrede)* Mrs **I**
Fräulein *(Anrede)* Miss **III U2**, 33
frei free **I**
Freiheit freedom *(no pl)* **III U2**, 36
Freiluft- outdoor **II**
Freitag Friday **I**
Freizeit free time; leisure **I**
Freizeitzentrum leisure centre **I**
fremd strange **I**
Fremdsprache foreign language **II**
fressen *to eat **I**
Freude fun **I**
Freudenfeuer bonfire **I**
sich freuen auf to look forward to **II**
sich **freuen** an to enjoy **II**
Freund/-in friend **I**
Dafür sind **Freunde** da. That's what friends are for. **I**
Freundin *(in einer Paarbeziehung)* girlfriend **II**
freundlich friendly **II**
Freundschaft friendship **II**
Freundschaft schließen *to make friends **II**
frisch fresh **I**
uns frisieren *to do our hair **I**
froh happy **I**
fröhlich happy; fun **I**
Frucht fruit **I**
früh early **I**
so **früh** this early **III AC2**, 53
Frühling spring **III TS2**, 77
Frühstück breakfast **I**
frühstücken *to have breakfast **I**
Frühstückszerealie cereal *(no pl)* **I**
Fuchs fox **II**
fühlen *to feel **I**
sich **fühlen** *to feel **I**
sich ausgeschlossen **fühlen** *to feel left out **II**
sich schlecht **fühlen** *to feel sick **II**
führen to guide **III TS1**, 49; *to lead **III U3**, 61
Führer/-in guide **II**
(sich) füllen to fill **III U3**, 60
Füller pen **I**
fünf five **I**
fünfzehn fifteen **I**
funktionieren to work **II**; to work out **III U2**, 39
für for **I**
für mich on my own **II**
Für wen …? Who … for? **I**
Furcht fear **II**
furchtbar awful **I**
Fuß foot, feet *(pl)* **I**
zu **Fuß** on foot **II**
Fußball football **I**
Fußboden floor **I**
Fußbodenheizung underfloor heating *(no pl)* **III U4**, 84
Fußgelenk ankle **II**
Fußknöchel ankle **II**
Futter food **III TS2**, 77
füttern *to feed **III U1**, 21

G

Gabel fork **III AC2**, 52
Gälisch Gaelic **III U1**, 14
gälisch Gaelic **III U1**, 14
ganz all **I**
den **ganzen** Tag all day **II**
ganz whole **I**
Garage garage **I**
garstig nasty **II**
Garten garden **I**; backyard **III TS3**, 107
Gast guest **III U2**, 34
Gastfamilie host family **III AC2**, 52
Gaststätte restaurant **I**
Gattung genre **III TS3**, 106
Geächtete/-r outlaw **III AC1**, 24
Gebäude building **I**
geben *to give **I**
es **gibt** there is/are **I**
Gebiet area **II**
geboren werden *to be born **III U4**, 91
gebrauchen to use **I**
gebrochen broken **I**
Gebühr fee **III U1**, 12
Geburtstag birthday **I**
Alles Gute zum **Geburtstag**! Happy Birthday! **I**

Herzlichen Glückwunsch zum **Geburtstag**! Happy Birthday! **I**
Gedächtnis memory **II**
Gedanke thought **II**
Gedicht poem **I**
gedruckt print **II**
Sehr **geehrte** Dame, sehr **geehrter** Herr Dear Sir or Madam **III U1**, 13
Gefahr danger **III U3**, 66
gefährlich dangerous **I**
Mir **gefällt** … I like … **I**
Gefängnis prison **II**
Gefühl feeling **II**
gegen against **II**; versus (vs.) **III U3**, 69
Gegend region **II**
sich **gegenseitig** each other **I**
Gegenstand object **III U4**, 85
gegenüber opposite **I**
Gegenwart present **II**
Gegenwarts- present **III U3**, 64
Gehege run area **III TS2**, 77
geheim secret **III U4**, 95
Geheimnis secret **II**; mystery **III U4**, 96
geheimnisvoll mysterious **III AC1**, 24
gehen *to go; to walk **I**
aus dem Weg **gehen** to avoid **III TS2**, 77
ins Bett **gehen** *to go to bed **I**
nach unten **gehen** *to go down **I**
zu jmdm. nach Hause **gehen** *to go over to **II**
Wie **geht** es dir? How are you? **I**
Wie **geht** es euch? How are you? **I**
Wie **geht** es Ihnen? How are you? **I**
nicht **gehorchen** to disobey **III TS3**, 107
gehören (zu) to belong (to) **II**
gehören zu *to go with **I**
zueinander **gehören** *to go together **I**
Geist ghost **II**; mind **III TS3**, 109
gelangweilt bored **I**
gelb yellow **I**
Geld money **I**
Geld sammeln to raise money **II**
Geld verdienen *to make money **I**
Gelee jelly **I**
Gelegenheit chance **II**
Gemälde painting **II**
gemein nasty **II**
Gemeindezentrum community centre **I**
gemeinsam together **I**
gemeinsam haben *to have in common **III TS3**, 110
Gemüse vegetable **III U3**, 59
genau exactly **II**
genau hier right here **II**
genauso wie the same way as **II**
Generation generation **III U4**, 87
Genie genius **II**
genießen to enjoy **II**
Gentleman gentleman, gentlemen *(pl)* **III U4**, 96
genug enough **I**
genügend enough **I**
Geocaching geocaching **III U1**, 18
geöffnet open **I**
Geografie geography **III U1**, 14
gerade just; at the moment **I**; right now **II**
geradeaus straight on **I**
Gerät machine **I**; tool **III U1**, 19; gadget **III U2**, 35
Geräusch sound **I**; noise **II**
gerecht fair **I**
Gern geschehen. You're welcome. **I**
gern haben to like **I**
gern mögen to love **I**
hätte/-st/-n/-t **gern** would like **I**
hätte/-st-/-n/-t sehr **gern** would love **I**
würde/-st/-n/-t **gern** would like **I**
würde/-st/-n/-t sehr **gern** would love **I**
Gerümpel rubbish **I**
Geschäft shop **I**; business **III U2**, 29
geschehen to happen **I**
Geschenk present **I**
Geschichte story, stories *(pl)* **I**; history **II**
eine **Geschichte** langsam entwickeln to step into a story slowly **III TS3**, 111
geschichtlich historical **I**
Geschick skill **I**
Gesellschaft society **III U1**, 19; company **III U2**, 29
Gesetzlose/-r outlaw **III AC1**, 24
Gesicht face **I**
Gesichtsausdruck facial expression **III AC3**, 83
Gespräch dialogue; conversation **I**
ein **Gespräch** dominieren to hog a conversation **III AC3**, 82
ein **Gespräch** für sich in Beschlag nehmen to hog a conversation **III AC3**, 82
hier: das **Gespräch** am Laufen halten *to keep the ball bouncing **III AC3**, 82
gesprochen spoken **II**
Gestalt figure **II**
gestalten to design **II**
Gestaltung design **II**
gestern yesterday **II**
völlig **gestresst** sein *to be stressed out **III U2**, 28
gesund healthy **I**
Gesundheit health **II**
Getränk drink **I**
getrennt separate **II**
Gewalt violence *(no pl)* **III TS3**, 106
gewaltig huge **II**
gewaltsam violent **III TS2**, 80
gewalttätig violent **III TS2**, 80
Gewerbe industry **III U3**, 59
Gewicht weight **III TS2**, 77
Gewinn prize **I**
gewinnen *to win **I**
Gewinner/-in winner **I**; champion **III TS1**, 50
gewöhnlich usually **I**
gewohnt sein *to be used to *(+ -ing)* **III AC2**, 53
gewöhnt sein an *to be used to *(+ -ing)* **III AC2**, 53
Gig gig **III U3**, 58
Gipsverband plaster cast **III U4**, 96
Gitter grid **I**
glänzen *to shine **II**
Glas glass **I**
glauben *to think; to believe **I**
gläubig religious **I**
der/die/das **gleiche** the same **I**
gleich right away **I**
jetzt **gleich** right now **II**
gleichmäßig regular **I**
gleichzeitig at the same time **I**
Glocke bell **II**
Glück haben *to be lucky **II**
noch mal **Glück** gehabt saved by the bell **III U2**, 32
Was für ein **Glück**! What luck! **III U4**, 92
… hat/haben **Glück**. … is/are lucky. **I**
glücklich happy **I**
Glücksbringer lucky charm **I**
Gold gold **III U4**, 90
goldenes Zeitalter golden age **III U4**, 86
Golf golf **III U1**, 14
Götterspeise jelly **I**
graben *to dig **II**
Grammatik grammar **II**
grau grey **I**
grausam cruel **III AC1**, 24
greifen to grab **II**
Grenze limit **III U2**, 35
Griff knob **II**
groß big **I**; tall; high; large **II**
großartig great **I**; fantastic **II**
Großbuchstabe capital letter **I**
Größe size **I**
Großeltern grandparents *(pl)* **I**
Großstadt city **I**
großzügig generous **III TS1**, 46
grün green **I**
Grund reason **II**
Grund- basic **II**
gründen to found **III U4**, 86
hier: **gründen** to start **III U3**, 60
grundlegend basic **II**
Grundschule primary school **I**
Gruppe group **I**; team **II**
Gruppenzwang peer pressure **III U2**, 38
gruselig scary **II**
Gruß greeting **I**
Grüße ausrichten (an) *to say hello (to) **I**
Herzliche **Grüße** Best wishes **III U1**, 13
Herzliche **Grüße** *(am Briefende)* Love … **I**
Liebe **Grüße** *(am Briefende)* Love … **I**
Viele **Grüße** Best wishes **III U1**, 13

Viele **Grüße** ... *(am Ende von Briefen und Mails)* Yours ... **II**
grüßen *to say hello (to) **I**
Günstling favourite **III U4**, 88
Gürtel belt **III U4**, 85
gut good; fine **I**
gut sein in *to be good at **I**
Guten Morgen. Good morning. **I**
Mir geht's **gut**. I'm fine. **I**
Guthaben credit **II**
Gymnasium grammar school **III U1**, 13

H

Haar(e) hair **I**
Haarbürste hairbrush **III U4**, 86
unsere **Haare** machen *to do our hair **I**
haben *to have got; *to have **I**
hätte/-st/-n/-t gern would like **I**
hätte/-st-/-n/-t sehr gern would love **I**
nicht ganz unrecht **haben** *to have a point **III U2**, 34
Hafen harbour **III U1**, 9
Hafendamm pier **I**
Haggis *(schottisches Gericht aus in einem Schafsmagen gekochten Schafsinnereien und Haferschrot)* haggis **III U3**, 55
Hähnchen chicken **I**
halb *(bei Uhrzeitangaben)* half past **I**
eine **halbe** Stunde half an hour **III U4**, 97
halb half **I**
Halbjahresferien half-term break **I**
Halbschwester half-sister **I**
die **Hälfte** half, halves *(pl)* (of) **I**
Halle hall **II**
Hallo. Hello.; Hi.; Hey! **I**
Halskette necklace **III U4**, 86
Halt stop **II**
halten *to hold; *to keep **I**
halten von *to think of **I**
Haltestelle station **I**; stop **II**
Hamburger burger **I**
Hammer hammer **II**
Hand hand **I**
Klatsch/Klatscht in die **Hände**. Clap your hands. **I**
Handbuch planner **I**
Handbuch für TTS-Schülerinnen und -Schüler TTS planner **I**
sich **handeln** um *to be about **I**
Handgelenk wrist **II**
Händler merchant **II**
Handlung action **I**; plot **III TS3**, 106
Handlungsort location **II**
Handschuh glove **I**
Handy phone **I**; mobile **II**
jmdn. **hänseln** to tease sb **III U2**, 38
Happy End happy ending **III TS3**, 106
hart hard **II**
hassen to hate **II**
häufig often **I**
häufig gefragt frequently asked **I**
Haupt- main **I**; lead **III U2**, 28
die **Haupteinkaufsstraße** the high street **III U2**, 36
Hauptrolle lead part **III U2**, 28
Hauptstadt capital **II**
Hauptwort noun **I**
Haus house **I**
nach **Hause** home **I**
zu **Hause** at home **I**
zu jmdm. nach **Hause** gehen *to go over to **II**
Hausarrest haben *to be grounded **III U2**, 36
Hausaufgabe(n) homework **I**
Haustier pet **I**
Haustür front door **II**
in jmds. **Haut** stecken *to be in sb's shoes **III TS3**, 108
He! Hey! **I**
Heim home **I**
heimlich in secret **II**
heiraten to marry **III U4**, 86
heiß hot **III TS2**, 79
Ich **heiße** ... My name is ... **I**
Wie **heißen** Sie? What's your name? **I**
Wie **heißt** du? What's your name? **I**
Heizung heating **III U4**, 84
Held hero, heroes *(pl)* **III AC1**, 24
Heldin heroine **III AC1**, 24
helfen to help **I**
heranzoomen (auf) to zoom in (on) **III U4**, 96
heraus out **I**
herausfinden *to find; *to find out **I**; to work out **II**
Herausforderung challenge **II**
herausschneiden to edit out **III U4**, 97
Herd cooker **I**
herein in **I**
hereinkommen *to come in **III U1**, 18
Herr lord **III U4**, 85
feiner **Herr** gentleman, gentlemen *(pl)* **III U4**, 96
Herr der Raben raven master **II**
Sehr geehrte Dame, sehr geehrter **Herr** Dear Sir or Madam **III U1**, 13
Herr *(Anrede)* Mr **I**
herrisch bossy **III U2**, 32
Herrschaft reign **III U4**, 90
herrschen to rule **III U1**, 16; to reign **III U4**, 91
die **Herrschenden** those in power **III TS2**, 80
herstellen to produce **III U3**, 57
um ... **herum** around **I**
herumschleichen to sneak around **II**
sich **herumtreiben** (mit) *to hang out (with) *(infml)* **III U2**, 36
herunter down **II**
herunterfallen *to fall off **II**
herunterkommen *to come down **I**
herunterladen *(aus dem Internet)* to download **II**
herunternehmen *to take off **I**
herunterrollen to roll off **II**
Herz heart **II**
Herzliche Grüße Best wishes **III U1**, 13
Herzliche Grüße *(am Briefende)* Love ... **I**
heute today **I**
heute Abend 2nite *(= tonight)* **I**
heute Nachmittag this afternoon **II**
heutig present **III U3**, 64
Hi. Hi.; Hey! **I**
hier here **I**
genau **hier** right here **II**
Hier ist ... Here's ... **I**
Highlight highlight **II**
Hilfe help **I**
ohne fremde **Hilfe** alone **I**
hilflos helpless **I**
hilfreich useful; helpful **I**
hilfsbereit helpful **I**
Himmel sky **III U3**, 66
hinauf up **II**
hinaus out **I**
hinausfließen to flow out **II**
hinausgehen *to go out **III U1**, 18
hinein inside **I**
hineingehen to enter **II**
hineingelangen *to get into **I**
Hin- und Rückfahrkarte return ticket **III U1**, 12
hinfallen *to fall over; *to fall **I**
hinkommen *to get there **I**
sich **hinsetzen** *to sit down **I**
hinten at the back of **II**
hinter behind **I**
Hintergrund background **I**
Hintergrund- backing **III U2**, 28
hinterhergehen to follow **II**
Hinterhof backyard **III TS3**, 107
hinüber over; across **I**
hinübergehen zu *to go over to **II**
hinunter down **II**
hinunterfallen *to fall off **II**; *to fall down **III TS1**, 50
hinuntergehen *to go down **I**
hinunterrollen to roll off **II**
Hinweis clue **II**; hint **III AC3**, 83
hinzufügen to add **I**
historisch historical **I**; historic **III U3**, 54
Hobby hobby, hobbies *(pl)* **I**
hoch tall; high **II**
hochleben lassen *to give the bumps **I**
Hochzeit wedding **I**
Hockey hockey **II**
Hofdame lady-in-waiting **III U4**, 96
hoffen to hope **I**

Hoffnung hope **II**
hoffnungsvoll hopeful **I**
höflich polite **I**
Sei/Seid **höflich**. Be polite. **I**
Höhepunkt highlight **II**
Höhle cave **III U1**, 21
holen *to get **I**
Holz wood **III U3**, 67
aus **Holz** wooden **III U3**, 66
hölzern wooden **III U3**, 66
Homepage homepage **I**
Honig honey **III TS1**, 47
Hoppla! Oops! **I**
Hör- audio **I**
horchen auf to listen for **I**
Hören listening **I**
hören *to hear **I**
Ich habe **gehört**, dass … I hear … **I**
Horn horn **III TS2**, 80
Horror horror **III TS3**, 106
Horrorfilm horror **III TS3**, 106
Horrorgeschichte horror **III TS3**, 106
Hör-/Sehverstehen viewing **I**
Hose trousers *(pl)* **III U1**, 18
kurze **Hose** shorts *(pl)* **II**
Hosentasche pocket **III U3**, 66
Hospital hospital **II**
Hotel hotel **II**
hübsch beautiful **II**; pretty **III U2**, 37
Huch! Oops! **I**
Hügel hill **III U1**, 18
Huhn chicken **I**
Hülle wrapping **I**
Humor humour *(no pl)* **III U3**, 64
Sinn für **Humor** sense of humour *(no pl)* **III U2**, 39
Hund dog **I**
den **Hund** ausführen to walk the dog **I**
mit dem **Hund** spazieren gehen to walk the dog **I**
Ich bin **hundemüde**. I'm dog-tired. **I**
Hunderte (von) hundreds of **III U3**, 61
hungrig hungry **I**
hüpfen to bounce **III AC3**, 82
Husten cough **II**
Hut hat **I**
hüten to look after **I**
Hymne anthem **III U3**, 58

I

ich I; me **I**
Ich bin aus … I'm from … **I**
Ich bin Engländer/-in. I'm English. **I**
Ich bin … I'm … **I**
Ich heiße … My name is … **I**
Ich mache … nicht gern. I don't like … **I**
Ich mag … nicht. I don't like … **I**
Ich möchte … I'd like to … *(= I would like to)* **I**
Ich weiß (es) nicht! I don't know! **I**
Ich würde gern … I'd like to … *(= I would like to)* **I**
ich würde lieber I'd rather **III U4**, 99
Idee idea **I**
sich **identifizieren** mit to identify with **III TS3**, 106
Identität identity **II**
Idiot/-in idiot **II**
Igel hedgehog **III TS2**, 76
ignorieren to ignore **III U2**, 37
ihm him **I**
ihn him **I**
ihnen them **I**
ihr you; u *(= you)* **I**
Ihr/-e your **I**; yours **II**
ihr/-e her; its **I**
ihr/-e *(Pl.)* their **I**
Ihr wisst, wie man … You know how to … **I**
illegal illegal **III TS2**, 80
im in; on **I**
im Innern inside **I**
im Moment at the moment **I**
im Weg sein/stehen *to be in the way **I**
Imbiss snack **I**
Imbissstube snack bar **I**
immer always **I**
für **immer** forever **II**
immer noch still **I**
immer wieder over and over again **III TS1**, 50
immerhin after all **I**
in in; on; at; to; into; inside **I**
in Cornwall Cornish **III U1**, 10
in der Nähe von near **I**
in der Straße in the street **I**
in Not in need **II**
in … hinein into **I**
in Ordnung OK; fine **I**
indem as **I**
Inder/-in Indian **I**
indisch Indian **I**
individuell individual **II**
Industrie industry **III U3**, 59
Infinitiv infinitive **I**
Informatik IT *(= Information Technology)* **III U2**, 28
Information information *(no pl)* **I**
Informationen information *(no pl)* **I**
Informationstechnik IT *(= Information Technology)* **III U2**, 28
Inlineskates fahren to skate **I**
Inlineskatefahren inline skating **I**
Inlineskates skates *(pl)* **I**
inmitten among **III TS3**, 107
innen inside **I**
inoffiziell unofficial **III U3**, 58
Insel island **III U1**, 9
Installateur/-in plumber **III U1**, 18
Instruktion instruction **I**
intelligent smart **III U2**, 27
interessant interesting **I**
Interesse interest **II**
(sich) **interessieren** to interest **II**
sich **interessieren** (für) to care (about) **II**
sich **interessieren** für *to be interested in **II**
interessiert sein an *to be interested in **II**
Interkulturelles Across cultures **I**
international international **I**; multi-ethnic **II**
Internet internet **I**
Internetauftritt website **I**
Internettagebuch blog **III TS2**, 79
Interview interview **I**
interviewen to interview **I**
irgendein/-e/-er any **I**
irgendwelche any **I**
irgendwo anywhere; somewhere **II**
Irisch Irish **III U1**, 14
irisch Irish **III U1**, 14
sich **irren** *to be wrong **I**

J

ja yes; yeah *(infml)* **I**
Jacke jacket **III U3**, 59
jagen to chase **I**
Jahr year **I**
Jahrbuch yearbook **II**
Jahrhundert century **II**
18-**jährig** 18-year-old **II**
11-**Jährige**/-r 11-year-old **II**
Januar January **I**
je … desto the … the **II**
jedenfalls anyway **II**
jede/-r/-s every; each **I**
jede Menge lots (of) **I**
jedes Mal, wenn whenever **II**
jeder everyone **I**; everybody **II**
jemals ever **II**
jemand somebody **I**; someone **II**
jemand anderes anyone else **II**
jene those **I**
jenes that **I**
jetzt now **I**
jetzt gleich right now **II**
Job job **I**
Joghurt yoghurt **I**
Jonglieren juggling **II**
jubeln to cheer **II**
Jugend- teen **II**
Jugendliche/-r teenager **I**; teen **III TS3**, 106
Juli July **I**
jung young **I**
Junge boy **I**
Juni June **I**
Juwel jewel **III U4**, 95

K

Kaffee coffee **I**
Kaiser emperor **III U4**, 84
Kaiserreich empire **III U4**, 84
Kalender planner **I**; calendar **III U4**, 86
kalt cold **II**
  kalt stellen *to leave it to cool **I**
Kamelrennen camel racing **II**
Kamera camera **II**
  mit der **Kamera** festgehalten caught on camera **II**
Kameraeinstellung shot **II**
Kamin chimney **III U1**, 18
Kampf fight **II**; battle **III U4**, 88
kämpfen *to fight **II**
Kanada Canada **I**
Kaninchen rabbit **I**
Kapitän/-in captain **I**
Kapitel unit **I**
kaputt broken **I**
Karneval carnival **II**
Karotte carrot **I**
Karriere career **III U2**, 28
Karte card **I**
Kartenschalter ticket office **III U3**, 66
Kartoffel potato, potatoes *(pl)* **III U3**, 60
Kartoffelchip crisp *(BE)* **I**
Kartoffelpüree mashed potatoes *(pl)* **III U3**, 60
Käse cheese **I**
Kasten box **I**
Katastrophe disaster **II**
Kategorie category **II**
Katze cat **I**
kaufen *to buy; *to get **I**
Käufer/-in buyer **I**
Kaufmann merchant **II**
kein/-e no **I**
  keine Ahnung no idea **II**
  Keine Sorge! Don't worry! **I**
kein/-e/-en not … any **I**
Keks biscuit **I**
Kelte/Keltin Celt **III U4**, 89
keltisch Celtic **II**
kennen *to know **I**
kennenlernen *to get to know **III U1**, 14
Kerl guy **II**
Kerze candle **I**
Kerzenlicht candlelight *(no pl)* **II**
Kfz-Mechaniker/-in mechanic **II**
Kilometer kilometre (km) **III TS3**, 109
Kilt kilt **III U3**, 55
Kind child, children *(pl)* **I**
Kino cinema **I**
Kirche church **I**
Kiste box **I**
Klang sound **I**
klappen to work out **III U2**, 39
klar clear **I**
Klasse group; class **I**
Klasse *(in einer englischen Schule)* tutor group **I**
  Ausstellung in der **Klasse** class display **I**
Klassenarbeit test **I**
Klassenkamerad/-in classmate **I**
Klassenlehrer/-in tutor **I**
Klassenposter class poster **I**
Klassenzimmer classroom **I**
klatschen to clap **I**
  Klatsch/Klatscht in die Hände. Clap your hands. **I**
Kleid dress **III U4**, 88
Kleider clothes *(pl)* **I**
Kleidergröße size **I**
Kleiderschrank wardrobe **I**
Kleidung clothes *(pl)* **I**; outfit **II**
klein small; little **I**; tiny **III U3**, 64
Klempner/-in plumber **III U1**, 18
Klettern climbing **II**
klettern to climb **I**
Klick click **II**
Klicken click **II**
Kliff cliff **III U3**, 64
klingeln *to ring **I**
klingen to sound **I**
Klippe cliff **III U3**, 64
klonen to clone **III U3**, 60
Klub club **I**
klug clever **II**; smart **III U2**, 27
Knacken crack **III U3**, 67
knackend cracking **III U3**, 66
knapp close **I**
  Das war **knapp**! That was close! **I**
sich den **Knöchel** verrenken to twist your ankle **II**
Koala koala **III TS2**, 79
Koch-AG Cooking Club **I**
Kochen cooking **I**
kochen to cook **II**
Kofferraum boot **III U4**, 97
Kokosnuss coconut **II**
Kollektion collection **II**
Köln Cologne **I**
Kolonie colony **II**
komfortabel comfortable **II**
Komiker/-in comedian **II**
komisch funny **III U2**, 32
  jmdn. **komisch** anschauen *to give sb funny looks **III U2**, 32
kommen *to come **I**
  kommen nach *to get to **I**
  kommen zu *to get to **I**
  Komm jetzt! Come on! **I**
  Komm schon! Come on! **I**
Kommentar comment **II**
kommentieren to comment (on) **II**
Kommunikation communication **II**
kommunizieren to communicate **II**
Komödie comedy **III TS3**, 106
Komparativ comparative **II**
Kompositum *(zusammengesetztes Wort)* compound word **II**
Kompromiss compromise **II**
  Kompromisse eingehen to compromise **III U2**, 27
Konfitüre jam **III AC2**, 52
konfus confused **III U2**, 38
König king **I**
Königin queen **II**
königlich royal **I**
  königlicher Leibgardist Beefeater **II**
konkurrieren (mit) to compete (with) **III U2**, 27
konkurrierend competitive **III U2**, 31
können can **I**; *to be able to (do sth) **II**
  könnte/-n could **II**
  kann nicht can't **I**; cannot **II**
  können nicht can't **I**; cannot **II**
  (vielleicht) **können** may **II**
  Es **könnte/-n** auch … sein. It might as well be … **III TS3**, 109
  konnte/-n could **III U2**, 36
Kontakt contact **II**
  in **Kontakt** bleiben (mit) to stay in touch (with) **II**
kontrollieren to check **I**
  gegenseitig **kontrollieren** to peer-edit **II**
Konversation conversation **I**
sich **konzentrieren** (auf) to focus (on) **II**
Konzept draft **I**
Kopf head **I**
  etw. aus dem **Kopf** bekommen *to get sth out of one's head **III TS1**, 50
Kopfhörer headphones *(pl)* **II**
Kopfschmerzen headache *(no pl)* **II**
Kopfweh headache *(no pl)* **II**
kopieren to copy **I**
Korbball netball **I**
Koreaner/-in Korean **II**
Koreanisch Korean **II**
koreanisch Korean **II**
Körper body **III U2**, 27
  menschlicher **Körper** human body **II**
korrekt correct; right **I**
Korridor hall **III U1**, 18
Korrigiere/Korrigiert … Correct … **I**
kosten *to cost **I**
  Es **kostet** …/Sie **kosten** … It's …/They're … **I**
  Wie viel **kostet/kosten** …? How much is/are …? **I**
kostenlos free **I**
Kostüm costume **I**; fancy dress **II**
Krachen crack **III U3**, 67
Kraft power **III AC1**, 24; energy **III TS3**, 109
  die **Kraft** der Wörter *(Wortschatzübung)* Word power **I**
Krampf cramp **II**
Kran crane **III U3**, 61
krank sick **II**; ill **III TS2**, 77

Krankenhaus hospital **II**
Krankenpfleger nurse **III U4**, 97
Krankenschwester nurse **III U4**, 97
Krankenwagen ambulance **III U4**, 97
kreativ creative **I**
Kreis circle **I**
  sich im **Kreis** drehen *to go round in circles **III U3**, 66
kreischen to scream **II**
Kreuz cross **III U1**, 14
kreuzen to cross **II**
Krieger warrior **III U1**, 18
Krimi detective **III TS3**, 106
Kriminalfilm detective **III TS3**, 106
Kriminalität crime **III AC1**, 24
Kriminalroman detective **III TS3**, 106
Kriminelle/-r criminal **III AC1**, 24
Kritik rating **III U4**, 94
Krone crown **III U4**, 88
Kronjuwelen crown jewels **II**
Küche kitchen **I**
Kuchen cake; pie **I**
Küchenschrank cupboard **I**
Kuh cow **III U1**, 21
Kühlschrank fridge **I**
Kultur culture **I**
Kummerkastentante agony aunt **II**
sich **kümmern** (um) to care (about) **II**
  sich **kümmern** um to look after **I**
  sich um jmdn. **kümmern** *to take care of sb **III U4**, 96
Kunde/Kundin customer **III U1**, 16
Kunst art **II**
Kunstunterricht Art **I**
Kurs course **II**
kurz short **I**
  kurz vor on the brink of **III TS2**, 80
Kurzantwort short answer **I**
Kurzform short form **I**
Kurznachricht text (message) **I**
Küste shore **II**; coastline **III U1**, 14
Küstenverlauf coastline **III U1**, 14
Küstenweg coastal path **III U1**, 18

L

Lächeln smile **I**
lächeln to smile **I**
lachen to laugh **I**
Laden shop **I**
Lady lady **III U4**, 96
Lage location **II**
Lage (aus) layer (of) **III TS2**, 77
Lagerfeuer bonfire **I**
Lamm lamb **I**
Lämmchen lamb **I**
Lampe light **II**
Land country, countries *(pl)*; land **I**; countryside **III U1**, 10
landen to end up; to land **II**
landesweit national **I**
Landkarte map **I**
Landschaft landscape **III U1**, 8
Landwirt/-in farmer **II**
lang long **I**
  (nicht) **länger** (not) any longer **III U1**, 10
… **lang** for … **II**
langsam slow **I**
  eine Geschichte **langsam** entwickeln to step into a story slowly **III TS3**, 111
langweilig boring **I**
Laptop laptop **II**
Lärm noise **II**
lassen *to let **I**; *to leave **II**
  Lass/Lasst uns … Let's … **I**
Lassi lassi **I**
Lauf run **II**
Laufbahn career **III U2**, 28
Laufen running **II**
laufen *to run; to walk **I**; *to be on **II**
  ins Foto **laufen** to photobomb **III U4**, 97
Läufer/-in runner **II**
Laune mood **II**
laut loud **I**; noisy **III U4**, 87
  laut vorlesen/vorsingen *to sing out loud **III TS1**, 47
läuten *to ring **I**
Layout layout **III U2**, 35
Leben life, lives *(pl)* **II**
leben to live **I**
lebendig lively **II**
Lebensmittel food **I**
Lebensstil lifestyle **III U4**, 87
hier: **Leckerli** treat **III TS2**, 78
leer empty **III U3**, 66
legen *to put **I**
  Lege/Legt es in … Put it in … **I**
Legende legend **III AC1**, 24
jmdm. eine **Lehre/Lektion** erteilen *to teach somebody a lesson **II**
lehren *to teach **II**
Lehrer/-in teacher **I**; instructor **II**
königlicher **Leibgardist** Beefeater **II**
leicht easy **I**; light **III AC3**, 82
leid tun *to be sorry **I**
  Tut mir **leid**! Sorry!; I'm sorry! **I**
leihen *to lend **III U2**, 37
leise quiet **I**
sich **leisten** to afford **III U4**, 99
leistungsorientiert competitive **III U2**, 31
leiten to guide **III TS1**, 49
Leiter ladder **II**
Lektion unit **I**
  jmdm. eine Lehre/**Lektion** erteilen *to teach somebody a lesson **II**
Lernen studies *(pl)* **II**
lernen *to learn **I**; to study **III U2**, 28
  viel zu **lernen** a lot to learn **I**
  auswendig **lernen** *to learn … by heart **I**
Lesen reading **I**
  vor dem **Lesen** pre-reading **I**
lesen *to read **I**
Leser/-in reader **I**
letzte/-r/-s last **I**; final **III U3**, 64
letztlich finally **II**
Leute people *(pl)* **I**; guys **II**
Licht light **II**
Lichtblitz flash **III U4**, 97
lieb nice **I**
  Lieber … Dear … **I**
  Liebe … *(Anrede in Briefen)* Dear … **I**
  Liebe Grüße *(am Briefende)* Love … **I**
Liebe love **III U1**, 21
lieben to love **I**
  Ich **liebe** dich. I love you. **I**
  Ich **liebe** … I love … **I**
lieber better **I**
  ich würde **lieber** I'd rather **III U4**, 99
Liebesfilm romance **III TS3**, 106
Liebesgeschichte romance **III TS3**, 106
Lieblings- favourite **I**
  Mein/e **Lieblings** … My favourite … **I**
  Was ist dein/-e **Lieblings**…? What's your favourite …? **I**
Lied song **I**
Liedtext (song) lyrics *(pl)* **III TS1**, 46
liegen *to lie **II**
Lifestyle lifestyle **III U4**, 87
lila purple **I**
Limit limit **III U2**, 35
Limonade lemonade **I**
Lineal ruler **I**
Linie line **I**
Link link **II**
linke/-r/-s left **I**
  auf der **linken** Seite on the left **I**
links on the left; left **I**
Liste list **I**
Liter litre (l) **III U3**, 57
live live **III TS3**, 110
Loch hole **II**
locker laid-back **III U2**, 28
Löffel spoon **III TS1**, 47
Logik logic **III U2**, 27
lokal local **III U1**, 15
LOL LOL (= laughing out loud) **II**
Londoner/-in Londoner **I**
Lord lord **III U4**, 85
Los ticket **I**
löschen to delete **III U2**, 39
lösen to solve **III U1**, 18
losgehen *to leave **II**
loslassen *to let go (of) **II**
Lösung solution **II**
Löwe lion **II**
Lücke gap **I**
Luft air **III TS1**, 48
  Luft holen *to take a breath **III TS3**, 109
Lüge lie **III U2**, 38
lügen to lie **II**
die **Lunge** the lungs *(pl)* **III TS3**, 109
lustig funny; fun **I**

M

Maat mate **I**
machen *to do; *to make **I**
Fotos **machen** *to take photos **I**
sich Notizen **machen** *to take notes **I**
Machst du so …? Is this how you (do) …? **I**
Mir **macht** es nichts aus (zu) … I don't mind … *(+ -ing)* **III U2**, 34
Macht power **III AC1**, 24
mächtig powerful **III AC1**, 24
Mädchen girl **I**
Magen stomach **II**
magisch magical **III AC1**, 24
Mahlzeit meal **II**
Mai May **I**
mailen to mail **II**
Mal time **II**
malen to paint **I**
Malerei painting **II**
Mama mum **I**; mummy **III U2**, 37
Mami mummy **III U2**, 37
manchmal sometimes **I**
Manga *(japanischer Comic)* manga **II**
Mango mango **I**
Mann man, men *(pl)* **I**
wie der **Mann** aussah what the man looked like **II**
Mannschaftsführer/-in captain **I**
Mäppchen pencil-case **I**
Mappe folder **I**
Marathon marathon **II**
Markt market **I**
Marmelade jam **III AC2**, 52
Marmelade aus Zitrusfrüchten marmalade **III AC2**, 52
marschieren to march **III TS2**, 80
März March **I**
Maschine machine **I**
Match match **II**
Material material **II**
Mathe Maths **II**
Mathematik Maths **II**
Matrose sailor **I**
Mauer wall **I**
Maus/Mäuse mouse *(sg)*, mice *(pl)* **I**
Mechaniker/-in mechanic **II**
Medien media **II**
Medikamente medicine *(no pl)* **III TS2**, 80
Medizin medicine *(no pl)* **III TS2**, 80
Meer sea **I**
Meerschweinchen guinea pig **I**
mehr more **I**
(nicht) **mehr** (not) any longer **III U1**, 10
mehr … als more … than **I**
mehrere several **II**
Mehrzahl plural **I**
meiden to stay away from **II**; to avoid **III TS2**, 77
Meile *(brit. Längenmaß)* mile **II**
mein/-e my **I**
Mein/e Lieblings… My favourite … **I**
mein/-er/-e/-es mine **II**
meinen *to mean **II**
Meinung opinion **II**
anderer **Meinung** sein to disagree **III U2**, 27
einer **Meinung** sein (mit) to agree (with) **II**
seine **Meinung** ändern to change one's mind **III U4**, 88
die **meisten** (the) most **I**
der/die/das **meiste** (the) most **I**
meistens usually **I**
Meldung report **II**; news report **III TS2**, 76
melken to milk **III U1**, 21
Melodie tune **III TS1**, 47; melody **III TS1**, 50
eine **Menge** a lot of **I**
jede **Menge** lots (of) **I**
Mensch person, people *(pl)* **I**
Menschen people *(pl)* **I**
Menschenmenge crowd **II**
menschlicher Körper human body **II**
sich **merken** to remember **I**
merkwürdig strange **I**; weird **II**; funny **III U2**, 32
sich **messen** (mit) to compete (with) **III U2**, 27
Messer knife, knives *(pl)* **III AC2**, 52
Meter metre **II**
mich me **I**
mieten to rent (out) **III U3**, 65
Milch milk **I**
Milliarde billion **III U2**, 29
Million million **II**
Ich habe das schon eine **Million** Mal gemacht. I've done this a million times before. **II**
Millionär/-in millionaire **III U2**, 28
mindestens at least **II**
Mine mine **III U1**, 18
Mini- mini **II**
Minute minute **I**
mir me **I**
Mir geht's gut. I'm fine. **I**
mischen to mix (up) **III U4**, 96
missverstanden misunderstood **III U2**, 34
mit with **I**
mit *(dem Fahrrad)* by *(bike)* **I**
mitbekommen *(ugs.)* *to catch **III AC3**, 82
mitbringen *to bring; *to take **I**
miteinander together **I**
Mitglied member **II**
mithalten (mit) *to keep up (with) **II**
mitkriegen *(ugs.)* *to catch **III AC3**, 82
Mitleid haben mit *to feel sorry for **III U2**, 39
mitmachen *to be in **II**
hier: **mitmachen** to enter **II**
mitnehmen *to take **I**; to pick up **III U4**, 92
Mitschüler/-in classmate **I**
mitsingen *to sing along **III TS1**, 46
Mitspieler/-in player **II**
Mittagessen lunch **I**
Mittagspause lunch break **I**
Mitte middle **I**
mitteilen *to tell **I**
mittelalterlich medieval **III U1**, 8
mitten in … stecken stuck in the middle of … **III TS1**, 49
Mitternacht midnight **III U3**, 60
Mittwoch Wednesday **I**
Mix mix **III U2**, 37
Mobiltelefon mobile **II**
Modalverb modal **II**
Mode fashion **II**
Model model **I**
Modell model **I**
Modeln modelling **III U2**, 28
Moderator/-in presenter **I**
modern modern **II**
mögen to like; *to be into; to want (to) **I**
gern **mögen** to love **I**
nicht **mögen** to hate **II**
Du **magst** … You're into … **I**
Ich **mag** dich. I love you. **I**
Ich **mag** … I like … **I**
Ich **mag** … nicht. I don't like … **I**
Ich **mag** … total gern. I love … **I**
Ich **möchte** … I'd like to … *(= I would like to)* **I**
Möchten Sie …? Would you like …? **II**
Möchtest du …? Would you like …? **II**
Möchtet ihr …? Would you like …? **II**
möglich possible **I**
möglicherweise probably **II**
Möglichkeit chance **II**
Möhre carrot **I**
Moment moment **II**
im **Moment** at the moment **I**
Monarch/-in monarch **III U4**, 86
Monat month **II**
Mondlicht moonlight **III U3**, 66
Monster monster **I**
Montag Monday **I**
montags on Mondays **I**
Monument monument **III U1**, 14
Mord murder **III U4**, 92
Morgen morning **I**
Guten **Morgen**. Good morning. **I**
morgen tomorrow **I**
morgens in the mornings **I**
motivieren to motivate **I**
Motto theme **I**
Mountainbikefahren mountain biking **III U1**, 9
müde tired **I**
sich **Mühe** geben to push oneself **III U2**, 32
Müll rubbish **I**
Mund mouth **I**
Training für den **Mund** mouth jogging **I**
Münze coin **I**

Museum museum **I**
Museumsrundgang gallery walk **I**
Musik music **I**
Musik- musical **III U3**, 59
musikalisch musical **III U3**, 59
Musiker/-in musician **II**
Musikgruppe band **III U3**, 56
Müsli muesli **III AC2**, 52
müssen must **I**; *to have to **II**
(tun) **müssen** to need (to do) **I**
nicht **müssen** needn't **I**
mutig brave **I**
Mutter mother **I**
Muttersprache first language **II**
Mutti mummy **III U2**, 37
mysteriös mysterious **III AC1**, 24
Mysterium mystery **III U4**, 96

N

nach to **I**
nach draußen outside; out **I**
nach drinnen inside **I**
nach Hause home **I**
nach oben up; upstairs **II**
nach unten down; downstairs **II**
nach *(bei Uhrzeitangaben)* past **I**
nach *(zeitlich)* after **I**
Nachbar/-in neighbour *(BE)* **I**
Nachbarschaft neighbourhood **III U3**, 69
nachdenken *to think **I**
Warte/Wartet und **denk**/**denkt nach**. Stop and think **I**
nacherzählen *to retell **I**
nachjagen to chase **I**
Nachmittag afternoon **I**
heute **Nachmittag** this afternoon **II**
nachmittags *(Uhrzeit)* p.m. **I**
Nachricht message **I**
eine **Nachricht** entgegennehmen *to take a message **I**
eine **Nachricht** hinterlassen *to leave a message **I**
Nachrichten news *(sg)* **II**
Nachrichtenbeitrag news report **III TS2**, 76
nachschauen to look up **I**
nachschlagen to look up **I**
nachspielen to act out **II**
nachspüren to trace **I**
nächste/-r/-s next **I**
der/die **Nächste(n)** next **I**
als **Nächstes** next **I**
am **nächsten** Tag the next day **II**
Nacht night **I**
die ganze **Nacht** all night **I**
über **Nacht** overnight **III U2**, 37
Nachtisch pudding **I**
Nachtwanderung night walk **II**
nackt bare **III TS1**, 47
Nahaufnahme close-up **II**
in der **Nähe** von near **I**
nahe near **I**; close **II**
Name name **I**
Namenstag name day **I**
Nase nose **II**
die **Nase** voll haben (von) *to be fed up (with) **III U2**, 36
Nashorn rhino **III TS2**, 80
nass wet **II**
national national **I**
Natur nature **II**
natürlich of course **I**
Naturwissenschaften Science **II**
neben next to **I**; besides **III U1**, 14; by **III U1**, 18
(von) **nebenan** next door **III AC3**, 82
negativ negative **III U1**, 8
(ein Bonbon) **nehmen** *to have *(a sweet)* **I**
nehmen *to take **I**
neidisch sein (auf) *to be jealous (of) **I**
nein no **I**
benennen to name **I**
nennen to name; to call **I**
jemandem auf die **Nerven** gehen *to get on people's nerves **I**
nervös nervous **II**
nett nice **I**; friendly **II**
Netz net **II**; web **III U3**, 68
soziales **Netzwerk** social network **II**
neu new **I**
Neuigkeiten news *(sg)* **II**
neun nine **I**
nicht not **I**
nicht gehorchen to disobey **III TS3**, 107
nicht mehr not any more **I**
nicht mögen to hate **II**
noch **nicht** not ... yet **II**
nicht- non- **II**
nichts nothing; not ... anything **I**
Nichts zu danken. You're welcome. **I**
nie never **I**
niederbrennen *to burn down **III U4**, 91
niedlich cute **I**
niedrig low **II**
niemals never **I**
niemand nobody **II**
niemand anderes nobody else **III U1**, 20
nirgendwo nowhere **III U1**, 10
nirgendwohin nowhere **III U1**, 10
noch still **I**; yet **II**
noch ein/-e another **I**
noch einmal again **I**
noch mal again **I**
noch nicht not ... yet **II**
noch mal Glück gehabt saved by the bell **III U2**, 32
Nomen noun **I**
Nord- north **II**
Norden north **II**
im **Norden** north **III U3**, 64
nördlich north **III U3**, 64
Nordsee North Sea **III U1**, 9
normal normal **II**
normalerweise usually **I**
Normanne/**Normannin** Norman **III U4**, 85
normannisch Norman **III U4**, 85
in **Not** in need **II**
Note mark **III U2**, 28
notieren to note down **II**
Notiz note **I**
Notizen machen *to make notes **I**
sich **Notizen** machen *to take notes **I**
notwendiger Relativsatz defining relative clause **II**
November November **I**
Nudeln pasta **I**
null zero **I**
null *(bei Telefonnummern und Uhrzeitangaben)* oh **I**
Nullmeridian Meridian Line **I**
Nummer number **I**
nun now **I**
nun well **I**
nur only; just **I**
Nuss nut **I**
nützlich useful **I**
nützliche Ausdrücke Useful phrases **I**

O

O! Oh! **I**
o.k. OK **I**
ob if **I**
oben on top **I**; above; upstairs **II**
nach **oben** up **II**
obendrauf on top **I**
oberer Teil top **I**
oberes Ende top **I**
im **Obergeschoss** upstairs **II**
Objekt object **II**
Obst fruit **I**
oder or **I**
offen open **I**
öffentlich public **II**
offiziell official **III U3**, 58
offline offline **II**
öffnen to open **I**
oft often **I**
so **oft** whenever **II**
ohne without **I**
ohne fremde Hilfe alone **I**
Oje! Oh dear! **III U1**, 18
Öko- Eco **II**
Oktober October **I**
Oma grandma; granny **I**
Onkel uncle **I**
Online-Pinnwand wall **III U2**, 39
online stellen to post **II**
online online **II**
Opa grandad **I**
optimistisch optimistic **III U2**, 39
Orange orange **I**

orange orange **I**
Ordner folder **I**
Ordnung order **I**
in **Ordnung** fine **I**
in **Ordnung** bringen to tidy *(a room)* **I**
organisieren to organise **I**
Ort place **I**; space **II**
örtlich local **III U1**, 15
Ost- east **I**
Osten east **I**
Ostern Easter **I**
Outdoor- outdoor **II**
Outfit outfit **II**

P

Paar pair **I**; couple **III U1**, 16
ein paar some; a few; a couple of **I**
Päckchen packet; parcel **I**
Packung packet **I**
Paket packet; parcel **I**
Palme palm tree **III U1**, 9
panisch werden to panic **II**
Papa dad **I**
Papier paper **I**
Stück **Papier** piece of paper **I**
Paradies paradise **II**
Paragraf section **II**
Park park **I**
Partei party **III U3**, 57
Partizip past participle **II**
Partner/-in partner **I**
Partnerarbeit pair work **II**
Party party **I**
passen to fit **II**
passen zu *to go with; to match **I**
zueinander **passen** *to go together **I**
passieren to happen **I**
Pasta pasta **I**
Pastete pie **I**
Pause break **II**; pause **III U2**, 32
PC PC *(= Personal Computer)* **II**
Pech haben *to be unlucky **I**
peinlich embarrassing **II**
Pence *(brit. Währungseinheit)* penny, pence *(pl)* **I**
Peng! Bang! **II**
Penicillin penicillin **III U3**, 60
Penny *(brit. Währungseinheit)* penny, pence *(pl)* **I**
perfekt perfect **I**
Periode period **III U3**, 57
Person person, people *(pl)* **I**
berühmte **Person** celebrity **III TS2**, 79
pro **Person** each **I**
persönlich personal **I**
hier: **persönlich** face-to-face **II**
Persönlichkeit personality **III U2**, 27
Perspektive perspective; point of view **II**
Pfandhaus pawn shop **III U4**, 99
Pfandleihe pawn shop **III U4**, 99
Pfeife pipe **II**
Pfeil arrow **III TS1**, 48
Pferd horse **I**
Pfirsich peach **III TS1**, 47
Pflanze plant **III U1**, 14
pflanzen to plant **II**
Pfund *(brit. Währungseinheit)* pound (£) **I**
Picknick picnic **I**
Pick-up pick-up **I**
Pier pier **I**
Pille pill **II**
Pilot/-in pilot **II**
pink pink **I**
Online-Pinnwand wall **III U2**, 39
Pizza pizza **I**
Placemat placemat **I**
Platzdeckchen placemat **I**
Plan plan **I**
planen to plan **I**
Planet planet **II**
Plattform platform **III U1**, 12
Platz place **I**; space; pitch **II**
Platz! *(Befehl für Hunde)* Sit! **I**
plaudern to chat **I**
plötzlich suddenly **I**
Plural plural **I**
Polen Poland **I**
Polizei police **II**
Polizeibeamter police officer **II**
Polizist/-in police officer **II**
Pommes frites chips *(pl) (BE)* **I**
Pony pony **I**
Ponyreiten im Gelände pony trekking **III U1**, 9
populär popular **I**
Porträt profile **I**
positiv positive **II**
Possessivform possessive form **I**
Post *(Eintrag im Internet)* post **I**
Poster poster **I**
Postkarte postcard **III U1**, 20
prägnant to the point **III AC3**, 83
praktisch practical **II**
Präposition preposition **I**
Präsens present **II**
Präsentation presentation **I**
präsentieren to present **I**
Praxis surgery **I**
Praxisräume surgery **I**
Preis price; prize **I**; award **II**
preiswert cheap **I**
pressen to press **II**
Privatdetektiv/-in private detective **III AC1**, 24
pro per **III U1**, 11
pro Person each **I**
pro Stück each **I**
probieren to try **I**; to taste **III U4**, 88
Probier mal … Try … **I**
Problem problem **I**
Probleme trouble **II**
produzieren to produce **III U3**, 57
Profil profile **I**
Profileinstellungen account settings **III U2**, 39
Programm programme **II**
Projekt project **I**
Prominente/-r celebrity **III TS2**, 79
Prosa fiction *(no pl)* **III TS3**, 106
Prospekt brochure **I**
Protest protest **III TS2**, 80
prüfen to check **I**; to check out *(coll)* **III AC3**, 82
Prüfung test **I**; exam **II**
Publikum audience **II**
Pudding pudding **I**
Punkt point **II**
Punktestand score **II**
pünktlich on time **II**
Puzzle puzzle **I**
Pyjama pyjamas *(pl)* **II**

Q

Qualifikation trial **II**
Qualität quality **I**
quer durch across **I**
Quiz quiz **I**

R

Rabe raven **II**
Herr der **Raben** raven master **II**
Rad wheel **I**
Radfahren cycling **I**
Radiergummi rubber **I**
Radio radio **II**
Rahmen setting **II**; set **III AC1**, 25
am Rande von on the brink of **III TS2**, 80
Rand- fringe **III U3**, 55
Rap rap **I**
rappen to rap **I**
Raster grid **I**
Rat advice **II**
raten to guess **I**
Ratespiel guessing game **II**
Ratschlag tip **I**; advice **II**
Rätsel puzzle; quiz **I**; mystery **III U4**, 96
Ratte rat **I**
Räuber/-in robber **III AC1**, 24
Rauch smoke **III TS3**, 107
Raum room **I**; space **II**
Raumschiff spaceship **II**
rauschen to roar **III TS3**, 109
reagieren to react **III U2**, 39
Reaktion reaction **II**
realisieren to realise **III U3**, 66
realistisch realistic **II**
recht haben *to be right **I**
rechte/-r/-s right **I**
rechthaberisch bossy **III U2**, 32
rechts on the right; right **I**

auf der **rechten** Seite on the right **I**
Rechtschreibung spelling **I**
rechtswidrig illegal **III TS2**, 80
Recycling recycling **II**
reden to talk **I**
reden mit to talk to **I**
Redensart saying **III U2**, 26
Redewendung phrase **I**
Redner/-in speaker **I**
Referendum referendum **III U3**, 55
Referenzartikel reference article **III TS2**, 76
Regel rule **I**
Was ist die **Regel** für ...? What's the rule for ...? **I**
regelmäßig regular **I**
Regenbogen rainbow **III TS1**, 47
Regenmantel raincoat **III U3**, 60
Regieanweisung stage direction **III AC3**, 83
regieren to rule **III U1**, 16; to reign **III U4**, 91
die **Regierenden** those in power **III TS2**, 80
Regierungszeit reign **III U4**, 90
Region region **II**
regnen to rain **II**
Reich empire **III U4**, 84
reich rich **III U2**, 28
die **Reichen** the rich **III AC1**, 25
Reihenfolge order **I**
Reim rhyme **I**
(sich) **reimen** to rhyme **III TS1**, 46
rein in **I**
reinigen to clean **I**
Reise trip; travel **II**; journey **III U1**, 9
Reisebericht travel report **II**
Reisebüro travel agent's **III U1**, 11; travel agency **III U3**, 65
Reisebus coach **II**
Reiseführer guide **II**
(das) **Reisen** travel **II**
reisen to travel **II**
Relativpronomen relative pronoun **II**
notwendiger **Relativsatz** defining relative clause **II**
Religion *(Schulfach)* RE *(= Religious Education)* **II**
religiös religious **I**
Rennen race; running; run **II**
rennen *to run **I**
reparieren to fix **II**
Reporter/-in reporter **II**
Requisite prop **III AC1**, 25
reservieren to book **III U1**, 12
der **Rest** the rest **I**
Restaurant restaurant **I**
Resultat result **II**
retten to save **I**; to rescue **III TS2**, 79
Rettung rescue **II**
Rettungsboot lifeboat **I**
Rettungsring lifebuoy **I**
Rezept recipe **III TS2**, 76
Rezept *(für Arzneimittel)* prescription **II**
Rhinozeros rhino **III TS2**, 80
Rhythmus rhythm **I**
richtig correct; right **I**; real **II**
Richtung direction **I**
in **Richtung** towards **II**
riechen *to smell **III U4**, 85
riesengroß huge **II**
riesig huge; large **II**
Ring circle **I**; ring **III U4**, 84
Ritter knight **III AC1**, 24
Rock skirt **III U1**, 18
Rock *(Musik)* rock **III U3**, 66
Rock 'n' Roll rock 'n' roll **II**
Rohr pipe **II**
Rohrleitung pipe **II**
Rolle role **I**; part **III U2**, 28
Rollen tauschen to swap roles **I**
Rollenkarte prompt card **II**
Rollenspiel role play **I**
Rollschuhe skates *(pl)* **I**
Rollstuhl wheelchair **II**
Rolltreppe escalator **I**
Römer/-in Roman **II**
römisch Roman **II**
rosa pink **I**
rot red **I**
Route route **II**
Rückblende flashback **III U4**, 98
Rücken an Rücken back to back **I**
Rückenschmerzen backache **II**
Rückenweh backache **II**
Hin- und **Rückfahrkarte** return ticket **III U1**, 12
Rückmeldung feedback **II**
Rucksack backpack **III U3**, 56
rufen to shout; to call **I**; to cry **II**
Rugby rugby **II**
Ruhe silence *(no pl)* **III TS3**, 109
ruhig quiet **I**; silent **III TS3**, 107
die Beine und Hände **ruhig** halten *to keep one's feet or hands still **III TS1**, 50
Rühr- sponge **I**
ruinieren to ruin **II**
Rumäne/Rumänin Romanian **II**
Rumänisch Romanian **II**
rumänisch Romanian **II**
rumhängen (mit) *to hang out (with) *(infml)* **III U2**, 36
Runde round **II**
Rundgang tour **II**
Rutschbahn slide **I**

S

Saal hall **II**
Sache thing **I**
Saft juice **I**
Sage legend **III AC1**, 24
sagen *to say; *to tell **I**
Sahne cream **I**
Salat salad **I**
Salbe ointment **II**
sammeln to collect **I**
Geld **sammeln** to raise money **II**
Sammlung collection **II**
Samstag Saturday **I**
Sand- sandy **III U1**, 9
Sandale sandal **III U4**, 86
sandig sandy **III U1**, 9
Sandwich sandwich **I**
Sänger/-in singer **II**
Sanitärarbeit plumbing **III U1**, 19
Satz phrase; sentence **I**
Satzgegenstand subject **II**
Satzstellung word order **I**
sauber clean **III TS2**, 77
säubern to clean **I**
sauer sein (auf) *to be fed up (with) **III U2**, 36
Säugling baby **I**
Saxofon saxophone; sax **I**
scannen to scan **II**
Schach chess **II**
Schachtel box **I**
Schade! Too bad! **I**
Schaf sheep, sheep *(pl)* **II**
schaffen to create **I**
Du **schaffst** es! You can do it! **III TS1**, 50
Wir haben es **geschafft**! We did it! **II**
Schälchen bowl **I**
Schale bowl **I**
Schalter switch **III U3**, 69
scharf sharp **III TS3**, 108
Schatten shadow **III TS3**, 107
Schatz treasure **II**
Schau show **II**
schauen to look **I**
Schau/Schaut mal! Look! **I**
Schau(t) genau ... Look closely ... **II**
Schauplatz setting; scene **II**
Schauspieler actor **II**
in **Scheiben** schneiden to slice **I**
scheinen *to shine **II**; to seem **III U2**, 35
schenken *to give **I**
scherzen to joke **II**
Schicht (aus) layer (of) **III TS2**, 77
schicken *to send **I**
schieben to push **II**
Schiedsrichter/-in official **II**
jmdn. **schief** anschauen *to give sb funny looks **III U2**, 32
schiefgehen *to go wrong **I**
schießen to kick **II**
schießen (auf) *to shoot **III TS1**, 48
Schiff ship **I**
Schiffsbau shipbuilding **III U3**, 59
Schiffsjunge cabin boy **I**
Schiffsoffizier mate **I**
Schild sign **II**

Schinken ham **III AC2**, 52
Schinkenspeck bacon **I**
Schlacht battle **III U4**, 88
Schlafanzug pyjamas *(pl)* **II**
schlafen *to sleep **I**; *to be asleep **II**
Schlafzimmer bedroom **I**
schlagen *to hit; to whip **I**; *to beat **II**
Schläger racquet **II**
Schlagzeile headline **III TS2**, 76
Schlagzeug drums *(pl)* **III U3**, 58
Schlamm mud **II**
schlammig muddy **II**
Schlange queue **I**
schlau clever **II**; smart **III U2**, 27
schlecht bad **I**
der/die/das **schlechteste** the worst **II**
sich **schlecht** fühlen *to feel sick **II**
schließen to close **I**
Schließfach locker **I**
schließlich at last; after all **I**; in the end; finally **II**
schlimm *(ugs.)* bad **I**
der/die/das **schlimmste** the worst **II**
Schlittschuh laufen to skate **I**
Schlittschuhbahn ice rink **I**
Schlittschuhe skates *(pl)* **I**
Schloss castle **II**
Schluchtenklettern gorge scrambling **II**
Schluss end **I**
zum **Schluss** in the end; finally **II**
Schluss *(einer Geschichte)* ending **I**
Schlüssel key **II**
Schlüsselanhänger key ring **III U3**, 67
Schlüsselbegriff key word **I**
Schlüsselbund key ring **III U3**, 67
schmal narrow **III U3**, 61
schmaler Durchgang close **III U3**, 61
schmecken to taste **III U4**, 88
Schmerz pain **II**
Schmuck jewellery; decorations *(pl)* **I**
schmücken to decorate **I**
Schmutz dirt **III U4**, 92
schmutzig dirty **II**
Schnäppchen bargain **I**
schnappen to grab **II**
schnarchen to snore **I**
Schnee snow **III U4**, 90
schneiden *to cut (off) **II**
in Scheiben **schneiden** to slice **I**
schneidend sharp **III TS3**, 108
schnell fast; quick **I**
schnell quickly **II**
Schock shock **II**
Schokolade chocolate **I**
schön nice; fine **I**; beautiful **II**
schon already **I**; yet **II**
schon einmal before **II**
Schornstein chimney **III U1**, 18
Schotte/**Schottin** Scot **III U3**, 60
Schottenkaro *(bestimmtes Muster eines Clans)* tartan **III U3**, 55
Schottenrock kilt **III U3**, 55
karierter **Schottenstoff** tartan **III U3**, 55
schottisch Scottish **III U1**, 9
Schrank cupboard **I**
schrecklich awful **I**
Schreiben writing **I**
schreiben *to write **I**
schreien to shout **I**; to scream; to cry **II**
Schritt step **I**
Schritt halten (mit) *to keep up (with) **II**
Schritt-für-**Schritt**- step-by-step **II**
Stück **Schrott** piece of junk **III U2**, 37
schubsen to push **II**
schüchtern shy **II**
Schuh shoe **I**
Schule school **I**
Schüler/-in student **I**
Schüleraustausch student exchange **III AC3**, 83
Schulfach subject **II**
Schulgebühren school fees *(pl)* **III U4**, 99
Schulgeld school fees *(pl)* **III U4**, 99
Schuljahr year **I**
Schulklasse class **I**
Schulstunde lesson **I**
Schultasche schoolbag **I**
Schulter shoulder **II**
Schüssel bowl **I**
schütten to pour **I**
Schwanz tail **I**
schwarz black **I**
schwarz werden *to go black **II**
schwarzes Brett noticeboard **II**
Schweif tail **I**
Schweigen silence *(no pl)* **III TS3**, 109
schweigsam silent **III TS3**, 107
Schwein pig **I**
schwer hard **II**; heavy **III U3**, 67
Schwerpunkt focus **III TS3**, 110
Schwester sister **I**
schwierig hard; difficult **II**
Schwierigkeit problem **I**
Schwierigkeiten trouble **II**
in **Schwierigkeiten** bringen *to make trouble **I**
Schwimmbecken swimming pool **III TS3**, 109
Schwimmen swimming **I**
Schwimmen gehen *to go swimming **I**
schwimmen *to swim **I**
Science-Fiction *(Zukunftsdichtung)* science fiction **II**
sechs six **I**
Vier plus **sechs** ist zehn. Four and six is ten. **I**
Second-Hand-Laden charity shop **I**
See lake **I**
See zum Rudern boating lake **I**
Seemann sailor **I**
die **Segel** einholen to reef the sails **I**
Segelboot sailboat **III U1**, 20
segeln to sail **III TS1**, 49
sehbehindert partially sighted **II**
sehen *to see; to look **I**
Sehenswürdigkeit sight; attraction **II**
sehr very; very much **I**
Sehr geehrte Dame, **sehr** geehrter Herr Dear Sir or Madam **III U1**, 13
Hör-/**Sehverstehen** viewing **I**
Seil rope **III U3**, 67
sein *to be **I**; *to be like **III U3**, 54
Sei/**Seid** höflich. Be polite. **I**
sein/-e his; its **I**
seit for *(+ Zeitraum)* **III U3**, 56
seit since *(+ Zeitpunkt)* **III U3**, 56
seitdem since *(+ Zeitpunkt)* **III U3**, 56
Seite page **I**; side **II**
auf der anderen **Seite** von across; opposite **I**
selber yourself **I**; himself; myself **II**; yourselves **III U1**, 13
das **Selbst** self self, selves selvz *(pl)* **III U2**, 27
selbst even **I**
du/dir/dich/Sie/sich (**selbst**) yourself **I**
ihr/euch/Sie/sich (**selbst**) yourselves **III U1**, 13
er/sich (**selbst**) himself **II**
ich/mir/mich (**selbst**) myself **II**
selbstbewusst confident **II**
Selbsteinschätzung self-evaluation **I**
selbstkritisch self-critical **II**
selbstsicher confident **II**
selbstverständlich of course **I**
Selfie selfie **II**
seltsam strange **I**; weird **II**
senden *to send **I**
Sender station **II**
Sendung programme **II**
separat separate **II**
September September **I**
Serie series, series *(pl)* **III TS3**, 106
Sessel chair **I**
setzen *to put **I**
sich **setzen** *to sit down **I**
Shinty *(eine Art Hockey)* shinty **III U3**, 57
Shorts shorts *(pl)* **II**
Show show **II**
Comedy **Show** comedy show **II**
sich each other **I**
sicher sure **I**; safe **II**
Ich bin mir (nicht) **sicher** … I'm (not) sure … **III AC2**, 53
Sicht view **II**
Sie you; u *(= you)* **I**
Sie sind … You're … **I**
sie her; she **I**
sie *(Pl.)* they; them **I**
sieben seven **I**
siegen *to win **I**
Sieger/-in winner **I**; champion **III TS1**, 50

Sightseeing- sightseeing **II**
Signal signal **III U3**, 66
Signalwort signal word **I**
Silber silver **II**
simpel simple **III TS1**, 48
singen *to sing **I**
Ich **singe** und tanze gern. I like singing and dancing. **I**
sinken *to sink **III TS3**, 109
Sinn meaning **II**; sense **III TS3**, 108
jmdm. in den **Sinn** kommen *to rise up in one's mind **III TS3**, 109
Sinn für Humor sense of humour *(no pl)* **III U2**, 39
Situation situation **I**
Sitzbank bench **III U2**, 39
Sitz! *(Befehl für Hunde)* Sit! **I**
sitzen *to sit **I**
sich gegenüber **sitzen** *to sit face to face **I**
Skateboard skateboard **II**
Skateboardfahren skateboarding **I**
Sklave/Sklavin slave **III U4**, 90
Skript script **III AC3**, 83
Slogan slogan **II**
Smalltalk small talk **III AC3**, 82
Smartphone smartphone **II**
SMS text (message) **I**
eine **SMS** schicken to text **II**
Snack snack **I**
so like this; so; like that **I**; that's how **II**
so oft whenever **II**
so ... wie as ... as **I**
so viel that much **III AC2**, 53
so früh this early **III AC2**, 53
sobald as soon as **II**
Sofa sofa **I**
sofort right away **I**; right now **II**
sogar even **I**
Sohn son **III U3**, 56
solch such **II**
solche/-r/-s such **II**
Soldat/-in soldier **III U3**, 58
sollte should **II**
sollte(n) nicht shouldn't **II**
sollten should **II**
solltest should **II**
solltet should **II**
Sommer summer **II**
Sommerferienlager summer camp **II**
Sonderangebot special offer **I**
sonderbar weird **II**
Song song **I**
Sonne sun **II**
Sonnenblume sunflower **III TS1**, 47
Sonntag Sunday **I**
sonst noch else **III U2**, 35
Sonst noch etwas? Anything else? **I**
Keine **Sorge**! Don't worry! **I**
sich **Sorgen** machen to worry **II**
für jmdn. **sorgen** *to take care of sb **III U4**, 96
sorgfältig careful **II**
Sorte kind **I**
Soße sauce **III U3**, 60
Souvenir souvenir **II**
sowieso anyway **II**
soziales Netzwerk social network **II**
Sozialwissenschaften Humanities *(pl)* **II**
Spalt gap **I**
die **Spanier** Spanish **III U4**, 86
Spanisch Spanish **III U4**, 86
spanisch Spanish **III U4**, 86
spannend exciting **I**
sparen to save **III U2**, 29
Spaß fun **I**
Spaß haben *to have fun **I**; to enjoy oneself **III U2**, 32
Es macht **Spaß**. It's fun. **I**
spät late **I**
zu **spät** late **I**
zu **spät** kommen *to be late **I**
Wie **spät** ist es? What's the time? **I**
zu **spät** dran sein *to be late **I**
kleiner **Spaten** trowel **II**
später later **I**
spazieren gehen *to go for a walk **II**
mit dem Hund **spazieren** gehen to walk the dog **I**
Speck bacon **I**
Speer spear **III U1**, 18
spektakulär spectacular **III U3**, 64
sperren to ban **III U3**, 60
speziell special **I**
Spiegel mirror **III U4**, 86
Spiel game **I**; match **II**
spielen to play **I**
einen Streich **spielen** to play a trick (on) **I**
spielen *(Theater)* to act **I**
eine Theaterszene **spielen** acting a scene **I**
Spieler/-in player **II**
technische **Spielerei** gadget **III U2**, 35
Spielfeld field; court; pitch **II**
Spielkarte card **I**
Spielstand score **II**
Spielzeug toy **I**
Spind locker **I**
Spinne spider **III U3**, 68
Spinnennetz web **III U3**, 68
Spitze top **I**
Sport sport **I**
... ist ein toller **Sport**. ... is a great sport. **I**
Sportart sport **I**
Sportunterricht PE *(= Physical Education)* **II**
Sprache language **I**
Sprachmittlung mediation **I**
Sprechblase speech bubble **I**
Sprechen speaking; talking **I**
sprechen *to say; to talk; *to speak **I**
sprechen über to talk about ... **I**
Sprecher/-in speaker **I**; talker **III AC3**, 82
Sprechgesang chant **II**
Sprichwort saying **III U2**, 26
springen to jump **I**; to bounce **III AC3**, 82
Spur clue **II**
Staatsoberhaupt head of state **II**
Stadion stadium **II**
Stadt city; town **I**
Stadtplan map **I**
Stadtteil part **I**
Stamm tribe **III U4**, 84
Stammbaum family tree **I**
Standbild still **II**
ständig always **I**
Standort location **II**
Standpunkt point of view **II**
Star star **I**
hier: **stark** hard **II**
stark strong **II**; powerful **III AC1**, 24; heavy **III U3**, 67
Stärke power **III AC1**, 24
starren to stare **I**
Start start **III U4**, 99
starten to start **I**
Startpunkt starting place **III U1**, 12
Station station **I**
stattdessen instead **III U2**, 36
stattfinden *to take place **I**
Steak steak **I**
stechen *to sting **III TS3**, 109
mitten in **stecken** stuck in the middle of ... **III TS1**, 49
stehen *to stand **I**
stehen auf *to be into **I**
Du **stehst** auf ... You're into ... **I**
stehlen *to steal **II**
steigen to climb **I**; *to rise **III TS3**, 109
Stein stone **III U3**, 66
Stein- stone **III U3**, 66
steinig rocky **III U1**, 9
Stelle place **I**
an Jays **Stelle** in Jay's shoes **III U2**, 30
an jmds. **Stelle** sein *to be in sb's shoes **III TS3**, 108
stellen *to put **I**
online **stellen** to post **II**
Stelle/Stellt es in ... Put it in ... **I**
sterben to die **III TS1**, 50
Stern star **I**
Steuer wheel **I**
Steuerrad wheel **I**
Stichwort key word **I**
Stichwortkarte prompt card **II**
Stiefel boot **III U4**, 86
Stiefmutter stepmum **I**
still quiet; still **I**; silent **III TS3**, 107
Stille silence *(no pl)* **III TS3**, 109
Stimme voice **I**

Stimmung mood; atmosphere **II**; humour *(no pl)* **III U3**, 64
stolz (auf) proud (of) **II**
stoppen to stop **I**
stören *to get in the way **II**
Story story, stories *(pl)* **I**
stoßen to push **II**
Stoßzahn tusk **III TS2**, 80
Strand beach **II**
Straße road **II**
Straße *(in der Stadt)* street **I**
auf der **Straße** in the street **I**
in der **Straße** in the street **I**
Strecke route **II**
Streich trick **I**
einen **Streich** spielen to play a trick (on) **I**
Streit fight **II**; argument **III U2**, 36
(sich) **streiten** *to fight **II**
streng strict **III TS3**, 108
streng mit jmdm. sein *to be hard on sb **III U2**, 33
strikt strict **III TS3**, 108
Strom electricity **III U1**, 18
Stromausfall power cut **II**
Stück piece **I**
pro **Stück** each **I**
Stück Papier piece of paper **I**
Stück Schrott piece of junk **III U2**, 37
Student/-in student **I**
Studie survey **I**
studieren to study **III U2**, 28
Studium studies *(pl)* **II**
Stufe step **I**
Stuhl chair **I**
stumm silent **III TS3**, 107
Stunde hour **II**
eine halbe **Stunde** half an hour **III U4**, 97
Stundenplan timetable **I**
Sturm storm **I**
stürzen *to fall down **III TS1**, 50
Such- search **II**
Suche search **II**
suchen nach to look for **I**
Süd- south **II**
Süden south **II**
Südkoreaner/-in South Korean **II**
Südkoreanisch South Korean **II**
südkoreanisch South Korean **II**
summen to hum **II**
super great; cool **I**
Es ist **super** zum/für … It's great for … **I**
Superlativ superlative **II**
Supermacht superpower **II**
Supermarkt supermarket **I**
Surfen surfing **III U1**, 9
süß cute; sweet **I**
Süßigkeiten sweets *(pl)* **I**
Swimmingpool swimming pool **III TS3**, 109
Symbol symbol **II**
Szene scene **I**; in-crowd **III U2**, 36

T

Tabak tobacco *(no pl)* **III U4**, 88
Tabelle grid **I**
Tablet tablet **II**
Tablette pill **II**
Taekwondo taekwondo **II**
Tafel board **III TS1**, 46
die **Tafelrunde** the Round Table **III AC1**, 25
Tag day **I**
am nächsten **Tag** the next day **II**
den ganzen **Tag** all day **II**
ein **Tag** in … a day out in … **II**
eines **Tages** one day **II**
Tagebuch diary **III U1**, 20
Tagebucheintrag diary entry **III U1**, 20
Takelage rigging **I**
Talent talent **I**
Talentwettbewerb talent show **I**
Talisman lucky charm **I**
Tante aunt **I**
Tanz dance **III U2**, 28
tanzen to dance **I**
tanzen zu to dance to **III TS1**, 50
Ich singe und **tanze** gern. I like singing and dancing. **I**
Tänzer/-in dancer **II**
Tanzveranstaltung dance **III U2**, 28
tapfer brave **I**
Tasche bag **I**; pocket **III U3**, 66
Taschengeld pocket money **I**
Taschenlampe torch **II**
Tasse cup **III AC2**, 52
Tätowierung tattoo **III U2**, 34
Tatsache fact **II**
Tatsachenbericht news report **III TS2**, 76
Tattoo tattoo **III U2**, 34
Rollen **tauschen** to swap roles **I**
tausende (von) thousands of **I**
Taxi taxi **II**
Team team **II**
Technik Technology **II**
technische Spielerei gadget **III U2**, 35
Technologie technology **II**
Tee tea **I**
Teebeutel tea bag **III U4**, 99
Teenager teenager **I**; teen **III TS3**, 106
Teich pond **II**
Teil part **I**
im hinteren **Teil** at the back of **II**
teilen to share **II**
teilnehmen to participate **II**
teilnehmen (an) *to take part (in) **II**
Telefon phone; telephone **I**
Telefon mit Wählscheibe rotary phone **III U3**, 69
Telefonanruf phone call **I**
Teller plate **III AC2**, 52
Tennis tennis **I**
Teppich carpet **II**
Test test **I**
einen **Test** machen *to take a test **II**
teuer expensive **I**
Text text **I**
Theater theatre **I**; drama **II**
Theaterstück play **III U4**, 86
eine **Theaterszene** spielen acting a scene **I**
Thema theme **I**; topic **II**; subject **III U2**, 27
Therme baths *(pl)* **III U4**, 84
Ticket ticket **I**
tief deep **III U1**, 9
Tier animal **I**
Tierarzt/**Tierärztin** vet **I**
Tierheim animal shelter **III TS2**, 79
Tierpark zoo **II**
Tierwelt *(in freier Wildbahn)* wildlife **II**
Tipp tip **I**; hint **III AC3**, 83
Tisch table **I**
Titel heading **I**; title **II**
Titelblatt cover **III U2**, 26
tja well **I**
Toast toast **I**
Tochter daughter **III U4**, 86
Tod death **III TS3**, 106
Toilette toilet **I**
toll great **I**; amazing **II**
… ist ein **toller** Sport. … is a great sport. **I**
Tomate tomato, tomatoes *(pl)* **I**
Tombola raffle **I**
Ton sound **I**
Tonmodell model **I**
Tonpfeife clay pipe **II**
Tonstudio recording studio **I**
Tor goal **I**
Torte cake **I**
Tortenguss jelly **I**
tosend roaring **III TS3**, 109
tot dead **II**
töten to kill **III TS2**, 80
Tour tour **II**
Tourismus tourism **III U1**, 14
Tourist/-in tourist **I**
Touristeninformation tourist information centre **I**; tourist board **III U1**, 13
Tradition tradition **I**
traditionell traditional **III U3**, 54
tragen to carry **III AC1**, 25
tragen *(Kleidung)* *to wear **I**
Trainer/-in coach **I**
trainieren to practise **I**; to train **II**
Training training **II**; practice **III U2**, 26
Training für den Mund mouth jogging **I**
Transport transport **III U1**, 10
Er **traute** seinen Augen nicht. He couldn't believe his eyes. **II**

Traum dream **II**
Traum- fantasy **I**
traurig sad **I**
treffen *to meet; *to hit **I**
sich auf halbem Weg **treffen** *to meet halfway **III U2**, 34
sich **treffen** *to meet **I**
sich **treffen** (mit) *to hang out (with) *(infml)* **III U2**, 36
treffend to the point **III AC3**, 83
Treppe stairs *(pl)* **III U3**, 66
treten to kick **II**
Trick trick **I**
Trifle *(englischer Nachtisch)* trifle **I**
trinken *to drink **I**
Trip trip **II**
trocken dry **III TS2**, 77
trotzdem anyway **II**
Tschüss! Bye! **II**
T-Shirt T-shirt **I**
Tudor- Tudor **III U4**, 86
tun *to do; *to make **I**
tun als ob to act like **II**
Tunnel tunnel **I**
Tür door **I**
Türklingel doorbell **III U2**, 32
Turm tower **III U3**, 66
Turnier competition **II**
Turnschuh trainer **III U2**, 36
Turteltauben lovebirds *(pl)* **II**
Tüte bag **I**
Typ guy **II**
Typ *(ugs.)* bloke *(fam)* **III U2**, 36
typisch typical **I**
typisch typically **III U3**, 55

U

U-Bahn underground **II**
die Londoner **U-Bahn** the Tube **II**
Übelkeit verspüren *to feel sick **II**
Üben practising **I**
üben to practise **I**
über about; over; across **I**
über Nacht overnight **III U2**, 37
überall everywhere **I**
überall (in) all over **I**
überall (egal, wo) anywhere **II**
überfallen to invade **III U4**, 88
überfliegen to skim **II**
überhaupt at all **I**
überleben to survive **III TS1**, 50
übernachten to stay **III U1**, 10
Übernachtung sleepover **I**
überprüfen to check **I**
überqueren to cross **II**
überraschen to surprise **II**
überraschend surprising **II**
überrascht sein *to be surprised **II**
Überraschung surprise **I**
überreagieren to overreact **II**
überreden to persuade **II**
Überschrift heading **I**; title **II**
übersetzen to translate **I**
Übersetze/Übersetzt nicht … Don't translate … **I**
Übersetzung translation **I**
überzeugen to convince **II**
üblich usual **III U2**, 37
übrig left **I**
Übung exercise **I**; practice **III U2**, 26
Übungsheft exercise book **I**
Ufer bank; shore **II**
UFO UFO **II**
Uhr clock **I**
Um wie viel **Uhr**? What time? **I**
Wie viel **Uhr** ist es? What's the time? **I**
Uhr *(Zeitangabe bei vollen Stunden)* o'clock **I**
um *(bei Uhrzeitangaben)* at **I**
um halb acht at 7:30 **I**
um … herum around **I**; round **II**
Um wie viel Uhr? What time? **I**
umarmen to hug **I**
umbringen to kill **III TS2**, 80
(sich) **umdrehen** to turn round **II**; to turn **III TS3**, 107
Umfrage survey **I**
Umgebung environment **III U1**, 14; set **III AC1**, 25
umgehen mit *to deal (with) **II**
umher around **I**
umkehren to turn back **II**
umkippen *to fall over **I**
sich **umschauen** to explore **I**
umsegeln to sail **III TS1**, 49
umsteigen (in) to change (onto) **II**
Umwelt environment **III U1**, 14
umziehen to move (house) **III U1**, 10
unabhängig independent **III U3**, 55
Unabhängigkeit freedom *(no pl)* **III U2**, 36; independence *(no pl)* **III U3**, 55
unbekannt unfamiliar **III AC2**, 52
und and **I**
unfair unfair **II**
Unfall accident **II**
unfreundlich unfriendly **II**
ungefähr about **I**
ungefährlich safe **II**
Ungeheuer monster **I**
ungehorsam sein to disobey **III TS3**, 107
unglaublich amazing **II**
Unglück disaster **II**
unheimlich scary **II**
unhöflich rude **I**; impolite **III AC2**, 53
Uniform uniform **I**
unordentlich messy **III U2**, 32
unrecht haben *to be wrong **I**
nicht ganz **unrecht** haben *to have a point **III U2**, 34
unrechtmäßig illegal **III TS2**, 80
unregelmäßig irregular **I**
uns us **I**
unscharf out of focus **III U4**, 97
unser/-e our **I**
unten below **I**; downstairs **II**
nach **unten** down **II**
nach **unten** gehen *to go down **I**
unter under **I**
untergehen *to sink **III TS3**, 109
im **Untergeschoss** downstairs **II**
unterhalb below **I**
Unterhaltung conversation **I**; entertainment *(no pl)* **III U4**, 91
Unternehmen company **III U2**, 29
unternehmen wegen *to do about **II**
hier: **Unterricht** class **II**
Unterricht lesson **I**
unterrichten *to teach **II**
Unterrichtsstunde lesson **I**
Unterschied difference **I**
unterschiedlich different **I**
unterwegs out and about **II**
unverschämt rude **I**
unwohl sick **II**
Urlaub holiday **I**
Seid ihr im **Urlaub**? Are you on holiday? **I**
Sind Sie im **Urlaub**? Are you on holiday? **I**
ursprünglich originally **II**
usw. *(= und so weiter)* etc. *(= et cetera)* **II**

V

Vanillepudding custard **I**
Vanillesoße custard **I**
Vater father **I**
Vegetarier/-in vegetarian **III U3**, 59
vegetarisch vegetarian **III U3**, 60
Veränderung change **III U1**, 19
Veranstaltung event **I**
die **Verantwortung** tragen (für) *to be in charge (of) **III U2**, 32
jmdn. **verärgern** *to make sb angry **III AC2**, 53
verärgert angry **I**
Verb verb **I**
verbessern to improve **I**
sich **verbessern** to improve **I**
verbieten to ban **III U3**, 60
verbinden *to put through **I**; to join; to link **II**
Verbindung link **II**; connection **III U1**, 12
Verbrechen crime **III AC1**, 24
Verbrecher/-in criminal **III AC1**, 24
verbrennen *to burn **III U4**, 91
verbringen *(Zeit)* *to spend **II**
verdienen to earn **I**; to deserve **II**
Geld **verdienen** *to make money **I**
die Augen **verdrehen** to roll one's eyes **III U4**, 96

Verein club **I**; society **III U1**, 19
Verfasser/-in writer **III U4**, 88
verfolgen to trace **I**
Vergangenheit past **II**
Vergangenheitsform simple past; past form **II**
vergeben *to forgive **II**
vergessen *to forget **I**
Vergleich comparison **II**
vergleichen (mit) to compare (with/to) **I**
verhaften to arrest **II**
sich **verhalten** to behave **III U2**, 32
sich **verirren** *to get lost **III U1**, 21
Verkauf sale **II**
verkaufen *to sell **I**
Verkäufer/-in assistant **II**
Verkäufer/-in *(auf einem Flohmarkt)* seller **I**
Verkehrsmittel transport **III U1**, 10
öffentliche **Verkehrsmittel** public transport *(no pl)* **II**
Verkleidung fancy dress **II**
verlassen *to leave **II**
sich **verlassen** (auf) to rely (on) **III U2**, 28
verlegen embarrassed **II**
verleihen *to lend **III U2**, 37
verletzen *to hurt **II**
verletzt hurt **II**; wounded **III U3**, 66
Verletzung injury **II**
verlieren *to lose **II**
verloren gehen *to get lost **III U1**, 21
vermeiden to avoid **III TS2**, 77
vermieten to rent (out) **III U3**, 65
vermischen to mix (up) **III U4**, 96
vermissen to miss **III U1**, 10
vermuten to guess **I**
verneint negative **III U1**, 8
verneinte Form negative form **I**
Vernissage gallery walk **I**
Verpackung wrapping **I**
verpassen to miss **II**
verraucht smoky **III U4**, 84
sich den Knöchel **verrenken** to twist your ankle **II**
verrückt crazy **I**; mad **II**
verrückt werden *to go crazy **II**
Versammlung assembly **II**
versäumen to miss **II**
verschieden different **I**; separate **II**
verschiedene several **II**
Verschmutzung pollution **II**
verschwenden to waste **II**
verschwommen blurred **III U4**, 99
verschwunden missing **II**
verschwunden sein *to be gone **II**
sich **versichern** *to make sure **I**
versorgen to supply **III U1**, 16
versprechen to promise **III U1**, 11
Verstand mind **III TS3**, 109
sich **verständigen** to communicate **II**
Verständnis understanding **II**
(sich) **verstecken** *to hide **III AC1**, 24
verstehen *to understand **I**
versuchen to try **I**
Versuch es mal mit … Try … **I**
vertrauen to trust **III U2**, 36
vertrauen (auf) to rely (on) **III U2**, 28
nicht **vertraut** unfamiliar **III AC2**, 52
verursachen to cause **II**
Vervollständige/Vervollständigt … Complete … **I**
verwenden to use **I**
verwirrt confused **III U2**, 38
verwischt blurred **III U4**, 99
verwundet wounded **III U3**, 66
verzeihen *to forgive **II**
verzieren to decorate **I**
Video video **II**
Videochat video chat **II**
viel much **I**
so **viel** that much **III AC2**, 53
viel/-e lots (of); a lot of **I**
Viele Grüße Best wishes **III U1**, 13
viel a lot **I**
viel zu lernen a lot to learn **I**
viele many **I**
vielleicht maybe **I**; perhaps **III U3**, 66
Vielvölker- multi-ethnic **II**
vier four **I**
Vier plus sechs ist zehn. Four and six is ten. **I**
Viertel nach/vor quarter past/to **I**
Viktorianer/-in Victorian **III U4**, 87
viktorianisch Victorian **III U4**, 87
violett purple **I**
Vitamin vitamin **III U4**, 99
Vogel bird **II**
Vogelbeobachtung birdwatching **II**
Vokabular vocabulary **I**
Volksentscheid referendum **III U3**, 55
Volksstamm tribe **III U4**, 84
voll (von) full (of) **I**
Volleyball volleyball **I**
völlig absolutely **II**; completely **III AC1**, 24
vollkommen perfect **I**
von from; about; of **I**; by **III U3**, 60
von … bis from … to **I**
vor in front of **I**
vor dem Lesen pre-reading **I**
vor *(bei Uhrzeitangaben)* to **I**
vor *(zeitlich)* before **I**; ago **II**
vorbei over **II**
vorbei (an) past **I**
vorbereiten to prepare **I**
sich **vordrängeln** to jump the queue **I**
vorgeschichtlich prehistoric **III U1**, 14
vorhaben *to be up to **II**
vorher before **II**
laut **vorlesen** *to sing out loud **III TS1**, 47
Vormittag morning **I**
vormittags in the mornings **I**
vormittags *(Uhrzeit)* a.m. **I**
Vorschlag suggestion **I**
Vorsicht! Be careful! **I**
vorsichtig careful **II**
Vorsingen audition **III U2**, 31
laut **vorsingen** *to sing out loud **III TS1**, 47
Vorsprechen audition **III U2**, 31
vorstellen to present **I**
sich (etwas) **vorstellen** to imagine **I**
Stelle/Stellt … **vor**. Introduce … **I**
Vorstellung introduction **II**
Vorstellungskraft imagination **III U2**, 27
Vortanzen audition **III U2**, 31
vortäuschen to fake **II**
Vortrag presentation **I**
vorüber over **II**
vorüber (an) past **I**
vorwärts forward **III U4**, 92

W

Wache guard **II**
Wachs wax **II**
wachsen *to grow **III U1**, 9
Wachsfigur wax figure **II**
Wächter/-in guard **II**
wackelig wobbly **II**
Wackelpudding jelly **I**
Waffe weapon **III U4**, 95
Wahl choice **II**
wählen to vote **I**; *to choose **II**
Telefon mit **Wählscheibe** rotary phone **III U3**, 69
wahr true **II**
während *(+ Nomen)* during *(+ noun)* **II**
während while; as **I**
wahrnehmen to notice **II**
wahrscheinlich probably **II**
Wald forest **II**; wood **III TS3**, 107
Wäldchen wood **III TS3**, 107
Waliser/-in Welsh **II**
Walisisch Welsh **II**
walisisch Welsh **II**
Wand wall **I**
Wandern walking **II**; hiking **III U1**, 9
Wanderweg walking trail **III U1**, 14
wann when **I**
wann immer whenever **II**
warm warm **III TS2**, 77
warten (auf) to wait (for) **I**
Warte/Wartet und denk/denkt nach. Stop and think **I**
Warte ab! Wait and see! **I**
Warteschlange queue **I**
warum why **I**
was what **I**
was für ein what **I**
Was fehlt? What is missing? **I**
Was für ein Glück! What luck! **III U4**, 92
Was geht ab? What's going on? **III U2**, 36

Was hast du? What's the matter? **III U1**, 18
Was ist das? What's that? **I**
Was ist dein/-e Lieblings...? What's your favourite ...? **I**
Was ist die Regel für ...? What's the rule for ...? **I**
Was ist los? What's the matter? **III U1**, 18; What's up? **III U2**, 32; What's going on? **III U2**, 36
Was ist mit ...? What about ...? **I**
was man ... what to ... **I**
was noch what else **I**
was sonst what else **I**
Was um alles in der Welt ...? What on earth ...? **II**
... **was** ich tun soll. ... what to do. **II**
waschen to wash **I**
sich **waschen** to wash **I**
Waschmaschine washing machine **II**
Wasser water **I**
Wasserrutsche water slide **I**
Wau! Woof! **I**
Webdesigner web designer **III U2**, 32
Webseite site **II**
Website website **I**
Wechsel change **III U1**, 19
wechseln to change **II**
Wechselt euch ab. Take turns. **I**
Wecker alarm clock **II**
Weg way **I**
im **Weg** sein/stehen *to be in the way **I**
im **Weg** stehen *to get in the way **II**
weg away **I**
weg sein *to be gone **II**
Es ist **weg**. It's gone. **II**
wegen because of; for **II**
wegfahren *to drive off **III U4**, 97
wegführen *to lead off **III U3**, 61
wegnehmen *to take **I**
wegrennen *to run away **I**
wegwerfen *to throw away **I**
weh tun *to hurt **II**
Weide field **II**
Weihnachten Christmas **I**
weil because **I**
eine **Weile** a while **II**
Wein wine **I**
weinen to cry **III TS1**, 49
auf andere **Weise** in other ways **II**
weiß white **I**
weit far **II**; wide **III U1**, 9
weiter (weg) further **III U3**, 64
weitere more; other **I**
weiterführen *to go on **I**
weitergeben to pass (on) **I**
weitergehen *to go on **I**
weitermachen *to go on **I**
welche/-r/-s what; which **I**
Welche Farbe hat ...? What colour is ...? **I**
Welche ... sind es? What are ...? **I**
Welle wave **I**
Welt world **I**
aus aller **Welt** from around the world **III U1**, 14
Was um alles in der **Welt** ...? What on earth ...? **II**
wem who **I**
wen who **I**
Für **wen** ...? Who ... for? **I**
wenden to turn round **II**
sich **wenden** an to turn to **III U1**, 19
Wendung expression **II**
wenige a few **I**; few **II**
weniger less **III U4**, 87
ein **wenig** a little **I**; a bit **II**
wenigstens at least **II**
wenn when; if **I**
wer who **I**
Wer ist dabei? Who's in? **II**
Wer ist es? Who is it? **I**
Wer macht mit? Who's in? **II**
Werbespot advert **III TS1**, 46
Werbespruch slogan **II**
werden *to become **II**; *to get **III U1**, 18
werden *(futurisch)* will **III U1**, 9
würde/-st/-n/-t would **III U2**, 27
werfen (nach) *to throw (at) **I**
Werk factory **III U4**, 87
Werkzeug tool **III U1**, 19
wert sein *to be worth **I**
das **Wesentliche** gist **II**
West- west **I**
Westen west **I**
im äußersten **Westen** in the far west **III U1**, 14
westeuropäische Zeit Greenwich Mean Time *(= GMT)* **I**
Wettbewerb contest **I**; competition **II**
in **Wettbewerb** treten (mit) to compete (with) **III U2**, 27
ich **wette** I bet **II**
Wetter weather **I**
Wettervorhersage weather forecast **III U1**, 12
Wettkampf contest **I**
Wettlauf race **II**
Whisky whisky **III U3**, 57
wichtig important **I**
wichtig nehmen to care (about) **II**
wie like **I**
wie as **II**
wie how **I**
Wie viele ...? How many ...? **I**
Wie alt bist du? How old are you? **I**
Wie alt sind Sie? How old are you? **I**
wie das ist what it's like **II**
wie der Mann aussah what the man looked like **II**
Wie geht es dir? How are you? **I**
Wie geht es euch? How are you? **I**
Wie geht es Ihnen? How are you? **I**
Wie heißen Sie? What's your name? **I**
Wie heißt du? What's your name? **I**
Wie man ... How to ... **I**
Wie spät ist es? What's the time? **I**
Wie viel (kostet/kosten) ...? How much is/are ...? **I**
Wie viel Uhr ist es? What's the time? **I**
Wie war es? What was it like? **III U4**, 84
Wie wär's mit ...? What about ...? **I**
wieder again **I**
Wiederaufbereitung recycling **II**
Wiederaufnehmen pick-up **I**
wiederholen to repeat **II**
Wiederholung revision **II**
auf **Wiedersehen** goodbye **I**
wiegen to weigh **III TS2**, 77
Wiese field **II**
wild wild **III U1**, 14
Wilderei poaching *(no pl)* **III TS2**, 80
Wildnis bush **III TS2**, 79
Willkommen! Welcome! **II**
willkommen heißen to welcome **II**
Wind wind **III U1**, 18
Windsurfen windsurfing **III U1**, 9
Winter winter **III TS2**, 77
Winterschlaf hibernation **III TS2**, 77
winzig tiny **III U3**, 64
wir we **I**
Wir sind aus ... We're from ... **I**
wirklich really **I**; real **II**
wirr confused **III U2**, 38
wissen *to know **I**
Du **weißt**, wie man ... You know how to ... **I**
Ich **weiß** (es) nicht! I don't know! **I**
Ihr **wisst**, wie man ... You know how to ... **I**
Wissenschaftler/-in scientist **III U3**, 60
Witz joke **I**
witzig funny; fun **I**
wo where **I**
Woche week **I**
Wochenende weekend **I**
am **Wochenende** at the weekend **I**
Wochentag weekday **II**
Woher ...? Where ... from? **I**
wohin where **I**
... **wohin** ich gehen kann. ... where to go. **II**
Wohlfahrt charity **I**
wohltätige Zwecke charity **I**
Wohltätigkeitsverein charity **I**
wohnen to live **I**
wohnen bei to stay with **II**
Wohnung flat **I**
Wohnzimmer living room **I**
Wolke cloud **III U1**, 18
wollen to want (to) **I**
Workshop workshop **I**
Wort word **I**

die Kraft der **Wörter** *(Wortschatzübung)* Word power **I**
Wortbildung word-building **II**
Wörterbuch dictionary **I**
Wörternetz *(eine Art Schaubild)* mind map **I**
Wörterwolke word cloud **II**
Wortschatz vocabulary **I**
Wortschlange word snake **I**
Wortspiel play on words **III TS1**, 50
Wortstellung word order **I**
Wortverbindung collocation **II**
Worum geht es in/im …? What is … about? **I**
Wow! Wow! **I**
wunderbar beautiful; wonderful **II**
Wunsch wish **I**
sich etwas **wünschen** *to make a wish **I**
Ich **würde** gern … I'd like to … *(= I would like to)* **I**
würde/-st/-n/-t gern would like **I**
würde/-st/-n/-t sehr gern would love **I**
Würfel dice **II**
würfle zweimal throw the dice twice **II**
Würfle/Würfelt mit zwei Würfeln. Roll two dice. **I**
Wurm worm **I**
Wurst sausage **III AC2**, 52
wusch whoosh **I**
Wut anger *(no pl)* **III U2**, 37
wütend angry **I**
jmdn. **wütend** machen *to make sb angry **III AC2**, 53

Z

z.B. *(= zum Beispiel)* e.g. *(= for example)* **I**
Zahl number **I**
zählen (auf) to count (on) **I**
Zauber- magical **III AC1**, 24
Zauberer wizard **III AC1**, 24
auf **Zehenspitzen** gehen to tiptoe **II**
zehn ten **I**
Vier plus sechs ist **zehn**. Four and six is ten. **I**
zehnmal ten times **I**
Zeichen sign **II**
Zeichentrickfilm cartoon **III AC3**, 82
zeichnen *to draw **I**
Zeichnung drawing **I**
zeigen to show **I**
Zeige/Zeigt auf … Point to … **I**
Zeige/Zeigt darauf. Point. **I**
Zeile line **I**
Zeit time **I**; tense **II**
(Zeit) brauchen *to take **II**
zur selben **Zeit** at the same time **I**
die ganze **Zeit** all the time **II**
Es ist **Zeit** aufzustehen! Time to get up! **I**
goldenes **Zeitalter** golden age **III U4**, 86
Zeitfenster time slot **II**
Zeitform *(grammatisch)* tense **II**
Zeitpunkt point **II**
Zeitschrift magazine **I**
Zeitspanne period **III U3**, 57
Zeitstrahl time line **I**
Zeitung newspaper **III TS2**, 77
Zelten camping **II**
zelten to camp **III U1**, 20
zentral central **II**
Zentral- central **II**
hier: **Zentrum** heart **II**
Zentrum centre **I**
zerbrechen *to break **I**
zerstören to ruin **II**
Zeug stuff **I**
Zeuge/Zeugin witness **II**
ziehen to pull **I**
Ziel goal **I**
Ziellinie finish line **II**
Zimmer room **I**
Zimmergenosse/Zimmergenossin roommate **I**
Zinn tin **III U1**, 18
Zitrone lemon **II**
zögern to hesitate **III TS3**, 107
Zoo zoo **II**
Zorn anger *(no pl)* **III U2**, 37
zornig angry **I**
zu too **I**
Zu dumm! Too bad! **I**
zu to **I**
zu Hause at home **I**
zubereiten to prepare **I**
züchten *to grow **III U4**, 85
Zucker sugar **III AC2**, 52
zuerst first **I**; at first **II**
Zug train **I**
Zuhause home **I**
zuhören to listen (to) **I**
Hör/Hört noch einmal **zu**. Listen again. **I**
Zuhörer/-in listener **II**
zujubeln to cheer **II**
Zukunft future **III U1**, 9
zum Beispiel for example **II**
zumachen to close **I**
zunächst at first **II**
hier: ein Feuerwerk **zünden** *to set off **III U3**, 60
zuordnen to match **I**
zupassen to pass **II**
(ein Foto) **zurechtschneiden** to crop (a photo) **III U4**, 97
zurück back **I**
zurückfahren to return **III U1**, 12
zurückgehen to turn back **II**
zurückgehen auf *to go right back to **III U1**, 18
zurückkehren to return **III U1**, 12
zurücklassen *to leave behind **III U3**, 61
hier: **zurückschrecken** to jump back **II**
zurückspringen to jump back **II**
zurzeit these days **III U2**, 36
zusammen together **I**
zusammenfassen to sum up **II**
in **Zusammenhang** stehen *to be connected **II**
zusammenhängen *to be connected **II**
zusammenstoßen to crash **III U4**, 97
zusätzlich extra **I**; additional **II**
zuschauen to watch **I**
Zuschauer/-in viewer **II**
zuspielen to pass **II**
zuständig sein (für) *to be in charge (of) **III U2**, 32
zustimmen to agree (with) **II**
Zutat ingredient **III AC1**, 24
zuvor before **II**
sich **zuwenden** to turn to **III U1**, 19
zwei two **I**
Zweifel doubt **III U2**, 27
zweisprachig bilingual **II**
zweite/-r/-s second **I**
Zwilling twin **III U1**, 19
Zwillings- twin **III U1**, 19
zwischen between **I**
zwölf twelve **I**

In the classroom

Tip

Die Wörter und Ausdrücke auf diesen Seiten musst du nicht auswendig lernen. Aber in vielen Situationen im Klassenzimmer wirst du sie nützlich finden!

Asking for help and information

Can you help me, please?	Kannst du / Können Sie mir bitte helfen?
How do you do this exercise?	Wie macht man diese Übung?
How do you spell …, please?	Wie schreibt man …, bitte?
Is this right? I'm not sure.	Ist das richtig? Ich bin mir nicht sicher.
Is it OK to …?	Ist es in Ordnung, wenn ich / wir …?
Is it true or false?	Ist das richtig oder falsch?
Sorry, I don't know. Ask …	Tut mir leid, das weiß ich nicht. Frag …
Sorry. Can you say that again, please?	Wie bitte? Können Sie das bitte wiederholen?
What does that mean?	Was bedeutet das?
What's for homework?	Was haben wir als Hausaufgabe auf?
What's that in English / German?	Was heißt das auf Englisch / Deutsch?

Vocabulary for instructions and activities

Act (out) one of the scenes. / Act (out) the dialogues.	Spiele eine der Szenen. / Spiele die Dialoge.
Add more words / ideas.	Füge weitere Wörter / Ideen hinzu.
Ask your partner questions.	Stelle deinem Partner / deiner Partnerin Fragen.
Answer your partner's questions.	Beantworte die Fragen deines Partners / deiner Partnerin.
Check your partner's text.	Überprüfe den Text deines Partners / deiner Partnerin.
Choose a character / one of the situations / options.	Wähle eine Figur / eine der Situationen/Optionen.
Collect ideas.	Sammle Ideen.
Compare English and German.	Vergleiche das Englische und Deutsche.
Complete the answers.	Vervollständige die Antworten.
Copy the grid / the mind map.	Schreibe die Tabelle / das Wörternetz ab.
Correct the wrong sentences.	Korrigiere die falschen Sätze.
Describe what you see / how it makes you feel.	Beschreibe, was du siehst / wie du dich dabei fühlst.
Decide who writes which part.	Entscheidet, wer welchen Teil schreibt.

Discuss different ideas.	Diskutiert verschiedene Ideen.
Divide your class up into two groups.	Teilt eure Klasse in zwei Gruppen auf.
Draw a picture.	Zeichne ein Bild.
Exchange your flyers / questions.	Tauscht eure Flyer / Fragen untereinander aus.
Explain your answer. / Explain why.	Erkläre deine Antwort. / Erkläre warum.
Fill in your grid / the form.	Fülle deine Tabelle / das Formular aus.
Find the rule / the right word order.	Finde die Regel / die richtige Wortstellung.
Finish your brochure.	Stelle deine Broschüre fertig.
Form expert groups.	Bildet Expertengruppen.
Get organised.	Organisiert euch.
Give reasons. / Give examples / feedback.	Nenne Gründe. / Gib Beispiele / ein Feedback.
Go back to your home group.	Gehe zurück zu deiner ersten Gruppe.
Guess the new words.	Errate die neuen Wörter.
Imagine you're one of the people in the story.	Stelle dir vor, du bist eine der Personen in der Geschichte.
Improve your text / part of the report.	Verbessere deinen Text / Teil des Berichts.
Learn your text by heart.	Lerne deinen Text auswendig.
Listen to the sentences / the dialogue.	Höre dir die Sätze / den Dialog an.
Look at the picture / the examples.	Schau dir das Bild / die Beispiele an.
Look up the words.	Schlage die Wörter nach.
Make a poster / a grid / a mind map / notes.	Fertige ein Poster / eine Tabelle / ein Wörternetz / Notizen an.
Match the sentence parts.	Ordne die Satzteile einander zu.
Note down what is missing.	Notiere, was fehlt.
Plan the scenes.	Plane die Szenen.
Practise your scenes / the dialogues.	Übe deine Szenen / die Dialoge.
Present the information from your text.	Präsentiere die Informationen aus deinem Text.
Put in the correct forms.	Setze die richtigen Formen ein.
Put the verbs in the right / correct form.	Bringe die Verben in die richtige Form.
Read your text aloud. / Read your text out loud.	Lies deinen Text laut vor.
Record your final report / dialogue.	Nehmt euren fertigen Bericht / Dialog auf.
Repeat the sentences / the dialogues.	Wiederhole die Sätze / die Dialoge.
Report what the people say.	Berichte, was die Leute sagen.
Say the words / the sounds.	Sage die Wörter / die Laute.
Scan the text for details.	Suche den Text nach Details ab.
Share the information with your partner.	Teile die Informationen mit deinem Partner / deiner Partnerin.
Skim the text for the gist.	Überfliege den Text und finde die wichtigsten Aussagen.
Sum up / Summarise what happens in the story.	Fasse zusammen, was in der Geschichte passiert.
Swap roles.	Tauscht die Rollen.
Take notes.	Mache dir Notizen.
Take turns.	Wechselt euch ab.
Talk with / to your partner (about …).	Sprich mit deinem Partner / deiner Partnerin (über …).

Tell your partner about your experiences.	Erzähle deinem Partner / deiner Partnerin von deinen Erfahrungen.
Think - pair - share.	Nachdenken - Paare bilden - teilen / austauschen.
Think about different problems.	Denke über die verschiedenen Probleme nach.
Think of ideas for …	Überlege dir Ideen für …
Translate the words / sentences.	Übersetze die Wörter / Sätze.
Underline the words that change.	Unterstreiche die Wörter, die sich ändern.
Use the ideas / the vocabulary.	Verwende die Ideen / die Vokabeln.
Watch the film.	Sieh dir den Film an.
Work with a partner or in a group.	Arbeite mit einem Partner / einer Partnerin oder in einer Gruppe.
Write dialogues / a short text / a reply / a summary.	Schreibe Dialoge / einen kurzen Text / eine Antwort / eine Zusammenfassung.
Write about your friends.	Schreibe über deine Freunde.
Write down your ideas / key words.	Schreibe deine Ideen / Schlüsselwörter auf.

Useful words

activity – Aktivität	presentation – Präsentation; Vortrag
answer – Antwort	prompt card – Rollenkarte
class display – Ausstellung in der Klasse	puzzle – Rätsel; Puzzle
collocation – Wortverbindung	pros and cons – Vor- und Nachteile
description – Beschreibung	question – Frage
dialogue – Dialog	quiz – Quiz; Rätsel
dice – Würfel	quote – Zitat
draft – Entwurf; Konzept	report – Bericht
drawing – Zeichnung	revision – Wiederholung
example – Beispiel	rhyme – Reim
fact – Tatsache; Fakt	role play – Rollenspiel
folder – Ordner; Mappe	rule – Regel
game – Spiel	scene – Szene
grid – Gitter; Tabelle; Raster	signal word – Signalwort
heading – Überschrift	slogan – Slogan; Werbespruch
information – Information(en)	speech bubble – Sprechblase
key word – Schlüsselwort	story – Geschichte; Erzählung
list – Liste	task – Aufgabe
mind map – Wörternetz	theme – Thema
order – Reihenfolge	title – Titel; Überschrift
perspective – Perspektive	unit – Lektion; Kapitel
phrase – Redewendung; Ausdruck	useful phrases – nützliche Ausdrücke
picture story – Bildergeschichte	vocabulary – Vokabular; Wortschatz
point of view – Standpunkt; Ansicht	word bank – Wortsammlung

Irregular verbs

■ ■ ■ Grundform, *simple past* und *past participle* sind identisch
■ ● ● Grundform unterscheidet sich vom *simple past* und *past participle*
■ ● ■ Grundform und *past participle* sind identisch, nur das *simple past* hat eine andere Form
■ ● ▲ Grundform, *simple past* und *past participle* haben alle eine andere Form

■ Grundform	■ simple past	■ past participle	Deutsch
cost [kɒst]	cost [kɒst]	cost [kɒst]	kosten
cut [kʌt]	cut [kʌt]	cut [kʌt]	schneiden
hit [hɪt]	hit [hɪt]	hit [hɪt]	schlagen, treffen
hurt [hɜ:t]	hurt [hɜ:t]	hurt [hɜ:t]	verletzen, sich weh tun
let [let]	let [let]	let [let]	lassen
put [pʊt]	put [pʊt]	put [pʊt]	legen, setzen, stellen
set up ['set ˌʌp]	set up ['set ˌʌp]	set up ['set ˌʌp]	erbauen, errichten
upset [ʌp'set]	upset [ʌp'set]	upset [ʌp'set]	aus der Fassung bringen

■ Grundform	● simple past	● past participle	Deutsch
bring [brɪŋ]	brought [brɔ:t]	brought [brɔ:t]	(mit)bringen
build [bɪld]	built [bɪlt]	built [bɪlt]	bauen
burn [bɜ:n]	burnt [bɜ:nt]	burnt [bɜ:nt]	(ver)brennen
buy [baɪ]	bought [bɔ:t]	bought [bɔ:t]	kaufen
catch [kætʃ]	caught [kɔ:t]	caught [kɔ:t]	fangen; mitbekommen
feel [fi:l]	felt [felt]	felt [felt]	fühlen
find [faɪnd]	found [faʊnd]	found [faʊnd]	finden
get [get]	got [gɒt]	got [gɒt]	holen, bringen, bekommen; werden
hang [hæŋ]	hung [hʌŋ]	hung [hʌŋ]	hängen
have [hæv]	had [hæd]	had [hæd]	haben
hear [hɪə]	heard [hɜ:d]	heard [hɜ:d]	hören
hold [həʊld]	held [held]	held [held]	halten
keep [ki:p]	kept [kept]	kept [kept]	(auf)bewahren, behalten
lead [li:d]	led [led]	led [led]	(an)führen
learn [lɜ:n]	learned [lɜ:nd] / learnt [lɜ:nt]	learned [lɜ:nd] / learnt [lɜ:nt]	lernen
leave [li:v]	left [left]	left [left]	(ver)lassen
lend [lend]	lent [lent]	lent [lent]	(ver)leihen
make [meɪk]	made [meɪd]	made [meɪd]	machen, tun
meet [mi:t]	met [met]	met [met]	treffen
pay [peɪ]	paid [peɪd]	paid [peɪd]	(be)zahlen
read [ri:d]	read [red]	read [red]	lesen
retell [ˌri:'tel]	retold [ˌri:'təʊld]	retold [ˌri:'təʊld]	nacherzählen
say [seɪ]	said [sed]	said [sed]	sagen
sell [sel]	sold [səʊld]	sold [səʊld]	verkaufen
send [send]	sent [sent]	sent [sent]	senden, verschicken
shoot [ʃu:t]	shot [ʃɒt]	shot [ʃɒt]	schießen (auf)
sit [sɪt]	sat [sæt]	sat [sæt]	sitzen

sleep [sli:p]	slept [slept]	slept [slept]	schlafen
smell [smel]	smelt [smelt]	smelt [smelt]	riechen, duften
spell [spel]	spelt [spelt]	spelt [spelt]	buchstabieren
spend [spend]	spent [spent]	spent [spent]	ausgeben, verbringen
stand (up) [stænd]	stood (up) [stʊd]	stood (up) [stʊd]	(auf)stehen
sting [stɪŋ]	stung [stʌŋ]	stung [stʌŋ]	stechen
tell [tel]	told [təʊld]	told [təʊld]	erzählen
think [θɪŋk]	thought [θɔ:t]	thought [θɔ:t]	(nach)denken, glauben
understand [ˌʌndəˈstænd]	understood [ˌʌndəˈstʊd]	understood [ˌʌndəˈstʊd]	verstehen
win [wɪn]	won [wʌn]	won [wʌn]	gewinnen, siegen

■ Grundform	● simple past	■ past participle	Deutsch
become [bɪˈkʌm]	became [bɪˈkeɪm]	become [bɪˈkʌm]	werden
come [kʌm]	came [keɪm]	come [kʌm]	kommen
run [rʌn]	ran [ræn]	run [rʌn]	laufen, rennen

■ Grundform	● simple past	▲ past participle	Deutsch
be [bi:]	was / were [wɒz / wɜ:]	been [bi:n]	sein
blow (out) [bləʊ]	blew [blu:]	blown [bləʊn]	(aus)blasen, (aus)pusten
break [breɪk]	broke [brəʊk]	broken [ˈbrəʊkn]	(zer)brechen, kaputt machen
choose [tʃu:z]	chose [tʃəʊz]	chosen [tʃəʊzn]	(aus)wählen
do [du:]	did [dɪd]	done [dʌn]	machen, tun
draw [drɔ:]	drew [dru:]	drawn [drɔ:n]	zeichnen
drink [drɪŋk]	drank [dræŋk]	drunk [drʌŋk]	trinken
drive [draɪv]	drove [drəʊv]	driven [ˈdrɪvn]	fahren
eat [i:t]	ate [et]	eaten [i:tn]	essen
fall [fɔ:l]	fell [fel]	fallen [ˈfɔ:lən]	fallen
fly [flaɪ]	flew [flu:]	flown [fləʊn]	fliegen
forget [fəˈget]	forgot [fəˈgɒt]	forgotten [fəˈgɒtn]	vergessen
give [gɪv]	gave [geɪv]	given[ˈgɪvn]	geben
go [gəʊ]	went [went]	gone [gɒn]	gehen, fahren
grow [grəʊ]	grew [gru:]	grown [grəʊn]	wachsen; anbauen
know [nəʊ]	knew [nju:]	known [nəʊn]	kennen, wissen
rise [raɪz]	rose [rəʊz]	risen [ˈrɪzn]	steigen, sich erheben
see [si:]	saw [sɔ:]	seen [si:n]	sehen
show [ʃəʊ]	showed [ʃəʊd]	shown [ʃəʊn]	zeigen
sing [sɪŋ]	sang [sæŋ]	sung [sʌŋ]	singen
sink [sɪŋk]	sank [sæŋk]	sunk [sʌŋk]	sinken, untergehen
speak [spi:k]	spoke [spəʊk]	spoken [ˈspəʊkn]	sprechen
swim [swɪm]	swam [swæm]	swum [swʌm]	schwimmen
take [teɪk]	took [tʊk]	taken [ˈteɪkn]	nehmen
throw [θrəʊ]	threw [θru:]	thrown [θrəʊn]	werfen
wake up [ˌweɪk‿ˈʌp]	woke up [ˌwəʊk‿ˈʌp]	woken up [ˌwəʊkn‿ˈʌp]	aufwachen; aufwecken
wear [weə]	wore [wɔ:]	worn [wɔ:n]	anhaben, tragen
write [raɪt]	wrote [rəʊt]	written [ˈrɪtn]	schreiben

Grammar solutions

Unit 1

G1 I'll miss you so much!

1. Olivia: I hope Dave **will love** his new school.
2. Holly: I'm sure the Prestons **will visit** Granny Rose and Aunt Frances in London soon.
3. Luke: I don't think the new home **will be** a problem for Sid. There **are** lots of fields and he **will be able to run around**. He **will make** new cat friends quickly. He **won't get bored**!
4. Gwen: I hope Dave **won't forget** us.

G2 If you look at a map of Great Britain, you'll find Cornwall in the far west.

Lösungsvorschlag:
If you visit Hamburg, you should see the harbour and try a fish burger.
If you go to Cologne, climb to the top of the Dome.
If you're interested in cars, you could go to Stuttgart and visit the Porsche Museum/Mercedes Museum.
If you go to Eisenach, you should visit the Wartburg and try Thüringer Bratwurst/sausages there. You could also visit the Bachhaus/Lutherhaus.

Unit 2

G3 If Jay practises a lot, he will be a better singer.

1. If we **don't leave** now, we'**ll miss** our train.
2. If we **miss** our train, we **won't get** to the cinema on time.
3. If we **don't get to** the cinema on time, they probably **won't let** us in.
4. And I'**ll be** really upset if that **happens**, Shahid. So, please hurry up!

G4 They wouldn't worry if they didn't care.

Jay: If Mum and Dad **tried** to understand me, we **wouldn't fight** so often.
Shahid: They're just worried about you, Jay. You **wouldn't have** so many fights if you **worked** harder for school and **got** better marks.
Jay: The problem is that they don't believe in me, Shahid. If they **believed** in me, they **wouldn't worry** about my marks.
Shahid: They only worry because they care about you, Jay. Maybe if you **weren't** so laid back, they **wouldn't have to** worry so much.

G5 You have to push yourself.

Olivia: Claire, I'm hungry. Can I make **myself** a sandwich?
Lucy: That's a good idea, Olivia. Can you make **me** one too?
Olivia: No, I can't. You can do that **yourself**.
Claire: Hey you two, please behave **yourselves**. You know I hate it when you fight with **each other**.

Unit 3

G6 How long have they been chatting?

1. How long **has** Mr Wilson **been working** in a hotel? → He **has been working** there **since** 2012.
2. How long **has** Mrs Wilson **been teaching** (English)? → She **has been teaching** (English) **for** five years.
3. How long **have** their children Sam and Jack **been going** to school? → Sam **has been going** to school **for** three years, Jack **(has been going to school) since** last year.

G7 Is Haggis made with meat?

Shinty is one of the oldest games in the world. Some people think that it **was invented** in Ireland 2000 years ago and that it **was brought** to Scotland by the Irish in the 6th century. Others say that it **has been played** in Scotland since Celtic times. Shinty is similar to field hockey but faster and more dangerous. In the past, whole villages played against each other. Today, Shinty is a club sport which **is played** between two teams of 12 players.

Unit 4

G8 He hadn't finished his game

Henry VIII and the Church of England

In 1509, seven weeks after Henry VIII **had become** the new king of England, he **married** Catherine of Aragon. She had been the wife of his older brother Arthur, who **had died** in 1502. Together, Henry and Catherine **had** a daughter, Mary. But Henry **needed** a boy who could become the next king. So, in 1533, after Catherine **had become** too old to have any more children, Henry **decided** to marry Anne Boleyn, who he **had met** and fallen in love with in about 1525. When the Pope **said** "no", Henry **broke** with Rome and **founded** his own Church – the Church of England.

G9 If I hadn't talked so much

And all because of a problem with the hot water

If there **hadn't been** a problem with the hot water, she **wouldn't have left** the house late.
She **wouldn't have missed** her train if she **had arrived** at the station on time.
If she **had had** time for breakfast, she **wouldn't have gone** to the café.
If a nice young man **hadn't sat down** opposite her, they **wouldn't have started** to chat.

Unit solutions

Unit 2, Story: Alternative endings

→ page 38, ex. 4

Hang out with us instead!

Alternative ending 1:

Shahid was on his way home on the train when he received a text message from his best friend, Dan, who was also a DJ:

> *Hi Shahid. Hope your weekend went well. Just to say, that was a great idea you had last week to copy all of our music onto each other's hard drives. I've really enjoyed listening to all your tracks – and it's great to know that we don't have to worry about losing all our music! Dan*

Alternative ending 2:

When Shahid arrived home the next morning, Jay was waiting for him at the door. "I've got something to tell you," he said sadly. Jay told his story while Shahid listened quietly – he never shouted but sometimes that made you feel worse. Finally, Shahid spoke. "You know how important my music is to me – without it I can't do my DJ work. So, you can guess how you're going to spend all your weekends for the next two or three months, can't you? I need you to record all my songs again. All of them!" How could Jay argue? He knew he had no choice. Shahid was really disappointed in him and now he couldn't go out for weeks! How much worse could life be?

Bildquellennachweis
Umschlag.1 YERMAN FILMS (Andrea Artz), London; **Umschlag.2** shutterstock.com (Nataliya Hora), New York, NY; **2.1** 123rf (kotenko), Nidderau; **2.2** shutterstock.com (Helen Hotson), New York, NY; **4.1** Getty Images (Oxford Scientific), München; **4.2** Corbis (Paul A. Souders), Berlin; **6.1** Ullstein Bild GmbH (ArenaPAL), Berlin; **8.1** Alamy Images (Melissa Gaskell), Abingdon, Oxon; **8.2** Alamy Images (Jeff Morgan 06), Abingdon, Oxon; **9.3** Alamy Images (Peter Horree), Abingdon, Oxon; **9.4** Thinkstock (versevend), München; **10.1** February Films (Andrew Kemp), London; **13.1** Klett-Archiv (Weccard), Stuttgart; **14.1** iStockphoto (MattStansfield), Calgary, Alberta; **15.1** Alamy Images (Kevin Britland), Abingdon, Oxon; **16.1** shutterstock.com (antb), New York, NY; **18.1** shutterstock.com (Helen Hotson), New York, NY; **20.1** Fotolia.com (acceleratorhams), New York; **21.1** February Films, London; **23.1** Picture-Alliance (dpa/Armin Weigel), Frankfurt; **23.2** shutterstock.com (iurii), New York, NY; **23.3** Getty Images, München; **24.1** February Films, London; **24.2** February Films, London; **24.3** February Films, London; **26.1** Corbis (KidStock/Blend Images), Berlin; **26.2** Corbis (Brian Mitchell), Berlin; **27.1** Getty Images (Matthias Hangst), München; **27.2** Thinkstock (Andrii_Oliinyk), München; **27.3** Thinkstock (arabes), München; **27.4** Thinkstock (Nixken), München; **27.5** Thinkstock (nuranvectorgirl), München; **27.6** Thinkstock (pking4th), München; **27.7** Thinkstock (nosopyrik), München; **27.8** Fotolia.com (alexghidan89), New York; **27.9** Thinkstock (comzeal), München; **28.1** YERMAN FILMS (Andrea Artz), London; **28.2** YERMAN FILMS (Andrea Artz), London; **29.1** Getty Images (Bloomberg), München; **30.1** YERMAN FILMS (Andrea Artz), London; **30.2** Thinkstock (iStock/kadmy), München; **31.1** shutterstock.com (George Dolgikh), New York, NY; **31.2** Getty Images (THOMAS COEX/AFP), München; **34.1** Corbis (Sandra Hoever), Berlin; **36.1** Corbis (Mark Scoggins), Berlin; **37.1** YERMAN FILMS (Andrew Kemp), London; **39.1** February Films, London; **39.2** February Films, London; **39.3** February Films, London; **40.1** iStockphoto (PeopleImages), Calgary, Alberta; **42.1** shutterstock.com (Yuri Arcurs), New York, NY; **42.2** Thinkstock (iStockphoto), München; **44.1** Avenue Images GmbH (Banana Stock), Hamburg; **44.2** www.CartoonStock.com (Madden, Chris), Bath; **44.3** www.CartoonStock.com (Farris, Joseph), Bath; **45.1** Getty Images (Blend Images), München; **46.1** Weisshaar, Harald, Bisingen-Zimmern; **47.1** shutterstock.com (visionaryft), New York, NY; **48.1** Avenue Images GmbH (Banana Stock), Hamburg; **49.1** Getty Images (Steve Jennings/WireImage), München; **50.1** Getty Images (GREG WOOD/AFP), München; **50.2** shutterstock.com (Syda Productions), New York, NY; **51.1** 123rf (kotenko), Nidderau; **51.2** shutterstock.com (Joshua Resnick), New York, NY; **52.1** February Films, London; **52.2** February Films, London; **53.1** February Films, London; **53.2** February Films, London; **54.1** plainpicture GmbH & Co. KG (Fancy Images), Hamburg; **55.1** Getty Images (Panoramic Images), München; **55.2** Alamy Images (Ian Dagnall), Abingdon, Oxon; **55.3** iStockphoto (George Clerk), Calgary, Alberta; **55.4** iStockphoto (TT), Calgary, Alberta; **56.1** iStockphoto (abzee), Calgary, Alberta; **56.2** YERMAN FILMS (Andrea Artz), London; **56.3** YERMAN FILMS (Andrea Artz), London; **57.1** Corbis (Kristian Buus/In Pictures), Berlin; **58.1** YERMAN FILMS (Andrea Artz), London; **58.2** Corbis (BPI/Richard Lee/BPI), Berlin; **59.1** YERMAN FILMS (Andrea Artz), London; **60.1** Corbis (Najlah Feanny/SABA), Berlin; **61.1** iStockphoto (code6d), Calgary, Alberta; **61.2** Alamy Images (John Peter Photography), Abingdon, Oxon; **62.1** Corbis (Adam Burton/Robert Harding World Imagery), Berlin; **62.2** Corbis (Colin McPherson/Sygma), Berlin; **62.3** Alamy Images (David Kilpatrick), Abingdon, Oxon; **62.4** iStockphoto (Gim42), Calgary, Alberta; **62.5** iStockphoto (kodachrome25), Calgary, Alberta; **62.6** iStockphoto (Mnieteq), Calgary, Alberta; **63.1** Alamy Images (Thornton Cohen), Abingdon, Oxon; **63.2** Getty Images (Andy Buchanan/AFP), München; **63.3** iStockphoto (Martin McCarthy), Calgary, Alberta; **63.4** iStockphoto (jenifoto), Calgary, Alberta; **64.1** Getty Images (DEA/PUBBLI AER FOTO/De Agostini), München; **65.1** shutterstock.com (Ron Dale), New York, NY; **65.2** shutterstock.com (Gepardu), New York, NY; **65.3** shutterstock.com (Vectomart), New York, NY; **69.1** February Films, London; **69.2** February Films, London; **70.1** Ullstein Bild GmbH (Stiebing), Berlin; **70.2** Getty Images (Sean Gallup), München; **71.1** shutterstock.com (Matyas Rehak), New York, NY; **71.2** shutterstock.com (Rainer Albiez), New York, NY; **71.3** shutterstock.com (Rainer Albiez), New York, NY; **72.1** shutterstock.com (Ints Vikmanis), New York, NY; **73.1** iStockphoto (miss_elli), Calgary, Alberta; **74.1** iStockphoto (Chris Jackson/EdStock), Calgary, Alberta; **74.2** iStockphoto (hansenn), Calgary, Alberta; **76.1** Corbis (Jim Craigmyle), Berlin; **77.1** Getty Images (Oxford Scientific), München; **77.2** shutterstock.com (Denisa Doudova), New York, NY; **77.3** shutterstock.com (Elena11), New York, NY; **78.1** shutterstock.com (David Dohnal), New York, NY; **79.1** Corbis (Joel Sartore/National Geographic Creative), Berlin; **79.2** iStockphoto (PandaWild), Calgary, Alberta; **79.3** shutterstock.com (Adam Filipowicz), New York, NY; **79.4** Getty Images (Hulton Archive/James Pozarik/Liaison), München; **80.1** shutterstock.com (Graeme Shannon), New York, NY; **80.2** shutterstock.com (Catfish Photography), New York, NY; **80.3** Thinkstock (Stockbyte), München; **82.1** www.CartoonStock.com (McNeill, Geoff), Bath; **83.1** February Films, London; **83.2** February Films, London; **83.3** February Films, London; **83.4** February Films, London; **84.1** Picture-Alliance (Becker & Bredel), Frankfurt; **84.2** Alamy Images (Lenscap), Abingdon, Oxon; **84.3** 123rf (Zvonimir Atletic), Nidderau; **85.1** shutterstock.com (Thomas Owen Jenkins), New York, NY; **85.2** shutterstock.com (Sytilin Pavel), New York, NY; **86.1** Corbis (Stapleton Collection), Berlin; **87.1** Corbis (The Print Collector), Berlin; **87.2** Corbis (I Love Images), Berlin; **87.3** shutterstock.com (George Dolgikh), New York, NY; **87.4** shutterstock.com (Monkey Business Images), New York, NY; **88.1** YERMAN FILMS (Andrea Artz), London; **88.2** Imago (EntertainmentPictures), Berlin; **91.1** shutterstock.com (Anneka), New York, NY; **92.1** shutterstock.com (Kamira), New York, NY; **94.1** Fotolia.com (babsi_w), New York; **94.2** ddp images GmbH (interTOPICS/LMK Media), Hamburg; **95.1** Getty Images (Fine Art Images/Heritage Images), München; **97.1** YERMAN FILMS (Andrea Artz), London; **97.2** YERMAN FILMS (Andrea Artz), London; **98.1** YERMAN FILMS (Andrea Artz), London; **99.1** February Films, London; **99.2** February Films, London; **100.1** Thinkstock (Jupiterimages), München; **100.2** iStockphoto (miskolin), Calgary, Alberta; **100.3** iStockphoto (fcafotodigital), Calgary, Alberta; **100.4** shutterstock.com (Sergios), New York, NY; **100.5** shutterstock.com (CHANG JO-YI), New York, NY; **100.6** Thinkstock (Hemera Technologies), München; **105.1** Getty Images (Time Life Pictures/Mansell/The LIFE Picture Collection), München; **106.1** Corbis (Jim Craigmyle), Berlin; **107.1** Corbis (Paul A. Souders), Berlin; **107.2** Corbis (Kelly-Mooney Photography), Berlin;**109.1** shutterstock.com (Photobank gallery), New York, NY;

111.1 Ernst Klett Sprachen GmbH, Stuttgart; **111.2** Ernst Klett Sprachen GmbH, Stuttgart; **113.1** Fotolia.com (Kristina Afanasyeva), New York; **114.1** shutterstock.com (M R), New York, NY; **115.1** Corbis (Samantha Mitchell), Berlin; **115.2** YERMAN FILMS (Andrea Artz), London; **116.1** shutterstock.com (javi_indy), New York, NY; **119.1** iStockphoto (DenisZbukarev), Calgary, Alberta; **122.1** YERMAN FILMS (Andrea Artz), London; **122.2** YERMAN FILMS (Andrea Artz), London; **123.1** Getty Images (Photolibrary), München; **124.1** Getty Images (Getty Images Sport), München; **124.2** akg-images (EON/UA/Album), Berlin; **125.1** Getty Images (Hans Georg Eiben/Photolibrary), München; **126.1** Getty Images (Cultura), München; **128.1** Corbis (Andreas von Einsiedel), Berlin; **128.2** Corbis (Jimmy Collins), Berlin; **128.3** shutterstock.com (marekuliasz), New York, NY; **128.4** Corbis (GraphicaArtis), Berlin; **132.1** Alamy Images (CJG - UK), Abingdon, Oxon; **135.1** Fotolia.com (Michael Rogner), New York; **140.1** Thinkstock (Comstock), München; **143.1** shutterstock.com (Dmitry Kalinovsky), New York, NY; **144.1** shutterstock.com (Kues), New York, NY; **148.1** ddp images GmbH, Hamburg; **148.2** dreamstime.com (Edward Bartel), Brentwood, TN; **149.1** akg-images (Album), Berlin; **149.2** Getty Images (Matt Cardy), München; **149.3** Ullstein Bild GmbH (pwe Verlag GmbH), Berlin; **154.1** Thinkstock (BananaStock), München; **155.1** YERMAN FILMS (Andrea Artz), London; **159.1** YERMAN FILMS (Andrea Artz), London; **161.1** Getty Images (Lonely Planet Images/J. Smith), München; **162.1** shutterstock.com (Michaelpuche), New York, NY; **162.2** Thinkstock (Alan Crawford), München; **163.1** shutterstock.com (JASPERIMAGE), New York, NY; **166.1** February Films (Andrew Kemp), London; **169.1** Fotolia.com (Jaroslaw Grudzinski), New York; **171.1** iStockphoto (Grafissimo), Calgary, Alberta; **171.2** Fotolia.com (micromonkey), New York; **175.1** Getty Images RF (Cultura/Juice Images), München; **183.1** shutterstock.com (Pressmaster), New York, NY; **188.1** Fotolia.com (konstan), New York; **188.2** iStockphoto (luoman), Calgary, Alberta; **188.3** Thinkstock (Vrabelpeter1), München; **188.4** iStockphoto (jeangill), Calgary, Alberta; **188.5** shutterstock.com (NemesisINC), New York, NY; **188.6** iStockphoto (blackjake), Calgary, Alberta; **191.1** shutterstock.com (wallix), New York, NY; **191.2** shutterstock.com (Targn Pleiades), New York, NY; **201.1** gemeinfrei; **203.1** Avenue Images GmbH (Ingram Publishing), Hamburg; **261.1** shutterstock.com (YanLev), New York, NY; **267.1** Fotolia.com (Michael Rogner), New York; **Timeline.1** Corbis (Stuart Forster/Robert Harding World Imagery), Berlin; **Timeline.2** Alamy Images (CJG - UK), Abingdon, Oxon; **Timeline.3** iStockphoto (Andrew Gosling), Calgary, Alberta; **Timeline.4** Corbis, Berlin

Sollte es in einem Einzelfall nicht gelungen sein, den korrekten Rechteinhaber ausfindig zu machen, so werden berechtigte Ansprüche selbstverständlich im Rahmen der üblichen Regelungen abgegolten.

Textquellen:
16 "The Romans in Britain": From www.poetryarchive.org/ poems/ romans-britain, © Judith Nicholls; **31** "Holiday" Text: Stevens, Lisa/Hudson, Curtis Lee © House of Fun Music Inc, Sony/ATV Music Publishing (Germany) GmbH, Berlin; **47** "Happy Poem": From Time Travelling Underpants, Macmillan Children's Books, 2007, 978-0-330-44709-6, p50; **49** „Count on me" Text: Hernandez, Peter Gene/Lawrence, Philip Martin/Levine, Ari © BMG Gold Songs/Bughouse/Mars Force Music/Round Hill Songs/Toy Plane Music BMG Rights Management GmbH, Berlin Northside Independent Music/Roc Nation Music/WB Music Corp./Neue Welt Musikverlag GmbH, Hamburg; **51** "I loved my friend" by Langston Hughes © 1994 Estate of Langston Hughes published by permission of Harold Ober Associates, New York; **58** "Flower of Scotland" Text: (OT) Williamson, Roy, Copyright Variena Music Inc./Edition AIM Publishing; **77** Brent Lodge Wildlife Hospital, 2014; **80** Ben Pulsford, First News, 03.10.2014; **107** Reprinted with the permission of Simon & Schuster Books for Young Readers, an imprint of Simon & Schuster Children's Publishing Division from AMONG THE HIDDEN by Margaret Peterson Haddix. Copyright © 1998 Margaret Peterson Haddix.; **109** Excerpt from Pig-Heart Boy by Malorie Blackman, Doubleday, an imprint of Random House Children's Books, London, 1997 © Oneta Malorie Blackman, 1997

Time line of British history

We don't know much about **the earliest people** who lived in the British Isles, but we can still see some of the famous stone rings they built, like Stonehenge. We also know that their priests were called Druids.

From around 500 BC, the **Celts** came from Europe to live in the British Isles. They lived in round houses with fires in the middle and built high walls to keep out wild animals. They had many gods.

A typical Celtic round house

500 BC

After the **Romans** had arrived, the Celts moved north and west to Scotland, Ireland and Wales. The Romans built Hadrian's Wall to keep the Scots out of their part of the island of Britain.

43–410 AD

5th, 6th cent.

After the Romans had left, Germanic tribes called **Saxons and Angles** conquered England. The Angles gave England its name: It means 'Land of the Angles'.

1066–1154

At the battle of Hasti William, Duke of Normandy defeated Harold, King of the Saxons. The **Norman** ruled England for th next 88 years.

1485

Industrialisation started in England in the 18th century. Factories with machines were built all over Britain and the invention of the steam engine meant that people could travel much more than before.

After the two world wars, Britain rebuilt itself, and people started to enjoy themselves again. British music and fashion became popular around the world. Even today, the music of the Beatles and Rolling Stones still has a major influence.

Powerful symbol of the Industrial Revolution: the steam train

After 1945

18th, 19th cent.

1973

1837–1901

ry VIII and his wives, as wax res at Madam auds

Queen Victoria reigned for almost 64 years

louse of Tudor** was important in English ry. Henry VIII changed England from a Catholic Protestant country, and founded the Navy. aughter Elizabeth was perhaps the biggest of the Tudor family. While she was queen, nd became rich and powerful and started to ise North America. It was a 'golden age' for c, literature and the theatre too.

During the reign of **Queen Victoria**, Britain had so many colonies around the world that people said the sun always shone somewhere in the British Empire.

The UK joined the European Community (later the European Union), but the British kept their own money: the pound.

SCOTLAND
SHETLAND ISLANDS
Atlantic Ocean
ORKNEY ISLANDS
OUTER HEBRIDES
Highlands
Inverness
Loch Ness
ISLE OF SKYE
Aberdeen
Balmoral Castle
Ben Nevis
Dunnottar Castle
Tay
Dundee
Firth of Forth
Loch Lomond
Glasgow
Edinburgh
Edinburgh Castle
Clyde
Tweed
ARRAN
North Sea